HISTORY OF THE POPES.

VOL. IV

CONTENTS OF VOL IV.

B
Ɔ

.4

TABLE OF CONTENTS OF VOLUME IV

BOOK I.

CHAPTER I

ELECTION OF PAUL II

CHAPTER II.

PAUL II. AND THE RENAISSANCE.

CHAPTER III

THE WAR AGAINST THE TURKS.

CHAPTER IV

EUROPEAN POLICY OF PAUL II   REFORMS

CHAPTER V.

THE NEW CARDINALS.   CHURCH QUESTIONS IN BOHEMIA

CHAPTER VI.

PAUL II.'S CARE FOR THE STATES OF THE CHURCH.

CHAPTER VII

DEATH OF PAUL II

BOOK II

CHAPTER I

ELECTION OF SIXTUS IV.

CHAPTER II

RISE OF THE ROVERE AND RIARIO FAMILIES.

CHAPTER III.

THE KING OF DENMARK IN ROME

CHAPTER IV.

THE JUBILEE YEAR

CHAPTER V

BEGINNING OF THE RUPTURE WITH LORENZO DE' MEDICI

CHAPTER VI.

THE CONSPIRACY OF THE PAZZI.

CHAPTER VII.

THE TUSCAN WAR.

CHAPTER VIII.

THE TURKISH WAR.

CHAPTER IX

ALLIANCE BETWEEN THE POPE AND VENICE ITALIAN WAR

CHAPTER X

THE POPE'S STRUGGLE WITH VENICE AND THE COLONNA   DEATH
OF SIXTUS IV.

CHAPTER XI

SIXTUS IV. AND ECCLESIASTICAL MATTERS

CHAPTER XII

SIXTUS IV AS THE PATRON OF ART AND LITERATURE

LIST OF UNPUBLISHED DOCUMENTS
IN APPENDIX.

— — — ——

BOOK 1.

PAUL II.   1464–1471

CHAPTER I.

THE Cardinals in attendance on Pius II. had hastened to
Rome as soon as it was decided that the election should be
held in that city. The period of the vacancy of the Holy
See was one of great disquiet, as it had often been before.
The Sienese in Rome suffered much, and were assailed
by a hostile crowd wherever they appeared *

Cardinal Roverella returned from his Mission to Naples
on the 23rd August, and Cardinal Gonzaga reached Rome
on the 24th   The Sacred College assembled in the morning
of the 25th in the house of Cardinal Scarampo   In this
preliminary meeting, doubts were expressed as to the
prudence of holding a Conclave in the Vatican while
Antonio Piccolomini, Duke of Amalfi, still kept possession
of the Castle of St. Angelo, and many Cardinals advised

---

* **Letter from Cardinal Gonzaga to his father, dated Rome, 1464,
Aug. 25. See *Despatch of G P Arrivabene, dated Rome, 1464,
Aug 27 "Quelli de Fermo hanno brusato quello castello de S.
Petro de Laio, vituperato le donne, menato via li fanciulli et usato
mille crudelitate etiam contra li luochi sacri, che è uno stupore ad
udire. Li Senesi dove se trovano sono a furia perseguitati." Jacobus
de Aretio writes on the 27th Aug, 1464, to Marquess Lodovico Gonzaga . *"Molti latrocinii et correrie se fanno vacante questa benedetta
sedia et maxime per la strada de Ancona a Roma " All these letters
are in the Gonzaga Archives, Mantua.

that the Election should take place in the Minerva or at the Capitol *

The Duke of Amalfi, who was at this time absent from Rome, seems to have been an object of suspicion, principally because of the close relations which existed between him, the Orsini, and King Ferrante of Naples. Some of the Cardinals feared that, in the event of a Pope being chosen who was not agreeable to the King, he might make difficulties about giving up St. Angelo. On the other side, it was maintained that Antonio Piccolomini had given the most positive assurances, and that regard for his brothers, one of whom was a member of the Sacred College, would deter him from doing anything that could interfere with the liberty of the Conclave. This consideration prevailed, and it was determined that the Election should be held in the Vatican †

On the evening of the 28th August,‡ the Cardinals went

* **Letter from Cardinal Gonzaga on the 25th Aug., 1464, *loc. cit.* For Roverella's arrival, see *Acta Consist, f 33b, Secret Archives of the Vatican

† See AMMANATI, Comment. 347 , **Letter of the 25th Aug, from Cardinal Gonzaga , and a **Despatch of J. P. Arrivabene of the 27th Aug, 1464 (Gonzaga Archives, Mantua), also the *Report of Jo An. Ferrofinus to Cecco Simoneta, dated Rome, ex palatio S. Petri die xxix. Augusti, 1464. State Archives, Milan, Cart Gen

‡ AMMANATI, *loc cit.*, says the 27th August   This date, which is repeated by CANCELLIERI, Stagioni, 15 ; GREGOROVIUS, VII, 206, 3rd ed. ; REUMONT, III, 1, 152; and ROHRBACHER-KNOPFLER, 232, is wrong, as is also that given by PETRUCELLI, 285, the 26th August   The Cron. Rom., 30, name the 22nd , the Diario Nepesino, 141, has the 18th ; Infessura, 1139, the 24th August ; CREIGHTON, III., 3, follows this last   The 28th is established as the day of entrance into Conclave by the following authorities :—(a) *Despatches of J. P. Arrivabene of the 27th Aug and 1st Sept , 1464 , (b) *Despatch of Jacopo de Aretio of the 1st Sept , 1464 (Gonzaga Archives) , (c) the *Report of J. A Ferrofinus of the 29th August : "Heri sera da

into Conclave. We have a graphic account of the proceedings from the Duke of Mantua's Envoy. The little Chapel of the Palace was chosen for the actual Election. The doors and windows were walled up The chambers to be occupied during the election were like monks' cells, they were twenty-five feet square, and were so dark that artificial light was almost constantly necessary. The cells were marked with a letter of the alphabet, and assigned to the different Cardinals by lot. Each Cardinal had his meals brought to him at regular hours by his servants, in a coffer called a cornuta, adorned with his coat of arms. These coffers had to pass three sets of guards who surrounded the Conclave. The first was composed of Roman citizens, the second of Ambassadors, and the third of Prelates, they carefully examined the contents of the coffers, so that no letters should be introduced with the provisions.*

Bessarion was invested with the dignity of Dean, and for a long time it seemed likely that the tiara would fall to his share.† After him the most notable among the Cardinals were, d'Estouteville, the head of the French party ; Carvajal, with his untiring zeal ; Torquemada, who was looked upon as the first theologian of his time ; and the two antipodes, Scarampo and Barbo. Of the more youthful members of the Sacred College, Roderigo Borgia was distinguished by his position of Vice-Chancellor.

---

le xxiii a le xxiv hore li rev^mi S^n cardinali intrarono in conclave numero xix che'l rev card de Theano nondum venit et S. Sisto propter infirmitatem nondum e venuto o rectius stato portato fin a questo matina si che adesso sonno xx^ti" (State Archives, Milan) ; (*d*) Cronica di Bologna, 758 , (*e*) *Acta Consist , f 33b, Secret Archives of the Vatican.

* **Report of Arrivabene of the 1st Sept , 1464 Gonzaga Archives.
† VESPASIANO DA BISTICCI, 192 ; CORTESIUS, De cardinalatu, CXXI b

His private life, like that of Francesco Gonzaga, was anything but edifying. Cardinals Filippo Calandrini, Francesco
Todeschini Piccolomini, Juan de Mella, Angelo Capranica,
Lodovico Libretto, and Bartolomeo Roverella,* by their
irreproachable conduct formed a great contrast to Borgia
and Gonzaga. In Ancona, Roverella had, like Capranica,
Carvajal, and Calandrini, been named as a candidate for
the papacy.† On the other hand, even in June, 1464,
when the condition of Pius II. had become worse, Cardinal
Barbo's prospects had been highly thought of.   The
Milanese Ambassador advised his master at that time to
make a friend of this Cardinal‡

On the 27th August, one of the Ambassadors then in
Rome wrote as follows : " The negotiations regarding the
Papal Election are being carried on in every direction in
secret, and with great zeal. God grant that the Holy
Spirit, and not human passions, may preside ! Some few
persons conclude, from certain predictions, that Cardinal
Torquemada will be Pope, but he is very suffering, and
this morning was said to be dead, which, however, I do not
believe. Others are of opinion that the choice will fall on
one who is not a member of the Sacred College, and, in
virtue of some prophecies, Battista Pallavicini, Bishop of
Reggio, is named."§

* AMMANATI, Comment 348b seq.; GASPAR VERONEN., 1028–
1038 ; GREGOROVIUS, VII., 205-206, 3rd ed.; CIAMPI, Forteguerri,
17-18.

† So Raphael Caymus informs us in a *Letter of the 15th August,
1464. State Archives, Milan

‡ *O. de Carretto to Fr. Sforza, dated Rome, 1464, June 14th.
Ambrosian Library.

§ **Despatch of J. P. Arrivabene, dated Rome, 1464, Aug 27th.
See the **Letter of Jacopo de Aretio, dated Rome, 1464, Sept 1.
(Gonzaga Archives, Mantua) At Ancona it was believed that
d'Estouteville's Election was very probable , see *Despatch of

The statements regarding Cardinal Torquemada's prospects of election are confirmed by one of the Duke of Milan's Envoys. On the 29th August he informed his master of the general impression that Cardinal Torquemada, who had that morning been carried into the Conclave, would never return to his own dwelling, but would either become Pope or die, as he was so old and feeble.* After Torquemada, Scarampo was thought by many likely to be the favoured candidate.†

The discourse pronounced by Domenico de' Domenichi, the eloquent Bishop of Torcello, in St. Peter's, before the Conclave began, gives a picture of the general state of affairs, and describes the disposition of the Electors ‡ The

S. Nardini to Fr. Sforza, dated Ancona, 1464, Aug 16th. (State Archives, Milan) For an account of the pious and learned B Pallavicini, who was a disciple of Vittorino of Feltre, see AFFO, Scritt. Parmiz, II , 242 *seq* ; MARINI, II , 181, 199

* "*Communis est opinio che'l rev. Monsig S. Sisto, quale questa matina fu portato al conclave, piu non debia tornare ad casa essendo aut creato pontifice aut posto in sepultura, adeo est senex et infirmis." Despatch of J A Ferrofinus of the 29th Aug , 1464. State Archives, Milan.

† *Letter from Jacopo de Aretio to Marchioness Barbara of Mantua, dated Rome, 1464, Sept 1 Gonzaga Archives, Mantua

‡ **Rev. patris Dominici episcopi Torcellani ad rev^mos dominos S. R E. cardinales oratio pro electione summi pontificis habita Romae in basilica S Petri. I am acquainted with four MS. copies of this Discourse, three of which are in the Vatican Library . (1) Cod. Vat , 3675 , (2) Cod. Vat , 4589, f 25-48 ; (3) Ottob , 1035, pp. 10-18b ; (4) Cod. CXXXIV., f. 105 *seq* , of the Library at Turin The last MS. states that the Discourse was pronounced on the iv. Cal. Sept MSS. N. 2 and 3, give viii Cal Sept =25th Aug , N. 1, v. Cal Sept.=28th Aug. As the customary Discourse de eligendo s. pontifice was pronounced before the Cardinals went into Conclave, and Cod Vat , 4589, expressly speaks of the Discourse as "habita in basilica S Petri," the last named date must be the correct one. On the 28th, the Cardinals heard the Mass of the Holy Ghost in St. Peter's , see

preacher took for his text the words of Jeremias, "To
what shall I equal thee, O virgin, daughter of Sion? For
great as a sea is thy destruction: who shall heal thee?"
and applied them to the state of Christendom. He recalled the fall of Constantinople, and the Christian losses,
in the East, which followed on that deplorable event.
Things had now, he said, reached such a point that tidings
of defeat were frequently, indeed almost daily, received;
and yet the Princes took no heed, and were, as had been
evident during the life-time of Pius II., deaf to the exhortations of the Supreme Head of Christendom After an
affecting picture of the dangers from without, Domenichi
turned to the contemplation of the ills which the Church
had to suffer from her own sons The clergy, he said, are
slandered, the goods of the Church plundered, ecclesiastical
jurisdiction impeded, and the power of the keys despised.
He frankly blamed the Popes for their compliance with
the unjust demands of Princes, and attributed the sad
condition of the times to the fact that those in authority
had sought their own interests, and not those of Jesus
Christ. Help, he maintained, could be looked for only
from a Chief Pastor who would give back to the Church
her former liberty, and would not fear the power of
Princes.* He pointed out that the relations between the
Pope and the Bishops had also been impaired. "Burdened
by you," exclaimed the Orator, addressing the Cardinals,
"the Bishops favour your enemies; oppressed by the
Princes, they turn, not to the Mother who appears to them
in the guise of a step-mother, but seek the favour of those
into whose power they have been allowed to fall" Finally,
Domenichi declared that the position of the Sacred College

*Report of J A Ferrofinus of the 29th August, 1464. State Archives,
Milan.

 * *Cod Vatic , 4589, f 38b, 39.

itself was not what it had been　"Where," he asked, "is the former splendour of your authority? where is the Majesty of your College?　Once, whatever was to be done, was first laid before your Senate, hardly anything was determined without your counsel."　Domenichi concluded by lamenting the complete change that had taken place, and pronouncing the existing state of things to be insupportable, inasmuch as the authority, dignity, and splendour of the Sacred College had well-nigh disappeared.*

These last words were hailed with delight by those Cardinals who sought as much as possible to limit the Papal authority.　On the first day of the Conclave this party framed an Election Capitulation, which all the Cardinals, except Scarampo, signed, and swore to observe †

The provisions of this document would necessarily have involved a transformation of the monarchical character of the Church's Constitution, and have reduced the Pope to the position of the mere President of the College of Cardinals.

The Capitulation began by binding the future Pope to prosecute the Turkish war, and to devote to this purpose

* *Cod. Vatic, cit f 40b, 42　There is a passage on this subject in GREGOROVIUS, VII , 206-207, 3rd ed

† Despatch of Arrivabene of Sept 1, 1464. (Gonzaga Archives, Mantua)　The Election Capitulation is in AMMANATI, Comment 350-51, and has often been published from his version, as in RAYNALDUS, ad an. 1464, N　55; CIACONIUS, II , 1071 ; QUIRINI, Vind , XXII-XXIX , DOLLINGER, Beitrage, III , 344.　HOFLER, Zur Kritik und Quellenkunde Karls V., 2nd Abth. (Wien, 1878), prints it, pp. 62-3, from a very incorrect MS. in the Court Library at Munich (Cod Lat , 151), as if it had not previously been published. Otto de Carretto promises soon to send the Duke of Milan a copy of the Election Capitulation, which, when he wrote, he had not himself seen. *Despatch, dated Rome, 1464, Sept. 11. Ambrosian Library, Milan, Cod Z.—219, Supp

all the revenue derived from the Alum quarries. He was, moreover, to reform the Roman Court, was not to remove it to any other Italian city without the consent of the majority of the Cardinals, nor to any place out of Italy without the consent of the whole body. A General Council was to be summoned within three years time. This Council was to reform Ecclesiastical affairs, and to summon the temporal Princes to defend Christendom against the Turks. It was further decided that the number of the Cardinals should never exceed four and twenty, and that one only should be of the Pope's kindred, no one was to be admitted into the Sacred College under the age of thirty, and also no one who did not possess the requisite amount of learning Creations of new Cardinals, and nominations to the greater benefices, were only to be made with the express consent of the Sacred College. The Pope was further to bind himself not to alienate any of the possessions of the Church, not to declare war, or enter into any alliance without the consent of the Cardinals ; to confer the more important fortresses in the Patrimony of St. Peter exclusively on Clerics, who, however, were not to be his kinsmen, no relation of his was to occupy the position of Commander-in-Chief of his troops. In State documents, the formula, "after consultation with our Brethren," was only to be used when the Cardinals had actually been summoned together in Council. Every month these resolutions were to be read to the Pope in Consistory, and twice in the year the Cardinals were to examine whether he had faithfully observed them ; should this not be the case they were, "with the charity due from sons towards their parents," to remind him three times of his promise What was to take place, in the event of these warnings being unheeded, is not stated. Schism was the only course open.

The arrangement of the Election Capitulation was followed by the Election, which, on this occasion, was very
rapidly concluded.   The first scrutiny took place on the
30th August.*   Scarampo had seven votes, d'Estouteville
nine, and Pietro Barbo eleven   The last-named Cardinal,
who, six years before, had almost obtained the tiara,† now
at once received three more votes by way of *accessit.*   His
election was accordingly secured.   The other Cardinals
also agreed, invested him with the Papal robes, and did
him homage.   Thus the high-born but needy Sienese Pope
was succeeded by a rich Venetian noble.   The populace
assembled in front of the Vatican received the news with
joy.   The Pope was then carried to St. Peter's, where the
throng was so great that it was most difficult to find a
passage through it.‡

* The principal authority for the completely new information given
above is **Despatch of Arrivabene of the 1st Sept, 1464   (Gonzaga
Archives, Mantua)   See, in the same Archives, the *Despatch of Jacopo
de Aretio to Lodovico Gonzaga of the 1st Sept, and Cardinal Gonzaga's
Letter of the 13th Sept, 1464.

† See our account, Vol II , p 322

‡ Various dates are given, not only for the beginning of the Conclave
but also for the actual Election of Paul II , and this even by con-
temporaries who ought to have been well informed   In a *Letter from
Albertino de Cigognara to Marchioness Barbara, dated Rome, 1464,
Sept 1, the Pope is said to have been elected on the 28th August.
(Gonzaga Archives)   PLATINA, 762, and the Istoria di Chiusi, 994,
name the 31st August, and are followed by CHEVALIER, 1740, and
KRAUS, 802, while L'ÉPINOIS, 435, mentions the 29th   The 30th August,
however, is established by the testimony of many chroniclers , see
Cronica di Bologna, 758 , Diario Nepesino, 141 ; NOTAR GIACOMO,
107 ; Chron Eugub , 1008 ; PH DE LIGNAMINE, 1310 ; *GHIRARDACCI,
Cron. di Bologna (see our Vol. III , p 354), and a number of other well-
informed contemporaries, such as Gaspar Veron in MARINI, II , 178 ; F.
HANKO, Polit. Corresp. Breslau's, IX , 94 ; *Arrivabene, *Jacopo de Aretio
(see preceding note*) , and Cardinal Gonzaga, in a Letter of the 30th
August to his father , also by the College of Cardinals itself in a *Letter

The unusual rapidity of Cardinal Barbo's Election was looked upon by many as a miracle, for an Election preceded by less than three scrutinies had not occurred within the memory of man; but a little consideration enables us to understand the motives for the haste of the Cardinals * The first of these was the anxious state of public affairs, together with fear of the King of Naples and of the Duke of Amalfi, the latter of whom had his troops encamped on the frontiers of the States of the Church,† moreover, Torquemada, Scarampo, and Barbo were very ailing, and Rodrigo Borgia had not yet recovered from his illness; he appeared in the Conclave with his head bound up ‡ The confinement and privations of the Conclave must necessarily have been doubly irksome to these invalids, and made them desirous to get through the Election without delay.

Cardinal Ammanati says that Barbo at first wished to take the name of Formosus; the Cardinals, however, objected, on the ground that it might seem to be an allusion to his good looks Barbo, who had been Cardinal Priest of St Mark's, then thought of selecting Mark, but this was the war-cry of the Venetians, and was therefore deemed unsuitable. Finally, he decided to be known as Paul II.§

to Lodovico Gonzaga, d. d. Romae die sexta Sept. A°, 1464, assumptionis dom nostri pape prefati die octava (Gonzaga Archives) To these may be added the statement in the *Acta Consist, *loc. cit*, of the Secret Archives of the Vatican.

* Besides CANENSIUS, 32, see the *Despatch of Jacopo de Aretio of Sept. 1, 1464: "Facta questa electione al mio parer miraculosa- mente, perho che tutti dicono non esser mai fatto meno che tre scruptinii." Gonzaga Archives

† **Despatch of J P. Arrivabene to Marchioness Barbara, dated Rome, 1464, Aug 27 Gonzaga Archives

‡ **Despatch of the same, 1st Sept, 1464

§ AMMANATI, Comment. 348 This historian, who certainly was

The new Pope was, as Ammanati in a confidential autograph letter informed the Duke of Milan, indebted for his elevation to the elder Cardinals, that is to say, to those who had been members of the Sacred College before the time of Pius II.; they were of opinion that the late Pope had shewn so little regard to the Cardinals, because his own experience as a member of the Sacred College had been very short. Some of the younger Cardinals, and amongst them Ammanati, joined the party of the elders.*

The Prelate so quickly elevated to the Supreme dignity of Christendom was at this time in the 48th year of his age.† His pious mother was sister to Eugenius IV., !

not prejudiced in favour of Paul II, writes : "Indiderat autem sibi Formosi pontificis nomen secutus credo religionem animi quandam qua historiam eius legens innocentiam adamarat." It is, however, not true that Paul II. wished to be called Formosus on account of his personal beauty, as PALACKY, IV., 2, 237, and others have stated. This writer charges Paul II, who would never allow a capital sentence to be carried out (see Platina in VAIRANI, I., 34) with cruelty (p 326), and also affirms that the Election Capitulation required the immediate summoning of a Council. Two names are spoken of in the *Despatch of Jacopo de Aretio to Marchioness Barbara, dated Rome, 1464, Sept. 1 (Gonzaga Archives), which is unfortunately mutilated   Otto de Carretto and the Archbishop of Milan, in their *Letter to Fr. Sforza, dated Rome, 1464, Aug. 30, only mention the name of Mark. State Archives, Milan.

* *Letter of Card Ammanati to Fr Sforza, written on the 1st Sept, 1464 (Ambrosian Library): see Appendix, N. 1. GREGOROVIUS' assertion, VII, 208, 3rd ed, that "he owed the tiara to the alliance of the Roman Court with Venice against the Turkish war," lacks proof.

† AMMANATI, 348, expressly says : "Annos 48 natus " REUMONT, III., 1, 153, GREGOROVIUS, VII, 207, 3rd ed. ; CHEVALIER, 1740, ZOPFFEL in Herzog, Real-Encykl, XI., 318, 2nd ed. , MUNTZ, II , 129; Rohrbacher-Knopfler and others must therefore be mistaken in giving 1418 as the year of his birth. CANENSIUS' statement (p 9) that Barbo was born on the 23rd February, 1417, agrees with that of Ammanati.

and the youth, originally destined for a mercantile career, had been very carefully brought up, and owed his education, as well as his ecclesiastical advancement, to that Pope * The teachers selected by Eugenius IV. for his nephew were men of ability,† yet the progress of the latter was but slow, he took no interest in Humanistic studies, History and Canon Law had more attraction for him Barbo's favourite pursuit at that time was the collection of coins, gems, and other antiquities ‡

As early as 1440, Barbo was, together with his rival Scarampo, raised to the purple, he also became Cardinal Deacon of Sᵗᵃ Maria Nuova (now Sᵗᵃ Francesca Romana), which Church he afterwards exchanged for S. Marco.§ Under Nicholas V and Calixtus III., he continued to occupy the same influential position as he had enjoyed

Regarding his family, which, of course, was in no way connected with the Domitii Aenobarbi, see LITTA, 146, where are given engravings of the coat of arms, of a ring, and of a Bust of Paul II, now in a Palace in Venice

* CANENSIUS, 9

† Barbo, when Pope, shewed his gratitude to them. See PLATINA, 763, CANENSIUS, 11, and a *Despatch from Otto de Carretto, dated Rome, Oct. 9, 1464   State Archives, Milan, Cart Gen.

‡ MUNTZ, II, 2, 3, 129. It may here be remarked that the Venetian nobles as a class were indifferent towards Humanism, see VOIGT, I, 416, 2nd ed

§ See our Vol I, 302   The nomination took place in Florence, and, on the 8th Sept, 1466, Paul II gratefully alluded to it in writing to the Florentines . "Insuper cum in minoribus agebamus, multum familiariter in ea urbe versati sumus et consuetudinem multorum habuimus ibique dignitatem cardinalatus accepimus, ut profecto eam patriam quasi nostram omni dilectione et paterna caritate complectamur." Cl X. Dist. II., N. 23, f 148b–149b   In a *Brief d. d Rom, 1468, Maii 16, Paul II. again declares his affection for Florence " ubi adolescentiam summa consolatione et benivolentia omnium bonorum civium egimus ac demum cardinalatus honorem suscepimus ;" ibid., f. 172   State Archives, Florence

during the pontificate of his uncle.* His relations with
Pius II. were not of so agreeable a character The
Cardinal of S. Marco† derived a princely income from
his numerous benefices, and made a most generous use
of it, sometimes for the benefit of less wealthy colleagues,
such as Cusa and Æneas Sylvius. A lover of splendour, like
all Venetians, he began in 1455 to build a great palace,
and in 1458 undertook the restoration of his titular Church
He was also a diligent collector of antiques and artistic
treasures, and in this respect, rivalled even the Medici ‡

The Cardinal of Venice, as Barbo was also styled, was
one of the most popular personages in the Court and City
of Rome His generosity, liberality, affability, and gentleness, soon won all hearts His devotion to his friends was
manifested on the occasion of the fall of the Borgia §
Any one who enjoyed his patronage was deemed fortunate.
He used to visit the sick in his neighbourhood with kindly

* See PLATINA, 764 , and B JUSTINIANUS in LUNIG, Orat. I, 8.
Barbo's appointment as generalis gubernator in prov Campanie et
Maritime, dat. 1456, prid Non Julii A° 2°, is in Regest 458, f 4b
Secret Archives of the Vatican

† His contemporaries generally called him by this title The
Cardinal in his *Letters used to sign himself

P tit s Marci presb. } episc Vicentin.
Car^hs Venetiar }

I found *Letters with this heading, but unimportant in their contents,
in the Gonzaga Archives, Mantua (to Lodovico Gonzaga, dat Rome,
1456, May 15 and Dec. 20), and in the State Archives, Milan (to Fr.
Sforza, d d ex urbe, 1454, March 11, 1455, Febr. 3. Autogr. pontif 1.)

‡ REUMONT, III , 1, 153 seq ; Lorenzo de' Medici, II , 131, 2nd ed.
Regarding the glorious choir-books, restored by Barbo, and now in
the Archives of the Papal Chapel, see HABERL, Bausteine zur Musik-
gesch , Fasciculus II

§ See our Vol II., p 477 The great "humanita" of Barbo is particularly praised by Jacopo de Aretio in a letter of the 1st Sept , 1464,
to Marchioness Barbara. Gonzaga Archives, Mantua

solicitude, and had a little pharmacy from which he dispensed medicines gratis The poor were loud in their praises of the open-handed and tender-hearted Prince of the Church, and strangers were delighted with the kindness of his welcome and his readiness to serve them. Any one who had matters of business at the Roman Court, might reckon on success if Barbo took an interest in him. Genial wit and good humour reigned at his table, and he used to say in jest that when he became Pope each Cardinal should have a beautiful villa, to which he might retire during the heat of summer.*

Cardinal Barbo added to his amiable qualities the charm of an imposing appearance ; he was tall, well-made, and his bearing was dignified, advantages which have always been greatly valued by the Italians. For half a century, says a chronicler, a handsomer man had not been seen in the Senate of the Church.† The weak points in his character were his jealousy, his vanity, and an overweening love of pomp, which betrayed his Venetian and mercantile origin.

According to the rude custom of the age the Romans used to plunder the abode of a new-made Pontiff, even Cardinals who had not been elected, frequently suffering on these occasions, Barbo and Scarampo had taken the precaution of placing military guards in their Palaces. An attack made on Scarampo's Palace, when a report of his election had been circulated, was repulsed ‡ After Barbo's

* VOIGT, Enea Silvio, III., 507, CHRISTOPHE, 110-119; BARBO'S "humanita, amore et benivolentia" towards his friends and servants are praised by Jacopo de Aretio in a second *Letter of the 1st Sept, 1464, addressed to the Marquess of Mantua. Gonzaga Archives.

† N. DELLA TUCCIA, 89, see 100, N 1; ÆN. SILVIUS, De viris illustr, 2 (Stuttgart, 1842), Gaspar Veron, in MARINI, II., 187, and SCHIVENOGI IA, 136

‡ *Jacopo de Aretio to Marchioness Barbara, dated Rome, 1464, Sept 1. Gonzaga Archives.

elevation became known, his Palace, which was full of treasures and works of art, was besieged by the rabble. Nothing but a haystack, however, fell into their hands. Some of the marauders then rushed to the Convent of Sta Maria Nuova, under the erroneous impression that property belonging to the newly-elected Pope was hidden there Defensive preparations had, however, been made, and the mob returned to the Palace. They seemed about to storm it, but were pacified by a present of 1300 ducats *

Extensive preparations for the Pope's Coronation were undertaken by three Cardinals chosen for the purpose † Even before this solemnity took place, he was delivered from the anxiety which had beset the first days of his reign in regard to the Duke of Amalfi. After the Election, the Castle of St Angelo and the fortresses of Tivoli, Spoleto, and Ostia, were still held by Sienese captains in the Duke's name ; the garrisons declared that they would not give up these strongholds until the sum of 30,000 ducats, which he said he had advanced to the Roman Church, had been repaid ‡ In order to guard against the recurrence of such a danger, the Pope entrusted St. Angelo, which was finally given up to him on the 14th September, to the learned Spaniard, Roderigo Sancio de Arevalo In compliance with the stipulations of the Election Capitulation, the Pope also arranged that for the future the governors of all the fortresses in the States of the Church should be Prelates §

* See the *Letter cited in the previous note Paul II was, however, unable to hinder the plunder of his chamber in the Conclave ; see *Arrivabene's Letter of the 1st Sept., 1464 Gonzaga Archives.

† See the two *Letters already cited, written by Jacopo de Aretio, 1st Sept, 1464 , and a *Despatch of this Ambassador, dated Rome, 1464, Sept 14

‡ *Despatch of W. Molitoris of 9th Sept , 1464.   Gonzaga Archives

§ *Report of J P. Arrivabene of the 16th Sept , 1464, *loc cit.*

The Pope's Coronation took place on the 16th September.* Cardinal Borgia, as the senior of the Cardinal Deacons, was entitled to perform the ceremony, but, as he was indisposed, Cardinal Fortegueiri acted in his stead † The ceremony took place on a tribune erected in front of St. Peter's. It was observed that Paul II did not, like other Popes, get a new tiara made for himself, but used the old one, which is said to have belonged to Pope St Sylvester

After his Coronation the Pope took possession of the Lateran It was long since the Romans had witnessed more splendid festivities. More than 23,000 florins were spent on this occasion, according to the accounts of the Apostolic Treasury.‡ The Pope rode from St Peter's to Sᵗᵃ Maria Nuova on a palfrey adorned with crimson and silver, which had been presented to him by Cardinal Gonzaga Ancient custom gave the Roman populace a claim to the horse ridden by the Pope to the Lateran, and, after the Coronation of Pius II., as well as on many other occasions, a riot had been the result. To avoid this,

According to the Diario Nepesino, 142, the Castle was not given over until the 16th Sept.

* Hitherto nothing has been known of Paul II's Coronation and the *Possesso*, save the date ; see CANCELLIERI, Possessi, 44-5. The description we give is founded on Arrivabene's Report, cited in preceding note, together with the *Despatches of Jacopo de Aretio and W Molitoris, dated, respectively, the 17th and 21st Sept, both of which are in the Gonzaga Archives, Mantua See also *Acta Consist, f 33b Secret Archives of the Vatican

† The statement of REUMONT (III, 1, 154) and HOFLER (Rod de Borgia, 24) that Card Borgia crowned the Pope is mistaken. Jacopo de Aretio, writing on the 17th Sept, expressly says . *" Et perche lo revᵐᵒ Monsig Vicecancelliere, a cui spectava porre la cor[ona] in testa a N Sʳᵉ come a piu antiquo diacono cardinale, non se sentiva bene perche an[cora non] è ben guarito, Monsig. de Thyano suppli e fece la incoronatione " Gonzaga Archives.

‡ MUNTZ, II , 124-6

Paul II. dismounted at the Convent of Sta Maria Nuova, leaving the palfrey there, and having himself carried in a litter the rest of the way. The function in the Lateran was followed by a banquet The Pope spent the night in the Palace of Sta Maria Maggiore, and on the following morning, after he had heard Mass, returned to the Vatican.*

Many Embassies soon arrived to pay homage to the new Pontiff. The first was from the King of Naples, which was admitted to an audience two days after the Coronation, when Paul II. reminded the Envoys of the benefits received by King Ferrante from the Apostolic See † The Neapolitan Embassy was followed by others from Lucca, Siena, Mantua, Milan, and Florence, this latter being remarkable for its magnificence. All these were received in public, but the Embassies from the States of the Church in Secret Consistories ; which furnished an opportunity for making complaints and asking for favours. Paul II., who, especially at the beginning of his reign, appeared to think a good deal of his own importance,‡ was not very ready to comply with these requests, and disputes with the Bolognese arose in consequence § Some of the speeches made by the

* *Acta Consist, *loc. cit.* Secret Archives of the Vatican.

† *Despatch of W Molitoris of 21st Sept., 1464. See Jacopo de Aretio's **Letter of the 29th Oct, 1464. Gonzaga Archives.

‡ See NOTAR GIACOMO, 107.

§ Besides Jacopo de Aietio's *Letter, cited in note †, see *Letter written by him on the 9th Oct, 1464, Polit Corresp. Breslau's, IX, 97, and a *Letter of W Molitoris, dated Rome, 1464, Oct. 28. (Gonzaga Archives) Regarding the complaints brought forward by the Ambassadors from Ascoli, see the *Letter of the Archbishop of Milan to Fr. Sforza, dated Rome, 1464, Dec 14 (Ambrosian Library, *loc. cit.*) The *Oratio of Giulia della Mirandola's Ambassador ad pontif summ. Paulum, II., 1464, is to be found in the Campori Library, Modena,

Ambassadors were masterpieces of Humanistic eloquence, filled with quotations from the ancient authors. That of the Jurist, Francesco Accolti, who was attached to the Milanese Embassy, was specially admired.* On the 2nd December the Ambassadors of the Emperor Frederick III. arrived ; they were commissioned to treat also of the affairs of Bohemia †

Some of the Articles of the Election Capitulation were so obnoxious that even a Pope less imbued with a sense

App Cod 169 (saec, 15) The *Instruction for the Florentine Embassy, dated 1464, Oct 6, is in the State Archives, Florence, X -I -53, f 125 GUIDICINI, Miscell., 16, speaks of the relations between Paul II. and Bologna See LA MANTIA, I, 316; CIPOLLA, 541

* A MS copy of Accolti's discourse is in the Chapter Library at Lucca ; it is printed in BALUZE-MANSI, Miscell, III, 166 seq. See VAHLEN, 415–16 , and MAZZUCHELLI, I, 1, 68 seq. Vahlen makes Accolti arrive in Rome at the end of 1464 This is incorrect. He delivered his discourse in the October of that year . *" Il nostro Missei Francesco d'Arezo ha facto il dovere cum grande comendatione dogni peisona che l ha udito" Otto de Carretto to Fr Sforza, dated Rome, 1464, Oct 22 (Ambrosian Library, loc. cit) The *Speeches of the Ambassadors of Naples, Lucca, Siena, Ferrara, Venice, and Florence are in Cod 537 of the University Library, Padua

† PALACKY, IV , 2, 328 seq. "To-day the Emperor's Ambassadors arrived," says Jacopo de Aretio in a *Despatch of the 2nd Dec , 1464 (Gonzaga Archives) The Archbishop of Milan, in a *Letter of the 14th Dec., 1464, Ambrosian Library, loc cit, mentions a night attack upon the Imperial Embassy, which greatly displeased the Pope (The war-cry of the rioters was "Austria ") In November, the Knights of St John, at Rhodes, sent an Embassy to offer their homage ; see BOSIO, 228. Regarding a French Embassy which, perhaps, was connected with this occasion, see JEAN DE REILHAC, I , 183. He is mistaken in asserting that the Acts of the French Nunciature in the Secret Archives only begin some years after the commencement of Paul II 's Pontificate.

of his own importance than Paul II. would have been driven to resist this fresh attempt to introduce an oligarchical character into the government of the States of the Church, and, as a necessary consequence, into that of the Church itself. As a Venetian, the Pope was only too well-acquainted with the defects of this system, and was firmly resolved not to allow himself to be reduced "to the helpless position of a Doge, controlled by Committees of the Nobles."* He was encouraged in this resolve, if we may believe Ammanati, by two Bishops who were aspiring to the purple †

The Pope, himself, prepared the Ambassadors for an alteration in the Election Capitulation To one of them he bitterly complained that its stipulations tied his hands so that he could hardly do anything without the consent of the Cardinals. " I perceive," wrote the Duke of Milan's Ambassador on the 21st September, "that His Holiness will endeavour, if he possibly can, to mitigate the Election Capitulation "‡

One of the reasons which, from Paul II's point of view, compelled him to take this course was, that, under existing circumstances, any limitation of the Monarchical power of the Pope in the States of the Church would necessarily interfere with the free exercise of that power in matters purely ecclesiastical.

* GREGOROVIUS, VII, 3rd ed ; CREIGHTON, III, 6

† Stefano Naidini, Archbishop of Milan, and Teodoro de Lelli, Bishop of Treviso AMMANATI, Comment. 351 ; see Epist, 114 Nardini's efforts to become a Cardinal are mentioned in a *Letter to Fr Sforza of the 6th Dec, 1464, which we shall cite, and in a *Despatch from Otto de Carretto, dated Rome, 1464, Sept. 21. Ambrosian Library, loc cit.

‡ **Letter of Otto de Carretto to Fr. Sforza, dated Rome, 1464, Sept 21 (Ambrosian Library, loc cit) See *Arrivabene's Letter of 1st Sept, 1464. Gonzaga Archives.

According to the Catholic Doctrine, the Constitution of
the Church is, by Divine appointment, monarchical ; any
attempt, therefore, to alter it was unlawful, and the oath to
observe the Election Capitulation invalid. It is, moreover,
an article of Faith that each Pope receives the plenitude of
power as directly from God as when it was first conferred
by the Divine Founder of the Church. Prescriptions of
limitation, therefore, whether contained in an Election
Capitulation or in the enactments of a predecessor, can
only affect the new Pope as counsels or directions, not as
binding obligations.*

According to trustworthy contemporaneous testimony,
the intentions of many of the Cardinals in framing the
Election Capitulation were far from disinterested   In
reality, their aim was, not the removal of prevailing abuses,
but an unlawful elevation and extension of the authority
of the Sacred College. At the head of this party was the
worldly-minded Cardinal d'Estouteville, who would have
had much to apprehend from a genuine reform † A very

* See our Vol. I, 179 *seq.*, 282. Papa subsequens non potest
ligari constitutione praedecessoris sui   See Declaratio Innoc III,
c 20, de electione. Bonif. VIII, c. fin. de rescriptis in VI —juncta
glossa ad "nostris successoribus indicamus" Eugen. IV, Constit,
"Quum ad nos" an. 1433, ap. RAYNALDUS. The Pope ought not
without reason to neglect such indications, accordingly, some Cano-
nists hold that he is bound *honestatis* not *necessitatis causa* to be
guided by them : *honestatis causa*, that is to say, non sine rationabili
causa ab illis constitutionibus recedere potest ; ita tamen ut penes
ipsum pontificem (et non penes alios) sit judicare de existentia et
rationabilitate causae recedendi a statutis praedecessorum. If this
holds good in the case of enactments of a predecessor, far less has
the College of Cardinals power to establish limitations See BENE-
DICTUS XIV, De synod dioec., XIII., c. 13, N 20 PHILLIPS, V, 900.

† **Report of Otto de Carretto of the 26th Sept, 1464. (Ambrosian
Library.) VAST (283) attributes the origin of the Election Capitulation
to Bessarion, but gives no decisive evidence to support this statement.

well-informed Ambassador, writing on the 11th September, 1464, says that the stipulation regarding the Council was not made in good faith by the Cardinals, but adopted by them as a means of keeping the Pope in fear, and inducing him to comply with their demands* Paul II, who thoroughly understood these designs, soon made it clear how much this resolution displeased him.

The Pope was required to publish a Bull, confirming the Election Capitulation, on the third day after his Coronation; but the Bull did not appear and, instead of framing it, Paul II. was occupying himself in devising means of recovering the free exercise of the Monarchical power.† He caused several legal authorities to draw up opinions on the question, whether the articles to which he had sworn in the Conclave were binding on him. These authorities answered in the negative,‡ and the Pope then

* **Report of Otto de Carretto of the 11th Sept, 1464 (Ambrosian Library) FRANIZ, Sixtus IV, 23, is therefore mistaken in considering the Election Capitulation as an expression of serious purposes of reform.

† **Report of Otto de Carretto of the 26th Sept., 1464 Ambrosian Library

‡ See ANDREAS DE BARBATIA, Consilia, I, c 1 (see SCHULTE, II, 306-311 ; and Jahrb. d preuss. Kunsts., II, 37), and the treatise dedicated to Paul II. in the MS. Theol Lat quart, 184, of the Royal Library, Berlin · *"Ad beatiss. Paulum P. M contra supercilium eorum, qui plenitudinem potestatis Christi vicario divinitus attributam ita cardinalibus communicatam censent, ut Romanum pontificem nec quae sunt fidei terminare nec cardinales creare nec ardua quaeque sine eorum consilio et consensu asserant posse disponere libellus" Lib, II., cap XIII, defends the principle "quod nulla pactio facta sede vacante etiam si voto vel jurejurando ante vel post electionem firmata fuerit Romani pontificis auctoritatem vel circa creationem cardinalium vel regimen universalis ecclesiae possit astringere" The copy in the Berlin Library, bound in red velvet and adorned with Miniatures, and with the arms of Paul II, is the one presented to the

laid a document, differing very essentially from the Election
Capitulation, before the Cardinals, and persuaded, or constrained, them to sign it. All yielded, with the exception of the aged Carvajal, who was immovable in his
opposition *

The excitement in the Sacred College reached such a
height that Cardinal Alain, brother of the Admiral of
France, told the Pope to his face that his whole life for
twenty-four years had been nothing but a plot to deceive
them † Cardinal Gonzaga, whose relations with Paul II.
were in general friendly, and who had received many
favours from him, wrote word to his father, on the 4th
September, that the Pope was very much taken up with

Pope The treatise of an unknown author in DOLLINGER, Beitiage,
III, 343–6, is directed against Barbatia Dollinger is certainly mistaken in ascribing this to the time of Paul II.; SOUCHON (Die
Papstwahlen, Braunschweig, 1888, p 16), believes Paris de Grassis,
Master of the Ceremonies to Julius II, to have been its author. The
*Disceptatio an capitula jurata a cardinalibus sede vacante obligent
futurum pontificem D Clementis Tosii monachi et abbatis Silvestrini
et s congreg indicis consultoris ad Alexand VII, P. O M, appeals
to Barbatia, Cod J–II–36 (not 31, as it is printed, Vol I, p' 283),
f 425–443, Chigi Library, Rome. The treatise of Domenico de'
Domenichi An papa ligetur vinculis sui juramenti, &c, also belongs
to this matter, Turin Library, Cod. 134, f. III seq. See PASINIUS,
II, 30

* AMMANATI, Comment, 351, see Epist, 113b seq Ammanati's
representation is not sine ira et studio, and it is much to be regretted
that the version of the other party is not before us. The following
passage from an Ambassador's Report is, however, interesting, and
gives us the date of the abolition of the Capitulation (which Ammanati
does not mention) *"Come per l'altra mia (unfortunately not to be
found), ho dicto ad V. Ill S. dopoy se sonno tolti in parte et in parte
modificati questi capituli del conclave, che e stato una saluberrima
cosa" Letter from Archbishop S Nardini of Milan to Fr Sforza,
dated Rome, 1464, Dec. 6. Ambrosian Library, loc cit.

† AMMANATI, Epist, 115.

his dignity, and was proceeding in a most dictatorial manner. "Possibly," he added, "the council which is to take place in three years may humble him"* Even in October, it was reported at the French Court that a schism had begun †

Happily this danger was averted, but the relations between the Pope and the Cardinals continued for a long time far from friendly No improvement took place, even though he granted pensions to the poorer members of the Sacred College, and to all Cardinals in general the privilege of wearing the red biretta, and a large mitre of silk damask, embroidered with pearls, such as had hitherto been worn only by the Popes ‡

Cardinal Ammanati, who now fell into complete disgrace, was the most bitter in his complaints of Paul II. "All," he wrote, "is suddenly changed, affability has given place to harshness, friendliness to a distant and repellent behaviour, a happy commencement to an evil progress" §

* Cardinal Gonzaga to his father, dated Rome, 4th Sept , 1464 , see Appendix, N. 3   Regarding the kindness shewn by Paul II. to Gonzaga, see Arrivabene's Despatch of the 1st Sept , cited *supra*, p 15, note §.

† **Despatch of the Milanese Ambassador in France to Fr Sforza, of the 5th Oct , 1644   National Library, Paris

‡ The following Reports from Ambassadors which I have found, have served to supplement the former account of this matter (in PHILLIPS, VI . 279 *seq*), and to settle its date · (*a*) *J P Arrivabene to Marchioness Barbara, d d. Roma, 1464, Sett. 13   "Vole el papa che da qui inanti li cardinali habbiano le lor mitre bianche raccamate de perle" (*b*) *Jacopo de Aretio, d d Roma, 1464, Sett 14   "Vole N Sre che differentia sia fra le mitre de questi S cardinali et altri prelati et per tanto ha ordinato quelle de li cardinali sieno de domaschino et cum alcune perle." (*c*) *Cardinal Gonzaga to his mother, 1464, Dec 28 ; see Appendix, N 7 , (*d*) B Suardo to Marchioness Barbara, dated Rome, 1465, Jan 7, regarding the Cardinals' red biretta   All these are in the Gonzaga Archives, Mantua

§ AMMANATI, Epist , 113b, f 93

The estrangement was aggravated by the Pope's inaccessibility, induced by his peculiar manner of life. Changes, which he considered necessary for the sake of his health, were made in the arrangements of the Court; day was turned into night, and night into day.* Audiences were only granted at night. A German Ambassador writes: "His Holiness gives no more audiences by day, and, as mine was the first, I sat all night in the Pope's chamber until 3 o'clock in the morning." † Other accounts say that even good friends of the Pope had to wait from fifteen to twenty days before they could see him.‡ To obtain an audience, the Envoy from Breslau writes, has now become quite an art. He had recently spent as much as five hours in the Palace, and had then been put off till the following evening. "It has now become three times as difficult to have an audience as it was under Papa Pio," says this same Ambassador, adding that he had often seen even Cardinals obliged to go away, after waiting two hours, without having obtained their object.§ It is not astonishing to find that business was greatly delayed and continued to accumulate

* Besides CANENSIUS, 48 and 69; PLATINA, 767-93, AMMANATI, Comm, 350, Cronica di Bologna, 788, and N DELLA TUCCIA, 100, n. 1, 269; see, in regard to the nocturnal habits of Paul II, *Otto de Carretto's Letter of the 9th Oct, 1464, and a *Despatch of Augustinus de Rubeis, dated Rome, 1465, June 18 Ambrosian Library, *loc. cit*

† VOIGT, Stimmen, 158. See BARROCIUS, in Anecdot Veneta, ed. Contarini, 266

‡ See the *Despatch of the Milanese Ambassador of the 9th Oct, 1464 (Ambrosian Library) *J P. Arrivabene, writing on the 3rd Oct, 1464, says that the old Secretaries of the Pope are much displeased, most of them not yet having had an audience Gonzaga Archives

§ Polit Corresp Breslau's, IX, 110; see 100-101. See *Jacopo de Aretio's Despatch of the 31st Jan, 1465. (Gonzaga Archives) See Appendix, N. 10 Augustinus de Rubeis in a *Despatch, dated Rome, 1466, Dec 6, complains of the difficulty of obtaining an audience State Archives, Milan

The progress of affairs was further hindered by the slowness, indecision, and distrustfulness which were natural to Pope Paul II.* In many cases he went so far as to instruct the Chancery not to accept authentic copies of documents, but to require the originals†

The Ambassadors also lamented the difficulties which the Pope made in granting dispensations and important favours.‡ All these causes tended seriously to diminish the incomes of the officials, and discontent soon prevailed amongst them.§ This dissatisfaction led to the expression

* All the Ambassadors repeatedly complain of these hindrances. See, amongst others, the Reports of Otto de Carretto of the 9th Oct., 1464 ; of Augustinus de Rubeis, dated Rome, 1465, May 12 (Ambrosian Library, *loc. cit*), of Jacobus Trottus, dated Rome, 1467, Dec. 1 (State Archives, Modena); of W. Molitoris, dated 1464, Dec. 20 (Gonzaga Archives, Mantua) *Augustinus de Rubeis on the 18th June, 1465, tells Fr. Sforza that the Pope is "longo, tardo et suspectuoso." (Ambrosian Library) In a *Letter of the 22nd Oct., 1464, Otto de Carretto complains of the inconstancy of Paul II The same reproach is made by Augustinus de Rubeis in a *Despatch, dated Rome, 1466, Nov 29 State Archives, Milan

† VOIGT, Stimmen, 158 In a *Letter to Fr. Sforza, dated Rome, 1465, Oct 24, Otto de Carretto speaks of the "suspicione mirabile che ha (Paul II) quasi dogniuno" (Ambrosian Library, *loc. cit*) Jacobus Trottus in a *Despatch, dated Rome, 1467, July 13, says the Pope is slow, wishes to do everything himself, and trusts no one State Archives, Modena

‡ See *Despatch of Jacopo de Aretio of the 31st Jan, 1465 (Gonzaga Archives), and the Milanese Ambassador's Reports, especially the *Letter of Augustinus de Rubeis, dated Rome, 1465, May 12 (Ambrosian Library) Jacobus Trottus writes on the 2nd Sept, 1467, to Ferrara . *"Voglio che V. Ex sapia che *il papa* (the words are in cipher) non serve ni fa conto de servire ni de far piacere a potentia alcuna de Italia indifferenter" He gives an example State Archives, Modena

§ Polit Corresp. Breslau's, IX , 103 , Cronica di Bologna, 788 ; *Letter of Augustinus de Rubeis, dated Rome, 1465, June 18 Ambrosian Library.

of unfavourable opinions regarding the Pope, which have not always been received with due caution

There is certainly no foundation for the charge of parsimony so often made and repeated against Paul II   Cardinal Ammanati, who originated it, must have had many opportunities of witnessing the Pope's generosity   He granted 100 florins a month to Cardinals whose income was under 4000 golden florins; he was most liberal in assisting Bishops who were poor or exiled from their Sees   Impoverished nobles, destitute widows and orphans, the weak and the sick, and especially the members of the dethroned families from the East, who had taken refuge in Rome, were all partakers of his princely beneficence *

Almost every page of the account books of his reign furnishes documentary proof of his magnificent benevolence Entry after entry records alms bestowed on needy widows and maidens, on nobles, on invalids or fugitives from the countries which had fallen under Turkish domination, from Hungary, and from the East.† He made admirable arrangements for the care of the poor of Rome, and by his orders the Apostolic Treasury, every month, "for the love of God" (amore Dei), distributed 100 florins to those in want ‡

* AMMANATI, Comment, 350; CANENSIUS, 66 seq , Gasp Veron. in MURATORI III , 2, 1019, 1047   See CHRISTOPHE, II , 177 seq.; MUNIZ, II , 12. See infra, Chap III.

† State Archives, Rome. *Div Pauli II , Vol I , 1464-1466. Payments, f 104· pro duobus pauperibus Ungaris fugitivis a captivit Turcor., 18th Sept. 1465, f 113 . pro honest mulieri Felicie pauperrime et egrote, Oct , 1465 , f 139: pro duobus pauperibus Indis, 5th Dec., 1465 ; f 163 . pro pauperibus Indis, Mart 1466 ; pro pauperibus personis, Mart 1466 ; f. 208 pro pauperibus Indis qui hodie projecerunt se ad pedes, S D N pape eundo ad S Petrum, 29 Junii, 1466, *Lib II , Bulletar Pauli II.; f 80   100 duc pro pauperibus puellis, 12th Dec , 1466, &c

‡ These 100 florins are entered every month , see loc cit , *Vol. 1 , f 175, 199; *Bullet, II., f. 1, 17b, 41, 75, &c ; *Bullet, III.

Fixed sums were also received at regular intervals by a
number of poor Convents and Churches in Rome , as, for
example, S Agostino, S. Marcello, Sᵗᵃ Maria sopra Minerva,
Sᵗᵃ Maria Ara Celi, Sᵗᵃ Maria del Popolo, Sᵗᵃ Sabina, S
Martino ai Monti, S Giuliano, S. Clemente, S. Onofrio,
SS. Giovanni e Paolo, Sᵗᵃ Susanna, S. Alessio, S. Francesco
in Trastevere, S. Cosimato and S Pietro in Vincoli ; but
his bounty was not confined within the limits of the
Eternal City , the Hospital of S Matteo at Florence looks
upon Paul II. as, after Leo XI., one of its chief bene-
factors.*

From the beginning of his Pontificate, Paul II devoted
much care to the concerns of the City of Rome,† a care
rendered all the more necessary on account of the series
of calamities, floods, tempests, and earthquakes by which
it had then been visited.‡ These were followed by pestilential epidemics, which raged in the autumn of 1464 to
such a degree that one of the Ambassadors says that all
the Cardinals' houses had become hospitals § This Plague

(March 1468 to March 1469), *Lib quart Bullet. (April 1469 to July
1470) ; *Lib. V Bullet (Aug 1470 to July 1471), regularly on the first
of each month See also in the Secret Archives of the Vatican.
*Introit. et Ex. 466 ; and CANENSIUS, 67.

* RICHA, VII, 92. Evidence regarding the support given to the
Roman Convents in the State Archives, Rome *Div Pauli II ,
Vol I., f. 175, 188, Bullet, II, 1467, Jan 11, April 2, &c

† Arch d Soc Rom, IV, 268 seq , MUNTZ, II, 8

‡ INFESSURA, 1141 , AMMANATI, Epist, 49 See also a *Letter from
Jacopo de Aretio to Marchioness Barbara, dated Rome, 1465, Jan 20,
in which he speaks of a violent storm which had visited Rome during
the previous night, and goes on to say " Caschò secondo intendo la
saetta in casa de Mons Vicecancelliere (R Borgia), ma non ha fatto
danno " (Gonzaga Archives, Mantua) An account of an earthquake
in the neighbourhood of Rome on the 15th Jan , 1466, is to be found in
Cod Δ, a XV, at Grottaferrata. See ROCCHI, Cod. 316.

§ *J. P Arrivabene to Marchioness Barbara, dated Rome, 1464,

lasted on into the colder months, and returned in the
following years.*   Paul II. rightly judged that the sanitary
condition of the city could only be improved by a greater
attention to cleanliness; he accordingly caused the streets
to be purified, and sewers and aqueducts to be repaired †

A great benefit was conferred on Rome by Paul II, in
the revision of its Statutes, which was completed in 1490,
and had for its object the better and more rapid administration of justice. The revised Statutes were printed in
the time of this Pope, probably in the year 1471. They
are divided into three books. Civil Law, Criminal Law,

Oct. 3: many died of the Plague; "Quasi in ugni casa de cardinali e
uno hospitale." See the *Despatches of Jacopo de Aretio of the
9th Oct. (Plague and fever prevail, many courtiers are dying) and
16th Oct, 1464. Gonzaga Archives

* See the *Despatch of Jacopo de Aretio, dated Rome, 1464, Nov.
13, and Arrivabene's of the 16th Nov (Scarampo fled from the Plague
to Albano) A *Letter from Cardinal Gonzaga to his parents, dated
Rome, 1465, Feb 12, speaks of the continuance of the Plague, which,
during May (see the *Despatch of Jacopo de Aretio of the 21st May,
Gonzaga Archives) and June (see AMMANATI, Epist., 69b, 70, 71, 72b),
continually claimed fresh victims. It again visited Rome in 1468 and
1469; see AMMANATI, loc. cit, 145-6, 175   The question whether
it was right to flee from an infectious malady was then discussed
It is dealt with in the *Epistola Dominici episcopi Torcellani quod
liceat pestem fugere ad rev, &c, Jacobum S R E. card S. Crisogoni Papien nunc in Cod B-51 of the Chapter Library, Padua
A little work against the Plague was also written in the time of
Paul II . it begins with the following words: "*Jesus* Questo è un
consiglio optimo contra lo morbo pestilentiale, Cioè anguinaglie;
Carbunculi antrace: apostemie . et altri mali cativi et apostemosi
Composto per Mastro Francesco da Siena doctore nell arte medicinale
In fine. Laus omnipotenti Deo Finis s l et a" A copy of this very
rare little volume, which I do not find mentioned by bibliographers,
was sold in 1888 in Florence by the Bookseller, Franchi (Cat. 66,
N. 1006).

† CANENSIUS, 99; MUNTZ, II, 96 seq.

and Administrative Law. This reform did not materially
alter the principles of the Statutes of 1363, and the
external and internal rights of the city remained
unaltered *

Paul II. took great pains to win the affection of the
Roman people. In 1466 he gave them the Golden Rose,
and the precious gift was borne in triumph through the
streets.† But they appreciated still more the variety and
splendour with which the popular festivals, and especially
the Carnival, were now celebrated.

Hitherto the Carnival had been confined to the Piazza
Navona, the Capitol, and Monte Testaccio. In 1466, Paul
II. allowed the races to be held in the principal street of
Rome, which from that time came to be called the Corso.
The triumphal Arch of Marcus Aurelius, near S. Lorenzo
in Lucina, was the starting point, and the Palace of S.
Marco was the goal‡ Games and prizes were multiplied.

* LA MANTIA, I, 173-8, GREGOROVIUS, VII, 213 *seq*, 3rd ed.
The ed princeps of the Statutes reformed by Paul II, is, however,
not so rare as CORVISIERI, Arch Rom, I, 484, supposes; LA
MANTIA, I., 176, enumerates eight copies See also Riv Europ,
XII., 456 (1879) Regarding the form of the oath taken by the Roman
Senate under Paul II, see Arch d Soc Rom, IV, 268 *seq*.

† "*La rosa heri foe data al populo de Roma e cussi tuto hoggi
cum gran triumpho l'hanno per la citade accompagnata; queste
cose molto gratificano questo populo, el quale se ne piglia piacere
assai" J. P. Arrivabene to Marchioness Barbara, d. d. Rom, 1466,
Mart 17. (Gonzaga Archives) To complete the account of the
Golden Rose, given in Vol I, 320 and 321, note 1, we may here
observe that the "Meisterwerke Schwabische Kunst aus der kunst-
historischen Abtheilung der Schwabisch Kreisausstellung" (Munchen,
1886), Plate XXI, N. 5, gives a very good Phototype (a quarter the
size of the original) of the Rose presented by Nicholas V, in 1454,
to Duke Albrecht of Bavaria, and now in the possession of the
Benedictine Priory of Andechs

‡ ADEMOI LO, Il Carnevale di Roma, 1 (Roma, 1883), is wrong

"In order," writes Canensius, in his Life of Paul II, "that none of the elements, out of which Roman society was formed, might be left out, he instituted races for Jews, for boys, for grown men, and, finally, for old people, each with its suitable prize. The palls which it was customary to bestow as prizes on the successful race-horses were, by his directions, made of more costly materials." The great banquets, in the Square of S Marco, to which the Pope invited the magistrates and the people, formed a new feature in the festivities. From a window of his Palace, Paul II. looked down upon these entertainments, and at their conclusion money was distributed amongst the people. To give greater variety to the scene, donkey and buffalo races were added * Amusement of a higher grade was provided in the magnificent processions "which represented the triumphs of the ancient Roman Emperors, a favourite theme of the imagination of the period" No doubt these "pictures of old Roman days were, in all archæological simplicity, clad in the brightest colours of the style of the early Renaissance, but that only gave more life and variety to the scene."† These worldly proceedings were even at the time condemned by some, but Paul II. paid no heed. He counted much on these popular amusements for counteracting the evil influences of the revolutionary

in giving the year 1467 as the date of Paul II's regulation ; see the testimony of the contemporary, Cron Rom, 31 ; see NATALI, Il Ghetto di Roma, 98 *seq* (Roma, 1887). Besides the materials collected by *CANCELLIERI, Il Carnevale di Roma (the MS is in the Archives of the Capitol), I found other unpublished Documents relating to the history of the Roman Carnival, these I intend to publish in a separate work, as to treat this subject adequately would lead me too far from the purpose of the present volume

* CANENSIUS, 50 *seq.* , BAYER, Aus Italien, 158

† BURCKHARDT, I, 230, II, 160, 163, 3rd ed ; BAYER, Aus Italien, 191.

demagogues.* How much the festivities were generally appreciated may be gathered from the detailed and enthusiastic descriptions given by different chroniclers.†

The care with which Paul II. promoted the better supply of provisions for the City, and his measures against the robbers who infested its neighbourhood, gave him a further title to the gratitude of the Romans‡ The Pope likewise endeavoured to check the vendettas and blood-feuds, to which so many lives were sacrificed in Rome and in all the Italian cities §

Paul II. hated violence, and made it his special object to ensure the preservation of peace in the City. His government displayed a happy combination of firmness and gentleness No malefactor escaped punishment, but the sentence of death was hardly ever carried out. The Pope met remonstrances against this great leniency by asking whether it were indeed a small thing to take the life of so wonderful a work of God as is man,—and a being upon whom Society has for many years expended so much pains. Criminals who had deserved death were generally sent to the galleys, but he gave express orders that they should not be treated with cruelty. The Pope was so tender-hearted and compassionate that he could not bear to see beasts led to the slaughter, and often bought them back from the butchers It is said that he had great difficulty in refusing any request, and was obliged to shun

* ROHRBACHER-KNOPFLER, 235

† Cron Rom , 31-4 ; see N DELLA TUCCIA, 90

‡ N DELLA TUCCIA, 89, N 2 , CANENSIUS, 35 , Gasp Veronen in MURATORI, III , 2, 1006 *seq.* In a poem of the year 1468, published by P. L GALLETTI, Verona, 1787, D Galletti celebrates the restoration of peace, both in Rome and outside it.

§ L'ÉPINOIS, 436 , BURCKHARDT, II , 207, 3rd ed From CHMEL, Materialien, II , 306, we learn that Paul II. insisted also on the Jews being justly treated

doubtful petitioners lest he should, against his own better judgment, grant what they asked *

Paul II. was a true friend and benefactor, not only to the Romans, but to all his other subjects He was zealous in the promotion of all useful public works In poor places such as Cesena† and Serra San Quirico,‡ he contributed towards the repair of the harbours and the city walls. He repeatedly took measures to protect the Bolognese territory from being flooded by the Reno.§ In the second year of his reign, he issued very salutary regulations for the better organisation of the Mint in the States of the Church. For a long time the rule prevailed that money should be coined nowhere but in Rome; afterwards, however, the privilege was extended to the cities of Fermo, Ancona, Ascoli, and Recanati, with the stipulation that the conditions previously laid down should be exactly observed.‖ In 1471 the Senate of the City of Rome was strictly enjoined to be diligent in proceeding against all who coined false money, or clipped the silver from the Papal mint.¶

* CANENSIUS, 39-40 ; CORTESIUS, LIIII.

† *Brief to Cesena of the 29th April, 1471, Lib brev 12, f. 139-139b. Secret Archives of the Vatican.

‡ *Document in the Archives of the place. The people of Ancona also received a grant "in reparationem murorum vestrorum"; see **Brief of Paul II, dated Rome, 1464, Sept 25 Archivi Comm. at Ancona

§ See the *Briefs of the 29th April, 1466, and 6th March, 1469 (Bologna Archives), see Appendix, N 13 and N 27

‖ For the subject in general, see PERUZZI, Ancona, 371 *seq*. The *Permission for Fermo and the other cities is dated Febr. 4 and July 4, and is to be found in the State Archives of Venice. Regarding the erection of a Mint in Rome, see AMMANATI, Ep, 61 ; and, in relation to the great number of coins of the reign of Paul II., see CINAGLI, 42 *seq* , and MUNTZ, II, 6

¶ Secret Archives of the Vatican, Lib brev 12, f 90 *Senatori urbis, dat. Romae, 1471, Febr. 1 ; see *ibid.,* fol 180 · *Brief for

A very wholesome Decree of this Pontiff forbade all Legates, Governors, and Judges to receive presents, and their conduct in this matter was closely watched * In grateful recognition of his excellent government the inhabitants of Perugia determined, in the year 1466, to erect a bronze statue of the Pope in their city †

Joh Bapt de Sabellis prov Marchie gubernatori, dat Romae, 1471, Febr 7 Similar *Orders concerning the exact observance of the ordinances for the coinage were sent on the 25th July, 1471, to all Rectors and Legates in the States of the Church

* See Appendix, N. 34 Bull to the Governor of Spoleto of the 5th April, 1471. Secret Archives of the Vatican

† PELLINI, 690 , and BONAZZI, 682. A *Brief from Paul II , dated 15th Dec , 1466, thanking the people of Perugia for their proposal to erect the statue, is preserved in the Municipal Archives of the city.

CHAPTER II.

PAUL II. AND THE RENAISSANCE —THE CONSPIRACY OF 1468, AND THE ABOLITION OF THE ROMAN ACADEMY —PLATINA AND POMPONIUS LAETUS —THE ART OF PRINTING IN ROME — THE POPE'S COLLECTION OF WORKS OF ART IN THE PALACE OF S. MARCO, AND HIS CARE FOR ANCIENT MONUMENTS.

THE great intellectual movement of the Renaissance was at the time of Paul II, still expanding and developing Through each one of its phases the two currents of heathen and Christian tendency are always clearly discernible, but the attentive observer cannot fail to recognise a considerable difference between its condition under Nicholas V and under Paul II

In the time of Nicholas V. the genuine and noble Renaissance, which had grown up on Christian principles, and, while embracing classical studies with enthusiasm, had made them subordinate and subservient to Christian aims and ideas, still thoroughly held its own against the other tendency. Subsequently, a change took place, and the school which inclined to substitute the heathen ideal of beauty for the central sun of Christianity, became predominant. In the second generation of Humanists that one-sided devotion to classical antiquity, which led to a completely heathen view of life, gained considerably in extent and importance.

Opposition on the part of the highest ecclesiastical authority was inevitable Even before the accession of Paul II. the Church and the heathen Renaissance would already have come into collision, had it not been so extremely difficult to lay hold of this tendency by any external measures. A formal heresy might be condemned, but it was much harder to discern the many byways into which this new, and, in itself, lawful and salutary form of culture had strayed, and any interference with its course would almost necessarily have destroyed not only that which was evil, but also much that was excellent. Moreover, the partisans of the heathen Renaissance carefully avoided any appearance of conflict between their learning and theology, and altogether contrived to assume such an innocent air of dilettanteism that it would have seemed ridiculous to attempt to deal seriously with them.

If, however, a case arose which did not admit of being excused as mere harmless classicism, the Humanists at once made the strongest professions of submission to the dogmas of the Church, and either altered or abandoned the theories which had been called in question. Thus, by their very frivolity and utter want of principle, the Literati were able to avoid any serious conflict with authority.*

But however complaisant the Literati might be in matters of this kind, it was quite another affair wherever their material interests were concerned. Any one who failed to treat them in this respect with the greatest indulgence and consideration must be prepared for the most violent attacks. Neither age nor rank were any protection against the envenomed tongues and pens of the disciples of Cicero. Lies and slanders pursued Calixtus III and Pius II, even to their graves. And the same fate in a yet greater degree befell Paul II.

A measure passed in the very beginning of his Pontificate gave occasion to a calumny which has not even yet completely died out, and which represents him as a

* See our Vol I, pp 21 and 38.

barbarous enemy of classical studies and of all intellectual
activity, in fact a "hater of learning."*

The measure in question affected the College of the
Abbreviators of the Chancery   In November, 1463, Pius II.
had made a Decree that this body should be composed
of seventy members, of whom only twelve were to be
appointed by the Vice-Chancellor.   The work and the
pay were to be distributed only amongst these seventy,
and not directly by the Vice-Chancellor   In May, 1464,
Pius II. reorganised the College, the former officials
were suppressed, and a number of Sienese, chosen from
the Humanist party, were appointed, some by favour and
others by purchase †   Paul II., who had always kept up
friendly relations with the Cardinal Vice-Chancellor, re-
instated him in his former powers, and reversed the
arrangements made by his predecessor.‡   Thus the

* GEIGER, 149. Similar unjust judgments on the part of other
modern historians have been collected by L'ÉPINOIS, Paul II , 278
seq.

† CIAMPINI, 25 seq ; VOIGT, Enea Silvio, III , 553 ; VAHLEN, 411
See in Appendix, N. 5, the *Despatch of Jacopo de Aretio of the
9th Oct , 1464   (Gonzaga Archives)   Regarding the Abbreviators,
see PHILLIPS, IV., 394 seq. , OTTENTHAL, Bullenregister, 49 seq. (Innsbruck, 1885) ; BRESSLAU, Urkundenlehre, I , 235 (1889)

‡ The Decree of Paul II , dated 1464, Dec. 3, is in CIAMPINI, 31.
It may be questioned whether the date of "Dec. 3" is correct, for
the **Letters of J. P. Arrivabene and Jacopo de Aretio of the 15th
and 16th October, 1464 (Gonzaga Archives), speak of the change
as having already taken place.   The time mentioned by PLATINA,
766, (statim ubi magistratum iniit), accords with October rather
than December   To this may be added the testimony of the
*Despatch of Jacopo de Aretio of the 9th Oct , 1464 (Gonzaga
Archives), which we print in Appendix, N 5.   It is much to be
regretted that we have not the key to the *Cipher Letters of Otto
de Carretto of the 15th and 21st, 1464, in the State Archives at
Milan, Cart Gen   GREGOROVIUS, VII , 210, 3rd ed ; REUMONT,

Abbreviators, who had enjoyed the favour of Pius II, lost both their places and their means of living This was undoubtedly a hardship to those who had bought their positions, although an order was given that the purchase money should be refunded.*

The indignation of those affected by this change was extreme. The secretaries, poets, and Humanists at the Roman Court really considered themselves the most important persons in the world ; they seriously believed that they " conferred on the Papal Court as much honour as they received from it," and were firmly persuaded that " men of their stamp were absolutely necessary to the Pope, and that he must seek them out from all parts of the world, and attach them to himself by the promise of rich rewards."†

The distress of these self-important men was equal to their astonishment They resolved, in the first instance, to have recourse to friendly representations ; and even the lowest members of the Papal Court were importuned for assistance to obtain them an audience For twenty consecutive nights they besieged the entrance to the Palace without gaining access to the presence of Paul II.

One of their number, Bartolomeo Sacchi da Piadena (a small place between Cremona and Mantua), known as an author by the name of Platina, the Latin form of Piadena, then resolved on a desperate measure.‡ He

III, 1, 155, ZOPFFEL, in HERZOG, Real-Enc, XI, 318, 2nd ed ; ROHRBACHER-KNOPFLER, 234 ; L'ÉPINOIS, 435, &c., are undoubtedly wrong in placing this event in the year 1466. This error may have arisen from the fact that Raynaldus relates the matter under that year (N. 21)

* See in Appendix, N. 5, the record of this order

† PLATINA, 766 , BURCKHARDT, I , 273, 3rd ed

‡ See in CHEVALIER, 1850, a notice of the literature regarding Platina , the important work of Vairani is here omitted. See also

wrote a pamphlet in the form of a letter, and, by his own
confession, addressed the Pope in the following terms .—
" If it is permissible for you to despoil us, without a hearing, of that which we had justly and fairly purchased, it
must be allowable for us to complain of so undeserved an
injury. Since we find ourselves contemptuously repulsed
by you, we will address ourselves to the Kings and Princes,
and urge them to assemble a Council, before which you
will be constrained to justify yourself for having robbed
us of our lawful possession" The letter concluded with
the subscription —" Servants of Your Holiness, if the new
regulations are cancelled "*

Platina gave this letter sealed to the Bishop of Treviso,
the Pope's most confidential Counsellor, remarking that it
was written by the Humanist, Ognibene da Lonigo †

Hitherto Paul II. had kept silence, now he acted.
Platina was summoned to the Papal Palace, where he
appeared with a defiant air, and, when the Bishop of
Treviso called him to account for his conduct, answered
very insolently. He was committed to St Angelo, where,
notwithstanding the intercession of Cardinal Gonzaga, he had
that same evening to undergo an examination by torture,
" I am very anxious on his account," wrote one of the
Ambassadors, then in Rome, on the 15th of October, " for
the Pope has spoken very violently about him to many,
and no one ventures to take the part of a man guilty of so

SCHMARSOW, 25 *seq*, 338 *seq*. The account given by BISSOLATI,
15 *seq*, is very unsatisfactory

* PLATINA, 767, and **Arrivabene's Despatch of the 16th Oct,
1464 (Gonzaga Archives) According to Platina, it was on this
occasion that Paul II. said "Omnia iura in scrinio pectoris nostri
collocata esse." The character of the reporter makes it very uncertain whether these words were ever really uttered

† **J P Arrivabene's Letter of the 15th Oct, 1464. Gonzaga
Archives, Mantua.

great a crime."* On the following day another writer mentions that Paul II. had talked of having him beheaded. "As Platina is an excellent author," he adds, "every one laments this mischance, more particularly Cardinal Gonzaga, in whose service he was at one time; but he is unable to help him in this matter. It is true, however, that when the Pope spoke to the Cardinal, he excused Platina as a madman. This deed of folly, indeed, proves him to be such "†

In the cold solitude of St. Angelo, Platina had full time for reflection. When, after four months of confinement, Cardinal Gonzaga's persevering intercession procured his release, he could hardly stand   He was obliged to promise that he would not leave Rome ‡ The Papal enactment was never repealed, and the ejected Literati, and more especially, their ill-starred leader continued to meditate vengeance

The meeting of these malcontents, and of the heathen-minded Humanists, took place in the house of a scholar well known throughout Rome for his intellectual gifts and for his eccentricity.   Julius Pomponius Laetus § was an ille-

---

* See the **Letter cited in preceding note.

† **Letter of Jacopo de Aretio, of the 16th Oct, 1464. Gonzaga Archives

‡ PLATINA, 768, GREGOROVIUS, VII., 211, 3rd ed, wrongly refers to Card. Gonzaga the words "admonet ne ab urbe, &c."

§ Regarding P Laetus and his studies, see AP. ZENO, Diss Voss, II., 232 seq., TIRABOSCHI, VI, 1, 92 seq, 185 seq.; A ZAVARRONI, Bibl Calabra, 59 seq (Neapoli, 1753), TAFURI, Scritt Nap, II, 2, 364 seq., TOPPI, Bibl Nap., 213 seq, NAEKE, De Julio Pomponio Sabino, Virgilii interprete (Bonn., 1824), VILLARI, I, 128, NOLHAC, in Mél. d'Arch et d'Hist, VI, 139 seq. (1886); DE ROSSI, Inscript, II, 401 seq, and in Studi e Doc, III, 49 seq, VII, 129 seq, also Arch d Soc Rom, X, 635 seq., 696 seq   A critical Biography of P Laetus, drawn from original sources, would be a great boon   I have been dis-

gitimate scion of the princely house of Sanseverino, had
come to Rome at an early age from his home in Calabria,
and had become Valla's disciple, and afterwards succeeded
him as Professor in the University. " Of all the worshippers
of antiquity, whose exclusive ideal was ancient Rome
and the oldest words of the Latin tongue," he was the most
extreme *   No scholar, perhaps, ever lived so completely in
the heathenism of the past ; " the present was to him a mere
phantom , the world of antiquity was the reality in which
he lived and moved and had his being "†

Pomponius Laetus lived in antique style, in haughty
poverty, like a second Cato.   In the cultivation of his vine-
yard he followed the rules of Varro and Columella   He
would often come down, with buskined feet, before day-
break to the University, where the hall could hardly contain
the crowd of his eager scholars.   The vivacious little man
might frequently be seen wandering alone through the
ruins of ancient Rome, suddenly arrested, as if in a rapture,
before some heap of stones, or even bursting into tears.
He despised the Christian religion, and passionately
inveighed against its adherents.   As a deist, Pomponius
believed in a Creator, but, as one of his most devoted
disciples tells us, as an antiquarian he revered the " Genius
of the City of Rome," or what would, in modern language,
be called " the Spirit of Antiquity."‡

appointed with the Memorie di P. Leto in the Cod G , 285, Inf, of the
Ambrosian Library, cited by DE ROSSI, Roma Sott , I., 7 , they contain
nothing new.

    * VOIGT, II., 239, 2nd ed.

    † HORSCHELMANN, 150-51 , see SCHMARSOW, 26

    ‡ "Fuit ab initio contemptor religionis, sed ingravescente aetate
coepit res ipsa, ut mihi dicitur, curae esse," says Sabellicus   See
P CORTESIUS, De Cardinalatu, LXXXVII ; CREIGHTON, III , 42 ;
GREGOROVIUS, VII , 566 *seq* , 3rd ed , GEIGER, 158   "Even from a
by no means rigorous point of view, P Laetus can hardly be any

His house on the Quirinal was filled with fragments of ancient Architecture and sculpture, inscriptions and coins.* Here, in an atmosphere charged with the spirit of heathen Rome, he assembled his disciples and friends   Disputations were held on ancient authors, and philosophical questions, discourses and poems were read, Comedies of Plautus and Terence were sometimes performed, and an infatuated admiration for the old Republic was cherished

Such was the origin of a "literary sodality," called the Roman Academy, whose object was the cultivation of pure Latinity, and of the ancient national life of Rome   "Pomponius, the founder of the Society, went so far as to refuse to learn Greek, lest he should injure the perfection of his Latin pronunciation"†

Around Pomponius, the representative of pagan Humanism, soon gathered a number of young freethinkers, semi-heathen in their views and morals, who sought to make up for their lost faith by a hollow worship of antiquity.

The members of the Academy looked upon themselves as a Confraternity , they laid aside their ordinary names, and adopted ancient ones instead.   The original name of Pomponius, who was venerated by all as their leader and teacher, is not even known.   Bartolomeo Platina and Filippo Buonaccorsi, who was called Callimachus, are the most noted of the other members   We also hear of Marcantonio Coccio of the Sabine country, called Sabellicus ; Marcus Romanus, or Asclepiades ; Marinus Venetus,

longer considered a Christian," according to GEBHARDT, Adrian of Corneto, 79 ; JANITSCHEK, 19, is of the same opinion

* "Leto's chief merit, in the judgment of posterity, is the initiation of a practical interest in antiquity," says REUMONT, III , 1, 341 , VILLARI, I , 129, expresses a similar opinion

† HORSCHELMANN, 151

or Glaucus ; a certain Petrus or Petrejus ; Marsus Demetrius, Augustinus Campanus, &c *

It may be admitted that this use of heathen names was a mere fancy, for which a parallel may be found in the increasing preference for such names, and even those which were of evil repute, in baptism. But other practices of the Academicians cannot be thus explained   The fantastic "enthusiasm of the adherents of the old Calabrian heathen" found vent in religious practices which seemed like a parody of Christian worship   The initiated constituted their learned Society into "a formal Antiquarian College of Priests of the ancient rite, presided over by a pontifex maximus, in the person of Pomponius Laetus"   The sentiments and the conduct of these "pantheistic votaries of Antiquity" were certainly more heathen than Christian.† Raphael Volaterranus, in his Roman Commentaries, dedicated to Julius II., plainly declared that the meetings of these men, their antique festivities in honour of the birthday of the City of Rome and of Romulus, were "the first step towards doing away with the Faith"‡

There was certainly some ground for the charges brought against the Academicians of contempt for the Christian religion, its servants and its precepts, of the worship of

* PAPENCORDT, 513, CORSIGNANI, II, 494, and NOLHAC in Mél. d'Arch, VI, 140 *seq*

† See SCHMARSOW, 26 ; REUMONT, III, 1, 342, CANTÙ, I, 187 GREGOROVIUS, VII, 568, 3rd ed, writes. "Among the Academicians there was scarcely a trace of Christianity . .   They despised the dogmas and the hierarchical constitution of the Church, for they were of the School of Valla and Poggio." In another passage he speaks of the Academy "as a classical Freemasons' lodge"   Regarding Platina's immorality, see *infra*. Sabellicus died in 1506, leaving an illegitimate son , see CORSIGNANI, II, 494-5

‡ Commentarii, XXI, f 246 ; see GEBHARDT, Adrian of Corneto, 79.

heathen divinities and the practice of the most repulsive vices of ancient times Pomponius Laetus was the disciple of Valla, and was certainly an adherent and dis- seminator of the destructive doctrines of his master. A heathen idea of the State, hostility to the clergy, and the dream of substituting for the existing government of Rome a Republic of the ancient type, prevailed in this circle, together with Epicurean and materialistic views of life " Experience had already sufficiently shewn that the enthusiastic veneration of the old Roman commonwealth was not unlikely to have practical consequences "*

This heathen and republican secret society seemed all the more dangerous in the increasingly excited state of the Roman populace. Many of the youths of the city were ready for any sort of mischief, and numerous exiles lurked on the Neapolitan frontiers. In the June of 1465, when Paul II went to war with Count Everso of Anguillara, there was a decided movement in favour of the tyrant.† A year later, many adherents of the Fraticelli were dis- covered ; their trial revealed the opposition of their rites and doctrines to those of the Church Further inquiry shewed that the partisans of this sect were at work not only in the March of Ancona, but also in the Roman Campagna and in Rome itself There is no proof of any connection between these heretics and the Roman Academy ‡ It is, however, certain that various fanatical demagogues, and some of the angry Abbreviators, held

* ROHRBACHER-KNOPFLER, 321 ; VOIGT, II , 239, 2nd ed , also thinks it very probable that P Laetus and his disciples may have had their heads full of heathen and republican aspirations Regarding Valla's doctrine, see our Vol I , p 12 *seq*.

† CANENSIUS, 56-9 , see also AMMANATI, Epist , 54b.

‡ It is even improbable that such existed Platina only condemns the excessive pomp of the Church "ecclesiae pompam " Regarding the Fraticelli, see *infra*

intimate relations with the Academicians, and that in their assemblies strong language against the Pope was freely indulged in. Thus " all the hostile elements of Heathenism, Republicanism and Heresy seemed to have their centre in the Academy "*

In the last days of February, 1468,† the inhabitants of Rome suddenly learned that the police had discovered a conspiracy against the Pope, and had made numerous arrests, chiefly among the Literati and members of the Roman Academy ‡

Disquieting reports of various kinds had, for some time, been prevalent in the city, and predictions of the Pope's speedy death had been circulated § Paul II. had attached

---

* GREGOROVIUS, VII, 570, 3rd ed ; CREIGHTON, III, 44; SCHMARSOW, 27. It need not surprise us, REUMONT observes (III, I, 345 and 509), that the Academy was looked upon with suspicion, when we see how, subsequently, in the 16th century, the Academy sided with the party of opposition in politics. In that of Florence, for example, a jargon, known only to the initiated, was framed for party purposes. See also REUMONT, Gesch Toskana's, I, 258 *seq* (Gotha, 1876).

† Not 1467, as CIAMPI, I, 27, and ZOPFFEL in Herzog, Real-Enc., XI, 318, 2nd ed, state, nor in 1469, as REUMONT, III, I, 344; MAR-CELLINO, III, 78, L'ÉPINOIS, Paul II, 27, CHRISTOPHE, 192; ROHRBACHER-KNOPFLER, 320; SCHMARSOW, 27, and others have it

‡ The chief authorities for the following details are the Despatches of the Milanese Ambassadors. Hitherto none was known but that of J. Blanchus of 28th Febr, 1468, which MOTTA published in the Arch. della Soc Rom., VII, 555-9 I succeeded in finding two other *Reports of J Blanchus of 28th and 29th Febr, as well as Aug. de Rubeis' Despatches of the 28th Febr and 4th March, in the State Archives, Milan See Appendix, N 19-22

§ A *Prognostic of Gistoldus de Melodia, for the year 1469, speaks of "mundi evacuacio, cleri decisio, christianitatis deposicio, &c" Cod 4764, f 193b, of the Court Library, Vienna A long *Prognostic for 1470, by a Servite, Paulus Venetus, is preserved in the State Archives, Milan, Astrologia

no importance to these rumours, but, after receiving a
warning letter from a temporal Prince, he looked on the
matter in a more serious light   His anxiety increased,
and his determination to act was confirmed, when some of
the Cardinals also made communications of an alarming
character   On the same night an order was issued for
the arrest of the ringleaders of the Conspiracy. Four
members of the Roman Academy, viz., Callimachus,
Glaucus, Petrejus, and Platina, had been named to the
Pope as the chiefs. The first three, having received intimation of the danger which threatened them, succeeded
in making their escape. Callimachus, himself, in a letter
subsequently written for his own justification, declares that
he had at first remained hidden in Rome, and then fled
secretly to Apulia.*

Others who had been connected with the Academicians
were, together with Platina, incarcerated in St Angelo,
and afterwards examined by torture   "Every night some
one is arrested," wrote the Milanese Ambassador, Johannes
Blanchus, on the 28th February, "and every day the
matter is better understood, it is not, as Cardinal
Ammanati supposed, a dream, but a reality. The plan
would have succeeded if God had not protected the
Pope "†

It is most interesting to observe the manner in which
Paul II. himself took the whole affair   Hitherto, we have
had little save the somewhat scanty account of his
biographer, Canensius, to guide us. He informs us that
the Pope had taken measures to make an example
of an infamous band of young Romans of corrupt

* ZEISSBERG, 352   Pomponius Laetus was in Venice at the time
when the conspiracy was discovered

+ Arch. della Soc Rom , VII. 557   PLATINA, 781, says that about
twenty persons in all were imprisoned

morals and insolent behaviour. They had maintained
that the Christian religion was a fraud, trumped up by
a few Saints, without any foundation in facts. Hence, it
was allowable to copy the Cynics, and give themselves up
to the gratification of their passions. "These persons,"
Canensius goes on to say, "despise our religion so much
that they consider it disgraceful to be called by the name
of a Saint, and take pains to substitute heathen names for
those conferred on them in baptism   The leader of this
Sect, whom I will not here name, was a well-known teacher
of Grammar in Rome, who, in the first instance, changed
his own name, and then those of his friends and disciples in
this manner. Some abandoned men associated themselves
with him : as, for example, the Roman, Marcus, who is
called Asclepiades ; the Venetian, Marinus, who is called
Glaucus , a certain Petrus, who has styled himself Petrejus ;
and Damian, a Tuscan, who is known as Callimachus.
These had bound themselves to murder the Pope."*

This account enables us to look at the affair from the
point of view of the Pope's position as " Guardian of Faith
and Morals," and recently discovered Reports of the
Milanese Ambassadors serve yet more clearly to eluci-
date its significance in this respect   Their independent
character, and the direct nature of their testimony, entitle
them to be considered as documents of the greatest importance.†

It was not easy for the Ambassadors of the League,

---

* CANENSIUS, 78–9 VOIGT, II , 240 *seq* , 2nd ed , observes that
this account is all the more unprejudiced, inasmuch as it is written
without a suspicion of the deeper significance of these events.

† The Milanese Ambassadors were by no means prejudiced against
Platina, and PLATINA, himself, says (789) that the Venetian and
Milanese Ambassadors afterwards made interest on his behalf with
Paul II.

then in Rome, to obtain really authentic information regarding the events which had just taken place there, for the most varied and fantastic accounts were circulated.*

Many different statements were made as to the day fixed upon for carrying the plot into effect. Some said that Paul II. was to have been murdered on Ash-Wednesday, at the Papal Mass, others that the crime was to have been perpetrated on Carnival Sunday, when all the people, and even the Papal Guards, would have gone to Monte Testaccio for the accustomed festivities. Others again declared Palm Sunday to be the day selected. It was further reported that the conspirators had, with a view to the accomplishment of their purpose, associated with themselves Luca de Tocio, a banished Roman, belonging to the party of the Orsini, who was a member of the Council at the Court of Ferrante I at Naples. This man was believed to be in league with other banished persons. Four or five hundred of them were to enter the city secretly, and to hide themselves in the ruins of the houses which had been pulled down in order to enlarge the Papal Palace. On the other side, forty or fifty partisans were to join the conspirators, and begin an attack on the attendants of the Cardinals and Prelates, who would be waiting in the Square in front of the Palace. By this means the Pope's small Guard would be occupied, and the conflict was to serve as a signal to the hidden outlaws, who would then make their way into the Church and murder the Pope and those about him. General pillage was to ensue, and Luca de Tocio was to establish a new Constitution.†

* The following description is from the *Reports of A de Rubeis and Joh Blanchus of the 28th and 29th Febr, 1468, given in Appendix, *loc cit.* State Archives, Milan

† The resemblance between this plot and that of Porcaro is obvious ; see our Vol II , p 224 *seq*

Even more alarming than the plot itself was the reported extent of its ramifications.   The King of Naples was accused of taking part in it, and some were of opinion that the King of France was also engaged, while others declared Sigismondo Malatesta to be one of the conspirators *

These varied accounts led the Ambassadors of the League to seek from the Pope himself more accurate information, and, at the same time, to express their sympathy and offer assistance on behalf of their several masters   An account of the Audience was drawn up by the Milanese Ambassadors personally, and in duplicate †   This document makes it perfectly evident that, from the very first, the Pope clearly distinguished between the Anti-Christian and immoral life of many Academicians, or their " heresy," as the Ambassadors shortly style it, and the Conspiracy against his person ‡

On the first of these points Paul II. made some very important statements, representing the Academicians as complete heathens and Materialists   They deny, he said, the existence of God, they declare that there is no other world than this, that the soul dies with the body, and that, accordingly, man may give himself up to the indulgence of his passions without any regard to the law of God, all that is

* J BLANCHUS in the Arch della Soc Rom, VII., 559.

† See Appendix, N 20 and 21 (State Archives, Milan)   The Perugians, according to PELLINI, 695, also sent an Ambassador to Rome to offer Paul II assistance against the conspirators, and to invite him to come to Perugia   This Ambassador must, no doubt, have written home, but I have not been able to find the Letters in the Perugian Archives ; another may, perhaps, be more fortunate

‡ Paul II did not alter the accusation in the tenth month after the imprisonment of the conspirators, as PLATINA, 785, would have us believe.

needed is to avoid coming into collision with the temporal power *

Paul II had much more to tell of the evil deeds of these Epicureans, who seem, indeed, to have adopted the doctrines promulgated by Valla in his book "on pleasure." They despised the commands of the Church, he said, ate meat on fast-days, and reviled the Pope and the Clergy They said that the priests were the enemies of the laity, that they had invented fasting and forbidden men to have more than one wife † Moses, they taught, deceived the Jews, his law was a forgery, Christ was a deceiver, Mahomet a great intellect, but also an impostor.‡ They were ashamed of their Christian names and preferred those which were heathen, and they practised the most shameful vices of antiquity Some of these free-thinkers are said to have contemplated an alliance with the Turks. Predictions of the speedy death of the Pope were circulated by them ; then there would be a new Election and a complete change in the state of affairs.

Paul II. named Callimachus, Petrejus, Glaucus, and Platina as the ringleaders of the Conspiracy He deeply regretted that the first three had escaped beyond the reach of justice. He evidently considered the matter to be most important, and expressed to the Ambassadors his determination to root out this " heresy," and his regret that he had not sooner become aware of its existence

In regard to the Conspiracy against his person, the Pope said he had heard the prevalent reports, but added that he

---

* It will be observed that this account agrees with that of Canensius, mentioned p 48

† It is known that, in the above-mentioned work, Valla advocated the community of women desired by Plato , see our Vol I , p 16

‡ This teaching is concealed beneath the leading idea of the work De tribus impostoribus. See WELLER'S edition, Heilbronn, 1876

could form no decided opinion as to whether they were
well-founded or not, because those believed to be the leaders
in the plot had escaped. According to the report of one of
the Ambassadors, Paul II. had, at first, a suspicion that
Podiebrad, the Hussite King of Bohemia, might be impli-
cated, it appeared to him not improbable that one heretic
might help another *

The Pope was particularly disquieted by the rumour
about Luca de Tocio, who had taken part in the troubles
in the time of Pius II.   He at once sent a courier to
Naples to ascertain whether he had really left that city.
As it was also affirmed that Tocio had given 1000 ducats
to the guards of St Angelo, as a bribe to induce them
to deliver up the fortress, the Pope caused searching
enquiries to be made, but very little information was
obtained   Even at the time, it was suspected that these
reports had been set afloat by persons whose interest it
was to raise a cloud of dust as a stratagem to escape
punishment †

A reward of 300 ducats was offered for the discovery of
the whereabouts of Callimachus, Glaucus, and Petrejus, and
500 for that of Luca de Tocio. The Pope hoped to get
hold of some, if not all, of the conspirators ‡ On the 29th
February, it was believed that a clue to Callimachus' abode
had been found; he was considered next in importance
to Luca de Tocio §

The houses of the fugitives were, of course, searched, and

* *Despatch of Joh Blanchus of the 29th Febr., 1468. (State Archives,
Milan) See Appendix, N. 21.

† *Loc. cit.*

‡ *Report of Augustinus de Rubeis of the 28th Febr., 1468. (State
Archives, Milan) See Appendix, N. 20.

§ *Report of Joh Blanchus of the 29th Febr, 1468 (State Archives,
Milan) See Appendix, N. 21.

the licentious poems which were found furnished fresh proof of the immorality of the Academicians.*

"We cannot wonder that the Pope did not consider the existence of such a Conspiracy as in itself incredible He had incurred the bitter hatred of the aggrieved Abbreviators Stefano Porcaro, the head of the conspiracy against Nicholas V., had also been a Humanist, and had dreamed of the restoration of the ancient Republic   The Ghibelline bands in Rome were still in existence, and their alliance with the party-chiefs of the city, and with the fugitives and exiles beyond its limits, constituted an abiding danger.   Again, in the days of Pius II., young Tiburzio, at the head of a similar Catiline band, had stirred the people up to cast off the priestly yoke, and revive the ancient liberty of Rome.   By his decided action, Paul II, at any rate, repressed disorder, and provided himself with material for investigation."†

Until the official documents are brought to light, it will be impossible to give an exact account of these proceedings, which were conducted by Cardinal Barbo, and watched with the greatest interest by Paul II. They would furnish us with the means of checking the detailed relation of Platina, whose participation in the events renders it necessary to receive his statements with the greatest caution.‡ In many cases they are, moreover, at variance with facts otherwise established §

He certainly is guilty of gross misrepresentation in his

* See the *Report cited in preceding note

† Voigt, II , 240, 2nd ed

‡ For critical observations on Platina, see Zeissberg, 351 seq , Voigt, II , 237 seq , 2nd ed ; Burckhardt, II., 277 seq , 5th ed ; Gregorovius, VII , 571, 3rd ed , L'Épinois, Paul II , 278 seq.; Creighton III , 274 seq , Tripepi, Religione e Storia, Roma, 1872

§ See especially Zeissberg, 351.

Life of Paul II., when he affirms that, in his examination, he had shewn the indolent Callimachus to be incapable of independently originating a Conspiracy In Platina's letters, written during his imprisonment, we find him, on the contrary, laying the whole blame on the blustering folly of Callimachus. "Who," he asks, in one of these letters, "would believe that the drunken dreams of this man, whom we mocked at and despised, could have brought us into such trouble? Alas! for us, poor wretches, who must pay for the silly temerity of another! That crazy bestower of treasures and kingdoms roams about freely, drunk with wine and glutted with food, while we, for being imprudent enough not to reveal his mad dreams, are tortured and shut up in dungeons" In almost all the other letters of this period Platina reiterates these accusations *

The constancy with which Platina claims to have undergone examination and endured torture must also be relegated to the domain of fiction

The letters written during his imprisonment also testify against him Anything more abject than his petitions addressed to the Pope can hardly be imagined His error, in not shewing up the drunken Callimachus, had been one of negligence, not of malice. For the future, however, he promised, whenever he hears anything against the name or the welfare of the Pope, even from a bird of the air, at once to report it to His Holiness. He approves of the measures taken for the repression of Humanistic license, inasmuch as it is the duty of a good shepherd to preserve his flock from contagion. He confesses that, when turned out of his office, he accused God and man ; he repents of this, and will not again so far forget himself Finally, he promises, if restored to liberty and secured from want, to

* VAIRANI, I , 30, 32, 33, 37.

become the Pope's most ardent panegyrist, to celebrate
in prose and verse "the golden age of his most happy
Pontificate"; he is even ready to abandon classical studies
and devote himself entirely to Holy Scripture and
Theology. The Humanist, however, again comes out when
he reminds the Pope that poets and orators confer immortality on Princes: Christ was made known by the
Evangelists, and Achilles by Homer. The prevailing tone
of the letter is expressed in its concluding words: "Only
give hope to us who, with clasped hands and bended knees
humbly await your mercy."*

Utterly broken and crushed, Platina in his distress
built much on the assistance of Rodrigo Sanchez de
Arevalo, Bishop of Calahorra and Prefect of St. Angelo,
and besieged him with elegant letters Rodrigo had the
courtesy to grant Platina's request that he would refresh
him with a letter This led to a brisk correspondence
between the two Humanists, one of whom was a representative of the Christian and the other of the heathen
Renaissance. Rodrigo sought to calm and elevate Platina's
mind by presenting to him religious motives of consolation.
It is curious to see how difficult the latter found it to
respond to the Bishop's thoughts. In spite of some
convulsive snatches after Christian reminiscences, the
antique element is the one that predominates in his letters,
and certain fatalistic observations which escaped from his
pen, induced Rodrigo to enlighten him as to the manner
in which a Catholic ought to speak of Fortune and of
Fate.†

The letters in which Platina invoked the intercession

* See the original text of this Letter in VAIRANI, I., 30-32.

† See VAIRANI, I , 45-66 Concerning Rodrigo Sanchez de Arevalo,
see, besides the works cited in our Vol II., p. 44, SAXIUS, Onom.,
II , 460 , CHEVALIER, 2036, and *supra*, p 17

of a number of the Cardinals and Prelates are as deplorable as the "abject and fulsome flatteries" with which he overwhelmed his gaoler. All these letters are full of the praises of those to whom they are addressed, and of Paul II. and Sanchez de Arevalo. In one of them Platina confesses that he contemplated suicide. In answer to the accusation of irreligion, he maintains that, as far as human frailty permitted, he had always fulfilled his religious duties, and denies that he had ever impugned any article of Faith. He is conscious of no crime save his silence regarding the babble of Callimachus *

Pomponius Laetus, who was delivered up to the Pope by Venice, during his detention at St Angelo's shewed little of the ancient Roman stoicism which he had so ostentatiously professed. At first he seems to have given some sharp answers to his examiners ; † but he soon followed the example of his friend Platina, and sought by obsequious flattery to win the favour of his gaoler and of the Pope.‡ He protested in the strongest terms that he was innocent, and, at the same time, begged for some books to read in his solitude Instead of Lactantius and Macrobius, for which Pomponius asked, Rodrigo de Arevalo sent him his treatise on the errors of the Council of Basle. Pomponius was little gratified by the substitution, but thanked him in an offensively fulsome letter. This was meant to pave the way for another petition, and, on the same day, he expressed a wish for a cheerful companion, with whom he

---

* See especially the Letter to Cardinal Ammanati in VAIRANI, I., 36-7

† This appears from a Letter of Platina's to P. Laetus, in VAIRANI, I , 38

‡ CREIGHTON, III , 44-5, 276-284 ; here the original text of the letters is given from Cod 161, of the Library of Corpus Christi College, Cambridge.

might interchange ideas   In support of his request, he quoted the words of Scripture : " Bear ye one another's burthens, and so you shall fulfil the law of Christ " This application was granted.

The Apology drawn up by Pomponius Laetus, while in prison, is also a pitiful production *   He meets an accusation, in regard to his relations with a young Venetian, by an appeal to the example of Socrates.   He had withdrawn from all intimate intercourse with Callimachus from the time he had become aware of his wickedness.   Everywhere, and especially in Venice, he had extolled Paul II. He confesses with regret that he had spoken strongly against the clergy; he had said these things in anger because he had been deprived of his maintenance; he begs to be forgiven for the sake of the sufferings of Christ.   He brings forward witnesses to prove that he had fulfilled his Easter duties, explains his disregard of the law of fasting by the state of his health, and declares that he had received the necessary dispensation.   Finally, in evidence of his Christian sentiments, he refers to the verses which he had composed on the Stations of the Cross, to his discourse in honour of the Blessed Virgin, and his treatise on the Immortality of the Soul   He concludes by a penitent admission that he has done wrong, and prays that, for the sake of the Risen Saviour, mercy may prevail over justice

This pitiful document seems to have decided the fate of Pomponius   Paul II. came to the conclusion that the

---

* **Defensio Pomponii Laeti in carceribus et confessio.   Cod Vatic , 2934, P. I, p. 305-308b   (Vatican Library.)   This Document was not, as GEIGER, 150, supposes, discovered by Gregorovius , DE ROSSI first drew attention to it (Roma Sott, I , 7).   GREGOROVIUS' extracts, VII , 571-2, 3rd ed , are more perfectly accurate , the correct reading must be " *effusissimo* ore laudavi," and " ignoscate " should be " ignoscite "

writer of such a letter was incapable of originating a Conspiracy, and, with regard to the other charges against him,
he probably considered that the severe lesson which he
had received was sufficient to reform him. The reason of
Platina's far longer detention in prison was evidently that
the suspicions against him were stronger, owing to his
former conduct *

Paul II. still hoped that the ringleaders of the Conspiracy would fall into his hands, and, if we may believe
Platina, Petrejus was actually apprehended, but confessed
nothing †

That the affair had a political side is evidenced by the
fact that, immediately on the discovery of the plot, the Pope
transferred his residence from St Peter's to S. Marco, "in
order to remove from the neighbourhood of the Orsini and
place himself near the Colonna." " But," as the Ambassador,
from whom we learn of this change, remarks, " danger is
everywhere "‡

Things, however, did not now seem so alarming. The
report of the departure from Naples of Luca de Tocio, the
partisan of the Orsini, and of his participation in the Conspiracy, proved to be mistaken   Paul II., nevertheless, considered it well to surround himself with a strong guard.
The Carnival amusements, as Augustinus de Rubeis, on
the 4th March, informed the Duke of Milan, took place just
as usual. "Regarding the Conspiracy against the Pope's
person," writes the same Ambassador, " enquiries have been
most carefully made, but as yet nothing has been discovered but some blustering talk of murdering the Pope,
which may easily have arisen in the way I have already

* CREIGHTON, III , 46 , VOIGT, II , 240, 2nd ed

† PLATINA, 784.

‡ *Report of Joh Blanchus of the 28th Febr., 1468 ; see Appendix,
N. 19.   State Archives, Milan.

described. As the populace and the whole Court are discontented, it was only necessary for some one to make a beginning in order to carry all with him." *

The obscurity in which this Conspiracy is involved will never be completely cleared away. Platina and Pomponius Laetus, "with touching unanimity concur in laying all the blame on the cunning of the fugitive who was not there to defend himself." Even in distant Poland, where he hoped to find sure refuge with Paul II.'s enemy, King Casimir, Callimachus had good cause to guard his lips, for the Pope made great, though ineffectual, efforts to get him into his power. Again, in the year 1470, the Papal Legate, Alexander, Bishop of Forli, urged the General Diet at Petrikau to deliver up the conspirator, who only escaped through a combination of favourable circumstances †

Although enquiries regarding this Conspiracy were finally abandoned in Rome for want of evidence, yet the prosecution of what was designated as the "heresy" of the Academicians, was carried on, and this with all the more reason, inasmuch as Platina himself had not ventured to deny the charge of heathen practices. Unfortunately, trustworthy information on this subject is but scanty. From many sources, however, we learn that Paul II. meditated measures of extreme severity against the heathen and philosophical extravagances of the Professors and Literati.

· "If God preserves my life," said the Pope to one of the Ambassadors very soon after the discovery of the plot, " I will do two things ; in the first place, I will forbid the study of these senseless histories and poems, which are full of heresies and blasphemies, and, secondly, I will prohibit the

* See Appendix, N 21

† See ZEISSBERG, 354 and *seq* , Acta Tomic., I , Appendix ; and CARO, V , I, 322 *seq*

teaching and practice of Astrology, since so many errors
arise thence." "Children," continued the Pope, "when
hardly ten years old, even without going to school, know a
thousand villanies. What, then, must they become when,
later on, they read Juvenal, Terence, Plautus, and Ovid?
Juvenal certainly makes a shew of blaming vice, but he
leads his readers to the knowledge of it."* There are
many other books, he added, through which a sufficient
amount of learning may be attained; it is better to call
things by their true names and to avoid poetical circum-
locution. These Academicians are worse than the heathen,
for they believed in God, while these deny Him. The
Ambassadors expressed their agreement with the Pope,
especially Lorenzo of Pesaro, who delighted him by
demonstrating the faith of the ancients with a great display of learning The Ambassadors also considered it
very advisable to forbid Ecclesiastics to study Poetry and
Astrology. The Pope concluded by declaring that he also
meant to take measures against the Roman habit of
spreading false reports.†

* This admirable discourse furnishes a fresh proof that Paul II
was not so unlearned as Platina represents him

† For the above, see the interesting *Report of Joh. Blanchus of 29th
Febr, 1468. (State Archives, Milan) See Appendix, N. 21 Amongst
other reproaches brought by Ammanati (see FRIEDRICH, Astrologie
u Ref, 20 seq, Munchen, 1864) against Paul II, is that of having,
in 1465, firmly believed in Astrological predictions. I have not yet
found any confirmation of the statement of this witness, who is certainly
open to suspicion the assertion, however, cannot be an absolute invention, and the general prevalence of Astrology in the Renaissance
age must be borne in mind See BURCKHARDT, II, 279 and 346, 3rd
ed, concerning Sixtus IV., see also GOTHEIN, 446, and PASTOR in
the Freib. Kirchenlexikon, I, 1525 seq, 2nd ed. In 1441, Domenico de
Domenichi even pronounced a *Discourse in laudem astrologiae et
confutationem opinionum ei adversantium (Manuscript in the Mantua
Library, see ZACHARIAS, Iter, 135)

In the consultations, which were held during this time, to devise the best means of attacking the false Renaissance, the Pope may have had in his mind a treatise which Ermolao Barbaro, the excellent Bishop of Verona, had dedicated to him in 1455. This author, looking at the matter exclusively from a moral point of view, vehemently protests against the undue estimation in which the ancient poets were commonly held, and in some places altogether condemns the whole of the old heathen poetry He goes through the whole series, first of the Greek, and then of the Latin poets, and cites a number of extracts from the writings of the Fathers, in which immoral poets are condemned. In his opposition to the fanatical admirers of ancient poetry, Barbaro sometimes flies to the other extreme, and completely condemns the art in itself. The conclusion which he deduces is, that if the study of these heathen writers, even by the laity, requires much circumspection, this must be still more necessary in the case of religious and priests *

One of the Ambassadors expressly states that, in the middle of March, 1468, all the teachers in Rome were, on account of the danger of heresy, forbidden to make use of the old poets; further details are wanting.† It is,

---

* Ad rev. in Christo patrem et dominum dom. Petrum tit S. Marci presbiterum card. dignissimum Hermolai dei paciencia episcopi Veronensis oratio contra poetas The preface is dated ex Verona, Cal. April. 1455. I found this remarkable treatise in Cod. Reg., 313, f. 167–192, of the Vatican Library. Barbaro looks only at one side of the question, and his adversaries at the other, the former blaming, and the latter praising, the poets. He dwells almost exclusively on the bad poets, and the evil contained in the writings of the good ones, while his opponents only mention the good. Barbaro died in 1471 ; see OROLOGIO, Canonici, 23

† The *Despatch of " Laurentius de Pensauro" to Fr. Sforza, unfortunately a very short one, which, in accordance with the Pope's

however, probable that the Papal prohibition was confined to the schools   At any rate, it did not apply to all poets, but only, as the Pope clearly explained to the Ambassadors of the League, to those who were objectionable on the score of morals.   Every one must admit that the moral aspect was the one which a Pope was bound to consider in form-ing a judgment on the Classics.   The vindication of the Christian moral law in this domain was, therefore, a most salutary act.   Poison is poison still, even if contained in crystal vials.

As regards the issue of the trial, we have only Platina's report, and it cannot be looked upon as trustworthy. According to him, the Academicians were acquitted from the charge of actual heresy, nothing more than flippancy and undue licence in language being proved against them Accordingly, the prisoners were now no longer shut up, but merely detained in the Papal Palace, then within the precincts of the Vatican, and finally, at the intercession of some of the Cardinals, especially Bessarion, only in the City of Rome , * but the Academy was dissolved, and certain limitations were imposed upon classical studies.

The severe lesson given by Paul II to the wanton insolence of the Humanists, was no doubt a salutary one   No one can deny that the Pope was acting within his rights when he took measures against the practical heathenism of the Academicians.   Platina, himself, in a letter to Pomponius Laetus, confessed that the heathenish practices of the Academy must, necessarily, give offence.

explanation, must refer to the immoral poets only, runs as follows: " Il papa ha prohibito a tutti li maestri de scole che non vole S Sta che legano poeti per la heresia era intrata in certi che se delectavano de questi poeti   Dat Romae, xvi. Martii, 1468 "   State Archives, Milan, Cart Gen.

* PLATINA, 788.

"And so," he adds, "we must not complain if the Pope defends himself and the Christian religion."*

The action of Paul II. towards the Roman Academy has received a remarkable justification from recent investigations in the Catacombs.

Until the 15th century the subterranean necropolis of the early Christians had, with the exception of the Catacomb of St Sebastian, been completely forgotten Traces of visitors begin to reappear from the year 1433 First, we have names of Monks and Pilgrims, led there by devotion   "I came here," writes Brother Laurentius of Sicily, "to visit this holy place, with twenty companions of the Order of the Friars Minor, on the 17th January, 1451." Then, suddenly, we come upon the autograph scratches (Graffiti) of Humanists and Roman Academicians of Pomponius, Platina, Volscus, Campanus, Pantagathus, Ruffus, Histrius, Partenopaeus, Perillus, Calpurnius, &c. They call themselves "a company of venerators and students of Roman antiquity, under the leadership of the pontifex maximus, Pomponius." Pantagathus describes himself as "Priest of the Roman Academy"† These men were in search, not of Christian, but of heathen, antiquity. In his large collection of inscriptions Pomponius inserted but

* "Justus fuit pontificis dolor; honesta tanta suspicione questio Proinde et nos ferre aequo animo debemus, si saluti suae, si christianae religioni cavit" VAIRANI, I, 38   See GEBHARDT, A of Corneto, 79 ; FRIEDRICH, J Wessel, 63 seq , and JANITSCHEK, 19 The last-named author says : "I do not believe the charge to be false, that the Academicians were enemies of the Christian religion and intended to bring back the heathen worship "

† DE ROSSI, Roma Sott, I , 3 seq , REUMONT, III , I, 342 seq   "The date 1475," observes Reumont, "points to the time of Sixtus IV , when, the meaning of these things being known, the danger was at an end. But, undoubtedly, this was a repetition, in a more public manner, of what had formerly been connected with a sort of secret society."

one which is Christian, and this one because it was metrical,
and its polished form had a flavour of heathenism *   Even
more characteristic is the fact that these "modern heathens"
ventured, in the venerable vaults of the Catacombs, where
the very stones preach the Gospel, to scrawl flippant inscriptions on the walls! †   With this evidence before us, therefore,
we cannot wonder that, even after their liberation from
prison, the contemporaries of the Academicians should
persist in maintaining that they were heathens rather than
Christians.‡

Of all the Academicians no one had been treated with
more severity than Platina.   After his release he cherished
the hope that his cringing flattery would, at least, have
secured him some appointment from the Pope.§   Paul II.
however, did not see any necessity for employing the pen
of this violent and immoral man.‖   This disappointment

* DE ROSSI, Inscript, II, 402.

† DE ROSSI, Roma Sott, I., 6.   The inscriptions have no individual
character, and are written in the ordinary capitals.

‡ KRAUS, Roma Sott, 3 (Freiburg, 1879).

§ BALAN, V, 196, concludes from a letter of Platina's that he had
been set at liberty some time before the September of 1469   A *Letter
of the Cardinal of Ravenna's of the 7th July, 1469, in the Gonzaga
Archives, proves this unfortunate man to have been at liberty at that
date.

‖ At this time Platina intended to dedicate to Paul II. his work, "De
falso ac vero bono."   In the printed version, however, it is dedicated
to Sixtus IV. (see ARISIUS, I., 317; and SCHMARSOW, 338 seq), but
Cod 805 of the Trivulzio Library, Milan, shews that Platina originally
offered or intended to offer it "divo Paulo II, P. M."   Testimony as
to Platina's immorality is furnished by the *Letter of the Bishop of
Ventimiglia, from which DE ROSSI, I, 3-4, has only given the passage
cited above.   The Bishop here complains that Platina had recently
loaded him with abuse in his own house   The cause of the quarrel
was Platina's jealousy of a member of the Bishop's household, who
was, he feared, likely to turn away his mistress from him . " vereris ne

intensified the hatred of the Humanist. He swore that he would have his revenge, and took it, after the death of Paul II., in his wide-spread "Lives of the Popes."

In this work he describes his enemy as a monster of cruelty, and a barbarian who detested all learning. This "biographical caricature" * has for centuries imposed itself on history. Even scholars, well aware of Platina's bias, have not succeeded in avoiding the influence of the portrait, drawn with undeniable skill and in a bright and elegant style. Some few over-partial attempts to vindicate his character have only served to increase the confusion, until, at length, recent critical investigation of the Archives has brought the truth to light †

It must always be remembered that Paul II was not an

illa tua adolescentula a tuis amoribus abducatur." The young person in question is then characterised as "puellam turpissimam monstroque similem," and Platina is reminded that he is no longer young. Cod. Vatic , 9020, f. 11 Vatican Library

* BURCKHARDT, II , 50, 3rd ed.; BAYER, Aus Italien, 160, calls Platina's Biography of Paul II 'a pamphlet.'

† The merit of this investigation is due to E. MUNTZ, II., 1 *seq* , where the new literature on the subject is quoted. See also GEOFFROY, 383 *seq*. "Platina," observes CREIGHTON, III., 274, "without saying anything that is obviously untrue, has contrived to suggest a conception of Paul II. which is entirely contrary to known facts, yet which is so vivid, so definite, so intelligible, that it bears the stamp of reality." The influence of this work on Gregorovius is, therefore, quite comprehensible, especially as its sentiments accord with the prejudice against the Popes which even the Sybels'chen Zeitschr , N. F., XXI , 358, admits to exist in his mind The great authority of Platina and Pomponius Laetus with their contemporaries has also had its effect, and so has the unfavourable opinion of Ammanati and of the author of the Cronica di Bologna, in regard to Paul II. The party feeling, which colours the writings of the Cardinal and the chronicler, has not been duly taken into account. See CREIGHTON, 273 *seq*. The disputes between Paul II. and Bologna warped the mind of the chronicler.

opponent of the Renaissance in itself, yet he is not to be looked upon as a Humanist, like Nicholas V. The boastfulness and conceit of its adherents repelled him : he preferred men of practical knowledge and practical tendencies. Poetasters had little to expect from him, and, in view of the pseudo-classical rhymes of a Porcello or a Montagna, this was not much to be regretted.*

The favours which Paul II granted to the Roman and other High Schools,† as well as his generosity to a number of learned men, prove him to have been no enemy of culture and learning. While still a Cardinal he repeatedly visited Flavio Biondo in his last sickness, gave him assistance, and promised to provide for his children. As Pope, he fulfilled this promise by giving the charge of the Registers to Gasparo Biondo, in recognition of his father's deserts ‡ When the pious and enthusiastic scholar, Timoteo Maffei, fell ill, Paul II. sent him a present of money and a skilful physician, and, on his recovery, he conferred on him the Bishopric of Ragusa. Bishoprics were also bestowed on the three former preceptors of the Pope, and one of them, Amicus Agnifilus, was even raised to the purple   Learned men,

* MUNTZ, II , 3, where there is proof from the *Epigrams of L. Montagna   Cod 103 of the Bibl de l'Institut, Paris

† RENAZZI, I , 175, 185, 193 , PAPENCORDT, 515   In regard to the other Universities, see DENIFLE, I., 514 ; PRANTL, I., 15–18 ; FROMMANN, Zur Gesch. d Buchh., II., 23 , BULAEUS, V., 674 *seq.* ; Ungar. Revue, 1881, p 503   "Hatred of learning" is not indicated by the fact that Paul II. excommunicated those who removed the books from the Library of S. Spirito in Florence (RICHA, IX , 58), or, by his command, that the Bishop of Modena should take care that the MSS. to be transferred from Monte Cassino to Rome suffered no injury on the way from rain or from any other cause. *Brief of the 20th March, 1471, in the State Archives, Venice

‡ Gott Gel Anz , 1879, p 1501 *seq*   Regarding Atti camerali rogati dal notaro G Biondo, see Studi e Doc , 1886, VII , 59 *seq.*

like Perotti, were promoted to positions of some importance in the States of the Church. Niccolo Gallo, Professor of Jurisprudence, when seriously ill, asked for a Confessor furnished with faculties to absolve from every sin; the Pope granted his request, and added a present of 20 ducats.* He summoned to Rome many scholars whose acquaintance he had made while a Cardinal; for example, Domizio da Caldiero and Gasparo da Verona, who was subsequently his biographer.† The Florentine, Lionardo Dati, was made Bishop of Massa, and Sigismondo de' Conti and Vespasiano da Bisticci bear witness to the Pope's affection for him, the latter declares that, if the life of Paul II. had been prolonged, Dati would have been a Cardinal.‡ In the year 1470, Paul II shewed the interest he took in historical studies by causing some Chronicles to be copied for him §

Among the scholars advanced by Paul II. to the Episcopal dignity, was Cardinal Cusa's intimate friend, Giovan Andrea Bussi of Vigevano, a man who deserves the highest praise for his labours in the diffusion of printing throughout Italy. The numerous books dedicated by this Prelate to the Pope prove the interest taken by Paul II in the

* CANENSIUS, 66-7; QUIRINI, XIII See also MUTIUS PHOE-BONIUS, Hist. Marsorum cum catal. episcop, p 35 (Neapol. 1678); and CORSIGNANI, II, 559 Regarding Maffei, see, besides the account in our Vol I, 8, note 1, and Vol II, 205 seq, GIULIARI, 39, 163, 167 seq., MONTFAUCON, Bibl bibl, I, 98; and ENGEL, Gesch von Ragusa, 184 seq.

† RENAZZI, I, 234; see 211, and GIULIARI, 40-44.

‡ MAI, Spic, I., 275. Sigismondo de' Conti, in his *Treatise pro secretariis addressed to Sixtus IV, wrote: *"Gratus jocundusque fuit Paulo II, pontifici sapientissimo Leonardus Dathus Massanus praesul vir summa innocentia, summa prudentia, summa in rebus omnibus temperantia, stilo praeterea erudito et gravi praeditus." Vatic, 2934, P. II, f 600, Vatican Library.

§ MUNTZ, Bibl., 133, 134; see CANENSIUS, 97-8

introduction of the newly discovered "divine art" "Your pontificate, most glorious already, will never be forgotten," says Bussi, "because this art has been taken up to your Throne."*

It is impossible to say, with certainty, who it was that summoned the first German printers—Conrad Schweinheim from Schwanheim, opposite Hochst on the Maine, Arnold Pannartz from Prague, and Ulrich Hahn from Ingolstadt— to Italy. Cusa was deeply interested in the important discovery, but he died before these Germans arrived in Italy. There can be no doubt that to Subiaco, "the Mother

---

* QUIRINI, 135 ; see MUNTZ, Bibl , loc cit, who, like PAPENCORDT, 515, and FALKENSTEIN, 209, maintains that the Pope patronised the new discovery. It is evident that Bussi's dedications were acceptable to the Pope, as the Bishopric of Aleria was conferred upon him in 1469 (regarding which, compare MAZZUCHELLI, I , 2, 701 seq. , MOTTA, P Castaldi . . . ed il vesc. d'Aleria, Torino, 1884 , and Riv. St. Ital , I.) ; and, moreover, a dedication to the Pope always implies his consent ; it is, therefore, somewhat surprising to find H. V. D. LINDE, I., 165, assert that "Paul II. was by no means a friend to the innovation ,' and that Bussi had provided his editions with letters of dedication to the Pope in order to convince him of the utility of typography. Tiraboschi's account of the Pope's proceedings against the heathen Academicians is quoted by H. v. d. Linde in support of his theory. Those proceedings cannot be understood to imply any aversion on the part of Paul II to the art of printing, for Bussi, in one of his dedicatory epistles (QUIRINI, 134), speaks of the humbling of these restless men as favouring his efforts. A great many other passages in these epistles (QUIRINI, 115, 152, 194, 196, 233) not only exclude the idea of Paul's aversion to printing, but shew it to be absolutely at variance with facts FALK, Die Druckkunst, &c., draws a vivid picture of the manifold encouragements afforded by the Church, in all European countries, to Gutenberg's invention during its first decades His work is founded on materials gathered from a very wide field, many of which have as yet been hardly, if at all, turned to account This view has since prevailed, even on the Protestant side, over the prejudices of former days , see, e.g , B HASE, Die Koberger, Leipzig, 1885, 2nd ed

House of the Benedictine Order, which has done so much for the cause of learning, is due the honour of having given a home to the first German printers."* Constant relations between this great seat of Western culture and Germany had been maintained ever since the days of the excellent Abbot Bartholomaus III. (1362, &c), who, in his zeal for the improvement of the monastic spirit, had invited from beyond the Alps many German monks, remarkable alike for their learning and their austerity of life.† Again, also, in the middle of the 15th century there were many German Benedictines at St. Scholastica

In the retirement of Subiaco, Schweinheim and Pannartz printed, first the Latin Grammar of Donatus, which was extensively used in the Middle Ages, then Cicero's work on Orators, and the Instructions of Lactantius against the Heathen. The last of these books was completed on the 29th October, 1465. Two years later, an edition of St. Augustine's "City of God" issued from the Convent printing press at Subiaco ‡ The States of the Church may therefore claim, after Germany, the honour of first producing printed books.

---

* GREGOROVIUS, VII., 515, 3rd ed.

† Cronaca Subl, 394, 396-7. The holy life of the monks in their solitude is described by PIUS II. Comment. 168. Cod. 211, Juvenal, written in 1455 by Peter Paul Dominici de Subiaco, bears witness to the cultivation of classical studies in the monastery of Subiaco.

‡ See C FUMAGALLI, Dei primi libri a stampa e specialmente di un Codice Sublacense impresso avanti il Lattanzio e finora creduto posteriore, Lugano, 1875, see FALKENSTEIN, 209, LAIRE, Specimen Hist Typogr Rom, Romae, 1778, AUDIFFREDI, Cat Rom edit. saec., XV, Romae, 1783, and OTTINO in the review, L'Arte della Stampa, 1870-71. Of the first edition of Lactantius but one copy now exists at Subiaco (before the French Revolution there was, according to BLUME, II, 241, a second); see the description in GORI, II, 325. The copy in the Casanatense Library, valued at 15,000 francs, dis-

Of Ulrich Hahn's labours at Subiaco no trace now remains   The learned Cardinal Torquemada induced him to come to Rome, and here, in 1467, Hahn, who is generally known by the name of Gallus, finished printing the " Contemplations" on the picture in the Court of Sta Maria sopra Minerva, which his patron had composed.*   In the September of the same year, 1467, Schweinheim and Pannaitz had also migrated to the Eternal City†   Here

appeared in 1885. The theft was, according to the "Frankf Ztg." supposed to have been perpetrated by one of the officials of the library, and they were all severely punished, the last of the Dominicans had a short time previously been removed   BERLAN'S opinion (La invenzione della stampa a tipo mobile revendicata all' Italia, Firenze, 1882), that Italy was the first country to make use of moveable type, is briefly refuted in the Jahresberichten der Geschichtswissenschaft, VI , 2, 268.

* Thirty-four folio pages with thirty-three woodcuts. LINDE, III , 715   See FALKENSTEIN, 211; and SCHMARSOW, 57   FROMMANN, Zur Gesch. d. Buchh , II., 5, says · "With the aid of the German monks, Torquemada caused the German printers, Schweinheim and Pannartz, to come to Subiaco and set up a printing press in the monastery"   This is a conjecture for which evidence is wanting.   Moveover, Falkenstein ought not to have confounded Cardinal Torquemada with the Spanish Inquisitor.

† The time when the German printers arrived at Subiaco cannot exactly be determined (FROMMANN, II., 5, thinks it was about the beginning of 1464, and so does VILLARI, 1 , 130, but Ph de Lignamine does not agree with them) ; I can, however, confidently give 1467 as the date when they settled in Rome. GASP. VERONEN, Paulus II , 1046, adds to his account of Carvajal's return from his mission to Venice, the remark: " Hac tempestate ad sanct. Romam quidam juvenes accesserunt et ii quidem Teutonici qui Lactantium Firmianum de hominis opificio, de Dei ira necnon contra gentiles mense uno formaverunt et ducentos hujusmodi libros quoque mense efficiebant." Carvajal's return took place on the 17th Sept, 1467, as we learn from the ·*Acta Consist., f 35b   (Secret Archives of the Vatican) PH DE LIGNAMINE, loc cit., relates the arrival of Schweinheim and

in the Massimi Palace, near the German National Hospice,
they established their printing press.   Its first production
was the " Letters of Cicero to his Friends."   In the course
of a few years this was followed by two editions of Lactantius, a second edition of Cicero's Letters, St Augustine's
City of God, the works of St. Jerome, the Holy Scriptures,
St Cyprian's Letters, the Catena of St Thomas, and,
amongst other classical works, those of Cæsar, Livy, Virgil,
Ovid, Pliny, Quintilian, Suetonius, Gellius and Apulius.*

The corrector, or, as we should now say, the editor, of
these works was the indefatigable classical scholar, Bussi.
Almost all the books we have mentioned had fervid dedications to the Pope from his pen, and contained verses
written by him.   On one occasion he thus alludes to the
names of his typographers, which had to the ears of his
countrymen a barbarous sound —

> The harsh-sounding German names awaken a smile .
> Let the admirable art soften the unmelodious tones.†

The friendly attitude of the Pope towards the new art,
and the extraordinary liberality with which he allowed
Bussi to make use of the precious Manuscripts in the
Vatican Library, greatly contributed to promote the success of the Bishop's efforts ‡

The important post of Corrector—with whom scientific
textual criticism had its beginning—was also filled at
Hahn's printing-house by a Bishop, Giantonio Campano, a

Pannartz in Rome, in June, 1465, but this must allude to their first
visit, after which they went to Subiaco

* QUIRINI, 107 *seq*   The Roman types were not so fine as the
older ones employed at Subiaco

† REUMONT, III, I, 347, 510   Most of Bussi's prefaces are in
QUIRINI, *loc. cit.*   See BOTFIELD, Prefaces to the first editions of
the Greek and Roman Classics, London, 1861

‡ QUIRINI, 188.

fact which shews the esteem in which typography was held at this period.*

After the death of Torquemada, Caraffa became a warm patron of the art of printing , nor did he stand alone among his colleagues in this respect. In 1469 Bussi writes, "We have as yet found no one in the Sacred College of Cardinals who has not been favourable to our efforts, so that the higher the dignity the greater has been their zeal in learning. Would that we could say as much for other orders."† As time went on, the Roman clergy maintained an unflagging interest in the "sacred art" which, in the dedication to Paul II prefixed to the letters of St. Jerome, is said to be "one of the most auspicious of all the Divine gifts bestowed during his pontificate on the Christian world, enabling even quite poor men at small cost to procure books"‡

The account-books of Paul II's pontificate, which have lately been brought to light, shew how little he can be charged with systematic hostility towards classical anti-quity. They lead us to the conclusion that this so-called barbarian watched over the preservation of ancient remains even more carefully than the scholarly Pius II. The triumphal arches of Titus and Septimius Severus, the Colossus of Monte Cavallo, and the equestrian statue of Marcus Aurelius were restored by his desire, and many forgotten and neglected relics of antiquity were brought to the Palace of S. Marco.§

The magnificent collection of antiquities and works of art, which Paul II had brought together in this Palace while yet a Cardinal, contained the most important treasures

* FALKENSTEIN, 211 ; FALK, 18 , GREGOROVIUS, VII., 517, 3rd ed.
† QUIRINI, 202.
‡ QUIRINI, 135 , FALK, 19-20 , LINDE, III , 705
§ MUNTZ, II , 4, 92-5.

of this kind from the time of the destruction of the Roman Empire. It contained numerous rare and most precious examples of antique Cameos and engraved gems, medals, and bronzes. From Byzantium there were pictures with golden backgrounds, little domestic altars with mosaics, reliquaries, ivory carvings, and gorgeously embroidered vestments. To these objects, whose value was enhanced by their age or their origin, was added a splendid selection of more recent works of art, such as Flemish tapestries, Florentine work in gold, vases and jewels. An inventory of this collection, taken in 1457, while Barbo was still a Cardinal, is one of the most interesting documents in the Roman State Archives,* and is of great value in connection with the history of art and civilisation in the Renaissance period. A comparison of the objects here mentioned with those in the Museums of the present day, enables us to realise the wealth of the Collection at S. Marco's The Museum of Vienna contains about 200 ancient Cameos, and the Paris Library about 260 ; the inventory of Barbo's collection mentions 227. The Cardinal collected about a hundred' ancient gold, and a thousand ancient silver, coins. He had twenty-five domestic altars with mosaics, a number greater than that now possessed by all the Museums of Europe together.†

But all these ancient, modern, and Eastern treasures were not sufficient to satisfy the soul of a collector like Paul II On the contrary, now that the means at his disposal were greater, his schemes assumed yet larger propor-

* Published with some later additions by MUNTZ, II , 181–287. Regarding Paul II as a collector, see *ibid.*, 128 *seq.* ; and MUNTZ, Précurseurs, 159, 170, 184, 193. His long sojourn in Florence, of which Paul II speaks with so much enthusiasm in his *Letter of Sept 8, 1466, cited on p 14, must have had an important influence on his taste for collecting

† MUNTZ , II , 140, 143.

tions. He seems to have seriously entertained the idea of transferring the whole of the library of Monte Cassino to his palace, and he is said to have offered to construct a new bridge for the inhabitants of Toulouse in exchange for a Cameo.*

The Pope, however, was not merely an enthusiastic collector, but also an expert in matters of art His memory was so extraordinary that he never forgot the name of a person or a thing, and he was able at a glance to tell where an ancient coin came from, and give the name of the Prince whose image it bore.†

The Churches of the Eternal City shared the care which he bestowed on the ancient monuments ; works of restoration, of a more or less extensive character, were carried on at the Lateran, S Lorenzo in Piscibus, Sᵗᵃ Lucia in Septemviis, Sᵗᵃ Maria in Araceli, Sᵗᵃ Maria Maggiore, Sᵗᵃ Maria sopra Minerva and the Pantheon. The bridges, gates, walls, and many of the public buildings in Rome were repaired by his command. Similar benefits were conferred upon Tivoli, Ostia, Civitavecchia, Terracina, Viterbo and Monte Cassino.‡

The progress of Architecture, under Paul II., was most

* Proof of this statement is to be found in MUNTZ, II , 133.

† Gasp. Veronen in MARINI, II , 179 , CANENSIUS, 31-2

‡ MUNTZ, II , 85-90, 94, 96, 98-107   See MUNTZ, Les Anciennes Basiliques, 8, 17, 18, 19, 20-21, and Rev Archéol, VII , 339, IX , 171 FORCELLA, XIII., 6. Regarding the Artists employed by Paul II , see also the Doc e Stud , published by the Deput. di St Patria, I. (Bologna, 1886), Studi, p 4 seq. On one of the doors of the Palazzo Pubblico, at Viterbo, I saw the arms of Paul II., with the inscription : PA PP II 1465   Paul II also contributed to the rebuilding of the Cathedral of Loreto , see TURSELLINUS, 133 seq (SCHMARSOW, 122), and the *Brief of this Pope to the "episcop Parentinus, eccl Rachanaten. vicarius," dated Romae, 1 Martii, 1471   Lib. brev. 12, f. 12' Secret Archives of the Vatican

remarkable,* and in this branch of creative art the Pope
appears as the champion of the Renaissance.   In the erection of the magnificent Palace of S. Marco he was the first
to apply the theories of Vitruvius and definitely to break
with the Gothic style.   The splendid and extensive buildings
at the Vatican secured the triumph of the new style in
Rome †   The fact that Paul II reverted to Nicholas V's
grand scheme for the reconstruction of St. Peter's, and
proceeded with the erection of the Tribune, is of the higest
interest.   A medal and a couple of lines in Canensius'
Biography of the Pope were, until lately, our only sources
of information on this subject, and, accordingly, it came to
be supposed that only works of restoration were alluded to.
The accounts preserved in the Roman State Archives,
however, furnish absolute proof of the magnificent projects
entertained by the Pope.   A passage, unfortunately very
laconic, in a letter from Gentile Becchi to Lorenzo de'
Medici, confirms this statement.‡

The transportation of the Obelisk on St. Peter's square—
another scheme of his great predecessor's—was also taken
in hand by Paul II.   The distinguished architect, Ridolfo
Fioravante degli Alberti, one of the first men of his day,

---

* Painting was not at this time very flourishing   See MUNTZ, II.,
30 seq , 32, 107-108, and JANITSCHEK'S Repert , VI , 215 seq.

† MUNTZ, II , 8, 32-43.

‡ "*Sam Marco si sta.   La tribuna di Sam Piero diseguita "
Gentile Becchi to Lorenzo de' Medici, 1470 (stil. flor), da Roma a
di III di Gennaio (Ricevuta a di V detto)   The Original is in the
State Archives at Florence.   Av il princ. filza 61, fol 119.   This
recently discovered information perfectly agrees with the extracts
from accounts given by MUNTZ, II , 45 seq , and with his conjecture
regarding the date of the medals given by Litta (note 11)   The
juxtaposition in these of the works at S Marco an   S Peter's, leads us
to conclude that a great new building had also   in contemplation
on the site of the latter

had prepared the plans, and the work had already been commenced when the Pope died *

The Palazzo di S. Marco, now Palazzo di Venezia, is the most magnificent creation of Paul II. Recent investigations of the Archives have thrown some light on the history of this gigantic work, but many questions regarding it are still unanswered.† Medals struck on this occasion, and frequently found during restorations in earthenware caskets, together with an inscription on the façade, bear witness that these extensive works were begun in the year 1455 ‡ This magnificent building was designed in truly Roman proportions. A whole quarter had to be pulled down in order to make room for it, and, although the works went on during the whole of Paul II.'s pontificate, the Palace "within which the newly decorated Basilica of St. Mark was contained like a chapel" was not completed at the time of his death. But even in its unfinished state it is one of the grandest of Roman Monuments,§ and, in a remarkable manner, exhibits the transition from the mediæval

* MUNTZ, II., 4, 24–5   See our Vol II., p 184. To the works concerning Fioravante, cited by MUNTZ, I , 83, may be added the Arch. St. Lomb , 1882, and the Giornale dell' Ingegnere Architetto of 1872.

† Here again the investigations of MUNTZ, II., 49 *seq* , are our principal authority , they are supplemented by his articles in L'Art (1884), and in Gli Studi in Italia, A°, VII , 1, fasc. 2 (which also appeared separately at Rome in 1884). See also SCHMARSOW, 62 *seq* , and Studi c Doc , VII , 67 *seq* (1886)

‡ BONANNI, I , 71. The inscription is as follows "Petrus Barbus Venetus cardinalis S Marci has aedes condidit A° Chi , 1455"

§ All contemporary writers mention this building with admiration. Fi Ariostus, in his *Description of Borso's elevation to the cakedom of Ferrara, which we shall hereafter quote, says, in regard to the passage of this Prince through Rome, that he came "per quella regione dove si fabrica quello alto e superbo pallazo pontificale a S Marco cum tanta incomparabile spesa, cum tanto maravegloso

fortress to the modern Palace, and from the Gothic to the Renaissance style. In the Palace proper, the character of a fortress predominates. "It is," to quote the words of a gifted historian of art, "a speaking monument of an age of violence, presenting to the mob a stern and imposing aspect, devoid of all grace or charm, jealously concealing all the beauty of its spacious and decorated halls, destined to be the home of a luxurious life, and the scene of many a gorgeous spectacle." * The grand unfinished court, with its portico ornamented with pilasters in the Doric-Tuscan style below and Corinthian above, the Palazzetto, begun in 1466, joining it at the right-hand corner, and the vestibule of S. Marco, connected with the Palace, are all in the Renaissance style.

From 1466, Paul II. had, during a great part of the year, taken up his abode in this stupendous Palace, which was

artificio, cum più ingegno, cum più magnificentia che per adriedo si sia usitado edificare in Roma " Cod. J, VII, 261. Chigi Library, Rome

* SCHMARSOW, 63, who conjectures that the purpose of this edifice was to put an end to the banishment of the Popes to the Leonine City. That political motives actually induced Paul II. frequently to dwell in the new Palace, is evident from the *Despatch in the Archives at Milan, cited *supra*, p 58. See PAPENCORDT, 516 *seq.*; GSELL-FELS, 188, BURCKHARDT-BODE, 98; REDTENBACHER, 155; BURCKHARDT, Gesch. der Renaiss, 55, 160 Regarding S. Marco, see ARMELLINI, 327. Calixtus III, in 1458, tertio Non Mau A° 4°, granted an Indulgence to promote the restoration of S. Marco, and, on this occasion, mentioned the care and expense bestowed by Card Barbo on this Church. Regest, 452, f. 40 (Secret Archives of the Vatican) Compare also Stevenson's remarkable treatise, " Sur les tuiles de plomb de la basilique de S. Marc, ornées des armoires de Paul II et des médaillons de la Renaissance," in the Mél. d'Arch, p 439 *seq* (1888). The area of the Palace, together with the Church and the Palazzetto, is (as the Architect, F. Pokorny, kindly informs me) 12,174 square metres The Ecclesialogist, XXIX, 160.

situated in the middle of the City, at the foot of the Capitol
and in the domain of the friendly Colonna family   The
Apostolic Treasury was also transferred there *   Subsequent Popes frequently, as their Bulls bear evidence, lived
there   Just a century after the Election of Paul II, this
grand building was given by Pius IV. to the Republic of
Venice †   Afterwards, when Venice fell into the hands of
Austria, it became the property of that Empire, whose
Ambassadors now occupy it.

* See GOTLOB, Cam Apost.   Especially in summer, when the
neighbourhood of the Vatican is infested with fever, the Pope lived
at S Marco, which is accordingly called by Fr Ariostus in the MS
cited *supra*, p 76, the 'stantia estiva de la Sta de N S.'   His sojourn
there was often prolonged into the winter months , in 1464, Paul II
was still at S Marco on the 16th November, as appears from the
*Acta Consist , f 34a.   (Secret Archives of the Vatican.)   The investi-
gations of MUNTZ (Arts, II , 13, 15, 16, 53 , Palais, 9) shew that
Giacomo da Pietrasanta, who first came into notice in the time of
Nicholas V., may justly claim to be considered the architect of this
Palace.   See REDTENBACHER, 146   Giuliano da San Gallo, then
a youth, Meo del Caprino, and Giovannino de' Dolci, were all fellow-
workers with him   Blocks of Travertine freestone, taken from the
Colosseum, were employed in the building   See MUNTZ, II., 7.   Over
and over again, valuable ancient stones were also sent out of Rome.
On the 16th Sept , 1464, *Cardinal Gonzaga writes from Rome to
his mother, Barbara · "Mando etiam per questo mestiere alcuni
pezzi de alabastri et altre antiquitate tuolte qui " (Gonzaga Archives,
Mantua)   A metrical inscription on the Church and Palace of S
Marco, which has not previously been published, will be found in
Appendix, N 9.

† See CECCHETTI, 1 , 333, note.   The transfer was symbolised by the
shutting and opening of the gates , see the *Act regarding the Traditio
of the Palace by Card. Guido Ascanius Sforza, Procurator of Pius IV ,
to the Orator Jacobus Superantius, dated 1564, 2, VII , in the State
Archives, Venice.   (Kindly communicated by Prof F. Kaltenbrunner)

CHAPTER III.

THE death of Pius II. inflicted a heavy blow upon the Church, more especially because its effect was to arrest the movement for the defence of Christendom against Islam, which had then just commenced. Cardinal Bessarion, one of Greece's noblest sons, gave expression to his sorrow in touching words.* The Crusade was, for the time, at a standstill, but the idea lived on in the minds of the Popes. Paul II. had, even while a Cardinal, taken a deep interest in the Turkish question, and his friends hoped great things from him.†

The first steps taken by the new Pope in no way disappointed these expectations. In the letters by which he informed the Italian Princes of his election, he gave expression to his zeal for " the defence of the Christian Faith against the fury of the Turks."‡ One of the principal

* Report of the Milanese Ambassador of the 23rd Oct, 1464 Ambrosian Library

† JAGER, II, 428 The letter of Paul Morizeno, of the 4th Sept., 1464, here cited, is no longer to be found in the Government Archives of Innsbruck.

‡ CONTELORIUS, 57–9 (see RAYNALDUS, ad an 1464, N. 59). The Letters to Florence (of which a copy exists in the Archives of that city) and to the Marquis of Mantua (Original in the Gonzaga Archives) are similar to that here published In a *Brief to Bologna, dated Rome, 1464, Sept 20, Paul II. also asserts his intention of carrying on the war against the Turks which Pius II. had begun (State Archives, Bologna, Q 3) See also THEINER, Mon Hung, II, 398

hindrances in the way of Pius II.'s magnificent schemes
had been his constant financial difficulties. Paul II., the
practical Venetian, sought to remedy this state of things,
by removing the charge of the revenue derived from the
Alum monopoly, and, in virtue of the Election Capitulation, destined for the Holy War, from the Apostolic
Treasury to a Commission composed of Cardinals Bessarion,
d'Estouteville and Carvajal.* These Cardinals, who were
styled "Commissaires General of the Holy Crusade," were
to deliberate on all measures necessary for the prosecution
of the war, and to report accordingly. "Also the income
from Indulgences and from the tithes paid by the clergy
for this purpose, as far as it had hitherto been at the disposal of the 'Camera Apostolica,' was now, for the most
part, directly handed over to the Commission, or expended
according to its decision." † The magnificent support
afforded by the Commission to the brave Hungarians has
won for it an abiding and honourable remembrance.‡

In the autumn of 1464, when the Envoys of the Italian
States came to Rome to do homage, the Pope took the
opportunity of bringing forward the Turkish question.§

* Letter of Cardinal Gonzaga to his Mother, dated Rome, 1464, Nov.
23 (Gonzaga Archives, Mantua.) See *ibid*, *Letter of Jacopo de
Aretio of the 1st Sept, 1464, AMMANATI, Epist, f 26, 60 ; and
CANENSIUS, 47.

† GOTTLOB, Cam. Ap.

‡ Further particulars will be found, *infra*, p. 83. A Papal Bull, " Ad
sacram," dated Romae, 1465, III. Id April (=11 April), renews the
prohibition of trade with the Infidels and of any interference with
the alum trade (Regest, 519, f. 153, Secret Archives of the Vatican.
Copy in the State Archives, Milan.) GOTTLOB, Cam Ap, shews that
Paul II. called upon the other powers to protect the Papal monopoly
of Alum.

§ See Paul II's Brief to Louis XI in D'ACHERY, III, 824, and
the *Letter of the Milanese Ambassadors of the 14th Oct, 1461,
Ambrosian Library.

Special negotiations were set on foot with the splendid Embassy of the Venetian Republic.* They proceeded to treat with the Commission of Cardinals, and a fresh scheme was proposed for the Italian States, according to which the Pope and Venice were each to contribute 100,000 ducats, Naples 80,000, Milan 70,000, Florence 50,000, Modena 20,000, Siena 15,000, Mantua 10,000, Lucca 8,000 and Montferrat, 5,000 †

The plan was by no means well received by the Italian powers. The Pope, who declared himself ready to pay the 100,000 ducats, even if he should have to take it out of his household expenditure,‡ had great difficulty in obtaining a promise to let the matter be again brought under discussion in Rome. The deliberations lasted for six months No one was prepared to pay the appointed contributions, which the Pope intended to devote to the assistance of the Hungarians. Each sought to diminish his own share, and the more powerful States attached onerous conditions to their compliance. Venice, Florence and Milan demanded the remission of the Papal tax of the tenth, twentieth and thirtieth, and the King of Naples the complete remission of the tribute which he owed to the Holy See. In order to enforce his request, Ferrante informed the Pope that the Sultan had made offers of alliance to him, with a sum of 80,000 ducats, if he would stir up a war in Italy. Subsequently, when the relations between Rome and Naples had become still more un-

* Regarding this Embassy, see ROMANIN, IV, 321.

† AMMANATI, Epist, 41. See Mon. Hung, II, 234, where the document on the subject is wrongly assigned to the year 1471, instead of the autumn of 1464 The proposal is also interesting as giving an idea of the wealth of the Italian States See the Table of 1455 in MUNTZ, Renaiss., 50.

‡ Mon Hung, II, 234.

friendly, he openly threatened to ally himself with the Turks *

The Ambassadors assembled in Rome displayed a true Italian talent for evasion and procrastination. It was evident that not one amongst them would do anything † This "hopeless state of things" induced Paul II. to lift the veil, and let all the world know whose fault it was that, after six months of deliberation, not a single step in advance had been made. The just displeasure of Paul II found vent in bitter complaints. " The outcry against the burdens imposed is only raised in order to avoid giving support to the Venetians. May it not prove that, in thus forsaking the Venetians, people are forsaking themselves and all the faithful." They desire to discharge their obligations with the money of the Church, and thus to render it impossible for her to assist the Hungarians. The consequence will be that Hungary will be compelled to make peace with the Turks What is left for the Venetians but to take the same course, especially as Mahomet has offered them tolerably favourable conditions ? When both these champions are removed, the way to Italy by land and sea lies open to the enemies of Christendom ‡

These complaints were as powerless to rouse the Italian powers from their lethargy as the tidings of the immense

* Besides the authorities cited by CHRISTOPHE, II , 120 *seq* , 152 *seq* , see the *Letter of Augustinus de Rubeis to Fr. Sforza, dated Rome, 1465, Febr 20 (Ambrosian Library.) Particulars regarding the conflict between Rome and Naples will be found in Chapter VI

† Jacopo de Aretio, one of the Ambassadors, writes (dat. Roma, 1465, Marzo 18), regarding the negotiations with the Commission of Cardinals : *" Secondo a mi parse comprendere in quelle volte che me so ritrovato in simil congregatione non compresi alcuno che vollese offerire alcuna cosa." Gonzaga Archives, Mantua

‡ AMMANATI, Epist , f 6ob , ZINKEISEN, II , 309 *seq.*

naval preparations of the Turks, which reached Rome in May, 1465, denoted immediate danger to Italy.* Yet at this very time Florence refused the payment of a yearly contribution for Hungary demanded by the Pope †

Even in the States of the Church the Pope encountered obstinate opposition to the payment of the Turkish tithes. Not only the smaller towns, like Viterbo, Toscanella and Soriano, but even the wealthy city of Bologna had to be seriously admonished to fulfil the obligation ‡ Tivoli and Foligno begged for a remission of the tax ; Ferentino lay for a long time under an Interdict for resisting the claims of the Apostolic Treasury ; the Counts of Conti in the Campagna were utterly recalcitrant Ecclesiastical penalties proved useless, and in the end it was necessary to resort to force §

Meanwhile, Paul II. maintained the war against the enemies of the Faith as well as his own resources permitted, making great sacrifices, especially on behalf of Hungary. A modern historian,‖ after mentioning 42,500 (or 40,000) ducats given to Matthias Corvinus at Ancona, speaks of "some smaller" sums of money sent by Paul to Hungary This statement is directly contradicted by the testimony of the Pope's contemporary, Vespasiano da Bisticci, who says that Paul II. sent about 80,000 ducats to Hungary in 1465, and also promised an annual contribution ¶ The

* *Letter of J. P. Arrivabene of the 21st May, 1465 Gonzaga Archives, Mantua

+ MULLER , Docum , 202-3

‡ *Brief to Bologna, dated Rome, 1464, Sept 20. (State Archives, Bologna, Q 3) Regarding the other cities, see *Cruciata Pauli II , f. 10b State Archives, Rome.

§ GOTTLOB, Cam. Ap

‖ HUBER, Gesch. Oesterr., III., 212

¶ MAI, Spic , I , 297

account-books preserved in the Roman State Archives shew that on the 23rd May, 1465, the Commissaries General of the Crusade paid 57,500 golden florins to the Ambassadors of King Matthias of Hungary from the proceeds of the Alum monopoly alone, and, on the 28th April, 1466, a further sum of 10,000 Hungarian ducats * The expense of the mercenaries meanwhile was so heavy that the Hungarian Monarch felt obliged to give up all offensive warfare against the Turks. Venice, also, at this time thought of making peace with the enemy   The deplorable policy of the Italian States, which Paul II had vainly endeavoured to gain to the common cause, explains this universal discouragement. " Naples and Milan kept on good terms with the Porte, Genoa and Florence hankered after the reversion of the commerce of Venice in the Levant." Under these circumstances, it was well that the heroic Skanderbeg and the war in Asia Minor, " by which the feudatory kingdom of Caramania was annexed in 1466," fully occupied the Turkish forces †

To prevent the conclusion of a peace with the Turks, Paul II. made large offers of money, and resolved to send Cardinal Carvajal, the most distinguished member of the

---

* *Cruciata Pauli II. See GOTTLOB, Cam Ap, and GORI, Aich, III, 39   I will not blame Huber for having overlooked the last mentioned treatise, but I ask why he has completely ignored the statements of Vespasiano da Bisticci in a work which is generally accessible. It is absolutely incomprehensible that HUBER, *loc cit*, should speak of "some few smaller sums of money also sent" by Paul II, while he himself cites the Brief of that Pope of May 26th, 1465, published by TELEKI, XI, 124 *seq*, in which the transmission of 57,500 florins is expressly mentioned   The zeal of Paul II. in resisting the Turks has been generally acknowledged, even by the Venetians, who were not favourably disposed towards him   See Mon Hung, I, 321, *ibid.*, 324, 332, 339, 343, 375

† HERTZBERG, Griechenland, II, 591. See ROMANIN, IV, 324 *seq*

Sacred College, to Venice. This prelate, who had through life ardently espoused the cause of the Holy War, was of all others the best fitted to accomplish so difficult a mission. His appointment as Legate for Venice took place on the 30th July, 1466; he left Rome on the 20th August, and did not return till the autumn of the following year.*

In November, 1466, a Diet, energetically promoted by Paul II., was held at Nuremberg† to consider the Turkish question. The despatch of an army to the assistance of Hungary was discussed at great length, but neither this Assembly nor those which followed had any definite result.‡

* GASP VERONEN, 1046, expresses himself in a very mysterious manner regarding Carvajal's Mission, but declares that the Cardinal accomplished the object in view. MALIPIERO, 38, says even more. The above dates, which have hitherto been unknown, are from the *Acta Consist. of the Secret Archives of the Vatican, f. 34b–35 ; the purpose of the journey is here mentioned in the following terms "sollicitaturus aliqua contra nephandissimum Turcum et alia etc " Concerning his return, see *infra*, p 140, note †. From a *Letter of Card. Gonzaga's, dated Rome, 1466, July 31, in which the 30th July is mentioned as the day of his appointment, we learn that Carvajal was to enter into negotiations not only about the Turkish War, but also concerning the other matters then in dispute between Rome and Venice. (Gonzaga Archives, Mantua) See *infra*, Chap IV Carvajal had also to treat of the entry of Venice into the Italian League ; see *Report of A de Rubeis, dated Rome, 1466, December 6 State Archives, Milan

† The Cardinal of Augsburg sent out the Papal Briefs, in which the "great peril of the Christian Faith ' was laid before the States, and they were called upon to send delegates to Nuremberg. The Original of a *Letter to Frankfort-on-Maine (dated Dillingen, 1466, Oct. 15) is in the Archives of that City, Reichssachen, 5537. Paul II. himself also exhorted the powers to attend the Diet appointed, also to meet at Nuremberg on the 15th June, 1467 See JANSSEN, Reichscorr , I , 251, and Cod Dipl Sax , 170-171 A list of those who at this time received these Papal Briefs is in the City Archives of Strasburg, AA 205

‡ See REISSERMAYER, I., 20 *seq* , where the dignity of Cardinal is

In July, 1466, the Pope invoked the assistance of the European Princes on behalf of Skanderbeg. For two years had this hero resisted all the attacks of the Turks, who had been repeatedly defeated by him * To avenge this disgrace, the Sultan determined on an expedition against Albania. In the spring of 1466 a Turkish force, 200,000, or, as some few writers say, 300,000 strong,† began its march against Croja, the capital city   At the end of May a messenger reached Ragusa with the news that Skanderbeg had been defeated by treachery, and that a number of Christians had been slain ; a second Turkish army was also said to threaten Hungary ‡   The Italians were panic-stricken. Piero de' Medici shed tears over the fate of Albania and promised help §   The Pope, who had already aided Skanderbeg, again sent money,‖ and lost no time in calling on the Christian powers to bestir themselves.   He spoke in moving terms of the affliction of Christendom, of the terror of the nations on the Adriatic coast, and of the fugitives who were constantly arriving from the East.   " One cannot without tears behold those ships that flee from the Albanian shore

wrongly ascribed to Fantinus   Besides the Acts of the Electoral Chancery in the State Archives of Vienna, the *Handelung auf dem papstlichen und kaiserlichen Tage zu Nurnberg, A° 66, in the City Archives at Oberehenheim, may be consulted in regard to this Diet

* PAGANEL, 327 seq., 349 seq.

† **Letter from the Ambassador of Mantua to Rome, 31st May, 1466 Gonzaga Archives

‡ **Letter of Bartol. de Maraschis to the Marchioness of Mantua, dated Rome, 1466, May 31   Gonzaga Archives

§ *Letter of T. Maffei of the 15th May, 1466, according to the Florentine State Archives, in Appendix, N 14   See the complaints of the Venetians in MAKUSCEV, Slaven in Albanien, 108.

‖ Documentary evidence of this fact, taken from the Roman State Archives (*Cruciata Pauli II), is given by Bertolotti in GORI, Archivio, III., 39, and also by GOTTLOB, who was unacquainted with Bertolotti's work, in Hist Jahrb , VI., 443

to take refuge in Italian harbours; those naked, wretched families, driven from their dwellings, who sit by the sea, stretching out their hands to heaven and filling the air with lamentations uttered in an unknown tongue." The account-books of his pontificate bear witness to the magnificent liberality with which Paul II. succoured these unhappy creatures The Pope might indeed say that he had done what lay in his power; the Hungarians alone had in the preceding year received 100,000 golden florins, but he could not do everything, effectual support from the Christian powers was more than ever a necessity.*

Happily the apprehensions regarding the fate of Albania were not realised. The heroic valour of its champion rendered Croja invincible "Skanderbeg pursued his ancient, well-tried tactics, and from the woodlands of Tumenistos he ceaselessly harassed the besiegers, inflicting so much loss and disgrace on the Turkish army, that the Sultan, finding corruption and force alike useless, left Balaban with 80,000 men to continue the siege of Croja and starve it into sub-mission, and himself retired with the bulk of his troops into winter quarters at Constantinople."†

The fate of Albania depended on the deliverance of Croja, which Balaban had encircled with a girdle of fortresses, and the task was beyond the unassisted powers of the Albanians and Venetians. Skanderbeg, therefore, resolved to go in

---

* Papal Letter to the Duke of Burgundy in AMMANATI, Epist., 102b–104, and in RAYNALDUS, ad an. 1466, N 2–6. The date, July 1466, wanting in CIPOLLA, 535, may be gathered from the contents, and from a comparison with the Brief cited by LICHNOWSKY, Urkunden, p CCCLXVIII, addressed to Duke Sigismund of the Tyrol. I have, however, vainly sought for this Document in the Ferdinandeum at Innsbruck

† FALLMERAYER, 87. See HOPF, 156, and MAKUSCEV, Slaven, 109.

person to Italy to beg for money and arms from Rome and Naples *

In the middle of December, 1466, the Albanian champion reached Rome, where he was received with honours. " He is," to quote the words of an eye-witness, "an old man in his sixtieth year , he came with but few horses, in poverty ; I hear that he will ask for help."†

It has been again and again falsely asserted that, in consequence of his "too Venetian sympathies," Skanderbeg obtained nothing from the Pope beyond the Indulgence and the Proclamations addressed to the deaf ears of Western Christendom, together with some pious exhortations and the renewal of the never fulfilled promise of the crown of Epirus and Macedonia.‡

His biographer, on the contrary, not only relates the honourable and friendly reception of the hero in Rome, but expressly observes that the Pope, like the Cardinals, had generously responded to his requests. "With many

* MALIPIERO, 38 , BARLETIUS, I , XII., p 355.

† PAGANEL, 356, gives 1465 as the date of Skanderbeg's journey to Rome , ZINKEISEN, II , 393, places it in the beginning of 1466 ; FALLMERAYER, 87, and HOPF, 156, in the summer of that year. They are all mistaken The Cron. Rom , 32, expressly mention his arrival in the December of 1466, and the *Account-books of Paul II in the Roman State Archives, as well as a *Letter of Card Gonzaga's of the 15th Dec , 1466 (Gonzaga Archives), concur in the statement In the Gonzaga Archives a *Letter from J. P Arrivabene, dated Rome, xiv. Decemb , 1466, contains the following words —*" El S. Scanderbeo gionse qui veneri [=12 Dec] et incontra li forono mandate le famiglie de' cardinali. È homo molto de tempo passa li 60 anni , cum puochi cavalli è venuto e da povero homo Sento vorrà subsidio " Beneath the Quirinal, Vicolo di Scanderbeg No. 116-117, is to be seen on the house where he is said to have dwelt, his image with the inscription · " Geor. Castriota a Scanderbeg princeps Epiri||ad fidem iconis rest. an. dom. MDCCCXLIII." See BELLI, Case, 58.

‡ FALLMERAYER, 88, where the Pope is twice called Paul III !

presents, and with a considerable sum of money," says
Barletius, "Skanderbeg returned cheered and encouraged
to his people "* Other authentic documents give fuller
particulars as to the results of the journey to Rome   In
the account-books of Paul II. we find that first of all
Skanderbeg received for his maintenance on one occasion
250, and on another, 200 ducats, and that furthermore on
the 19th April, 1467, 2700, and on the 1st September
1100 ducats were paid to him.† Regarding the Secret
Consistory of January 7th, 1467, in which the assistance to
be given to the Albanian hero was considered, we have
the testimony of Cardinal Gonzaga, who took part in it ‡
He says that the Pope at once declared his readiness to
pay 5000 ducats ; the necessity of protecting his own
country was his reason for not contributing yet more
largely ; Cardinal Orsini, who was hostile to Paul II,
ventured to observe that the Pope had nothing to apprehend from any quarter.   This remark greatly angered the
Pope, and provoked some interesting disclosures as to his
relations with Naples. He said that he knew with certainty that Ferrante was eager to attack the States of the
Church   One of the King's five confidants on this matter
had given information to Rome   It is evident that, under
these circumstances, the Holy See could not do more for
the champion of Albania   A Secret Consistory of the 12th
January, 1467, determined that in any case Skanderbeg
should have 5000 ducats § Not only Venice, but also

* BARLETIUS, I, XII, p. 358   The speech of Skanderbeg here
related is no more genuine than that which the hero is said to have
made on his death-bed

† Authorities are given in the articles by BERTOLOTTI and GOTT-
LOB, cited p. 86, *supra*   See also CANENSIUS, 74

‡ See in Appendix, N. 18, the text of this *Document, which I found
in the Gonzaga Archives.

§ *"Questa matina de novo foe havuto ragionamento in consistorio

Ferrante, whose relations with Skanderbeg had long been
of an intimate character, received him and sent money,
provisions and munitions * On his return to his beloved
country he soon won fresh laurels ; in April, 1467, the
Turks were defeated and Balaban's brother taken prisoner.
A second victory quickly followed, in which Balaban fell
and his troops took to flight † Croja was saved. The
danger, however, was not at an end ; a second Turkish
army appeared, and Skanderbeg had to keep the field
throughout the whole year. In the midst of these conflicts, death overtook the Albanian champion ; on the 17th
January, 1468, Skanderbeg succumbed at Alessio to the
effects of a fever ‡
   No greater loss had befallen Christendom since the
death of Hunyadi and St. John Capistran. This was but
too plain to the enemies of the Faith. It is said that when
the Sultan heard the news, he exclaimed, "At last Europe
and Asia are mine. Woe to Christendom ! she has lost
her sword and her shield !"

secr [eto circa] li fatti de Scandarbeo al qual se daranno pur li cinque-
milia ducati." Letter from Card Gonzaga to his father, dated Rome,
12 Januarii, 1467 Gonzaga Archives, Mantua.

   * TRINCHERA, I , 90.

   † This is related by Zacharius Barbarus, writing on the 10th May,
1467, from Letters from Alessio. See MAKUSCEV, Slaven, 110.

   ‡ HAMMER, II , 91, 94, makes Skanderbeg die in 1466 ; PAGANEL,
377 , ROHREACHER-KNOPFLER, 227, and CIPOLLA, 539, fix 1467
as the date ; and REUMONT, III , 1, 189, February, 1468 The date
we have given above, to which FALLMERAYER, 95, also adheres, is
confirmed by the Letter of Condolence in TRINCHERA, I., 439, and
the Milanese Report in the Mon. Hung, II , 93 See also HOPF,
Griechenland, 157. Skanderbeg's helmet, with a goat's head erect
embossed, and his sword, with the inscription in Arabic, "God's hero,
Iskender Beg," are preserved in the Ambras Collection at Vienna ;
see VON SACKEN, Ambras Sammlung, 211–212 (Wien, 1855).

The effect of the blow was felt at once by the hard-pressed Albanians The Turks overran their country—" in the whole of Albania we saw nothing but Turks," says a contemporary account—8000 unhappy creatures were sent away as slaves within a few weeks * But Albania was not yet completely vanquished : Scutari and Croja, whose garrisons were strengthened by Venetian troops, continued to hold out. The enthusiastic honour paid by the afflicted people to the memory of their departed chief was most touching. " Choirs of Albanian maidens," Sabellicus informs us, "though surrounded with the din of battle and the clang of barbarian arms, assembled regularly every eighth day in the public squares of the cities of the principality to sing hymns in praise of their departed hero." † The valour with which the little nation resisted the overwhelming power of Mahomet for more than a decade is a proof that the spirit of Skanderbeg still survived amongst them, though he himself had passed away.

* HOPF, Griechenland, LXXXVI., 157
+ SABELLICUS, Decad , III., 568 ; FALLMERAYER, 100

CHAPTER IV.

STRUGGLE AGAINST THE DOMINEERING POLICY OF THE VENETIANS
AND LOUIS XI OF FRANCE.—EFFORTS TO GIVE GREATER
EXTERNAL SPLENDOUR TO THE HOLY SEE.—REFORMS.—
PUNISHMENT OF THE FRATICELLI —REGULATIONS REGARDING
THE JUBILEE. — ATTEMPT TO UNITE RUSSIA WITH THE
CHURCH.

THE independent attitude which the island city of Venice
maintained towards the other Italian States is equally
marked in the domain of ecclesiastical politics. In no
portion of the Appenine Peninsula do we meet with such
early and persistent efforts for the extension of the
authority of the State at the expense of the liberty of the
Church   The Popes were the natural opponents of these
efforts, and more than once found themselves under the
sad necessity of inflicting the sharpest ecclesiastical
penalties on the proud Republic.*

The great piety of the Venetians, to which their numerous
churches still bear silent witness, seems to contrast strangely
with these efforts to subjugate the Church to the State.
A deeply religious spirit no doubt existed among the
people, and of this the rulers of the Republic, who loved
to call it by the name of St Mark, were obliged to take
some account   Yet this St. Mark was almost constantly

* See *Collect. Scripturar spectantium ad interdictum reipubl
Venetae inflictum a variis summis pontificibus. Cod. L 27 of the
Vallicell Library, Rome

in conflict with the Holy See, because it strove in every
way to degrade the freeborn Church into the position of
handmaid to the State.   Further contests with Rome
were also occasioned by the efforts of the Republic to
obtain possession of the Romagna   In 1441 the Venetians
had gained a footing in Ravenna, and ever since that
period they had been constantly bent on the extension of
their dominion to the detriment of the States of the
Church.   These more external disputes, however, were
driven into the background, by the contests which arose
from the pretensions of the Venetian oligarchy to absolute
dominion over the whole life of its subjects, even in regard
to ecclesiastical matters *

Even while a Cardinal, Paul II had come into collision
with the government of his native city.   In 1459, on the
death of Fantin Dandolo, Bishop of Padua, Pius II. had
conferred the See on Cardinal Barbo † By this appointment he intended to please both the Cardinal and the
Republic,‡ which had always been glad to see her Bishoprics
occupied by the sons of her noble families   The Venetian
government had, however, on this occasion selected another
candidate, Gregorio Correr, and now made every effort to
give effect to their choice.   It was resolved that, unless the
Cardinal should within twenty days renounce his Bishopric,
all his revenues derived from Venetian territory should be
sequestrated.   Moreover, Paul Barbo was to put pressure

* FRIEDBERG, II., 688 *seq*., follows almost exclusively the unsatisfactory article of SAGREDO, in Arch St. Ital, 3 Serie, II, 92 *seq*
See also LEBRET, II, 2, 668 *seq*.   Many fresh details are given by
CECCHETTI, V, e la C di Roma, 2 vols, but ill-arranged and very
defective

† May, 1459, see DONDI OROLOGIO, Canonici, 24.

‡ Pii II Comment 44   See DONDI OROLOGIO, Dissert. nona s.
l'Istoria Eccl. Padovana, 50 *seq*   (Padova, 1817.)

on his brother in the same direction, and if he failed to
induce him to resign, was to be banished from the Venetian
territory and deprived of his possessions!* Soon afterwards,
the Signoria wrote many urgent letters on the matter to
the Pope and to various Cardinals † As Cardinal Barbo
did not yield, the Venetian Ambassador was strictly
charged not to visit him.‡ So firmly did the Signoria
adhere to their purpose § that the Cardinal was at last
obliged to give way. Jacopo Zeno, however, not Gregorio
Correr, became Bishop of Padua. He was required to pay
2000 ducats yearly to Cardinal Barbo, and the resolutions
against Paul Barbo were rescinded.‖

Great was the embarrassment of the Venetian statesmen
when, a few years later, the Cardinal who had been treated
in this manner was elevated to the Papal throne No elec-

* *Decision of the 5th March, 1459 Sen Secr. XX, f 177b-178
State Archives, Venice

† *Letters to Pius II , dated 1459, March 8 and 27, and to Card
Scarampo, dated 1459, March 27 Sen Secr. XX, f. 178-9, *loc cit.*

‡ *"Bene autem commemoramus et mandamus vobis, quod desistere debeatis a visitatione rmi card S. Marci ex causis et respectibus
vobis notis " *Instruction for the Envoys for Mantua, 17th Sept,
1459 Sen Secr XX, f 190. DARU, and after him VOIGT, III , 70,
are mistaken in speaking of a prohibition to speak to the Pope or to
salute him

§ See especially the discourteous *Letter to the Envoys to the Pope
of the 4th January, 1459 (st fl), in Sen Secr XX , f 203.

‖ See SANUDO, 1167 , CANENSIUS, 97. The resolution against
P Barbo was repealed on the 5th March, 1460 , see *Sen Secr XX ,
f. 177b Memmo's Memoir of 1709, printed in Arch St Ital , 3 Serie,
II , 120 *seq* , incorrectly gives 1443 as the date, and speaks of a
Cardinal of Mantua instead of S Marco FRIEDBERG, II , 692, has
simply adopted the chronological error, although any list of Bishops,
e g , UGHELLI, V , 456, might have served to correct it CAVACIUS'
opinion (Hist coenobii D Justinae Patav , p 228, Venetiis, 1606) that
Barbo was Bishop of Padua for a year is a mistake.

tion could have been less agreeable to them   They were,
however, prudent enough carefully to conceal their vexation.
Arrangements for public rejoicings were made immediately,
and an Embassy of surpassing splendour was sent to Rome
to proffer obedience to Paul II. The usual number of
Envoys on such occasions was four. In the case of Eugenius
IV., who was a Venetian, this number was doubled ; but
now ten were sent.* The Pope perfectly understood the
value of these outward tokens of honour. Even before
the arrival of the Mission he spoke in bitter terms to the
Milanese Ambassador about the arrogance and the personal
hostility of certain Venetian statesmen, and expressed his
opinion that before the Envoys had been a fortnight in
Rome, disputes would break out.† In fact, unpleasant
explanations began almost immediately,‡ and the tension
kept on growing from day to day, for no European power
was viewed in Venice with such jealousy as the Roman
See.§ At the end of 1465, Paul II poured forth a whole
list to the Milanese Ambassador of charges against his
fellow-countrymen. In the Turkish matter, he said, they
had, by a simple act of arbitrary power, imposed a tithe on
the clergy. They claimed tribute from Cardinals visiting
Venice, a thing which no Christian Prince had ever done.
They were perpetually incurring reprimands for contemp-
tuous conduct towards their Bishops. They had forbidden

* MALIPIERO, 32 , SANUDO, 1181 ; Ist Bresc , 900. The Pope knew
that the festivities in Venice were intended to obliterate the memory of
former injuries , see Carretto's *Letter to Fr. Sforza, dated Rome,
1464, Oct. 24 (Ambrosian Library.) Regarding the Embassy to do
homage, see also *GHIRARDACCI, ad an. Cod. 768 of the Library at
Bologna

+ See Appendix, N. 6 Ambrosian Library

‡ *Letter of S Nardini to Fr Sforza, dated Rome, 1464, Dec 6
Ambrosian Library

§ LEBRET, II , 2, 670 ; Gesch d Republik Venedig

the Archbishop of Spalatro to enter his See   They were seeking to take possession of the Morea, which belonged to Thomas Palæologus   The Venetian Merchants, by buying alum from the Turks, put Christian money in the pockets of their enemies   The penalty of Excommunication would have to be pronounced against them.   Assuming the position of mistress of the Adriatic, Venice oppresses Ancona ; she holds wrongful possession of Cervia and Ravenna. The Knights of St. John at Rhodes, and the Emperor, complain of the Republic, and indeed every one has some grievance against her.   The law which prohibits any one who has a relation among the clergy from being a member of the Council is absolutely intolerable , the infidels themselves could not do worse ; this measure must be repealed.*

Nothing of the kind was contemplated in Venice ; the remonstrances of the Pope were utterly unheeded †   In the following spring the appointment to the Patriarchal Throne gave occasion for further conflicts with Rome, which were aggravated in the summer, when the Signoria took advantage of the scare about the Turks again arbitrarily to impose taxes on ecclesiastical property.   Many in Rome were of opinion that this was done with the object of concealing a secret understanding with the Sultan ‡   It is quite certain that a powerful party in Venice favoured a peace with the Porte ; some few Venetians, according to

* **Report of S. Nardini, Archbishop of Milan, to Fr. Sforza, dated Rome, 1465, Dec 11. (Ambrosian Library.) Concerning the dispute about the tithes, see NAVAGIERO, 1125 ; the notice in CECCHETTI, I , 154 , and also ROSMINI, Milano, IV , 67

† See in Appendix, N 8, the undated *Brief to the Doge   Cod. Ottob. of the Vatican Library

‡ Cardinal Gonzaga mentions this on the 5th July, 1466 (Gonzaga Archives, Mantua) See Appendix, N. 15. For further particulars relating to the question of the Patriarchate, see Arch. St. Ital, *loc. cit*, 121 *seq*

the report of the Milanese Ambassador, even went so far
as to say that it would be well, not merely to make peace
with the Turk, but also to open the way to Rome for him,
that he may punish these priests ! * In the summer of
1466 the Republic raised the question of the Council.
This so incensed Paul II that he spoke of excommunicating them, and laying them under Interdict.† Several
Consistories took place, in which these extreme measures
were seriously considered. Two grave motives weighed
against a breach with Venice · in the first place, the
necessity of previously securing the support of an Italian
Power,‡ and secondly, the fear that the Signoria might
actually conclude peace with the Infidels Even in July
the Milanese Ambassador was persuaded that, notwithstanding the threats which had been pronounced, the Pope
would in the end endeavour to come to an amicable understanding § This difficult undertaking was entrusted to
Cardinal Carvajal, who, however, was empowered, in case
of necessity, to pronounce the Interdict. What has trans-
pired of the instructions given to him, makes it evident
that the Pope sincerely endeavoured to bring about a
satisfactory understanding. Cardinal Gonzaga believed
Paul II. to have contemplated an alliance with Venice, as

* Mon Hung , II , 14

† *Report of the Milanese Ambassador, dated Rome, 1466, Aug 4.
Paul II., he says, fears the Council "piu che l'inferno" Fonds Ital ,
1591, f. 362-3, of the National Library, Paris.

‡ See in Appendix, N. 16, Card Gonzaga's *Letter of July 19,
1466

§ "*Questi signori preti faranno ogni cosa per abonizare dicta signoria." *Letter of A. de Rubeis to the Duke and Duchess of Milan,
dated Rome, 1466, July 20 (Fonds Ital , 1591, f 358 of the National
Library, Paris.) The presence of the Duke of Urbino, who is spoken of
in the *Report of 4th August, cited above, was no doubt connected
with the Venetian dispute

a protection against the animosity of the King of Naples.*
Details regarding the protracted negotiations carried on
by the distinguished Cardinal are unfortunately wanting.
He is, however, said to have admirably discharged his
arduous mission. If he was not successful in bringing all
questions between Rome and Venice to a solution, he at
any rate prevented the conclusion of a peace with the
Porte, and prepared the way for better relations between
Paul II and the Republic.† The question of the tithes
having been settled in 1468, in a manner which contented
the Venetians, in the May of the following year the Pope
and the Signoria entered into an alliance directed chiefly
against the treacherous Roberto Malatesta. The double
game which the Venetians subsequently played,‡ and fresh
disputes regarding the Turkish tithes, again caused discord
between the allies   When Paul II. died, things had reached
such a pass that there was no Venetian Ambassador at the
Roman Court.§

Paul II. had repeated differences with Florence on
matters connected with the liberty of the Church, and in

* *Letter of Card Gonzaga to his father, dated Rome, 1466, July
31. (Gonzaga Archives, Mantua.) The Milanese Ambassador, in the
*Report of August 4th, 1466, which we have already cited, expresses
his belief that Carvajal was charged to bring about a reconciliation
between the Republic and the Holy See

† See *supra,* Chap III , and also the two very short notices in
CECCHETTI, I , 154, regarding the solution of the tithe question   See
also Mon Hung , II , 33, 35, 63

‡ See *infra,* Chap. VI

§ MALIPIERO, 239   Regarding the joy of the Venetians at the death
of Paul II , see Arch d Soc Rom , XI , 254.   In the year 1472, Paul's
sister, Isabella Zeno, mother of the Cardinal, was imprisoned and
banished because she was said to have revealed State secrets to the
Roman Court   Isabella subsequently came to Rome.   Her last resting-
place was in St Peter's ; see REUMONT, III , 1, 494, and CECCHETTI,
I , 419 *seq.*

1466* and 1469 about the arbitrary taxation of ecclesiastical property The obstinacy of the opposition encountered by the Pope may be estimated by the frequency of his remonstrances.† One was published but a few days before his death.‡ Beyond the Italian frontier the appointment to the See of Brixen also gave rise to a conflict §

The omnipotence claimed by the State was also the occasion of considerable tension in the relations between the Pope and the French King. Louis XI. wished to reign alone, alike in State and Church, his will was to be in all things supreme ‖ Even in the beginning of November, 1464, fresh anti-Roman measures of the King were reported in Rome. It was said that Louis XI had announced that the

---

* *Paul II's Brief to Florence, dated 1466, March 25 State Archives, Florence, X, II., 23 f., 141 *seq.*

† *Paul II's Brief to Florence, dated 1469, Aug 25, *loc cit.*, X, II., 25, f. 14b-15.

‡ Paulus II., Florentinis, dat 1471, Julii 23 Lib brev 12, f. 180 (Secret Archives of the Vatican) *Ibid*, f 45b, is a *Brief which must here be mentioned, inasmuch as it treats of the protection of ecclesiastical rights · * "Regi Aragonum. Non absque magna admiratione intelleximus quod adhuc possessionem monasterii S Victoriani ac prioratus de Roda Ilerd dioc. dil fil noster L [udovicus] tit s. 4 coronator. S R. E. presb card^lis assequi non potuit" Threats follow Dat. 1470, Dec 5.

§ The account given of this matter by EGGER, I , 595, is very imperfect; the author's attack on his own fellow-countrymen speaks for itself Regarding Paul II.'s measures for the protection of ecclesiastical liberty in Hungary, see TELEKI, XI , 133 *seq* , 139 *seq.*, 141 *seq.* I am indebted to the kindness of Dr Fraknói, Vice-President of the Hungarian Academy, for having made known to me a *Brief of Paul II. to the Abbot of the Convent of S Maximiani extra muros Trev, in which the latter is blamed for having invoked the assistance of a layman in a dispute : "Hoc enim non videtur ius suum velle defendere, sed monasterium et ecclesiam laicis ipsis quodammodo subicere."

‖ See FIERVILLE, 137

publication of Apostolic Bulls throughout the whole of his
kingdom must depend on his permission, and had also prohibited *expectances*. "These things," wrote the Milanese
Ambassador, "are poor tokens of obedience; these measures
are worse than the Pragmatic Sanction, which formerly
prevailed in France." No wonder that Paul II. distrusted
the French Monarch, whose tyrannical and ambitious disposition was well known to him.*

A treatise, written by Thomas Basin about the end of the
year 1464, shews the state of feeling which then prevailed
at the court of Louis XI. He twisted the words in which
homage was paid to Louis XI. so as to deduce from them
that this document only bound the King to Pius II. personally. By the death of that Pope, Louis XI. was freed from
all further obligation. Basin also insisted on the necessity
of speedily convening a French National Synod.†

Evil counsels of other kinds came to the French King
from Milan. In March, 1466, an Envoy from that State
was charged to advise Louis XI. to defer his profession
of obedience as long as possible, on the ground that, while
this matter was in suspense, the Pope would be obliged to
shew himself pliable.‡ The French Monarch, however,
did not take this view; his honour, he thought, allowed of
no further delay, and that which had already taken place
had been injurious to him.§ When, however, the representative of Milan again brought forward his request, the

* **Letter from O. de Carretto to Fr. Sforza, dated Rome, 1464,
Nov. 6. (Ambrosian Library.) See also BULAEUS, V., 671 *seq.*;
Ordonnac., XVI., 244 ; GUETTÉE, VIII., 24.

† BASIN-QUICHERAT, IV., 69, 73–90.

‡ See in Appendix, N. 12, the *Instruction of the 3rd March, 1466,
to the Milanese Envoys. National Library, Paris.

§ Paul II. had not granted the concessions asked by the French
Ambassador, Pierre Gruel, in the name of Louis XI.; see FIERVILLE,
136.

King consented to procrastinate as long as possible. "As
the French fear the heat and the Plague," adds the
Milanese Envoy, "the Embassy which is to do homage
in the usual form will not start before September   The
Archbishop of Lyons, Charles of Bourbon, will be its
leader, Cardinal Jouffroy, who is to accompany and
support the Envoys, will not, his people say, begin his
journey before September"* This last piece of news
was untrue, for Jouffroy reached Rome on the 4th October,
1466† The great Embassy, however, did not leave Lyons
until the end of the month‡ In a letter to the Pope
the King excused his tardiness on the plea of the troubles
in his kingdom. The instructions given to the Envoys
seemed to promise a favourable change in the ecclesiastical
policy of France. They were desired, in the first place, to
express the sincere devotion of the King to the Holy
See, of which the decree abrogating the Pragmatic Sanction, in spite of the opposition of almost all the kingdom,
was a token. Besides making the profession of obedience
in the form which, since the days of Martin V, had been

* *Letter of Joh Petrus Panicharolla to the Duke and Duchess of
Milan, dated Montargis, 1466, June 25. Fonds ital, 1611, of the
National Library, Paris

† *Acta Consist of the Secret Archives of the Vatican   Jouffroy's
Biographer, Fierville, fails to give us any information regarding these
dates

‡ "*Li rev^{mi} arcivescovo di Lione, fratello del duca di Borbon et
monsig. da Mans, fratello del conte San Pollo et li altri ambassatori
che vanno a Roma di presente sono per partire da Lione." Emanuel
de Jacopo and J P. Panicharolla to the Duke and Duchess of Milan,
dated Orleans, 1466, Oct 26 (Cod 1611 of the Fonds Ital of the
National Library, Paris) FIERVILLE, 137, is mistaken in his statement that the Embassy started as early as "towards the end of 1465
or beginning of 1466" See also Lettres de Louis XI, III, 99, 107 *seq*
112 *seq*

in use, the Ambassadors were charged to apologise in
Louis's name for the anti-Roman ordinances of 1464 ; and
to explain that they were not the act of the King, but due
to the Bishop of Bayeux and the Patriarch of Jerusalem.
The King would be an obedient son of the Holy See;
in return he asked for the right of appointing to twenty-
five Bishoprics.*

Paul II was not deluded by these fair words, for he was
well aware that the Bishop of Bayeux had acted by the
directions of the King. The Ambassadors obtained nothing.
At this time, Jean de La Balue, Bishop of Evreux, and
afterwards of Angers, another favourite of Louis, took part
with Cardinal Jouffroy in the negotiations concerning
the ecclesiastical policy of France † This designing man,
who was exactly of the same stamp as Jouffroy and his
apt pupil, sought, like him, to win the purple by means
of the question of the Pragmatic Sanction.‡ For a while
Paul II. resisted the admission of such a man into the
Senate of the Church, but the hope that Louis XI would
now really suppress the Pragmatic Sanction induced him
at last to yield. "I know the faults of this priest," he is
reported to have said, " but I was constrained to cover them
with this hat."

In return for the red hat conferred upon his favourite,§

---

* RAYNALDUS, ad an 1466, N. 15–16, and FIERVILLE, *loc cit.*

† For the literature regarding La Balue, see CHEVALIER, 214 and
2439. Also Lettres de Louis XI , III , 225–6.

‡ GUETTÉE, VIII , 27.

§ 18th Sept , 1467, according to the *Acta Consist of the Secret
Archives of the Vatican. FRIZON, 517, is mistaken in making Balue
Cardinal as early as 1464 For satires concerning this nomination,
see Bibl de l'École d. Chartes, Series IV., I , 565 The Harenga facta
per rev. card. Albiensem in eccl Paris , A° 1468, qua die cardinalatus
dignitatem recepit dom. card. Andegavens. in D'ACHERY, nov. edit ,
III., 825 to 830 See FIERVILLE, 141–6. Cardinal Alain took part in

Louis XI. issued a declaration against the Pragmatic
Sanction of a more stringent nature than those which
had preceded it.   When La Balue, on the 1st October, 1467,
appeared in Parliament with this document, the Procurator-
General refused to register it.   In order to work upon the
mind of the King, much stress was laid upon the abuse of
commendams,* and the large sums of money sent to Rome
from France †

The University of Paris, like the Parliament, declared
against the abrogation of the Pragmatic Sanction   An
appeal to a future Council was even issued.   Now, however, the Procurator-General resigned his post, and the
Royal Declaration remained in full force, although not
registered.‡   The ecclesiastical policy of France, nevertheless, remained as unsatisfactory and disquieting as ever,
for the King never relaxed his efforts to bind the Church
fast within the toils of the State.   His favourites, Jouffroy
and La Balue, turned the position of affairs to their own
advantage.   His acceptance of the anti-Roman project of
a Council, put forward by the Hussite King of Bohemia,
enables us to estimate the value of the " filial obedience " to
the Holy See so often spoken of by his Envoys in Rome.
In 1468, when the French demand for a general Council
was again mentioned to Paul II., he said that he would
hold one that very year, but that it should be in Rome §

the ceremony of giving the red hat. His Recessus versus Galliam is
noted in the *Acta Consist., Secret Archives of the Vatican, as taking
place on the 12th June, 1468.

* Paul II. looked into this abuse, and gave advice regarding its
abolition.   It was not, however, thoroughly remedied   See AMMANATI,
Epist., f. 59 , FIERVILLE, 18.

† PICOT, I , 426, note 2, considers the statements respecting the
money made by the excited Parliament of 1467 to be exaggerated

‡ GUETTÉE, VIII , 29-32

§ This is stated by the Milanese Ambassador, Joh. Blanchus, in the

Meanwhile, in the person of the new Duke of Burgundy, Charles the Bold, the King encountered so dangerous a political adversary, that ecclesiastical affairs were again for a time completely in abeyance Ever since the subjugation of Liège, Charles had reigned more absolutely than any of his predecessors, and his immense financial resources gave him a great advantage over the French King Louis fought his enemy with the weapons of treachery and corruption He had an interview with him at Peronne, during which tidings arrived of a fresh rising of the Liégeois, excited by the agents of Louis. The Duke of Burgundy was furious, and, it is said, contemplated the murder of the King, who was in his power. The demands which the Duke now made would have appeared to a high-minded man worse than death: Louis was to proceed in person against Liège, which he had himself incited to revolt. Utterly destitute of every feeling of honour, he made no difficulty, and at once consented to join the Duke in his expedition against the Netherlands, and thus witness with his own eyes the barbarous sack of Liège.*

The immediate consequence of these events was the downfall of La Balue, by whose advice the meeting at Peronne had taken place His good fortune was short-

---

Postscript to a *Despatch, dated Rome, 1468, March (the date effaced), State Archives, Milan, Cart Gen Regarding the Bohemian project of a Council, see the next Chapter.

* See SCHMIDT, Gesch Frankr, II, 432 *seq.*, HENRARD, Les Campagnes de Charles-le-Téméraire contre les Liégeois (Bruxelles, 1867) Paul II had, in 1468, sent Onofrius de S Cruce, Bishop of Tricarico, as Legate to Liège to appease the discord between Bishop Louis of Bourbon and his subjects, and to prevent Charles the Bold from turning his victory to the prejudice of the liberty of the Church ; this mission failed. The Legate wrote a Memorandum in his own justification. It is published in BORMANS, Mém du Légat Onofrius sur les affaires de Liège en 1468 (Bruxelles, 1886).

lived, and the King thought that he had before him
evidence of a treacherous understanding between the
Cardinal and the Duke of Burgundy He resolved to
take signal vengeance on the man whom he had raised
from nothing to be the first of his subjects. La Balue was
despoiled of his possessions and imprisoned. A like fate
befell the Bishop of Verdun, who was believed to be in
league with him. Even a tyrant like Louis XI. saw that
a Cardinal could not be tried without the Pope, and two
Envoys were charged to enter into negotiations on this
subject with Rome The conditions which the Pope laid
down for the trial were perfectly in accordance with the
prescriptions of the Canon law, but they were not to the
King's taste Under these circumstances, it was deferred,
and La Balue remained in prison.*

The hostility of Louis XI to the Holy See was further
evinced by the efforts which he made, in the year 1470,
to induce the Pyrenean Princes, as well as those in the
Appenine Peninsula, to support his Conciliar projects,
which were aimed directly against Paul II.† All these anti-
Roman machinations, however, led to no definite result.

* Details are given in AMMANATI, Comment, I., VII., GUETTÉE,
VIII, 33; LEGEAY, II, 8-9 Regarding the canonical prescriptions,
see PHILLIPS, VI, 283 seq

† See Mariana in FIERVILLE, 198, and MOUFFLET, Étude sur une
négociat. dipl. de Louis XI (Marseilles, 1884). Here is given the text
of the Speech addressed to the Duke of Milan and other Italian
Princes by Guillaume Fichat on the question of the Council. Corrections and additions to Moufflet's work were furnished by GHINZONI
(G Maria Sforza e Luigi XI, in Arch St. Lomb, Series II, part 1,
1885). It is evident, from a *Report of the Milanese Envoys, dated
Rome, 1468, April 27, that even at that period Louis XI. was seeking,
by threats of a Council, to extort concessions from Paul II. The
same Report informs us that similar threats were used by Charles the
Bold State Archives, Milan

Paul II. was a steadfast defender of the privileges of the Holy See, not only against the temporal power, but also against ecclesiastical encroachments On the 1st June, 1466, he strictly prohibited the use of the Tiara* by the Archbishop of Benevento, and reserved the right of consecrating the Agnus Dei to the Holy See† In 1469 a stop was put to the loss inflicted on the Apostolic Treasury by the frequent practice of uniting benefices to each other which were subject to Annates It was decided that henceforth all ecclesiastical Corporations were, every fifteenth year, to contribute what were called "Quindennium," instead of Annates, for the benefices united by them ‡

This last measure, and the great delight which the Pope took in pomp and splendour, have been made the subject of severe strictures It cannot be said that these reproaches are altogether unfounded ; but, on the other hand, the surrounding circumstances must be taken into account. In a time of such general magnificence as the period of the Renaissance, the Papacy could not, without a loss of dignity, be clothed in Apostolical simplicity. Paul II was firmly persuaded that the Pope ought to appear in a style befitting the highest position on earth His private life§ was as simple as his appearance in public

* MARINI, II , 161.

† Bull V., 199-200. The Agnus Dei, which hold the first place amongst all Sacramentals, are little tablets of wax with the image of the Lamb of God imprinted. Their use is extremely ancient See Breve notizia dell' origine, uso e virtù degli Agnus Dei (Roma, 1829); Freib Kirchenlexikon, I , 344 *seq* , 2nd ed , MORONI, I , 127 *seq*.

‡ PHILLIPS, V., 2, 581 *seq*.

§ Paul II , as a rule, ate only plain dishes ; he always mixed water with the wine he drank. See CANENSIUS, 98-9 ; CHRISTOPHE, II , 179 ; GEBHART, 183

was sumptuous. He always went in state from the Vatican to his Palace at S Marco, scattering money amongst the crowd.* All Church Festivals in which he took part were celebrated with exceptional magnificence. His coronation and the ceremony of taking possession of the Lateran had given the Romans a foretaste of future glories.† The following Christmas the Pope appeared in gorgeous vestments and wore the Tiara ‡ It was then reported that a new Tiara, more costly and splendid than any that had yet been seen, was to be made. At the Easter of 1465 the Pope wore this work of art, which was the wonder of his contemporaries § Holy Week and Easter were always celebrated with great pomp and solemnity. Thousands of foreigners crowded on these occasions to the tombs of the Apostles.‖ The Pope had a new litter made for the Christmas of 1466, and it must have been a marvel of workmanship. It is said to have cost more than a palace.¶

* See the *Description given by Augustinus de Rubeis in a *Letter, dated Rome, 1465, Oct 28 Ambrosian Library

† See *Letter of Jacobus de Aretio, dated Rome, 1464, Nov 13. Gonzaga Archives, Mantua

‡ *Letter of J P Arrivabene to Marchioness Barbara, dated Rome, 1464, Dec 26 Gonzaga Archives

§ See Appendix, N. 11 : Letter of A de Rubeis of the 21st April, 1465. Ambrosian Library.

‖ Bart. Marasca, writing from Rome, 1467, May 30, mentions this to Marchioness Barbara, and adds *"lo officio d'heri fu molto solenne cum quello regno in modo che a hora 20 fu finito." (Gonzaga Archives, Mantua) The importance attached to great functions by Paul II. and also by Sixtus IV. (BURCKHARDT, I., 149, 3rd ed) cannot be deemed surprising by a Catholic If the magnificent Liturgy of the Church is the mantle of the mysteries of religion, its worthy celebration is an efficacious means of promoting the honour that is due to her.

¶ " *Ha similiter facto fare una cadrega da farse portare a questo natale che es dice costa piu che non faria uno bono palazo. Et

At these great festivals all beholders were deeply impressed by the noble figure and countenance of the Pope, the magnificence of his vestments, and his majestic bearing. Even on the lesser festivals the ceremonial was very carefully carried out * The love of splendour which belonged to his artistic temperament led him to surround the person of the Vicar of Christ with corresponding magnificence. We have already mentioned the measures taken at the beginning of his reign to give greater external dignity to the Cardinals.† Another change was made at the same time Any one who has seen the Papal leaden seals will be able to recall the ancient type : the heads of SS. Peter and Paul are on one side, and on the reverse the name of the Pope of the day. In the time of Paul II., we find on the face of the seal the Pope himself enthroned and dispensing graces, with two Cardinals by his side, and in the foreground a number of other persons ; on the reverse are the full-length figures of the Princes of the Apostles, seated ‡ This alteration, however, was

demum Sua Sta è tutta piena di magnanimita et magnificentia quemad modum se po intendere per le cose grande chel fa " Augustinus de Rubeis from Rome, 1466, December 6. State Archives, Milan.

* See the *Letter of Giacomo d'Arezzo to Marchioness Barbara, describing the distribution of candles by the Pope, of whom he observes . "molto è ceremonioso " This letter is dated Rome, 1465, Febr 13 (Gonzaga Archives) See Gasp Veronen in MARINI, II , 178, and in MURATORI, III , 2, 1009

† See *supra*, p 25.

‡ COMTE DE MAS-LATRIE, Les éléments de la dipl pontificale, in the Rev d Quest Hist , XLI , 434 (April, 1887), considers these leaden seals of Paul II 's to be " sceaux spéciaux soit pour confirmer les décisions des conciles soit pour d'autres usages moins définis," and cites the Bull of 13th June, 1468, confirming the privileges of the University of Paris as an example " de ce *rare* type " (Archives Nat Paris, Bull. L., 234, N. 3.) All the seals of Paul II. are, however, of this design, as, for instance, that affixed to a Bull of 17th Sept., 1464, in the Innsbruck

not maintained, and the ancient type reappears under Sixtus IV.*

The necessity of reforms, especially in Rome, had been insisted on by Paul II , immediately after his election,† and soon the question as to the manner in which they were to be accomplished arose. In the very first Consistory the matter was seriously considered, and a number of wholesome regulations were framed. It was on this occasion that several Cardinals declared themselves in favour of the abolition of *reservations*, no less a personage, however, than the excellent Carvajal adduced such weighty reasons against this measure that it was abandoned ‡   It is certain that Paul II. was anxious to introduce a thorough reform amongst the officials of the Court, and also that, at the very outset of his reign, he opposed the simoniacal and corrupt practices which prevailed there.§

Archives (L. 3, 16 A). That the measure was a general one, adopted by the Pope immediately after his Election, is evident from J P Arrivabene's *Report of the 3rd Oct, 1464, in Appendix, N 4   Gonzaga Archives, Mantua

* See, *e g*, the *Bull of Sixtus IV regarding the appointment of Georgius Golser, decretor. doctor. et canonicus Brix, to the Episcop. ecclesiae Brix, dated Romae, 1471, 17 Cal. Jan A° 3°, from the Brixen Archives in the Government Archives, Innsbruck, L 3, 21d

† *Letter of J P Arrivabene, dated Rome, 1464, Sept 1   Gonzaga Archives, Mantua

‡ AMMANATI, Epist , 58b–59 ; PHILLIPS, V , 530.

§ In the Corp jur can (C 2, de simonia) [l. 5 tit 1] Paul II's Constitution of the year 1464 against simoniacal persons was adopted   See also ROD. SANCIUS, Hist Hispaniae, IV., c. 40 ; see FRANTZ, Sixtus IV., 18, and GREGOROVIUS, VII , 211 *seq* , 3rd ed. Regarding the corruption which prevailed among the Roman officials, see SS rer. Siles . IX , 97, 101, 103, 104, 111, 114, 115   ÆGIDIUS of Viterbo, in his *Hist., XX. secul , greatly praises Paul II for the strict morality which he tried to enforce amongst those immediately around him. Cod C 8, 19, f 308b. Angelica Library, Rome

If, in the sequel, the Venetian Pope did not prove such a zealous reformer as the sad state of affairs perhaps required, he cannot be charged with absolute inaction " The abuse of the *commendams* and *expectances* was, if not removed, yet practically much restrained , simoniacal practices were combated, the receiving of gifts by Legates, Governors and Judges was forbidden, and also the alienation of Church property, or leasing it for more than three years ; and the interests of benevolent foundations were protected."* In the matter of refusing presents, the Pope himself set a good example. When the Ambassadors who came to congratulate him on his elevation offered the customary gifts, he steadfastly declined them all, whatever their value might be He desired nothing, he said, but perfect fidelity to the Holy See † During the whole of his reign he adhered to this practice In the spring of 1471, the Archbishop of Trèves sent him an ornament composed of diamonds and rubies, and the Pope, who did not think it possible to refuse the present, at once sent in return a cross adorned with similar stones, adding that it was not his habit to receive gifts ‡

The high and fixed principles on which Paul II acted in making appointments to ecclesiastical offices was greatly calculated to improve the condition of the Church. In other matters, he is reported to have said, the Pope may be a man, but in the choice of Bishops he must be an Angel, and in that of members of the Sacred College, God.§ Canensius expressly informs us that he conferred ecclesi-

* REUMONT, III , I, 155   See Bull. V., 183-6, 194-5, and Bull Ord Praed , III , 458
† CANENSIUS, 31
‡ See the *Brief of the 19th April, 1471, in Appendix, N. 36   Venice Archives
§ Ægidius of Viterbo in RAYNALDUS, ad an 1471, N 63.

astical dignities only after mature and impartial deliberation, having strict regard to the merits of the recipients,
and he adds that many excellent men were appointed
Bishops without their previous cognisance and in their
absence *

Paul II. did much to promote monastic reform, particularly in Lombardy, Modena, Ferrara and Venice ;† as also
in Western and Southern Germany, especially in Cologne,
Bavaria and Wurtemberg ‡ In 1469 he issued a Bull for
the better regulation of the Augustinian Congregation in
Lombardy.§ A few months before his death the Pope
exhorted the Patriarch of Venice to proceed against all
clergy and monks who led irregular lives, without respect
of persons,‖ and also took measures for raising the standard of education amongst the clergy in the Diocese of
Valencia.¶ The evil star which presided over the Briefs
of Paul II. has consigned much interesting information on
this subject to unmerited oblivion.

The fact that Paul II. was always surrounded by men of
worth is one that speaks well for his own character In the
autumn of 1466 the Milanese Ambassador mentions the
Archbishop of Spalatro, Lorenzo Zane, who became Treas-
urer, Stefano Nardini, Archbishop of Milan, and Teodoro de'
Lelli, Bishop of Feltre and, after the 17th September, 1466,

* CANENSIUS, 48, 99

† RICHA, IX, 187; Bull Ord Praedic., III., 469; *Lib. brev. 12,
f 111b ; see below, note ‖

‡ Bull. Ord Praed , III , 449 , Anal Francisc , 413, 417 seq , where is
also information regarding the reform of the Convents of St Francis
and St. Clare at Eger.   See also Deutsche Chroniken aus Bohmen,
III , 12, 277 seq

§ KOLDE, Augustiner Congregation, 106 seq.

‖ *Patriarchae Venetiarum, VI. Martii, 1471   Lib. brev. 12, f 111b
Secret Archives of the Vatican

¶ *Brief dated Romae, 1471, 28 Martii, loc cit , 251.

of Treviso, as possessing much influence with the new Pope.
The Bishop of Aquila, who had been his preceptor, is also
named amongst those who occupied positions immediately
about him   Lelli, as it was at once surmised, took the first
place *   No letter, or decree of importance, was issued until
it had been examined by this excellent man.† On his
death in 1466, the Pope took his nephew Marco Barbo, and
Bessarion into his confidence.   Agapito Cenci de' Rustici,
Bishop of Camerino, who had been greatly valued by both
Pius II and Paul II., had passed away in October, 1464 ‡
Giovanni Barozzi, Patriarch of Venice from the year 1465;
the learned Angelus Faseolus, Lelli's successor in the See
of Feltre, Valerius Calderina, Bishop of Savona, Pietro
Ferrici, Bishop of Tarasona, afterwards a Cardinal;
and Corrado Capece, subsequently Archbishop of Bene-

---

* *Letter of O de Carretto to Fr Sforza, dated Rome, 1464, October
9   (State Archives, Milan, Cart Gen)   Nardini was at once given a
lodging in the Papal Palace , see the *Despatch of J. P. Arrivabene,
dated Rome, 1464, Sept 1   In this Ambassador's *Reports of the 11th
Sept and 3rd Oct , 1464, we have evidence that the Pope's relations with
Lelli were of a very intimate character   These three documents are
in the Gonzaga Archives, Mantua   Fr. Sforza, writing from Rome
on the 11th Sept, 1464, informs Jo Jacobus de Plumbo Parmen that
Lelli is one of the 'principali homini' about the new Pope. (State
Archives, Milan)   Regarding Lelli's appointment as Bishop of
Treviso, see *Reg Bull Pauli II, A. 2, tom II, f. 203   (Secret
Archives of the Vatican) See Appendix, N. 4

† AMMANATI, Epist , 109b   See also, regarding Lelli, A. M
QUIRINI, Ad S D. N. Benedictum XIV Monum lit. episc Venetor
ditionis, 1742

‡ "*A questi di mori lo rev mons vescovo de Camerino notabilis-
simo prelato pianto da tutta la corte per la integrita et virtu sue . . . fu
in somma gratia di papa Pio" [see Vol III , p 41], who entrusted to him
the Signatura delle supplicationi   Paul II also loved him and visited
him during his illness   *Jacopo de Aretio, dated Rome, 1464, Oct. 9
(Gonzaga Archives) See also MARINI, II , 157.

vento,* were also in the Pope's confidence   Most of the
Sienese had left Rome , many of them were called to account
by the Pope for extortion or embezzlement †   Even Platina
bears witness to the strict order and discipline which he
maintained in his Court and among his dependents ‡   Moreover, at the very beginning of his pontificate it was observed
that Paul II. engaged no Venetians among his guards §

The disorders of the Fraticelli (fraticelli de opinione)
were, like the abuses at the Court, energetically repressed
by Paul II.   In the summer of 1466 it became evident
that the partisans of this sect had gained a footing, not
only in the March of Ancona and the adjacent district of
Romagna, but also in the Campagna, and even in Rome
itself || The headquarters of these dangerous heretics were
Assisi and the little town of Poli near Palestrina, where
Stefano de' Conti was accused of being in league with
them ¶   The Pope caused this Baron and all the rest

* Gasp Veronen. in MARINI, II , 192 seq   See CHRISTOPHE, II ,
205 seq.

† See VOIGT, III , 556   ‡ PLATINA, 794

§ In Carretto's Letter of the 9th Oct., 1464, cited supra, p 112, he
observes *"Scuderi ce sono Milanesi, Alexandrini, Monferrini, Man-
tuani e daltre natione   Fina qui non ce nullo Venetiano bence ne sono
de Friuoli e Vicentini "   State Archives, Milan.

|| DRESSEL, Documente, IV. , INFESSURA (1140-1141) wrongly
assigns the prosecution of the Fraticelli to the year 1467   So does
LEA, III , 178, who is unacquainted with Dressel's Documents and
with Canensius !   Besides the pieces published by Dressel, may be
cited for the year 1466 the *Letter of B. de Maraschis of Sept 1, 1466,
in Appendix, N. 17. (Gonzaga Archives, Mantua)   It is, however, true
that some of these heretics were punished in 1467 , this appears from
*Lib II , Bullet Pauli II , where, on the 6th July, 1467, are entered
payments for " xii vestibus, ferram lignis et aliis oportunis rebus . . .
emendis in faciendo cert act nonnullor hereticor"   State Archives,
Rome

¶ CANENSIUS, 78, and DRESSEL, Documente, 9.

of the accused to be confined in St. Angelo, where they
were tried.   Five Bishops were appointed to conduct the enquiry.*   Many statements made by the accused are extant,
but as most of them were extorted by the rack their value
may be questioned.   One of their principal doctrines seems
to have been, that of all the successors of St. Peter, no one
had really been the Vicar of Christ who had not imitated
the poverty of his Chief, from the time of John XXII,
who spoke against the poverty of Christ, in particular, all
Popes had been heretics and excommunicate, as also had all
Cardinals, Bishops and Priests consecrated by them.   Paul
II. was no true Pope   These heretics were, moreover,
charged with immoral practices in their assemblies, and
other crimes   In the record of the trial, mention is made
of a small codex found in the possession of a priest of this
sect, which confirmed the truth of these allegations.   A
Fraticelli bishop is named in this, thus a formal Church
must have been contemplated.   The Hussite principle, that
unworthy priests lose their powers,† was also a part of their
teaching   It is certain, at any rate, that the movement was
one which threatened great danger to the Papacy, and
which had for a long time been making progress in the
locality we have named.   One of the women accused said
that St Jacopo della Marca had converted her, and that she

---

* "*Cum apud Asisium plures deprensi fuerint fraticelli della
oppinione vulgariter nuncupati, ii autem ad urbem vincti ducti sunt
et in castro s Angeli duris carceribus mancipati per summum pontificem Paulum II, causa Mediolanen archiepiscopo, Zamorensi,
Farensi, Tarraconensi et mihi Ortano episcopi commissa, &c"   Nic
PALMERIUS, De paupertate Christi. (Cod Vatic., 4158, f. 1, Vatican
Library)   See DRESSEL, Doc 24

† Processus contra haereticos de opinione dampnata A° 1466, from
Cod Vatic, 4012, in DRESSEL, Documente, 7, 12, 17, 20-22, 25, 31;
see NIEDNER'S Zeitschr, 1859, III, 436 seq

had again relapsed into error.* All these heretics, Platina says, were punished : those who continued obstinate, with the greatest severity. Such as acknowledged their errors, and sought for pardon, were treated more leniently.†

The extent to which these doctrines had spread, and the serious manner in which they were viewed in Rome, may be estimated from the numerous refutations which at once appeared, although the Franciscan, St Jacopo della Marca, had already published a work dealing thoroughly with the subject.‡ Nicholas Palmerius, Bishop of Orte, one of the prelates who took part in the enquiry, composed a treatise on the poverty of Christ, and dedicated it to Cardinal Jouffroy.§ Rodericus Sancius of Arevalo offered his work on the same subject to the Pope himself, in this treatise he shews that there is no contradiction between the statements of Nicholas III. and John XXII. in regard to the poverty of Christ.‖ There are also treatises on this sub-

---

* *Loc. cit*, p. 46.

† PLATINA, 776, CANENSIUS, 78. In 1471 the Fraticelli reappeared on the coast of Tuscany

‡ Dialogus contra fraticellos in MANSI, Miscell., IV, 595–610 See JEILER in the Freiburg Kirchenlexikon, IV, 1930 *seq*, 2nd ed, who, however, is mistaken in saying that after 1449 the name of the Fraticelli vanishes from history

§ Rᵈᵒ J[oan.] tit. s [Stephani in monte Coelio] presb card Albiensi nuncupato de paupertate Christi (Cod Vatic, 4158.—70 pages). This beautifully adorned copy is evidently the one presented to the Cardinal

‖ In the Vatican Library, *Cod Vatic, 969, I found the copy presented to Paul II, adorned with his arms and with miniatures Ad sanct et clem. patrem et dom d Paulum papam II pont. max libellus incipit de paupertate Christi creatoris et dominatoris omnium nec non apostolor eius . . editus a Roderico episc. Zamoren eiusdem Sanctᵘˢ in castro suo s Angeli de urbe fidelissimo castellano et referendario.

ject from the pens of Torquemada* and of Fernando of
Cordova †

At this time tidings reached Rome of the discovery in
Germany of a sect similar to that of the Fraticelli ‡ The
copy of a letter, addressed to Bishop Henry of Ratisbon
by Rudolf of Rudesheim, Bishop of Lavant and the Papal
Legate, on the 11th June, 1466, contains details regarding
these dreamy fanatics, whose chiefs were Brothers John
and Livin of Wirsberg A member of this sect called
himself John of the East; he was to be the forerunner of
the anointed Redeemer, the One Shepherd of whom Christ
had spoken These heretics declared the Pope to be Antichrist, and all Catholics who did not believe in the
"anointed Redeemer" to be members of Antichrist. "John
of Wirsberg promulgated his doctrines in Eger as well as
in the country, and even in the Bishopric of Eichstatt; his
most zealous adherent, however, was his brother Livin,"
who died in prison in 1467, after having abjured his
errors §

It is very probable that Paul II. also took measures

---

* *Libellus velociter compositus et editus contra certos haereticos
noviter impugnantes paupertatem Christi et suorum apostolorum
(Cod Vatic, 974, f 55 seq.) MONTFAUCON, Bibl, II, 1382, saw this
work also in the Library at Metz, where it is no longer to be found

† Fernandi Cordubensis (see regarding him, HAVET in the Mém
de la Soc. d'Hist. de Paris, IX, 193 seq.), adversus haereticos qui
fraterculi dela opinione vulgo appellantur ad rev in Christo patrem
et illi dom. G episcop Hostiensem S R E card. Rotomagens. vulgo
appell. tractatus I found this work, which FABRICIUS, I, 570, does not
cite, in the Cod Vatic, 1127, it occupies 166 pages

‡ See in Appendix, N. 17, the *Letter of B de Maraschis of the 1st
September, 1466 Gonzaga Archives, Mantua

§ JANNER III, 564–71, and GRADL, Die Irrlehre der Wirsperger,
in the Mittheilungen des Vereins fur Gesch. der Deutschen in Bohmen
(1881), XIX, 270 seq.

against these sectaries Direct evidence, however, is wanting, for the Secret Archives of the Vatican only contain
Briefs belonging to the second half of the seventh year
of his pontificate These Briefs shew that he proceeded
against heretics in the Diocese of Amiens, and afterwards
in Bologna *

The solicitude of Paul II. for the spiritual welfare of the
faithful committed to his charge is manifested by his
decision that the Jubilee should, for the future, be celebrated
once in every twenty-five years The Bull on this subject
was published on the 19th April, 1470. " The thought of
all that the Church had suffered from schism at two
periods, and all that it had cost her to end it , the terror of
Western Christendom when, by the fall of Constantinople,
the Turks gained a footing in Europe ; the alarming outbreaks of devastating maladies , finally, the ruin which
ceaseless wars had wrought in the very life of the Western
kingdoms, led men to turn their eyes to Heaven, and
shewed that, in order to avert the strokes of the chasten-
ing hand of God, it was needful that all should tread the
paths of penance." Moved by considerations such as
these, and by the fact that, under the former regulations,
but few could partake of the Jubilee Indulgence, the Pope
made the Decree we have mentioned, which was at once
solemnly announced throughout Christendom † But Paul

* Lib. brev 12, f. 26 · *heret pravit inquisitori in prov Remen. et in
dioc Ambianen , dat Romae, xviii Oct , 1470, A° VII°, f 121 *Simoni
de Novaria Ord Praed prof. heret pravit inquisitori, dat xiii Martii,
1471 Here is also mentioned a letter to the Bishop of Bologna,
which has not been preserved (Secret Archives of the Vatican) See
also Annal Bonon , 897

† Bull V , 200-203 (in RAYNALDUS, ad an 1470, N 55, the beginning
is wanting, and there is an error in the date). See NOTHEN, 65 seq ,
and FESSLER, Schriften, 23 Regarding the publication, see N.
DELLA TUCCIA, 98, and Istoria di Chiusi, 995-6. The Bull is to be

II was not destined to see the beginning of the new Jubilee year.

Towards the end of this pontificate a remarkable effort was made to prepare the way for the union of the Russian with the Roman Church, and also to gain the Grand Duke Iwan III. as a champion against the Turks. The idea originated with Bessarion, and found great favour with Paul II., who had just at that time expressed to the Maronites his wish that they should conform more closely to the Roman ritual * An Ambassador was sent to Moscow to propose a marriage between the Grand Duke and Zoe (Sophia), the daughter of the unfortunate Thomas Palæologus Iwan entered into the project, and the Ambassadors were at once sent back to Rome to bring a portrait of the bride. After a time things were so far settled that a Russian Embassy was sent to Rome to conduct Zoe to her new home. When this Embassy, bearing letters to Bessarion and to the Pope, reached Italy, Paul II. had ceased to live. His successor, however, took up the matter with equal zeal †

found in many Manuscripts, as, *e g*, in Cod 12,262 of the State Library, Munich (see Catal, IV, 2, 63), Cod 3496, f 6a-8b, Court Library, Vienna; and in Cod LXXVI, f 159a-160b, of the Cathedral Library, Zeitz.

  * RAYNALDUS, ad an 1469, N. 28 *seq*

  † See FR. PIERLING'S remarkable article, " Le Mariage d'un Tsar," 353 *seq*, which is much better than the account of FIEDLER (Sitzungsberichte der Wiener Akademie, XL., 29 *seq.*), or PICHLER, II , 54, and PELESZ, I., 261

CHAPTER V.

(THE NEW AND THE OLD CARDINALS — CHURCH QUESTIONS IN BOHEMIA)

THE NEW AND THE OLD CARDINALS —CHURCH
QUESTIONS IN BOHEMIA

THE appointment of new Cardinals was spoken of in
the earliest months of Paul II.'s pontificate. At the
Christmas of 1464, or, at the latest, in the following Lent,
he seems to have contemplated an increase of the members
of the Sacred College. Marco Barbo, Bishop of Vicenza,
and Stefano Nardini, Archbishop of Milan,* were named
as candidates No nomination, however, according to
Canensius, actually took place until the second year of his
reign, and Teodoro de' Lelli, Bishop of Treviso, and Giovanni
Barozzi, Patriarch of Venice, the only Prelates then
elevated to the purple, both died before their publication.† A creation of Cardinals was positively announced for
December, 1466 ,‡ but it did not take place. The consent

* *Letter of Stefano Nardini to Fr Sforza, dated Rome, 1464, Dec
6, in which he asks for his good offices with Paul II. Ambrosian
Library.

† CANENSIUS, 100. Although the *Acta Consist. are silent regarding this nomination, we cannot, like CONTELORIUS, 63, completely
reject it Canensius was in all matters very well-informed PAN-
VINIUS, 315, is mistaken in assigning the first nomination to the year
1464 Regarding the death of the two who were created, see GAMS,
792 and 804

‡ *Despatch of J P Arrivabene, dated Rome, 1466, Dec 19, who
says it was believed that L Zane, Archbishop of Spalatro, would be
made Cardinal. Gonzaga Archives, Mantua

of the Sacred College probably could not be obtained.
At last, in the beginning of the fourth year of his reign,
on the 18th September, 1467, Paul II. was able to create
a large number of Cardinals *   Three of the eight then
admitted to the Sacred College were foreigners: Thomas
Bourchier, Archbishop of Canterbury ; Stephan de Varda,
Archbishop of Colocsa,† and Jean de La Balue, Bishop of
Angers   The last-named prelate, who, "by his cleverness
and cunning," had risen from a very obscure position, was
at this time Louis XI's Ambassador to Rome, and was
engaged in negotiations regarding the repeal of the Pragmatic Sanction ; this explains his appointment.

Of the five Italians promoted, one of the most distinguished was Olivieri Carafa, Archbishop of Naples.
"He was a jurist, a theologian, an antiquarian, and a
statesman ; he had even taken part in warfare as Admiral
against the Turks   Highly esteemed and influential in his
own country, he was remarkably popular in Rome.   His
popularity was due to the use which he made of his ample
income and to his affability.   He was generous in supporting learning and learned men ; many youths were won by
him for the Church and for serious studies." ‡   Paulus

* *Acta Consist , f 35b, Secret Archives of the Vatican   See
*Despatch of J Trottus of the 18th Sept , 1467   " N. S. ha facto hoggi
li cardinali descripti ne la presente cedula" (State Archives, Modena),
and *Letter of Card Gonzaga of the 18th Sept., 1467   " Questa matina
sono pronuntiati octo cardinali cioè, etc." (Gonzaga Archives, Mantua.)
N DELLA TUCCIA, 271, is mistaken in naming the 19th December

† The King of Hungary had, from the year 1464, exerted himself on
his behalf ; see Mon Hung , I., 305 ; also Arch. St. Ital (Series 3),
XX , 311

‡ REUMONT, III., 1, 259-60.   See CHIOCARELLUS, 286 *seq.* ;
CIACONIUS, II , 1097 *seq.* , CARDELLA, 159 *seq* ; TOPPI, Addiz alla
Bibl. Neapolit., 189 *seq* (Neap. 1683) ; MUNTZ, II., 87   MIGNE,
622, and CHEVALIER, 392, are mistaken in stating that 1464 was the

Cortesius praises his great discretion, his uprightness, and his blamelessness.*

The character of Paul II.'s nephew, Marco Barbo, Bishop, first of Treviso (1455-64) and afterwards of Vicenza, was still more admirable † A singular sweetness of disposition and deep piety were in his case united with a rare capacity for business and great learning He was absolutely dis-interested. During his lifetime he gave almost all his income to the poor, to whom he afterwards bequeathed what remained, " for," he said, " the goods of the Church are, according to the teaching of the Fathers, the inheritance of Christ's poor." His fine library was the only gratification he allowed himself ‡ Of all the Pope's relations, he was the one most closely united with him , his " inexhaustible power of work and his consummate prudence" were of great use to Paul II.§

year of Carafa's appointment. Regarding Ferrante's exertions for Carafa, see TRINCHERA, I , 33 *seq.*

* CORTESIUS, De cardinalatu, f LXIb and CCXXXVIb

† In the Library at Wurzburg, I found in Cod Q , 1 · *Leonelli Chieregati oratio in laudem Marci Barbi episc Vicentini pio ingressu suo in civitatem, dat Vicentiae, Kal. Octob , 1464.

‡ LITTA, Famiglie · Barbo , MUNTZ, II , 153 ; MAZZUCHELLI, II., 1, 318-19 ; Tiara et pulp Venet , 31 *seq* , 66 *seq* , 368. In the Lib confrat b Mariae de anima, p 23, is the entry · " Marcus episc. Prenest. card hospitalis nostri protector et singularis promotor, 1479 " Barbo's sweetness is particularly praised by P CORTESIUS, De Card , CCXXXVII. , see CXXb A work dedicated to him by Amelius Trebanus, De felicitate, is in Cod Vat , 2924. See ABEL, I , CXXX On the 15th March, 1471, *Paul II informs the Doge that he has con-ferred the Bishopric of Vicenza on Cardinal M Barbo Lib brev. 12, f. 113. Secret Archives of the Vatican

§ See SCHMARSOW, 25. The confidential relations of Barbo to the Pope are mentioned by the Ambassador of Este, J. Tiottus, in a *Despatch of the 19th Sept , 1467, in which he advises his master to congratulate the Cardinal of Vicenza " il quale è lo ochio destro del

Amicus Agnifilus, the third of the Cardinals nominated
on the 18th of September, 1467, had been a member of
the household and a friend of Domenico Capranica, and
subsequently tutor to Paul II. When raised from low
estate to be Bishop of Aquila, he had chosen, for his
armorial bearings, a lamb and a book. His epitaph praises
his generosity to the poor, his discretion, and his thorough
knowledge of Canon Law *   Little has been handed down
concerning the fourth Cardinal, the Protonotary, Marquess
Theodore of Montferrat,† and even less concerning Francesco della Rovere, the General of the Franciscans, on the
occasion of whose elevation to the purple Paul II is said
to have observed that he had chosen his successor.‡

On the 19th September, the Red Hat was conferred on
those among the newly-created Cardinals who were at the
time in Rome.   On the 2nd October, the mouth of Cardinal
Barbo was opened, and S. Marco assigned to him as his
titular Church.   On the 22nd of the month, Agnifilus
reached Rome; the Cardinal's Hat was at once given to
him in a Public Consistory, and, on the 13th November, he
received the Church of Sta Balbina, which, on the 13th
October, 1469, he exchanged for that of Sta Maria in
Trastevere   S Pietro in Vincoli was the titular Church of
Francesco della Rovere, and SS Pietro e Marcellino that
of Carafa, who arrived in Rome on the 3rd December, 1467.

papa e ragiona in concistorio de darli il suo titulo de S. Marco," in
order that his palace may be left to him.   See also a *Despatch of
this Ambassador, dated Rome, 1469, Sept 30.   State Archives,
Modena

* CIACONIUS, II., 1111 ; CARDELLA, 172 seq., CHEVALIER, 39, is
mistaken in regard to the appointment as well as the title of Agnifilus

† CARDELLA, 174-5   The Hist Monteferrat (MURATORI, XXIII.,
136) is wrong in giving 1466 as the date of his nomination   The
Cardinal had a benefice in Mayence , see JOANNIS, II., 288

‡ FULGOSUS, I. c. 2.

Cardinal Theodore of Montferrat did not make his entry into Rome until the 21st April, 1468, when S. Teodoro was assigned to him *

On the 21st November, 1468, Paul II. created two more Cardinals, who, like Marco Barbo, were of his own kindred : these were Battista Zeno and Giovanni Michiel, the sons of two of his sisters   They received the Red Hat, and the Churches of Sta Maria in Porticu and Sta Lucia, on the 22nd Nov., and the ceremony of the opening of their mouths took place on the 9th December.† The Popes nephews were both men of unblemished character.   None of the Cardinals were excessively wealthy or influential ‡

Towards the end of his reign, Paul II. created four other Cardinals   This was done in a secret Consistory, and with the proviso that, in the event of his death, they were to be considered as published §   They were Johann Vitéz, Archbishop of Gran, Pietro Foscari, Giovan Battista Savelli, and Francesco Ferrici ‖

---

* All these statements are from the *Acta Consist. of the Secret Archives of the Vatican   From the same authority it appears that, on the 13th May, 1468, Bourchier, S. de Varda, and La Balue received respectively the Churches of S   Ciriaco, SS   Nereo ed Achilleo, and Sta Susanna   The Cardinal's hat was not transmitted to S de Varda until 1471 ; see Appendix, N 28

† *Acta Consist , f 39   Secret Archives of the Vatican

‡ CREIGHTON, III , 50, who, at p 51, observes   " In the creations of cardinals, Paul II shewed his general impartiality and his good intentions." For a further account of Zeno and Michiel, see Tiara et purp Venet, 34 *seq* , 369 ; CIACONIUS, II , 1112 *seq* , and CARDELLA, 175 *seq*.

§ CONTELORIUS, 62-3 ; CIACONIUS, II , 1114   The publication was deferred out of consideration for the French King ; see *Letter of J. P Arrivabene, dated Rome, 1471, June 8.   Gonzaga Archives

‖ Regarding Vitéz, who died in 1472, see REUMONT, in Arch. St. Ital , 1874, and the Monograph of FRAKNÓI (Budapest, 1879), regarding the others, see *infra*, for Foscari, see Tiara et purp Venet , 39 and 371.

Between the Cardinals created by Paul II, who were called the " Pauleschi," and the " Piischi,"* who owed their elevation to his predecessor, a certain opposition existed. Of the latter number, Ammanati fell into complete disfavour, while Forteguerri, Roverella, and Eroli enjoyed the good graces of Pope Paul II, and the first of these three Cardinals enjoyed great influence with him † At the beginning of the pontificate, Richard Longueil,‡ who, on the 1st October, 1464, was sent as Legate to Perugia, was also at the French Court believed to have considerable influence § Cardinals Borgia and Gonzaga also received marked favours; the latter, however, was not a friend of the Pope‖ On the 18th February, 1471, he was appointed Legate at Bologna, possibly with the object of removing him from the Court ¶

The relations which existed between the Pope and

Frederick III sought in vain to obtain the elevation of Domenico de Domenichi (DOMINICUS, De dignit episc, 32), and King René that of the Archbishop of Arles, his Ambassador to Rome; see LECOY DE LA MARCHE, I., 542.

* These appellations are, as far as I know, found for the first time in a *Despatch, which I shall speak of later, written by Joh Blanchus on the 29th July, 1471. State Archives, Milan.

† N DELLA TUCCIA, 98. Concerning Ammanati, see *supra*, p 25.

‡ *Letter of A Malletta to Fr Sforza, dated Abbeville, 1464, Oct. 8. Fonds Ital, 1611, National Library, Paris.

§ *Acta Consist   Secret Archives of the Vatican

‖ See *supra*, p 24, and Appendix, N 2   Gonzaga Archives

¶ Card Gonzaga to his father, dated Rome, 1471, Febr 18. *" Questa mattina è piaciuto a la Sta de N S deputarmi legato ad Bologna " (Gonzaga Archives.)   See *Acta Consist. of the Secret Archives of the Vatican   According to this authority, Card. Gonzaga did not set off until the 5th July.   *Ghirardacci speaks of his entry on the 21st July.   A *Bull granting numerous faculties for his new sphere of work, dated Rome, 1471, tertio Non Julii A° 7°, is in the State Archives, Bologna, Q 22

Cardinal Scarampo were of a peculiar character.   The
latter, whose contemporaries deemed him remarkable for
his cunning, had, shortly after his rival's elevation, made
peace with him.   The reconciliation seems to have been
tolerably complete, for, in September, 1464, the Pope had
no hesitation in granting to Scarampo the full exercise of
his post of Cardinal-Camerlengo   " Neither Calixtus III.,
nor Pius II , nor even Nicholas V., would have done this,"
observed a secretary in Cardinal Gonzaga's service.*   The
fact that, after the death of Cardinal Pierre de Foix, Paul
II. conferred the Bishopric of Albano upon Scarampo
shews that some degree of friendly feeling existed.†   That
there was, however, a certain amount of friction in the
relations between the former rivals, is far from improbable.
For instance, in answer to a pointed remark of the
Cardinal's regarding the cost of the Palace of S. Marco,
the Pope is said to have declared that it was far better to
spend his money in buildings than to play it away.‡

At the beginning of March, 1465, Scarampo fell ill, and,
on the 22nd, he died.§   He was a thoroughly worldly man,

* "*Item dom papa voluit quod rev dom. camerarius debeat
officium suum exercere libere in curia Romana quod tempore pape
Calisti et pape Pii (see VOIGT, III , 544) et eciam pape Nicolai facere
non potuit." W Molitor, in a *Letter, dated Rome, 1464, Sept 21.
Gonzaga Archives, Mantua

† *Report of Giacomo d'Arezzo to Marchioness Barbara, dated
Rome, 1465, January 9   Gonzaga Archives.

‡ CORTESIUS, De cardinalatu, CXXXIIII

§ VOIGT, III., 508, attributes Scarampo's death to vexation at the
election of Paul II *J. P. Arrivabene, writing on March 1, 1465,
reports Scarampo to be suffering from gout Cardinal Gonzaga
seems to have been on good terms with Scarampo, for in a *Letter to
his parents, dated Rome, 1465, March 21, he expresses his sorrow
that Scarampo "laborat in extremis ne se gli ha speranza alcuna."
Gonzaga Archives, Mantua

and was known at the Roman Court by the name of Cardinal Lucullus As a Prince of the Church, his example was bad As a statesman and politician, however, by restoring regular government in Rome, by promoting employment, and looking after the welfare of the people, by his consummate skill in the conduct of the negotiations with the Italian Princes, as well as by his care for the army and fleet, he did good service to the restored Papacy at a critical period *

The close of Scarampo's career was followed by a somewhat painful episode. He had availed himself of the right conceded to him of making testamentary dispositions to bequeath his whole property, amounting to 200,000, or, according to some accounts, to 400,000 golden florins, to his nephews Scarcely anything was left to the Church in whose service he had amassed these riches To the general satisfaction, Paul II set aside this will and devoted the whole of the property to charitable purposes, such as churches, the poor, and refugees from the countries which had been conquered by the Turks The nephews of the deceased were also remembered , even Platina here admits the kindness of the Pope.†

* Such is the opinion of GOTTLOB, Cam Ap See our Vol I , p 301 seq

† CANENSIUS, 40 seq ; FULGOSUS, VII , c. 7, see VI , c. 10; GREGOROVIUS, VII , 210, 3rd ed According to *GHIRARDACCI, Cronica di Bologna, 759, the Cardinal left 600,000 ducats. Here there is a mistake as to the day of his death the date we give is established by the *Acta Consist., Secret Archives of the Vatican. See Annal Bonon , 895, and Cronica Borselli (GUIDICINI, Miscel , 44), which add, "Oh ! Che buon elemosiniere !" *Carlo de Franzoni, writing to the Marchioness of Mantua, speaks of the "infinita di denari e goije ' left by the Cardinal (Gonzaga Archives) For an account of Scarampo's tomb in S Lorenzo in Damaso, see MUNTZ, II , 81 seq. ; GATTULA, II , 568 , and FORCELLA, V , 171.

His friendship for Cardinal Bessarion speaks well for
Paul II   The dispute about the Election Capitulation had
temporarily estranged them, but, in the year 1468, the
Duke of Este's Ambassador spoke of Bessarion as enjoying
more consideration than all the other Cardinals, and, in
the following year, he wrote word that Barbo and the
Greek Cardinal were much in the Pope's confidence, and
were the only men trusted with the most secret affairs.*
In fact, "in the history of this period Bessarion stands
forth almost like a father of the Church ; his majestic
presence, his noble Greek profile with his long flowing
beard, also contributed to enhance the esteem and deference
which were everywhere accorded to him."†

Bessarion, who was an ardent patriot, not only took the
deepest interest in the proposed Crusade, but also endeavoured in every way to awaken the compassion of Western
Christendom on behalf of his exiled countrymen   The
unselfishness with which he assisted the scattered fugitives,
and his "noble efforts to preserve and render profitable
whatever it had been possible to rescue from a vanishing
civilisation, call upon us to deal leniently with his weak-
nesses "‡

* Report o Jacobus Trottus, dated Rome, 1468, Nov 2 (*Niceno.
Rohano e S Angelo son contra il Re a moisi et a calci et piu Niceno
che è tuto Venetiano et che ha piu auctoritate chal resto de cardinali),
and 1469, Sept 30   (State Archives, Modena) See Vespasiano da
Bisticci in MAI, I., 193, and CANENSIUS, 101.

† SCHMARSOW, 4   See also our Vol I , p 319 *seq* , Vol II , 69
seq   I have since had an opportunity of seeing the Russian Monograph of Alex Sadov (St Petersburg, 1883) there mentioned, and it
has disappointed my expectations   The author brings forward no new
documents or authorities, but rests exclusively on foreign literature
As Vast's work is also unsatisfactory, a new life of the Greek Cardinal
based on original sources, is still greatly to be desired

‡ GOTHEIN, 400–401.

The Greek Cardinal's state of health became so much worse during Paul's reign that, in 1466, he caused the simple tomb, which is still well-preserved in the Church of the SS Apostoli, to be prepared.* In the following year he stayed for a considerable time at Viterbo, where he had on former occasions taken the baths† In spite of his bodily sufferings he devoted himself as zealously as ever to study , his celebrated work in defence of Plato appeared at this time   He was also in constant intercourse with the Humanist Scholars in Rome   His house at SS Apostoli was common ground for the most noted Greeks and Italian Hellenists, where all were welcomed by their learned host with the most winning kindness‡   " Here Andronikos Callistos, Constantine Laskaris, and Theodore Gaza held brilliant and genial converse with the Cardinal in friendly rivalry with his pupil and favourite, Niccolo Perotto, who translated Polybius, and composed a metrical poem." Francesco della Rovere, afterwards Sixtus IV., Domizio da Caldiero, Johannes Muller Regiomontanus, the great astronomer and geographer, and many others, also frequented his house,§ and Bessarion

* VAST, 293 *seq*

† N. DELLA TUCCIA, Pref XX and 91   That Bessarion was also at Viterbo, in 1468, is shewn by his Letter to the Doge, dated from that city, giving his valuable library to the Republic of Venice ; see Serapeum, II , 94 *seq*. Regarding this gift, see also Arch St. Ital , 3 Series, IX , 2, 193 *seq* (here, p 198, is also an account of a College, founded by Bessarion in Candia, for the education of clergy of the Greek Rite), and OTTINO-FUMAGALLI, Bibl. bibliograph. Italica, 350 *seq* (Roma, 1889)

‡ CORTESIUS, De cardinalatu, LXXIII , says that Bessarion, like Torquemada and Cusa, was always most courteous to the learned men who visited him

§ SCHMARSOW, 26. See VOIGT, II , 130 *seq*, 2nd ed ; GASPARY, 110 , VAST, 308 *seq* , Arch St Ital, 1887, XIX , 314 *seq*. Among the learned men whom Bessarion assisted we must also mention Michael

took part in their learned disputations with unfailing interest.*

As Protector of the Basilian Order, the Greek Cardinal's labours were both extensive and important. The reforms which the Order at this time required, and which Martin V. had already attempted, were energetically taken in hand "Persuaded that the extent of the malady demanded a comprehensive remedy, Bessarion began by drawing up a Rule in Italian and in Greek, which he strictly imposed upon the Monasteries in Italy and Sicily. He increased their revenues by recovering lands which had been alienated, and by regulating their household expenses, and endeavoured to give new splendour to the Order by beautifying its ancient buildings and by constructing on the old lines skilfully arranged additions." Bessarion everywhere insisted on serious study; he encouraged the monks to apply themselves to the Greek classics, to transcribe and collect Manuscripts and to establish good schools. Among these, the Gymnasium of Messina acquired a great reputation. Laskaris, whom Bessarion appointed Professor at this Institution in 1467, soon attracted scholars from all parts of Italy.†

In recognition of these important services Pius II, in August 1462, nominated Bessarion Commendatory Abbot of Grottaferrata. This celebrated Abbey, which had long been considered as a link uniting East and West, had, at the period of which we are speaking, fallen into a state of dilapidation. Bessarion at once devoted himself most ardently to the work of restoration, and quickly succeeded in effecting a thorough renovation, both material and

Apostolios, concerning whom see LEGRAND, Bibl. Hell, I, LVIII. seq, and NOIRET'S work, Lettres inéd de M A. (Paris, 1889).

* CORTESIUS, De Cardinalatu, XXXIX

† VOGEL, C Laskaris in the Serapeum, VI, 45 seq., VAST, 224 seq., LEGRAND, I., LXXIX

spiritual, in this interesting spot, so rich in classical associa-
tions and Christian memories * His chalice, his famous
Inventory (Regestum Bessarionis †), and some valuable
Manuscripts, presented by him to his Abbey, are still preserved at Grottaferrata ‡

The Vatican Basilica, the Camaldolese Abbey at Avel-
lana, and the Church of the Holy Apostles in Rome, were
also generously enriched by Bessarion § The last-named
Church, which Eugenius IV had assigned as his title, was
the special object of his paternal solicitude In the beginning of Paul II.'s pontificate the Cardinal caused the
Chapels of the Archangel Michael, of St John the Baptist,
and of Saint Eugenia, at the left of the High Altar, to be
completely restored and decorated by the painter Anto-
nazzo Romano. " In the centre of the vaulting appeared
the figure of Our Lord, enthroned and surrounded with nine
choirs of Angels, in a blue firmament strewn with stars and
encircled by a frieze. In the corners were the four Evangelists, with a Latin and a Greek Father of the Church writing
in his cell beside each On the upper part of the wall behind
the Altar was the apparition of the Archangel Michael on
Monte Gargano, and beneath this the birth of St John the
Baptist On the side walls, between two real and two painted
windows, stood two Archangels above, and the third with St
John the Baptist below. From half-way up the wall down
to the ground, curtains ornamented with patterns in flowers

* ROCCHI, Grottaferrata, 38 *seq* , 65, 80, 138, 162 The Catalogue of
the Manuscripts of Grottaferrata, commenced by order of Bessarion in
1462, has been published by BATIFFOL in DE WAAL'S Quartalschrift,
III , 39 *seq*

† Description in ROCCHI, Cod Crypt , 513

‡ A liturgical Manuscript, Γ β 1 , which Cesarini gave to his friend
Bessarion, and the magnificent Codex Z δ 1 , are particularly worthy
of notice See ROCCHI, Cod Crypt , 220 and 500.

§ MUNTZ, II , 298 *seq* , MALVASIA, 80 *seq* , 83 *seq*

and gold were painted.   On each of the six pilasters was the figure of a Saint under a canopy.   The framing-arch was adorned with a frieze, and three shields with the arms of the founder "*

Amongst the nearest and dearest of Bessarion's friends was Juan de Carvajal, the most devoted of all the sons of the Church.   His motto was " To suffer all things for Christ and His Church ! "   In consequence of his extreme modesty, and utter disregard of fame, the memory of this distinguished man has not been honoured as it deserves   The student of history can discover but scanty records of the life of this saintly Cardinal, who proved his fidelity and self-sacrificing devotion to the cause of the Church in twenty-two Legations and " from all his journeys brought back nothing but the reputation of an unspotted priesthood "†

Since the autumn of 1461 Carvajal had again been living in Rome   " The vigorous man, whom Pope Calixtus had sent to Hungary at the time when Belgrade was threatened by the Turks, had grown old and feeble in that severe climate, amid the turmoils of the Court and camp, and the fatigues of travel.   His teeth were so loose in his mouth that he could only use them with the aid of artificial appliances.   Yet it was political reasons rather than considerations of health, which at last induced him to abandon this bleak country of moorlands and marshes.

* SCHMARSOW, 57   See MALVASIA, 36 *seq.*; MUNTZ, II, 82 *seq.* The first of these writers draws attention to the similarity of these frescos, which were whitewashed over in the 17th Century, and Fra Angelico's paintings in the Vatican

† See our Vol II, p 7 and p. 390 *seq*   The scarcity of materials for a life of Carvajal is evident from the Monograph of LOPEZ, Rome, 1754 A College, which he founded at Salamanca, is mentioned by DENIFLE, I , 813   FRAKNÓI, in an article which has just appeared, and which I have not yet seen, gives the history of the Cardinal's Legations in Hungary

He left behind him the memory of a pure and beneficent
life, and his merits, which have never been questioned by
any historian, met with an honourable appreciation in
Rome. No other Cardinal, it was justly observed, did so
much and endured such sufferings as Carvajal in the six
years during which he was Legate for Hungary, while
championing the Church's highest interest, the purity of
her faith "* Extreme simplicity and exemplary order
prevailed in his modest dwelling near S. Marcello † His
ascetic manner of life enabled him to be very liberal to
the poor, and to provide for needy churches He was
never absent from any great ecclesiastical function or
from a Consistory. In Consistory he expressed his
opinion freely, but in a conciliatory manner. In their
" brevity, simplicity, and clearness, their strict logic and
their utter absence of rhetoric," his discourses form a
striking contrast to the bombastic and artificial productions of the literary men of his day, his Reports while
a Legate have the same " restrained and impersonal
character '‡

Though always genial in his intercourse with others,
there was a something about Carvajal which inspired a
certain awe in all who saw much of him   Cardinal

* VOIGT, III, 511-12, who remarks that Carvajal would have been
a Pope suited to the period, after the Tridentine Reforms In regard
to the date of his return, which is given wrongly by all writers, see our
Vol III, p 225, note §, the extract from the *Acta Consist, Secret
Archives of the Vatican

† Carvajals mortal remains found their last resting-place in this
church The inscription on the monument, erected by Bessarion, has
the following lines —

　　" Pontificum splendor iacet hic sacrique senatus ;
　　Namque animo Petrus, pectore Caesar erat "
　　　　　　　　　　　　　—CIACONIUS, II, 926.

‡ VOIGT, I, 260

Ammanati observed of him. "our age may rightly place him by the side of the ancient Fathers of the Church," and these words expressed the general opinion of the members of the Sacred College. It might be said that Rome did not contain a single man who had not done homage to "the height and depth of his character." Pomponius Laetus, "who admired nothing in ruined Rome but the heroic grandeur of its earliest founders; who hardly deigned to bestow a glance on the Barons and Prelates of the Papal City,—the proud Platonist, the cynic scorner of all flattery and of every kind of dignity, who never uncovered his head, or bowed to any one, made but one exception, and that was the aged Cardinal of S. Angelo."*

Subsequent historians have unanimously endorsed the esteem and admiration of his contemporaries for Carvajal The latest biographer of Pius II, who is generally disposed to believe the worst of men,† speaks of Carvajal with the greatest reverence. Even the Hussite historian of Bohemia says of him: "Not only in zeal for the Faith, in moral purity and strength of character, was he unsurpassed, but he was also unequalled in knowledge of the world, in experience of ecclesiastical affairs, and in the services which he rendered to the Papal authority. It was chiefly due to his labours, prolonged during a period of twenty years, that Rome at last got the better of Constance and Basle, that the nations returned to their allegiance, and that her power and glory again shone before the world with a splendour that had not been seen since the time of Boniface VIII. Carvajal's colleagues knew and acknowledged this, and in

* M Fernus, J Pomp Leti Elogium Hist, in FABRICIUS-MANSI, VI., 630, VOIGT, III., 514. We have shewn, *supra*, p 57, that P Laetus had his hours of weakness

† This is the opinion of VAHLEN, Valla, LXI, 371.

all important matters were guided by his counsels. Paul
II himself feared him, and yielded to all his wishes   Thus,
his personal influence, and his opinion regarding King
George and the doctrine of the Hussites, had great weight
in Rome."*

As a member of the Commission appointed by Paul II
to consider the state of ecclesiastical affairs in Bohemia,
Carvajal was associated with Bessarion and d'Estouteville.†
From the beginning he advocated stern measures. The
ill-advised conduct of the King of Bohemia, who omitted
to send any one from his Court to offer the congratulations
usual from Princes to a new Pope, had confirmed the
Cardinal in the conviction "that it would be absolutely
necessary to employ the knife in the case of wounds which
admitted ·of no other remedy, and to guard against fatal
corruption by severing the decayed members from the body
of Holy Church "‡

The Pope at first hoped that gentleness might be
successful with George Podiebrad.   The proceedings which
Pius II. had commenced were at once suspended.   Paul II.
declared that, if the Bohemian King fulfilled his promises,
he would be to him not a Pope, but a loving brother §   It
soon became evident that the double-tongued monarch had
no thought of keeping his oath.   When all Christian
Princes sent Ambassadors to Rome, none appeared from
Bohemia.   Fresh complaints were constantly made by the

* PALACKY, IV, 2, 372   Regarding Carvajal's influence with Paul
II , see CANENSIUS, 101

† BACHMANN, I , 548, and other historians mention Cardinal
"William of Ostia," without giving his real name   This is not a
scientific way of speaking

‡ PALACKY, IV., 2, 325   See Fontes Rer. Austr , XLIV, 589.

§ This is related by Johann Rohrbacher to Procopius von Rabenstein in PALACKY, Urkundl Beitr , 338, Gesch , IV , 2, 329

Catholics   The "pacific inclinations" of Paul II. gradually
vanished   The letter which the King of Bohemia sent to
Rome on the 7th March, 1465, only apologises in a passing
way for the delay of the Embassy , its main purpose is to
explain the reasons why George did not think it well to
comply with the Pope's desire, and raise the siege of the
fortress of Zornstein, which belonged to the Catholic
Heinrich von Lichtenburg.   Paul II.'s reply to this letter was
not addressed to the King himself, but to the Bohemian
Prelates and Barons (13th May, 1465),* a fact which shews
the change in his feeling   By the middle of the summer of
this year the stern views of Carvajal had completely
prevailed, and from henceforth guided the Pope in all his
decisions.   On the 2nd August, Podiebrad was summoned
by Cardinals Bessarion, Carvajal and Eroli, who were
entrusted with the management of the Bohemian affair, to
appear at Rome within 180 days to answer charges of
heresy, of relapse into heresy, of perjury (in regard to the
breach of his coronation oath), of spoliation of churches,
and of blasphemy.   "In order, however, to guard against a
further outbreak of heresy during the trial, and to protect
the oppressed Catholics," the Pope, on the 6th August,
empowered the Legate Rudolf, Bishop of Lavant, to inflict
ecclesiastical censures on all George's adherents, and to
declare all engagements entered into with him null and
void †

Meanwhile George's position had become much worse,
the chief lords of Bohemia, dissatisfied with his arbitrary
government, having become more and more hostile to him
He therefore made new proposals of accommodation with
Rome , but Rome was weary of these endless negotiations

* BACHMANN, I , 549 *seq* , 553

† SS Rei Siles, IX , 135-9 , PALACKY, Urk. Beitr , 362-6 , FRIND,
IV , 65

" Long years of prevarication had destroyed all confidence in George, so that even those who had once depended upon his word now turned from him with feelings embittered by disappointment, and firmly resolved never again to be deceived by him "* As early as the 8th December, 1465, Paul II had released George's subjects from their oath of allegiance ; on the 6th February, 1466, the proposals made through Duke Louis of Bavaria in favour of the King of Bohemia were absolutely rejected

In order to understand the severe language of this document, we must remember the shameful manner in which George had trifled with Calixtus III. and Pius II. regarding the Turkish question It is strange to find the King now bringing forward this question, and demanding to be rewarded beforehand for his return to the Church, and his participation in the Crusade, by the title of Emperor of Constantinople for himself, and the Archbishopric of Prague for one of his sons. Is a relapsed heretic, a perjured man, Paul II remarks, to ask, instead of penance and punishment, for a reward such as could hardly be granted to the most Christian Princes, who had rendered the greatest services to religion ? He desires to traffic with his conversion to the Faith, and sell his conscience for gain His feigned obedience would indeed be a precious boon to the Church, while the old leaven would still ferment throughout the kingdom. Is the Apostolic See to beg for this, while he reserves to himself the right to accept or reject what is offered ? The proposed Archbishop is a youth, scarce twenty years of age, who has grown up in the midst of his father's crimes and deceits, in

* BACHMANN, I , 574 Regarding the League among the Lords, see Markgraf's article in SYBEL'S Hist Zeitschr, XXXVIII , 49 *seq* , where, however, at pp. 54 and 65, the date of Paul's accession and Pius II.'s death are wrongly given.

ignorance of all law, either human or Divine, he has but
just ceased to be a heretic, and is now to be made a
Bishop!   Equally obnoxious is the request that the
Archbishop should have as assistant an Inquisitor who will
prosecute all "heresies outside the Compact." That is very
cunningly devised   is it not equivalent to a covert demand
that the Compacts should be re-established?   Again, what
is the meaning of the petition for the Imperial Crown of
Constantinople?   Evidently its object is only to secure an
easier passage from one Confession of Faith to another (the
Greek)   But the dominion of the Infidels, who have never
known the truth, is a lesser evil than the rule of a heretic
and schismatic, who has apostatised from that which he
professed   The Church has not yet fallen so low as to be
compelled to seek the protection of heretics and robbers of
churches.*

The fact that Podiebrad, in the summer of 1466, took the
excommunicated Gregor Heimburg into his service is a
proof that the Pope had not judged him too severely   His
connection with this unscrupulous man, who, "for twenty
years, had been at the head of every opposition offered
outside the limits of Bohemia to the restoration of the
Papal power," was equivalent to a renunciation of all idea
of reconciliation with the Church.†   Even on the 28th
July, Heimburg, who had formerly made a parade of his
German sympathies, published a manifesto in defence of
the "honour and innocence" of the Czech monarch, who

---

* Paul II to Duke Louis of Bavaria, 1466, Febr. 6. SS Rer Siles,
IX, 156–63 See PALACKY, IV, 2, 375 *seq*, BACHMANN, I, 575
seq, KLUCKHOHN, Ludwig, 261 *seq*, JORDAN, 195 *seq*, Markgraf
in SYBEL'S Hist Zeitschr, XXXVIII, 72 *seq*. Paul II's Brief to the
people of Breslau (Fontes, XLIV, 593), which Bachmann erroneously
assigns to the year 1465, refers to this occasion

† BACHMANN, I, 583, PALACKY, IV, 2, 391

had been treated by Rome worse "than the fratricide Cain and the Sodomites!" George, he said, was no private individual whom the Pope might summon to Rome at his pleasure, but a King, and a King of great merit. This advocate found excuses for everything, even for the imprisonment of Fantinus, which was a breach of the law of nations. The Pope was accused of credulity, and his conduct characterised as hasty, as an offence against Divine and natural law, and opposed to reason and Scripture. He further insisted that a Diet should be summoned, at which the Envoys of the temporal Princes should, in the presence of a Legate, deliberate on the ecclesiastical affairs of Bohemia * As this manifesto was at once sent, not only to all the German Courts, but also to the King of France and the other Princes of Christendom, it was impossible for the Papal party to be silent. The autumn had not passed before letters in answer appeared from Rudolf von Rudesheim, Bishop of Lavant, and from Cardinal Carvajal. The former sought to surpass his opponent in violence of language, and lost himself in prolix explanations, while Carvajal, in his brief, simple and logical style, exposed the treacherous arts of the Czech monarch and of his advocate. In particular, he brought forward the sacrilegious manner in which George had violated the right of nations by his conduct towards Fantinus and the double-faced policy by which he had trifled with the Holy See What Rome now commanded was the result of mature deliberation, and was in accordance with justice. George's intrigues are unmasked, the axe is laid to the roots , he must prove his innocence or else experience the rigour of justice †

* SS Rer Siles , IX , 181–90, MULLER, Reichstagstheater, II , 250–58 ; BROCKHAUS, 286 *seq.* , JORDAN, 227 *seq*

† Instead of "ut penas juris paciatur oportet" (SS Rer. Siles , IX , 209) we must surely read "aut penas," as the copy in Cod. 4, f 74b–76b,

Heimburg soon wrote a second apology for King George, in which he gave vent to his violent hatred of the two heads of Christendom and for the Cardinals. All manner of false charges were here made against both Pope and Emperor, and amongst others that of immorality. The " very violence and indecency of these accusations destroyed their effect."* The only result of this letter was entirely to put an end to the friendly relations which had existed between George Podiebrad and Frederick III The action of George's counsellor was certainly not that of a states-man.

of the Library at Kremsmunster has it This Manuscript also gives f 45a–68b, the above-mentioned *Letter of Rudolf von Rudesheim contra venenosum hereticum Georgium I also found in a collection formerly belonging to the Convent of Ebrach *Scripta in causa G Podiebradii Bohemiae regis, f 53–79, now Cod Q 15, of the University Library, Wurzburg

* MARKGRAF in SS Rer Siles, IX, 190, where it is observed that PALACKY, who (Urkundl Beitr., 647 *seq*) publishes the Apology, is mistaken in giving 1467 as its date. The charges of immorality made by Heimburg against Paul II. are also to be found in B. CORIO, 264 SCHMARSOW, 14, had not been able to receive this man's evidence because of its very general character (uomo molto dedito alla libi-dine), and because of the close relations which existed between him and Galeazzo Maria Sforza, who was hostile to Paul II , in the earlier parts of his history he is very untrustworthy (see ANNONI, Un plagio dello storico B Corio, a reprint from the Rivist Ital , and Arch St Lomb , II , 155), and also in the later period tells his readers many incredible stories and reports (see the example from the time of Alexander VI in DOLLINGER, Papstfabeln, p 32, note, 2nd ed) Nor is Janus Pannonius a more credible authority , according to VOIGT, II , 325, 2nd ed , he brought "all the moral filth of Italian Humanism into Hungary," and derided the precepts of the moral law and found pleasure in turning ecclesiastical things and persons into ridicule The passage on the subject (in WOLF, II , 112) is, for all purposes of historical criticism, properly characterised as a biting epigram JANUS, 372, rightly perceives that in such a case the testimony of partisans

The decided measures advocated by Carvajal did not meet with universal approval at the Roman Court Looking at the matter from a merely human point of view, some urged that there was no one who could carry into effect the sentence of the Holy See. Nothing was to be expected from the irresolute Emperor, and Poland also displayed little inclination to be of use. King Matthias of Hungary had, indeed, given the best assurances of good-will, but it was generally desired that he should reserve his forces for the Turkish war. It was doubtful whether the power of the Bohemian nobles was equal to the occasion. In the face of these grave difficulties, Carvajal remained unmoved in his opinion that justice ought to take its course, and that there was a duty to be accomplished. God would, he believed, provide for all.*

After Carvajal had left Rome as Legate to Venice, on the 20th August, 1466, Cardinals Ammanati and Piccolomini were the chief advocates of strong measures. After long deliberations their opinion finally prevailed.† On the

like Heimburg (see BROCKHAUS, 369) and Corio, or the obscene Pannonius, is inadmissible, that adduced from Attilio Alessio (in BALUZE-MANSI, IV, 519) must also be rejected, inasmuch as he wrote after 1530 .In the numerous Ambassadorial Reports in the Archives of Milan, Mantua, and Modena, which I have gone through, there is no trace of a charge against the moral character of Paul II., although his other faults are by no means concealed The silence of his bitterest enemy,—Platina,—who, if grounds of accusation had really existed, would certainly not have passed them over, ought to be deemed conclusive

* See Fabian Hankos Report of the 17th July, 1466, in SS Rer. Siles, IX, 181. Further particulars regarding the attitude of Poland will be found in CARO, V, 1, 269 *seq*, 273 *seq*.

† AMMANATI, Comment, 401-402 (Frankfort ed, p 437), speaks as if the energetic words of Carvajal had at once, and of themselves, brought about the Consistory of Dec 23, 1466 PALACKY, IV., 2, 419, and BACHMANN, I., 592, who follow this later account, might have

23rd December a Consistory was held, in which George Podiebrad was deposed from his dignities of King, Marquis and Prince, his posterity declared disqualified for any honour or inheritance, and his subjects absolved from their oath of allegiance *

The Papal Bull announcing this decision made a deep impression on loyal Catholics, and in order to lessen its effect, Podiebrad, on the 14th April, 1467, published a solemn appeal to a General Council, which ought properly, he said, to have been assembled before this time, and

learnt from the final sentence of 23rd Dec, 1466 (SS. Rer. Siles, IX, 211), that Carvajal was not at the time in Rome. The *Acta Consist in the Secret Archives of the Vatican also expressly declare that Carvajal was absent from Rome from the 20th August, 1466, until the 17th Sept, 1467. See also HOFLER, Geschichtsschr. der Husitischen Bewegung, III, 224, and Cardinal Gonzaga, who wrote from Rome on the 18th Sept, 1467 *" Heri sera tornoe el rev mons de S Agnolo" (Gonzaga Archives) Probably the Cardinal was exerting himself in opposition to Podiebrad in Venice, while Heimburg was endeavouring to gain the Republic over to the Bohemian side. (BACHMANN, I., 584, note 3) The above-mentioned controversial letter must also have originated there

* Besides Balthasar of Piscia's Report in SS Rer Siles, IX, 214–215; see *J P. Arrivabene's letters from Rome   (1) Dat 1466, Dec 19 "P S Fornito el consistorio de hoggi niente si è saputo de cardinali Sono stati sopra questa materia del Re de Bohemia" Probably a Public Consistory was to be held on the Monday   (2) Dat 1466, Dec. 23 : "P S Nel consistorio publico che foe differito ad hoggi è sta dechiarato quello Georgio che se pretende Re de Bohemia heretico e privato d'ugni dignitate regale ducale e marchionale e d'ugni bene spirituale e temporale e inhabilitato li figlioli e l'acto foe sollenne secundo el stilo de ragione   Ad' esso che è xxiv hore e giunto Alexio" (Gonzaga Archives, Mantua)   A *Commentary on the Bull of Deposition was written by Rodericus Sancius de Arevalo, and dedicated to Paul II. Bessarion's Copy of the Document is preserved at the Marciana in Venice (see ANDRES, Cartas, III, 73 [Madrid, 1790]); present number, Z L. CXCIV

had been put off only by the Pope's negligence This
document, which attacked the Pope personally, was drawn
up by Heimburg It was immediately sent to all the
German Princes.* At the same time an Ambassador
was despatched from Prague to the Court of the French
King He was to propose the conclusion of an offensive
and defensive alliance between Louis XI. and Podiebrad,
into which the Poles and a number of the German Princes
were to be drawn, especially the rulers of Saxony and
Brandenburg, whose sympathies were with Bohemia The
immediate object of the allies was to be the humiliation
of Burgundy When this was accomplished, Louis XI.
was to summon a Council, "which should be held by the
nation," and which should put down all strife and all
arrogance, especially the pretensions of the Pope and the
Emperor, who were to be brought low and punished! At
the French Court the Ambassador maintained that the
Pope was endeavouring "to get both swords into his hands,
and thus subject all rulers to himself, so that the clergy
might have their way in everything" Words like these
found a ready access to the ear of a tyrant like Louis XI.
He promised to exert himself in Podiebrad's favour in
Rome, and also to use his influence "to maintain the
Compacts of the Holy Council of Basle in force", he further
advised that the German Princes should be persuaded to
advocate the assembling of the Council. George's efforts
in this matter were unsuccessful, and complications in his
own dominions, and with England, so fully occupied the
French King, that he was unable to pursue his anti-
Roman project of the Council.† The close relations which

* Fontes Rer. Austr Dipl, XX, 454–8, XLII, 410, SS Rer Siles.,
IX, 226.

† J Pažout, G. v Bohmen und die Concilsfrage im Jahre 1467,
in the Archiv fur Œsterr Gesch, XL, 333 *seq* See *supra*, p 104.

continued to exist between Louis XI. and the Bohemian
monarch is evidenced by the fact that when, in the following
year, Paul II. wished to have the Bull of Maundy Thursday,
in which Podiebrad was mentioned by name, published
in France, the French King at once raised objections, and
the Duke of Milan did the same.*

While Podiebrad was somewhat unsuccessfully labouring
to elevate his personal contest with Rome into a matter
of general importance to all the temporal powers, the
opposing party within his kingdom did not remain idle
Nothing decisive, however, was done, even after the formation of a great Catholic League in the December of
1467 It became more and more evident that the League
could only hope to prevail against George if assisted by
some powerful Prince.   All efforts to obtain such aid proved
fruitless, and accordingly in the end no alternative remained
to the Pope and the League, save to listen to the overtures
made to them by the King of Hungary †

The adversaries of George greatly rejoiced when Matthias
Corvinus (1468, March 31) declared war against Bohemia.
Cardinal Ammanati's letters to Paul II and Carvajal bear
witness to their satisfaction ‡ The necessary interruption

* DAUNON, 265 *seq* See FRIEDBERG, Grenzen, 479 From a
command on the subject to the Archbishop of Lyons on the 25th
Febr, 1469, we find that Paul continued his efforts to have Podiebrad's
Excommunication published in France D'ACHERY, III, 834 (nov edit).
The Maundy Thursday Bull, expressly naming Podiebrad, was also disseminated in the vernacular in Italy I found a contemporary Italian
translation of the Bull *Cœna Domini*, of 1469, in the State Archives
at Modena , Bolle. In reference to the opposition made by the Duke
of Milan, see a contemporary *Notice on the copy of the Maundy
Thursday Bull in the State Archives, Milan

† This is the opinion of HUBER, III., 208, see 215 ; and CARO, V ,
1, 293

‡ AMMANATI, Epist , f 151b, 152b, pp 655-6 (Frankfort ed)

of the war with the Turks was looked upon as a lesser
evil   The Apostolic Faith was deemed to be in imminent danger unless the Bohemian King should voluntarily
abandon his schismatic position, or be forcibly deprived
of the power of doing harm.* On the 20th April, 1468,
the Pope had again pronounced the severest ecclesiastical
penalties on all the adherents and abettors of George, and
had moreover promised a number of Indulgences to those
who should either personally, or by pecuniary contributions,
take part in the war against him † Lorenzo Roverella,
the Bishop of Ferrara, who had but lately returned to
Rome, was again sent to Germany to publish these Indulgences, and furnished with fuller powers ‡

During the year 1468 the fortunes of war favoured the
King of Hungary   In the following February, Matthias
advanced into Bohemia, but was completely shut in by
Podiebrad in the defiles near Wilimow, and his case seemed
hopeless   He then began to negotiate for a truce, and
promised to obtain from the Pope the toleration of the
Compacts for the Bohemians. On the 24th March, the
two Kings purposed to meet at Olmutz, and conclude a
permanent peace   The Papal Legate, Roverella, hastened
to the spot to prevent this, and succeeded in doing so §

* See the passage from Joh von Rabenstein's Dialog in the Archiv
fur Œsterr Gesch , LIV , 382

† SS Rer Siles , IX , 265-9

‡ RAYNALDUS, ad an 1468, N 2-3 A *Letter of Credentials,
given by Paul II to L Roverella for the City of Ratisbon, dated
1468, April 20, is in Regensb R-T-A in the Records Office in
Munich Even on the 8th April, 1468, there appears in *Cruciata
Pauli II , f 84, an entry of 1000 ducats, " pro dom episc Ferrariensi,
nuncio et oratori S D N papae in partibus Alamanniae pro negotiis
Bohemiae rem fidei concernentibus ituro "   State Archives, Rome.

§ PALACKY, IV , 2, 573 *seq*.   See Urkundl Beitrage, 569 *seq*., and
Fontes, XLIV , 661 *seq*.

In July, 1469, the war broke out afresh, Matthias having been two months previously solemnly elected King of Bohemia No decisive advantage was gained by either party during that year or the next. The war was one of mutual devastation, and seemed likely to be endless. Notwithstanding all the efforts of his opponents, George held his ground, paying his partisans out of the spoils of the Church. He failed, however, to accomplish his plan of founding a Czech dynasty by securing the succession to one of his sons.*

Meanwhile, the "greatest, and, in regard to his moral character, the most estimable, of the enemies of Bohemia in the Sacred College," Juan Carvajal, had died in Rome (6th December, 1469).† At the same time it was reported that one of the Cardinals had advocated a pacific arrangement with Podiebrad, this induced the latter to express to the Cardinal in question, whose name is unfortunately unknown, his desire for reconciliation with Rome. He declared that he had never intended to injure the Holy Father, and yet had undeservedly to endure his severe displeasure. He had never believed himself to be outside the Holy Church, in which alone is salvation. If in any way he had departed from the unity of the Faith, he had done it in ignorance. Although he had already entrusted his reconciliation with Rome to King Casimir of Poland, he

* FRIND, IV, 73, GRUNHAGEN, I, 321, 324

† RAYNALDUS, ad an 1470, N 48, and PALACKY, IV., 2, 657, both give 1470 as the year of Carvajal's death They are contradicted by AMMANATI, Comment, lib VII, and the precise statement of the *Acta Consist, that on the 6th Dec, 1469, at the first hour of the night, the Card Joannes tit S. Angeli episc Portuens, Camerlengo of the Sacred College, died "cuius anima per dei misericordiam propter sua infinita benemerita requiescat in pace" (Secret Archives of the Vatican) A complete and really critical biography of Carvajal would be a very valuable work

now sent another Ambassador, whom he hereby accredited to the Pope *

If these endeavours at reconciliation were really sincere, the increasing danger from the Turkish power gave them a prospect of success   But when matters had gone so far a higher Hand intervened.   On the 22nd February, 1471, Rokyzana, "the soul of all the anti-Catholic efforts of the Utraquists," died in Prague, and on the 22nd March George Podiebrad followed him.   The opinion that the King was, before his death, reconciled to the Church is erroneous.†   It is, however, certain that Gregor Heimburg, the man who had exercised so potent an influence on his anti-Roman policy, did, before his death (1472), make his peace with the Church.‡

The struggle about the Compacts, which were not really observed in any of the Utraquist Churches, was not terminated by the deaths of the spiritual and temporal chiefs of the party ; the Polish Prince Wladislaw, when elected by the Bohemians in May, 1471, as their King, was obliged expressly to bind himself to uphold them.   The hopes cherished by the father of the newly-elected sovereign, that

---

* PALACKY, IV , 2, 657 *seq* , see Urk Beitrage, 639 *seq*

† FRIND, IV , 75, speaks decidedly of George's conversion, and considers his interment in the Cathedral to be evidence of his reconciliation with the Church ; see, on the other hand, PALACKY, IV , 2, 665, N 458   The testimony of COCHLAEUS, 1 XII (followed by PESSINA, Phosphorus septicornis, 292 [Prag., 1673], and VOIGT, III , 501, who does not reject the statement), cannot be considered of weight in this question , every doubt, however, is removed by the Letter of Paul II to Roverella (in THEINER, II., 425), where he expressly mentions "Georgius de Podiebrad *damnate memorie.*"

‡ Heimburg applied by letter to Sixtus IV., who, inasmuch as the Holy See is not wont to refuse forgiveness to penitent sinners, gave the Bishop of Meissen full power to absolve him   BROCKHAUS, 383-4 ; and Cod. Dipl. Sax , 211 *seq*

the Bohemian position would be recognised by Rome were accordingly without foundation ; for this was no mere question of externals, but a deep-seated and essential separation which might be for a time concealed by a formula of union, but could not be conclusively settled by any such means.*

* See HOFLER, Gesch der Husitischen Bewegung, I., xxxvi. ; III., 205   The fanaticism which possessed many of the Bohemians appears in the "Manifesto of Satan," written in the time of Sixtus IV., and published by JORDAN, 520 *seq*. This letter begins as follows "We, Lucifer, by the power of fraud, King of the Kings of earth, holding the sceptre of the most illustrious Roman Emperor by virtue of our presence and residence near the tombs of the Holy Apostles Peter and Paul, where we have achieved the complete abandonment of the doctrine of Jesus and trodden His faith under our feet."

CHAPTER VI.

PAUL II 's CARE FOR THE STATES OF THE CHURCH.—DESTRUC-
TION OF THE BANDIT FAMILY OF ANGUILLARA —THE PEACE
OF 1468 —THE POPE'S DIFFERENCES WITH FERRANTE OF
NAPLES.—SECOND JOURNEY OF FREDERICK III TO ROME —
THE STRUGGLE REGARDING RIMINI.

PAUL II., who was by nature anything but warlike, was in
the early part of his reign more successful in his conflicts
with tyrants in the States of the Church than in his
expeditions against the Turks and Hussites * The robber
Knights of Anguillara were the first to claim his attention

The cruel Count Everso of Anguillara had already given
great trouble to his immediate predecessors. "During the
Pontificate of Pius II. he had taken possession of all the
territory formerly held by the Prefects, and there in his
mountain fortresses securely guarded the spoils gathered
from the plunder of towns, pilgrims, and merchants Like
Malatesta, he had been the ally of all the enemies of the
Pope" Cardinal Ammanati says that he despised God and
the Saints and yet made pious foundations † Much has

* Jacobus Trottus, Ambassador of Este, in a Postscript to a
*Despatch, dated Rome, 1469, Sept. 6, remarks of Paul II , "non e de
natura bellicosa" (State Archives, Modena.) See also CANENSIUS,
83.

† GREGOROVIUS, VII., 218, 3rd ed See AMMANATI, Comment ,
351b , MASSIMO, Torre Ang , 12 seq.; ADINOLFI, Laterano e Via
Maggiore (Rome, 1857), Doc. 4 , ROHAULT, Pl. 63 , ARMELLINI,
272.

lately been heard of the portion of his Palace which still exists, a gloomy tower in Trastevere, which was in danger of falling a sacrifice to a destructive work of restoration. Happily this interesting building, which commands a splendid view of the City, has for the present escaped ; who can say, however, how long it may be spared ?

Count Everso, who had to the last defied Pius II., died on the 4th September, 1464 * His two sons, Francesco and Deifobo, began by making the fairest promises to the Pope, but soon betrayed a disposition to follow in the footsteps of their father, and ruin the peace of the whole neighbourhood. Paul II. then determined to make war upon this race of tyrants, who had braved the authority of four successive Popes, and were a scourge to that portion of the States of the Church. His prudence and caution enabled him to take the Counts completely by surprise.

At the end of June, 1465, the sentence of Excommunication was pronounced against them, and Cardinal Niccolo Forteguerri, Federigo of Urbino, and Napoleone Orsini,† at once advanced with an armed force. They were joined by troops from the King of Naples, who had a personal quarrel with Deifobo. Thirteen castles, some of which had been deemed impregnable from their position and fortifications, were taken almost without a blow. In these robbers' nests were found implements for coining Papal money, correspondence of a compromising character, and numbers of unhappy captives, doomed by the tyrants to perpetual

* Not on the 3rd September, as GREGOROVIUS, VII , 218, 3rd ed , says, following INFESSURA (1140), who is most unreliable, especially as to dates , see in MASSIMO, 15, Everso's epitaph, which was formerly to be found in Sta Maria Maggiore , this agrees with the statement in the Diario Nepesino, 141.

† See Paul II.'s Brief to Cesare de Varano, 10th June, 1465. State Archives, Florence (Urbino).

imprisonment. Deifobo escaped to Venice; Francesco was imprisoned, together with his children, but was soon liberated at the instance of Stefano Colonna.* Twelve days sufficed to break the power of the Anguillara; the conquered towns and fortresses came under the immediate rule of the Holy See †

The year 1465 also witnessed an extension of Papal authority in the Romagna. By virtue of the treaty concluded in 1463 with Pius II., the towns possessed by the Malatesta were, on the extinction of their line, to revert to the Holy See. Malatesta Novello, Lord of Cesena, dying childless on the 20th November, 1465, his nephew, Roberto, sought to occupy Cesena and Bertinoro. His efforts were, however, frustrated by the loyalty with which these cities adhered to the promise given to the Holy See. The inhabitants had good reasons for preferring immediate

---

* "*Francescho fiolo che fu del conte de Aversa è cavato de presone mediante la intercessione de Stefano Colona, quale ha fatto securtate de cento milia ducati," writes Bartholomaus de Maraschis to Marchioness Barbara, under date Rome, 1465, July 24 (Gonzaga Archives, Mantua). Francesco seems to have been again imprisoned subsequently, for, on the 13th Aug., 1471, Sixtus IV set him at liberty. This we learn from *Petrus de Modegnano in his Report of August 14. (State Archives, Milan.) REUMONT, III., 1, 175, gives 1475 as the year of Francesco's death. The epitaph in SCHRADER, Mon. Ital., 129, and GALLETTI, III., 156, however, have 1473; and FORCELLA, IV., 385, agrees with them. I found in Cod. Vat 939, Vatican Library, an *Epistola ad nob. vir. Franc de Anguillara exhortatoria ad pacientiam (belonging to the time when he was in confinement at S Angelos).

† For an account of the war against the Anguillara, see AMMANATI, Comment., 355 seq., Epist, 71b, 77, Gasp. Veronen. in MURATORI, III., 2, 1014 seq.; N. DELLA TUCCIA, 270; CANENSIUS, 51-64, Diario Nepesino, 149-52, PLATINA, 772-3, Cronica di Bologna, 760-61; Chron. Eugub, 1009; BALDI, Fed. di Montef., III., 71 seq., CIAMPI, Forteguerri, 14, ROSMINI, Milano, IV., 65; Arch. d Soc Rom, VII, 117-18, 179-82, X, 425-6.

dependence on the government of the Church, which allowed them far greater liberty, and did not harry them with oppressive taxation. In order to conciliate and win over the warlike Robert, Paul II invested him with the fiefs of Meldola, Sarsina, and some other small places, and took him into his service as a captain of mercenaries *

Not long after the downfall of the Anguillara, the Pope came into conflict with the King of Naples, "the terrible and faithless Ferrante." †

The unreasonable demands of the King, and his prevarications about the payment of his tribute, had, even at the beginning of the Pontificate, caused some estrangement between Naples and the Pope ‡ Although, according to the Bull of Investiture granted by Pius II, the severest penalties—such as Excommunication, Interdict, deposition from the throne, and forfeiture of his fief—were to be incurred by non-payment of the tribute, Ferrante steadily neglected it "When called upon to pay, he never failed to find some excuse; at one time he pleaded the great difficulties occa-

---

* SUGENHEIM, 341; REUMONT, Lorenzo, I, 179, 2nd ed, BALDI, III, 86 *seq*, TONINI, V, 308 *seq*; L'ÉPINOIS, 437 Rob. Malatesta's pay is entered on the 10th Oct, 1466, in *Div Pauli II, Vol II, f 43 State Archives, Rome.

† Thus designated by GREGOROVIUS in the Augsburg Allg Zeitung, 1870, N. 146. See GOTHEIN, 32 Bartholomaus de Maraschis, in the *Despatch of the 24th July, 1465, cited on p 150, note*, tells how the Neapolitan troops, immediately after the downfall of the Anguillara, oppressed the Romans.

‡ See the *Letter of Otto de Carretto to Fr Sforza, dated Rome, 1464, Oct. 14 and 24 (Ambrosian Library, Milan), and a *Letter of the 21st Oct, 1464, from the same Carretto in the State Archives at Milan. See the passage from a *Despatch of Nicodemus of the 31st Oct, 1469 (State Archives, Milan), given *infra*, p. 172, note *. When Federigo, the son of the King of Naples, came to Rome in April, 1465, he was treated with great honour *Div Pauli II, 1464-66, fol 82b, contains records of money expended on this occasion State Archives, Rome

sioned by internal troubles, at another the expenses in which
he had been involved by his share in the war against the
Anguillara." The tension constantly increased. When
Ferrante, who already owed the Pope 60,000 golden ducats,
sent the customary palfrey, but not a farthing with it, the
Pope returned it   The King went so far as to threaten
that, if the claim were still insisted upon, he would enter
into alliance with the Turks, whereupon the Pope answered
that he would provide for having Ferrante driven from
his kingdom, and the Turks expelled from the Christian
dominions *

The complicated relations which existed between Naples
and the Apostolic See made it possible for the King to
keep the Pope in perpetual alarm, by constantly making
fresh demands   The real ground of Ferrante's hostility
was the jealousy with which he viewed the consolidation
of the Papal power in the States of the Church, and
accordingly he harassed the Pope in every way that he
could.

The energetic measures of Paul II against the lawless
Barons in the Roman territory "had not perfectly restored
peace ; feuds were constantly breaking out amongst them,
as well as amongst the lesser nobles, while bloody and
barbarous revenges were of frequent occurrence   Yet
much had been gained   The Pope laboured unremittingly,
by means of his Cardinals and Prelates, to bring about
reconciliations "†   At the same time he did what he could

* CANENSIUS, 74-5 , GASP VERONEN , 1041 , REUMONT, Lorenzo,
I., 220, 2nd ed ; BORGIA, Dom temp nelle Sicil , 196-7, Rome, 1789,
2nd ed   According to GOTTLOB, Cam. Ap , Part 3, the *Introitus-
register of Paul II 's pontificate records no payment of tribute by
Ferrante.

† REUMONT, III., 1, 157   See L'ÉPINOIS, 436   Regarding the
Pope's efforts to promote peace in Orvieto, see the documents in

to maintain among the Italian powers that peace which
the danger of Turkish invasion rendered so necessary
His prompt action at the critical moment of the death of
Francesco Sforza, which occurred on the 8th March, 1466,
after an illness of but two days, was specially judicious
and effective.   This unexpected event caused the greatest
consternation at the French Court,* as well as in Florence
and in Rome, where the news arrived on the 16th March.†
A Consistory was at once held, in which, at the Pope's
suggestion, it was determined that the Holy See should
use every possible means for the maintenance of peace.
Paul II forgot all previous differences with Milan, and
sent a special Ambassador to express his sympathy, and
declare his intention of standing by the Duchess and her
children.‡ He also addressed Briefs to all the Italian
Governments, informing them of his determination to
maintain peace in the Peninsula, and earnestly exhorting
them to avoid all disturbances §   The warning was needed,

FUMI, 724-8   Paul II's *Briefs of the 17th Nov, 1470, to Card
S. Clementis (Ravenna), and the Episc Fumanus, deal with troubles
in the dominions of Todi and Spoleto   Lib brev, 12, f 36, Secret
Archives of the Vatican.

* See the *Despatches of Panigarola and Em de Jacopo to the
Duchess of Milan, dated Orleans, 1466, March 23   Fonds Ital, 1611,
National Library, Paris

† *Letter of J P Arrivabene, dated Rome, 1466, March 17.
(Gonzaga Archives) See BUSER, Beziehungen, 134 seq

‡ See A de Rubeis' Report of the 18th March   Fonds Ital, 1613,
National Library, Paris.

§ See PLATINA, 775 ; *PARENTI, Hist Fiorent (Original Manuscript
in the National Library, Florence) ; MAGLIAB, XXV -2-519, f 2 , and
CANENSIUS, 70 seq. ; see also DESJARDINS, I., 137.   A *Brief of
Paul II to Florence, dated Rome, 1466, xiii. Cal April, and relating
to this subject, is in the State Archives, Florence (X -II -23, f. 142-3):
the Republic is here urged to maintain peace in Italy.   In the State
Archives, Milan, I found a copy of a *Brief of similar import addressed

especially in regard to the Republic of St Mark, whose
policy had given the Pope just cause for dissatisfaction *
Many exiles from Florence had at this time betaken themselves to Venice to hatch in safety conspiracies against
the rule of the Medici   The Signoria, ever ready to fish
in troubled waters, while avoiding any open breach of
the peace, by no means discouraged these plots. " The
old grudge against Florence, on account of the defeat of
their schemes against Milan by Cosmo, revived.   The
resentment of the banished Florentines was to be turned
to account to establish a government there, which should be
dependent on the support of Venice, and to overthrow the
Sforzas in Milan."†   Bartolommeo Colleone, an ambitious
and avaricious Condottiere, was to be the instrument employed for the accomplishment of these designs.   In order
to enable the exiled Florentines to avail themselves of
his services, the Signoria dismissed him with promises of
money ‡

In face of the threatening attitude of Colleone, the
Ambassadors of Florence, Naples and Milan, on the 4th
January, 1467, entered into a defensive alliance at Rome,
under the protection of Paul II., with a view of securing the

by Paul II to the Doge of Venice, dated 1466, April 17, with an
observation appended to the effect that letters of the same character
had been sent to Naples, Ferrara, Mantua, and Siena.

* See Appendix, N 14   *Letter of T. Maffei of the 15th June, 1466,
and *supra*, p 96 *seq*.

† REUMONT, Lorenzo, I., 173–4, 182, 2nd ed.   See BUSER,
Beziehungen, 135 *seq*. Regarding the conspiracy in Florence, see
PERRENS, 313 *seq*   Paul II wrote a *Letter of condolence, dated
Rome, 1466, Sept 8, to the Florentine Government in reference to
these troubles, which he characterises as dangerous to the city, and
injurious to the peace of Italy and the war against the Turks.   State
Archives, Florence, X –II –23, f. 148b–149b.

‡ See PERRENS, 328.

peace of Italy.* This was a time of great anxiety for the
Pope, he placed no confidence in Ferrante, who shewed
symptoms of meditating an attack on the temporal possessions of the Holy See † In the month of March the
Ambassador of Modena was of opinion that Ferrante would
declare war on the Pope ‡

Besides Colleone, the Florentine exiles took Ercole of
Este, Alessandro Sforza of Pesaro, Pino degli Ordelassi,
Lord of Forli, the Lords of Carpi and Galeotto de' Pici
della Mirandola into their pay   An army, 14,000 strong,
was assembled. The Republic of Florence engaged the
services of the Count of Urbino, while Ferrante sent
auxiliary troops, and Galeazzo Maria himself hurried to the
front, at the head of 6000 men   The two most famous
Italian Generals of the day, Colleone and Federigo of
Urbino, thus stood opposed to one another, each at the
head of a considerable force. On the 23rd July, 1467,
they met at La Molinella, in the territory of Imola; but
the battle led to no decisive result §

After this action, more than half a year was spent "in
useless marches and entrenchments, and in wrangling,

* See MALIPIERO, 212 , TRINCHERA, I , 1 *seq* , 6 *seq* , BUSER, Beziehungen, 139; DESJARDINS, I., 144 *seq* , REUMONT, Lorenzo, I., 173,
183, 2nd ed   GREGOROVIUS, VII , 221, 3rd ed , is wrong in giving the
2nd January as the date of the conclusion of the League   A *Letter of
Augustinus de Rubeis, dated Rome, 1466, Dec. 6, throws important
light on the negotiations which preceded the treaty   State Archives,
Milan.

† *Letter of Card Gonzaga of the 7th Jan , 1467   Gonzaga Archives ,
see Appendix, N. 18

‡ "*Il me pare vedere che Re Ferrando [ha] voglia di guerra col
papa" Report of Jacobus Trottus, dated Rome, 1467, March 15
State Archives, Modena.

§ LEO, III , 410 *seq* , REUMONT, Lorenzo, I , 183 *seq* , 2nd ed. ,
PERRENS, 331

recriminations and negotiations "*   At last Paul II. determined, on the Feast of the Purification, 1468, after Mass at
Araceli on the Capitol, to proclaim peace by his own
authority +   The Bull published on this occasion first
insists on the necessity of peace in face of the danger from
Turkey, then relates the efforts made by the Pope for the
restoration of tranquillity, and requires Venice, Naples, Milan,
and Florence, within the space of thirty days, to come to terms.
Colleone was named General of the Christians, with a salary
of a hundred thousand florins, to which all the Italian States
were to contribute, and he was to carry on the war with the
Turks in Albania ; the territory which he had won from the
Florentines, and from Taddeo Manfredi of Imola, was to be
restored within fifty days ‡

---

* REUMONT, Lorenzo, I , 188, 2nd ed   See SYBEL s Hist Zeitschr ,
XXIX , 329 seq , and CIPOLLA, 541 seq   Further lights are needed to
explain the attitude of Paul II during these negotiations   AMMANATI,
Comment , lib IV , is by no means an absolutely trustworthy authority ;
nor can we, like SISMONDI, X , 324 seq , place complete confidence in
G B. PIGNA, l VIII , who wrote in the time of Alfonso II.

+ Until this time war had been threatening ; not till the 28th Jan ,
1468, could Card Gonzaga declare : * ' Heri matina in concistoro secreto
la Sta de N S concluse che omnino voleva pronunciare questa pace el
di de la purificatione " Gonzaga Archives, Mantua

‡ RAYNALDUS, ad an 1468, N 14-21 ; Bull V , 189-94, where the
Bull is wrongly assigned to the year 1467. See AMMANATI, Comment.,
l IV ; N DELLA TUCCIA, 272 , MALIPIERO, 231 seq , PALMERIUS,
250-51 , SANUDO, 1185 , Chron Eugub , 1015 , also SUMMONTE, IV ,
564 , and Arch St Napol., IX , 217. The Brief to Colleone, which
accompanied the Bull, is in the Istor. Bresc , 911-12 On the 2nd
February the Florentines were also informed by a *Brief of the conclusion of peace , a Copy is in the State Archives, Florence, X -II -
23, f 170. A detailed account of the proclamation in Araceli is given
in a *Report of Aug de Rubeis and Joh Blanchus, dated Rome, 1468,
Febr. 3 (State Archives, Milan, Cart Gen) Expenses pro luminaribus
pro pace publicanda are entered on the 1st Febr , 1468, in *Div.

Milan and Naples, however, would not do anything towards paying Colleone A chronicler sums up their reply in the following words : " We desire peace, but as to Colleone, we will not give him even a biscuit." * Other difficulties were also raised , and for some time it seemed as if the war must break out again. Paul II. was obliged to give up the stipulation regarding Colleone On the 25th April peace was proclaimed in Rome, and soon afterwards in Florence, and celebrated everywhere with brilliant festivities Some fresh obstacles were now created by Venice,† but finally these, too, were happily overcome, and on the Feast of the Ascension peace was proclaimed in the territories of the Republic ‡ By the 8th May the conditions

Pauli II , Vol I I. (State Archives, Rome) Gold medals were struck to commemorate the conclusion of peace (MALIPIERO, 233). Domenico Galletti, on this occasion, addressed several poems to Paul II., these are preserved in Cod Vat , 3694 and 3695 ; Piero Luigi Galletti published them in a very rare pamphlet (Nozze-Publ), Verona, 1787

* Chron. Eugub , 1015.

† RAYNALDUS, ad an. 1468, N 22 , LANDUCCI, 10 , Cr di Bologna, 773 , TRINCHERA, I., p LVIII seq , *Letter of August Patritius to Campanus, dated Rome, 1468, April 27 , Cod. S 1 1., f 117, of the Angelica Library, Rome , *Letter of Card. Gonzaga, dated Rome, 1468, April 25 (Gonzaga Archives, Mantua) , and *Despatch of Lorenzo da Pesaro to the Duke of Milan of the same date. This last Document begins with the words · *" Ad laude et gloria del omnipotente dio, de la sua madre madona S Maria semper vergine et de S Ambroscio, de S. Agnese, de S. Petro matiro et de tucta la corte celestiale, ad exaltation et grandeza del stato de V J. S , &c, hoggi havemo firmata la pace in lo infrascr. modo " The Original and Copy are in the State Archives, Milan Regarding the festivities in the States of the Church on occasion of the peace, see also PERUZZI, Ancona, 376 ; BONAZZI, Perugia, 683 As to the Republic of Florence, see P BIGAZZI, Miscell. Stor , N 3, p 25 seq (Florence, 1849)

‡ Ist Bresc, 912 See CIPOLLA, 584 seq., and ROMANIN, IV, 332, for the ratification

had been officially drawn up in Rome in the Pope's presence *

On Ascension Day there was a magnificent procession, in which Paul II himself took part on foot Hymns were composed for the occasion by Lionardo Dati and an eloquent discourse was pronounced by Domenico de' Domenichi †

Paul II's satisfaction at the advent of peace was enhanced by the hope which it encouraged that Italy would now offer a serious resistance to the Turks. For this object he had already expended no less than the sum of two hundred thousand florins,‡ and his disappointment, when clouds again overspread the political horizon, must have been in proportion to his interest in the cause.

Ferrante of Naples was the disquieting element. In the summer of 1468, when Paul II. had attempted to occupy the important fortress of Tolfa, which commanded the alum mines, he had been prevented by the Neapolitan troops, who not only supported the Orsini, who were the lords of the soil, in their resistance, but even threatened Rome itself. The Pope was so much alarmed that he meditated flight. His most valuable property had already been hidden in St. Angelo, when the Neapolitan army turned against Sora §

---

* Secret Archives of the Vatican   *Lib rubeus (see our Vol III, p. 245), f 81 *seq*, and *Cod B-19, f 49, of the Vallicellana Library, Rome. RAYNALDUS, ad an 1468, N 25, makes use of the latter manuscript See also MITTARELLI, Access Faventinae, 337 (Venet, 1771).

† CANENSIUS, 82 ; AMMANATI, Epist., f 143 *seq*, 165, 166b, 167. Domenichi's *Discourse, which QUIRINI, 287, intended to publish, is preserved in Cod A 44, N. 9, of the Chapter Library, Padua, and in Cod Ottob, 1035, f. 46-53, Vatican Library. Disbursements for the peace rejoicings on Ascension Day appear in the *Lib III, Bullet. Pauli II, on the 22nd May, 1468. State Archives, Rome.

‡ See the *Brief of the 16th May, 1468, addressed to Florence. State Archives, Florence, also Appendix, N 23.

§ CANENSIUS, 84. See REUMONT, Diplomazia, 371.

During the contest for the throne of Naples, Pius II had become Sovereign of this important Duchy, and he had maintained his rights over it against all the efforts of Ferrante. On the accession of Paul II., the King had again endeavoured to recover Sora He now deemed the moment to have arrived for the forcible accomplishment of his object, and certainly the opportunity seemed favourable. Paul II, who always shrank from outlay for military purposes, was almost defenceless ; in vain did he reproach the faithless Monarch with ingratitude towards the Holy See, to whose favour he owed his crown Fortunately for him, Cardinal Roverella was successful in persuading Ferrante not to advance any further In October, 1468, the Pope gave orders that fresh troops should be levied, to occupy the frontier between the States of the Church and Naples, which shews how little confidence he had in his neighbour.* Paul II. was unsuccessful in his attempts to obtain possession of Tolfa ; subsequently, an amicable arrangement was arrived at, and in June, 1469, the Apostolic Treasury purchased the place for 17,300 golden ducats †

Ferrante was also the Pope's chief opponent in regard to the territory of Malatesta.

In the October of 1468, Sigismondo Malatesta, who had

---

* Jacobus Trottus in a *Letter, dated Rome, 1468, October 28, says : *"Il papa ha molto ben forniti de fanti quelli suoi luoghi de confine dove el dubitava del Re " (State Archives, Modena.) See CONTA-TORE, 239-40 Blanchus, in a Report of the 28th March, 1468, in LAMANSKY, 765, speaks of the labours of Bessarion in favour of the Venetians. Regarding the claims of Ferrante, see Chron. Eugub., 1016.

† PLATINA, 774, 791, AMMANATI, Comment , 368 seq., CANENSIUS, 83-8 ; THEINER, Cod 456-8. *Lib III, Bullet Pauli II., contains entries of payments for war material for the conquest of the castrum Tolphe as late as August, 1468 State Archives of Rome

not long returned from the Turkish war, died without
leaving any legitimate heir, and accordingly, in virtue of
the treaty which had been made, Paul II. justly claimed
Rimini Sigismondo's wife, Isotta, however, assumed the
government of the city.   Roberto Malatesta, who was at
the time in Rome, promised the Pope, by oath and in
writing, that he would deliver up Rimini to him.*   Upon
this he was at once commissioned to take possession of the
city on behalf of the Holy See.   But no sooner had he
succeeded, with the assistance of the inhabitants, and by
means of the subsidies granted by Paul II., in getting rid of
the Venetian garrison and making himself master of the
citadel, than he informed the Pope that he did not consider
himself bound by the promise he had given.   A secret
alliance with the King of Naples encouraged him to venture
on this step.   "The Pope, finding himself thus betrayed,
collected an army, and in a short time nearly all the Italian
States were involved in the war about Rimini"†

Such was the political situation of the Italian Peninsula
when Frederick III. determined to undertake a pilgrimage
to Rome, in fulfilment of a vow which he had made in 1462,
while a prisoner in the Castle of Vienna, and of which
he had repeatedly postponed the accomplishment ‡   The

* On the 16th June, 1469, the Pope communicated copies of this
promise to the King of Naples, the Duke of Milan, and the Florentines
*Transcripts of the letters, which are all of similar import, are in the
State Archives at Venice and Florence

† GREGOROVIUS, VII., 220 *seq.*, 3rd ed. , SUGENHEIM, 342 ; LILIUS,
Hist di Camerino, II., 215 ; UGOLINI, I , 485 *seq.* ; TONINI, V , 325
seq , YRIARTE, 341 *seq.*

‡ Regarding the postponement of the journey, see LICHNOWSKY,
VII , 113, and also TRINCHERA, I , 106, where is given a letter of the
8th April, 1467, from the King of Naples ; but even on the 16th
February, 1467, J. P. Arrivabene wrote *"La venuta del imperatore
da octo di in qua se fa piu dubia che prima " Gonzaga Archives.

Emperor's suite was not a large one, it consisted of fourteen Princes and Counts, and a number of knights, and
amounted altogether to 700 horsemen   All were in mourning garb on account of the death of the Empress.*

Frederick travelled by the same route as that which he
had followed sixteen years before, it led through Treviso
to Padua, where the Venetian Ambassadors met him and
paid their respects, then by Rovigo to Ferrara †   At Fran-
colino on the Po, Borso d'Este welcomed his noble visitor ‡
From Ferrara the pilgrims continued their journey by
Ravenna along the coast to the Sanctuary of Loreto §
The gates of Rimini were closed by Robert Malatesta, who
distrusted the Emperor   This obliged him to alter his
route, but the swampy character of the ground compelled
him again to approach the city.   The inhabitants at once
armed themselves and hastened to the walls, where they
remained until the travellers were out of sight ‖   He
met with even greater rudeness from the Ambassadors
of Duke Galeazzo Maria Sforza, who, when informed by
Frederick that he looked upon Milan as belonging to
the Empire, had, we are told, the audacity to reply,
that Galeazzo's father had won the Duchy by the sword,

* Gesch W. von Schaumburg, 7, and GRAZIANI, 641. *LANDO
FERRETTI, Storia d'Ancona (original Manuscript in Cod. H, III., 70,
of the Chigi Library, Rome), f 304, mentions " sei cento cavalli ben
guarniti et molto all' ordine "   The Diario Ferrar, 215, and CANENSIUS,
88, speak of only 500 as accompanying the Emperor.

† See in Appendix, N. 25, Tommaso Soderini's *Letter of the 29th
Nov, 1468   State Archives, Florence

‡ For an account of the honour paid to the Emperor in Ferrara, see
Diario Ferrar, loc cit., Cronica di Bologna, 776, Annal Bonon
897.

§ On the 18th December, Frederick III. was at Ancona. See
CIAVARINI, I., 186 (see PERUZZI, 373), and *L FERRETTI, loc. cit.

‖ TONINI, V., 329, where for 1464 read 1468

and that his son would not lose it save by the sword.*

Paul II looked forward with some apprehension to the Emperor's arrival   He took precautions against possible disturbances in Rome by bringing large bodies of troops into the city.† Special Briefs were sent to all the officials of the States of the Church, desiring them to receive Frederick III. with honour, and to entertain him at the expense of the Holy See ‡   The Governor of the March of Ancona, by order of the Pope, accompanied the Emperor to Rome,§ and a number of members of the Papal Court were appointed to meet him || On Christmas Eve Frederick approached the walls of Rome. He had proceeded by water from Otricoli to Castell Valcha, where Cardinals d'Estouteville and Piccolomini met him with a numerous escort.¶

He was met at Ponte Molle by the Vice-Camerlengo, the City Prefect, the Conservators, and the rest of the municipal authorities, with the Roman nobles, by command of the Pope   The Sacred College had a long time to wait at the Porta del Popolo   The late hour at which Frederick arrived made it difficult to carry out the order of the procession, every detail of which had been arranged by Paul II.**

* Chronic Eugub , 1017

† Chronic Eugub., 1016 ; PLATINI, 785, and *Report of J P Arrivabene of Dec 26, 1468, Gonzaga Archives, Mantua ; see Appendix, N. 26

‡ *Brief to "Joh Bapt. de Sabellis notario nostro civit. nostre Bononien gubernatori," dated Romae, ap. S Petrum, 1468, Dec 6 (State Archives, Bologna.) Bolle e brevi, Q 22   See also CANENSIUS, 89

§ *L FERRETTI, loc. cit., f 305. Chigi Library, Rome.

|| See Paul II's Brief to the Emperor, in MULLER, II., 320.

¶ *Report of J. P. Arrivabene ; see Appendix, N 26

** PATRITIUS, 207.

At this gate of the city, Bessarion made a speech, and he and Cardinal d'Estouteville then took their places, one on each side of the Emperor   They then proceeded first to S Marco, all the streets through which they passed being richly decorated. The Emperor clad in black, rode with the Cardinals under a baldacchino of white silk damask, embroidered with gold, and bearing the Papal and Imperial arms   One of Frederick's suite estimated the number of torches in the procession at 3000 *

The Imperial pilgrim was met in front of St. Peter's by the clergy of the city bearing a cross and relics   At the fifth hour of the night he entered the venerable Basilica, and, going at once to the tomb of the Prince of the Apostles, knelt " for a long time in prayer' The Pope, who was very exact in matters of the kind, had most minutely arranged the ceremonial to be observed at the meeting of the two chief powers of Christendom. This appeared to their contemporaries so significant as a token of the relations then existing between them, that Augustinus Patritius, the Papal Master of Ceremonies, carefully transcribed the whole in a special note-book.†

"As soon," Patritius says, "as the Emperor beheld the

* Gesch W von Schaumburg, 8   See AMMANATI, Comment, Lib 7, Storia Napolit, 235 , INFESSURA, 1141 , and the *Report of J P Arrivabene in Appendix, N 26   (Gonzaga Archives) Payments ad explanandum et mundandum stratam de Ponte Mollo ad portam populi et . .   palatium s Marci are noted in *Lib III., Bullet Pauli II   State . Archives, Rome.

† First made use of by RAYNALDUS, ad an. 1469, N 1, from Cod F., N. 73, of the Vallic Library, and afterwards published from the same MS by MABILLON, II , 256-72 , PEZ, II , 609-622 , and MURATORI, XXIII , 205 seq   I cite from this last   Patritius' account is also in Cod Vat , 8090   There is nothing of interest to us in the Notula hist de Frid. III. Imp. Romam, 1469, visitante in Cod 4455, f 366, of the Court Library, Vienna

Pope upon his throne, he bent the knee before him, and repeated this act several times during his approach. When he had got up to the Pope, he did homage to the Vicar of Christ by kissing his feet. Paul II. bent his eyes upon Frederick with an expression of great benevolence, put his arms round him, and permitted him to kiss both his knees, then he rose a little and embraced him warmly. He pointed out to him the place he was to take on his right hand above the Cardinals. The Emperor's seat, which had a back, was covered with green cloth, embroidered with gold; the Papal throne was so placed that the Emperor's seat was at the same height as the feet of the Pope." After the conclusion of the ceremonies in St. Peter's, which were accompanied with chanted psalms, "the Emperor departed to a noble palace, hung with cloth of gold and precious tapestry, wherein he was to have his abode, and every one of his people, according to his rank and dignity, was conducted to a well-appointed chamber therein."*

The Christmas festival was celebrated with great splendour "When it came to the holy Gospel," says Wilwolt von Schaumburg, "the Emperor put on a dalmatic The Pope gave him, as was fitting, a costly hat, they say that it must have been worth 8000 ducats And when the Emperor was to begin singing the Gospel, one of the highest of his servants, who was appointed for the purpose, took the hat from his head, and put the naked sword, which was commonly carried before him, into his hand. The Emperor held it solemnly aloft, and ever and anon, while he sang the Gospel, he brandished the sword lustily."

After the Offertory, the Emperor was incensed next

* Gesch. W von Schaumburg, 8   The Emperor lived in the part of the Palace which he had occupied in 1452. PATRITIUS, 209

after the Pope, Paul II., having given him Holy Communion with his own hand, bestowed on him the kiss of peace. The Pope administered the Blessed Sacrament to the Emperor, Deacon and Sub-Deacon, under the species of Bread only, although it was usual to give the Chalice in such cases to all who communicated with him. On this occasion the practice was discontinued on account of the erroneous teaching of the Hussites.[*]

After the conclusion of Mass, the Pope and the Emperor venerated the veil of St. Veronica. Then Paul II. solemnly imparted his Blessing, and an Indulgence was proclaimed. After the customary form, the words, "and for our Emperor Frederick, that the Lord God may grant him victory over the heretical Bohemians, the Turks, and the other enemies of the Christian name," were added.

Throughout these solemnities, and during the days which followed them, Frederick III. behaved towards the Pope with the utmost respect and deference. When Paul II. returned his visit, he accompanied him back to his chamber, and, on New Year's Eve, when they quitted the Lateran together, Frederick sprung forward to hold the Pope's stirrup. The Pope, however, declared that he would not allow this, and refused to mount until the Emperor had dispensed him from receiving, and himself from rendering, this service "The Pope's affability," Patritius observes, "was thought all the more of, because the credit of the Papacy is no less than in former times, and its power is far more considerable, for God has so disposed things, that the Roman Church, through the sagacity of her Pontiffs, and especially of the present Pope, has so increased in power and wealth, that she can hold her own by the side

* PATRITIUS, 212   See AMMANATI, *loc. cit.*   Heimburg's Apology in PALACKY, Urkundl Beitrage, 657, shews that the Pope's precaution was not uncalled for

of kingdoms of the first rank. The Roman Empire, on the other hand, has fallen into such deep decay, that nothing but the name is left to its chief Under these altered circumstances, the smallest mark of honour comes to be very highly regarded" In the sequel he lays much stress on the Pope's courtesy towards the Emperor, and says that he treated him in all points as an equal.*

The ceremony at which, in presence of the Pope, the Emperor conferred knighthood on 125 Germans in the middle of the bridge over the Tiber, provided an imposing pageant for the Romans. On this occasion Frederick III also declared Galeazzo Maria to have forfeited the Duchy of Milan, and granted investiture of this fief to his grandson.†

The first point to be discussed between Frederick III and the Pope was the war against the Turks and the Hussites A Public Consistory for this purpose was held but four days after Christmas The Emperor began by declaring, through his spokesman, that it was not merely his vow which had brought him to Rome, but also his concern for the general good, and that he desired to learn the views of the Holy Father in regard to the measures to be adopted against the Turks. Paul II caused all the efforts of the Holy See for this great object to be related, saying that his resources were now exhausted, and it had become the duty of the Emperor to counsel and to act When Frederick explained that he had come to receive, and not to give, counsel, the Pope repeated what he had

* PATRITIUS, 215-6 See CANENSIUS, 89, and the *Report of J P Arrivabene of the 26th Dec, 1468, Gonzaga Archives, see Appendix, N. 26. Regarding the visit to the Lateran, see ROHAULT, 251 *seq*, 500, 502

† CANENSIUS, 90, Chron Eugub, 1017, PLATINA, 785 ; Gesch. W. von Schaumburg, 9, GREGOROVIUS, VII., 223, 3rd ed. See ADINOLFI, I., 16-17.

already said The Emperor then, with his Counsellors and all the Ambassadors who were present, withdrew into an adjoining hall to deliberate on the subject, and remained there for an hour. As the result of heir consultation, he proposed that a general assembly should be held at Constance, in the presence of the Emperor and the Pope. Afterwards, Ammanati informs us, most of those who were accustomed to weigh matters at that period doubted whether the proposal had originated from the Emperor, who might have been anxious to shew his zeal for the Faith, or from the politic Venetians The Pope and the Cardinals, however, were agreed that the existing state of affairs did not demand such a measure, which past experience had shewn to be dangerous It was at last settled that the Ambassadors of all the Christian Princes should be invited, in the name of the two heads of Christendom, to a Congress, to be held in Rome in September, and that the Venetians should be allowed to levy a tenth part from the clergy, the twentieth part from the Jews, and the thirtieth from the laity, in their dominions.*

It is equally hard to ascertain the exact nature of the claims which Frederick at this time made on the Pope, and the special purpose of the Imperial pilgrimage. According to Dlugoss,† he sought, but did not obtain, from the Holy See the confirmation of the succession in Hungary and Bohemia to himself and his son Maximilian. He would "seem also to have tried unsuccessfully to procure the transfer of the electoral vote belonging to the Crown of Bohemia to the house of Austria The

* AMMANATI, Comment , I , 7, and Frederick III's letter in BONELLI, III , 271. See GEBHARDT, 46 As to the negotiations now carried on regarding the Birxen affair, see SINNACHER, VI , 558

† DLUGOSSI Hist Pol , II , 439

Court of Rome looked upon King Matthias as its principal
champion in Christendom, and would consent to nothing
that would be distasteful to him. In reference to the
Crown of Bohemia, moreover, its views differed wholly
from those of the Emperor, as it desired the suppression
of this dignity."* The Emperor, on the other hand,
obtained the confirmation of the Order of St. George, as
also the commencement of the process of canonisation
of Margrave Leopold of the house of Babenberg, and the
erection of two Bishoprics, one at Vienna and one at
Wiener-Neustadt.† This last measure fulfilled a desire
which had been ardently cherished by Rudolf of Hapsburg.

On the 9th January, 1469, the Emperor left Rome,
enriched with many Indulgences, relics, precious stones,
and pearls ‡ The Pope had borne all the expenses of
his suite § Cardinals Capranica and Borgia escorted him

* PALACKY, IV, 2, 554, RAUCH, 34.

† GAMS, 321–2 ; POTTHAST, Bibl Suppl, 440 ; and WIEDEMANN,
Beitr z Gesch d Bisthums Wiener-Neustadt, in the Œsterr Viertel-
jahrschrift fur Kath Theol, 1864, III, 514 seq, all give the year 1468
as that of the foundation of the Bishopric. The Bull in Cod. 9309
of the Court Library, Vienna, which the last-named author cites,
is certainly dated Romae, anno 1468, Jan. 18, but the note "pontif
nostri anno quinto" shews the document to belong to the year 1469
The Bull for the erection of the Bishopric of Vienna, whose original
is in the Consistorial Archives of the Archbishop at Vienna, has
also "pont nostri a° quinto" (this Bull is printed in Bull V, 195 seq,
but wrongly placed in the year 1468). On account of the opposition
of the Bishop of Passau it was not solemnly published until 1480;
see details in the exhaustive Study of Prof KOPALLIK, in Wiener
Diocesanbl, 1887, N 2, and KEIBLINGER, I, 659.

‡ PATRITIUS,216, INFESSURA,1141, GRAZIANI,641 The Cion Rom,
34, gives a wrong date, 19th, which is repeated by LICHNOWSKY, 115.

§ According to GOTTLOB, Cam Ap, the festivities, the lodging,
and entertainment of Frederick's suite cost 6000 flor auri, the Pope
contributed 3690 florins from his private purse

as far as Viterbo   Here, as well as in Rome and throughout his return journey, Frederick III. conferred many
honours *

Soon after the Emperor's return, the war, which Roberto
Malatesta's treacherous usurpation of Rimini had rendered
inevitable, broke forth. The Pope and the Republic of
Venice, formerly rival claimants for the possession of the
city, now united against Roberto, who had deceived them
both. On the 28th May, 1469, an alliance was concluded,
by which Venice undertook to assist the Pope energetically,
both by land and sea †   Paul II. made haste to collect
troops, and took Napoleone Orsini and Alessandro Sforza
into his service ‡   Lorenzo Zane, Archbishop of Spalatro,
was appointed Legate for the Papal army.   The war began
in the month of June, and it seemed as if the crafty
Malatesta was doomed to destruction.§

Things, however, took a different turn.   Roberto's escape
was principally due to " Federigo of Montefeltre, an ancient

* N DELLA TUCCIA, 94. For an account of Frederick's homeward
journey, see SANSI, Storia, 64-5 ; PELLINI, 69 *seq.*, BONAZZI, 684 ,
CRISTOFANI, 327; CINELLI, L'Imperiale castello presso Pesaro,
1881 ; Jahrb der Preuss Kunstf, IX, 166, BURCKHARDT, I,
18 *seq*, 3rd ed , MURATORI, Ann ad an   Regarding his sojourn
in Venice, see SANUDO, 1188 , MALIPIERO, 237; Gesch W. von
Schaumburg, 10 *seq* ; MITTARELLI, 1015, and TODERINI, 13 *seq*.

+ DUMONT, III , 1, 405; RAYNALDUS, ad an 1469, N. 24;
ROMANIN, IV , 333, N 2

‡ A *Letter of Napoleone Orsini (S R E armorum generalis
capitaneus) to Piero de' Medici, d d ex felicibus castris S D N
apud flumen Toppini prope Fulgin. die II. Aug , 1469, is in the
State Archives, Florence, Av il princ , f 17, f 736

§ J. P Arrivabene wrote from Rome to Mantua on the 20th June,
1469 *"La impresa de Arimino per quanto se comprende dara
occasion de rumpere in tuto la guerra, perche se sente pur chel Re
fa adunare le gente suoe al Tronto" Gonzaga Archives, Mantua.

enemy of his house, who unexpectedly became his friend
and helper" Federigo, "the most powerful feudal lord in
the States of the Church," looked upon "the Pope's zealous
and successful efforts to diminish the number of feudal
potentates in his territory" as a danger to himself.* For
the same reason, not only the King of Naples, who was
almost always more or less at variance with the Pope,† but
also Milan and Florence, declared against him.‡ All these
powers were agreed that "any increase of the authority of
the Popes in their temporal principality," at the expense of
its feudal nobility, was to be strenuously resisted. "The
element of weakness, caused by the partition of the States
of the Church among a number of feudal nobles," must be
retained §

The support of these allies emboldened Roberto Malatesta
to command his General, Federigo of Montefeltre, to assume
the offensive. On the 30th August, just when Rome was
celebrating the sixth anniversary of Paul II 's elevation to

* SUGENHEIM, 345

† Jacobus Trottus, writing on the 15th April, 1469, says that the
Pope was disposed for war, and only contemplated the ruin of the
King Another Ambassador from Este, Agostino de Bon, wrote on the
14th April, 1469. *"Questo papa me pare ogni dì ingrossa le sue
gente Lo cardinale de Napoli, che fu mio compagno in studio, me
ha ditto, che lo Re de Napoli ha mandato a dire al papa che el volle
intendere che homo el debba esser o de dio o del diavolo, queste sono
le parole formale e par voria fare certi capituli cum el papa, non sa
ancora se se poterano acordare, ma pure me pare che lo Re ogni otto
dì ge da una spelazata" State Archives, Modena

‡ On the 16th June, 1469, Paul II. wrote to Florence *"Hortamur
in domino et summopere rogamus devotionem vestram ut tametsi
Robertus ipse ad vestra stipendia conductus existit, nihilominus in hac
re nihil ipsum iuvetis aut presidis prosequamini contra nos et S R E"
State Archives, Florence, 11, X, dist. II, 25, f. 10–11.

§ SUGENHEIM, 344; UGOLINI, I, 487, 496, REUMONT, Diplomazia,
372 seq

the Chair of St. Peter,* he attacked the Papal army, and
completely routed it.   Three thousand prisoners, a number
of guns and other booty from the enemy's camp, were
seized by the victors.   Amongst the spoils was all the
Legate's silver plate †

The consequences of this victory might have been
serious, but Federigo of Montefeltre shrank from attacking
the actual territory of the Holy See   He contented himself with subjugating thirty castles and the territories of
Rimini and Fano to the authority of Roberto Malatesta,
and then, in November, 1469, disbanded his troops ‡

The co-operation of Florence and Naples, which had
made this successful resistance on the part of his rebellious
vassal possible, deeply incensed the Pope.   Before the
assembled Consistory he broke forth into bitter complaints
of the Medici and of Ferrante.   " The King," he said to
the Milanese Ambassador, " immediately after my elevation,
demanded the surrender of Ascoli and other things so
preposterous that I can never be his friend.   He is so

* J Trottus' account in a **Letter of the 30th August, 1469   State
Archives, Modena.

† See AMMANATI, Comment , I., 5, f. 375 *seq* , Epist , 174 *seq*., 176 *seq*
Vespas da Bisticci in MAI, I , 107–108 , TONINI, V , 336 *seq* , SUGEN-
HEIM, 344 , REUMONT, III , 1, 157 , and ROHRBACHER-KNOPFLER,
236, follow Muratori in naming the 23rd August as the day of the
battle.   The date given above is that in the Annal Forliv , 228, and in
the document in REUMONT, Diplomazia, 373   The Cronica di Bologna,
777, has the 29th , CANENSIUS, 92, and NOTAR GIACOMO, 116–17, mention the 31st August   On the 5th Sept , 1469, *J. Trottus declares that
the Pope had received a letter concerning the defeat. (State Archives,
Modena)   *Angelus Azaiolus informs Pietro Dietisalvi, ex Ferrara,
2nd Sept , 1469, that the army of the Church had been defeated, " e
forsi piu grossamente che non si dice qui "   State Archives, Florence,
Strozz , 365, f 88

‡ Cronica di Bologna, 777.

crafty and malignant that no one can trust him.   Moreover, he is no son of King Alfonso's, Pope Calixtus told me the names of his real parents."*

The confederates were in no way intimidated either by Paul II.'s complaints or by the warlike preparations which he carried on with much energy † On the contrary, in July, 1470, Naples, Milan, and Florence renewed their alliance, and determined, with their united forces, to protect Malatesta against the Pope, not only in the possession of Rimini, but also "in that of all the conquests which he had since made in the States of the Church or might yet make, unless within two months the Pope should agree, on his restoration of these spoils, to be reconciled to him and to invest him with the remainder of his family dominions."‡

Hard as it was for Paul II., he was compelled to yield, for he knew that his Venetian countrymen and allies were

---

* I find this statement, which has not hitherto been made public, in a *Letter from Nicodemus de Pontremoli, dated Rome, 1469, Oct. 31 Speaking of Paul II, he says · *"Poi disse de le stranie cose havia volute da lui fui ad havergli facto domandare Ascoli quamprimum fo assumpto al pontificato et altre domande adeo enorme che mai gli poria esser amico, ne persona se posseva fidare de lui, tanto è ficto e de mala natura, fin a dirmi non è figliolo del Re Alphonso et como papa Calisto gli havia dicto el patre et la matre, quali ha dicti ad me " State Archives, Milan, Pot Est

† In a *Despatch, dated Rome, 1469, Sept. 14, J P Arrivabene says *"Qui non se attende ad altro se non a le provision de remetter queste gente eccles " (Gonzaga Archives, Mantua.)   The preparations were considered very onerous   "All the Cardinals," wrote *Angelo Acciaioli from Rome on the 12th Dec., 1469, "wish for peace, but with honour to the Pope and the maintenance of the States of the Church " On the 20th Dec, 1469, he wrote · *"La S. de N. S non può lasciare Arimino sanza gran vergogna e carico suo e damno della chiesa" Both these *Despatches are in the State Archives, Modena.

‡ DUMONT, III , 1, 354 seq., 408 , MORBIO, VI , 377, 393 seq. ; SUGENHEIM, 345

playing a very double game, " more intent on the extension
of their own power in the Romagna than on the support of
the Papal government."* A yet more decisive influence was
exercised by an event which now filled Christendom in
general and Italy in particular with fear : Negropont was
taken by the Turks.†

* REUMONT, III , 1. 157-8 , BALAN, V , 198 Regarding the delay
of the Venetian subsidies, see the *Letter of J. Trottus of the 30th
Aug , 1469 State Archives, Modena

† Malatesta was not actually put in possession of the fief of Rimini
and its territory until after the death of Paul II , see TONINI, V . 347
seq ; BALDI, III., 208.

CHAPTER VII.

The Fall of Negropont, and the Negotiations in Italy and
Germany regarding the Turkish Question.—The Dignity
of Duke of Ferrara Conferred upon Borso d'Este.—
Sudden Death of the Pope.

Ever since the naval fortunes of Venice had under the
command of Niccolò Canale (1468), taken a more favourable
turn, Sultan Mahomet, with the energy which was his
characteristic, had laboured to increase and improve his
fleet Many new ships of war were built, and numerous
Jews and Greeks, then deemed the best seamen, were
engaged to man them In the spring of 1470, he thought
that the favourable moment had arrived for avenging his
former defeat and dealing a crushing blow to the Venetian
power. Mahomet himself set out for Greece at the head of
an army more than 100,000 strong, while Mahmoud Pasha,
with a fleet of about 400 vessels, 100 of which were men-of-war,
put to sea. In the latter half of June the tidings that this
great expedition was on the way reached Venice, and from
thence passed on to Rome.* It was not yet known for
certain that Euboea, "the pearl of the Italian dominions in

---

* **Letter of Cardinal Gonzaga to his father, dated Rome, 1470,
June 30 (Gonzaga Archives, Mantua), here, as well as in Malipiero,
51, the number of Turkish vessels is given at 400 , other authorities
mention 300 , see Cronica di Bologna, 779 , *Letter of A Hyvanus of
the 19th Aug , 1470, Cod 3477, f. 3b, of the Court Library, Vienna
See also Magistretti, 341.

Greece," was its goal, but the greatness of the peril was manifest. A Consistory was at once summoned in an unusual manner by the Pope ; Cardinal Gonzaga informs us that he was prepared, for the sake of restoring peace in Italy, to renounce his claim to Rimini and the other places taken from him in the war, and that a Congregation of Cardinals was appointed to take counsel regarding further measures * In view of the confusion prevailing in the whole of Europe, and more particularly in Italy, and the failure of all former attempts † at combination against the ancestral enemy of Christian civilisation, the task was somewhat hopeless.   Yet Paul II. at once issued an urgent general appeal for help.   King Ferrante of Naples, who, next to Venice, seemed the most immediately threatened, declared his readiness not only to join a general alliance of all the Christian powers, but also to enter into a special agreement with Venice and Rome   As the bitter enmity which existed between Venice and Milan left little prospect of a general alliance among the Princes of Christendom, Paul II., forgetting the injuries which he had received from

* This Consistory, which has hitherto remained unknown, is mentioned by Cardinal Gonzaga in the **Letter cited in note on previous p

† The accounts of the Congress held in Rome, in the autumn of 1469, to deliberate on the measures to be taken against the Turks and Hussites, are very scanty. Frederick III sent Hinderbach on this occasion as his representative (BONELLI, III , 270–71). The passage of many Envoys is mentioned by N DELLA TUCCIA, 97   It appears from a *Letter of the City of Cologne to Dr "Wolter van Bilssen," dated 1469, June 22 (Cologne City Archives, Letter-book 29, f 33b), that even the German cities were called upon by Frederick III to send Envoys Nicodemus de Pontremoli, the representative of Milan, who was himself devoid of zeal for the Turkish war (see BUSER, Beziehungen, 153), in a *Letter dated Rome, 1469, Nov 20, admits that the Pope had the cause much at heart (ha molto al core) State Archives, Milan.

the Neapolitan monarch, accepted his second proposal
He gave orders that eight of the Cardinals, postponing all
other business, should assemble once in every four days to
take counsel regarding the measures to be adopted.   Their
first meeting was held on the 8th August, at which time no
answer had yet been received from either Milan or Florence
to the Papal Briefs despatched to them at the same date
as that to Naples   From the outset it was evident to all
experienced persons that the negotiations were likely to be
extremely protracted *   On the 3rd of August a fresh Brief
had been addressed to Florence, and also to Milan, insisting
on the imminent danger with which the siege of Negropont
threatened Italy, and exhorting these powers to despatch
Envoys.†

Meanwhile, the growing power of Islam had again given
proofs of its strength , on the 12th July, after a desperate
resistance on the part of the besieged, Negropont, which
had been accounted impregnable, had fallen into the hands
of the Turks.‡   The terrible tidings caused the greatest
consternation throughout Italy, and nowhere was the
feeling more intense than in Venice   The Milanese
Ambassador to that city, in a despatch of the 7th August,
said that he had seen the proud nobles weep as if their
own wives and children had been slain.   " All Venice,"

* **Report of Jacobus Trottus to Borso of Este, dated Rome, 1470,
Aug 8   State Archives, Modena

† MULLER, Doc , 211–12 ; where is also to be found the answer of
the 8th of August expressed in terms of general goodwill.

‡ ZINKEISEN, II , 322 seq.; VAST, 379 seq., ROMANIN, IV., 337
seq , Rivista Maritt, 1886, Luglio-Agosto, and Arch   Veneto,
XXXII, P. II, p 267   The Brief concerning Niccolo de Canale,
given in part and without date by RAYNALDUS, ad an. 1470, N 17,
is in *Lib brev. of the Secret Archives of the Vatican, 12, f. 61, dated
24th Dec , 1470. See Bibliofilo, VII., 40

he added, some days later, "is struck with dismay ; the inhabitants, half-dead with fear, say that the loss of all their possessions on the mainland would have been a less disaster "* " The glory and credit of Venice are destroyed," wrote the chronicler Malipiero, " our pride is humbled "†

The conquest of Euboea by the Turks was in fact an event of such importance that the latest historian of Greece considers it as the close of an epoch. All the Greeks, with the exception of a small fraction, were now in the clutch of the Sultan. Venice "was driven back into Crete and a few small islands and fortresses on the outer rim of Greece."‡

The alarm of the Venetians was increased by the strained relations which existed between them and the Pope, the Emperor and the King of Hungary, as well as by the openly hostile attitude of Duke Galeazzo Maria Sforza, who was the centre of a party which sought to take advantage of the misfortunes of the Republic, and recover the territory surrendered in 1454 In Bergamo, Crema, and Brescia an immediate invasion of Milanese troops was apprehended , guards were doubled, and the work of strengthening the defences was carried on day and night.§ Happily, the King of Naples declared to the representative of Milan that, in presence of the actual danger from Turkey, he would take no part in any attack upon Venice || The attitude of the King of

* See the Despatch from the Milanese State Archives in MAGIS-TRETTI, 347, see 101

† MALIPIERO, 59 The terror was great in Naples and Sicily, where all the harbours were placed in a state of defence ; see BLASI, Storia di Sicilia, II , 648.

‡ HERTZBERG, II , 603 , see III , 3 seq.

§ MAGISTRETTI 81, 89, 92-4, 101, 106

|| Ibid., 114, 116.

Hungary, on the other hand, was by no means reassuring.
Paul II., however, with a true sense of his high position,
laid aside all resentment against Venice, and laboured
earnestly for the restoration of peace and the conclusion
of an alliance against the Turks * On the 25th August
he informed all the Christian powers of the fall of Negropont, drew a vivid picture of the danger which lowered
from the East, and urgently implored assistance. prompt
action on their part, he said, would give him the greatest
consolation.† The Pope earnestly entreated the Duke
of Milan, who had attacked the Lords of Correggio, to
lay down his arms, and urgently admonished the Venetians
to desist from the works they had begun on the Mincio,
which were a menace to the Marquess of Mantua, and
were calculated to excite fresh troubles ‡ Paul II
himself set a good example, by determining to waive
his rights regarding Rimini, and to refrain from punishing
the Neapolitan King. On the 18th of September an
invitation was addressed to all the Italian powers, calling
upon them to send Ambassadors as soon as possible to
Rome, in order to consult on measures for the general
defence and the preservation of their own liberties §

* See Paul II's *Brief to Florence of the 23rd Aug., 1470. State
Archives, Florence, X -II.-25, f 25-6

† **Brief to Frankfort-on-Maine, dat Romae, 1470, Octavo Cal.
Sept, in the Archives of that City. A similar Letter to Joh. de
Sabaudia comes Gebennensis is in the State Archives, Turin, and
the one to Cologne in the City Archives, Or Pgm, arrived with
the appended Bull, according to the entry in the Chancery,
Nov 23, 1470 I found in the R T A, I (Sect V.), f 135, of the
Kreisarchiv, Bamberg, a German translation of the Brief, also
addressed to Margrave Albrecht of Brandenburg on the 25th August,
1470.

‡ RAYNALDUS, ad an. 1470, N 39-40.

§ Ibid, ad an 1470, N 41 The reports prevalent at this time

The Pope had no more zealous supporter in his labours than Cardinal Bessarion, who addressed several long circular letters to the Italian Princes and people, vividly representing the magnitude of the common peril and the necessity for unanimous action against their cruel foe * With the impression of his soul-stirring words fresh on their minds, the Italian Envoys commenced their deliberations in Rome There were apprehensions to be removed and disputes to be settled, but at length the efforts of Paul II. were crowned with success † On the 22nd December, 1470, a general defensive alliance of the Italian States against the Turks was concluded, on the basis of the League of Lodi, Roberto Malatesta being included among its members ‡ Public thanksgivings were offered and bonfires kindled throughout the States of the Church by desire of Paul II.§

concerning a defeat of the Turkish fleet were not confirmed, see the *Letter of Jacobus Azzarolus to Pietro Dietisalvi, dated Rome, 1470, Sept 20 "Le novelle vostre della ropta della armata del Turcho non graniscono" C STROZZ, 365, f 106 State Archives, Florence

* VAST, 385 seq. On the 13th Dec, 1470, Bessarion sent them to Guillaume Fichat, Prof in Paris See the *Cardinal's Letter of that date in Cod. Vat, 3586, Vatican Library

† See RAYNALDUS, ad an 1470, N. 38; and WURDTWEIN, Nov Subs, XIII, pp 68-70. Paul II also speaks of his labours to promote a league of Italians in the *Brief of the 20th Dec., 1470, to the Duke of Modena, and explains that the representative of Modena, Jacobus Trottus, had been unjustly calumniated. Lib brev, 12, f 58, Secret Archives of the Vatican

‡ LEIBNIZ, Cod 429-30; DU MONT, III, 2, 29-30, RAYNALDUS, ad an 1470, N 42 See TRINCHERA, I, LX

§ RAYNALDUS, ad an 1470, N 43 In the State Archives at Bologna I saw the original of the Brief published by Raynaldus from Lib brev, and also by LUNIG, Cod Dipl Ital, IV, 184-5 It bears the address. Joh Bapt de Sabellis, gub Bononiae (The Cr. di Bologna, 783, speaks of the joy which it awakened) Similar

"But this time again the hopes of the Pope were far from being realised. Sforza did not ratify the treaty, ostensibly because his wishes were disregarded in some unimportant points in the draft of the document, but in reality because he disliked committing himself to a war against the Turks Although the Florentine Signoria sent their ratification, Guicciardini put it aside, because Lorenzo, who desired to hold with Milan, and, like his grandfather, not to break with the Sultan, had secretly instructed him not to sign "*

In France and Germany the prospect was not any brighter The Pope sent special envoys to both countries † Cardinal Francesco Piccolomini, the Legate for Germany, left Rome on the 18th March, 1471,‡ to proceed in the first instance to Ratisbon, where a Diet was to open at the end of April

Piccolomini was chosen for this mission, first, on account of his "distinguished personal qualities," and secondly, because he could speak German,§ and was "a nephew of Pius II., whose memory was still warmly cherished at the Imperial Court."||

---

*Documents were sent to gubernat Marchie, rect. Campanie, gub Fani, Cesenae, Sore, &c (Information kindly furnished by Dr Fraknói, Vice-President of the Hungarian Academy.)

* REUMONT, Lorenzo, I , 222, 2nd ed.

† CANENSIUS, 95

‡ *Acta Consist, f 42, Secret Archives of the Vatican. Piccolomini's nomination as Legate in Alemaniam had taken place on the 18th February, *loc cit.*

§ See A Patritius in FREHER, II , 145. In a letter of 1485, the Cardinal again alludes to his knowledge of the German language , see JANNER, III., 543 It was, at this time, the custom of the Roman Court, when possible, to send representatives acquainted with the language of the countries to which they were accredited , the contemporary French Nuncio understood French , see AMMANATI, Comment , I VII.

|| REISSERMAYER, I., 28-9 ; see II , 15

He entered Ratisbon on the 1st May, where all his energies had first to be applied to the allaying of the ill-feeling occasioned by the prolonged delay of the Emperor. His position was by no means an easy one : " he desired and was even bound to defend the Emperor, and yet he could not altogether deny the justice of the complaints made by the impatient Assembly."* At last, on the 16th June, Frederick III. arrived, and "the great Christian Diet" began on the 24th During the deliberations which ensued, the zeal displayed by Cardinal Piccolomini fully justified the repeated commendations of the Pope.† But neither his acknowledged eloquence, nor the urgent entreaties of the unhappy victims of the Turkish invasion from Croatia, Carniola, and Styria, sufficed to remove the manifold obstacles in the way of unanimous and energetic action. "The question of aid against the Turks proceeds so slowly," wrote an Italian Ambassador on the 7th July, "that the Cardinal Legate is wearied to death, and looks for little result from this Diet, on which he had built such great hopes."‡ After fully four weeks of negotiations, no decisive resolution binding all the states of the Empire had been arrived at "All went well till it came to the determination of the amount to be contributed by each power, because, up to that point, general promises and offers sufficed , but when definite engagements were to be set down in black and white, difficulties of all kinds were raised, absurd pretexts invented, conditions imposed, and fresh proposals made to escape the obnoxious task." For a little while, to the delight of the Cardinal, things seemed again to take a more favourable turn ; but the issue of this

* REISSERMAYER, I , 54–5

† See in Appendix, N 37 and 39, the two *Briefs from the Secret Archives of the Vatican

‡ Report of A Bonattus in REISSERMAYER, II , 126

Diet, the largest within the memory of man, was no better than that of those which had preceded it. " Private interests on all sides outweighed the general interests of the Empire."* Only two among the Princes—Ernest, Elector of Saxony, and Albrecht of Brandenburg, who had made his peace with the Pope at Ratisbon†—sent troops to the threatened frontiers, none of the others stirred

" O the blindness of men !" exclaims Rodericus de Arevalo " The Catholic Princes see the blazing torch of the infidel at their very doors, ready to set fire to all the kingdoms of Christendom, while they are squabbling each one for his portion. With their own eyes they behold the destruction of the Faithful, while every heathen jeers at their struggles to conquer each other, without thinking of saving themselves "‡

Besides the threatened danger from Turkey, the year 1471 had brought many other troubles to Paul II At its very outset, disturbances had broken out in the Bolognese territory ;§ in Florence, as well as in Venice, there had

---

* REISSERMAYER, II , 73 *seq* , 113 *seq*   See SCHWEIZER, Vorgesch. des schwab Bundes, 55 *seq* (Zurich, 1876) , and GOTHEIN, Volksbewegungen, 3 *seq*. and 42.

† See in Appendix, N 41, the *Brief of 20th June, 1471.   Secret Archives of the Vatican.

‡ " O mortalium ingenia sinistris passionibus tenebrata   vident catholici principes commune omnium regnorum incendium ab infidelibus parari, dum ipsi inter se super regnis concertant.   Cernunt omnium fidelium naufragium, ipsi vero non de salute, sed ut ethnicus ille dicebat aut potius irridebat super gubernatione contendunt   Rodericus episc Calagurritan. ad rev patr. et dom d Rodericum Borja S. R E. diacon card et vicecanc. liber de origine et differentia principatus imperialis et regalis et de antiquitate et iusticia utriusque "   Cod Vat , 4881, f. 1, Vatican Library   This MS. is richly adorned with miniatures, and is no doubt the copy presented to the Cardinal.

§ See Paul II 's *Brief to Alex de Perusio episcopatus nostri Bonon. vicarius, dat Romae, 1471, Jan. 11.   State Archives, Bologna, Q 22.

been "troublesome discussions" about the contributions
for the Turkish war, and scarcely anywhere, either in
Italy or elsewhere, was any genuine zeal for the defence
of Christendom to be found * Tidings of a very anxious
nature had come from the Knights of St. John at Rhodes
It would appear that, for some time past, the Christians in
that island had completely lost heart. Paul II hastened
to encourage the Knights to stand firm, promised assistance,
and exhorted them to put the fortifications of the island
into a state of thorough repair † A serious attack
of the Turks might, under the actual circumstances of
the island, have been successful. Happily, no such
attempt was made, the attention of Mahomet being
at that time much engaged by the Turcoman Prince
Usunhassan

Of all the Italian Princes, no one was on more friendly
terms with Paul II. than Duke Borso of Modena ; there
was much intellectual sympathy between them, both were
warm patrons of Art, and had a taste for external splendour,
which the Duke, as well as the Pope, believed to have a
great effect on the popular mind ‡ Borso's most ardent
desire was to add the ducal title of Ferrara to that of
Modena , during the pontificate of Pius II he had vainly

* In the *Brief of the 20th Dec , 1470, to the Duke of Modena,
mentioned in *supra*, p 179, note †, Paul II dwells on the confidence with
which he had hoped for aid from the Italians   Secret Archives of the
Vatican

† See in Appendix, 30, 31, and 33, the *Briefs of 20th Jan and 12th
March, 1471   With regard to the General Chapter of the Knights
of St John, held in Rome, and the appointment by Paul II of
Giambattista Orsini as Grand-Master (1467), see BOSIO, 234 *seq* ,
243 *seq*

‡ See MUNTZ, Renaissance, 328   Regarding Borso's promotion of
Art, see Atti d Romagna, III., 388 *seq* , 3rd Series , and VENTURI in
the Rivist. St. Ital , II., 689-749.

laboured for the realisation of this wish.*   Under Paul II.
further negotiations were carried on, and, in the spring of
1471, they were brought to a successful conclusion †

Borso came to Rome to receive his new dignity.   On
the 13th March he left Ferrara with an almost royal train.
The Lords of Carpi, Correggio, Mirandola, and Scandiano
formed part of the company, and a host of nobles and
knights ; there were more than 700 horses and 250 mules, all
adorned with costly trappings, and some of them bearing the
arms of Este   Paul II. sent his friend, the Archbishop of
Spalatro, to welcome the Duke,‡ who, on his arrival in
Rome, was received by Cardinals Barbo and Gonzaga, all
the great Barons, the Ambassadors, the Senate, and all
the other city dignitaries   A contemporary informs us
that, in the opinion of the Romans, no such honours had
ever been accorded to any King or Emperor as were now
paid to Borso §   Festal music resounded through the
richly-decorated streets which he traversed on his way
to the Vatican   Shouts of " Paulo, Paulo ! Borso, Borso !"

* See a *Letter from Card Gonzaga to his father, dated Rome, 1463,
Feb 15   Gonzaga Archives, Mantua.

† Considering the good relations which existed between Paul II
and Borso, it is somewhat strange to find a *Brief addressed to him
on the 31st Dec , 1470, admonishing him to pay his tribute, inasmuch
as the Apostolic Treasury has to meet great expenses in the defence
of the Catholic Faith   Lib biev, 12, f 63b.   Secret Archives of the
Vatican

‡ See in Appendix N 32, the *Brief of 31d March, 1471, from the
State Archives, Modena

§ Atti d deput p le prov Moden , II , 307 (1864)   Besides the
description here given from the Archives of Modena, see the continuation of the Chron Estense in MURATORI, XV , 542 ; INFESSURA,
1142, and especially a very detailed *Report from the Jurist Franciscus
Ariostus to Ercole d'Este, dated Rome, 1471, April 3 (not 1, as
GREGOROVIUS, VII , 224, 3rd ed , has it)   Cod. J., VII , 261, Chigi
Library, Rome.

from the crowd mingled with the clang of the trumpets
The Pope received his visitor seated on a throne adorned
with gold and ivory, and the Palace of Cardinal Castiglione,
which adjoined the Vatican, was assigned to him as his
residence.* The rest of his followers were provided for,
at the expense of the Apostolic Treasury, in the numerous
inns which then existed in Rome.†

On Palm Sunday, after Mass, Paul II. assembled the
Cardinals and informed them of his intention regarding
Borso They all approved of the Pope's decision, and
the Duke was then called in. Paul II told him what
had passed, and Borso warmly expressed his gratitude.‡

* "*Questo e uno magno regale et eminente pallazo non molto
distante dal pontificale quale gia la recolenda memoria de monsignor
Constanciense haveassi fabricado cum spesa non vulgare e cum
admirabile inzegno." F. Ariostus in the *Report cited in note § on
preceding page I intend elsewhere to publish his description of the
street decorations, which is of value as bearing on the history of
Renaissance Art and culture.

† *Lib quintus Bullet. Pauli II, p. 205 *seq.*, gives the payments
pro infiascriptis personis hospitibus in alma urbe et pro expens fact d.
march Ferrarie—in all flor aur de cam septem millia noningentos
triginta octo, b XLIIII, d XII. This sum represents only a part of
the outlay, which, according to CANENSIUS, 96, amounted to 14,000
golden florins , in the same *Lib quintus other payments are entered,
e g, "pro luminaribus in dicto castio [S Angeli] pro adventu ill ducis
Mutine" 1st April, 1471 These records have a special interest from
the fact that they give the names of the Roman inns of the period
We have *Hospes ad solem, ad spatam, ad turrim, ad navim, ad stellam,
ad navim in campo florae, ad camellum, ad coronam, ad lunam, ad
scutum, ad angelum, ad S Catherinam, ad galeam* and *Hospitissa ad
dalphinum* and *ad S. Triffonem* (State Archives, Rome) Some of
these names are still kept up See the unhappily incomplete Notizie
storiche intorno alla origine dei nomi di alcune osterie, etc., di Roma,
by A Rufini, Roma, 1855

‡ *Letter of Cardinal Fr Gonzaga of 1st April, 1471 Gonzaga
Archives, Mantua

Easter Sunday (14th April) was the day fixed for Borso's solemn investiture with the title of Duke of Ferrara.* All the Cardinals, Bishops, and Prelates then in Rome, together with all the members of the Court, were assembled in the Basilica of the Prince of the Apostles, where Borso was in the first place made a Knight of St. Peter. The Pope himself handed him a naked sword, saying "Take this in the name of the Father, the Son, and the Holy Ghost, and use it for your own defence and that of God's Holy Church, and for the destruction of the enemies of the holy Cross and of the Faith" The High Mass then began, the music being rendered by the Papal Choir.† When the Epistle had been sung, Borso took the oath of allegiance to the Pope. After the Communion, he and his followers received the Sacred Host from the hands of Paul II., who then bestowed on Borso the

* For the following account, see, besides Borso's short letter of the 16th April, 1471, which was known to PIGNA, Hist d princ. d'Este, 617 (Ferrara, 1570), and is published in the Atti d st. patr. d. prov. Mod., II, 307–308, (a) Lettera inedita di Borso d'Este scritta in Roma il di 15 Aprile 1471, al suo segretario Giovanni di Compagno, printed in honour of a wedding, Ferrara, 1869; (b) a *Description (Latin and Italian) of all the festivities by the Ferrarese, Franciscus Ariostus, dated ex urbe Roma Cal. Man, 1471, and dedicated to Duke Ercole (regarding F Ariostus, see MAZZUCHELLI, I., 2, 1058), in Cod J, VII., 261 (not T VII, as CORVISIERI, in his otherwise correct description of the MS in Arch. Rom, I, 467, has it), Chigi Library, Rome My copy of this MS occupies 160 quarto pages, which may give an idea of the detailed character of the Report It is of special interest in connection with the history of civilisation, and I shall again revert to it

† "*Non altramente haresti sentido, magnanime signore divo Hercule, ussire di quel choro de più excellentissimi cantori un concerto de tante melodie nello intonar quello sancto introito ricevendo cum maravigliosi signi de letitia la S Sanctita." F. Ariostus, *loc. cit.*

Ducal robes and the other insignia of his new dignity.
The veneration of the Veil of St. Veronica, the Papal
Benediction, and the proclamation of a Plenary Indulgence
closed this imposing function, which was witnessed by
an immense multitude gathered from far and near * When
Borso sought to accompany the Pope back to his apartments, his Holiness desired the Cardinals to pay that
token of respect to the Duke, who was enchanted with
the distinctions heaped upon him He wrote to his
Secretary · "We have been treated as if we were a
King or an Emperor"

On the following day Borso accompanied the Pope to
St Peter's, and there received the Golden Rose. From
there he rode, carrying the Rose, to the Palace of S.
Marco, where a great banquet was prepared During the
ensuing days the same pomp and ceremony were displayed
in various other entertainments provided for the new Duke,
especially at a grand hunting-party, in which many of the
Cardinals took part.†

After all these festivities were over, the Duke still lingered
in Rome The extraordinary honours of which he was
the object, and his frequent interviews with the Pope, had,
from the time of his arrival, attracted general attention
Even the Cardinals were kept in the dark as to the subjects
of these conversations With a view of obtaining some
information, Cardinal Gonzaga told Borso of the pleasure
which it had given him to hear it said at the Court that
the Pope meant to accompany the Duke back to Ferrara ,
and further expressed his opinion, that, considering the
dispositions of Germany and the perpetual demands of

---

* The Diario Ferrar, 228, and F Ariostus give 200,000 as the
number of those present, but this is certainly an exaggerated estimate
† CANENSIUS, 96

France for a Council, such an Assembly might with advantage be held in that City Borso replied that the Cardinal's view was most reasonable, adding. "Would to God that every one thought the same." "These words," wrote the Cardinal to his father, "make me think that something of the sort may be in the wind." In a second conversation the Duke expressed his confident hope of bringing the Pope to Ferrara. Cardinal Battista Zeno, the Pope's nephew, at this time said that it would be wise to hold a Congress at some suitable place in Italy, for that by doing so in time, and of his own accord, the Pope would avoid the danger of having it forced upon him, when also some undesirable place would probably be selected.*

The learned Bishop of Calahorra, Rodericus Sancius de Arevalo, had some years previously, in a treatise dedicated to Cardinal Bessarion, declared against the holding of a Council, the demand for which had always been the war-cry of the opposition Nothing of the sort was required to deal with either the Turkish question or that of Reform Hard fighting, not a Congress, was the means by which the Infidels must be repelled. From the outset of his pontificate, Paul II. had done everything in his power to protect Christendom against them. The example of the Synod of Basle was not one to encourage another attempt of the kind. And as to the Congress of Mantua, it had

* These particulars, previously unknown, are taken from a *Letter of Cardinal Gonzaga, written on the 10th April, 1471, which I found in the Gonzaga Archives, Mantua, and have printed in Appendix, N 35 The first half of the *Considerationes de concilium generale congregandi utilitate et necessitate, belonging to the year 1471, in Cod 4 of the Kremsmunster Library, deals with the demand for a Council See thereon H SCHMID, Cat Cod manuscript, Bibl Cremf, I, 66 From ROMANIN, IV., 353, where, unfortunately, the exact quotation is wanting, it appears that Venice also at this time asked for a Congress or Council

been utterly fruitless, and even prejudicial, for it had made the disunion of Christendom patent to the Turks *

Another project to which Paul II had turned his mind seemed far more likely to prove beneficial than the meeting of a Congress. This was an alliance with the enemies of the Sultan in the East, and especially with the Turcoman Prince, Usunhassan, who was now at the summit of his power † Following the example of the Venetians and of his predecessors, Calixtus III. and Pius II., Paul II leagued himself with this Prince, the only one among the Oriental rulers who could venture to measure swords with Mahomet. Usunhassan indeed made such solemn promises of co-operation against the common foe,‡ that powerful aid from the East seemed a certainty. At this crisis Paul II. suddenly died.

The Pope, whose constitution was naturally strong, had appeared to be in excellent health. At the beginning of his reign he had suffered from the dangerous Roman fever ; § in 1466, and again in 1468, he had been ill, but had quite recovered ;|| at this moment there seemed no cause for apprehension.

* *Roderici Calaguritani, De remediis afflictae ecclesiae, Cod Z.-L.-XC, f 11 and 27b, St Mark's Library, Venice. Regarding other manuscript copies of this work, see our Vol II, p 55, note *. In the year 1466 Rodericus Sancius dedicated to Pope Paul II his *Defensorium ecclesie et status ecclesiastici contra querulos, detractores et emulos sublimitatis, auctoritatis et honoris Romani pontificis nec non praelatorum et ceterorum ministrorum ecclesie Cod Vat, 4106 Vatican Library

† MULLER, Islam, 325 *seq*, 340, HLYD, II, 326

‡ RAYNALDUS, ad an 1471, N 48

§ *Despatch of Laurentius de Pensauro to Fr Sforza of 27th Oct, 1464 (State Archives, Milan) See also *Card Gonzaga's Letter of 8th Oct, 1464 Gonzaga Archives

|| See CANENSIUS, 101, and the *Letter of Barth de Maraschis of 1st Sept, 1466, in the Gonzaga Archives, Mantua, see Appendix, N. 17

On the morning of the 26th July the Pope was perfectly
well, and had held a Consistory lasting for six hours, he
then dined bare-headed in the garden* and freely indulged
his taste for melons and other indigestible food.   At the
first hour of the night he felt ill, and his chamberlain
advised him to postpone the audiences usually granted at
that time, and to rest for a while.   Paul II. was suffering
from a sense of oppression and lay down on a bed, while
the chamberlain left the room to dismiss those who were
waiting without   After an hour had passed, he heard a
knocking on the door of the bed-chamber, hurried in, and
found the Pope half-insensible and foaming at the mouth
With difficulty he lifted the sick man on to a bench and
rushed out to summon assistance.   By the time he returned
the Pope had expired, having died of a stroke.   Cardinal
Barbo was at once called, and the corpse, accompanied by
a few torches, was borne to St Peter's †   Here the obsequies

In reference to the illness of 1468, Giacomo Trotti, in a *Despatch,
dated Rome, 1468, May 21, says   *"N S hora non da audientia ni a
cardinali ni a persona del mondo   Il se ha sentito malo e se medecina."
According to a *Despatch of 15th June, the indisposition of the Pope
continued up to that time   no audiences were granted   The Plague
was then raging in Rome, see in Appendix, N 24, the *Letter of G
Trotti of 8th July, 1468   All these letters are in the State Archives,
Modena

  * CANENSIUS, 103

  † See in the Appendix, N. 42, Nicodemus of Pontremoli's Report,
which I found in the State Archives at Milan   One of the last cares
of Paul II regarded the health of the Duke of Ferrara, see in
Appendix, N 38 and 40, the *Briefs of the 10th and 20th July, 1471
(Secret Archives of the Vatican)   On the 27th July the Archbishop of
Milan, writing to Galeazzo Maria Sforza, to inform him of the Pope's
death, said, "che è stato uno stupore maraviglioso ateso che era sanis-
simo piu fosse stato gran tempo fa "   The Cardinals at once assembled,
made some preliminary arrangements, and summoned their absent
colleagues.   Nardini reluctantly undertook the "governo di Roma"

for the departed took place , * the mortal remains of Paul II. were deposited in an imposing monument erected by Cardinal Barbo in the Chapel of St. Andrew. It was the work of Mino da Fiesole, " an artist who exercised a very important influence on sepulchral decoration, and with whom began a new and brilliant epoch in monumental art." Fragments of the tomb are still to be seen scattered about in the Grotto of St. Peter's †

" Pope Paul," says the chronicler of Viterbo, " was a just, holy, and peaceable man ; he established good government in all parts of his dominions " ‡ His labours, as a practical ruler, to strengthen and consolidate the authority of the Holy See throughout the States of the Church, may indeed be considered one of the chief characteristics of his reign. A modern historian sums up his judgment of the Pope in the following words. " Paul II was certainly a born ruler, and one animated by the most noble intentions. It may be regretted that the mitre was compelled to give way too much to the tiara, and that his pontificate displayed an excess of worldly splendour, but it cannot be said that ecclesiastical interests suffered in any direct way from this. In many

(State Archives, Milan) On the 27th July the Cardinals announced the death of the head of the Church Letters to this effect are to be seen in the Archives of Florence (X –II –25, f. 35a, b), and in those of Milan ; the latter is marked, *cito, cito*

* According to information kindly furnished by Dr Gottlob, 13,610 pounds of wax, costing about 1852 florins, were consumed on this occasion ; 6062 flor 10 bolog were also paid pro broccato auri ac pro pannis lane ac aliis rebus eiusmodi . . ratione exequiarum fe. ie. dom. Pauli pape II " State Archives, Rome

† REUMONT, III , 1, 399 *seq* See GREGOROVIUS, Giabmalei, 98. BURCKHARDT, Cicerone, II , 372 *seq* , 4th ed , speaks in less favourable terms of this monument. See also MUNTZ, II., 48-9

‡ N DELLA TUCCIA, 98

matters he was a zealous reformer   Witnesses who are
above suspicion attest his determination in opposing all
simoniacal practices.   If, weighed down beneath the burden
of affairs, he was not always successful in accomplishing
the good he desired, we must not be harsh in our judgment
of one whose uprightness is admitted even by his enemies
The nepotism from which he was not free, never took
the offensive and mischievous form which we have to
lament in his immediate successor.   Even his enemies
do not venture to say that it was ever hurtful to the
Church." *   In opposition to Platina's calumnies, it must
be remembered that Paul II. opposed only that heathen
abuse of learning which seemed dangerous to religion ;
apart from that he encouraged it.   It was not the learning
of the Humanists that he hated, but that tendency which
Dante characterised as the stench of heathenism †   All
Platina's other charges against the Pope are merely in-
sinuations, not facts   " How virtuous," concludes a non-
Catholic scholar, " must he have been when so diligent
and malicious an enemy as this Humanist could bring
forward so little against him " ‡

The statement that Paul II did not realise the Turkish
danger is also unjust   It is true that this war was not
the one all-engrossing object of his life, as it had been
with Pius II., but the silence of those who hated him
most is in itself a proof that no cause of complaint can be
found against him on this head.   Recent investigations,
moreover, have brought to light many facts which are
much to his credit §   It is impossible that a conclusive
judgment can be formed until our information is completed

* ROHRBACHER-KNOPFLER, 238 ; REUMONT, III., 1, 160

† Parad , XX , 125

‡ CREIGHTON, III., 275

§ See GOTTLOB in the Hist Jahrb , IV , 443, and Cam. Apost

by further examination of the Archives. We have, as yet, before us but scanty particulars as to the negotiations which took place in 1471 for the purpose of organising defensive measures against the Osmanli   A newly-discovered letter of Cardinal Gonzaga, written on the 17th of January in that year, shews that Paul II. was prepared to devote 50,000 ducats, the quarter of his annual income, to the expenses of the Turkish war.*   This sum does not include the revenue derived from the Alum monopoly, which, from the beginning of his reign, he had assigned to the objects of the Crusade. Subsidies and pensions were provided out of these funds for all the unfortunate exiles who had been driven by Turkish conquests to take refuge in the States of the Church. The account-books of his pontificate are full of entries of this description, sometimes reaching the annual amount of 20,000 to 30,000 ducats. The name of Thomas, the dethroned Despot of the Morea, appears as the recipient of a monthly pension of 300 florins. After the death of Thomas, the Pope continued this allowance to his children, who were brought up under the care of Cardinal Bessarion.†   Catherine, Queen-Mother of Bosnia, who migrated to Rome in 1466, from that time received 100 florins a month, and in the following year a further annual allowance of 240 florins was made to her for the rent of her house.‡   To the Despot Leonard of Arta, were

* The Venetians were dissatisfied with these offers of the Pope See Appendix, N 29

† FALLMERAYER, Morea, II , 404   See our Vol III , p 251, and also, for an account of the death of Thomas, **J de Aretio's Despatch of the 21st May, 1465. (Gonzaga Archives) In the *Div Pauli II , 1464–1466, f. 100 (also f 112, 126, 135, &c), payments are entered "pro filiis bon mem olim dom Thome Paleologi Amoree despoti" from Sept 5, 1465. State Archives, Rome.

‡ She lodged with the "prudens vir Jacobus Mentebone" For

granted, "as assistance in the war against the Turks,"
1000 golden florins on the 12th March, 1465, 1200 on the
18th July, 1466, and another 1000 on the 2nd April, 1467.
Monthly pensions were likewise bestowed on Queen
Charlotte of Cyprus, Prince John Zacharias of Samos,
Nicolaus Jacobus, a citizen of Constantinople, Thomas
Zalonich, and many others. From the year 1467 the
Archbishop of Mitylene and the Despot of Servia also
received regular allowances, which were supplemented by
occasional presents.*

These facts prove the princely liberality of Paul II. It
is also worth noting that now, as on many subsequent
occasions, possession of the States of the Church enabled
the Holy See to offer an asylum to the persecuted and
exiled, and to succour the oppressed and unfortunate.
"The dominions of the Church have a characteristic which
distinguishes them from all other kingdoms ; in contra-
distinction to the exclusiveness of other States, they partake
of the Catholicity of the Church. They form a separate
realm ; but as their Monarch is the Supreme Head of
Christendom, this realm is the common patrimony of all
Christians. No nationality is excluded from its offices and
dignities, and its educational institutions and Convents are
open to all races." †

these particulars I am indebted to the kindness of my friend, Dr.
Gottlob, who intends to publish a complete list of those assisted by
the funds of the Cruciata, founded on accurate study of the *Account-
books preserved in the Roman State Archives. Hist. Jahrb , VI , 443
See *supra*, p 28

* As on 17th Dec , 1467, 200 gulden   State Archives, Rome

† PHILLIPS, V , 708   In regard to the international character of the
Roman Court in the 15th Century, see our Vol. I , p. 242 *seq*. Amongst
Pius II.'s officials we find numerous Germans, several Englishmen, a
Burgundian, Bohemians, and Spaniards   At the Court of Paul II
there were three Henrys, all of them Germans , see MARINI, 152, 202

BOOK II.

SIXTUS IV. 1471–1484.

CHAPTER I.

THE death of Paul II. had occurred at a most critical
moment. Steadily, like an advancing flood, the Turks
streamed on to overwhelm the distracted West   It was
not Italy alone which now found all barriers swept away
between her coasts and the enemy. The defenceless
frontiers of the Holy Roman Empire were overrun by
these barbarian hordes, carrying rapine, murder, and devastation in their train as they pressed through Croatia
into Styria. The terrible tidings of the destruction which
threatened Italy and Germany alike, were well calculated
to startle the most slothful from their slumber. Nevertheless, at the Diet which met at Ratisbon, under the "influence
of the Turkish panic," next to nothing was accomplished ;
the Papal Legate, Piccolomini, preached to deaf ears.* ·
Italy, like Germany, was rent by internal dissensions : no
one seemed to realise the serious character of the times.
"As wave follows wave upon a storm-swept sea, so one
political combination was perpetually giving way to another

* See *supra*, p 181. Regarding the inroads of the Turks, see
ZINKEISEN, II , 362 *seq.* , HASELBACH, 42 , ILWOLF in the Mittheil.
des Historischen Vereins fur Steiermark, X , 222 *seq.*, and HUBER,
III , 224

in a restless, aimless succession. This everlasting change
of relations, this possibility of being at once mutually
friendly and hostile ; the impossibility of having any clear
certainty of the position, at any given moment, of any
State towards its neighbour, became more and more the
characteristic of Italian political life "*

During the vacancy of the Holy See in 1471, the Province
of Romagna, always more or less unquiet, gave special cause
for anxiety † Considerable excitement also prevailed in
Rome   Immediately after the death of Paul II , the Secular
Canons of the Lateran had, with the assistance of their
Roman friends, driven out the Regular Canons introduced
by the deceased Pontiff.   On the 28th July a deputation
from the people of Rome appeared in front of the Minerva,
where the Cardinals had assembled, demanding, amongst
other things, that, for the future, benefices in Rome should be
conferred on none but Romans, and that the income destined
for the Roman University should no longer be diverted to
other objects   The Cardinals answered in a conciliatory
manner, whereupon an order was issued that all should lay
down their weapons, and that the outlaws should leave
Rome.   This did much to soothe the popular feeling.
Other concessions were also made to the Romans   On
the morning of the 29th, forty prisoners, confined in the
Capitol for minor offences, were set at liberty.   The
Cardinals released two citizens of Ascoli and a Baron
suspected of heresy, who were imprisoned in the dungeons
of St Angelo, on condition that they should not depart
from Rome before the Coronation of the new Pontiff.‡

* BUSER, Beziehungen, 155

† *Letter of J. P. Arrivabene, dated Rome, 1471, Aug. 6. (Gonzaga
Archives, Mantua.) See N. DELLA TUCCIA, 100

‡ **Letter of Joh Blanchus de Cremona to the Duke of Milan, dated
Rome, 1471, July 29 (State Archives, Milan) The imprisoned Baron

The City continued tolerably quiet during the ensuing days.*

Sixteen Cardinals were in Rome when Paul II. died.   Of those who were absent, none but Roverella and Gonzaga were able to reach the City in time for the Election. Roverella, Legate of Perugia, arrived on the 1st, and Gonzaga on the 4th August.† Many persons expected that the latter would be Pope, others thought the election of Cardinal Forteguerri more probable.‡ A Milanese Ambassador insists on the importance of the Turkish question in regard to the Election; he mentions the persons apparently best fitted to bring about its solution, in connection with the two parties, the Piischi and Pauleschi, already existing in the Sacred College. Of the former, he names in the first place, Forteguerri, then Eroli, Ammanati, and Roverella.   Among the Pauleschi he looks upon Amicus Agnifilus and Francesco della Rovere as the most likely candidates.§

The preponderance of the Italian element on this occasion was very remarkable. Of the eighteen electors, all but three (Bessarion, d'Estouteville, and Borgia) were Italians The thirteen years which had elapsed since the Conclave of

was probably the nobleman from Poli mentioned *supra*, p. 113.   For a further account of the Canons of the Lateran, see CANENSIUS, 45 ; ROHAULT, 253 , MAZZUCHELLI, I., 2, 882

* *Letter of the same Ambassador, dated Rome, 1471, Aug 1 (State Archives, Milan.) See *ibid*, a *Letter from Nicodemus of the 2nd Aug , 1471

† *Acta Consist , f 42b, Secret Archives of the Vatican

‡ REUMONT, Lorenzo, I , 243, 2nd ed.   In regard to Forteguerri, J. Blanchus, in a *Despatch of the 1st Aug , 1471, wrote : " *La opinione grandissima del s pontificato persevera molto sopra Thiano " State Archives, Milan.

§ Second *Letter of J. Blanchus to the Duke of Milan, dated Rome, 1471, July 29. (State Archives, Milan) See *supra*, p 124, note *

Pius II. had brought great changes, and the ascendancy of the foreign Cardinals was at an end.*

Foremost among the aspirants to the Tiara were Cardinals d'Estouteville and Orsini. The former eagerly endeavoured to secure the support of the powerful Duke of Milan. A confidential person was employed to inform him that his brother, Ascanio Sforza, would receive the red hat, and that he himself might be the wearer of a royal crown in the event of d'Estouteville's success.† The wealthy Cardinal Orsini, a man of great capacity for business, was equally energetic in his efforts to obtain the supreme dignity. His brothers and relations had assembled in the neighbourhood of Rome, and it was reported that the former had determined to procure his elevation to the Papal Throne, whether by fair means or foul, and that the King of Naples favoured their design. The Ambassador of Mantua confirms this statement, and adds that Orsini, if his own cause seemed hopeless, would espouse that of Forteguerri and Eroli‡ Even before the beginning of the Conclave, serious differences occurred between Cardinals Orsini and Bessarion,

---

* The Conclave of 1458 was composed of eight Italian and ten foreign Cardinals, see our Vol III, p 6 The distribution of creations during the last four pontificates was as follows. four Italians, six Frenchmen, one Spaniard, and one German were raised to the purple by Nicholas V, four Italians, three Spaniards, one Portuguese, and one Frenchman by Calixtus III. (see our Vol II., p 457 *seq*, and PANVINIUS, 302 *seq*), eight Italians, two Frenchmen, one Spaniard, and one German by Pius II ; and seven Italians, one Englishman, one Hungarian, and one Frenchman by Paul II See our Vol III, p 293, and *supra*, p 119

† **Letter of Paulus Gazurrus de Novaria cap^{nus} d revm: Rhotomag. to Duke Galeazzo Maria, dated Rome, 1471, July 29. State Archives, Milan.

‡ Besides the **Letter of P. Gazurrus, cited above, see that of J. P. Arrivabene of the 6th Aug , 1471. Gonzaga Archives, Mantua

the latter declared that he would not, under any circumstances, suffer the Election to be carried out in the same way as the last had been. Controversies also arose regarding the admission of Cardinals Savelli and Foscari, who had not yet been published. Orsini desired their exclusion, and his opinion prevailed.*

On the morning of the 6th August, after the solemn obsequies of Paul II. had been concluded, the Mass of the Holy Ghost was sung, and the College of Cardinals went in procession into the Conclave in the Vatican. There were seventeen present, and on the following day Cardinal Ammanati, who had been delayed by indisposition, was added to the number †

On the morning of the 9th August, Francesco della Rovere, Cardinal of S Pietro in Vincoli, was elected Pope ‡ As the Conclave had commenced on the feast of Pope Sixtus II., the new Pontiff assumed the name of Sixtus IV.

A number of fresh documents regarding the proceedings of the Conclave are now before us; they do much to complete the scanty details hitherto known, but leave some important matters still obscure. By far the most valuable of these are in the State Archives at Milan. They consist of two lists of the Electors, with an exact account, on the one hand, of which candidate each Cardinal voted

* See *Despatch of Pietro de Modegnano, dated Rome, 1471, Aug 1 (State Archives, Milan) See PETRUCELLI DELIA GATTINA, 293.

† *Acta Consist, *loc. cit*, Secret Archives of the Vatican REUMONT, III, 1, 163, CHRISTOPHE, 209; and ROHRBACHER-KNOPFLER, 238, are mistaken in asserting that there were nineteen Cardinals VAST, Bessarion, 398, makes the Conclave begin on the 20th July !

‡ See the *Despatch of J P Arrivabene, dated Rome, 1471, Aug. 9. (Gonzaga Archives) Also Appendix, N 44

for, and on the other of the number of votes received by each, with the names of the voters *

The faithful and capable Nicodemus de Pontremoli managed to procure these lists for the Duke, his master, who had expressed a great desire for trustworthy Reports of the Conclave. The Ambassador himself was far from over-estimating their value, and, in order at the present day to appreciate them fairly, it is necessary to bear his observations in mind. After dwelling on the difficulty of obtaining these lists, he draws attention to the fact that most of the Cardinals in the Conclave voted for those whose votes they hoped by this means to win, and not for those whose Election they really desired , some few, he adds, reserved their votes to conceal secret engagements.† According to these lists, which, unfortunately, do not enable us clearly to distinguish the several scrutinies, Roverella and Calandrini were at first seriously thought of in the Conclave, each of them receiving seven votes , Bessarion ‡ and Forteguerri followed next, each with six ; d'Estouteville had only four in all, and Orsini but two   The same authority informs us that Cardinals Giovanni Michele, Teodoro of Montferrat, Battista Zeno, Roverella, Forteguerri, Agnifilus, Bessarion, Calandrini, and Orsini gave their votes for Francesco della Rovere , Borgia, d'Estouteville, and Barbo afterwards adding theirs.

* See Appendix, N. 43   These two lists agree, with only two exceptions , they are on separate sheets, and have hitherto escaped notice

† **Despatch of Nicodemus de Pontremoli, dated Rome, 1471, Aug. 20   (State Archives, Milan)   When transmitting the lists on the 28th August to the Duke, the Ambassador again refers to these explanations ; see Appendix, N 46.

‡ The Venetians had begged their friends in the Sacred College to give him their support , see G Colli's Despatch of the 2nd Aug , 1471, in Arch d Soc Rom , XI., 254

The omission of the name of Cardinal Gonzaga from among the supporters of Rovere in the report of Nicodemus is very strange, for all the other accounts are unanimous in asserting that his Election was chiefly due to Orsini, Borgia, and Gonzaga, and that they were liberally rewarded for their share in securing it.* Ample testimony exists in proof of the part taken by Cardinal Gonzaga. A Despatch from the Ambassador of Mantua to his mother details the reasons which had induced him to espouse the cause of Rovere. In the first place, there was the hope of winning the favour of the future Pope, secondly, Rovere was a person acceptable to the Duke of Milan, and thirdly, d'Estouteville had no prospect of success Accordingly, says the Ambassador, our most gracious Lord Cardinal has taken the greatest trouble on behalf of Cardinal della Rovere, so that it may be said that he, more than any one, has made him Pope. His Holiness has shewn his gratitude by confirming him in his appointment as Legate, and authorising him, if he chooses, to perform his duties by proxy. Moreover, the Abbey of S Gregorio in Rome has been conferred on the Cardinal, and I believe that he will also have the Bishopric of Albano. The Ambassador then expressly says that the tenth vote for Rovere was given by Cardinal Gonzaga, the eleventh by Barbo, and the twelfth by d'Estouteville.† The Duke of Milan's share in securing the election of Sixtus IV is confirmed by so many other authorities that we may look upon it as clearly established ‡

* Regarding Borgia's share in the matter, see AMMANATI, Epist. (Frankfort edition), N 534

† **Letter of J. P Arrivabene, dated Rome, 1471, Aug. 11 Gonzaga Archives, Mantua

‡ In a second *Letter of the 28th Aug, 1471, Nicodemus informs his master that the Pope was grateful to the Duke "vide

No mention, however, is made in the Ambassadorial
Despatches of the part which, according to two chroniclers,
the Franciscan Pietro Riario had in the election. Cardinal
della Rovere brought him into the Conclave, where he
was very useful to his patron in winning for him many
undecided votes * The Election Capitulation, to observe
which Sixtus IV. was obliged solemnly to bind himself, is
also only alluded to in these Despatches †

The election of Cardinal Francesco della Rovere caused
great joy throughout Rome, especially, Nicodemus informs
us, because the well-known piety and holiness of his life
led all to hope that he would be an excellent Pastor for
the Church and for the Christian Faith everywhere ‡
Francesco, like Nicholas V, owed his elevation to the
purple to his reputation as a learned theologian and a
man of blameless life. He belonged to an ancient, but
impoverished, Ligurian family, and was related to the

et intese quel fo operato pro lui in nome vestro" State Archives,
Milan

* COBELLI, 258, and INFESSURA, 1143.

† On the 13th Aug., 1471, J. A Ferrofinus relates that on the
aforesaid day the Pope had shewn to the Cardinals at St. Angelo
Paul II 's jewels "de le quali secondo m' ha detto Rhoano hanno
capitulato in conclavi che non possa disponere ma le conservi a li
bisogni de la fede" (State Archives, Milan) No doubt, then, an
Election Capitulation was drawn up in 1471. See also *infra*, p. 211,
and the *Despatch of B Bonattus of 13th Dec, 1471, given in
Chapter II, p 235, and the statement in MAI, Spic, I, 198, that
Roverella would not promise anything in the Conclave which might
refer to the Election Capitulation.

‡ *Despatch of the 9th Aug, 1471. (State Archives, Milan.) See
Appendix, N. 44 The election caused great satisfaction also in the
States of the Church , see Cr. di Bologna, 788, and *Ghirardacci;
also *infra*, p 206, note † N. DELLA TUCCIA, 100, speaks of Sixtus
IV as "omo umile e di buona complessione" See SIGISMONDO DE'
CONTI, I , 5.

Piedmontese Rovere, Lords of Vinovo * His father, Lionardo, lived in modest circumstances in the little village
of Abezzola, not far from Savona. To escape from an infectious disease which broke out there, he and his wife,
Luchina Monleone, migrated to Celle on the sea-coast,
and here Francesco was born.†

   In consequence of his repeated sicknesses, Francesco's
pious mother consecrated him by vow to St Francis ;
and, in spite of the opposition of some worldly-minded
relations, entrusted him, when nine years of age, to the
care of the Minorite, Giovanni Pinarolo. Under the
guidance of this excellent religious, the gifted boy learned
to know and esteem the monastic life to which he was
destined to devote himself. Later, he went to the High
School of Chieri, and finally to the Universities of Pavia
and Bologna, where he studied philosophy and theology
" His talent for dialectics was displayed for the first time
in the General Chapter of his Order held at Genoa when
he was only twenty. On that occasion he acquitted
himself so well in the Latin disputation, that the General,
Guglielmo Casale, embraced him."‡ After he had completed his philosophical and theological studies at Padua,
he undertook the duties of Professor, and taught with

   * Francesco's letter of 1468 in VILLENEUVE, 31, contradicts the
assertion in REUMONT, Lorenzo, I , 243, 2nd ed , that nothing was
heard of this relationship until he became Pope.

   † PLATINA, Vita, Sixti IV , 1053 seq , is the principal authority for
all the following particulars. His detailed narrative gives us what
those most nearly concerned then believed to be true , see SCHMAR-
SOW, 3, N. 1. We have also a poem, composed in 1477, and entitled
*Lucubraciunculae Tiburtinae cuiusdam protonotarii, which I generally
cite from the MS. in the Court Library, Vienna (Cod. 2403), where
I found it, and an *Oratio ad Sixtum IV , by Naldo Naldi in Cod. 45,
C. 18, f. 113b–117, in the Corsini Library, Rome

   ‡ FRANTZ, Sixtus IV , 132 , MAGENTA, I , 355.

great success at Padua,* Bologna,† Pavia, Siena, Florence,
and Perugia‡ The attendance at his lectures was so
great that Johannes Argyropulos and Bonfrancesco Arlati
subsequently declared that every learned man in Italy
had been a disciple of Rovere's Cardinal Bessarion is
expressly mentioned as having been among his hearers,
and ever after having held him in the greatest esteem
So much was this the case, that from that time he would
not publish any of his works until the great Franciscan
philosopher and theologian had revised and corrected
them §

Francesco was also a distinguished preacher, and was,
on many important occasions, a support to the General of
his Order. He was afterwards called to fill the post
of Procurator in Rome   When the General, Jacopo de
Sarzuela, felt the burden of office too heavy for his advanced age, he chose Francesco " as his Vicar for the whole
of Italy, and made him Provincial of the Ligurian Province of

* In Naldo Naldi's Oration, cited in preceding page, note †, he speaks
in the following terms of Francesco's labours in the City of Padua :
*" In ea enim cum homines min. ordinis domi theologiam edoceres,
tantus populariter ad te concursus audientium factus est, quod publicis
etiam illius civitatis institutis munus tibi philosophie precepta tradendi
demandatum esset, ut multi praestantes viri, quidam etiam ex ipsa
usque Grecia interessent " According to Naldo, Francesco also professed philosophy in Rome   Cod. 45, C. 18, f 114, Corsini Library,
Rome

† See *Ghirardacci, St. di Bologna, Cod 768, University Library,
Bologna   The affection of the Bolognese, many of whom were
personally acquainted with the new Pope, was, Ghirardacci informs
us, manifested in the splendid Embassy sent in 1471 to congratulate
him.

‡ See GRAZIANI, 644, and BINI, Mem. Ist della Perug Univ, I.,
I, 515 seq (Perugia, 1816).

§ See the testimony of L Carbo from Cod Vat., 1195, in SCHMAR-
SOW, 335-6, and CREIGHTON, III , 57

the Order, where he was very successful in carrying out measures of monastic reform." *

He won yet greater renown by the part which he took in the disputation regarding the Precious Blood, held in December, 1462, in the Vatican before Pius II.† The learning and controversial ability which he then manifested doubtless had a share in bringing about his Election to the Generalate, at the great Chapter of the Franciscans held at Perugia in May, 1464.‡ He at once determined vigorously to undertake the reform of his Order. A violent fever laid him low for a time, but did not hinder the accomplishment of his purpose The skill and care of Ambrosius Grifus § brought him safely through, and he hardly gave himself time to recover before beginning the work of visitation and reformation in the Franciscan Convents and the educational establishments connected with them.

Francesco so ably defended the privileges of the Institute over which he presided that Pope Paul II abstained from the measures he had intended to take against the whole Order. A General Chapter was consequently held at Florence in 1467 ‖ In the summer, the General went to his home to recruit his health, which had been impaired by his sojourn in Rome ; he then visited Pavia, and meant to proceed thence to Venice, and there to give theological lectures during the winter. He was ready to start on

* FRANTZ, Sixtus IV , 133.

† See our Vol III , p. 286

‡ WADDING, XIII , 344-5

§ See the **Letter of " Franciscus de Saona " to the Duke of Milan, dated Bologna, 1465, Jan 2, and also a *Brief of Sixtus IV. of the 15th Nov , 1471, to the same. Both documents are in the State Archives, Milan

‖ WADDING, XIII , 397. I saw in the State Archives at Milan an Autograph *Letter of Franciscus de Saona to Duke Galeazzo Maria Sforza, dated Florence, 1467, Febr 27

the journey, when, at the end of September, a letter
from Cardinal Gonzaga, accompanied by another from
Bessarion, informed him that he had been created Cardinal
on the 18th September, 1467, by Paul II *

On the 15th November, 1467, the new member of the
Sacred College reached Rome, where he received the red
hat, and had S. Pietro in Vincoli † assigned to him as his
titular Church   The condition of the Cardinal's Palace
adjoining this venerable Basilica was so dilapidated that
Francesco was at once obliged to restore it, a work which
his poverty would have rendered impossible, had it not been
for the assistance of his colleagues.   In the purple, the
Cardinal of S Pietro in Vincoli, as he was styled, continued
to be a simple Franciscan ; " in his house, which overlooked
a great part of the ancient and of the modern City, questions
of scholarship and ecclesiastical affairs were discussed, but
no politics." ‡   Whatever leisure his new dignity allowed
him was devoted to learned pursuits, and, during the four
years of his Cardinalate, he published a number of works
which brought him more and more into notice.

In the first place the Cardinal again took up the disputed
question regarding the Precious Blood ; his work on the
subject, dedicated to Paul II, was printed in Rome in
1470, together with a treatise " On the power of God."   A

* See *Acta Consist , Secret Archives of the Vatican, and *supra*,
p 122   On the 24th Sept , 1467, Francesco still wrote as General to
the Duke of Milan, and, on the 9th and 12th October, as Cardinal.   I
found these three Autograph *Letters, which are dated from Pavia, in
the State Archives at Milan   According to AMMANATI, Ep , 529, and
Vespas da Bisticci (MAI, I , 194), Bessarion induced the Pope to raise
Francesco to the purple , regarding the affection entertained by Paul
II for him, see COBELLI, 258.

† *Acta Consist., Secret Archives of the Vatican   the 20th November
is here named as the day of the *aperitio oris.*

‡ REUMONT, Lorenzo, I , 243, 2nd ed ; VILLENEUVE, 8 and 31

philosophical and theological dispute in the University of
Louvain was the occasion of a writing entitled " De futuris
contingentibus" A work on the Immaculate Conception
bears witness to that devotion to the Blessed Virgin which
continued unabated after his elevation to the Papal throne.
With a view of composing the frequent disputes between
the Dominicans and the brethren of his own Order, in which
the one party appealed to Duns Scotus and the other to St
Thomas Aquinas, he endeavoured to shew that the two
authorities, although differing in words, were really of one
mind. In the midst of these labours the voice of his
colleagues summoned him, at the age of fifty-seven, to fill
the Chair of St Peter.*

A portrait from the hand of his Court-painter, Melozzo
da Forli, which is still preserved, represents the new Pope
as a man of middle stature and strong, compact frame
The features are regular, the nose and forehead forming an

---

* SCHMARSOW, 6, where Duns Scotus is strangely confounded with
Scotus Erigena. Regarding the learned writings of Sixtus IV, see
CORTESIUS, XXXIX, Bibl pontif, 203 *seq.*, FABRICIUS, VI., 491 *seq* ;
CAVE, II, App, 187, QUIRINI, 283 *seq*, MUNTZ, Renaiss, 354. In
the eulogistic poem, *Lucubraciunculae Tiburtinae cuiusdam protonotarii, written in 1477, which has been mentioned at p. 205, occur the
following lines :—

> " Tris autem scripsit libros (ut opuscula nondum
> Edita praeteream), quibus in tribus eminet eius
> Ingenium excellens ingensque scientia rerum
> Ex iis unius titulis (si rite recordor)
> Est de posse Dei, de contingentibus alter,
> Tertius inscriptus liber est de sanguine Christi "

Cod 2403, f 5–5b, Court Library, Vienna It is hard to understand
how GEIGER, Renaissance, 152, can assert that Sixtus IV was no
scholar or respecter of mediæval theology, and that he had no right
to the place which Benozzo Gozzoli assigns to him in his picture as an
admirer and expounder of St Thomas Aquinas

oblique line, with a gentle curve between them The powerful head impresses us with an idea of uncommon energy and force, which difficulties could not daunt , while the lines on the brow bear witness to a life of hard and unremitting toil.

Sixtus IV. commenced his reign by conferring favours on the Cardinals, and in this proceeding formed such a contrast to his predecessor, that, as an Ambassador wrote, every one felt as if they were in a new world * In the first place, those who had brought about his Election were rewarded Cardinal Borgia received the Abbey of Subiaco *in commendam*, and Gonzaga that of S. Gregorio, while Orsini was made Camerlengo, and as such took the oath as early as the 12th August The position of Legate to the Marches was promised to Cardinal Forteguerri, but report said that he declined it, preferring to remain at the Court , it was accordingly conferred on Roverella, and Ammanati was sent to Perugia †

On the 13th August the Pope gave a banquet to the Cardinals at St. Angelo After its conclusion, the money and valuables collected by Paul II. were inspected Great

---

* "*Ad ugniuno pare vedere principio d'un novo mundo " Letter of J P Arrivabene, dated Rome, 1471, Aug 13 Gonzaga Archives.

† *Report of Nicodemus of Pontremoli, dated Rome, 1471, Aug 12. (State Archives, Milan) Borgia completed a wing of the Castle at Subiaco, and added the tower, still standing, where his coat of arms and an inscription may be seen , see GREGOROVIUS, Wanderjahre, II , 17 , GORI's Arch St , IV , 126 ; and JANNUCELLI, Subiaco, 230. According to the *Acta Consist., f 43 (Secret Archives of the Vatican), Bessarion's translation from the See of Albano to that of Porto took place on the 30th Aug , 1471 , Cardinal Borgia, who must then have been a priest, at the same time being appointed Bishop of Albano GAMS. XXIII , and BRESSLAU, Urkundenlehre, I , 211, are mistaken in giving 1468 as the date of Borgia's elevation to the episcopal See of Albano, as is CLEMENT, 133, in stating that it occurred in 1476.

interest was at this time felt regarding these treasures, which had hitherto been so carefully preserved, and, in conformity with the Election Capitulation, were to be expended on the cause of the Faith * The Pope and the Cardinals were occupied for the whole day in examining these precious stores. One of the Cardinals told the Duke of Milan's Ambassador that they had found, in the first place, fifty-four silver shells, filled with pearls, valued at 300,000 ducats. These were sealed up by all the Cardinals, and were to be sold to defray the expenses of the war with the Turks Next were seen the jewels and the gold belonging to the two tiaras which Paul II. meant to have had rearranged, worth about 300,000 ducats. A magnificent diamond, estimated at 7000 ducats, was pledged to Cardinal d'Estouteville for monies which he had advanced to the deceased Pontiff. The amount of gold, silver, jewels, precious objects, and other ornaments filled them with astonishment, and their value was deemed to be a million ducats " But," the Ambassador adds, "the worth of these things depends on the opinion of those who will buy them." The money found amounted only to 7000 ducats, and was chiefly in the form of carlini. Deposits of 100,000, 60,000, 80,000, and 30,000 ducats were entered in a note laid up in a chest. The place where these sums were concealed could not at first be discovered ; but their actual existence was certified by the fact that Paul II., in a Consistory held not long before his death, had spoken of half a million of ducats which he would expend on the war if the Christian Princes would undertake an expedition against the enemies of the Faith All these treasures, which the new Pope had

* Besides the passage from Ferrofinus' Despatch of the 13th August, quoted *supra*, p 204, note †, see two *Letters of J P Arrivabene, dated Rome, 1471, Aug 11 and 13 (Gonzaga Archives, Mantua) In regard to L Orsini, see SANSOVINO, Casa Orsina, 5 *seq*

sworn not to touch, were sealed up by the Cardinals, and placed in the custody of the Castellan of St. Angelo *

After Sixtus IV. had been consecrated Bishop, his solemn Coronation took place on Sunday, the 25th of August.† The tribune where the Pope received the tiara of St. Gregory the Great from the hands of Cardinal Borgia was so lofty that all the people could witness the ceremony.‡   According-ing to ancient custom, he then proceeded to take possession of the Lateran.   In the splendid procession were to be seen the Despot of the Morea and Scanderbeg's nephew.   A tumult occurred in front of the Lateran, the Pope himself was in danger, and Cardinal Orsini had much difficulty in appeasing the excited populace.   The impression made on Sixtus IV. by this untoward event was such that he returned to the Vatican at the first hour of the night §

* The above account is drawn from the hitherto unknown *Report which Petrus de Modegnano, apost. protonot, furnished to Duke Galeazzo Maria, dated Rome, 1471, Aug 14. See also a *Letter of Nicodemus de Pontremoli, dated Rome, 1471, Aug 20; both these documents are in the State Archives, Milan. As Dr. Gottlob has kindly informed me, the account-books shew that Sixtus IV. sold many of Paul II.'s jewels as early as 1471. On the 31st May, 1472, the Medici paid 23,170 florins, "pro valore plurium jocalium de diversis sortibus emptorum ab ipsis depositariis usque in diem 19 Sept proxᵉ pretenti;" a further sum of 12,000 florins was realised by the sale of jewels. The King of Naples lent 16,000 florins, and received jewels as security for their repayment.

† See Bull Vatic., 195. Here and elsewhere the 26th of August is wrongly named as the day of the Coronation, in contradiction to all the best authorities; see following note. FRANTZ, 134, is also mistaken in giving the 22nd August; and the Lib confrat b. M de Anima, 13, the 8th September.

‡ See the *Reports of Nicodemus de Pontremoli, dated Rome, 1471, Aug 25, and that of Blanchus de Cremona, dated Rome, 1471, Aug. 26th (State Archives, Milan), as well as the *Acta Consist. of Secret Archives, f. 43.

§ The *Letters of the Milanese Ambassadors which we have just

The letters by which the Pope made his elevation known to the temporal powers are dated on the day of his Coronation, in these he begs for the support of fervent prayers that he may rule the Church to the praise and glory of God, and the salvation of the people committed to his care.*

"When the tiara first rested on the brow of Sixtus IV. the figure of Nicholas V., amongst his immediate predecessors, must have presented itself most vividly to his mind, for he also was a native of Liguria, and like Sixtus himself, but unlike Pius II. and Paul II., had risen from a modest position. Again, he was by nature a scholar, and only after his elevation had developed the princely magnificence whose traces were visible wherever ruined Rome bore the aspect of a new city. That the new Pontiff should resolve to follow in his steps, and with the good fortune of the Rovere, to carry out the work begun

quoted, give more details than Infessura and Platina regarding Sixtus IV.'s *Possesso*. The Jews who stationed themselves on the Bridge of St Angelo are here mentioned Schmarsow, misled by Platina (see on the other side CANCELLIERI, Possessi, 45), makes the Coronation take place after the *Possesso* and after the tumult. PLATINA, Vita Sixti IV, 1057, estimates the expenses of the Coronation of Sixtus IV. and the obsequies of Paul II (see *supra*, p 191, note *) at 28,000 golden florins (see also MUNTZ, III, 1, 268 *seq*, and ROHAULT, 253 and 503). The sum is not so extravagant as SCHMARSOW, 8, imagines, for the Coronation alone of Paul II cost 23,000 florins

* RAYNALDUS, ad an. 1471, N. 70. I found letters of this description, with some textual variations, in the Gonzaga Archives, Mantua (original), in the Florentine State Archives (Copy, X-II-25, f 35b–36b), and in the Archives of Perugia VOIGT, Gesch Pieussens, IX, 41, mentions one addressed to the Grand Master of the Teutonic Order in the Archives of Konigsberg The letters of the Sacred College regarding the election are also dated on the 25th August; see CHMEL, Urkunden und Briefe, II, 267; a similar letter to the Duke of Saxony is in the State Archives, Dresden

by his energetic countryman, was but natural.   But he had
not the clear start from the first that Nicholas had
Nicholas V. had been freely elected, his actions were
untrammelled   Sixtus, in order to be elected, had permitted himself to be bound, and the conditions of the
Papal power also had undergone a complete change in the
interval." *

In Italy itself the Apostolic See had no trustworthy
friends. Sigismondo de' Conti tells us that the excessive
obstinacy of Paul II. had almost everywhere provoked
distrust and hatred.† The jealous fears of Italian
politicians in presence of the increasing power of the States
of the Church may have exercised a yet more potent
influence. Sixtus IV. at once sought to establish friendly
relations on all sides   Under Paul II the disputes with
Naples and Venice seemed to be interminable   Sixtus IV
at once came to an understanding with these two powers,‡
although at the cost of considerable sacrifice on his own
part   Without any great trouble Ferrante obtained the
satisfaction of seeing the rich Abbey of Monte Casino
conferred upon his youthful son, while the Protonotary
Rocha was made Archbishop of Salerno §

"This Pope evidently intends to be on good terms with
every one," wrote the Marquess of Mantua's Ambassador,||
briefly describing the beginning of Sixtus IV.'s pontificate.

* SCHMARSOW, 7

† SIGISMONDO DE' CONTI, I , 5

‡ *Loc. cit*, I., 6–7

§ *Letters of Nicodemus de Pontremoli, dated Rome, 1471, Aug 31
(State Archives, Milan), and of the Ambassador of Mantua, B Bonattus,
dated Rome, 1471, Sept. 2. (Gonzaga Archives, Mantua.) See also
GATTULA, II , 568, and TOSTI, Monte Cassino, III , 181.

|| "*Questo papa monstra voler star bene cum ognuno"   B.
Bonattus on the 2nd Sept., 1471. Gonzaga Archives

Before he had an idea of being Pope, or even Cardinal,
Sixtus IV had had amicable relations with the Duke of
Milan, and this in a measure explains the warm interest
taken by Galeazzo Maria Sforza in promoting the election
After it had been carried, he was one of the first to
congratulate the new Pope * Sixtus IV. replied at once
on the 16th of August by an autograph letter of the most
flattering character. He began by recalling their former
relations, praised the Duke's piety and devotion to the
Holy See, of which he had given proof in the Romagna
during the vacancy of the Chair of St. Peter, and finally
assured him that his pontificate should bring the Duke
nothing but happiness and blessing †

The bond between the new Pope and the Florentines was
even closer   " He looked upon the Medici, the patrons and
friends of the modest Thomas of Sarzano, as his natural
allies "‡   This was made very apparent when the Florentine
Embassy, headed by Lorenzo de' Medici, arrived in Rome
to pay homage on behalf of the Republic.   Its reception
was most cordial and honourable.   Two antique marble
busts were presented to Lorenzo, and he was allowed to
acquire gems and cameos from the collection of Paul II.

---

* In the State Archives, Milan, "Roma," I found the draft of this
*Letter of congratulation, dated 1471, Aug 11.

+ See Appendix, N 45   (State Archives, Milan) Nicodemus de
Pontremoli, writing to the Duke on the 20th Aug., 1471, says . * " As
I have already stated, His Holiness has repeatedly declared that he
places his chief hopes on your Excellency ; he expresses himself in
this manner, not only to me and to Cardinal Gonzaga, but also in the
Consistory, and on every occasion when your Highness is mentioned "
(State Archives, Milan.)   The Cronica di Bologna, 789, gives an
account of the great Milanese Embassy, in which Ascanio Maria
Sforza took part   See N DELLA TUCCIA, 101, and RATTI, I,
78, 89

‡ SCHMARSOW, 7.

at a very moderate price   The Pope's confidence and good-
will were also manifested in other very substantial ways.
The financial affairs of the Papacy were confided to the
Roman Bank of the Medici, by which arrangement a rich
source of wealth was opened to Lorenzo and to his uncle
Giovanni Tornabuoni.   Further concessions in regard to
the alum works were granted to him.   Emboldened by so
many favours, "the practical-minded Medici at last took
courage to remark that he had but one desire unfulfilled,
and that was to see a member of his family admitted into
the Sacred College.   To this request Sixtus IV. also lent
a favourable ear, for he was unwilling to refuse Lorenzo
anything   The latter soon left the Eternal City, laden with
all possible tokens of the Pope's good-will, which was soon
to be repaid with ingratitude."*

For a time indeed Filippo de' Medici, Archbishop of Pisa,
endeavoured to maintain good feeling between Florence
and Rome.   "The Pope has shewn me such honour," he
wrote on the 15th November, 1471, from Rome to Lorenzo
de' Medici, "that a hundred tongues would fail me to express
it.   He told me to rest assured that I might dispose of
Sixtus IV. as I would.   Had you not yourself been here
I would write yet more particularly regarding His Holiness'
affection for our house, but as you know it, I think it
unnecessary." †

On the 28th November the Venetian Envoys appeared

* Opinion of SCHMARSOW, 8   See REUMONT, Lorenzo, I , 243 *seq* ,
251 *seq* , 2nd ed. , MUNTZ, Précurseurs, 182 , FRANTZ, Sixtus IV , 135
seq , and PERRENS, 358. The *Oration on behalf of the Florentine
Embassy was deliver d on the 3rd Oct , 1471, by Donato Acciaiuoli
(see MAI, Spic , I , 440 ; MAZZUCHELLI, I , 1, 41), and is preserved in
Cod 541 of the Chapter Library, Lucca, and in a Manuscript in the
Riccardian Library, Florence, from which LAMIUS, 4-5, gives a passage.
  † BUSER, Lorenzo, 19 , see 23 and 27

in Rome. One of them, Bernardo Giustiniani, made an elaborate speech in the Pope's presence, the principal subject of which was the unspeakably deplorable condition of the East.* It was not indeed necessary to remind Sixtus IV of this, for he had already turned his attention to the terrible danger with which the steady advance of Islam threatened Christian civilisation. He aimed at the formation of a league of the European powers, to be directed exclusively against the Turks. A great Congress was to carry the idea into effect. During the days which immediately followed his Election, it was rumoured that, in accordance with the Capitulation, the Pope intended as soon as possible to convene such an Assembly. Cardinal Gonzaga † at the same time endeavoured to have his

---

* CIACONIUS, III, 120–26, LUNIG, Orat., I, 26–46, Orat clar. vir, 105 seq (Cologne, 1559). A *Letter from the Ambassador of Mantua, dated Rome, 1471, Nov. 29, speaks of the arrival of the Venetian Embassy. (Gonzaga Archives) The 16th November was the day appointed for the Florentines to pay their homage, see Filippo de' Medici's *Letter to Lorenzo, dated Rome, 1471, Nov. 15. (State Archives, Florence, F 27, f 522) The Embassy of Frederick, Count Palatine, which was admitted to audience on the 21st April, 1472, also dealt with the Turkish question ; see JACOB VOLATERR, 87. In November of the same year Envoys from Sigismund of the Tyrol were in Rome I found in Cod. Q, 41, of the Franciscan Library at Schwaz the Discourse pronounced on this occasion, *Pro Sigismundo Austrie duce illustr. ad Sixtum IV. P. M. Ludovici de Fryburgk utriusque juris doctoris oratio anno sal. septuagesimo secundo die veneris sexta Novemb. Romae in consistorio publico habita Ravenna sent a special Embassy to Rome, payments for which I find entered on the 21st October and 13th November in *Sixt IV., Lib. Bullet, 1471–73 (State Archives, Rome), where appear also payments on the 11th November, 1471, "pro oratoribus regis Ungarie," and on the 18th November, 1471, "pro nuntio regis Portugallie"

† See his *Letter of the 17th Aug., 1471, from which it appears that the Pope and the Milanese Ambassador had considered this

paternal city chosen as the place of meeting, and his proposal was favourably received, although Cardinal Orsini exerted himself on behalf of Florence.* Piacenza and Pavia were also spoken of† On the 30th of August the matter was discussed in Consistory. Bessarion and others among the older Cardinals sought to deter the Pope from leaving Rome, and to induce him to hold the Congress in the Lateran , others again preferred Mantua or Pisa   No definite decision was yet arrived at ‡ A letter was now received from the Emperor, who asked that Udine might be selected, but the Duke of Milan and other Italian Princes declared against this city.   Sixtus IV accordingly proposed, first Mantua and then Ancona—but all in vain , the Princes neither understood nor sympathised with the aims of the Holy See, and all proposals were wrecked on the rocks of their indifference and private interests.§

Sixtus IV was not as much distressed by this failure as he otherwise might have been, because at this moment a dangerous enemy was threatening Turkey in the rear. The Turcoman Prince, Usunhassan, "with the hope of completely supplanting the Sultan, seemed disposed to make common cause with European Christendom.   At the

plan (Gonzaga Archives) GROTEFEND, I , 217, speaks of the processions ordered by the Pope to avert the danger of Turkish attack

* *Despatch of Nicodemus de Pontremoli, dated Rome, 1471, Aug 20. State Archives, Milan

† *Letter of Nicodemus de Pontremoli, dated Rome, 1471, Aug. 29. State Archives, Milan

‡ *Report of Nicodemus of Aug 31, 1471, and that of the Mantuan Ambassador of Sept 2, 1471   (Gonzaga Archives) Regarding the reasons in favour of Rome, see PLATINA, Sixt. IV , 1056 *seq*

§ PLATINA, *loc cit* ; FRANTZ, Sixtus IV , 142   On the 21st Dec , 1471, the *Mantuan Ambassador, B Bonattus, wrote word that a Congress (dieta) was no longer talked of, but rather the despatch of Legates.

time of Sixtus IV.'s accession the conflict between Mahomet and Usunhassan in Caramania appeared to be tending to a great catastrophe, while the relations between Mocenigo, the Doge of Venice, and Usunhassan were such that they seemed only to need to be drawn a little closer to make the position of the Turks absolutely hopeless." The Turkish question might thus be said to have become a matter of world-wide importance, and accordingly the Pope "inaugurated his action in it with a certain magnificence."*

On the 23rd December a Secret Consistory was held, and five Cardinals were appointed Legates de latere, with the object, as the Consistorial Acts declare, of calling upon the whole Christian world to defend the Catholic Faith against the Turk, the enemy of the name of Jesus. Bessarion was sent to France, Burgundy, and England ; Borgia to Spain, Angelo Capranica to Italy, and Marco Barbo to Germany, Hungary, and Poland, while Oliviero Carafa was to command the naval forces which were to be assembled with the assistance of the King of Naples †

* CARO, V , I, 361-2 ; N. DELLA TUCCIA, 102, mentions the sending of Ambassadors from Great Caramania to Rome

† "*Die lunae xxii[i] decembris, 1471, idem S D N in dicto consistorio secreto creavit quinque legatos de latere cardinales per universas provincias et regna mundi ad requirendum reges, principes et alios christianos ad defensionem fidei Catholicae contra nefandissimum Turcum qui nomini Jesu infensus, etc. —

    Rev dom Nicenum apud regem Franciae, ducem Burgundiae et regem Angliae
      „   „ Vicecancellarium apud regem Yspaniae et alios
      „   „ S^{tae} Crucis apud principes et dominos Italiae
      „   „ S^{ti} Marci apud imperatorem et regem Ungariae et alios
      „   „ Neapolitanum apud regem Ferdinandum et per mare"

Acta Consist, f 44 (Secret Archives of the Vatican) See also **Bessarion's letter of the 23rd Dec, 1471, which I shall cite PALACKY, V., I, 74, and CARO, V, I, 362, mention only four Legates, in this

A few days later the Pope issued a solemn Bull, in which he described the Turkish preparations for the conquest of Christendom, and called on the powers to take common measures of defence.*

The aged Bessarion was certainly the most worthy of all the Legates   Although he feared that the burden would be beyond his strength, yet in the hope of being able, at least, to effect something, he had resolved to accept it †   On the 20th April, 1472, he left Rome, but instead of directly proceeding to France, he remained some time longer in Italy ‡   According to Ammanati, he lingered from dread of undertaking the arduous task ; other accounts attribute his delay to the fact that Louis XI kept him waiting a long time for a letter of safe conduct §   When once he had

following PLATINA, 1057.   The Venetian authorities (SANUDO, 1196 ; MALIPIERO, 70) correctly give five as the number

* RAYNALDUS, ad an 1471, N 72.

† See his **Letter of 23rd Dec., 1471, in the State Archives of Florence

‡ BANDINIUS, LV (MIGNE, CLXI), says that Bessarion left Rome at the beginning of the year.   The *Acta Consist of the Secret Archives of the Vatican record his departure from Rome for France on the 20th April, 1472 , and so does a *Despatch from the Milanese Ambassador of the 20th April, 1472   In Sixti IV., Lib Bullet, 1471–73, a sum is entered as paid for "cursori eunti ad regem Galliae et archiepisc, Lugdunen ," who were to announce Bessarion's appointment as Legate (State Archives, Rome)   On the 21st March, 1472, Sixtus IV had written to Charles of Burgundy regarding Bessarion's mission. BALUZE, IV, 527–31   On the 27th April the Cardinal was at Gubbio (Chronic Eugub, 1021), on the 10th May at Bologna (PIERLING, Le mariage d'un Tsar, 368), and on the 16th May at Piacenza (Annal Placent., 942)   The date of the letter in REUMONT, Lorenzo, I , 420, 2nd ed , must accordingly be wrong

§ VAST, 409   Ammanati's assertions regarding Bessarion's attitude on this occasion (see, especially, Epist , 437 and 534, and also 425 of the Frankfort edition) cannot now be individually verified ;

received it, he travelled as rapidly as his infirm health permitted   On the 15th August he wrote from Saumur to the French King, exhorting him to peace, and, on the same day, he also sent letters to the Dukes of Brittany and Burgundy.*

Shortly before this time an understanding had been arrived at, by direct negotiations with Rome, in regard to the abnormal condition of ecclesiastical affairs in France, but this agreement met with violent opposition in some quarters.   There can be no doubt that the Greek Cardinal touched on these matters in his interviews with the King. He also tried to obtain the release of La Balue, but his efforts proved unsuccessful, as did also those which he made to reconcile the French Monarch with Charles the Bold of Burgundy, and to win him for the Crusade.   Sick and disheartened, he started on his homeward journey   When he reached Ravenna, his illness assumed a dangerous character, fever came on and soon consumed the little strength which yet remained to him, and on the 18th November, 1472, he died.†   His mortal remains were

---

SCHMARSOW, 9, looks upon his authority as open to suspicion   Vespasiano da Bisticci's account (MAI, I., 195) is doubtful, his statement that Bessarion did not give his vote for Francesco della Rovere is in direct contradiction to the documents which we give in Appendix, N. 43

* D'ACHERY, III, 842, new edit, MIGNE, CLXI., 699, VAST, 413 seq, 459 seq   '

† BANDINIUS, LVI ; MALVASIA, 254 ; VAST, 430. By several writers, as, for example, REUMONT, Lorenzo, I, 420, 2nd ed, ROHRBACHER-KNOPFLER, 240, CIPOLLA, 565, CHEVALIER, 301, the 19th November is wrongly given as the day of the Cardinal's death, SCHMARSOW, 13, names the 6th November, ZINKEISEN, II., 400, even places it in the December of 1473   The *Acta Consist of the Secret Archives of the Vatican, amongst other authorities hitherto unknown, adhere to the date we have adopted in the text   So does *GHIRARDACCI, St di Bologna ; see our Vol III, p 243, note †.

borne to Rome, where they arrived on the 3rd December, and were deposited in the Church of the Holy Apostles.* Sixtus IV. was present at the obsequies.

Cardinal Borgia, who had been appointed Legate for the whole of Spain and the neighbouring islands, was not more successful in advancing the cause of the Crusade   On the 15th May, 1472, he went to Ostia, there to embark for his native land †   His task was no easy one, for the Peninsula was at this time in a state of great agitation and disorder. Ammanati speaks most unfavourably of Borgia's proceedings in Spain   He says that he shewed himself everywhere vain, luxurious, ambitious, and greedy   Yet, in a letter which is still extant, this same Ammanati writes to Borgia in the most flattering terms, and praises the way in which he had carried out his Spanish mission.‡   Such a writer has no claim to our credit.   It is, however, extremely probable that Borgia considered a Cardinal Legate as a very important person, and acted accordingly, in fact, treated his countrymen to a considerable amount of Spanish

---

* Acta Consist., *loc. cit.*   Regarding the monument, which was afterwards transferred to another position, and is still preserved, see VAST, 432 and 461–62   REUMONT, III, 1, 532, also gives the Epitaph, he is mistaken in asserting (III, 1, 316) that the Cardinal died in Rome   L MAZIO speaks of Bessarion's palace and of his tomb, Studi Storici, 275–77 (Roma, 1872); and p. 280 of the probable dwelling-place of Platina   See also, in regard to Bessarion's mission to France and d Estouteville's nomination as Legate for that country, S. LJUBIĆ, Dispacci di Luca de Tollentis vescovo di Sebenico e di Lionello Cheregato vescovo di Traù nunzi apostolici in Borgogna e nelle Fiandre, 1472–88, ZAGABRIA, 1876, 24 *seq*, 27 *seq*, 32.

† *Acta Consist (Secret Archives of the Vatican), by which CLEMENT, 118, is to be corrected   In *Sixti IV, Lib Bullet, 1471–1473, on the 12th Febr, 1472, occurs the entry "Roderico vicecan. legato ad regna Hispaniar flor duo millia octuaginta" State Archives, Rome

‡ Ep, 513, Frankfort edition.

pride   A recent historian, by no means prejudiced in Borgia's favour, speaks of the discharge of his diplomatic duties in terms which form a complete contrast to Ammanati's account   "The Legate," he says, " had, as far as lay in his power, fulfilled his mission to Spain.   It was time for him to return to Rome, and render an account to the Pope of the state of things which he had found on his arrival, of that which prevailed during his sojourn in the country, and of the result of his efforts   Matters had certainly improved in Aragon , in Castille the situation depended on factors which were entirely beyond the sphere of a Legate's authority, and which were working themselves out independently of him.   His task was fulfilled when he had done what he could in helping to direct affairs along the only path which could lead to peace and quiet."*

On the 11th September, 1473, Cardinal Borgia made his will, and began his return journey.   Off the coast of Pisa he encountered a fearful storm , one of his galleys sank before his eyes, and the ship in which he himself sailed almost met the same fate   More than 200 of his suite were drowned, and amongst them three Bishops , the loss of property was estimated at 30,000 florins, and was aggravated by the depredations of wreckers on the coast.†

There can be no doubt that the task entrusted to Cardinal Barbo was undoubtedly the most difficult of all, while at the same time the most important, for, with regard to the Turkish war, " nothing was more indispensable than the aid of Hungary, Poland, and Bohemia,—and these were

---

* HOFLER, R Borgia, 37. See also HERGENROTHER, VIII , 199-200.

† See AMMANATI, Ep , 534 , PLATINA, 1060 , PALMERIUS, 256-7 ; ZURITA, XVIII., c. 59   I found in the State Archives at Florence a **Letter of Cardinal Borgia's of the 12th Oct , 1473, in which he gives an account of his misfortune.   Regarding his Will, see THUASNE, III , App , p I -II.

involved in almost hopeless discord."* Barbo's zeal is
evidenced by the fact that he left Rome on the 21st
February, 1472, his instructions directing him to proceed
in the first place to the Emperor.† Until the autumn of
1474, the Cardinal Legate's labours in Germany, Poland,
and Bohemia were unremitting ‡ Even those who judge
him most severely, highly praise his persevering efforts for
the restoration of peace ; success, however, was not granted
him § The internal dissensions of the European nations
had reached such a pitch that it was beyond the power of
any individual to allay them. Frederick III., who, from
the point of view of that day, was the natural leader, was
extremely slow in his decisions, especially in cases where a
pecuniary sacrifice was in question.‖ Unbounded egotism
prevailed among laity and clergy ; their attitude towards
the great danger in the East was one of almost absolute
indifference.¶

* CARO, V , I, 362

† *Acta Consist (Secret Archives of the Vatican) The date
commonly given, 22nd February (PALACKY, V , I, 74 , SCHMARSOW,
11), is to be corrected by reference to this document On the 6th
Febr , 1472, Cardinal Barbo received 2083 florins for his journey.
*Sixti IV, Lib Bullet , 1471–1473. (State Archives, Rome) The
Cardinal's Instructions are to be found in Cod epist , 259 , in TELEKI,
XI., 459 seq ; and THEINER, Mon. Hung , 436 seq

‡ According to the *Acta Consist. (Secret Archives of the Vatican),
Card Barbo returned to Rome from Germany on the 26th Oct., 1474,
and not in November, as SCHMARSOW, 94, states.

§ PALACKY, V., I, 74 seq.; FABISZA, 98 seq. ; CARO, V , I, 365;
ZEISSBERG, 245 seq.

‖ "*Dominus Imperator tardus est admodum in [de]liberationibus
suis et in eis presertim in quibus pecuniam effundere oportet." These
words are taken from a Roman *Instruction of this period, but
unfortunately undated, in Cod S. 1, 1, f 21–24. Angelica Library,
Rome.

¶ Regarding the return of the Cardinal, whose amiability had won

Sixtus IV., however, did not permit the indifference of the great European powers to damp his zeal in regard to the war. During the earlier months of 1472 he was engaged in negotiations for the restoration of peace in Italy,* and particularly in the equipment of galleys Repeated letters were addressed to all the Faithful, urging them to contribute towards these warlike preparations, and at the same time the Pope made repeated efforts to awaken the interest of individual Princes in the cause †

Sixtus IV was all the more dependent on extraneous contributions for the naval preparations on account of the deplorable state in which he found the Papal finances at his accession The general belief that Paul II had left large sums of money had soon proved to be a delusion Treasure and jewels were not wanting, but of actual coin there was not more than 7000, or, according to other accounts, 5000 florins. The Cardinal-Camerlengo put the officials of the Treasury in prison, but nothing could be extracted from them Creditors of previous Popes took the opportunity of coming forward and demanding payment. Sixtus IV. had to sell many of the gems and works of art, handed down by his predecessors, to satisfy them. Some

the affection of the Germans (SCHMARSOW, 25), see AMMANATI, Epist, 595, Frankfort edition

* See the Letter of B Bonattus, dated Rome, 1472, Jan. 4 (Gonzaga Archives), and the **Brief of 5th Jan, 1472, to the Duke of Milan State Archives, Milan

† See RAYNALDUS, ad an. 1472, N 2 and 16 A *Brief to Cologne, dated Rome, 1471, Sept 24 (8 Cal. Oct is to be rendered by this date, and not, as ENNEN, III, 307, has it, by 8th October), mentions the despatch of a special Ambassador to Frederick III, to inform him of the equipment of a fleet for the Crusade by the Pope Or. Pgm, with seal appended, is in the City Archives, Cologne

few of the Cardinals, amongst them d'Estouteville, now presented old claims *

Notwithstanding these difficulties, the arming of the fleet proceeded. The account-books show that in 1471–72 144,000 golden ducats in all were devoted by Sixtus IV. to this object † A treaty was entered into with Venice and Naples, in accordance with which both these States equipped a fleet for the war. The Pope himself furnished twenty-four galleys and 4700 soldiers, who embarked at once on the Adriatic. Four ships came up the Tiber for Cardinal Carafa.‡ On the Feast of Corpus Christi, the 28th May, 1472, he sang a solemn High Mass at St Peter's, in presence of the Pope and the whole Court. Sixtus IV then blessed the banners for the fleet, which were presented to him on his throne by the Ambassadors. In the afternoon, a new and unwonted spectacle was witnessed ; the Pope on horseback, accompanied by all the Cardinals, went in procession from the Vatican to the ships, which lay at anchor in the Tiber below S Paolo. Sixtus " went on board the Legate's galley, and, from a platform at the stern, blessed the ships, the commanders with their followers, and the crews.

---

* PLATINA, 1057 , SCHMARSOW, 8 See the *Letter in the State Archives, Milan, cited *supra*, p. 212, note* On the 19th Sept , 1471, Bessarion received "ex precio jocalium, S R. E ," the amount of his expenses in the time of Paul II , and the cost of his journeys as Legate for Germany and Venice under Pius II. *Sixti IV., lib Bullet., 1471–73 State Archives, Rome.

† GOTTLOB, Cam Apost. Individual cities in the States of the Church, as, *e g*, Jesi, contributed to the cost of the fleet ; see BALDASSINI, Jesi, 175.

‡ GUGLIELMOTTI, 360–65. See CIPOLLA, 566. LANDO FERRETTI, *Storia d'Ancona, says, in agreement with Bernabei : " Delle galee del papa ne furono armate sei in Ancona " Cod H. III.. 70, f. 307 Chigi Library, Rome

He then bestowed a farewell embrace upon his lieutenant, and left him in the ship, himself returning to the Vatican as the sun was declining."*

The Cardinal-Admiral Carafa is described as a man " of resolute character and full of good-will." He went by way of Naples, where he was most honourably received, to Rhodes Having appeased some internal dissensions among the Knights of St. John, he joined the Neapolitan and Venetian ships † The whole fleet now numbered eighty-seven galleys, to which were added two from Rhodes ‡ In a Council of War, it was determined that an attack should, in the first instance, be made on the port of Satalia on the coast of Caramania The southern coast of Asia Minor was selected, on account of the alliance which existed between the Caramanian Princes and Usunhassan, who was also on very friendly terms with the Venetians, and with the Pope Another reason for commencing operations here was the opportunity it afforded for shewing the strength of the Crusaders' fleet to their Asiatic allies § The chains which defended

* SCHMARSOW, 11 To the authorities from which we have drawn our account may be added the *Acta Consist of the Secret Archives of the Vatican, and a *Letter of Arcimboldi's, dated Rome, 1472, May 30. (State Archives, Milan) According to this last Report, the Pope again blessed the galleys on the 30th May, and the next day Carafa sailed for Ostia In *Sixti IV lib Bullet , 1471–73, the following entries occur on the 23rd May, 1472 " Oliv Card Neapolit pro stipendio classis flor. auri de camera viginti quatuor millia unum." On the 9th June " archiepiscopo Pisar pro expedit. galear flor triamillia ducentos octo ," and on the 10th July, 1472, a sum " pro vexillis Sce † revmo card Neapolit " State Archives, Rome

† BOSIO, II , 334.

‡ GUGLIELMOTTI, 371-2 See FINCATI, L'armata Venez , 38, and CHIOCCARELLUS, 289.

§ HEYD, II , 326 From Malipiero, 79, it appears that Ambas-

the harbour of Satalia were burst, and serious injury was inflicted on the Turks by the destruction of its rich warehouses and suburbs, but the city proper, with its strong fortifications, successfully resisted the attack Jealousies between Naples and Venice soon reached such a point that the Neapolitan fleet returned home, yet it was resolved that the war should be carried on. The wealthy city of Smyrna was taken by surprise. Carafa wished to preserve it as an important basis of operations, but the Venetians were of a different opinion, and it was given up to plunder, and then set on fire. This dispute broke up the friendly relations which had existed between the Papal forces and their Venetian allies, and, when winter began, the fleet of the Republic retired to the harbours of Modone and Napoli di Romania, while Carafa returned to Italy On the 23rd January, 1473, he made his entrance into Rome, bringing with him a number of Turkish prisoners on camels The Cardinal hung up portions of the broken harbour-chain of Satalia on the door of St. Peter's; these trophies are now placed over the entrance which leads to the Archives of the Basilica*

Carafa's successor as Legate, Lorenzo Zane, Archbishop of Spalatro, and a Venetian by birth, sailed with ten galleys for the East at the end of April, 1473,† he was

sadors from Usunhassan came to Rome I found in *Sixti IV lib. Bullet, 1471-72, in the State Archives, Rome, an entry made on the 16th Aug, 1471, of payments for "tribus oratoribus Somcassani principis, etc, in alma urbe commorantib"

* GUGLIELMOTTI, 372 *seq*, F JULIEN, Papes et Sultans, 110 *seq*. (Paris, 1879).

† I take the above dates, in regard to which GUGLIELMOTTI (396), the most accurate student of these matters, gives no information, from a *Letter of the Milanese Ambassador, Sacramorus, dated Rome, 1473, April 25 "S Sᵗᵃ questa matina ha benedite et date le bandere al arcivescovo de Spalatro che va legato in Levante cum

not able to do anything, and Usunhassan's defeat at Terdschan (26th July, 1473) gave a decided advantage to the Turks. Moreover, the Venetian Commander, Mocenigo, held aloof from the Papal Legate, fearing that the latter would frustrate his designs on Cyprus *

Hopes had been entertained that the marriage of Princess Zoe, niece of the last Byzantine Emperor, with the Russian Grand Duke, Ivan III, would enlist a new champion for the Crusade, and bring about the reunion of the Russian with the Roman Church. These hopes were doomed to disappointment. On the 25th May, 1472, Sixtus IV. had received the Russian Ambassadors in Secret Consistory, and, on the 1st June, Zoe, who was acknowledged by her contemporaries to be the legitimate heiress to the Byzantine throne, was married by proxy to the Grand Duke What took place on this occasion, in regard to the question of religion, is not clear, but Rome was probably deceived by fair promises. The Pope gave the Princess rich presents and the sum of 6000 ducats, provided for her a suitable escort, and sent letters of recommendation to the different States through which she was to pass on her journey to the North †

The Greek Princess left Rome on the 24th June, 1472 ;

le X gallee che se armano in Anchona, cosa che a jaschuno etiam a li piu cardinali pare mala spesa et denaro gettato, ma per piu rispetti dio perdoni a chi l'ha persuaso" If victorious, Zane·was to receive the red hat   State Archives, Milan

    * GUGLIELMOTTI, 396 *seq*, and SISMONDI, X, 420 See also FINCATI, L'armata Venez, 57, and WEIL, Gesch. der Chalifen, V, 340

    † PIERLING, Le mariage d'un Tsar, 375, says that he has discovered only one of these letters, that addressed to the Duke of Modena. I am able to point out two others . (*a*) to Bologna, dated Rome, 1472, June 22 "Cum dil in Christo filia nob mulier Zoe" State Archives, Bologna ; (*b*) to Nuremberg, dated Rome, 1472, June 30 Kreis-archiv, Nuremberg.

everywhere, both in Italy and in Germany, the Pope's
letters procured for her a brilliant reception   His kindness
was but ill repaid, for, from the moment she set foot on
Russian soil, she shewed herself a schismatic.*   On her
entry into Moscow (12th November), the Papal Legate
who accompanied her was only admitted into the city in
incognito, for it was feared that his public appearance with
his cross would imply an acknowledgment of the Pope's
Supremacy.   The new Grand Duchess completely con-
formed to the Orthodox Church †

Four years later, we again hear of negotiations between
Sixtus IV. and the Russian Grand Duke, who was then
seeking to obtain the Crown.   Poland at the time dreaded
the consequences of their success, and worked against
the Union which it had supported at Kiew.‡   Michael
Drucki, the Metropolitan of that place, had, with the
consent of his clergy, sent an Embassy with a letter to
the Pope, expressly acknowledging his Primacy , and his
successor, Simeon, is said to have been in favour of Union.§

* PIERLING, *loc cit* , 376 *seq* , 379 *seq*

† STRAHL, Beitrage zur Russischen Kirchengeschichte, 89, 190
(Halle 1827, 2nd ed), and Gesch Russlands, II , 335 *seq* , KARAMSIN,
Geschichte des Russ Reiches, VI , 51 *seq* (Riga, 1824).

‡ See THEINER, Mon Pol, II , 230, PICHLER, II , 54-5 , HER-
GENROTHER, VIII , 265, N 7

§ PELESZ, I , 476-7 , HERGENROTHER, VIII , 266.   The letter
of the Kiew Clergy to Sixtus IV. was first published in 1605, and
was for a long time considered apocryphal ; recent and thorough
investigation on the part of Malychewski has established the genuine
character of this important document ; see Rev. d. Quest. Hist., XVII.,
274 (1875).

CHAPTER II.

Rapid Elevation of the Members of the Families of La Rovere and Riario — The Cardinal of San Sisto.

THE admirable energy with which, in the earlier years of his pontificate, Sixtus IV. devoted himself to the defence of Christendom, is, in great measure, clouded by the extravagance with which, from the moment of his accession, he heaped favours upon his numerous, and, in many instances, unworthy relations

Foremost among his kindred appear the sons of his brother Raffaello, Giuliano, Bartolomeo, and Giovanni della Rovere, of whom the first two embraced the ecclesiastical state, while Giovanni remained in the world, and, under Federigo of Montefeltre, studied the art of war.[*] Lionardo, who afterwards became City Prefect,[†] was the son of Bartolomeo della Rovere, another brother of the Pope's.

[*] Further details regarding him will be found, *infra*, p. 270 Bartolomeo della Rovere entered the Franciscan Order at an early age, was made Bishop of Massa Marittima in 1473, and of Ferrara in 1474 or 1475, see UGHELLI, II, 553, and GAMS, 695, also ADINOLFI, Portica, 116. His praises are sung by the author of the *Lucubrac. Tiburtinae, mentioned *supra*, p 205, note,† in Cod 2403, f. 19, of the Court Library, Vienna In the British Museum is a drawing by Melozzo da Forli, representing an old man without a beard, in complete profile, turned towards the right (Photogr Braun, N 61) SCHMARSOW, 391, supposes this to be the likeness of Raffaello della Rovere, the father of Julius II

[†] VILLENEUVE, 38-9

Three sisters of the Pope had respectively married into the families of Riario, Basso, and Giuppo, and from these marriages sprang a number of descendants, "over all of whom the oak spread its branches,* so that the golden fruit fell into their laps." † Bianca della Rovere, the wife of Paolo Riario, had two sons, Pietro and Girolamo, and one daughter, Violante; Violante married Antonio Sansoni and was mother of Cardinal Raffaello Riario Sansoni, well-known in connection with the Pazzi conspiracy. Luchina, the Pope's next sister, had, by her marriage with Giovanni Guglielmo Basso, five sons, Girolamo, Antonio, Francesco, Guglielmo, and Bartolomeo, and a daughter, Mariola Antonio was a man of pure and blameless life; and in 1479 he espoused a relation of the King of Naples ‡ The christian name of the Pope's third sister, who married Pietro Giuppo, is not known; a fourth, Franchetta, is mentioned as married to Bartolomeo Armoino, and dying in 1485 §

A new epoch for his kindred began with the elevation of Francesco della Rovere to the Throne of St Peter As early as the autumn of 1471, we find three of his nephews in the Papal service ‖ In the following spring, two of his

* The arms of Sixtus IV

† SCHMARSOW, 30

‡ VILLENEUVE, 36, 49–50 , SCHMARSOW, 178. As to Antonio Basso, see Civ. Catt., I , 679, 1868, where are given two hitherto unpublished Briefs relating to him.

§ VILLENEUVE, 51–3, partly from Acts in the Vatican Archives.

‖ On the 31st Oct, 1471, among the payments made by the Thesaurarius, is entered · *"mag[cis] dominis Leonardo, Antonio et Jeronimo S. D N[ri] pape nepotibus duc auri 3250 pro eorum presentis anni provisione" Exitus, 487, f 150 (Secret Archives of the Vatican) See *Sixti IV lib Bullet, 1471–73, where, f 20b, on the 30th Sept., 1471, is a payment "pro Leonardo nepoti ad stipendia S R. E nuper conducto," and on the 16th Oct , 1471, others " pro Leonardo, Antonio et Hieronymo nepotibus " State Archives, Rome.

sisters, probably Bianca and Luchina, migrated to Rome, where Sixtus IV had prepared for them a suitable dwelling * The arrival of the other relations was not long delayed.

All the members of the Ligurian colony which assembled around the Pope well understood how to take advantage of the fact that "Sixtus did not know the value of money, and, having grown up from his youth in a mendicant Order, gave with full hands as long as he had anything to give "† These relations, who had mostly been in very needy circumstances and humble positions, in the course of a few years found themselves in the enjoyment of wealth, and of ecclesiastical and temporal dignities such as hitherto they had never dreamed of.

Sixtus IV had not occupied the Papal throne for many months before two of his youthful nephews, Giuliano della Rovere and Pietro Riario, were admitted into the Sacred College. The Pope was deeply indebted to Paolo Riario of Savona, the father of the last-named young man. Leone Cobelli, in his Chronicle of Forli, has recorded some interesting particulars regarding their earlier relations ‡ A certain Franceschino of Savona, he tells us, of the Order of the Minorites, was studying in that town, and was on very friendly terms with Paolo Riario Paolo, a worthy and benevolent man, observing the young monk's love of learning, resolved to receive him into his house, and to

* See the entries of the 23rd of March and 8th April, 1472, in *Sixti IV lib Bullet., 1471-73 (State Archives, Rome) The sisters of Sixtus IV arrived on the 2nd April, 1472 , see the Milanese Ambassador's *Letter of that day in the State Archives at Milan, in which the nephew, Antonio, is spoken of as "homo de bona conditione," and his care of the Pope, who was suffering from the gout, is mentioned.

† SCHMARSOW, 30.

‡ L COBELLI, 257-8

support him   Franceschino accordingly instructed the
sons of his patron, and was enabled by the latter to
complete his own education. This generous assistance
could not have been better bestowed, for the needy student
became one of the best professors in his Order   In the
fulness of his gratitude to Paolo Riario, Franceschino said
to him : " I well know that to you, after God, I owe it that
I have become what I am , I will shew myself grateful , let
me have your son Pietro for my son   I will give him the
best possible education, and make a notable man of him."
Paolo gladly consented ; Francesco clothed his *protégé*
with the Franciscan habit, and shewed him the greatest
kindness *   When a Cardinal, he took Fra Pietro with him
to Rome, where he is said to have played an important part
in the Conclave.†   Almost immediately after his accession,
Sixtus IV. bestowed on Pietro an Abbey on the Franco-
German frontier, with a yearly income of 1000 ducats, and
the Bishopric of Treviso ‡   But he was destined ere long
to mount yet higher.

* According to the *Funeral Oration for Cardinal Riario in Cod 45,
C. 18, of the Corsini Library, Rome, which we shall hereafter cite, his
father died when he was twelve years of age ; Francesco della Rovere
was then lecturing on Holy Scripture in Siena, and made the orphan
come to him   From the same source, we also learn that Fra Pietro
studied at Pavia, Padua, Venice, and Bologna, and subsequently at
Siena and Ferrara. CIACONIUS, III , 43, says that the Oratio in
funere Petri card. S. Sixti habita a Nicolao episc. Modrusien has been
printed   A complete refutation of the fable, invented by political
enemies of Sixtus IV., to the effect that the Riario were his sons, is to
be found in the Civ. Catt , III , 417 *seq* , 1868   REUMONT, in the
Allgem Zeitung, p. 3836, 1877, expresses his astonishment that a man
like Villari (MACHIAVELLI, I , 61) should repeat charges so utterly
unfounded

† See *supra*, p 204.

‡ *Letter of Nicodemus de Pontremoli, dated Rome, 1471, Aug 31.
State Archives, Milan.

In the second week of December, 1471, it was reported that the Pope was about to create new Cardinals , that he purposed to make an alteration in the Election Capitulation, and meant to elevate his two young nephews to the purple * Sooner than had been expected, these anticipations were realised.

On the 16th December, 1471, a Consistory was held, and Pietro Riario, aged twenty-five, and Giuliano della Rovere, aged twenty-eight, were created Cardinals, though not immediately published † To the former was assigned, as his title, on the 22nd December, the Church of S Sisto, while Giuliano received that of S. Pietro in Vincoli, previously held by Sixtus IV. himself‡ On the following day, although not yet published, both of the young Cardinals appeared with the Red Hat, a thing which the Marquess of Mantua's Ambassador mentions as hitherto unheard-of.§

The promotion of these two nephews afforded to those

* "* De far cardinali se fa gran praticha et per quello sento al papa se consentirà de farne dui che siano aut de carne sua aut de natione cum far una aditione al capitulo del conclave de questa reformatione per non stringer el resto, et questi serano il vescovo de Carpentrasse suo ninodo [=nipote] ex fratre et il vescovo di Treviso suo alevo [=allievo]" *Letter of B. Bonattus, dated Rome, 1471, Dec 13. Gonzaga Archives, Mantua

† *Letter of B Bonattus, dated Rome, 1471, Dec 21 (Gonzaga Archives) The day of the creation, which is not here given, is learned from the *Acta Consist, Secret Archives of the Vatican The common statement that the nomination was made on the 15th December is erroneous SCHMARSOW (10) is also wrong in saying that this creation of Cardinals took place in "the same sitting" as that in which the Legates for the Turkish war were nominated, and REUMONT, III., I, 164, in speaking of this Consistory as the first

‡ *Acta Consist , Secret Archives of the Vatican.

§ "*Res inaudita che prima siano comparsi cum il capello che publicati" B Bonattus from Rome, 1471, Dec. 23 Gonzaga Archives

who had not approved of the first acts of Sixtus IV., and
had deemed themselves overlooked, a welcome occasion
for angry and injurious comments. Cardinal Ammanati
speaks of the elevation of two youths, now for the first
time brought out of obscurity, and altogether inexperienced,
as an act of imbecility   " He declaimed against the
nepotism of La Rovere, quite forgetting that his own patron,
Pius II , had been far from blameless in this particular."*

This first creation of Cardinals by Sixtus IV. was
certainly an infringement of the Election Capitulation,
"but the uncertain position of the new Pope, surrounded
as he was on all sides by experienced, influential, and
skilful prelates, who desired to use him as a tool for
their own selfish designs, justifies this step, to which Bessarion lent his approval and aid. Sixtus IV, to ensure
his independence, required the support of trustworthy
coadjutors, whose energies should be absolutely at his
disposal "†

Giuliano della Rovere was certainly the most remarkable
of the two nephews. "Even at an early age he gave
evidence of those qualities which rendered his long and
brilliant career so distinguished alike in the political
history of Italy and in the annals of intellectual culture.
If, like others, he profited by the abuse which had now
become a system, and allowed numerous Bishoprics and
Abbeys to be conferred upon a single individual, with the

---

* SCHMARSOW, 9

† With this opinion of SCHMARSOW, 10, may be compared the
justification of Sixtus IV. in his Brief to Charles of Burgundy
(BALUZE, IV , 528), and the declaration of GREGOROVIUS, VII , 230,
3rd ed , that nepotism " formed for the Pope a governing party, and a
bulwark against the opposition of the Cardinalate " As early as the
summer of 1472, Sixtus IV was completely "master of the situation,"
" potestate, abundat," says AMMANATI, Epist , 454.

sole object of enriching him; if his uncle made him
Archbishop of Avignon and of Bologna, Bishop of Lausanne, Coutances, Viviers, Mende, and finally of Ostia and
Velletri, and Abbot of Nonantola and Grottaferrata,
heaping benefice after benefice upon him, Giuliano manifested in the expenditure of his income, and in his whole
manner of living, a prudence and seriousness which
contrasted favourably with the conduct of many other
prelates. If his moral character was not unblemished, his
outward demeanour was always becoming, and, immediately after his elevation to the purple, he began to devote
that attention to the fine arts, and especially to architecture,
which won for him lasting renown. The serious character
of his other studies, although they were mostly directed to
secular subjects, contributed to develop those exceptional
abilities of which his labours in later life gave such signal
proof, and which had begun to manifest themselves even
during the pontificate of Sixtus IV."*

Giuliano della Rovere was born on the 5th December,
1443, at Albizzola, near Savona, where his parents were
living in very poor circumstances. Having entered the
Franciscan Order, he pursued his studies at Perugia
Sixtus IV, even while a Cardinal, treated him with exceptional favour. "The grave and resolute character of this
nephew justly inspired him with confidence. Like himself,
he had been trained in the strict discipline and privations
of the monastic life, and there had been an almost constant
interchange of thought between them." Giuliano's appearance was striking. Melozzo da Forli's fresco of " Sixtus IV,

* REUMONT, III, 1, 165 See SCHMARSOW, 177 *seq*, 369 *seq*
Regarding Giuliano's connection with Grottaferrata, see ROCCHI, 102
seq About the year 1475 the Abbey of Gorze was bestowed on him,
see LAGER, Gorze, 85, MARTÈNE, II., 1503-4. In reference to the
Bishopric of Lausanne, see Jahrbuch fur Schweiz Gesch, IX, 22 *seq*

surrounded by his Court, appointing Platina Librarian of
the Vatican" represents his tall figure, his face in profile,
looking down upon his uncle with great dark eyes full of
seriousness and dignity.   He wears the purple cape, lined
with ermine   His black hair is surmounted by a bright
coloured skull-cap.   The "round head, with its angular
cheek-bones, and the firmly closed mouth betoken the man
of deeds, who wastes no words, but acts."*

Pietro Riario was a very different character   He was
intelligent and cultivated, courteous, witty, cheerful, and
generous, but his good qualities were counterbalanced by
a lust of power, a boundless ambition and pride, and a love
of luxury, which rendered him utterly unworthy of the
purple   Unfortunately, Sixtus IV fostered these faults by
lavishing rich benefices on him, even more abundantly than
on the Cardinal of S Pietro in Vincoli.   The Archbishopric
of Florence, which had so lately been held by a Saint, the
Patriarchate of Constantinople, the Abbey of S. Ambrogio,
and a number of Bishoprics were soon concentrated in the
hands of this young man †   His yearly revenues before
long exceeded 60,000 golden florins ‡ (=about 96,000
pounds), but even this sum was far from satisfying his requirements, for Riario, "transformed in one night from
a mendicant friar into a Crœsus, plunged into the maddest
excesses "§   The Cardinal, says Platina, set himself to
collect together unheard-of quantities of gold and silver
plate, costly raiment, hangings and carpets, splendid horses,
and a multitude of servants in scarlet and silk.   He
patronised young poets and painters, and delighted in

---

* SCHMARSOW, 44.

† See CIACONIUS, III , 43.

‡ So says CORTESIUS, De cardinalatu, XLIV.   SCHIVENOGLIA, 176,
estimates the income at 50,000 ducats

§ GREGOROVIUS, VII , 231, 3rd ed.

contriving and carrying out pageants and tournaments on the most magnificent scale   He gave extravagant banquets to some of the Ambassadors, and to Leonora, daughter of the King of Naples. He was very generous to scholars, and to the poor. Moreover, he began a palace in the vicinity of the Church of the Holy Apostles, the extensive foundations of which bespoke a colossal superstructure. He seemed to vie with the ancients in pomp and grandeur[*] —and, it may be added, in vices   All morality was openly defied by this upstart. Instead of the habit of St Francis, he went about in garments laden with gold, and adorned his mistress from head to foot with costly pearls [†]

The ostentation of Cardinal Riario, says Ammanati, surpassed anything that our children will be able to credit, or that our fathers can remember [‡]

The Reports of Ambassadors then in Rome shew that Ammanati's expressions were not exaggerated , the Ambassadors of the Duke of Milan seem unable to say enough of the brilliant tournaments and the rich banquets given by the Cardinal, especially during the Carnival.[§]

---

[*] PLATINA, Sixtus IV, 1058   See FULGOSUS, VI , c 10   The *Funeral Discourse in Cod 45, C 18, of the Corsini Library gives, f 119, the number of his household as about 500.

[†] FULGOSUS, X , c. 1 . "Amicam Tiresiam non palam solum, sed tanto etiam sumptu alebat quantus ex eo intelligi potest quod calceis margaritarum tegmento insignibus utebatur temporis meliore parte inter scorta atque exoletos adolescentes consumpta "   See Cr di Viterbo di Giov di Juzzo, 104 ; Annal Placent., 944 , KNEBEL, II , 54 ; and the passage from the *Work of Sigismondo Tizio (Chigi Library) in Arch d. Soc Rom , I , 478.

[‡] AMMANATI, Epist , 548 (Frankfort edition).

[§] *Joh Ferrofinus, in a *Report, dated Rome, 1473, March 4, describes the "giostre ha facto fare in questi di de carnevale il cardinale S Sisto" (State Archives, Milan.) See also INFESSURA, 1144, and Una cena carnevalesca del Card. P. Riario. Lettera

Great astonishment was excited by a feast to which Riario invited four Cardinals, all the Ambassadors, and several prelates on the 1st February, 1473 * The sons of the Despot of the Morea, the City Prefect, and the Pope's nephews, Girolamo and Antonio, also took part in it. The walls of the dining-hall were adorned with precious tapestry, in the middle, on an elevated platform, was a table where the so-called King of Macedonia sat, in splendid robes, and attended by four Counsellors and an interpreter. At the left of this platform was the Cardinal's table, to which those of the guests were joined, there were two sideboards laden with silver, and a multitude of torches made a blaze of light. The feast lasted fully three hours Before every course the seneschal appeared on horse-back to the sound of music, and each time in a fresh costume The banquet was followed by a Moorish dance and other pastimes At its conclusion, came a Turkish Ambassador, bearing credentials, and accompanied by an interpreter, who complained that Cardinal Riario had bestowed on the King of Macedon a kingdom which belonged to the Turks, and threatened that unless he gave up his usurped insignia, war should be declared. The Cardinal and the King replied that they would let the matter be decided by arms Accordingly, on the following day, the combat took place in the square before the Church of the Holy Apostles, and the Turk—being taken captive by Usunhassan the King of Macedon's General—was led through the streets of Rome in fetters †

med a di Lud Genovesi 2 Marzo, 1473 Roma, 1885 (Nozze Vigo—Magenta.)

* I take the description of this feast from a **Report of Johannes Arcimboldus to Galeazzo Maria Sforza, dated Rome, 1473, Febr. 3, which I found in the State Archives, Milan

† This strange representation seems to have been so much admired

Before the year was over, Riario again gave an entertainment on a yet larger scale, surpassing in mad extravagance
anything that the sumptuous age of the Renaissance had
yet produced.   The occasion for this further display was the
passage through Rome of Leonora, the daughter of the King
of Naples, on her way to her husband, Ercole of Ferrara *

On the 5th June, 1473, after a short rest at Marino,
Leonora approached the walls of Rome.   Ercole's brothers,
Sigismondo and Alberto, together with many nobles from
Ferrara and Naples, accompanied her   Cardinals Carafa
and Ausio, and several Prelates, awaited her arrival at
the third milestone from the City, and conducted her to
the Lateran, where she partook of some refreshment, and
venerated the holy relics †   Meanwhile, the Pope's two
favoured nephews, Pietro Riario and Giuliano della Rovere,
had come to bid her welcome, and, escorted by them,
the Princess proceeded to the residence of the Cardinal
of S. Sisto by the Church of the Holy Apostles, where
preparations for her reception had been made in a style
of unprecedented magnificence ‡   " In the square before the

that it was repeated at the beginning of March, 1473   *" Heri," writes
Joh Ferrofinus on the 4th, "se fece uno bellissimo tornamento et
bagordo cum representatione de Ussoncassan da un canto et lo Turco
da l'altro quale tandem fo preso et menato per la briglia per Roma et
poy reducto ad casa de Mᵣᵉ."   State Archives, Milan

* See the Monograph of OLIVI, who, p 27, proves, in opposition to
Gregorovius, that Leonora was the legitimate daughter of Ferrante

† See CORVISIERI, I , 479 seq , and Sacramorus' **Report of the
7th June, 1473, which I found in the State Archives, Milan

‡ On the 5th June, 1473, Sacramorus writes   *" Questa duchessa
de Ferrara intrera hoggi a le xxi hore ; smonta in casa de S Sisto
como V. Ex. è advisata grande apparechio, ymo sumptuosissimo de
tappezarie, ornato e argenti li fa in casa sua."   The Cardinal, the
Ambassador adds, willingly shews his numerous precious possessions
State Archives, Milan

Church, Riario had caused to be erected a splendid house
constructed of wood, rivalling the Palaces of ancient times
It had three halls, with wreathed pillars, surmounted by
a rich frieze, on which the arms of the Pope, the Cardinal,
and the Duke of Ferrara were hung. The open sides of
these halls looked into the court, which, on its fourth
side, was closed by a stage prepared for the theatrical
representations which were to be given.   In the middle
of the court were two fountains, supplied with water from
the roof of the Basilica   The whole open space was
protected by an awning from the rays of the sun   Five
spacious sleeping rooms for the Princess and her ladies
opened into the first hall.   The gentlemen of her suite
were accommodated in fourteen chambers, similarly opening
into that of the opposite wing.   The middle hall, looking
across to the stage, was in front of the Church over
against its portico   Externally, the edifice was painted
to resemble stone; within, the walls, ceilings, and floors
were covered with gold-embroidered carpets and precious
tapestries and stuffs, so that the wood-work nowhere
appeared "*

The banqueting-hall of this palace was kept cool by
means of three bellows, out of sight, and here was to be
seen the marvellous tapestry, representing the creation
of the world, made by order of Pope Nicholas V., and
believed to be unequalled in Christendom   This masterpiece of art was afterwards hopelessly lost.†   The luxury
of the interior was indescribable, silk, damask, and gold
brocade were lavished in reckless profusion ; even the
meanest vessels were made of pure silver and gilt !   However highly we may estimate the extravagance of the age,

* SCHMARSOW, 51. To the authorities here cited may be added
the Reports in CORVISIERI, X , 645 seq
    † See KINKEL in the Allgem Zeitung, 1879, p 3003.

such senseless prodigality must necessarily have given cause for scandal and offence.*

On Whit-sunday, after the Mass at St Peter's, the Princess, attired with dazzling splendour, was received by the Pope, and in the afternoon the History of Susanna † was represented by a Florentine troupe.

On Whit-monday, Riario gave a banquet in her honour, which, in its sumptuous and unreasonable luxury, recalled the heathen days of Imperial Rome ‡ If the silk-clad servants, and the splendid decoration of the hall, the great sideboard, with its twelve épergnes and masses of silver plate, was enough to astonish the guests, the feast itself was even more marvellous. Before its commencement, sweetmeats, oranges encrusted with sugar, and malvoisie were offered to the company, and then rose-water for the hands. The guests took their places at the table to the sound of trumpets and fifes. Only ten persons sat at the principal table with Leonora, eight belonging to her suite, her host and Girolamo Riario The banquet lasted six

* See INFESSURA, 1144, who indignantly exclaims . "Oh guarda in quale cosa bisogna che si adoperi lo tesauro della chiesa." See also AMMANATI, Epist , 548, and the **Report of T Calcagnini of 7th June, 1473 University Library, Padua

† See Leonora's Letter of the 10th June, in CORVISIERI, X , 647 seq , and the **Reports of Sacramorus and T. Calcagnini , as also a Letter from the Ambassador of the Duke of Modena, dated Rome, 1473, June 7 (State Archives, Modena), now published by OLIVI, 26–7

‡ Besides the documents published by CORVISIERI, X , 648 seq , and, in particular, the Princess's Letter of the 10th June, we may here refer to the **Reports of Sacramorus (State Archives, Milan) and T Calcagnini, written on the 7th June, and already cited The latter of these, which I found in the University Library, Padua, is also interesting, as having furnished the foundation of Corio's account its length is such that I am obliged to publish it elsewhere. Of more modern writers, see SCHMARSOW, 52 seq , and MUNTZ, 50 seq.

whole hours , there were three courses, during which forty-
four dishes were served , amongst them were stags roasted
whole and in their skins, goats, hares, calves, herons,
peacocks with their feathers, and finally, a bear with a
staff in his jaws. Most of the dishes were for show, the
bread was gilt, the fish and other viands were brought to
table overlaid with silver. The sweets and confectionery
were countless, and all sorts of artistic shapes   Amongst
other devices, the labours of Hercules were represented the
size of life , and a mountain with a gigantic and apparently
living serpent. Sugar fortresses, with towers and citadels
from which banners waved, were borne in and thrown
amongst the people from the balcony   " Ten great ships
sailed in, made of confectionery and laden with sugared
almonds, which, in allusion to the arms of the Rovere, were
shaped like acorns   Next came the triumph of Venus,
drawn in a chariot by swans," then a mountain from which
a man emerged and expressed his astonished admiration
of the banquet   Allegorical figures also appeared during
the feast, amongst others, a youth who sang verses in Latin,
and announced: " At the command of the Father of the
Gods I am come, and bring you joyful news : Envy us no
longer the festivals of our Heaven, for Jupiter himself is a
guest at your board." *

Towards the end of the entertainment a ballet was
danced on a stage by ancient heroes with their mistresses ;
while it was going on, ten Centaurs suddenly burst in upon
the scene, with little wooden shields and clubs, and were
driven away by Hercules   Bacchus, and also Andromeda,
were represented, and " other things," says a writer belonging
to the Princess's suite, " which I do not remember or did

* See CORVISIERI, X , 649, where a colon should be inserted after
' jubet '

not understand, as I was not a proficient in Humanistic studies."*

Leonora received many costly gifts from Sixtus IV. and the Cardinals ; she remained in Rome until the 10th June.† Other spectacles, of a more Christian character, were provided in her honour, forming a striking contrast to the mythological representations we have described ‡

The splendid reception of the Neapolitan Princess had, in part, a political object , it was intended to make the alliance between the Pope and Ferrante evident to the world This agreement had cost the Pope considerable sacrifices, but it put an end to a ceaseless series of disputes, and, for a time, delivered the Apostolic See from apprehensions which had caused much distress to Paul II.§ A family connection was to confirm the alliance with Naples. In the spring of 1472, on the death of Antonio Colonna, Lionardo della Rovere had become City Prefect.‖ Soon afterwards, he married a natural daughter of Ferrante, and Sora, Arpino, and other territories were bestowed on the newly-married couple Both outwardly and inwardly, Lionardo was so poorly gifted that he was the laughing-stock of the Romans Thus the union was anything but an attractive one In order to bring it about, Sixtus IV. renounced his right of sovereignty over Sora, and Ferrante agreed to invest Rovere with that fief¶

* **Report of T Calcagnini in the University Library, Padua

† OLIVI, 29, is wrong in naming the 9th

‡ CORVISIERI, X , 653 For some account of similar feasts in that age of luxury, see MUNTZ, Renaissance, 225 *seq* , and in REUMONT, Lorenzo, II , 310 *seq* , 2nd ed , the description of B Salutati's banquet on the 16th February, 1476

§ Sixtus IV alludes to this fact in a **Brief of the 30th May, 1472 State Archives, Milan

‖ **Brief of the 17th Febr , 1472   State Archives, Florence

¶ SCHMARSOW, 12

Not satisfied with what he had already obtained, the
Neapolitan Monarch now brought forward the question of
the feudatory tribute, and, in this matter also, Sixtus IV.
shewed himself exceedingly complaisant, remitting the
whole tribute, together with all other debts   The King, in
return, bound himself to send a white horse yearly to Rome,
in recognition of the tenure of his fief, to take part in the
war against the Turks, to defend the coasts of the States of
the Church against pirates, and, if necessary, to support
the Pope, at his own expense, with an armed force[*]
Platina admits that this agreement was disapproved of
by many.[†]   Sixtus IV., in writing to the Duke of Milan,
quotes the advice of the Cardinals and the intention of
Pius II in justification of his renunciation of territory,
adding that the fief had brought the Church more trouble
than gain, and that the Duke himself had advised the
measure [‡]

"After this beginning, a crafty diplomatist like Ferrante
too clearly perceived the advantages promised by the
alliance with the Pope to refrain from making use of it
for his own ends   In the spring it was evident that
nothing would come of the Italian League. The King
soon succeeded in rendering the negotiations with the
agents of the different States, who had come to Rome,
ineffectual, and lost no time in writing to inform the

* See the *Letters of Sixtus IV to Ferrante, dated Rome, 1472,
Febr 28 and March 11, in Cod B 19, f 122b and 125 of the Vallicellana Library, Rome. Also RAYNALDUS, ad an 1471, N. 82, and
1472, N 57-8 ; GOTTLOB, Cam Apost and Mél d'Archéol , 185,
1888.

† PLATINA, Sixtus IV , 1059 , SCHMARSOW, loc cit In a *Letter,
dated Rome, 1472, April 2, Cardinal Gonzaga mentions the remission
of the Neapolitan tribute   Gonzaga Archives.

‡ **Brief of 30th May, 1472   State Archives, Milan.

Milanese of the dissolution of the compact between him and them." *

This disturbance of the relations between Milan and Naples was extremely disagreeable to the Pope, who earnestly endeavoured to prevent a breach between the two powers.† He had reason to hope for success, from the fact that his relations with Milan, which had always been good, had of late been drawn yet closer Platina informs us that, either from jealousy at Rovere's elevation to the post of City Prefect and to the Dukedom of Sora, or else in obedience to the wishes of the Lord of Milan, the Cardinal of S Sisto had exerted himself to promote the betrothal of his brother Girolamo with Sforza's grand-niece, the daughter of Conrad of Cotignola. Girolamo had hitherto been a grocer, or, some say, a public scrivener in Savona. The little town of Bosco was now purchased for him at the price of 14,000 golden florins Riario even went so far as to have Cardinal Giuliano's youthful brother secretly conveyed from Pavia to Rome, because Galeazzo Maria Sforza had cast his eyes upon him, and expressed a wish that this nephew of the Pope's should be connected with his family by marriage. When Giovanni della Rovere so suddenly disappeared from Pavia, Galeazzo changed his plans The Countess of Cotignola made difficulties about the dowry, with the result that this alliance was relinquished, and Girolamo Riario married instead Caterina Sforza, a natural daughter of the Duke, and was made Count of Bosco.‡

* SCHMARSOW, 12.

† **Brief of the 30th May, 1472, *loc cit*

‡ PLATINA, 1059; SCHMARSOW, 12-13   Cardinal P. Riario, in a *Letter, dated Rome, 1472, June 20, thanked the Duke of Milan for having invested his brother with Bosco (State Archives, Milan) *B Bonattus, writing from Rome on June 3, 1472, mentions 16,000 ducats

Meanwhile, all danger of war between Milan and Naples had ceased. On the 22nd June, the Pope had urged the Duke to keep on good terms with the King of Naples, assuring him that in no way could he give him greater pleasure * On the 17th July, he was able to express his satisfaction to Galeazzo in learning that he meant, for the future, to preserve amicable relations with Naples †

Cardinal Riario was now in the fullest enjoyment of the favour of the Pope. He seemed, says a contemporary, able to do whatever he wished. A chronicler speaks of him as being the first among the Cardinals, having the complete control of the Papal treasure, and the Pope himself entirely in his hands ‡ " Not the reserved, brusque Giuliano, but the versatile and agreeable Pietro was the one to conduct all negotiations, and, with undeniable skill, to assist Sixtus IV, who had little experience in diplomacy, in all the more important business of the State." § The influence of the Cardinal of S Sisto had in a very short time become so great that he was feared, not only by the Cardinals, but even by Sixtus IV. himself, to whom nothing but the

as the sum paid for Bosco, and says that the whole business was carried out "molto secreta" (Gonzaga Archives.) Girolamo went in person to Milan ; see in Appendix, N 47, the *Brief of the 22nd June, from the State Archives, Milan Regarding the splendid presents given by Girolamo to his bride, see MAGENTA, II , 351 seq.

* *Brief of the 22nd June, 1472 (State Archives, Milan) See Appendix, N 48.

† *Brief of the 17th July, 1472. State Archives, Milan.

‡ "*Card de S Sisto dicto fratre Pietro da Savona ord min primo cardinale di Roma lo quale havea ne le mane tutto el thesauro de papa Sisto et che gubernava la Sua Sta come voleva et ad minus cavalchava cum trecento cavali et era de estode de anni circa 23 in 24" U. CALEFFINI, Cronica Ferrariae, f. 38 Cod. I -I -4, Chigi Library, Rome.

§ SCHMARSOW, 10–11.

Papal dignity seemed left, while all real power was in the hands of the favourite *

The year 1473 was one of trouble for Sixtus IV. In February he was attacked by an illness,† in consequence of which he spent the hot season on the airy heights of Tivoli.‡ All through the summer he was harassed by political anxieties. In May, tidings came that the Duke of Milan had sold Imola to the Florentines for 100,000 florins, and, at the same time, he heard that the Hungarians had entered into an agreement with the Turks, and meant to attack the Venetians in Dalmatia§ The last of these reports was false, but the first proved correct.

The Pope was greatly, and very reasonably, disturbed by the sale of Imola. Neither he nor Ferrante could "calmly witness" the extension of Florentine domination "into the Romagna, which would introduce relations of a very different order from those maintained with the small existing dynasties. Moreover, the measure was also unwelcome, because it would obviously tend to stimulate the desire of Venice for further annexations."‖ On the 16th of May, a Brief of admonition and complaint was addressed to the Duke of Milan, informing him that the Pope would not, on

* NOTAR GIACOMO, 123 , Cr di Viterbo di Giov di Juzzo, 104. See CORIO, 264

† See in Appendix, N 49, the *Brief of the 24th February, 1473. State Archives, Milan

‡ According to the *Acta Consist. in the Secret Archives of the Vatican, the Pope was absent from Rome from the 19th July to the 13th November. AMMANATI, Epist , 478, 514, 518, condemns this sojourn of Sixtus IV at Tivoli "He forgot," remarks SCHMARSOW, 17, "when he said this, that Pius II. had loved to stay there." Regarding the care of Sixtus IV for Tivoli, see VIOLA, III , 108.

§ *Letter of Ol de Bonafrugis of 26th May, 1473 Gonzaga Archives.

‖ REUMONT, Lorenzo, I , 256, 2nd ed

any account, permit the sale of Imola * This declaration
was repeated in Papal Missives to Florence itself, to the
King of Naples, and to the Bolognese.† A week later,
Sixtus IV again begged the Duke to revoke the sale of
this city, which belonged to the Church. "O my son!" he
writes, in concluding his letter, "listen to your father's
counsel, depart not from the Church, for it is written:
'Whoever separates himself from thee, must perish'"‡
Shortly afterwards, on the 6th June, another Brief was
written to the Duke, who had meanwhile expressed his
willingness to comply with the Pope's desire. The importance attached by Sixtus IV. to the matter is manifested
by the fact that he again wrote with his own hand.§

On this occasion the Pope obtained all that he wished.
Galeazzo Maria Sforza restored Imola to the Holy See for
the sum of 40,000 ducats, and, with the consent of the
Cardinals, Sixtus IV. conferred it as a fief upon Girolamo
Riario ‖

There can be no doubt that these circumstances were
connected with the tour through Italy which Cardinal
Riario undertook, in the middle of the summer of 1473, as
Legate for the whole of that country.¶ The commence-
ment of this journey was far from propitious The
Cardinal's efforts to compose the party strife in Umbria

* See the **Brief of the 16th May, 1473 State Archives, Milan

† See the **Brief of 17th May, 1473, in the State Archives, Bologna.

‡ I also found this interesting **Brief, which is in Sixtus IV's own
handwriting, dated Rome [1473], May 23, in the State Archives,
Milan.

§ **Original in the State Archives, Milan

‖ RATTI, II, 35 *seq* , BURRIEL, III., XXIX *seq*., TONDUZZI,
Faenza, 506 , RIGHI, II , 229

¶ Not late in summer, as SCHMARSOW, 16, says, for, on the 6th
August, 1473, *Cardinal Riario writes "ex Tuderto" (State Archives,
Florence.) Arch. Med Filza, 46, f 263.

were unsuccessful. Spoleto and Perugia refused to obey
his commands. "The Legate indignantly turned to
Gubbio, whither he had summoned the petty princes of
the Flaminian and Pisan territory to meet him ; but
Niccolo Vitelli, who was practically tyrant of Città di
Castello, answered his invitation by saying that he was a
private individual, and a simple burgess of his native city ;
an assembly of Princes in no way concerned him, as he
had never coveted so high a title. Thus the Legate was
mocked, and the competency of his tribunal denied "*
The immediate punishment of the refractory Vitelli being
impossible, Riario proceeded to Florence,† to take possession of his Archiepiscopal See, amid great festivities ‡ On
the 12th September he entered Milan. The Duke received
him with royal honours, conducted him in triumph to the
Cathedral, and then to the Castle, where, as if he had been
the Pope himself, apartments were given him, and the
keys of the Citadel delivered to him each night In the

* PLATINA, Sixt IV, 1060, SCHMARSOW, 16. In regard to the
dispute concerning the marriage ring of the Blessed Virgin, which at
this time occupied the Perugians and then the Pope, see GRAZIANI,
644 , PELLINI, 712 seq , 726 seq , 731 seq , BONAZZI, 686 seq , FANTONI,
Del pronubo anello della Vergine, Perugia, 1673 , CAVALLUCCI, Istoria
del s anello, Perugia, 1783

† He announced his arrival to Lorenzo in the following words ·
*" Prest^me vir ut frater car^mo Proximo [die] lune ad vos venturi sum-
memus iter, quod scientes Tue Prest^ne gratum fore scribere voluimus.
Vale. Augusti xx , 1473, P[etrus] S. Sixti presb. caid , patriarcha
Constant Perusiae etc. legatus." Original in the Arch Med. Filza, 46,
f. 268, State Archives, Florence, where are also a number of *Letters
of Riario's, from which the further course of his journey may be
learned He dates ult Aug Florentiole, IV Sept Bononiae, 18 Octob.
ex sancto Cassano

‡ REUMONT, Lorenzo, I., 255, 2nd ed , where the "eulogistic verses"
of Angelo Poliziano, "with their evil bombast and profane idolatry,"
are mentioned.

negotiations which ensued, the Cardinal succeeded in securing the favour of the Duke for himself   Report, moreover,
spoke of a compact then entered into, by virtue of which
the Pope was to make the Duke of Milan "King of
Lombardy, and give him possession of all the cities and
provinces appertaining to this dignity"   The Duke, in
return, it was said, promised to help Cardinal Riario to
obtain the Tiara   It was even asserted that, on his return
to Rome, the Pope would resign the Chair of St Peter in
favour of his nephew!*

From Milan, Riario proceeded by way of Mantua† and
Padua to Venice, where further festivities awaited him.
By the end of October‡ he was again in Rome.   Soon
afterwards Sixtus IV thanked the Duke of Milan for
his splendid reception of Riario, and confirmed the arrangements entered into by the latter §

Two months more brought the scandalous life and

---

* SCHMARSOW, 16 seq , and BURCKHARDT, I , 101, 2nd ed , are
inclined to give credit to Corio's Report.   See also Arch. St. Lomb ,
III , 449, and VI , 721 seq   I have found nothing concerning this
matter in the Ambassadors' Despatches.

† SCHIVENOGLIA, 175-6.

‡ This appears from a *Brief of Sixtus IV to Bologna, dated Rome,
1473, Oct. 28, in which he says, "as soon as ever Cardinal Riario
returned, he told me of his splendid reception at Bologna ;" the
Pope then expresses his thanks   (State Archives, Bologna, Q 3)
With this accords the following notice in the *Cronica Ferrariae of
the Notary Caleffini . *" 1473 a di 13 de Octobre arivò in Ferrara il
card S Sisto cum circa 300 cavalli nominato frate Pietro da Savona ,
he had been in Lombardy and Venice , the Duke went to meet him,
and shewed him great honour   On the 15th, the Cardinal started
for Rome per la via de la Marcha"   Cod 1 -I -4, Chigi Library,
Rome.

§ See in Appendix, N. 50, the *Brief of 2nd Nov , 1473, from the
State Archives, Milan.   See CORIO, 276, whose manner of expressing
himself lacks exactness and clearness

ambitious projects of the Pope's nephew to an end. In
the third week of December, 1473, Riario was attacked
by a violent fever ; * on the 5th January, 1474, he was
a corpse † Venetian poison was spoken of by some, but
the statement of other contemporaries, who say that the
Cardinal, though only eight and twenty years of age, fell
a victim to his own excesses, is more probable ‡ The

* See the *Report of J P Arrivabene, dated Rome, 1473,
Dec 20, who speaks of "febre continua" and "gran indisposition
del stomacho", only the physicians were admitted to see him
(Gonzaga Archives, Mantua) Riario must soon have recovered ,
see the Despatch of the 30th Dec 1473, in Arch d. Soc Rom , XI ,
264, when a relapse ensued

† *Acta Consist, Secret Archives of the Vatican, and *Letter of the
Mantuan Ambassador, dated Rome, 1474, Jan. 5

‡ A highly-coloured apologetic article, " Il card fra Pietro Riario,"
in the Civ. Catt , III , 705, 1868, questions the testimony of Raph
Volaterranus, because he wrote his "Commentarii ' thirty years after
the death of the Cardinal ; this objection cannot be raised against that
of PALMERIUS, who expressly says, p. 257 . "morbo ex intemperantia
contracto moritur " See also Arrivabene's *Report of the 20th Dec ,
1473, cited above Riario was buried in the Church of the Holy
Apostles, where the well-known beautiful monument was erected in
his memory (see SCHMARSOW, 166 seq) The obsequies took place
on the 18th Jan , according to the *Acta Consist of the Secret
Archives of the Vatican In Cod 45, C 18, of the Corsini Library,
Rome, f 117–23, is the *Oratio in funere revdi d Petri card S Sixti
habita Romae a revdo patre d Nicolao episc Modrusien, a tissue
of flatteries which must be received with the greatest circumspection
The orator may be more easily credited when he praises Riario's
great "liberalitas" ; he then continues . "Extinctus jacet optimarum
artium dedicatissimus amator Interit omnium studiosorum prae-
cipuus fautor, cultor bonorum (!) curiae splendor, ornamentum civitatis
et huius urbis diligentissimus restaurator " The notice, f 119,
"Nullas a ministris impensarum exigebat rationes : nulla computa
exigere volebat," is interesting, as a proof of his neglect of money
matters CIACONIUS, III , 43, says that the "Oratio in funere Petri
card. S. Sixti habita a Nicolao episc Modrusien " has been published

Report of a Milanese Ambassador also informs us that Riario was converted before his end, received the holy Sacraments, and died truly penitent.*

All Rome wept with Sixtus IV over the untimely death of the pomp-loving Cardinal The feeling of the people is expressed by the Senatorial Secretary, Infessura, who says "Our delightful feasts all came to an end, and every one lamented the death of Riario"† In the short period of his cardinalate he had squandered 200,000, or, according to some accounts, 300,000 golden florins, and the debts which he left amounted to 60,000 florins ‡ Justice, however, requires us to add that Riario had also spent some of his wealth on noble objects. "In his love of splendour we trace the taste of the period for that artistic embellishment of existence, without which the temporal rulers of the day, even the wildest and most warlike of them, deemed it impossible to live. During his sojourn at his Palace of the Holy Apostles," continues Melozzo da Forli's biographer, "his love of the fine arts was evidenced by the way in which he attracted to himself, and gathered into his service, all the talent that Rome afforded"§ This account is confirmed by the statement of a Roman scholar, who, after a thorough investigation of the subject, asserts that every poet at

* Letter of Sacramorus, written on the 5th Jan, 1474, in Arch. d Soc Rom., XI , 262-4.

† INFESSURA, 1144 Many cutting satirical verses were also composed on the occasion , see CORIO, 276, and SCHMARSOW, 338 ; of this class is the Epitaphium rev. d Petri card^{lis} Sixti IV. in the rare little volume entitled "Epitaphia claror viror.," Strasburg, 1510

‡ Ci. di Viterbo di Giov di Juzzo, 104, and RAPH VOLATERRANUS, XXII , f 234

§ SCHMARSOW, 50 , see 54, 163, where it is shewn that, after critical investigation, the connection of Melozzo da Forli with Cardinal Riario, although very probable, is not absolutely proved.

that time living in Rome has commemorated the Cardinal as a patron of talent * The funeral discourse pronounced at his obsequies makes mention of the valuable library which he was preparing to establish in his Palace, and also his restorations and embellishments of churches at Treviso, Milan, Pavia, and Rome.†

* CORVISIERI, in Arch d Soc Rom , I , 478 *seq* See also COR-SIGNANI, II., 468, and Civ Catt., III., 696 *seq*., 1868

† In particular, S Gregorio in Rome , with regard to the Church of the Holy Apostles, the funeral discourse only declares that Riario intended to beautify it. Cod 45, C 18, f 121b-122 of the Corsini Library, Rome.

CHAPTER III

CHRISTIAN, KING OF DENMARK AND NORWAY, AND FEDERIGO OF URBINO IN ROME.— DISTURBANCES IN THE STATES OF THE CHURCH —CARDINAL GIULIANO DELLA ROVERE'S EXPEDITION INTO UMBRIA — FEDERIGO BECOMES DUKE OF URBINO, AND GIVES HIS DAUGHTER IN MARRIAGE TO GIOVANNI DELLA ROVERE —THE LEAGUE OF THE 2ND NOVEMBER, 1474.

SIXTUS IV. consoled himself more quickly than had been expected for the death of his beloved nephew.* For a few days he gave himself up to his sorrow, no one, not even the Cardinals, being admitted to his presence , † but on the 10th January, 1474, the Mantuan Ambassador was able to inform the Marchioness that the Pope was beginning to get over

* Even the *Brief of the 6th Jan , 1474, to Ercole of Este has a calm and collected tone · *"Sed quoniam ita fuit Dei voluntas, in cuius potestate omnia posita sunt, ferendum est equo animo iuxta illud Dominus dedit, dominus abstulit, ut domino placuit, sic factum est, sit nomen domini benedictum ·' The Original is in the State Archives, Modena The same quotation occurs in the *Briefs of like import dated Rome, 1474, Jan 6, which informed the Florentines and the Duke of Milan of P Riario's death, and commended Girolamo Riario to them (State Archives, Florence, X –II –25, f 59, and State Archives, Milan, Autogr) It may indeed be a question how far the official letters of the time represented the feelings of the Pope

† "His Holiness," Marquess Giov. Francesco Gonzaga writes from Rome on the 9th Jan , 1471, to Marchioness Barbara, *"sta molto strata et cum dolore et ad niuno se lasse vedere fin qui ne ad cardinali ne ad altri." Gonzaga Archives, Mantua

Riario's loss *   The question as to who would now exercise
the influence wielded by the late Cardinal, whose jealousy
had kept all others in the background, and on whom would
his wealth devolve, was eagerly and generally discussed
Some predicted the elevation of Girolamo Riario, while
others thought it would be Cardinal Orsini, who had now
no opponent †

Riario's possessions, regarding which fabulous stories
were circulated, passed to his brother, Girolamo, who
inherited with them much of his influence.‡   Cardinal
Giuliano della Rovere also became a prominent figure.
The conduct of this nephew of the Pope formed a happy
contrast to that of Pietro Riario.   Giuliano "was not
distinguished by brilliant intellect or fine literary culture,
but he was a man of serious disposition and great prudence,
though frequently rough in his manner and proceedings.
He did not surround himself with an extravagant number
of attendants, and indulged in no needless expense in
apparel or in living, yet his taste was good in his house
and furniture, and he loved excellent workmanship.   On
suitable occasions, he knew how to give free play to the

* "*Benche N S doppo la morte de frate Petro ne in lo giorno de
la epiphania uscisse fuori a la messa ne habia fatto consistorio ne
voluto udire cardinale che ·sia andato a palatio, nondimeno se
intende che de questo caso se ne porta piu constantemente che
la brigata pensava e dice che vol attendere a vivere. Le conte
Hieronymo sento gli fa persuasione assai a questo effecto." *Letter
of J P. Arrivabene, dated Rome, 1474, Jan 10. Gonzaga Archives,
Mantua.

† See J P. Arrivabene's *Letter of the 10th Jan, 1474, cited in
preceding note

‡ See N. Benededei's Report in CAPELLI, 252   *" De qua," to use
the words of J. P Arrivabene in a *Despatch, dated Rome, 1474,
March 5, "lo conte Jeronimo continua in grande favore e reputatione
e fa piu che tuti li altri" Gonzaga Archives, Mantua

largeness of his nature."* Such occasions presented
themselves when princely persons visited his uncle in the
Eternal City, and in 1474 and 1475 they were of frequent
occurrence.

Early in March, 1474, it was rumoured that King
Christian of Denmark and Norway was coming to Rome
Sixtus IV. at once declared his intention of shewing all
possible honour to the Northern Prince, and lodging him
in the palace formerly occupied by Frederick III ;† he
also wrote him a very cordial letter of welcome ‡ If, as
would seem probable from recent investigations, the motive
of the King's journey was principally religious, the joy
of the Pope and the attentions paid to his guest can
easily be understood § Moreover, Sixtus IV. hoped for

* SCHMARSOW, 18, where is also a good remark regarding the
authority of Jacobus Volaterranus. He also justly observes (see p 10)
that the description of Giuliano's first years as a Cardinal given by
BROSCH (5 seq.) needs many corrections

† *Letter of Card Gonzaga, dated Rome, 1474, March 3   Gonzaga
Archives

‡ RAYNALDUS, ad an 1474, N. 1   The date is not given by Ray-
naldus, and is also wanting in the MS B –19, f 220, of the Vallicellana
Library, Rome   Regarding the pilgrimage of Christian I to Rome
(which MANNI, 79, wrongly assigns to the year 1475), see, besides
CANCELLIERI, Notizie della venuta in Roma di Canuto II., e di
Christiano I, re di Danimarca negli anni 1027, e 1474, etc. (Roma,
1820), LOHER in the Hist. Taschenbuch, 1869, p 266 seq, and
HOFMANN, Barbara, 23, especially the Danish Monograph of F.
KROGH, published in Copenhagen in 1872   In this work the documents in the State Archives, Milan, are used but partially, and without
accurate references   Krogh is not acquainted with the *Letters from
the Gonzaga Archives, Mantua, which we shall cite.

§ KROGH, 7. In Germany, certainly, every one spoke only of the
political objects of this journey, and cities and Bishops heard of it
with anxiety. LOHER, loc cit, 267   There is no doubt that various
diplomatic negotiations were connected with Christian's pilgrimage.

the assistance of Christian I in the war against the Turks,
he was aware that the King believed in a prophecy which
had declared that a Northern Ruler was destined to
conquer and expel the Infidel.

The King, a grave man, with a long gray beard, came
with 150 followers; all were soberly clad, and pilgrims'
staves were embroidered on the housings of their horses *
On the 6th of April the travellers entered Rome   Christian I. was overwhelmed with tokens of honour; the whole
Court went to meet him and conducted him to St. Peter's.
Here Sixtus IV. would have embraced him at once, but
the King knelt down with all his followers, and begged
for the Papal blessing.   When he rose from his knees,
the Pope embraced him and conducted him to his Palace.
Cardinals Gonzaga and Giuliano della Rovere provided
for the hospitable entertainment of the visitors †

During the whole time of his sojourn in Rome, Christian I. paid such honour and attention to the Pope and
the clergy, that he was often cited as an example to the
Italians of the manner in which they ought to bear themselves towards the Church and her servants ‡   The Pope
gave the royal pilgrim a portion of the true Cross and
other relics, a portable altar,§ a splendid mule with a
bridle studded with gold, a valuable ring, and other

* See SCHIVENOGLIA, 177-8   The Italians wondered at the fair
hair and complexions of the Northerns, see N. DELLA TUCCIA, 111,
*Ghirardacci, Hist di Bologna, writes "Era questo re tutto vestito
di negro con una beretta rossa e portava nel petto un segno come
portono li pelegrini che vanno a S Jacomo di Galezia" Cod. 768,
University Library, Bologna

† KROGH, 46; SCHMARSOW, 18

‡ S AMMANATI, Epist, 556, of the Frankfort edition   The date,
April 4, also given in the Milan edition, f 276b, must be wrong,
perhaps it ought to be IV Idus April = 10th April

§ Now in the Museum at Copenhagen.

precious things. On Maundy Thursday, after Holy Mass, Sixtus IV bestowed his blessing on the King, and granted him an Indulgence. On Easter Sunday Christian received Holy Communion from the hands of the Pope, and the Golden Rose. He also received costly gifts from the Cardinals, and, in return, presented them with beautiful furs, and other choice products of his kingdom *

King Christian remained in Rome for three weeks, Sixtus IV. shewing him honour in every possible way.† The conversations between the Pope and the King dealt with the question of the Crusade, the affairs of the Northern Kingdom, and perhaps other political projects, such as the possibility of changing the Ducal Crown of Sforza into a Royal one ‡ As the Papal Bull for the foundation of the University of Copenhagen is dated 12th June, 1475, the erection of such an institution in the North must also, at this time, have come under discussion § The Pope shewed great readiness in meeting the wishes of his royal guest with regard to several other Bulls, and Christian was so much delighted with his sojourn in Rome that he had a medal struck to commemorate it ∥

* KROGH, 52-3   See Lubeckische Chroniken, published by GRAUTOFF, II., 358, where, in some cases, dates different from those of Krogh are given ; the latter, however, being supported by the Letters of the Milanese Ambassadors, deserves the preference.

† See the *Report of J P Arrivabene, dated Rome, 1474, April 19 Gonzaga Archives

‡ LOHER, loc cit, 267 seq , KROGH, 47

§ The University at Copenhagen was opened on the 1st June, 1479, the High School at Upsala having been inaugurated on the 22nd Sept, 1477 , see KROGH, 54, and C ANNERSTEDT, Upsala universitets historia. Forsta delen (Upsala, 1877)

∥ The only example of this Medal, possessed by the Royal Collection in Copenhagen, was lost in 1805 , KROGH, 55   How far Sixtus IV consented to the extension of Royal rights over the Danish Clergy, which, by the advice of Albrecht of Brandenburg, Christian

After again devoutly visiting the seven principal Churches,* Christian I started on the 27th April on his homeward journey.† The Milanese Ambassador informs us that all the Cardinals conducted him, with every token of respect, to the gate of the City Two members of the Sacred College accompanied him on his way, as far as the frontier of the Papal territory According to the same Ambassador, Christian was the bearer of important letters from the Pope to the Emperor, Frederick III , a fact which proves that the opportunity afforded by this pilgrimage for discussing political affairs had not been neglected ‡

Soon after the departure of Christian, Count Federigo of Urbino, a former friend of the Pope, arrived in Rome.§ On this occasion also, Cardinal Giuliano was splendid in his hospitality , " he had given up his residence in S Pietro in Vincoli to the City Prefect, and had moved to Bessarion's Palace, near the Church of the Holy Apostles "‖ On the 28th May, the Count was solemnly received by the Pope ; Sixtus IV. had "assigned him a place in the Chapel on the benches of the Sacred College, so that he sat immediately below the last Cardinal, an honour hitherto reserved for the eldest sons of Kings " Although d'Estouteville and Gonzaga were extremely annoyed at this arrangement, the Pope adhered to it.¶ His motive

sought to obtain, I am unable to say (See Archiv fur Œsterr Gesch , VII , 98–9)

* This is expressly stated by J P Arrivabene in a *Letter, dated Rome, 1474, April 24. Gonzaga Archives, Mantua.

† *Report of Sacramorus, dated Rome, 1474, April 28 State Archives, Milan, " Roma "

‡ See KROGH, 55.

§ BALDI, III , 208 , REPOSATI, I , 42

‖ SCHMARSOW, 18–19

¶ JACOBUS VOLATERRANUS, Diarium, 95. See two *Reports of J P Arrivabene, dated Rome, 1474, May 28 Gonzaga Archives, Mantua.

was soon evident. A marriage was in contemplation between a daughter of Federigo and Giuliano's younger brother, Giovanni della Rovere, who was to be given Sinigaglia and Mondavio. Even before it had been discussed in Consistory the Pope had impressed upon the Count the impossibility of obtaining the consent of the Cardinals to the project * Jacobus Volaterranus informs us that it was looked upon in the Sacred College as a dangerous example of nepotism. Federigo was obliged to depart without effecting his purpose †

During the Count's sojourn in Rome, and at the very time when the Pope was occupied in taking precautions against an impending dearth, tidings reached him of the murder of Gabriello Catalani, the Guelph Lord of Todi, and of the outbreak in that city of an insurrection which seemed likely to spread ‡ All the discontented from Umbria, and especially from Spoleto, with their partisans, flocked into Todi, and were headed by Giordano Orsini and the Counts of Pitigliano § Soon the whole of the province was in commotion. Rioting, murder, and incendiarism were the order of the day If the whole place was not to be given over to absolute anarchy, "it was necessary to act at once with a strong hand "‖

At the beginning of June, Sixtus IV. sent Cardinal Giuliano to restore peace in Todi by force of arms ¶ The

* *Letter of Cardinal Gonzaga to his father, dated Rome, 1474, May 27 Gonzaga Archives, Mantua.

† See *Cardinal Gonzaga's Letters, dated Rome, 1474, June 2 and 4, *loc cit*

‡ PLATINA, Sixtus IV, 1061.

§ The people of Spoleto had already, at the beginning of the year, given trouble to those of Ceretano. See the *Brief of 3rd Febr, 1474. State Archives, Florence.

‖ Opinion of SCHMARSOW, 20.

¶ See the **Letter of Cardinal Giuliano della Rovere to Lorenzo

task was one of great difficulty, but in selecting Giuliano the Pope had chosen a man well fitted to carry it out.* " Accustomed to privations, and to the stern discipline of the cloister, the Cardinal did not shrink from the hardships of a soldier's life. With the assistance of the valiant Giulio of Camerino, he forced his way into Todi. Giordano Orsini and the Count of Pitigliano withdrew, some of the insurgents were cast into prison and others banished, and all communication between the country people and the city was cut off " †

Cardinal Giuliano then turned his arms against Spoleto, which, at the time, was in the hands of the party of the Orsini. At 3000 paces from the city he halted, and, through Lorenzo Zane, Patriarch of Antioch, called upon the inhabitants to lay down their arms. Thereupon many of the citizens fled, carrying their most valuable possessions to the mountain fortresses in the neighbourhood ; the rest accepted the Ambassador's offers of peace, went to meet

de' Medici, dated Rome, 1474, June 1 (State Archives, Florence), and Sixtus IV.'s Brief to Perugia of the same day. Arch St Ital , XVI., 588 The day of Giuliano's departure from Rome is not mentioned in the *Acta Consist of the Secret Archives of the Vatican, which, for this period, are very fragmentary and incomplete. The Pope, at the same time, appealed to the friendly powers for their support , see the *Brief of the 1st June, 1474, in Appendix, N 51 (State Archives, Milan) The Cardinal's Mission to Todi was announced to the people of Spoleto by a Brief of the 3rd June, 1474 ; see SANSI, Saggio di Doc , 43-5.

* Even in 1472 Sixtus IV had endeavoured to appease disturbances which had broken out in Todi. Two *Briefs to Perugia, one dated 1472, April 16, and the other s die, are excerpted in Cod C IV 1, University Library, Genoa

† PLATINA, 1061 , FRANTZ, 153 , SCHMARSOW, 20 See also Sixtus IV's *Brief to Florence of the 20th June (State Archives, Florence, X -II -25, f 62b-63), and that to Ercole d'Este of the 14th July, 1474 State Archives, Modena

the Legate, and begged for pardon   Giuliano garrisoned
the gates of the city, and had already begun to endeavour
to reconcile the contending parties, when, in defiance of
his express command, the greedy mercenaries began to
plunder. Most of these men were from Camerino and
Ceretano, and were bent on retaliating on the people of
Spoleto the depredations which they had suffered at their
hands   The Legate's voice was powerless to restrain the
lawless troops , indeed, his own life was at one moment in
danger. He could only be thankful that he was able to
save the Episcopal Palace and the Convents, and to
preserve the women and maidens from outrage. "Such,"
observes Platina, "was the fate of the Spoletans, who had
despised the Pope's commands, and had filled their city
with the spoils of their neighbours "*

At the end of June, the Cardinal proceeded to the upper
valley of the Tiber, where Niccolo Vitelli, the tyrant
of Città di Castello, replied to all remonstrances from
Rome with words of open scorn. He was charged with
having lent assistance to the insurgents in Todi and
Spoleto : the time had come when he must be compelled
to submit. His contumacy seemed all the more dangerous,
because it found favour with his neighbours. "Whenever
any political dispute should break out with Rome, the
forcible alienation of the important district on the borders
of Tuscany was to be apprehended. The adjacent stronghold of Borgo San Sepolcro was still in the hands of the
Florentines, to whom it had been mortgaged by Eugenius
IV. The Pope was bound to put an end to this state of

---

* PLATINA, 1061–2. See SCHMARSOW, 20 , FRANTZ, 154 *seq* ;
CAMPELLO, lib XXXVII ; PELLINI, 740 ; SANSI, Saggio di Doc., 43-4,
and Storia, 68 *seq*. In the *Briefs of June 20 and July 14, 1474, already
mentioned, Sixtus IV speaks of Giuliano s resistance to the plunder
of Spoleto

things." Not till all peaceable means had been exhausted did he proceed to force.* And even to the last he declared that, if Vitelli would submit, he would again receive him into favour, for he only sought obedience, not vengance †

Vitelli, meanwhile, had no idea of submission ; he rejected the easy conditions offered by Cardinal Giuliano, who was accordingly compelled to lay siege to Città di Castello. Sorties were made every day, and the Papal troops repeatedly suffered serious losses But a far greater danger threatened them in the consequences of an alliance which Vitelli had succeeded in negotiating with Milan and Florence The Florentines, forgetful of benefits received from the Pope, even as recently as during the war of Volterra, had furnished the tyrant with money, and then, in spite of the absolute promise of Sixtus IV.‡ that their territory should remain inviolate, had sent 6000 men to Borgo San Sepolcro near Città di Castello, ostensibly for the protection of their frontier, but in reality with the object of assisting Vitelli whenever the situation should become critical.§ Sixtus IV justly complained of the shameful manner in which help was thus given to "a

* SCHMARSOW, 21, where details are given in regard to Vitelli's defiant bearing towards Paul II and Ammanati ; the latter pleaded in favour of Vitelli, and thereby incurred the displeasure of Sixtus IV See also REUMONT, Lorenzo, I , 257, 2nd ed.

† See in Appendix, N. 52, the *Brief of the 25th June, 1474 State Archives, Milan.

‡ "*Promittimus enim vobis in verbo pontificis neque nos neque legatum nostrum neque ullas copias que illuc profecte sunt aut proficiscentur minimam offensiunculam terris aut agris vestris illaturas," are the words of the *Brief to Florence of the 28th June, 1474 State Archives, Florence, X -II.-25, f 63b-64

§ FRANTZ, 155, SCHMARSOW, 22 See the opinion of REUMONT, Lorenzo, I , 257, 2nd ed

rebellious subject, whom no kindness had been able to win to obedience."*

During the siege of Città di Castello the attitude of Galeazzo Maria Sforza was very unsatisfactory. On the 5th June the Pope felt constrained to express his astonishment at the manner in which the Duke had written to him on this occasion, and to defend the justice of his action. The Pope said, "We ask nothing from Vitelli but obedience, if he will submit, and live as a private individual, We will be gracious to him, but no Prince can tolerate open rebellion. The excuse of the Florentines that they feared an attack on Borgo San Sepolcro, was hypocritical, for, on the 28th June, We had already pledged our word on this matter" †

In the middle of July, Milan and Florence began diplomatic action in favour of Vitelli, meanwhile, the Pope refused to accede to the request that he would withdraw his troops from Città di Castello, giving a full account of the motives which influenced his decision ‡ It is worthy of note that the King of Naples, who had received many benefits from Sixtus IV, also interfered on behalf of the rebels. Anarchy in the States of the Church was more in accordance with his wishes than peace and

* See *Brief to Ercole d'Este, dated Rome, 1474, July 14 State Archives, Modena.

† See the *Brief of 5th July, 1474, in Appendix, N. 53 (State Archives, Milan) On the same day Sixtus IV again wrote to Florence *" Monemus et hortamur vos pro mutua benevolentia, pro iustitia ipsa et honestate, desinite ab inceptis favoribus quos Nicolao prestatis ne indignationem Dei contra vos provocetis " State Archives, Florence, X.-II –25, f. 64b-65b.

‡ This appears from the *Brief to Naples, Milan, and Florence, dated Rome, 1474, July 18 (Copy in the State Archives, Milan and Bologna, Q 22), in which the Pope refuses the above-mentioned request.

order The ingratitude of the Duke of Milan seems to have been particularly distressing to the Pope, who, on the 28th July, 1474, sent him an autograph letter, reproaching him in touching language *

In this serious state of affairs Sixtus IV. turned to the warlike Count Federigo of Urbino In order to make yet more sure of his fidelity, he bestowed on him, on the 21st August, the Ducal dignity with the same pomp and ceremonies observed in the case of Borso of Este three years before † Two days after this, Federigo arrived at the Papal camp before Città di Castello. ‡ On the appearance of this General, "who was reputed to be invincible," Vitelli expressed a willingness to negotiate. His bearing, however, was still anything but submissive. He knew that he had powerful friends to fall back upon, and he was also aware that Federigo had no intention of strengthening the Papal authority on his own borders. The daring rebel was able so to manage the negotiations, that the capitulation was not a submission, but an honourable treaty. § It was decided that the Cardinal, with 200 soldiers, should be admitted into the city. The personal safety of the tyrant was guaranteed, Lorenzo Zane, Patriarch of Antioch, was to remain with a garrison in

* In Appendix, N. 54, I give this *Letter, which I found in the State Archives, Milan.

† Particulars are given in the Letter of J. P. Arrivabene of the 21st August, 1474, amongst AMMANATI, Epist , N. 568, of the Frankfort edition See PLATINA, Sixtus IV., 1062, and a *Letter of Card. Gonzaga, dated Rome, 1474, Aug. 21. (Gonzaga Archives, Mantua) REPOSATI, I , 250, wrongly gives the 23rd March, and REUMONT, Lorenzo, I , 259, 2nd ed , the 23rd August as the day when the Ducal dignity was conferred

‡ This we learn from a *Letter written by J P Arrivabene, and dated Rome, 1474, Aug 26 Gonzaga Archives

§ L'ÉPINOIS, 441 , SCHMARSOW, 23

the castle until the return of the exiles and the completion
of a fort, for the erection of which, Giuliano had given
orders.   The army then withdrew, and the Cardinal,
accompanied by Duke Federigo who brought Vitelli with
him, started for Rome.*

The tidings of the fall of Città di Castello were received
with great rejoicings in Rome; trumpets announced the
event from S Angelo, and more noise could not have been
made about the taking of a Spartacus or a Sertorius, yet,
adds Cardinal Gonzaga's Secretary, "I do not believe in a
real submission, for there are crafty people who know how
to mingle fire and water without disturbing any one"†

The capitulation was, indeed, calculated rather to encourage than to subdue Vitelli.   It was in harmony with
the whole course of this affair, which clearly shewed the
character of the confederates with whom Sixtus IV had
to deal.   "Surrounded by treachery, with such an ally as
the crafty Ferrante of Naples at his side, and with neighbours like Lorenzo de' Medici, can the Pope be blamed for
establishing his nephews firmly in the States of the Church,
where a Cesare Borgia and a Pope like Julius II. were needed
to purge it from its oppressors great and small?"‡

* SCHMARSOW, 23, who (p 21, note 3) draws attention to the fact that
Roberto Orsi's (De obsidione Tifernatum, Citta di Castello, 1538, and
in TARTINIUS, II, 671 seq —an Italian translation by E Manucci
appeared in 1866 at Perugia) account is that of a partisan of Vitelli's
See also UGOLINI, I, 507   In a Brief, dated Rome, 1474, Sept 2,
Sixtus IV. informs the Duke of Milan "deditionem civitatis nostre
Castelli." The original is in the State Archives, Milan, and it was
printed by MARTÈNE, II., 1468

† Letter of J P. Arrivabene of the 3rd Sept., 1474, in AMMANATI,
Epist, 574, Frankfort edition. See ibid, N 575, and a *Letter of
Cardinal Gonzaga to his father, dated Rome, 1474, Sept. 5   Gonzaga
Archives

‡ FRANTZ, 156-7

Platina informs us that the Legate, on his journey back
to Rome, was met by Envoys from many cities, who
congratulated him and brought him valuable presents
These the Cardinal either declined, not from pride, but as
unbefitting a servant of the Church, or else devoted to pious
objects, like the restoration of Churches and Convents *
" On the 9th of September, early in the morning, Giuliano
with the Duke reached the Porta Flaminia   All the
Cardinals had been commanded by the Pope to go and
meet him, but the hardy Ligurian was too early for them
Before the sun had risen he was in the Church of Sta Maria
del Popolo.   Thence he was conducted to his Palace with
great pomp   The Duke, the City Prefect, and Count
Girolamo rode in front, preceded by Vitelli amid some
nobles "   A Consistory was then held, and the vanquished
rebel did homage †   The Pope was prevented by indisposition from taking part in these proceedings ‡

During the Duke of Urbino's sojourn in Rome on this
occasion he received honours even greater than those
bestowed upon him in the spring   The rooms provided
for him were immediately above those of the Pope §   This
time the negotiations regarding the marriage were brought

* PLATINA, Sixtus IV, 1063   See SIGISMONDO DE' CONTI, I , 9

† Letter of J P. Arrivabene of the 9th Sept , 1474, in AMMANATI,
Epist , 578, Frankfort ed ; SCHMARSOW, 23

‡ On the 9th September, Arrivabene was full of conjectures as to
the Pope's malady, but on the 10th he was able to write · *" Lo mal
del papa per quanto se habia è piccol cosa ; ha havuto doi legieretti
parosismi de terzanetta, de la qual se munda e non ne fanno caso se
non per essere papa, e lo secundo de heri doppo'l disnare non fu piu
che tre hore." On the 16th of September, the same Ambassador
says *" La cosa è tardata per questa puocha febre del papa che fu
solamente doi parosismi, hora sta bene " Gonzaga Archives, Mantua.

§ *Letter of Card. Gonzaga, dated Rome, 1474, Nov. 2   Gonzaga
Archives.

to a satisfactory conclusion   On the 10th of October Sixtus
IV informed the Duke of Milan that "to-day the betrothal
of our nephew, Giovanni della Rovere, with the Duke of
Urbino's daughter, has been announced"*   Two days
later, the Vicariates of Sinigaglia and Mondavio, which,
after the death of Pius II., had revolted against Antonio
Piccolomini, Duke of Amalfi, were conferred upon Giovanni †   The document appointing him Vicar was signed
by all the Cardinals, including those who before had voted
against the measure, with the exception of Cardinal Piccolomini.   The yearly salary was fixed at 600 ducats.‡

In attaching to himself, by benefits and by bonds of
relationship, the warlike Federigo of Urbino, who might
have been a dangerous enemy, Sixtus IV. had achieved an
important political success   Indeed, the Pope had much
reason to congratulate himself on all that he had gained
during the summer of 1474.   The attempt "to keep his
hands full at home, by making troubles in the States of
the Church, had not succeeded for any time, and its authors
had been exposed.   The intrigues of Lorenzo de' Medici
were laid bare   He had most unwarrantably interfered in
a private affair of the Pope's.   Even Cardinal Ammanati,
who certainly was no partisan of the Rovere family,
thought it necessary to remonstrate with him.   Not content
with supporting the insurgents, he had, under cover of the
confederation, sent letters and messengers about to excite

* See Appendix, N 55.   State Archives, Milan
† SIENA, L , St. di Sinigaglia, 154.
‡ *Report of J P. Arrivabene, dated Rome, 1474, Oct 12   (Gonzaga Archives) SCHMARSOW, 343–4, gives extracts from Cod. Urb ,
1023, concerning the architectural works undertaken by Giovanni
della Rovere in Sinigaglia   *La vita e gesti della buona mem. sig. Johan
Prefetto auct Fra Garzia de Francia.   A good description is also here
given of Giovanni's person.

disturbances throughout the whole of Italy, with the view of compelling the Pope to desist from the chastisement of the rebels "*   His efforts had failed, and Lorenzo de' Medici saw that his hopes of assistance from Milan and Naples were vain †   He at once looked about him for new allies, and turned to Venice   The rulers of the Republic, however, felt that the league against the Turks bound them to Naples, and yet more to the Pope, who had sent money and provisions when Scutari was besieged ‡   The Signoria, Navagiero informs us, answered Lorenzo's overtures by declaring that they had already concluded a league with Naples, and with the Pope, and that he was free to join it.   The matter was to be dealt with in Rome, where Ambassadors from all parts would soon meet.   The hopes of the Pope, that his wish for a general alliance among the Italian powers might yet be fulfilled, began to revive. The failure of this scheme, so necessary in view of the warlike preparations of the Turks, was in no way his fault.§

The progress of the negotiations seemed at first to justify the brightest expectations   An agreement, which satisfied all parties, was framed.   But at the last moment, when the treaty was about to be signed, Ferrante, according to the testimony of a Venetian chronicler, instructed

* SCHMARSOW, 24.   SIGISMONDO DE' CONTI, I , 9, writes of Lorenzo "Nam praeterquam quod Nicolao pecunias et vires subministrabat, omnem Italiam literis nuncusque sub specie foederis sollicitavit ad opem illi ferendam, ut pontifex ab incepto turpiter desistere cogeretur "

† PLATINA, Sixtus IV , 1063

‡ SCHMARSOW, loc cit

§ An anonymous *Letter, ex Constant , III Julii, 1474, says · *" Imprimis in Constantinopoli publice divulgabatur che in el anno futoro il Turcho intende de uscire cum una potente armata in el golfo de Vinexia " (State Archives, Milan   Milit. Guerre, Turchia)   See also Mon Hung , II , 263

his Ambassadors to break off the negotiations * On the
2nd November, 1474, Florence, Venice, and Milan concluded a defensive alliance for twenty-five years † The
Duke of Ferraia, the Pope, and the King of Naples were
invited to join this league. The Duke alone consented
to do so.‡ Sixtus IV gave a decided refusal, accompanying it with a full explanation of the reasons which
induced it. He looked upon the league "as a coalition
against the Holy See, an attempt to isolate him and to
reduce him to the position of a mere tool for carrying out
the egotistical policy of the Tyrants"§ Such was the
condition of Italy immediately preceding the Holy Year
proclaimed by Paul II.

* Navagiero (in MURATORI, XXIII.), 1144

† *Renovatio et instauratio pacis et ligae inter Venetos, ducem
Mediolani et Florentinos cum infrascriptis capitulis In nomine s. et
ind trinitatis, etc. Aᵒ 1474 die II. mensis Novemb. Compertum est
pacem ut rerum optimam mortalibus a nostro redemptore imperatam,
ita maxime necessariam non posse in Italia esse diuturnam sola
cessatione bellorum, etc. Cod. B 19, f 156, Vallicell Library, Rome
RAYNALDUS, ad an. 1474, N 15, used this copy ; I saw another in
the State Archives, Bologna, lib Q 22. See also concerning the
proclamation of the League, SISMONDI, XI , 33 , ROMANIN, IV, 373 ,
REUMONT, Lorenzo, I., 261, 2nd ed ; TRINCHERA, I , p LX ; VIGNA,
II , 2, 473

‡ According to Califfini, *Cronica Ferrariae, Ercole joined the
League on the 14th February, 1475 Cod. I -I.-4, f. 51, Chigi Library,
Rome.

§ FRANTZ, 150. See CHMEL, Mon. Habsb , III , 471, and RAUSCH,
147.

CHAPTER IV.

The Jubilee Year, 1475 —Commencement of Works for the Embellishment of Rome —King Ferrante visits Sixtus IV.—The Fall of Caffa and the War with the Turks.

As early as the 26th March, 1472, Sixtus IV had confirmed his predecessor's decision that every twenty-fifth year should be a year of Jubilee, a further Bull of the 29th August, 1473, abrogated all other Indulgences and Faculties during the Jubilee Year.* In Rome itself the Pope at once began various works of embellishment in preparation for the approaching solemnity. "From the autumn of 1474," writes Platina, "Sixtus IV. devoted himself to the beautifying of Rome. The bridge, which, from its ruinous state, had long been called by the Romans the Ponte Rotto, was rebuilt from its foundations, at great cost, of square blocks of Travertine. This restoration was an immense boon, both to the Romans and to the strangers who came for the Jubilee, and Sixtus IV, with a justifiable pride, desired that it should bear the name of Ponte Sisto. It was a truly princely gift, and we appreciate it all the more, when we see that no Pope before him had ever attempted it In my opinion," continues Platina, "this was done principally to guard against the recurrence of the disaster which occurred on the Bridge of St. Angelo, in the time of Nicholas V., and which I have already related, when,

* Raynaldus, ad an 1472, N. 60, Manni, 76

owing to a panic, numbers of pilgrims were crushed to death "*

Infessura tells us that this bridge was begun in the spring of 1473. On the 29th of April the foundation stone was laid. The Pope, with the Cardinals and several prelates, proceeded to the bank of the Tiber, and, descending into the bed of the river, inserted, in the foundations, a square stone, with the inscription : "Built by Pope Sixtus IV. in the year of Salvation, 1473 "† Two years later the work was completed, so that this "most durable and solid," though not beautiful, bridge was ready for the use of the pilgrims in the Jubilee Year.‡ Two inscriptions on marble tablets also for many centuries bore witness to the care of Sixtus IV. for these pilgrims.§

Another work of great public utility, commenced in 1472, was finished in the Jubilee Year. The Aqueduct, conducting the Aqua Virgo to Rome, which had been almost stopped up, was cleared out and prolonged from the Quirinal to the Fontana Treve‖ "The architectural decorations at its mouth were entrusted to Antonio Lori

---

* PLATINA, Sixtus IV, 1064   The passage is important, as it shews that Platina's Vita Nicolai V was at this time completed, and furnishes a further argument in support of the belief that the Vita Sixti IV. in Muratori is really from the pen of Platina   See, on this subject, also *infra*, Chap XII. The beginning of the works in Rome coincides, according to Platina, with Barbo's return from Germany, which was in the end of October, 1474 , see *supra*, p 224, note †, the extract from the *Acta Consist , Secret Archives of the Vatican

† INFESSURA, 1143

‡ VASARI, IV , 136, is wrong in naming Baccio Pontelli as the architect , see MUNTZ, III., 201 , SCHMARSOW, 32

§ In the present day nothing is spared, and these memorials have been removed. For the text of the inscriptions, see REUMONT, III , I, 533, and FORCELLA, XIII , 54

‖ PLATINA, 1064 , MUNTZ, III , 174 *seq.*

of Florence and Giacomo of Ferrara. Here, as in many
other undertakings, Sixtus IV. continued what Nicholas
V. had begun. Opposite to the simple inscription left
by his predecessor, he placed one of his own, and surmounted it with a cornice which, with pillars, formed
the façade."*

The chief solicitude of Sixtus IV. was for the restoration
of those Churches and Sanctuaries which were the special
objects of the pilgrims. He had St Peter's thoroughly
cleaned, and inserted several windows to admit more
light. He caused a portion of the wall on the left side,
which was in a dangerous condition, to be strengthened
The Basilica of Constantine was cleansed, and the side
aisles were refloored and embellished † The Vatican Palace
was restored, the bronze equestrian statue of Marcus
Aurelius Antoninus, which was falling from age, was
repaired, and placed in front of the Lateran on a larger
marble pedestal decorated with trophies ‡ The Church
of the Holy Apostles was beautified, and many of the
smaller Churches, which, even in those days, were very
numerous in Rome, were renovated "There was hardly a
chapel in the whole City," says Sigismondo de' Conti, "to
which the Pope did not contribute something in the Jubilee
Year" Many inscriptions still remain which bear witness
to his energy in this respect.§

* SCHMARSOW, 33 FEA, Storia delle Acque, p. 16 (Roma, 1832),
and the *Poem in the Court Library, Vienna, 2403, f 10, cited p 209.

† PLATINA, Sixtus IV, 1064, SCHMARSOW, 34, ROHAULT, 254.

‡ Albertini Opusculum de mirabilibus Romae, 1509, ed Schmarsow,
Heilbronn, 1886.

§ MUNTZ, III, 154 seq, SCHMARSOW, 35 The passage in SIGIS-
MONDO DE' CONTI is I, p 205. See also FORCELLA, VIII, 301, IX,
263, 345, 531, X, 35, 219, 221, 319, 322, 323, ARMELLINI, 112, 133,
199, 245, 260, 577, 593

The Cardinals vied with the Pope in their care for the Sanctuaries of the Eternal City "The ancient saying, that the people copy their Princes, was verified," wrote Platina, in the year 1474, "for so much building is going on throughout Rome, that, if Sixtus lives, the whole City will soon be transformed. Inspired by these examples, Guillaume d'Estouteville, the Cardinal Archbishop of Ostia, had vaulted the side aisles of the Basilica of the Holy Crib, now called Santa Maria Maggiore, and so embellished it, that nothing finer can be found in Rome."*

In the early part of this pontificate the restoration of the ruined Hospital of Santo Spirito was begun. Here, also, care for the expected pilgrims was the chief inducement for taking the work in hand † Amongst many other instances of his solicitude for their welfare, we find exhortations addressed to the Italian Powers, calling on them to take care that the roads should be good and secure, to provide a sufficient number of inns for their accommodation, and not to burden them with tolls ‡

Similar considerations led Sixtus IV "to revert to the plans for the improvement of the streets, already contemplated by the patron of Leon Battista Alberti "§ In a Brief, addressed to the Papal Commissary, Girolamo de Giganti, on the 14th December, 1473, we find the following passage "Amongst countless other cares we must also

* PLATINA, Sixtus IV , 1064 , SCHMARSOW, 36 , PAULUS DE ANGELIS, Bas Mar Mag, Descriptio, 44 and 52 (Roma, 1621)

† Further details are given *infra*, Chap XII In 1475 the foundation stone of the new Church at the Hospice of the Campo Santo al Vaticano was also laid , see DE WAAL, National-Stiftungen d. Deutsch Volkes in Rom , 11 (Frankfurt, 1880).

‡ **Brief to Florence, dated Rome, 1474, Nov 25 (State Archives, Florence, X -II.-25, f 78-78b) See also MARTÈNE, II., 1476, and PEZZANA, III , 367.

§ SCHMARSOW, 33

attend to the purifying and beautification of our City; for, if any city should be clean and fair, certainly this one should be so, since, by reason of the Chair of St. Peter, it is the head of the whole world. Considering, then, that through the negligence of those whose duty it is to keep the streets in good order, they are in many places foul and unsightly, we command you for the future to pay special attention to this matter"*   Already in the year 1474 the paving of the streets between the Bridge of S Angelo and the Vatican was put in hand   The other principal thoroughfares were then paved with blocks of stone, the road from Monte Mario to the Borgo repaired, and the walls and gates of the City restored †

In the beginning of the Jubilee Year appeared the cele brated Bull, "which had, for its chief provision, the renovation of Rome"   It opens with the following sentences : "If it is a part of our common duty to see to the welfare of all the cities in the States of the Church, then, certainly, our best-beloved daughter, the chief City of the Church, hallowed by the blood of the Princes of the Apostles, has a special claim on our care and attention.   Unhappily, many calamities have befallen her, through which her buildings have fallen into decay, and the number of her citizens has been diminished   We therefore earnestly desire to see her population increased, her houses and palaces rebuilt, and all her other necessities duly provided for"   Many valuable proprietary rights and privileges are promised to all who will contribute to the accomplishment of these objects.‡

It may easily be understood that the Pope met with "great difficulties in carrying out his improvements, when

* MUNTZ, III, 179–80
† SCHMARSOW, *loc. cit*
‡ THEINER, Cod Dipl, III, 480–81, MUNTZ, III, 180–81; SCHMARSOW, 34

they involved clearances to be effected in the narrow streets beyond the Leonine City, belonging to the Roman burghers Haughty barons could not easily be induced to sacrifice their private property, or the unkempt comfort of their dwellings, to the higher end of the common good. Thus progress was necessarily slow, but the Romans dated the obnoxious measures from the visit of the King of Naples, who certainly encouraged the Pope in his plans, although he was not their originator "*

In December, 1474, an approaching visit from the Neapolitan monarch began to be talked of, the motives of which were rather political than religious.† Ferrante and Sixtus IV. had been drawn closer together by the League of November 2, 1474, which was a cause of grave apprehension to them both. A personal interview was now to afford the opportunity of deciding on the attitude to be adopted towards this new combination.

The reception of the King of Naples was honourable in the extreme   Rodrigo Borgia and Giuliano della Rovere,‡ two of the most distinguished among the Cardinals, welcomed him in Terracina, on the borders of the States

* SCHMARSOW, 170, is no doubt correct in thus understanding Infessura's well-known anecdote, according to which the King told the Pope that he was not lord of the City as long as the streets remained so narrow and so obstructed with porticoes, balconies, and erections of all kinds

† *Despatch of Cardinal Gonzaga, dated Rome, 1474, Dec 18. (Gonzaga Archives, Mantua) A *Letter from the Cardinal, preserved in the same Archives, and dated Rome, 1474, Dec 24, says that Ferrante's visit was to be expected on the 20th January, 1475   *On the 2nd January, 1475, he writes that the King would leave Naples on the 7th or 8th of the month

‡ They left Rome on the 14th January ; see *Letter of J. P Arrivabene, dated Rome, 1475, January 17. (Gonzaga Archives) See also NOTAR GIACOMO, 128

of the Church. When he entered Rome on the 28th January, 1475, all the Cardinals met him before the Porta S. Giovanni * Splendid festivities followed The King and his brilliant suite, however, remained but three days in Rome Infessura says that the numbers of falcons which the Neapolitans brought with them completely cleared the City and all the neighbourhood of owls

The King and the Pope interchanged rich presents, nor did Ferrante forget the Roman officials and the Churches † When he left Rome, on the 1st February, all the Cardinals accompanied him to the Porta S Paola, and four of their number as far as S Paola itself, where he heard Mass before starting for Marino, Rodrigo Borgia and Giuliano della Rovere being with him on this occasion, and Federigo of Urbino having also arrived ‡ At Grottaferrata he received the Order of the Garter, sent to him by the King of England.

On the 8th February, 1475, the Mantuan Ambassador wrote word that Ferrante was to return to Rome secretly by night. On the 5th a report was current that the King

---

* Not on the 6th January, 1475, as REUMONT, III , 1, 169, following the inaccurate INFESSURA, 1144, says , see Cron. Rom., 35 (where certainly 1475 should be read for 1476) ; SUMMONTE, III , 490, and the *Despatch of J. P Arrivabene, dated Rome, 1475, January 29 *" Heri introe in Roma la M^{ta} del Re al qual tuti li cardinali andorono contro un puocho fuora de la porta de S Janni " (Gonzaga Archives) The description of Ferrante's entry, given by Giovanni Santi in his *Reimchronik von Urbino (Cod Ottob, 1305, f. 211b), is, MUNTZ informs us (III , 279), inaccurate

† INFESSURA, loc. cit. NOTAR GIACOMO, 128-9, where Ferrante's entrance is assigned to the 25th February , a mistake repeated by REUMONT, Lorenzo, I , 262, 2nd ed See SUMMONTE, III , 490, and SCHMARSOW, 34

‡ So we learn from a *Letter written by J P Arrivabene, dated Rome, 1475, Febr. 1 Gonzaga Archives, Mantua

had come privately to the Pope.* According to Paolo
della Mastro's Chronicle, he was in Rome on the 13th and
14th February.†

The subject of these interviews between the Pope and
Ferrante was at first unknown to the majority even of
the Cardinals. On the 17th February, Cardinal Gonzaga
thought he had some inkling of it. On that day Sixtus
IV. summoned a Consistory, in which he announced that
the danger from Turkey called for a general League
of all the Italian Powers, and the levy of a tithe from
the clergy. This decision was then imparted to the
Ambassadors appointed to attend the Consistory, but the
Neapolitan Envoy was the only one who displayed any
alacrity in responding to the wishes of the Pope.‡ There
can be no doubt that negotiations had also been carried
on between Sixtus IV. and Ferrante regarding the attitude
to be adopted by them towards the League of the 2nd
November, 1474 §

The concourse of Jubilee pilgrims, which commenced
on Christmas Day of that year, did not at first equal the
great expectations entertained The wars in France,
Burgundy, Germany, Hungary, Poland, Spain, and other
countries were, according to the Chronicle of Viterbo, the
reason why so few people came ; also, respect for the
clergy had been much shaken by former experiences ‖
An encouraging token of a return to a better state of
feeling was, however, manifested by the much-decried

　*　*Despatches of J P. Arrivabene, dated Rome, 1475, Febr 5 and 8
Gonzaga Archives, Mantua

　† Cron. Rom , 35.

　‡ **Letter of Card Gonzaga, dated Rome, 1475, February 17.
Gonzaga Archives

　§ See PALMERIUS, 258

　‖ Cron di Viterbo di GIOV DI JUZZO, 411

courtiers, who eagerly availed themselves at Easter of the graces of the Jubilee* The pilgrims now became more and more numerous One of the Ambassadors gives 200,000 as the number present when the Pope solemnly blessed the people on Ascension Day.† This is, no doubt, an exaggerated estimate, but the report of this eye-witness fully establishes the fact that the concourse was immense.

Entries in the Confraternity-Book of the Church of the Anima shew that a great many pilgrims, both clerical and lay, came from Germany during the "golden year" ‡

Among the princely personages at Rome on this occasion we may mention Queen Dorothea of Denmark,§ Nicholas of Ujlak,‖ whom Matthias Corvinus had made King of

---

* "*Questi di sancti benche la Ex V soglia havere male opinione de cortesani se attesto tanto al spirituale et a visitar questi luochi sacri per guadagnar lo iobileo che le cose del mundo erano in tuto mese da canto" *Letter of J P. Arrivabene, dated Rome, 1475, April 1 (Gonzaga Archives, Mantua) LANDUCCI also went as a pilgrim to Rome in 1475, see Diario, 14.

† *Letter of J P Arrivabene, dated Rome, 1475, May 5 He further says * " Qua concorre gente asai a questo iobileo et piu che mai non se haveria veduto." Gonzaga Archives

‡ Lib confrat. b Mariae de Anima, 25 seq., 78, 105, 260 For an account of the pilgrimage of the Bishop of Ratisbon, see JANNER, III., 574 ; of that of the Abbot of Melk, KEIBLINGER, I , 644 seq Regarding the editio princeps of the tract entitled "Indulgentiae et reliquiae urbis Romae" of 1475, see ROSSI, I , 163.

§ DAAE, Kong Christian, 92, cites only the account of the Chronicle published by Gherens (Norsk Hist Tidsskr, IV, 105) The Queen's journey is mentioned also by SCHIVENOGLIA, 180 , GIOV DI JUZZO, 411 , and SIGISMONDO DE' CONTI, I , 204. See also KROGH, 25 ; and HOFMANN, Barbara von Hohenzollern, 23

‖ See ENGEL, Welthist, XLIX, 3, 431 , *Califfini, Cronica Ferrariae (Cod. I –I –4, f. 51-2, Chigi Library, Rome), says that the Re di Bossina arrived at Ferrara on the 21st February, 1475, with 110 horses (andava a Roma al perdono del jubileo), and was again there on the

Bosnia , Anthony of Burgundy, the " Great Bastard ", * and
finally, Charlotte of Lusignan.   Charlotte had left Rhodes
on the 4th July, 1474, and was never again to see that
island or Cyprus   She had gone first to her husband at
Montcalier, and now journeyed to Rome, where her rights
were recognised.†   In the latter part of May she reached
Civita Vecchia,‡ and on the 3rd June entered Rome   The
Cardinals went to meet the deposed Princess, and during
her stay in Rome she was entertained at the Pope's
expense §

Sixtus IV. caused the reception of Charlotte of Lusignan
to be portrayed among the frescoes in the Hospital of
S. Spirito.   "Beneath the picture, still visible, which
represents the Queen, adorned with the insignia of her
rank and surrounded by her attendants, kneeling before
Sixtus IV., is a somewhat fulsome inscription, which

5th April on his return journey   J. P. Arrivabene also says, in a
*Letter, dated Rome, 1475, March 24, that the King of Bosnia came
only on account of the Jubilee.   Who the "ill madama ducessa
d'Alemagna," mentioned in a *Letter of Arrivabene's, dated Rome,
1475, March 6, as then arriving in Rome, may be, I am unable to say.
Gonzaga Archives.

* Jahrbuch der Preuss. Kunstsammlungen, II, 253   Anthony's
visit to Naples in the month of April is mentioned by the Giornali
Napol , 1135, and his arrival at Ferrara on the 15th June, by Califfini,
loc cit., f 52   (Chigi Library, Rome)   Arrivabene, in a *Despatch,
dated Rome, 1475, May 22, also says, "to-morrow the bastardo de
Bergogna will depart"   Gonzaga Archives, Mantua.

† HERQUET, Konigsgestalten, 89-90, and Charlotta, 186 seq , who,
however, like MAS-LATRIE, III , 114, is ignorant of the exact time
of her arrival in Rome.   See also Bibl de l'École des Chartes,
p. 268 (1877)

‡ See *Letters of J P. Arrivabene, dated Rome, 1475, May 18 and
22. Gonzaga Archives, Mantua

§ *Letter of Arrivabene, dated Rome, 1475, June 8 (El papa li fa le
spese). Loc. cit.

declares that the Pope received the unhappy lady with
such kindness, that, in her overflowing gratitude, she was
incapable of words and could only weep"* Charlotte
spent the next year in Rome, supported by a pension from
the Pope; a house in the Leonine City, now the Palazzo
de Convertende, was assigned to her as a residence †

The Jubilee year closed sadly for the Pope. The City
Prefect fell ill at the end of October, and died on the 11th
November ‡ Sixtus IV. conferred the vacant post on his
nephew, Giovani della Rovere § During the same month,
the Tiber rose and overflowed a great part of the City
The mud, which it deposits more abundantly than almost
any other river, and the continued dampness of the flooded
quarter, produced malaria and pestilence.‖ Under these

* HERQUET, Konigsgestalten, 90, and Charlotta, 194.

† See ADINOLFI, Portica, 96 *seq*. Regarding the maintenance given
by the Pope, see MAS-LATRIE, III., 148 *seq* , and GOTTLOB, Cam Ap

‡ J. P Arrivabene wrote from Rome on the 3rd Nov , 1475 .
*"Heri sera lo prefetto laborabat in extremis destitutus omni spe
medicorum Nra Sre [=Card Gonzaga] fu a visitarlo . Sua Bne
fa mostra de haverne extrema passione" (Gonzaga Archives.) Regarding his death, see INFESSURA, 1145

§ On the 17th December, 1475, see Cod XXXIII-129, f. 115.
(Barberini Library, Rome) A *"Panegyricus cum Joannes Rovere
praefectus urbis creatus est," composed by D. Calderino, is preserved
in Cod 157 of the Chapter Library, Verona. Giovanni, by his
marriage with the Duke of Urbino's daughter, solemnised in 1478,
"with Persian pomp" (Palmerius), Lord of Sinigaglia, was, as
SCHMARSOW, 43, remarks, the most permanently prosperous of the
Pope's nephews, and his son, Francesco Maria della Rovere, became
heir to the Duchy of Urbino In regard to Giovanni's popularity in
Sinigaglia, see SIENA, Sinigaglia, III , 160.

‖ INFESSURA, 1145, and NOTAR GIACOMO, 130 See A DE WAAL,
Das Bohmische Pilgerhaus in Rom , p. 70 (Prague, 1873). The Plague
soon spread through a great part of the Italian Peninsula , see
HORSCHELMANN in the Allg Ztg , 1884, N 177 ; BONAZZI, 728 , and
MASSARI, 46 *seq*

circumstances, many were prevented from coming to Rome to gain the Jubilee Indulgence The roads had also become more insecure, and accordingly, to avoid exposing pilgrims from a distance to these risks, the Pope commanded that the Jubilee should be held at Bologna during the Eastertide of 1476, and granted the Plenary Indulgence to all who, besides fulfilling the usual conditions, should visit the Churches of S. Pietro, S Petronio, S. Antonio, and S. Francesco in that city * Countless pilgrims, therefore, flocked to Bologna, which had never before seen so many strangers within her walls.† Participation in the graces of the Jubilee Year, without leaving home, was also granted to several other foreign Princes and countries ; in most cases with the condition that the Jubilee alms should be devoted to the defence of Christendom from the Turks.‡

Besides his consultations with the King of Naples in the beginning of the Jubilee Year, the Pope was repeatedly occupied with the affairs of the Turkish war "Owing to the hostile complications in which Central Europe was involved through the Burgundian war, it had become powerless to resist the advance of the Turks." Sixtus IV., accordingly, on the 15th February, 1475, appointed Bishop Alexander of Forli Papal Legate for the restoration of

---

* NOETHEN, Gesch der Jubeljahre, p 67, is mistaken in stating that this change was made in the year 1475 Cardinal Gonzaga, in a *Letter of the 6th May, 1476, speaks of the concession in favour of Bologna as recently granted Gonzaga Archives

† See FALEONI, 510

‡ NOETHEN, 68, MANNI, 85 ; Freib Kirchenlexikon, II 317, 2nd ed , VITTORELLI, 317 See THEINER, Mon Hung, II, 449 seq.; Mon Slav, 503 seq , Mon Hibern 474-6 FINKE in the Zeitschr fur Gesch Westfalens, 45, p 113 seq , mentions a volume preserved among the *Libri decime* of the State Archives at Rome, with the Notaries' Deeds regarding the Jubilee alms in Burgundy and the adjacent countries.

peace * In the ensuing months the Pope made repeated appeals to the Italian Powers for help †   The state of affairs in the East was indeed calculated to cause the greatest anxiety.   Usunhassan had never been able to recover from his defeat, and thus the hand of the Sultan pressed more and more heavily on the Christians in Albania, the coasts of the Adriatic, and the Danubian Provinces ‡ At the end of 1474 a powerful Turkish army attacked the brave Woiwode of Moldavia, Stephen the Great, who refused any longer to pay tribute. Stephen, with great skill, decoyed the superior forces of the enemy on through the forest to the Lake of Rakowitz (north-west of Galatz), and there inflicted on them a severe defeat (10th January, 1475).§

Meanwhile, a fleet of 300 sail, with 40,000 men on board, had been made ready at Constantinople. Candia was, at first, supposed to be its destination, but it took an easterly

---

* CHMEL, Mon Habsb, III., 435 , RAUSCH, 135, see 146, in regard to the Legate's success

† On the 16th April, 1475, Sixtus IV commended Usunhassan's Ambassadors to the Florentines MULLER, Doc., 220 On the 1st July, 1475, he wrote to the Italian Powers, describing the increasing danger from Turkey, and claiming from them assistance. * " Quare eandem devotionem vestram per viscera, etc , hortamur in Domino ac deprecamur, ut iuxta vires vestras aliquam subventionem facere velitis " *Brief to the Florentines in the State Archives, Florence, and on the same day, 1st July, to the Marquess of Mantua Gonzaga Archives, Mantua

‡ HERTZBERG, Osmanen, 630

§ See the Letter of the 24th January, written from Torda, to King Matthias, and the Report of Woiwode Stephen of the 25th January in Mon Hung , II , 299–302 See MAKUSCEV, II., 13 seq , also HAMMER, II , 137, and Arch St. Lomb , I , 315 seq , besides the documents published by C. ESARCU in the year 1874 at Bucharest Stephen sent some of the banners he had taken from the Turks to Sixtus IV. ; see RAYNALDUS, ad an 1474, N. 10–11

course, ran into the Black Sea, and, on the 31st of May, appeared before Caffa in the Crimea, a rich and important Genoese colony. On the 6th of June the place was in the hands of the Turks, and its fate was soon shared by the whole southern coast of the Crimea *

Strenuous efforts for the preservation of this city had in former days been made by Popes Calixtus III., Pius II., and Paul II † The tidings of its fall reached Rome in September, 1475. Further details were soon received from the Knights of St. John,‡ and the accounts of the cruelties exercised by the Turks on its unfortunate inhabitants caused general horror and dismay, which were intensified by the impossibility, under the melancholy circumstances of the West, of that united defensive action which alone could have promised success. Discouraging as the result of his former attempts had been, the Pope again fulfilled his duty. He sent special Briefs to all the Princes of Christendom, informing them of the disaster, and calling on them to resist the indefatigable foe § Sixtus IV., at the same time, exhorted them to send Ambassadors

* VIGNA, II , 2, 163 *seq.*, 177, 474 *seq.*, 480 *seq.*; SERRA, 248 *seq.*; ZINKEISEN, II , 386 *seq.*, HERTZBERG, Osmanen, 633 , HEYD, II , 400 *seq* , CARO, V , 1, 445, N 2.

† See our Vol. II , p 435 *seq.*, VIGNA, II., 1, 164 *seq* , 559–60, 645 *seq* , 665 *seq.*, and THEINER, Mon Slav., I., 464 *seq*

‡ AMMANATI, Epist , 641, Frankfort edition. See RAYNALDUS, ad an 1475, N. 23–6, and VIGNA, II , 2, 176

§ Cardinal Gonzaga wrote from Rome on the 18th Sept , 1475 · * "La Sta de N. S. havuto mo la certeza de la perdita de Caffa ne da aviso a tuti li principi e potentie de Italia" Gonzaga Archives, Mantua, where is also the *Brief to Mantua, dated Rome, 1475, Sept. 12. I saw in the State Archives of Modena, and in those of Florence, X –II.–25, f 89b–90b, similar Briefs of the same date It appears from Mon Habsb , III , 437 *seq* , that Briefs were also addressed to other Princes besides those of Italy.

to Rome It would seem that he still hoped to bring about a League of all the Powers against the Osmanli, but he met with little response ! * In November negotiations began, and they lasted for months. "Their result may be learned from the fact that the flames of the places the Turks had set on fire were soon visible from the belfry of St. Mark's." † In March, 1477, Cardinal Ammanati wrote : "Our Pope is doing everything in his power He did not dismiss the Italian Ambassadors, as he wishes to obtain more than the tithe. The tithe from the clergy, and a twentieth part from the Jews, has been granted to him, but how little is that compared to such a war. What are a few hundred thousands for the defence of a needy king ‡ against the ruler of all Asia and a good part of Europe? The assistance of the laity, so anxiously desired by His Holiness, has not yet been afforded. We strive as far as in us lies, to copy the indefatigable zeal and courage of our Father. May God enlighten our minds and hearts, that we may not walk in darkness and the shadow of death, and, when we have lost this valiant champion, too late lament that we have not sooner known the way of our salvation." §

* Sixtus IV was obliged frequently to urge the sending of Ambassadors ; see his *Briefs of the 17th and 30th Sept., 1475, in the Gonzaga Archives, Mantua, and the State Archives, Florence, X -II -25, f. 91 and 91b-92 , ibid , 94b-95b, a long *Brief, dated Rome, 1475, Dec. 21, in which he earnestly prays that assistance may be sent against the Turks

† REUMONT, Lorenzo, I , 263, 2nd ed Regarding the persons of the Ambassadors, see PEZZANA, III , 378 PERUZZI, Ancona, 383, and SERRA, III , 252, shew that Sixtus IV cannot be accused of negligence as to the Turkish war.

‡ Matthias Corvinus of Hungary

§ AMMANATI, Epist., 644, Frankfort edition.

CHAPTER V

THE pestilence, which had already visited Rome in the Jubilee Year, returned early in the summer of 1476, with such violence that residence in the City became almost intolerable.* At the beginning of June the Pope determined to seek the heights of Viterbo,† on the 3rd he commended his States to the Protection of King Ferrante,‡ on the 10th he left Rome, accompanied by Cardinals d'Estouteville, Borgia, Carafa, Nardini, Gonzaga, and Michiel.§ Cardinal Cybò remained behind as Legate. Later on, the City was visited by terrible thunderstorms and tempests The Palace of the Senate was closed, and justice

---

* This epidemic, which broke forth with great virulence in March, was consequent on the inundations in January. See the Roman Letter of the 21st March, 1476, in KNEBEL, II, 408-9, Cron di Viterbo di GIOV DI JUZZO, 412, and a *Notice in Cod Vatic, 7239, f. 157. (Vatican Library.) In the course of the month of April, Duke Albrecht of Saxony came to Rome (ROHRICHT, Pilgerreisen, 160), where Girolamo Riario held a splendid tournament on the 25th (INFESSURA, 1145) On the 1st May, *Cardinal Gonzaga mentions the return of the Plague, which rapidly increased. See J P Arrivabene's *Letter, dated Rome, 1476, May 24. All these Papers are in the Gonzaga Archives.

† *Letter of J P. Arrivabene, dated Rome, 1476, June 5, *loc. cit.*

‡ MARTÈNE, II, 1452-3

§ See Acta Consist. of the Secret Archives of the Vatican in MARINI, II., 17, and INFESSURA, 1145.

was administered at the foot of the steps   Penitential
processions thronged the streets   Infessura mentions one
in July, in which the venerated image of our Lady from
S Maria Maggiore was carried with much devotion *

The Pope was obliged, immediately on starting, to alter
his route, for the terrible malady had appeared at Viterbo,
he went, therefore, first to Campagnano, then to Vetralla,
then for a time to Amelia and Narni, and finally settled at
Foligno † Thence he visited Assisi, where, in the month of
August, he celebrated the Feast of St. Francis, the founder
of his Order, and venerated his relics with great devotion ‡

* INFESSURA, 1145. A Brief of 5th Aug , 1476, commending Cardinal
Cybò, is given in MARTÈNE, II , 1548

† See MARINI, II , 217 *seq* , and Cron di Viterbo di Giov di Juzzo,
413.   See also the incomplete *Reports of the Bishop of Parma, S.
Sacramorus, which are in the State Archives at Milan.   One of these
*Letters, written in July (the date is effaced), speaks of the terrible
ravages of the Plague in Rome, whence every one had fled : it appears
"non ci sia rimasto quasi niuno"; the pestilence had also reached
Todi   A *Report by Sacramorus, written ex Amelia on the 8th July,
1476, shews that the Plague continued in Rome ; isolated cases had
occurred in Viterbo, Spoleto, and Todi , the Pope was suffering from the
gout   A Letter, dated Foligno, 1476, Sept 26, shews that the Pope was
then in that town.   See also, in reference to Sixtus IV.'s sojourn at
Foligno, the Cronica di Suor Caterina Guarneri in Arch St. p. le
Marche, I , 300 (Foligno, 1884)   Ammanati's Letter of the 13th July,
1476, in Anecd Litt , III., 372, speaks of the ravages of the Plague in
the Sienese district   In Perugia it was so violent that Sixtus IV , by a
*Brief of the 7th July, 1476, authorised the magistrate to pass important
resolutions when only two-thirds of the members of the Council were
present.   Regest in Cod. C.–IV–I , University Library, Genoa

‡ SCHMARSOW, 110, after WADDING, ad an 1476, XIV , 145 *seq*
See Cronich di S Francesco, III , 182   In a *Letter, dated Foligno,
1476, Aug 29, Bonfrancesco Ailotti also mentions that Sixtus IV. went
to visit the bodies of St Francis and St Clare   (State Archives
Modena.)   GRAZIANI, 647, says that Sixtus IV. left Assisi on the 25th
August on account of the Plague

As the pestilence abated very slowly, Sixtus IV remained at Foligno until the autumn. When Cardinal Giuliano della Rovere returned, on the 4th October, from his mission to France, he found the Pope still in this charming little town,* which he only left on the 7th of the month He spent the first night at Spoleto, and then, probably because the Plague was still claiming many victims,† travelled so slowly that he did not reach his capital until the 23rd of October.‡

Just as this calamitous year was closing, all Italy was struck with horror at the assassination of the Duke of Milan (26th December, 1476) This crime was a tyrant-murder of the ancient type, and was directly attributable to the influence of ideas zealously propagated by the false Humanist, Cola Montano The Annals of Siena expressly state that the conspirators had studied Sallust, and Sigismondo de' Conti also informs us that Lampugnani had, from early youth, chosen Catiline as his model.§

"The peace of Italy is at an end!" exclaimed the Pope, on hearing of the death of Galeazzo Maria Sforza ; and,

* *Acta Consist , Secret Archives of the Vatican.

† See a *Letter of Card Gonzaga of the 24th Oct , 1476. Gonzaga Archives, Mantua

‡ *Acta Consist., Secret Archives of the Vatican SCHMARSOW, 110, N. 5, has already pointed out the error of Infessura in giving the 27th December as the date of the Pope's return to Rome Many condemned his long absence, as we learn from the justification offered in the *Lucubrac. Tiburtin., Cod. 2403, Court Library, Vienna. To this subject also refers *Oratio habita ad pontif Xistum qua cohortatur ut remota sevitie pestis ab urbe dignetur repetere urbem Romam et ipsam presentia sua consolari. Cod Ottob , 2290, f 172b–173, of the Vatican Library

§ SIGISMONDO DE' CONTI, I., 17. See REUMONT, Lorenzo, I., 266, 2nd ed ; BURCKHARDT, I , 58, 134, 3rd ed , and, besides the literature alluded to in our Vol II , p 216 seq , Atti d deput p 1 prov di Romagna, 1869, VIII , 121 seq , and Arch St Lomb , II , 284 seq , XIII , 140 seq., 414 seq

indeed, the existing political system seemed entirely upset The Duke of Milan was the only Prince sufficiently rich and powerful permanently to counterbalance the ambitious King of Naples, his heir was still a child ; the Regency was in the hands of the Duchess Bona, a weak woman, entangled in the meshes of her intriguing brothers-in-law *

Fully alive to the dangers which threatened Italy, Sixtus IV., on the first day of the new year (1477), addressed a Brief to all the Italian Princes and Rulers, earnestly exhorting them to the maintenance of peace † Cardinal Giovanni Mellini was also sent as special Legate to Milan and Lombardy, and instructed to use every effort for the same object ‡ The newly-appointed Legate was a man venerable alike for his age, his learning, and his goodness ; he started on the 27th January, and returned on the 7th May §

The course of affairs in Milan was watched, not only by the Pope, but also by Lorenzo de' Medici, with the keenest interest. Peace was for the present preserved, and the Duchess remained in power,‖ but her authority rested on

* SCHMARSOW, 109, 111. See REUMONT, Lorenzo, I , 267 *seq* , 2nd ed   Duchess Bona's letter, informing the Pope of the murder, is given by MURATORI, Chron Est , XV , 546

† All these *Briefs are dated Rome, 1477, Jan 1, and their words are identical. I have seen the Originals in the Gonzaga Archives, Mantua, and the State Archives, Modena and Bologna (Lib Q 3), and a contemporary copy in the State Archives, Florence, X -II.-25, f 103b-104

‡ See *Acta Consist , Secret Archives of the Vatican, and a *Brief from Sixtus IV. to Florence, dated Rome, 1477, January 3   State Archives, Florence, *loc cit* , f 104b.

§ *Acta Consist , Secret Archives of the Vatican   See SIGISMONDO DE' CONTI, I , 17.

‖ See the **Letter of Ascanio Maria Sforza to Albrecht of Bonstetten of the 20th March, 1477, in Cod 719, N 51, of the Chapter-Library at St Gall

no solid foundation.   Lorenzo sought in every way to confirm it.   " But," as a friend of the Medici writes, " it is perfectly incomprehensible how, at so critical a moment, when
the support of Milan was most uncertain, he could think
of giving just cause of complaint to neighbours whom he
knew to be already dissatisfied with him.   Yet this is
what he did." *

At the beginning of his reign, Sixtus IV. had been very
favourably inclined towards the Medici, the reception
which Lorenzo met with in Rome, the fact that the
financial affairs of the Holy See were, much to their advantage, entrusted to their care, and that the Alum works
at Tolfa were farmed out to them, were plain proofs of
this good-will †   If these friendly relations were of brief
duration, it was only because Lorenzo openly manifested
his ungrateful purpose of making troubles for the Pope ‡

The Florentine Expedition against Volterra, in the year
1472, was the first occasion on which these differences
appeared.   The Pope had sent auxiliary troops to aid the
Florentines in suppressing the revolt of that city ; this act
of friendship towards Lorenzo led to disastrous results.
After twenty-five days of bombardment, the city capitulated,
on condition that the lives, honour, and property of the
burgesses should be spared.   No sooner, however, had
the undisciplined troops entered the place, than a general
plunder began   " In vain did Federigo of Montefeltre
remonstrate ; Volterra was sacrificed in the most shameful
manner.   This seemed to have delighted the Florentines
When the victor came, with a heavy heart, to their city,
they overwhelmed him with marks of gratitude to console

---

* REUMONT, Lorenzo, I , 270, 2nd ed.

† See *supra*, p. 215   From GOTTLOB, Cam. Apost , we learn that,
previously to 1478, the Medici farmed the customs in Rome.

‡ SCHMARSOW, 111   See *supra*, p 265 *seq* and 268 *seq*

him for the wound that his honour had sustained; but
the Pope saw his credit abused, and general compassion
excited on behalf of the ruined city. His magisterial hand,
which had been laid upon the balance in favour of the
Medici, was stained with blood."*

Then followed the purchase of Imola. The acquisition
of this territory from the Duke of Milan interfered with
the designs of the Republic, which had eagerly sought an
extension of its domain in that direction† Lorenzo had
made the greatest efforts to make it impossible to obtain
the money required Henceforth "the Court of Rome
could no longer employ him in a financial capacity That
which had once been so generously offered to him was
now withdrawn. The management of the Apostolical
Exchequer was transferred to the Bank of the Pazzi, who,
in spite of the Medici, had advanced the sum, that was all,
but it was enough."‡

* Such is the judgment of SCHMARSOW, 13 See REUMONT,
Lorenzo, I, 249, 2nd ed, and II., 455, where the special literature
on the subject is indicated FRANTZ, 141, believes the first alteration
in the relations between Sixtus IV and Lorenzo was due to the
Pope's decided refusal to elevate Giuliano de' Medici to the purple.
An ecclesiastical difference (taxation of the clergy) is mentioned in
the *Brief of 14th Sept, 1471 State Archives, Florence, X–II–25,
f 37b-38

† FRANTZ, 141

‡ SCHMARSOW, 24. See FRANTZ, 177, and BUSER, Lorenzo, 31
SIGISMONDO DE' CONTI, I., 16, speaks of the withdrawal of the
financial business in Rome from the Medici in 1476 "Fisci tamen
administrationem apud eum amplius esse non passus est, credo ne
posset sanctam Romanam ecclesiam viribus propriis oppugnare"
But a Letter of Lorenzo, of the 14th Dec, 1474 (in BUSER, Lorenzo,
132), implies that this had already been done According to information kindly communicated by Dr Gottlob, from July, 1474, the Medici
no longer appear as depositarii generales S R.E in the Libri introitus
et exitus of the Secret Archives of the Vatican DAUNON, I, 279, is

The tension between Sixtus IV and Lorenzo was also greatly increased by the faithless conduct of the latter at the time of the siege of Città di Castello He repaid the assistance rendered to him by the Pope, during the war with Volterra, by vigorously supporting rebellion in the States of the Church * The persistent aid accorded by Florence to Vitelli rendered his complete subjugation impossible. Thus the capitulation, which was at last brought about, is characterised by Cardinal Ammanati, favourably disposed as he was towards the Medici, as an insult to the victors, for the terms were dictated by the vanquished.†

The next dispute had to do with a more ecclesiastical question. On the death of Cardinal Riario, Francesco Salviati had aspired to the Archbishopric of Florence, but had been compelled to give way to Lorenzo's brother-in-law, Rinaldo Orsini ‡ In 1474, Filippo de' Medici, Archbishop of Pisa, a man much devoted to the interests of his relations, died. Without consulting the Florentines, the Pope now raised Francesco Salviati to the vacant throne § It is not to be supposed that the Pope made this appointment with the intention of wounding the Medici and the Republic, but " from a letter of Cardinal Giuliano to Lorenzo, it is evident that he knew it would not be welcome. The Cardinal commends the Archbishop-

altogether incorrect in saying " Un des premiers soins de Sixte IV. fut d'ôter à la famille de Medicis l'emploi de trésorier."

* FRANTZ, 160. See *supra*, p 265

† REUMONT, Lorenzo, I., 258, 2nd ed

‡ GAMS, 748, does not give the day of his appointment. A *Brief of Sixtus IV., dated Rome, 1474, quinto Cal. Mart, acquainted the Florentines with Orsini's nomination. State Archives, Florence, X.-II.-25, f 59b-60

§ On the 14th Oct, 1474, Sixtus IV. communicated the elevation to the Florentines, see the *Brief of that date in the State Archives, Florence, X.-II -25, f. 69b-70

elect to Lorenzo, and emphatically declares that there had
been no intention of offending his Magnificence by the nomination."* Girolamo Riario earnestly entreated Lorenzo
to overrule the opposition that would be made to the
acceptance of Salviati. As this letter was not answered,
Girolamo Riario wrote again on the 26th October, 1474,
and this time with his own hand. "If," he says, "you
would have me see that I am loved by you, and that my
friendship is agreeable to you, and would also have our
Master perceive that you are towards His Holiness all that
I have ever declared you to be, then deal with me in this
matter as you wish me to deal with you and your affairs."†

Two days before this letter was written, the Pope had
exhorted the Florentines to be reasonable, and to acknowledge the newly-appointed Archbishop; but neither the
Republic nor Lorenzo had any idea of yielding‡ Lorenzo,
writing to the Duke of Milan, declared that to consent to
recognise the Archbishop would be to betray the honour
of the city.§ Early in 1475 Girolamo sent his Chancellor
to Florence to enter into negotiations for an agreement;
but a long time passed without any settlement.‖ All the

* REUMONT, Lorenzo, I , 270–71, 2nd ed
† BUSER, Lorenzo, 30
‡ *Brief, dated Grottaferrata, 1474, Oct. 24. *"Nos quidem," it
says, "eo animo sumus, ut digne a nobis factam provisionem sub-
stineamus; vos quidem cum prudentes sitis nobiscum convenietis in
sententiam et electo ipsi statim possessionem tradi facietis." State
Archives, Florence, X -II -25, f 70–70b
§ BUSER, Lorenzo, 31 and 132.
‖ Regarding the result of the negotiations, see the Report of the
Milanese Ambassador , BUSER, Lorenzo, 32-3   J P Arrivabene
writes on the 13th April, 1475 *"Le cose de Lorenzo de Medici
dico de le rasone suoe de la depositeria qui presso al papa sono in
speranza d'acordo, el qual seguendo stimase che lui habia a venir qui in
brevi personalmente " Gonzaga Archives, Mantua.

Pope's exhortations failed to obtain Salviati's reception.* For three whole years the Florentines held out. Salviati remained in Rome, and the resentment which he cherished was soon shared by others "Lorenzo," says an historian by no means prejudiced against him, "could not fail to perceive that this affair was seriously disturbing his relations with the Pope and his adherents. It is easy to understand that the feeling of animosity was directed against Lorenzo personally, men had come to look upon him as the head of the Republic, and everything, whether good or evil, was ascribed to his influence "†

A fresh manifestation of the hostile disposition of the Florentines towards Sixtus IV. occurred in the autumn of 1475 Niccolo Vitelli was then endeavouring to regain his former position in Città di Castello The enterprise failed, but the Pope's request, that the faithless rebel should no longer be permitted to dwell in the territory of the Republic, was refused.‡

After all this, it is not surprising that Sixtus IV. did not grant the petition that a Florentine should be admitted into the Sacred College, but put off the Republic with hopes for the future §

In the spring of 1477 Lorenzo placed further difficulties

* On the 6th October, 1475, Sixtus IV wrote to Florence: *"Per integrum fere annum exspectamus, ut dil filio electo Pisano possessionem ecclesie traderetis", they must at last do this State Archives, X.-II.-25, f. 92-92b

† REUMONT, Lorenzo, I, 278, 2nd ed.

‡ SIGISMONDO DE' CONTI, I., 19. See in Appendix, N 56, the *Brief of 21st October, 1475. State Archives, Florence.

§ In a *Brief on the subject, dated Rome, 1476, Jan 12, Sixtus IV says *"Non tulerunt tempora quemadmodum nobis supplicastis ut ante hac ornare vestram rempublicam cardinali Ro. ecclesiae potuerimus", he then holds out hopes of the ultimate accomplishment of their desires State Archives, Florence, X.-II.-25, f 95b.

in the Pope's way, by encouraging the mercenary captain, Carlo Fortebraccio, to abandon the Turkish war and return to the Umbrian frontier   Carlo desired to win for himself the quasi free city of Perugia, where his father and brother had formerly ruled.* Without the consent of the Florentines this was impossible, as free passage through their States and maintenance for his troops were indispensable ; but they also had designs upon the city. They wished to draw it into their league, to alienate it from the Pope and to bring it under their own influence.   They therefore incited Carlo to attack the Sienese ; he nothing loth began, on the most frivolous pretexts, to plunder and to levy contributions in the valleys of the Chiana and the Arbia. The Medici viewed with satisfaction these troubles of their neighbours, hoping that they would tend to incline them to submit to their domination.   Moreover, it was desirable that the Pope's attention should be diverted from Perugia, until the conspiracy for the betrayal of the city should be mature †

The Sienese, thus attacked in time of peace, complained to the Pope and the King of Naples, and from both received promises of assistance.   Sixtus IV. remembered that Carlo's father had threatened to make Pope Martin say twenty Masses for a *bolognino* ‡ A division of the army, under Antonio of Montefeltre, advanced to chastise the mercenary chief, who had thus wantonly disturbed the peace of the

* In *Letters of the 3rd and 11th Jan , 1477, Sixtus IV had already forbidden the Perugians to admit Fortebraccio into their city   On the 22nd March he thanked them for having given a good reception to the Bishop of Rieti, whom he had sent as Governor.   Regest. in Cod C –IV –1, University Library, Genoa

† SCHMARSOW, 135 ; REUMONT, Lorenzo, I , 273, 2nd ed. ; LEO, IV , 388

‡ See Cronica di Viterbo di Giov di Juzzo, 414

district.* Carlo Fortebraccio made a feint of going to meet the enemy, but on a day agreed upon with some of the nobles who were in league with him, suddenly appeared before Perugia. Happily the plot was discovered, and the seizure of the place prevented. Carlo thus saw the scheme, for whose accomplishment he had come to Tuscany, frustrated, and, as the hostile army had meanwhile increased in strength, he retired first to Montone and afterwards to Florence. Duke Federigo of Montefeltre had, by this time, led a large force into the Perugian territory. Montone was surrounded. The stronghold of the Bracci stood on a steep height, and was defended by lofty walls and various outworks, erected by the old Condottiere. All the plunder amassed by Fortebraccio was collected in this mountain fortress, and his wife, who was in charge, appeared with dishevelled hair, urging the garrison to offer a brave resistance. Carlo himself also sent messengers and letters from Florence to encourage them, promising that a powerful army should soon arrive to raise the siege, for he was assured of the assistance of the Medici and their allies; but no castle had yet been able to hold out against Federigo, "a stormer of cities like Demetrius, the son of Antigonus". The troops sent from Florence were repulsed, and Montone compelled to capitulate. "As pardon had been promised to them," says Sigismondo de' Conti, "they remained unharmed from first to last, and were, moreover, through the Pope's goodness, indemnified for their losses,

* See L'ÉPINOIS, 441; REUMONT, Lorenzo, I, 273, 2nd ed. The *Brief in the State Archives of Florence, here cited, was already known by means of a Regest in Arch. St. Ital, XVI., 2, p. 588. *Briefs regarding the sending of troops to Perugia were addressed to that city by Sixtus IV on the 25th and 28th of June and the 6th July, 1477. Regest in Cod C-IV.-1, University Library, Genoa

but the walls were destroyed, and a nest of rebellion was thus rooted out."*

The Sienese from this time forth were greatly alarmed · they concluded a close alliance with Sixtus IV. and Ferrante of Naples (8th February, 1478). Lorenzo himself could cherish no illusions as to the untoward position in which his own fault had placed him. He looked round about him for allies He thought he might depend upon Milan, and then turned to Venice to ask if he might, in case of necessity, reckon on the troops of the Republic, the answer was in the affirmative. Interests and parties became more and more sharply separated. Sixtus IV, Count Girolamo, Ferrante, and Siena being on one side, and Florence, Venice, and Milan on the other.†

Lorenzo's attitude towards the Pope remained unchanged. " It is hard to discover in these proceedings his customary circumspection and political penetration. Even his bio-grapher, Niccolo Valori, is not able to reconcile his conduct towards Sixtus IV. with the claims of either statesmanship or gratitude."‡

* SIGISMONDO DE' CONTI, I, 20, SCHMARSOW, 136, where the date of the 2nd September, as that of the fall of Montone, is wrong. ALLEGRETTI, 783, mentions the 27th September, and in accordance with this is a *Brief of the 30th Sept, 1477, to the Marquess of Mantua, informing him of the surrender of the place. Gonzaga Archives, Mantua, where is a long *Brief of the 2nd Sept., 1477, in which the Pope speaks of the shameful conduct of Fortebraccio.

† BUSER, Lorenzo, 34

‡ REUMONT, Lorenzo, I, 274, 2nd ed.

CHAPTER VI.

The Conspiracy of the Pazzi, 1478

At the beginning of the year 1478 the tension between
Rome and Florence was such as to render a catastrophe
almost inevitable   Wherever the opportunity had occurred,
Lorenzo de' Medici had thwarted the Pope; he had done
everything in his power to prevent the consolidation of the
temporal principality of the Pope and to foster the elements
of weakness which existed in the States of the Church *
His ambition and masterfulness had increased beyond all
bounds. he would have been prepared to sacrifice even the
precious blessing of ecclesiastical unity to carry out his own
schemes   His confidential letter of the 1st February, 1477,
to Baccio Ugolini shews that he would have contemplated
a schism without shrinking.   In this letter he says, in so
many words   "For any one in my position, the division
of power is advantageous, and, if it were possible without
scandal, three or four Popes would be better than a single
one"†

The downfall of the Medici, who had become the very
soul of the anti-Papal agitation in Italy, appeared the only

---

* Sugenheim, 350-52

† The passage to which Buser, Lorenzo, 32, first called attention is
as follows   *"Per mia pari fa che la auctorita si distribuischa et se
potessi esser sanza scandalo sarebbono meglo tre o quattro Papa che
uno" Arch Medic innanzi il princ. F, 89, f 351   State Archives,
Florence.

hope of security for the future. No one maintained this view with more warmth and eloquence than the Pope's nephew, Girolamo Riario, who felt that, as long as that family governed Florence, his hold upon Imola must remain precarious. The weakness of Sixtus IV. allowed to Girolamo an overweening influence in public affairs, and his ambition had become absolutely unbounded since his marriage with Caterina Sforza (May, 1472), a woman of a spirit kindred to his own.* " I am not," she said, " Duke Galeazzo's daughter for nothing : I have his brains in my head."†

Lorenzo, more or less by his own fault, had made many enemies in Florence as well as in Rome. Eaten up with pride, " he cared for no one and tolerated no rival. Even in games he would always be first. He interfered in everything, even in the private lives of the citizens, and in their marriages ; nothing could be done without his consent In the work of casting down the mighty and raising up those of low degree, he refused to act with that consideration and discretion which Cosmo had always been careful to observe "‡ Among the old nobility, in particular, there was great dissatisfaction. It was an essential part of the policy of the Medici to prevent any family, even if allied

* See **Report of Sacramorus ex urbe, 1477, May 25 (State Archives, Milan), and Juzzo's Chronicle in the edition of N. DELLA TUCCIA, 414 , F. OLIVA, Vita di C Sforza, 2 seq (Forli, 1821) , and BONOLI, 248

† SCHMARSOW, 137, conjectures that it was Caterina Sforza's account of her father's assassination which suggested to Girolamo that the haughty Prince who stood in the way of his further advancement might be removed in a similar manner   FRANTZ, 178, is convinced that the Milanese conspiracy encouraged the Pazzi to follow in the same track.

‡ Thus VILLARI, I , 40, judges Lorenzo de' Medici   The documents subsequently brought to light by Buser are not calculated to modify his opinion

or related to their own, from becoming too powerful or too
rich   Lorenzo de' Medici carried out this principle to the
utmost.   The Pazzi soon perceived that he was planning
their ruin.   They saw themselves excluded from all honourable offices and influential positions in the Republic, and at
last found their property also attacked   Grievances such as
these drove them into the party of Lorenzo's opponents,
" whose motto was, the Liberty of the Republic "*

The enemies of the Medici soon formed themselves into
two groups, one of which gathered round the Pazzi, and the
other round Girolamo Riario.   The hostility of the Pazzi
towards the Medici was purely political, or, perhaps, social
and political, in its character.   With Sixtus IV. and his
right hand, Riario, its motives were chiefly ecclesiastical

The indignation of the Florentine nobility against the
purse-proud tyranny of the Medici was so deep and so
wide-spread that, independently of Roman influence or
co-operation, it must sooner or later have led to a catastrophe such as it had often already produced   The outbreak
was hastened on by the alliance of the Pazzi with Girolamo,
which had become closer since the purchase of Imola.

It is uncertain whether the idea of effecting a change in
the form of government in Florence by violent means
originated with the Pazzi or with Girolamo   However this
may be, Francesco de' Pazzi, the Roman banker, was quite
as active and as eager in the matter as Riario †   Together

* See REUMONT, Lorenzo, I, 278, 2nd ed, who thinks that the
Pazzi were not the principal offenders. See SCHMARSOW, 137, and
FRANTZ, 175 *seq*.

† See FRANTZ, 204.   According to a passing observation of JAC
VOLATERRANUS, 128, the Roman Palace of the Pazzi was near the
Bridge of S Angelo, therefore in the Street Canale del Ponte, now
Via del Banco di S Spirito, where the Sienese and Genoese bankers
also lived

they induced the Archbishop of Pisa, Francesco Salviati, who was living at the Roman Court, and very bitter against the Medici, to join them.

The first most important point was to discover what line the Pope would take in regard to their plan. "There was no doubt that, in his present state of irritation, he would favour any attempt to bring about a change of government in Florence. But Girolamo Riario was also well aware that his uncle would not lend himself to any undertaking which could imperil the honour of the Papacy. They must aim at securing a free hand to carry out the revolution, without letting the Pope know how it was to be accomplished "* He must be led to believe that the ill-will in Florence against the Medici was already so great that they could be easily overthrown in the usual manner, that is to say, by an insurrection without assassination. Giovan Batista da Montesecco, a vassal of Riario's, was selected, after the blow had been struck, to march into Florence with an armed force, and follow up the advantage gained. He consented, but warned the conspirators that the business might not be so readily accomplished as they thought †

* REUMONT, Lorenzo, I , 280-81, 2nd ed   When VILLARI, I., 40, writes of the Pazzi conspiracy "It was planned in the Vatican by Sixtus IV., and many members of the most powerful Florentine families took part in it," he, by an unworthy perversion of facts, falsely attributes the origination of the crime to one who was only drawn into connection with it afterwards. For there is no doubt but that "Salviati and Fr de' Pazzi, with Count Girolamo," were, as CIPOLLA, 582, says, "primi autori di tutta quella intricata matassa" , see Montesecco's confession in CAPPONI   Reumont, in his day, also protested, in the Allg Ztg , against Villari's violent condemnation of Sixtus IV   See supra, p. 234

† See Montesecco's depositions in CAPPONI, II , 548-58   This edition is henceforth cited, as being the only one taken from the

Montesecco had also another misgiving as to what the Pope would say to the plan   The answer given by Girolamo and Salviati is most significant   "Our Lord, the Pope," they said, "will always do what we persuade him, and he is angry with Lorenzo, and earnestly desires this." "Have you spoken to him of it?" "Certainly," was the reply, "and we will arrange that he shall also speak of it to you"[*]

This interview, at which Salviati and Girolamo alone were present, soon took place. According to the later and thoroughly credible statement of Montesecco, the Pope from the first declared that he wished for a change of government in Florence, but without the death of any man "Holy Father," replied Montesecco, "these things can hardly be done without the death of Lorenzo and Giuliano, and, perhaps, of others also." The Pope answered . "On no condition will I have the death of any man : it is not our

original MS Montesecco merely details the preliminaries of the conspiracy , as to the crime itself, see (a) Politianus, De conjurat. Pactiana commentarius, 1478 (published again in OPERA POLITIANI, Basil, p 636–43, 1553, and in an old Italian translation, in P 's Prose volgari, ed. G Adimari, Napoli, 1769), a contemporary work, substantially true, but written with great bitterness (see ROSCOE, Lorenzo, 155, and REUMONT, II , 456, 2nd ed) ; (b) LANDUCCI, Diario, 17–19 , (c) Strozzi's Report, first published by Bini e Bigazzi, Vita di Fil Strozzi il vecchio, 55–9 (Firenze, 1851), and afterwards by FRANTZ, 207 seq ; (d) *Parenti (see infra), used by REUMONT, I , 287, 2nd ed , in his excellent description As to further authorities, see CAPPONI, II , 379 ; REUMONT, II , 456, 2nd ed. , and PERRENS, 384 seq Diplomatic Reports regarding the crime were hitherto unknown , I was fortunate enough to find the *Reports of the Milanese and Mantuan Ambassadors, written two days after the event ; the text of these two important pieces is given in Appendix, N. 57 and 58. As the Milanese Ambassadors were invited by Lorenzo, we have here a fresh account from eye-witnesses

* CAPPONI, II., 550 , REUMONT, Lorenzo, I., 283, 2nd ed.

office to consent to the death of any, and, even if Lorenzo
is a villain (villano), and has wronged us, I in no way desire
his death , what I do desire is a change of government." *
Girolamo then said, "What is possible shall be done to
avoid such a casualty, but if it should occur, will your
Holiness forgive its authors?"   "You are a brute," rejoined
Sixtus, " I tell you I do not desire the death of any man,
but only a change in the government; and to you also,
Giovan Battista, I say that I greatly wish that the government of Florence should be taken out of Lorenzo's hands,
for he is a villain and an evil man, and has no consideration
for us, and if he were out of the way we should be able to
arrange matters with the Republic according to our mind,
and this would be a great advantage."   "What your
Holiness says is true," said Riario and the Archbishop.
" If, after a change of government in Florence, the State is
at your disposal, your Holiness will be able to lay down
the law for half of Italy, and every one will have an interest
in securing your friendship   Therefore, be content to let us
do all that we can for the attainment of this end."   Here-
upon Sixtus IV again spoke very decidedly, without any
reserve or ambiguity.   "I tell you," he said, "I will not
Go and do as seems good to you, but no one's life is to be
taken "†   At the close of the audience, he gave his consent

* "Io non voglio la morte de niun per niente, perchè non è offitio
nostro aconsentire alla morte de persona , e bene che Lorenzo sia
un villano e con noi se porte male, pure io non vorria la morte sua
per niente, ma la mutatione dello Stato sì." CAPPONI, II , 552 ,
FRANTZ, 199.

† "Io te dico che non voglio   Andate e fate chome pare a voi,
purchè non cie intervengha morte" CAPPONI, II , 552 ; FRANTZ,
200 , REUMONT, Lorenzo, I , 284, 2nd ed.   All these strong words of
prohibition, although spoken in a private audience and to confidants,
must, according to GREGOROVIUS, VII , 242, 3rd ed , have been a
mere farce   "If," writes this historian, "he" (Sixtus) "did not

to the employment of armed men. Salviati said, as he withdrew : " Holy Father, be content to let us steer this bark, we will guide her safely." The Pope said, " I am content." " Sixtus IV. could only understand that those present fell in with his views, and he gave his consent."

The Pope, who had grown up in the cloister, and was little acquainted with the world, evidently believed that the advance of the troops assembled on the frontiers of the Republic, to join the discontented Florentines, would make it possible to overpower and capture the Medici.* The conspirators had other views. After repeated consultations, Girolamo and Salviati determined to act in opposition to the clearly expressed desire of the Pope. Preparations were at once commenced.

It is important to observe that Sixtus IV. again sent a message through a Bishop to urge the confederates to consider the honour of the Holy See and of Girolamo himself.† Had he known anything of the purpose of assassination, such an exhortation would have been absolutely unmeaning. " For, even if it succeeded, if both the Medici fell at once, and the Republic declared itself free, the

---

expressly desire their " (the Medici's) "death, he cared little whether blood was shed or not " Dr. Joseph Schmid has very kindly communicated to me the following extract from the work of Dr. Kempter, a gifted writer, too early taken from us . " How," he says, " can such an assertion, which is not merely prejudiced, but utterly unfounded, be reconciled with history and justice ? According to the literal sense of the documents, we should be condemned by any tribunal as guilty of libel and calumny, if we were to say that Sixtus IV. intended the death of the two Medici in the year 1478 "

* FRANTZ, 203

† See Montesecco in CAPPONI, II., 555. It is hard to understand how Reumont's critic can maintain, in the Rev. Hist., XXVI., 164, that the words in question are not to be found in Montesecco's confession in Capponi.

honour of the Holy See would be compromised   Sixtus
IV. accordingly remained, as is perfectly clear from the
whole of Montesecco's deposition, under the impression that
the plan was to take both the Medici prisoners . Lorenzo
on his journey to or from Rome, Giuliano perhaps on
his way from Piombino, and then to issue a Proclamation
from the Republic.   An unprejudiced critic cannot arrive
at any other conclusion from the documents before us." *

Circumstances had hitherto been unfavourable to the
execution of the scheme.   As, however, many had been
initiated, it became necessary to act promptly, to avoid the
risk of discovery.   Francesco de' Pazzi had at last won
over his brother Jacopo, the head of the family: among the
other conspirators may be named, Bernardo di Bandini
Baroncelli and Napoleone Franzesi Jacopo, son of the well-
known Humanist, Poggio Bracciolini, two of the Salviati,
and two clerics, Stefano of Bagnone, a dependent of
Jacopo de' Pazzi, and Antonio Maffei of Volterra, "who
had been led to take part in the plot by grief at the
misfortunes of his native city, whose ruin he attributed to
Lorenzo" Francesco de' Pazzi and Bandini were to
murder Giuliano, while Lorenzo was to be killed by
Montesecco , Salviati was to seize the Signorial Palace,
and Jacopo de' Pazzi to arouse the Florentines †

Just at this time, in the spring of 1478, the young
Cardinal Rafaello Sansoni-Riario came to Florence, in
consequence of an outbreak of the Plague at Pisa, and
took up his abode at the Villa of the Pazzi.   According
to the original plan, the Medici were to be assassinated at
a banquet, but, as Giuliano was prevented by indisposition
from attending it, the murder was postponed.   Cardinal
Rafaello, who was but eighteen, had no suspicion of all

* FRANTZ, 206–7.

† REUMONT, Lorenzo, I , 286 *seq.*, 2nd ed. ; FRANTZ, 197.

that was going on, and held fiee and friendly intercourse with Lorenzo de' Medici. Lorenzo repeatedly urged him to visit his Palace and the Cathedral, and Rafaello Sansoni promised to do so on Sunday, the 26th April, 1478. The conspirators determined to take advantage of this favourable opportunity for carrying out their purpose.

Loienzo had invited a brilliant company to dinner in honour of the Cardinal. Many Ambassadors and Knights, among them Jacopo de' Pazzi and Francesco Salviati, were invited. On the morning of the eventful day, the Cardinal, with a few companions, among whom were the Archbishop and Montesecco, went into the city Giuliano de' Medici excused himself from the feast on the plea of ill-health, but promised to be present in the Cathedral. "This caused a change of purpose, and the church, instead of the banqueting-hall, was selected as the scene of the murder."[*] Montesecco, however, at the last moment refused to perpetrate the crime in the Cathedral, either because he shrank from shedding blood in a church, or, on maturer consideration, from the affair altogether.[†] In his stead,

---

[*] REUMONT, Lorenzo, I., 287, 2nd ed   Regarding the frequency of paid assassinations at this period, see, besides the work of Lamansky, GOTHEIN, 22 ; and BURCKHARDT, II, 222 seq, 2nd ed., who, in I, 56 seq, 2nd ed, also speaks of murders in churches; see VILLARI, I, 27, and GEIGER, Renaissance, 192.

[†] So says SIGISMONDO DE' CONTI, I, 23 (o fosse mosso da religione o piu attentamente considerando a che impresa si sarebbe sobarcato— in the very carelessly-given Latin text the Preface is omitted). POLITIANUS (Op, 638) only says . "Destinatus ad Laurentii caedem Joannes Baptista negotium detractarat." *PARENTI, f 9b, only remarks at first, "ricussolo poi dicendo nolle fare in chiesa *secondo che molti dichono*" Later on he speaks of Montesecco's refusal in the following words : "o che non li bastasse alhora la vista o che l'amicitia teneva con Lorenzo lo rattenesi o che religione l'impedisce o che altra occulta causa lo movessi in effetto lo recuso" National Library, Florence.

the two clerics, Stefano and Maffei, undertook the
deed

The beginning of the second part of the High Mass was
the signal of action for the conspirators.* With the cry
"Ah! traitor!" Bernardo di Bandini Baroncelli made a
rush at Giuliano, and plunged his dagger in his side.
Severely wounded as he was, he strove to defend himself,
and, in doing so, pushed against Francesco de' Pazzi, from
whom he received a thrust in the breast. After this he
staggered about fifty paces further, and then fell to the
ground, where Francesco de' Pazzi stabbed him repeatedly
till life was extinct.† Stefano and Maffei had meanwhile

* On no point do accounts vary so much as with regard to the
exact time appointed for the deed ; see the comparison of passages
in FRANTZ, 208, N 1.   The Milanese Ambassador, in his *Report,
says the *Agnus Dei*, the Mantuan and LANDUCCI, 17, mention the
Elevation, these two moments are so near that it was very easy to
confound them   Vespasiano da Bisticci (MAI, I, 448), writes · "levato
il corpo di Cristo circa la communione", the Synodus Florentina
expressly declares   "Evenit autem ut in ecclesia ab elevatione ad
communionem res differretur."   F Strozzi, on the other hand, observes,
"in sul dire missa est" ; whereupon PERRENS, 385, adds   "A ce
moment, quoiqu'il y ait encore quelques prières à dire, chacun se leve,
sort de sa place, s'achemine vers les portes   Il y a dans l'église un
va-et-vient, un brouhaha très favorable aux violences.   En outre les
cloches sonnent alors   elles devaient avertir l'archévêque Salviati," &c.
But the bells were also rung at the *Elevation* and the *Communion*
In opposition to Strozzi's statement is the fact, expressly mentioned by
himself and several other writers, that Giuliano and Lorenzo, according
to their custom, were then walking about in the church (see Appendix,
N. 57), which, at the end of the Mass, would be natural and not worthy
of notice, but during its continuance was unusual, and a bad habit of
a corrupt age   The conspirators cannot then have chosen the *Ite
missa est* as their signal, for their victim in that case might easily
have escaped.

† " *Venuto el tempo a hora circa xiv Bernardo Bandini secondo che
ciaschuno afferma perche fu chosa quasi invisibile si cacciò adosso a

attacked Lorenzo, but only wounded him slightly. While his servants and some youths warded off further blows with their cloaks, he fled into the old sacristy, and its bronze door was fastened at once by Angelo Poliziano.*

All this was the work of a moment. Very few persons could see exactly what took place. This, and the horror which paralysed the senses of the immediate witnesses, accounts for the many variations in the details which have reached us Those who were at a little distance did not know what was going on, and many thought that the dome of the Cathedral was about to fall in.†

Salviati's attempt to take possession of the Signorial Palace was equally a failure. Jacopo de' Pazzi's cry of liberty met with no response, while the people rose on all

---

Giuliano et con una coltella li menò nel fiancho dicendo : hai traditore Giuliano ispaurito si mosse per volersi aiutare et retornarne et rintoppò in Francesco che medisimamente li menò un altro colpo nel petto. Il perche discostatosi Giuliano qualche cinquanta passi dal primo luogho dove fu ferito cascò in terra et Francesco addossoli tante ferite li dette che lo lasciò morto. Similmente trasseno fuori l'armi alcuni famigli di Francesco intorno a Giuliano , in nella baruffa ferirono Francesco in una gamba et gravemente." PARENTI, f. 11. (National Library, Florence) Machiavelli's assertion, repeated by REUMONT, I., 288, 2nd ed , that Francesco wounded himself, is therefore erroneous ; see also PERRENS, 386, N. 2

* See, besides the authorities cited above and in PERRENS, 387, the detailed account of the attack on Lorenzo in the *Reports of Don Albertinus (Gonzaga Archives), and of the Milanese Ambassadors. (State Archives, Milan) Appendix, N 57 and 58.

† POLITIANUS, Op , 639 See also STROZZI's description (*loc. cit.*, 56), and PARENTI, who writes * " Fatto questo la confusione fu grande tra cittadini che si trovavano nella chiesa   Chi si fuggi di chiesa e corse a casa sua, chi per paura si noscosse nella calonica di S Reparata, chi nelle case vicine, chi ando per l'arme et tornò in chiesa in difesa di Lorenzo, chi pure vi si rimase senza suspetto per veder le cose dove restavano et chi prese un partito e chi un altro."

sides to that of "Palle" (the balls in the armorial bearings
of the Medici). The slaughter of the guilty at once began.
Archbishop Salviati, his brother, and his nephew Jacopo
Bracciolini, with Francesco de' Pazzi, were all hung up
together from the window-bars of the Signorial Palace
Then the ropes were cut, so that the bodies fell amidst the
crowd,* where they were torn in pieces, and the severed
heads and limbs borne in triumph through the streets.
All who were supposed to be enemies of the Medici,
whether guilty or innocent, were butchered † The two
assassins who had fallen upon Lorenzo had their noses and
ears cut off before they were killed.

Montesecco was seized on the 1st, and beheaded on the
4th, May. Neither his withdrawal at the last moment, nor
the disclosures which he made in regard to the ramifications
of the conspiracy, availed to mitigate his sentence.‡ His
statements are of the greatest importance in their bearing
on the question of the participation of Sixtus IV. in the
events of the 26th April "It is certain that he desired
that the Medici should be overthrown by force. It is
equally certain that he can have known nothing beforehand
of the details of the attempted assassination, for these were
only arranged in haste on the very morning of the deed,
when it had been found necessary to abandon the plan of
murdering the brothers at a banquet "§

The further question, whether Sixtus IV. approved of the
murderous intention of the conspirators, must be answered

* See the Milanese Ambassadors' *Report of the 28th April, 1478, in
Appendix, N 57 State Archives, Milan

† LANDUCCI, 19, POLITIANUS, Op, 640; REUMONT, Lorenzo, I,
291 *seq*, 2nd ed, PERRENS, 391 *seq*

‡ PERRENS, 393.

§ H HUFFER in the Allg Ztg, 1875, p 1010, indirectly against
RANKE, Papste, I, 31, 6th ed

in the negative. Had this been the case, " Montesecco, whose interest it was to make the least of his own share in the crime, would scarcely have concealed the fact. His depositions bear upon them the stamp of truth, they have sometimes been taken in their obvious sense, and sometimes arbitrarily interpreted. In face of such evidence, to continue to make the Pope an abettor in the murder is worse now than it was 400 years ago." *

It is, however, deeply to be regretted that a Pope should play any part in the history of a conspiracy. Lorenzo had given Sixtus IV. good ground for a declaration of war, the principle of self-preservation demanded active measures for future security, and amongst them, the overthrow of this malignant enemy, but open warfare would certainly have been more worthy of a Pontiff than participation in a political plot, even had it involved no bloodshed.

* Opinion of REUMONT, Lorenzo, I., 292, 2nd ed., see II, 456, 2nd ed , and CREIGHTON, III , 75, in regard to the credibility of Montesecco's statements, which have been well described as an honourable, soldierly avowal. See also HEFELE-HERGENROTHER, VIII., 214, N 2, against BROSCH, Julius II, p. 10.

CHAPTER VII.

The Tuscan War.—French Intervention in Favour of the Florentines.—Relations of Louis XI. with the Holy See.—The Pope's Reconciliation with Florence.

An unsuccessful conspiracy always strengthens the power against which it has been directed. Lorenzo, who shewed admirable skill and tact in making the most of his advantage, now rose to absolute power in Florence. "Even those who had hitherto been heartily opposed to him, from Republican convictions, came over to his side The baseness of this attack on his life, to which was added the abuse of the sacred place and the most solemn act of worship, and the presence of a Cardinal, had called forth the greatest indignation."* Immediately after the failure of the plot, this anger found vent in the indiscriminate slaughter of all the enemies of the Medici; and, as time went on, far too much license was permitted to the mob. Twenty-three days after the event, boys were allowed to drag the half-clad corpse of Jacopo de' Pazzi through the streets, and fling it, with ghastly jibes, into the Arno.† Cruel reprisals continued even into the year 1480 · a well-informed contemporary doubts the guilt of those then sentenced Renato de' Pazzi, a peaceful man, devoted to study, who had refused to take any part in the conspiracy,

* Frantz, 213
† Landucci's description of this scene (Diario, 21-2) makes one shudder.

was certainly innocent. Nevertheless, he was executed *
Bandini was pursued to Constantinople, where the Sultan
gave him up to Lorenzo. This circumstance, and, in a yet
greater degree, the letters of condolence which he received
from all sides, from Princes and Republics, Statesmen and
Cardinals, helped to make him haughtier than ever †

Many ecclesiastics who had nothing to do with the
conspiracy were also executed ‡ The Archbishop of Pisa
was brutally scourged, without trial of any sort, and
Cardinal Rafaello Sansoni-Riario, although perfectly innocent, was imprisoned. These things greatly angered Sixtus
IV. Sigismondo de' Conti thus describes his feelings
when the tidings first arrived from Florence. "The Pope
expressed his horror at the crime, in which the conspirators
had added sacrilege to murder He was also deeply grieved
at the danger of Cardinal Sansoni, the disgraceful slaughter
of innocent priests, and the ignominious death of the Archbishop. He saw that a serious indignity had been inflicted
on the Church. This latter point was specially distressing
to him, because it made peace impossible, for it would

* REUMONT, Lorenzo, I., 292, 2nd ed. PERRENS, 396, agrees with
Reumont in saying that the vengeance exceeded all bounds, and was
quite unparalleled , see also p. 391, where Perrens speaks of an *orgie
de vengeance*, and VILLARI, Machiavelli, I , 41.

† In the State Archives, Florence, X -II -25, we find *Letters of
condolence from Lucca, Perugia, and Venice, and also from Cardinal
d'Estouteville. The last of these *Letters is dated Rome, 1478, April
28, and contains the following words : * " Per l'antiqua affectione et
singulare amore che havemo portato et portiamo a quella E.S. non
sanza grande dolore et despiacere de animo havemo intesa questa
matina la novita che li e stata et dallo altro canto inteso el buon
fine per la V. tranquillita et pace che e seguito secundo el dolendo
caso , habiamo ringraziato dio," &c. Spoleto also condoled with the
Florentines ; see SANSI, Storia, 80, and Doc 46.

‡ SIGISMONDO DE' CONII, I , 24

be a dangerous example for the future, if those who had so gravely infringed her rights were to be left unpunished." *
Accordingly, Sixtus IV. claimed satisfaction from the Florentines for their violations of ecclesiastical immunities, and also demanded the liberation of Cardinal Sansoni, and the banishment of Lorenzo

The first two demands were undoubtedly just. Donato Acciaiuoli, the Florentine Ambassador in Rome, though he had been deeply affronted by Riario,† strongly advised his Government to fulfil the promise which they had made in writing to release the unoffending Cardinal. Florence, he observed, gained nothing by his detention, and the refusal to comply with the righteous request of the Pope must lead to serious danger. But "the reasonable representations of their trusty servant," and Ferrante's warning not to add fuel to the fire,‡ were alike unheeded

It was decided that the Cardinal should for the time be retained in captivity, as a hostage for the safety of the Florentines in Rome.§ On the 24th May, Sixtus IV sent the Bishop of Perugia to the city with a letter from the Cardinal-Camerlengo to Lorenzo, informing him that a commission was already appointed to commence proceedings against the Republic, unless the Cardinal was

* SIGISMONDO DE' CONTI, I., 25; see *ibid*, 39, Sixtus IV.'s circular letter. In 1476 the Pope had remonstrated against the practice, which prevailed in England and Wales, of summoning clerics to appear before secular judges, as a breach of ecclesiastical law HARDOUIN, Conc., IX, 1496 *seq* ; ROSCOVÁNY, Monum., **I**, 115-17; WILKINS, III., 609-10, Mon Acad Oxon, I, 348 *seq*.

† Sixtus IV. maintained that this had occurred without his knowledge, and regretted the incident ; see Vespasiano da Bisticci in MAI, I , 451

‡ BUSER, Lorenzo, 37 , FRANTZ, 218.

§ See *Letter from the Milanese Ambassadors, dated Florence, 1478, May 20, Ambrosian Library

at once set free. Venice also advised the Florentines not
to give their enemies just cause of complaint by keeping
Sansoni in prison.*   All, however, was in vain , although
there had been ample time to establish the innocence of
the young Prelate, they would not hurry themselves, and
matters daily grew worse.†

Sixtus IV. was at last weary of waiting.   He " would,
no doubt, have preferred a reconciliation with Florence,
but that had been rendered impossible." ‡   Accordingly,
on the 1st June, fully four weeks after the tragedy,
and, therefore, when the excitement of the first moment
had subsided, he issued a Bull excommunicating Lorenzo
and his adherents   The Bull began by enumerating the
whole series of Florentine offences . the protection afforded
to the Pope's enemies, the attack on the Papal territory,
the hindrances placed in the way of those who were going
to Rome, and the detention of convoys carrying provisions
to the Court there, finally their treatment of Francesco
Salviati   Passing on to the events which had succeeded
the conspiracy, Sixtus IV. declared that the vengeance
taken in the form of executions and banishments had been
cruel and excessive. Lorenzo, the Gonfaloniere, and the
Prior in their mad fury, and by the instigation of the devil,
had even laid hands on ecclesiastics.   They had hanged
the Archbishop at the window of the Palace in the sight
of the crowd, and, cutting the rope, allowed the corpse to
fall down into the street.   Other innocent clerics, of whom
some belonged to the suite of Cardinal Sansoni, had also
suffered death.   Finally, although the Bishop of Perugia
had been sent as Legate to apply, in the name of the
Pope, for the release of the Cardinal, he had not been

* ROMANIN, IV , 390 , FRANTZ, 219

† REUMONT, Lorenzo, I , 299, 2nd ed.

‡ REUMONT, loc cit, 300

released   On account of these crimes, the sentence of the greater Excommunication was pronounced against Lorenzo and the other functionaries, and, in the event of these guilty persons not being delivered up, the city would be laid under an Interdict and its Archiepiscopal dignity cancelled.*

In spite of the severity of this Bull the Cardinal was still kept in prison, though the rigour of his captivity was somewhat mitigated   Its character may be gathered from the description a Sienese chronicler gives of his appearance when he was at length set free. " On the 13th June," says Allegro Allegretti, " Cardinal Sansoni-Riario came to Siena, more dead than alive from the terror he had endured, and still feeling as if the rope were about his neck."†

On the 20th June the Cardinal arrived in Rome   The deadly pallor of his face bore witness to the torments he had undergone, and this he retained to the end of his life.‡ Francesco Gonzaga had left the City two days previously for Bologna, where the friendship of the Bentivogli with the Medici awakened some anxiety.   The instructions given to Gonzaga betray the Pope's " uneasiness, and his consciousness of the bad impression produced by Florentine events."   They also shew that there had been a possibility

* Bull, " Iniquitatis filius et perditionis alumnus Laurentius de Medicis," in RAYNALDUS, ad an 1478, N 4 *seq*, and FABRONIUS, II , 121 *seq*. See FRANTZ, 221 *seq* , HEFELE-HERGENROTHER, VIII , 216 , and L'ÉPINOIS, 444

† ALLEGRETTI, 784, who also says that the Cardinal had been repeatedly threatened with hanging   In regard to Sansoni's Letter to the Pope, " which was apparently dictated " (REUMONT, I , 299), see the excellent observation of CIPOLLA, 586

‡ *Acta Consist, f 55, Secret Archives of the Vatican. According to the same authority, the ceremony of opening the Cardinal's mouth was performed on the 22nd June, and on the 26th he went as Legate to Perugia.

of reconciliation ; for, after exhorting the Bolognese to be faithful, Sixtus IV. observes, " We have not taken it ill, nor do we blame our people for their friendliness towards the Florentines when the tidings of these disturbances first reached them. On the contrary, we approved of this manifestation of sympathy with their neighbours, as the Republic had as yet done nothing against the Church, and we ourselves wrote to Florence to express our regret at the occurrence But, now that they have committed such shameful outrages on the ecclesiastical state, and have incurred the censures of the Church for their persistent violations of her rights, the Bolognese can no longer in honour continue to stand by them. Such a course would constitute an attack upon us, and would not assist them."*

The long-deferred, but practically inevitable, release of the Cardinal, whose innocence could not be denied, was the only concession made by Florence to the Pope The Excommunication was despised ; the Interdict,† pronounced on the 20th June, was disregarded ; and the alliance of other Powers, especially that of France, was sought Memorandums, couched in violent language, and evading any real answer to the very definite charges made by the Pope,‡ threats of a Schism, and preparations for war were the only reply vouchsafed by the once pious and fastidiously refined Florentines to the exhortations of

* REUMONT, I., 303, 2nd ed The copy here used of the *Instructio pro R Card Mantuano in the Cod Capponi, XXII (now in the National Library at Florence), is without date , the date may, however, be gathered from the statement in the *Acta Consist, Secret Archives of the Vatican, that Gonzaga started on the 18th June on his Mission to Bologna

† See RAYNALDUS, ad an. 1478, N. 12-13

‡ See FRANTZ, 228 seq , and REUMONT, I , 318, 2nd ed

Sixtus IV., who was convinced of the 'justice of his cause.*

Although the Florentine Government set the Excommunication and Interdict at naught and constrained the clergy to perform their sacred functions, they still complained of the distress which these censures had occasioned. The document known by the name of the "Synodus Florentina" bears eloquent testimony to the fanatically anti-Roman temper of the party of the Medici   In it Sixtus IV. is called "the adulterer's minion" and the "Vicar of the Devil." He is loaded with accusations, and the hope is expressed that God may deliver His people from false shepherds who come in sheep's clothing, but inwardly are ravening wolves †

---

* See, in particular, the autograph Letter to the Duke of Urbino, of 25th July, 1478, in FABRONIUS, II, 130-31.

† See HEFELE-HERGENROTHER, VIII, 218, and FRANTZ, 242 *seq* There is no room for doubt as to the authenticity of the document known as the Synodus Florentina, and published in FABRONIUS, II, 136 *seq*, for the original, probably in the handwriting of Gentile Becchi, Bishop of Arezzo, is preserved in the State Archives, Florence (C STROZZ, 387). The further question, whether the Synodus Flor was the work of an actual and formal Conciabulum, or was a more or less individual production of Gentile Becchi, has been treated at length by FRANTZ, 237 *seq* This conscientious writer believes that, "to the shame of the clergy who had grown up under the Medici," we must admit "that the Council was really summoned, and asserted the principles of the Synodus Flor." Striking as are Frantz's observations in detail, and thoroughly as he analyses the document, his reasons do not seem to me, nor to the latest biographer of Lorenzo (REUMONT, I, 318, 2nd ed), sufficient to establish his conclusion   FABRONIUS, Dollinger, 354, CAPPONI, II, 385, and CREIGHTON, III, 287, are of opinion that there was no Synod; HEFELE-HERGENROTHER, VIII, 218 *seq*, and REUSCH, II., 969, believe that there was.   The lamented C. Guasti was kind enough, at my request, to make minute investigations regarding this matter, but neither in the State Archives, nor

War began in July. Ferrante, hoping by this means to gain Siena, espoused the Pope's cause. Lorenzo looked for support to Venice and Milan, and especially to Louis XI., King of France.

The relations between this monarch and Sixtus IV. had, from the first, been precarious. In 1472 he had, indeed, sent an Embassy to Rome* to do homage, but it soon became evident that the King adhered to his former policy of holding the Pragmatic Sanction and the Council over the Pope's head, to be used as a bait or a rod according to circumstances.† The agreement arrived at by direct negotiation with Rome, in the summer of 1472, lasted but a short time. The University resisted it as contrary to the Basle Decrees. Although Louis XI. ratified the Concordat on the 31st October, 1472,‡ the Pragmatic Sanction continued practically in force.§ The Mission of the Bishop of Viterbo to France made no change in the state of affairs ‖ In the following year the tension between France and Rome increased. At the French Court it was asserted that the

those of the Duomo at Florence, is there any notice of this supposed Synod. in the latter, however, the expenses incurred on such an occasion would necessarily appear, yet no trace of them is to be found.

* Regarding the reception given to the French Ambassadors in Rome, see LJUBIČ, *loc. cit*, 22. Cardinal Gonzaga gave them a splendid banquet. See MOTTA in Bollet. st. d. Suizz, VI, 21.

† REUMONT, I., 305, 2nd ed. See PHILLIPS, III, 328, Kirchen-lexikon, II, 754, 2nd ed., GUETTÉE, VIII, 36; FIERVILLE, 146–7; and LEGEAY, II, 90.

‡ CHARAVAY, Sur les lettres de Louis XI, 9 (Paris, 1881); PICOT, I., 425; and FIERVILLE, 147.

§ FIERVILLE, 147; BULAEUS, V, 701 *seq.*

‖ The *Acta Consist., Secret Archives of the Vatican, mention d'Estouteville's nomination as legatus in Gallias on the 12th October, 1472; but he declined the appointment, and the Bishop of Viterbo went in his stead See GINGINS LA SARRA, I, 3 *seq.*

creation of Cardinals by Sixtus IV on the 7th May, 1473, was simoniacal   The Pope justified himself in a letter addressed to the King on the 22nd August, 1473.* Louis' reply is a combination of reclamations and insults. He angrily complained that the Pope had passed over the names of those whom he had proposed for the purple, while the wishes of other Princes were taken into consideration. He thought that he deserved better treatment than this, after having abolished the Pragmatic Sanction in his kingdom. He concludes with an appeal to Almighty God and to St Peter and St Paul !

At the end of 1474 Sixtus IV. had remonstrated with the King about his breach of the treaty of 1472 †   Louis answered by issuing an Ordinance on the 8th January, 1475, " for the protection of Gallican liberties," making the Royal Placet necessary for the publication of all Papal Decrees ‡   Measures of a more hostile character soon followed   The King began to agitate for the holding of a General Council, in which the "Church might be reformed," and "a lawful Pope elected in the place of Sixtus IV, who had obtained his elevation by simony." Secret Despatches, taken from a Hungarian Envoy, shew that Louis was seeking to win over the Emperor Frederick to this scheme   The King of Hungary, upon this, represented to the Duke of Burgundy that he and the King of Naples thought that the only way of counteracting these manœuvres was for the Pope himself at once to summon a Council. He

* I found in the State Archives of Milan a contemporary copy of this hitherto unknown *Document, and will publish it elsewhere, together with the *Answer of the French King. GUETTÉE, VIII , 38, may be corrected by reference to these documents

† D'ACHERY, Spicil , III , 844 seq. (Paris, 1723).

‡ See Archiv fur Kirchenrecht, XVIII., 170, and DAUNON, II , 263.

had obtained the consent of Sixtus IV., and urged the Duke to join them *

In January, 1476, Louis XI. issued a decree convening an Assembly of the French Church at Lyons.† Thus, the Council so much dreaded in Rome threatened to assume a tangible form. There can be no doubt that the Mission of the Legate, Giuliano della Rovere, to France was connected with this movement ‡ His presence there was also rendered desirable by the state of affairs in Avignon,§ of which city Giuliano was Archbishop; to this dignity was now added that of Papal Legate.|| Louis XI., who was by no means favourably disposed towards the Cardinal,¶ did everything in his power to have the former Legate, Charles of Bourbon, reappointed. A violent dispute ensued, in which it seemed probable that Avignon would have been lost to the Holy See. At last the difficulty was settled

* DROYSEN, II, 1, 301 ; SEGESSER, Beziehungen der Schweizer zu Matth Corvinus, 72 seq. (Luzern, 1860), RAUSCH, 148 seq , MENZEL-SCHLIEPHAKE, Geschichte von Nassau, V, 424 (Wiesbaden, 1879), doubts, but without sufficient reason, whether this agitation for a Council was serious.

† GINGINS LA SARRA, I., 285, see 321

‡ Although this Mission of Giuliano's (see next page, note *) is mentioned in universally accessible publications, BROSCH, in his Monograph, 7–9, knows nothing of it ! SCHMARSOW, 110, has already observed that, in consequence of this gross ignorance, Brosch "takes upon himself to suggest that the Cardinal Legate may at this time have fallen under the Pope's displeasure " We have here a characteristic example of this writer's want of circumspection, and of his mania for hazarding injurious conjectures on every occasion.

§ Giuliano left Rome on the 19th February, 1476, as Cardinal Gonzaga and J P. Arrivabene concur in stating in their *Letters, dated Rome, 1476, February 20. (Gonzaga Archives, Mantua) See also the Brief of the 24th February in MARTÈNE, II., 1528.

|| FANTONI, I , 343.

¶ See LAGER, Gorze, 85 , MARTÈNF, II , 1503–4.

by the elevation of Charles of Bourbon to the purple *
Giuliano founded a College in Avignon for poor students,
and was received with great honour in Rome when he
returned in the autumn   In the difficult negotiations with
the French monarch, he received much assistance from his
skilful judicial adviser, Giovanni Cerretani.†

In March, 1476, while Giuliano was still in France, a
letter from Louis XI was affixed to the door of St. Peter's,
commanding all Cardinals, Prelates, and Bishops of his
kingdom to appear at Lyons on the 1st May, to deliberate
upon the assembling of a General Council ‡   In the latter
part of April a French Embassy presented to the Pope
the strange request that he would consent that a Council
should be held at Lyons, and would be present there in
person ! Naturally, this request was not granted § For a
considerable time it was reported that the Pope, in order to
be beforehand with the opposition, would himself summon
a General Council to meet in Rome.‖   In the end, neither
Assembly came to anything

* Besides FANTONI, *loc cit*, see, regarding Giuliano's Mission to
France, GINGINS LA SARRA, II, 33 *seq*, 97, 131, 185; N. DELLA
TUCCIA, 413, KNEBEL, II, 429, AMMANATI, Epist (Frankfort
edition), ep 877 and 886, MARTÈNE, II. 1529, 1547, SCHMARSOW,
109-10, REUMONT, Lorenzo, I, 305, 2nd ed, FRIEDBERG, II, 477,
CHARPENNE, Hist des réunions temp d Avignon, I., 10 (Paris, 1886)

† PALMERIUS, 259 According to the *Acta Consist. of the Secret
Archives of the Vatican, Giuliano reached Foligno on his homeward
journey on the 4th Oct., 1476, "ubi papa cum curia sua tunc residebat"
This date was hitherto unknown.

‡ KNEBEL'S Tagebuch, II., 391-2; RAUSCH, 150 See also
MARTÈNE, II, 1535, and the **Despatch of J P Arrivabene, dated
Rome, 1476, May 14 Gonzaga Archives, Mantua

§ Sixtus IV. explained his reasons in a **Brief to the Duke of
Milan, dated Rome, 1476, April 21. (State Archives at Milan) A
similar *Brief to Ercole d'Este is in the State Archives, Modena

‖ See KNEBEL'S Tagebuch, II, 408; also 405 and 406

Trusting in the schismatical tendencies of Louis XI., Lorenzo had, on the 2nd May, 1478, begged him to interfere in the contest between Florence and Rome, and a little later had recommended that the usual means of intimidation, the proposal to hold a Council, should be employed.* Louis XI. did not need much persuasion. "The King," writes a contemporary Ambassador, "has long cherished the plan of bringing about a schism in the Church. That which has taken place in Florence has furnished him with an excellent pretext He is, therefore, sending Philippe de Commines to Turin, Milan, and Florence Commines will not go to Venice, the King being persuaded that, in consideration of the close alliance existing between him and the Signoria, the intimation of his wishes by a simple letter will suffice."†

Sixtus IV. did not allow himself to be cast down by the threats of the French King. On the 11th July an outbreak of the Plague obliged him to betake himself to Bracciano,‡ where he was joined by the representatives of Venice, Milan, Florence, and Ferrara, together with two new French Envoys On the 1st August all the Envoys met together

* BUSER, Beziehungen, 193–4. See DESJARDINS, Polit. de Louis XI, 29, and Négociat, 171 *seq*

† Despatch of the Milanese Ambassador of the 16th June, 1478, in KERVYN DE LETTENHOVE, I, 173 *seq*. See FRANTZ, 261, and HEFELE-HERGENROTHER, VIII., 220 Nothing, unfortunately, is known of the negotiations with the Pope carried on by Commines ; even the time of his visit to Rome has not been exactly ascertained , see REUMONT, I , 310, 2nd ed

‡ *Acta Consist, f 55, Secret Archives of the Vatican. We learn from this authority that Sixtus IV did not return to Rome until the 17th September. HEFELE-HERGENROTHER, VIII., 223, is, accordingly, mistaken. The Plague, as J. P. Arrivabene in a *Despatch, dated Rome, 1478, May 24, declares, had broken out in May. Gonzaga Archives, Mantua.

in the Castle of the Orsini, and declared that the conduct
of Sixtus IV. towards Florence and towards Lorenzo was
a scandal to Christendom, because it hindered the Turkish
war. Repeated requests for the removal of the censures
had been made to him without any effect. For this reason,
and also because all countries, chiefly through the faults
of their rulers, needed thorough reform, they demanded
the assembly of a Council in France.* On the 16th
August Louis XI strictly forbade the transmission of any
money to Rome. In September the temporal and spiritual
magnates of France met at Orleans They left it to the
King's choice, "either in the following year to summon a
National Council at Lyons, or to prevail on the Pope to
hold an Œcumenical Council Louis XI. deemed it best
to attempt the latter alternative "†

At the beginning of December, 1478, Sixtus IV., with the
object of counteracting French intervention in the contest
with Florence, as well as the schismatic tendencies of Louis
XI and his Italian allies, sent two Nuncios to the Emperor
Frederick III, requesting his mediation and assistance ‡

* The *Document drawn up on this occasion, which GREGOROVIUS,
VII, 246, 3rd ed, was the first to point out, is in the State Archives,
Florence, Atti publ, CLXI. It begins with the words: "In nomine,
&c, 1 Aug, 1478 Cum Sixtus IV injuste," &c, and concludes as
follows · "Acta facta et gesta fuerunt predicta omnia et singula supra-
scripta Brachiani Sutrin dioc terrar (not territ, as Gregorovius reads)
dom Neapoleonis de Ursinis et in palatio sive fortitio dicti oppidi
Brachiani" The French Envoys were Tristanus comes Claramontis
and Gabriel Vives Regarding the unjust accusations made by the
King, see FRANTZ, 261 seq On the 5th Aug, 1478, entrance into
France was denied "à ung nommé Herosme Riaire, homme de bas
lieu," &c., see BASIN-QUICHERAT, III, 67.

† REUMONT, Lorenzo, I, 327, 2nd ed , GUETTÉE, VIII, 40 seq ,
LEGEAY, II, 318 , BUSER, Beziehungen, 478 , PERRENS, 413.

‡ Sixtus IV had already written to the Emperor about Lorenzo on

The Ambassadors of the King of France reached Rome in January, 1479, and at once presented a memorial desiring the assembling of a General Council. Sixtus IV. replied that, if it were possible, such a measure would be very agreeable to him. At the same time, he made it plain that the Pope presides in an Œcumenical Council, and that to him belongs the right to summon it. He pointed out that the Prelates, who are all bound to maintain the liberty of the Church, would sit in it. No one of them would say that Lorenzo had the right to cause the Archbishop of Pisa to be ignominiously executed. All would rather be of opinion that he ought first to have been sentenced by an ecclesiastical tribunal. No Council could be called without the consent of the Emperor and the other Princes. The summoning of such an Assembly belongs to the Pope, and he would take council with the Cardinals on the subject Sixtus IV. went on to speak in detail of the ecclesiastical policy of Louis XI. As to the Pragmatic Sanction, he said, either it was a just measure, in which case the King ought not to have revoked it, or an unjust one, in which case he ought not to think of reviving it In recalling the Prelates from Rome, he had done wrong their Superior is the Pope. The King would do better to lead Lorenzo to acknowledge his errors, and to persuade him to make fitting atonement , if he did this, he would obtain pardon, and all else would be easily settled. A Papal Ambassador had, moreover, been sent to France, and would be able to give the King further explanations. Numerous letters received from members of the clergy bear witness to the indignation that would be felt if the Pope did not appear

the 23rd May, and again on the 6th Aug., 1478 ; on the 1st December, he informed him of the arrival of L de Agnellis ; see Mon Habsb, 451, 454 The *Instruction for L. de Agnellis and A de Grassis are in Appendix, N. 59 Secret Archives of the Vatican.

as the avenger ot the insults offered to the Church in Florence *

On the 15th February another Consistory was held, and the Emperor's Ambassadors, who had meanwhile arrived, took part in it. They expressed themselves with decision regarding the rights of the Holy See, and did not think a Council necessary, but were of opinion that the Pope should deal mercifully with the Florentines, and conclude a peace, considering the present danger from the Turks †

Most of the Cardinals also desired the restoration of peace, but Count Girolamo and Ferrante laboured with all their might against it, and were at first successful ‡

The uncertain attitude of Bologna at this time caused the greatest anxiety to Sixtus IV., and Cardinal Gonzaga was sent there §

* RAYNALDUS, ad an 1478, N 18 *seq.* ; FRANTZ, 283 *seq* ; HEFELE-HERGENROTHER, VIII., 224 *seq.*

† HEFELE-HERGENROTHER, VIII , 227 *seq.*, GUETTEE, VIII , 41-2, where are details regarding the negotiations which followed DESJARDINS, Polit. de Louis XI , 31, sees the matter completely from the French King's point of view, and believes in his honourable feeling for Christendom !

‡ See N DELLA TUCCIA, 421, and in Appendix, N. 60 and 61, Pandolfini's *Letters of the 20th and 25th March, 1479   State Archives, Florence

§ See *Ghirardacci, St di Bologna, *loc cit* (see our Vol III , p 243), and an autograph **Letter of Sixtus IV to Cardinal Gonzaga, dated ex urbe 20 Martii, 1479 (Orig in the Episcopal Archives, Mantua), from which it appears that Gonzaga was also to go to Germany   This Mission, however, came to nothing; for on the 21st April, A tit S. Sabine card. Montisregalis [=Auxias de Podio] was appointed legatus de latere in partibus Alamanie , he set off on the 17th May   (*Acta Consist , f 57, Secret Archives of the Vatican)   On the last day of March Sixtus IV. commanded Card. Gonzaga, should the Bolognese continue obstinate in their disobedience, at once to leave the city *Brief of this day in the State Archives, Milan   By the end of the

In the struggle with Florence, things at last seemed taking a more favourable turn, for, on the 4th April, 1479, the ecclesiastical censures were suspended, and a temporary cessation of hostilities proclaimed by the Pope * Emboldened by this partial success, the Florentines, on the 28th April, rejected the terms of peace then proposed by him. In order to bring pressure to bear upon Sixtus IV., on the 27th May the League, through the Venetian Ambassador, declared that, unless within a period of eight days he should agree to a peace, their representatives should be instructed to leave Rome. Sixtus IV. was justly astounded at this communication, which "was tantamount to a refusal to make any concession to his demands. The limit of eight days, also, was an insult, since it was obviously impossible for him to conclude a peace without the consent of his allies, Naples and Siena."† On the 31st May the Ambassadors again assembled in the Pope's presence for further negotiations Sixtus IV. caused a long statement to be read, shewing that he had tried every possible means for the restoration of peace "The Venetian Ambassador replied in a speech in which he greatly incensed the Pope, by dwelling largely on the obnoxious topic of the Council" When the French Ambassador, in the name of his master, and in accord with the League, endeavoured to enter a protest against the

year, partly through the conciliatory action of the Pope (see *Letter of Joh. Angelus de Talentis, dated Rome, 1479, May 27, State Archives, Milan), matters were so far settled that in a *Brief, dated Rome, 1479, November 20, Sixtus was able to praise the Bolognese for their obedience   State Archives, Bologna

  * Sixtus IV and Giuliano della Rovere lost no time in informing the French Ambassadors of the fact   See in Appendix, N 62 and 63, *Letters of the 6th and 7th April, 1479, from the Milanese State Archives.

  † HEFELE-HERGENROTHER, VIII , 231.

failure of the negotiations, Sixtus IV. brought the meeting to a close.   Soon after this the Envoys of the League left Rome, unaccompanied, however, by those of the French King.*

The position of the Florentines grew much worse in the autumn.† Discontent was more and more openly expressed ; Lorenzo was told to his face that the city was weary of war and needed peace.   It became evident that there was no hope of assistance from Louis XI, and this conviction had a great effect on public feeling ‡

In his necessity Lorenzo boldly resolved to go himself as a suppliant to Naples (6th December, 1479).   The utter faithlessness of Ferrante now became evident   Regardless alike of the alliance concluded with the Pope, and of the loyalty which he owed to his suzerain, he did not hesitate to betray him.   The treaty of peace, which was the result of his negotiations with Lorenzo and Lodovico il Moro, regarded nothing but his own interests, although he had but recently sworn that he would lose ten kingdoms and his crown rather than let Lorenzo go without securing the conditions desired by Sixtus.§   The Pope bitterly complained that the victory which had been in his hands was filched away, as it were, behind his back ; but, that no one might accuse him of being an obstacle in the way of peace, he ratified the treaty, stipulating, however, that

* BUSER, Beziehungen, 208-12, and Lorenzo, 141 *seq.*, DESJARDINS, Négociations, I, 185-6, PERRENS, 426-7

† The Pope was at this time more than ever resolved on the expulsion of Lorenzo from Florence, see the *Briefs of the 20th and 22nd Sept, 1479, to Alfonso of Calabria and Federigo of Urbino State Archives, Milan.

‡ FRANTZ, 332 *seq*

§ FRANTZ, 351   Regarding Ferrante's artfulness and faithlessness, see GOTHEIN, 32, and SYBEL'S Hist Zeitschrift, N F, XXI, 365

Lorenzo should come in person to Rome, from this time "the Tuscan war languished "*

Meanwhile Otranto had been taken by the Turks, and this loss did more than anything else to turn attention from these internal disputes to the dangers in the East, and to remove the last obstacles in the way of a complete reconciliation. " The advantage which the Florentines derived from the altered condition of affairs was so manifest that many voices were heard which accused Lorenzo of having encouraged the Sultan to attack Apulia "† Florence decided to send a solemn Embassy to Rome, praying for the removal of the Interdict It arrived on the 25th November, 1480, and the negotiations for peace were promptly brought to a happy conclusion. On the 3rd December the Florentines were released from all ecclesiastical censures.‡

* HEFELE-HERGENROTHER, VIII , 236; GREGOROVIUS, VII , 247, 3rd ed
† REUMONT, Lorenzo, I , 368, 2nd ed , FRANTZ, 352.
‡ Particulars of the ceremonies and of the conditions of peace are given by JACOB. VOLATERRANUS, 113 *seq.*

CHAPTER VIII.

TURKISH EXPEDITIONS AGAINST RHODES AND OTRANTO —RESIST-
ANCE OFFERED BY SIXTUS IV.—DEATH OF SULTAN MAHOMET.
—THE POPE'S REPEATED ATTEMPTS AT A CRUSADE.

IT has always been a part of the policy of the Eastern
conquerors to profit by the quarrels of the Western Powers
From this point of view the last thirty years of the 15th
Century had been an exceptionally favourable period for
the Sultan   Half Europe was convulsed with wars, and,
from 1478, Rome, hitherto always the foremost in the
defence of Christendom, had been involved in an unholy
struggle, with the result that for a time Sixtus IV did
nothing in this direction.

From 1477 the outlook in the East had grown more
and more gloomy. " In May of that year, while a Turkish
army blockaded Lepanto and Leucadia, Achmed Bey
attacked Kroja, the capital of Albania, and, on the 15th
June, 1478, this stronghold was compelled to capitulate
Schabljak, Alessio, and Drivasto also fell into the hands
of the Turks ; only Antivari and Scodra continued to hold
out though besieged " *

Even more distressing than these losses were the barbarous incursions of the Turks into the Austrian Alpine
Provinces, † Friuli, and Upper Italy. The Tuscan war

* HERTZBERG, Osmanen, 630   See FALLMERAYER, Albanes. Element, 103 *seq*, and MAKUSCEV, Slaven, 115

† See HUBER, III, 234 *seq*, where are also details regarding the

deprived the Venetians of all hope of assistance from their fellow-countrymen , and an alarming outbreak of the Plague added yet more to their discouragement. The Signoria took the momentous resolution of abandoning the contest. On the 25th January, 1479, a treaty of peace was signed at Stamboul by Giovanni Dario, the Venetian Commissioner. The conditions were hard. Not only Kroja and Scodra, the Albanian chieftains, and the house of Tocco, but also even Eubœa and Lemnos were abandoned to the enemy ; however, the trade of the Republic with the Levant was preserved *   From this moment a period begins during which the whole policy of Venice is devoted to the one object of maintaining this advantage.†

In the very nature of things, for a conquering state there is no standing still. This was evident after the great successes gained by the Turks over the first naval power of the West. In the summer of 1479, Leonardo Tocco the Third was driven from Leucadia. The unfortunate man sought refuge in Rome, where the number of fugitives from the East was constantly increasing. Sixtus IV. generously gave him 1000 ducats at once, and allowed him twice that sum as a yearly pension, promising to do more when better times should come.‡

The next year an attempt was made to put an end to the rule of the Knights of St John in Rhodes. They had

conflicts in Moldavia and Wallachia Huber seems to have been unacquainted with Haselbach's work, Die Turkennoth im 15 Jahrhundert mit besonderer Berucksichtigung der Zustande Oesterreichs, Wien, 1864

* See ZINKEISEN, II, 432-7, HERTZBERG, 632 , HEYD, II., 327 seq. , HOPF, Griechenland, LXXXVI, 161 , Cal of State Papers, Venet, I, 139 seq

† ZINKEISEN, II, 441

‡ JACOB VOLATERRANUS, 102

long been the terror of the Turks, and the object of their bitterest hatred. As there was no Christian naval power now to be feared, the task seemed an easy one ; but the heroic valour of Pierre d'Aubusson and his Knights wrought marvels, and this last bulwark of Eastern Christendom was saved for a time (Summer of 1480).* Tidings of the approach of succour from the West hastened the departure of the Turks † Sixtus IV had granted a special Indulgence to all who should do anything to aid the Knights ; had called upon the Italian Powers to assist them, and besides himself sending two ships with provisions and war materials, was preparing for further exertions ‡

Western Christendom had not yet recovered from the agitation caused by the struggle in Rhodes, when a fresh disaster filled all hearts with terror and dismay

Mahomet had long been gazing with covetous eyes on the wealth of Italy, the seat of his great enemy, the Papacy.§ There can be no doubt that the insane jealousy of Venice at the increase of the power of Naples, hurried on the impending attack. If the Signoria did not actually invite the Turks into Italy, they certainly allowed them to believe that their arrival would be far from unwelcome to them ‖

The result appeared in the despatch of a Turkish fleet, with a number of troops on board, to Apulia On the 11th

---

* ZINKEISEN, II., 464 *seq.*, BERG, Die Insel Rhodus, 60, 133 *seq* (Braunschweig, 1862) The Knights were praised by all for the courage displayed in this war , see ROHRICHT-MEISNER, Pilgerfahrten, 22 (Berlin, 1880)

† SIGISMONDO DE' CONTI, I , 102

‡ RAYNALDUS, ad an 1480, N 2 *seq* , 24 ; JACOB VOLATERRANUS, 106 ; Diario Parm., 334, 345, 348 , FOUCARD, Dispacci, 104 *seq* , 106 *seq* , 118 *seq* , 131, 139, THEINER, Mon. Pol , II , 214 , GUGLIELMOTTI, 423.

§ See MAKUSCEV, Slaven, 90

‖ BROSCH, Julius II , p 18. See CIPOLLA, 605, and FOUCARD, Dispacci, 132.

August, 1480, Otranto was in the hands of the Infidel.[*] Of its 22,000 inhabitants, 12,000 were put to death with terrible tortures, and the rest carried away into slavery. The aged Archbishop, who, with heroic courage, had remained to the last before the altar imploring the help of God, was sawn in two, as was also the Governor. Indescribable horrors were perpetrated Many captives, who refused to become Mahometans, were slaughtered on a hill before the city, and their bodies thrown to the dogs[†]

The tidings that the victorious banner of the Crescent had been planted on Italian soil "produced unutterable consternation."[‡] "In Rome," says Sigismondo de' Conti, "the alarm was as great as if the enemy had been already encamped before her very walls. . Terror had taken such hold of all minds that even the Pope meditated flight. I was at that time in the Low Countries, in the suite of the Cardinal Legate Giuliano, and I remember that he was commissioned to prepare what was necessary at Avignon, for Sixtus IV had decided upon taking refuge with the French, if the state of affairs in Italy should become worse."[§]

---

* See *Copia della piesa d'Otranto da Turchi nel anno 1480 in Cod X -IV, 52, N 17   (Casanatense Library, Rome) See JAC VOLATER-RANUS, 110, FOUCARD, Dispacci, 85, 88, 92, 111, 153, 165 seq ; M SANUDO, 1213, Diar. Parm, 352, CIPOLLA, 604

† The height on which these victims died for their Faith has ever since borne the name of the Martyrs' Hill They were at once venerated as saints by the people, and ultimately canonised by Clement XIV Acta Sanctorum, 18th Aug, p 179 seq., ROHRBACHER-KNOPFLER, 248, SUMMONTE, III, 501 seq

‡ See BASIN-QUICHERAT, III, 68, SERRA, Liguria, 267, CIAVARINI, I, 195; BLASI, Sicilia, II, 665, see also his Storia dei vicerè, &c, di Sicilia, 118 (Palermo, 1842).

§ SIGISMONDO DE' CONTI, I, 107-9; SCHMARSOW, 142, GUGLIEL-MOTTI, 429. Ferrante had sent a special messenger to inform the Pope of the fall of Otranto, see FOUCARD, Dispacci, 86.

Ferrante's dismay was even greater than that of the Pope
His son, Alfonso, was immediately recalled from Tuscany,*
and the assistance of Sixtus IV , and all the other Princes
of Italy, vehemently invoked with the threat that, unless
active support were speedily given, he would throw in his
lot with the Sultan for the destruction of all the others.
We see, from the report of a contemporary historian on the
Papal side, how unfriendly were the relations between the
Pope and the King of Naples at this time   "Sixtus IV ,"
he writes, "would have witnessed with great indifference the
misfortunes and losses of his faithless ally, had Ferrante's
enemy been any one but the Sultan ; but it was a very
different matter when the common foe of Christendom had
actually got a footing on Italian soil, and speedily the Papacy
and Rome itself were threatened with utter ruin, unless he
were promptly expelled.   He at once sent all the money that
he could get together, permitted tithes to be levied from all the
clergy in the kingdom, and promised a Plenary Indulgence
to all Christians enlisting under the banner of the Cross. '†

Immediately on the landing of the Turks in Apulia,
Sixtus IV. had appealed to the Italian Powers, and his
cry for help was soon repeated in yet more pressing
terms ‡ " If the faithful," he said, " especially the Italians,
wish to preserve their lands, their houses, their wives,
their children, their liberty, and their lives, if they wish
to maintain that Faith into which we have been baptised,

* NOTAR GIACOMO, 146 , G A PECCI, Mem di Siena, I , 14 *seq*
(Siena, 1755) ; FOUCARD, Dispacci, 82, 121, 153 ; REUMONT, Lorenzo,
II , 368 *seq* , 2nd ed.

† SIGISMONDO DE' CONTI, *loc cit*.   See FOUCARD, Dispacci, 110 *seq* ,
142, 609 *seq*.

‡ Florence also received similar *Briefs, dated Rome, 1480, July 27
and August 5   (State Archives, Florence, X -II.-25, f 154b-156b)   The
Pope had already, in July, the intention to fit out a fleet in Genoa, and so to
meet the Turkish danger.   CHMEL, Briefe, 278 *seq* , 299 *seq*., 302, 325 *seq*

and through which we are regenerated, let them at last trust
in our word, let them take up their arms and fight "*

In a Consistory, held on the 14th August, it was determined that every possible effort should be made to expel
the Turks from Otranto †

On the 18th August Gabriele Rangoni was appointed
Cardinal Legate to Naples, and, on the 23rd, he started
for his post.‡   On the 22nd September fresh Briefs were
addressed to all the Italian States, desiring them to send
representatives to a Congress to be held in Rome at the
beginning of November §   The example set by Sixtus IV,
in his reconciliation with Florence, could not fail to have a
good effect on his efforts for the restoration of peace in
Italy.   One of the conditions of the treaty with the
Republic was that it should furnish fifteen galleys for the
war with the Turks.|| On the 4th December Cardinal
Savelli was sent to Genoa, to endeavour to reconcile the
contending parties there, and to superintend the equipment
of the Papal fleet in the harbour ¶

---

* See RAYNALDUS, ad an. 1480, N. 20–28, and Diar Parmen, 352

† FOUCARD, Dispacci, 98, 112

‡ *Acta Consist, Secret Archives of the Vatican   See FOUCARD,
Dispacci, 114, 142, and 154–5, Brief of Sixtus IV, of the 16th August,
regarding the purposed Mission of the Bishop of Terracina to Naples.
An undated *Brief of Sixtus IV., referring to Rangoni's Mission, is in
the Library at Bamberg (bound up with Incunabel, Q II, 24).

§ *Brief to Florence, dated Rome, 1480, Sept 22   State Archives,
Florence, X –II –25, f 158b ; a copy is in the State Archives, Milan,
Autogr.

|| REUMONT, Lorenzo, I , 370, 2nd ed.

¶ *Acta Consist., Secret Archives of the Vatican   The 20th December
is here mentioned as the day of Savelli's departure, while JACOB
VOLATERRANUS, 116, has the 19th. From the *Acta Consist we
learn that the Cardinal had only returned from Perugia on the 2nd
of the month.

The Divine assistance was invoked by an ordinance of the Pope, desiring that the Octave of the Festival of All Saints should henceforth be solemnly celebrated throughout Christendom.* The preparations for the Crusading fleet were at once commenced, twenty-five galleys were to be built, partly in Ancona, and partly in Genoa† As the Papal Treasury was empty, Sixtus IV was compelled to have recourse to extraordinary taxation. A tax of a gold ducat was, in the first instance, laid upon every hearth‡ in the States of the Church, and then a tithe imposed for two years on all churches and convents in the Papal territory §

A Brief of Sixtus IV. to Bologna, dated 3rd January 1481, furnishes detailed information regarding the delibera-tions of the Envoys assembled in Rome. The Pope explains that, as a tax for the expenses of the Turkish war has to be imposed on all Princes, he and the Cardinals, in order to set a good example, have undertaken to contribute the sum of 150,000 ducats, although so large an amount is almost beyond his powers 100,000 ducats of this is to be expended on the equipment of twenty-five triremes, and the remaining 50,000 to be sent to the King of Hungary He, moreover, engages to collect 3000 soldiers for the recovery of Otranto, to which place he has already sent troops. With regard to the building of the fleet, the Ambassadors

* RAYNALDUS, ad an 1480, N 29

† JACOB VOLATERRANUS, 115, GUGLIELMOTTI, 432.

‡ See the **Brief to Card Gonzaga of the 29th Nov., 1480. (State Archives, Bologna.) A Sienese Ambassador, whose *Report is, unfor-tunately, half-destroyed, writes, under date Rome, 1480, Nov. 20, that the Pope said *" Nos una cum istis venerab. fratribus nostris sumus parati pro posse et ultra posse facere debitum nostrum et exponere introitus nostros et omnia bona nostra et calices, &c." State Archives, Siena

§ See RAYNALDUS, ad an 1480, N 28, and a *Brief to Bologna, dated 1480, December 17 State Archives, Bologna, Lib Q 3

are of opinion that 100 triremes must be prepared, and 200,000 ducats be sent annually to the King of Hungary. The money required for these purposes is to be raised among the several Powers, he and the Cardinals having already contributed their share, the preparation should be completed by March. The Bolognese must not delay, for the danger was imminent.*

The action of the Pope was not confined to Italy He was unremitting in his endeavours to unite all the Princes of Europe against the common foe The results varied in different places King Edward IV. of England declared that it was unfortunately impossible for him to take part in the war † No help was to be expected from distracted Germany Even now, the States assembled to take counsel together were unable to come to terms ‡

Tidings of a more favourable nature arrived from France, where Giuliano della Rovere was at this time acting as Papal Legate.§ He had been charged to bring about a peace between Louis XI., Maximilian of Austria, and the Flemings, to obtain the release of Cardinal de La Balue, and procure French assistance for the Crusade.‖ Giuliano had

---

* MAKUSCEV, I, 311-12 See also the Milanese Report of 13th Dec, 1480, in CHMEL, Briefe, 347 *seq*

† Cal of State Papers, Venet, I, 142-3

‡ ENNEN, III, 308

§ BROSCH, Julius II., pp 15 and 304, following Jac Volaterranus, only mentions the 9th June as the date of Giuliano's departure. From the Acta Consist, Secret Archives of the Vatican, f 59, we learn that the Cardinal was appointed legatus de latere for France on the 28th April; the 9th June is also given here as the day when he left Rome Giuliano was at Parma on the 3rd July See Diar Parm, 343

‖ This appears from a *Letter, written by Giuliano della Rovere to Sixtus IV, dated Vendôme, 1480, Aug 24, in which he speaks of his favourable reception by Louis XI. I found a copy of this document in the State Archives, Milan.

been obliged to renounce the exercise of his full powers as
Legate, but he was in great measure successful in regard
to the Crusade.* On the 28th August he was able to
forward to the Pope a royal letter, containing the most
satisfactory assurances as to the share France would take
in the war.† Envoys were to be sent to Rome to settle
the details. In the instruction for this Mission, Louis XI.
says . "No sufficient resistance can be offered to the Turks
at less cost than at least 100,000 golden scudi a month.
He proposed himself to furnish 100,000 annually, and
twice that sum if the Pope would allow him to impose a
tribute on all ecclesiastics in his kingdom, and would send
him a Legate provided with all the faculties desired by the
King, and especially with full powers to absolve in cases
reserved to the Pope Other Christian Princes, however,
must also contribute their share. The King counted on
40,000 scudi annually from Italy and the States of the
Church ; on 200,000 from Germany, which had so many
rich Archbishops, Bishops and Beneficiaries, Princes and
cities , and on the same amount from Spain. The King of
England might contribute 100,000 scudi. Venice, he had
heard, would not be unwilling to declare war against the
Turks if help from Italy were certain. The plenipo-
tentiaries were accordingly authorised to unite with the
other Italian Powers in promising an annual subsidy of
300,000 scudi to the Republic. In the event, however, of
the other Kings and nations not giving any definite promise,
the French Envoys were only to undertake that their
Government would contribute its just share of the burden.

* Authenticated by BROSCH, Julius II , 16 See also FRIEDBERG,
II., 477.

† This *Letter of Louis XI to Sixtus IV , dated Vendôme, 1480,
Aug. 28, was hitherto unknown , I found a copy in the State Archives,
Milan

The Pope must also, above all, secure France against England "*

Soon after the arrival of the French Mission (8th March)† Sixtus IV. wrote a circular letter to the Italian Powers, laying before them the proposals of Louis,‡ as expressed in a Memorandum, in which the Envoys had embodied the result of their negotiations. It proclaimed a general peace throughout Italy, and decreed that speedy assistance against the Turks should be rendered with the least possible delay. France promised troops, and was to be included in the alliance The Emperor was also invited to join it, and a subsidy of 50,000 ducats was allotted to the King of Hungary. The Pope undertook to furnish twenty-five, and King Ferrante forty triremes. Genoa promised five galleys, Ferrara four, Siena three, and Bologna two, Lucca, Mantua, and Montferrat one each ; while Milan engaged to give 30,000 and Florence 40,000 ducats §

According to the testimony of a contemporary historian, the Milanese and Florentines were not remiss in contributing money ; the Venetians only held aloof, because they had concluded peace with the Sultan.‖

On Passion Sunday, the 8th April, 1481, Sixtus IV published an Encyclical, calling on all the Princes of Europe

---

* GOTTLOB in the Hist Jahrb, VI , 447.

† JACOB VOLATERRANUS, 123   See BASIN, III , 70.

‡ *Brief to Milan, dated Rome, 1481, March 23 (the Original is in the State Archives, Milan) , one of the same day to the Duke of Ferrara (Original in the State Archives, Modena), and to Florence (Copy in the Florentine State Archives).

§ RAYNALDUS, ad an. 1481, N. 4 seq. See GRASSO, 323

‖ SIGISMONDO DE' CONTI, I , 110   In a *Brief of the 3rd Jan , 1481, Sixtus IV. exhorted the Milanese Government to pay the tax , on the 10th April he again called upon them for aid against the Turks. Both these *Bulls are in the State Archives, Milan

to take part in the Turkish war.* Indulgences were proclaimed throughout Italy, and the tithe for the war was
levied. On the 9th April the tithe was announced in
France and Dauphiné, and Giuliano della Rovere appointed
Collector-General † Notwithstanding the daily increasing
danger, there was still in many places but little zeal. The
wealthy city of Bologna, for instance, declared that the
tribute of hearth-money and the equipment of two triremes
were too much for her, the Pope accordingly, on the 1st
February, 1481, forgave the tribute, but urged that the two
vessels should be prepared at once ‡ A Papal Brief of the
3rd May to the Vice-Legate at Bologna shews that the
city then professed itself willing to contribute 2000 ducats
towards the expenses of the war. The Pope considered the
sum very small, but had all the more hope that it would be
sent without delay. In June we hear of difficulties. On
the 7th of August it was still unpaid. At last, on the 11th
of September, it arrived ! § Several other cities behaved in
the same manner

Personally, Sixtus IV. gave the best possible example
He parted with his own silver plate, and sent a large
quantity of sacred vessels to the Mint to meet the expenses
of the Crusade.‖

* See RAYNALDUS, ad an. 1481, N 19, 20 *seq* , FABRICIUS, VI., 492 ;
and GRASSO, 351 A complete copy of the Bull of the 8th April,
beginning with the words, " Cogimur jubente altissimo," is in the State
Archives, Milan.

† GOTTLOB in the Hist Jahrb, VI , 448

‡ *Brief of Sixtus IV to Bologna, dated Rome, 1481, Febr. I.
State Archives, Bologna, Lib Q 3

§ *Briefs of Sixtus IV. to the Legate's representative at Bologna,
dated Rome, 1481, May 3, June 16, Aug 7, and Sept 11, *loc. cit* See
also on next page, note †.

‖ Diar Parm , 364-5 See CORTESIUS, De cardinalatu, f CXXIV ,
and Anecdot Litt, III , 258

In the midst of these anxious and hurried preparations came tidings of the death of the mighty conqueror, whose name, during one whole generation, had filled Europe and Asia with terror. By the end of May rumours of this event began to circulate in Rome, and, on the 2nd June, the report was confirmed by letters from the Venetian Government to its Envoys * Cannons were fired, and all the Church bells rang to announce the good news The Pope himself went at once in thanksgiving to the Vespers at Sta Maria del Popolo, which the Sacred College and all the Ambassadors also attended. As darkness came on, bonfires were lighted in all directions. On the 3rd of June, processions of thanksgiving were ordered during three successive days, and Sixtus IV. personally took part in them † Briefs, dated the 4th June, pointed out to all Christian Powers that this was the moment for dealing a decisive blow. Sixtus IV was able to announce that he had already equipped a fleet of thirty-four ships at Genoa, which would soon be in the Tiber, and that men-of-war were being built at Ancona and would be added to the Neapolitan fleet.‡

* **Despatch of B. Bendedeus of the 2nd June, 1481 (State Archives, Modena) See JACOB VOLATERRANUS, 134

† *Letter of B. Bendedeus, dated Rome, 1481, June 3rd (State Archives, Modena.) See NOTAJO DI NANTIPORTO, 1071, and INFES-SURA, 1147 Throughout all Italy similar rejoicings took place ; see Diar Parm , 374 In many instances the newly-kindled zeal for the Crusade grew cold. The Bolognese, seeking to withdraw from their promise of a subsidy, said "mortuo nunc Turcorum tyranno neces-sitatem amplius non imminere " Sixtus IV. expressed his astonishment at such language in a *Brief to the Vice-Legate, dated Rome, 1481, June 16. and urged them to take advantage of this opportunity of crush-ing the enemy. He was himself determined, he added, to do everything in his power to accomplish this end. State Archives, Bologna, Lib. Q 3.

‡ MULLER, Docum , 233

On the 30th June the Pope, with all the Cardinals, went
to S. Paolo for the blessing of this fleet, which brought the
Cardinal Legate Savelli back to Rome, and also its recently
appointed Admiral, Cardinal Fregoso.   After Vespers, the
Pope held a Consistory.   Savelli gave an account of his
mission, and the ceremony of opening the mouth of Cardinal
Fregoso then took place.*   Sixtus IV. made him an address
on the task which he was called upon to undertake, "gave
him his Legate's ring and the banner which he had consecrated for the fleet.   The captains of the ships then came in,
kissed the foot of the Pope, and were signed with the cross
on their breasts.   At the close of the Consistory, the Pope,
with the Cardinals and a great number of Prelates, proceeded to the river, where the galleys were lying at anchor,
went on board each of the vessels, and gave the Apostolic
blessing   The crew stood fully armed on the decks and
saluted when he appeared.   Weapons were brandished,
swords drawn and struck upon the shields, and military
evolutions executed as in actual battle.   Hundreds of
hoarse voices shouted the Pope's name amid the thunder of
artillery ; it was a feast for both eye and ear," writes the
chronicler, Jacobus Volaterranus †

On the ‡ 4th July the Cardinal Legate sailed by way of
Naples for Otranto, and, together with Ferrante and his
ships, took part in the siege of that place.   The resistance
of the Turks was most obstinate, and they did not lay down
their arms until the 10th September   Ferrante at once
informed the Pope of the happy event, and he, in his turn,
transmitted the news to all the Powers §

---

* *Acta Consist , f 62, Secret Archives of the Vatican

† SCHMARSOW, 181, according to JACOB VOLATERRANUS, 139   See
also Diar Parm , 377 , and NOTAJO DI NANTIPORTO, 1071

‡ *Acta Consist , f 62, Secret Archives of the Vatican.

§ Ferrante's letter in JACOB VOLATERRANUS, 146 *seq* , in regard to

Sixtus IV had, from the first, intended that, after
Otranto had been retaken, his fleet, joined by the ships of
the other Powers, should proceed to Vallona, and, with the
help of the Albanians, wrest this important fortress from
the Turks   As early as the 30th of August he had written
to Genoa to this effect *   The Portuguese fleet of twenty-
five vessels, which had appeared before Ostia, was to form
part of this expedition   Its Commander, the Bishop of
Elbora, begged permission to go to Rome and receive the
Pope's blessing, a favour which Sixtus IV could not refuse.
But his annoyance may be imagined, when, on his return
from a short absence, he found that the Portuguese officers
had preferred sight-seeing in Rome to going to the war,
while the sailors occupied themselves in robbing the
Roman vineyards.   It required stringent orders from the
Pope to induce them at last to weigh anchor and proceed
to Naples, but only to linger there in a similar manner,
under pretext of completing their equipment.†   Sixtus IV.

the Papal Brief of the 18th Sept, 1481 (National Library, Florence),
see Appendix, N. 64   Also GRASSO, 481 and 484-5. PRUTZ, Mittel-
alter, II , 553, gives a medal struck by Sixtus IV. to commemorate the
expulsion of the Turks from Otranto. Luca Pasi, in a *Letter, dated
Rome, 1481, Sept 20, speaks of the feasts and processions by which
this victory was celebrated   State Archives, Modena

    * "*Januensibus," dated Rome, 1481, Aug. 30   This Brief is one
of the first in the extremely important collection of Sixtus IV.'s Briefs
in Cod. Magliab, II.-III -256, of the National Library, Florence (in
future, where this Library is cited, this MS is to be understood.
RAYNALDUS, ad an 1481, N 19, laments the loss of the Register for
the year 1481 , we have here almost a complete collection of the Briefs
of Sixtus IV from the end of August, 1481, till the end of August, 1482.
The Florentine MS is from the Rinuccini Library, and no doubt
originally came from the Secret Archives of the Vatican , in the
University Library, Genoa, I found a fine copy of this valuable
collection , Cod B VIII , 17

    † JACOB VOLATERRANUS, 154 , SCHMARSOW, 185   In a *Brief to

repeatedly complained of the conduct of these Crusaders, and especially of that of their unprincipled chief.* But it was all in vain.

Meanwhile, still more deplorable events had occurred at Otranto   Disputes had arisen among the victors about the partition of the spoil.   On the 1st September the Cardinal Legate wrote word that the captains of the triremes were bent on leaving, because the Plague had broken out on board four ships, and, moreover, their pay had not arrived. Sixtus IV. wrote to the Legate on the 10th September, maintaining that he was in no way to blame, he had fulfilled all his promises , he also exhorted Fregoso to use every effort to retain these captains †   On the 18th September, after hearing that Otranto had been recaptured, Sixtus IV again urged his Legate to follow up the victory to the best of his power.‡   Great, therefore, was his surprise when he learned from the King of Naples that the Legate had given out that the Pope had desired him to return with his fleet after the capture of Otranto '   Sixtus IV. at once, on the 21st September, wrote to the King that he had, on the contrary, always intended and desired that the fleet, after delivering Otranto, should sail to Vallona §   At the same time, he sent strict orders to the Legate to proceed

the Bishop of Elbora, dated Bracciano, 1481, Sept 15, the Pope says *" Intelleximus frat tuam audita Hydronti recuperatione nolle ulterius progredi, sed statuisse istic morari   Miramur vehementer, &c" National Library, Florence.

* See **Briefs of the 17th September to the Cardinal of Lisbon and to the King himself   National Library, Florence.

† "*Tibi mandamus expresse et quemadmodum per alias litteras scripsimus omni studio, cura et ingenio enitaris ad continendos et refienandos animos eorum   Legato classis, 1481, Sept 10 "   National Library, Florence

‡ See Appendix, N 65.

§ *Regi Ferdinando, 1481, Sept 21   National Library, Florence.

thither at once, recapture the place, and destroy the
Turkish ships.* On the 23rd September Sixtus IV. sent
one of his naval captains to prevent the return of the
Papal fleet, and to urge the Legate to start for Vallona †

All the Pope's efforts were, however, fruitless By the beginning of October the Legate and his ships appeared before
Civita Vecchia Sixtus IV. hastened there to endeavour to
prevail upon him to turn back Protracted consultations ensued, in which the Pope presided, and the Legate, the Neapolitan Ambassador, and the captains of the ships took part.

---

* "*Volumus et ita expresse tibi praecipiendo mandamus ut   .
redeas omnino et unacum classe regia Vallonam proficiscaris ad eam
expugnandam et classem Turcorum comburendam, ita enim est firme
et immutabilis nostre voluntatis Cardᴸ Januensi, dat Bracciani, 1481,
Sept 22" (National Library, Florence) There is also a similar
*Brief from Sixtus IV to Fregoso, dated 23rd Sept, 1481, in Cod
Vatic 4103, P II, f 105, Vatican Library.

† *Cardᴸ Januensi and *Melchiori Zocho triremium nostrai.
capitaneo, dat Bracciani, 1481, Sept 23, *loc. cit.* GREGOROVIUS
completely misrepresents the facts of the case when, after dwelling
on the favourable opportunity for carrying on the war with the Turks
afforded by the deliverance of Otranto, he says (VII, 249, 3rd ed)
"Andreas, the last of the Palæologi, had at this time found an asylum
in Rome after appearing as a suppliant at the gates of every European
court Sixtus generously granted him a yearly pension of 8000 ducats ;
but he would hear nothing of the East (in the 2nd edition, here follow
the words, 'and continued completely engrossed by his territorial
policy') His fleet, with the Cardinal Legate, P. Fregoso, returned to
Civita Vecchia, and in vain did the Neapolitan Ambassador, Anello,
urge the prosecution of the war." Regarding Andreas Palæologus see,
in contradiction to Gregorovius, a *Brief of Sixtus IV to the Bishop
of Elbora, dated Bracciano, 1481, Sept. 15, in which he is directed to
assist Andreas to pass over to the Peloponnesus, so that he might be
able to reconquer his country (National Library, Florence) An
admirer of Gregorovius has lately observed that "he looks at the
deeds of the past with the eye of a poet"; this is evidently a doubtful
course

These last complained much of the conduct of the Duke of Calabria, while Fregoso represented, with all due deference, the impossibility of carrying out the undertaking. " The outbreak of the Plague on board the ships, the impracticability of the men, whom no amount of pay could persuade to serve any longer, the advanced season of the year, the essential difficulty of the enterprise, its immense cost—for the repair of the fleet alone, 40,000 ducats would at once be required —all these things were brought forward to prove the enterprise hopeless, but Sixtus IV. declared himself ready for every sacrifice. He would, like Eugenius IV, pawn his mitre, he would sell the rest of his silver plate. all was in vain " *
He was obliged to return to Rome without effecting his purpose, only leaving orders that the harbours of Civita Vecchia and Corneto should be thoroughly repaired †

* ZINKEISEN, II , 461, from JACOB. VOLATERRANUS, 147-52 See CIPOLLA, 608, N. 2, and BALAN, 221, both of whom express their disagreement with Gregorovius See also GUGLIELMOTTI, 459, 461 ; SERRA, Liguria, 268 seq , and GRASSO, 339 seq I have failed to find, either in Rome or in Florence, the ten letters of Sixtus IV belonging to this period, mentioned by Guglielmotti as published by de Romanis (Notizie istoriche della terra di Canino con alcune lettere di Sisto IV, Roma, 1843); the pamphlet is reviewed in Arch St. Ital, App VI, 412 seq. , but I have sought for it in vain in the editorial library of this Review.

† JACOB VOLATERRANUS, 152-3. The Pope returned to Rome on the 17th Oct., 1481. For an account of the Embassy of the Prete Gianni, which arrived in Rome in November, 1481, see the Report of the Milanese Ambassadors in Arch. St Lomb, 1889, p. 151 seq. which also treats of Turkish affairs.

CHAPTER IX.

WHILE Sixtus IV. was zealously devoting himself to the
Turkish war, Count Girolamo was occupied with matters
of a very different nature   His ambition soon involved the
too indulgent Pontiff in a new war in the immediate neighbourhood of Rome, and even in the City itself   Giuliano
della Rovere was at this time Legate in the Low Countries,
where he had been sent to make peace between Louis XI.
of France and Maximilian of Austria. His prolonged
absence rendered it easy for Count Girolamo to carry out
his plans and abuse the affection of the Pope *

It was intolerable to Girolamo that Lorenzo had not only
escaped the attempted assassination on the 26th April, 1478,
but that it had actually served to render his position more
secure   All his thoughts and desires were directed to the
one aim and object of obtaining some compensation for
this failure.   His uncle's advanced age urged him to
prompt action   "Wholly incapable of making himself a

* SCHMARSOW, 177 ; REUMONT, III, 1, 174, and Lorenzo, II, 182,
2nd ed   Regarding Giuliano's Mission, see the Report of his private
secretary, SIGISMONDO DE' CONTI, I., 108-9, also LEGEAY, II, 400
seq, and COMMINES-LENGLET, III, 574 seq, 595 seq, 598 seq., 600 seq.,
616 seq, 623 seq, 630 seq.

name by valorous deeds, Girolamo, who cared for nothing
but his own aggrandisement, was perpetually, by his schemes,
running counter to all statesmanlike plans of policy.   He
thus entangled a generous nature like that of Sixtus IV
in deplorable inconsistencies, and took advantage of his
uncle's affection to urge him further and further down the
steep incline which ends in ruin "*

Ferrante of Naples had, during the Tuscan war, faith-
lessly abandoned the Pope and constrained him to make
peace on very unfavourable terms.   From this time forth,
the chronicler says, the Pope's confidence, withdrawn
from Naples, was bestowed on the Venetians.   At the
beginning of February, 1480, negotiations were set on foot
which led to the conclusion of an alliance with Venice
Here Count Girolamo stepped in   Even during the war
of Otranto he had formed close relations with Venice.
Not content with Imola, he had taken advantage of the
dispute which broke out after the death of Pino of
Ordelassi, regarding the succession, and seized on the
Countship of Forli †   After this success he cast his
insatiable eyes on Faenza.   In January, 1481, Venice had
made known her willingness to gratify him in this point
also   The Council of Ten, however, warned him that
another project of his, which aimed at nothing less than
the expulsion of Ferrante from Naples, must be kept a
profound secret ‡   According to Sigismondo de' Conti, it
was Virginio Orsini, the heir of Napoleone, who urged
the Count on to this enterprise.   "Virginio claimed from
Ferrante the Countships of Alba Fucense and Tagliacozzo,
which formed part of his patrimony, and which the King

* Such is the opinion of SCHMARSOW, 178.

† See the detailed account of SCHMARSOW, 179 ; REUMONT, Lorenzo,
II., 365, 2nd ed ; BONOLI, 247 , and BURRIEL, III , p xliii

‡ BROSCH, Julius II., 21.

had sold for 12,000 ducats to Lorenzo Oddone Colonna
and his brother " Orsini was deeply wounded by this
transaction, because his family had always been true to the
King   He now hoped, by Ferrante's humiliation or downfall, to recover his rights.   He promised Girolamo that his
family would assist to the utmost in the war against the
King of Naples   Sixtus IV, in his irritation against
Ferrante, gave his consent to the scheme, but he and
Girolamo were well aware that the co-operation of Venice
was indispensable.   This could only be obtained by offering
some tangible advantage to the Republic   Ferrara was
accordingly held out as a bait   Sixtus IV. was incensed
with the Duke, because, in the Florentine war, he had been
at the head of his enemies, and because he persistently
strove to evade his yearly tribute.   Moreover, Ercole of
Ferrara had so far forgotten himself as to prohibit the
publication of several Apostolic Rescripts in his State,
which he governed in the name of the Holy See *

In September, 1481, Girolamo Riario went to Venice.
He was received like an Emperor, the Doge meeting
him at the foot of the Palace steps.†   In a Secret Council
the Count unfolded his plan for overthrowing Ferrante,
and promised the Venetians Ferrara if they succeeded in
conquering it.   They were only asked to furnish a fleet, to
keep the King in check, and a few troops.   Girolamo claimed
nothing for himself, except Lugo and Bagnacavallo, two

---

* SIGISMONDO DE' CONTI, I , 114 *seq.* , SCHMARSOW, 182 ; BALAN,
223   An admonitory Brief to the Duke regarding the tribute to be
paid, written as early as the year 1475, is given in MARTÈNE, II.,
1480   BROSCH'S statement, Kirchenstaat, I , 12, that Ferrara had
paid 5000 ducats as tribute, is, according to GOTTLOB, Cam. Ap ,
mistaken ; the *Introitus-Register of the Secret Archives of the
Vatican mention 4000 florins.

† FRANTZ, 370 ; BONOLI, 249.

cities in the Flaminia, on the border of his Countship of Imola.*

After the Pope's nephew had left the Council, deliberations began   Opinions were divided   The elder men, whose judgment was the clearest, objected to involving the Republic in a fresh war.   They represented the difficulty of taking Ferrara, a strong and populous city, surrounded by swamps and a wide river , they averred that Ercole d'Este was a skilful soldier , that his neighbours were bound to him by ties of kindred and friendship, and that he had at his disposal treasures amassed by a long line of ancestors   Doubts were also expressed as to the trustworthiness of Riario, who was not considered scrupulously truthful , it was further urged that Sixtus IV. was but mortal and had reached an age when death could not probably be distant, that he was a Ligurian and inconstant in his resolutions, that even if he adhered to his purpose the Sacred College would not stand by him, as they had never desisted from claiming the restoration of Cervia and Ravenna from the Venetians   The votes of the younger members of the Council, however, prevailed against these considerations, and war was decided upon.   Girolamo returned to Sixtus IV., after having received the freedom of the city and been admitted amongst her nobles †

The beginning of the year 1482 seemed to offer some hope that peace might still be maintained   Giuliano della Rovere returned at this time from his Mission to France, and Ercole d'Este and Lorenzo de' Medici sought, by

* Sigismondo de' Conti, I , 119 ; Schmarsow, 184

† Sigismondo de' Conti, I , 120   While Girolamo was occupied with these far-reaching projects, the ground under his feet began to give way.   Three conspiracies occurred in succession, and were with difficulty suppressed.   Florence persistently stirred up discontent against Girolamo   See Schmarsow, 274.

means of his powerful influence, to avert the war. They
were well acquainted with the Cardinal's opinion of the
ambitious and restless Riario,* who just then had scarcely
recovered from a violent fever,† and this fact also made it
more probable that the Pope might be induced to withdraw
his consent

In the middle of April the King commenced hostilities
by the advance of his troops into the States of the Church ‡
In Rome, preparations for war were but half completed,
and Venice would not be ready till the end of April   Two
fleets had been equipped by the Republic · one of them,
under Vettor Soranzo, was to commence operations on the
coast of Naples, while the other, under Damiano Moro,
was to penetrate to the States of Ferrara.   The land forces
were also divided into two armies, under the command of
Roberto Malatesta and Roberto da Sanseverino   At the
beginning of May Venice declared war against Ferrara.§
The Marquess of Montferrat, Genoa, and Pietro Maria
de Rossi, Count of San Secondo in the Parmesan territory, joined the Papal and Venetian league.   Ferrara
and Naples found powerful allies not only in Milan
and Florence, but also in the Marquess Federigo of

* SCHMARSOW, 188

† See *Letters of Alexander Arrivabene, dated Rome, 1482, January
23 and 26. Gonzaga Archives, Mantua

‡ BALAN, 228   On the 2nd April, 1482, Sixtus IV. had issued the
following *Order . "Gubernatori Reatis et Interamnis . .   volumus
ac tibi presentium tenore expresse mandamus ut omnia loca et passus
istius gubernii ex quibus transire solent aut possunt qui in regnum
proficiscuntur diligenter custodiri facias " , no troops were to be allowed
to pass without a written permission from him or Count Girolamo
"Simile gubernat. Campanie, praefecto urbis, Virginio de Ursinis."
National Library, Florence

§ See SANUTO, Commentarii della guerra di Ferrara nel 1482, 11–12,
and SIGISMONDO DE' CONTI, I., 121. See CIPOLLA, 612

Mantua, Giovanni Bentivoglio of Bologna and Federigo of Urbino *

Unhappily for the Papal cause, the ancient feud between the Colonna and the Orsini at this time broke out again

The immediate occasion of this outbreak was the hostility between the rich and noble families of della Valle and Santa Croce.   In the autumn of 1480 the whole City had been involved in this contest, the della Valle being supported by the Colonna, and the Santa Croce by the Orsini.   Not till April, 1481, did the Pope, after much trouble, succeed in restoring peace.   A Commission of three Cardinals was appointed to watch over its maintenance, and to arrange all differences that might arise.†

As most of the great Roman Barons, with the Pope's consent, had entered the service of Ferrante, and were fully occupied by the war at Otranto, tranquillity for a time continued, but after the recovery of that city, quarrels recommenced, and, fomented by the King of Naples, became more and more violent.

In consequence of the tension which existed between Rome and Naples in the spring of 1482, the Pope recalled the Barons who, since the war with the Turks, had remained in Ferrante's pay.   The Orsini, headed by Virginio, the intimate friend of Girolamo Riario, obeyed, and the Conti also, as well as Stefano Colonna of Palestrina, with his sons Giordano and Giovanni, re-entered the Papal service.   The Savelli, on the other hand, and the Colonna of Paliano-Genazzano cast in their lot with the King of Naples.   Their alienation was partly due to the enmity between them and the Orsini, which Ferrante took pains to foster, but partly

* Sismondi, XI, 227

† Jacob Volaterranus, 126   Sigismondo de' Conti, I, 134 seq., gives a full account of the origin of the animosity between Valle and Sta Croce

also to the domineering ways of Girolamo Riario. The Pope endeavoured, by gentleness and consideration, to repair the harm which his nephew had done, and several Cardinals, amongst whom were Giuliano della Rovere and Stefano Nardini, did their best to pacify the offended Colonna, even at the last moment, but all these efforts were fruitless.[*]

At the beginning of April a fresh incident occurred, which made matters worse. During the night of the 3rd of that month the Santa Croce, aided by the Palace guards, whom Girolamo had given them, attacked the house of the della Valle. Most unfortunately, in the struggle which ensued, Girolamo Colonna, an illegitimate brother of the Cardinal of S. Maria in Aquiro and of Prospero of Paliano, was killed [†] The Pope, in consequence, outlawed the Santa Croce, and caused their palaces to be destroyed. The exasperation of the Colonna from this time forth knew no bounds.

At this critical moment, several weeks before the Venetian declaration of war, the King of Naples commenced hostilities against Rome. In the middle of April his troops appeared in sight of the Papal residence at Marino, ostensibly for the purpose of defending the Colonna against the Orsini. Ferrante informed the Conservators that he was not taking up arms against Rome, but for the deliverance of the City and of Italy from the slavery to which the bad government of Girolamo Riario had reduced them.[‡]

---

[*] SIGISMONDO DE' CONTI, I , 132 *seq.* ; SCHMARSOW, 191, who very justly observes · "BROSCH, Julius II , 23, completely misapprehends the position of affairs when he considers Giuliano della Rovere to have been guilty of a breach of confidence in regard to the Pope" Brosch is very unfortunate in his most prejudiced conjectures ; see *supra*, p. 322.

[†] BALAN, 227, note 4.

[‡] *Ibid*, 228

On the 18th April the Pope admonished King Ferrante to withdraw his troops from Rome,* on the 23rd he complained in Consistory of the presence of the Neapolitans at Marino, and declared that he could not grant the request of the King's son, Alfonso of Calabria, for a free passage through the States of the Church to support Ferrara.†

The Ambassadors of Naples and Ferrara left Rome on the 14th May. They went, in the first instance, with great pomp to Lorenzo Colonna at Marino. Strengthened by the Savelli, and by constant reinforcements from Naples, Lorenzo now ventured to lead his men up to the very gates of Rome. On the 30th May his troops entered the City, but were driven back by the Orsini and Girolamo Riario. Prospero Colonna had previously gone over to the side of the Pope's enemies, and had received in Paliano (on the 22nd May) a garrison from the Duke of Calabria, who had meanwhile appeared before Rome as Commander of the Neapolitan troops.

Sixtus IV. was naturally much incensed by this treachery, and all the more so because Prospero had recently drawn a portion of his pay. The Pope also fully realised how injurious to him was the loss of these villages. Therefore, Sigismondo de' Conti informs us, he resolved on a hazardous step, which, however, the sequel proved to have been a judicious one.‡

A Consistory took place at mid-day on the 2nd June. Count Girolamo and Virginio Orsini attended it, and accused Cardinals Colonna and Savelli of treason   The

---

* *Sixtus IV. regi Ferdinando, dated Romae die XVIII Aprilis, 1482 National Library, Florence.

† BALAN, 228, from Despatches in the State Archives, Modena Here also are the particulars of a last attempt made by the Pope to win the Colonna

‡ SIGISMONDO DE' CONTI, I , 137

two Cardinals warmly defended themselves, openly condemning the conduct of their kinsmen and casting all the
blame upon them.   The meeting was stormy, and lasted
until the evening.   At last the Pope, to avoid worse evils,
gave orders that the accused Cardinals should be kept as
hostages for their disaffected families.   Cardinal Savelli's
brother, Mariano, who had a command in the Papal army, was
also arrested   As disturbances were apprehended from the
partisans of the Colonna, the Vatican was guarded by horse
and foot soldiers   The captured Cardinals were honourably
treated during the first day and the following night · Savelli
in the house of Giuliano della Rovere, and Colonna with
Girolamo Basso, who at that time lived in the Vatican.   At
the close of the second day an order arrived to transfer
them to St. Angelo *

Several hundreds of light Turkish horsemen from the
garrison of Otranto had gone over to Alfonso of Calabria,
and now formed part of his army, which was encamped
within sight of Rome.   These wild troops ravaged the
Campagna, and spread terror in every direction.   On the
6th of June the Papal force was ready.   Count Girolamo
was Commander-in-chief, and under him were Count Niccolo
of Pitigliano, Virginio and Giordano Orsini, Giovanni
Colonna, Giacomo and Andrea de' Conti, the Count of
Mirandola, and many others.†

Sigismondo de' Conti has left us a graphic picture of the
state of things in Rome at this crisis   " In the Pope's ante-
chambers," he says,‡ " instead of cassocked priests, armed

---

* FRANTZ, 375-6   In contradiction to the Venetian Documents
(see SCHMARSOW, 192), SIGISMONDO DE' CONTI, I , 137, maintains
the innocence of the Cardinals

† REUMONT, III , 1, 175

‡ SIGISMONDO DE' CONTI, I., 137-8   For "qui impar " *read*
"quia 1," and for "quoinm" *read* "quorum"   The Roman edition of

guards kept watch. Soldiers, equipped for battle, were drawn up before the gates of the Palace All the Court officials were filled with terror and anguish ; the fury of the populace was only restrained by the fear of the soldiers "

Thus, with the assistance of the Colonna, Alfonso of Calabria had succeeded in effecting his purpose, and transferring the war to Roman soil He was perpetually making raids in the vicinity of the City walls, and carrying off men and cattle The Papal army, encamped near the Lateran, did not venture out, either from a sense of its own weakness or from a fear that the angry townspeople, in whose vineyards it lay, might shut the gates and prevent its return. To add to all, the Plague again broke out in the City. Alfonso took Albano, Castel Gandolfo and Civita Lavinia, without encountering any resistance. His father, Ferrante, meanwhile was active. With a fleet of twenty triremes he harassed the shores of the Roman territory. He further succeeded in making himself master of Terracina and Benevento by treachery The Florentine army, under the command of Costanzo Sforza, took Città di Castello. The Pope was greatly alarmed, and commanded his chamberlains and domestics to take turns in keeping nightly watch. His anxiety increased from day to day, more particularly as the Venetian fleet, on which all his hopes rested, had not yet sailed *

this author, published in 1883, is far from perfect in this respect See also *supra*, p. 308, and GOTTLOB in the Hist Jahrb , VII , 303 *seq*.

* SIGISMONDO DE' CONTI, *loc. cit.* The Romans had much to suffer from Girolamo, whose soldiers even desecrated the Lateran Church On the 20th June Città di Castello fell into the enemy's hands, whereupon Sixtus IV sent troops against this city (*Brief of the 5th July to the City Prefect National Library, Florence) The citadel of Terracina was lost four weeks later, and Benevento in the middle of July; see the Despatches to Modena in BALAN, 229 Sixtus IV. then drew as many troops as he could into Rome , see his

Rome was insufficiently defended, and was shut in on every side by enemies * The perplexity and anxiety of the Pope were increased by accounts which reached him from the North of attempts which the Dominican, Andrea Zuccalmaglio, Archbishop of Carniola,† was making to revive the Council of Basle. He had come to Rome in 1478, as Envoy from the Emperor,‡ and received many presents and marks of distinction from the Pope § His ambition led him to aspire to greater dignities, and even to the purple, and, in October 1480, he induced the Emperor to address to the Pope and the Sacred College letters

*Briefs of the 11th, 12th, and 24th of July to the City Prefect (National Library, Florence) At the beginning of August the Pope even recalled his troops to Rome from Bologna, which was unsafe ; see *Brief to Perugia, dated 1482, Aug 3. Cod G -IV -1, University Library, Genoa

* In his necessity, Sixtus IV. even applied to France , see REUMONT, Lorenzo, II , 183, 2nd ed

† Recent students, such as BURCKHARDT, Andreas von Krain, and FRANTZ, 435, are certainly incorrect in adopting Hottinger's idea that Andreas lived at Laibach (Aemona), for, until 1788, Laibach was not an Archbishopric (GAMS, 283). From 1452-1525, seven, or possibly eight, Archiepiscopi Cramenses are known Andreas succeeded his predecessor on the 18th January, 1476 (loc. cit , 405). Several Slav provinces bear the name of Krains; according to FARLATTI, III. Sacr , IV , 189 seq , the coast about Macarsca is here meant (see Kirchenlex , I , 837, 2nd ed.); GAMS, loc cit., thinks that a somewhat more southerly district is to be understood

‡ BURCKHARDT, 25 ; FRANTZ, 434 , and GEBHARDT, 47, say that Andreas first came to Rome between 1480 and 1482 , the Briefs in Mon Habsb., III., 453, and II , 330, which certainly Burckhardt had not the means of consulting, shew this statement to be mistaken In his table of contents, p. xlii , CHMEL wrongly designates Andreas as Archbishop of Gran.

§ SIGISMONDO DE' CONTI, I , 157 ; Lib confrat. B M de Anima, 27 , and the Briefs of 10th Sept , 1481, and 4th May, 1482, to which we shall presently refer

recommending him in pressing terms.* In consequence
of these letters, Sixtus IV, who readily made promises,
seems to have given him some encouragement; but, as the
red hat did not arrive, Andrea soon began to pour forth
torrents of insolent abuse against the Pope, his nephews,
and the Roman clergy. Sixtus IV. admonished and
warned him, but in vain   There was nothing for it but to
call him to account for his calumnies. The Emperor's
mediation soon procured his liberation from confinement
in St. Angelo, where, out of consideration for Frederick
III, he had been treated leniently. The same motive
induced the Pope, in opposition to the desire of the
Cardinals, to abandon the suit which had been commenced
against him, and then to set him at liberty.† Sixtus IV.
soon had cause bitterly to regret his indulgence. Andrea
Zuccalmaglio went by way of Florence to Basle, where he
falsely announced himself as the Emperor's representative,
and even went so far as to assume the title of Cardinal of
S. Sisto. On the 25th March, 1482, he entered the Cathedral
of Basle during the celebration of Mass, and, with violent
invectives against the Pope, proclaimed a General Council,
to be held in that city. Even at this time, his secretary,
Numagen, clearly perceived that he was not quite right in
his head   He could not control himself, was incapable of
deliberation, and would listen to no one's advice.‡

In April, Andrea went to Berne, and was at first cordially
received by the authorities, but at the end of eight days

---

* Mon. Habsb., III., 48

† See the important Brief of the 10th Sept, 1481, published in the
Appendix to SIGISMONDO DE' CONTI, I, 410. This at last throws
some light on a matter hitherto involved in obscurity, and decides the
date of the conflict. BURCKHARDT, 25, has placed it at too late a
period

‡ HOTTINGER, 356, BURCKHARDT, A. von Krain, 28-89

the Bernese had discovered his real character. On the
4th May the alarmed Council sent a letter to Basle to
warn that friendly city against the danger of espousing his
cause. Berne apologised to Rome for having unwittingly
shewn honour to one who placed himself in opposition to
the Church and the Pope *

In Basle, also, Andrea's abuse of the Pope had awakened
some doubts, and a suspicion that he was influenced by
personal hatred. Nevertheless, he was left quite free when
he formally announced the assembling of a Council at the
beginning of May The Emperor was duly informed, but
did nothing, and waited to see what would come.

Sixtus IV was greatly disquieted, and, on the 4th May,
wrote to Frederick III., and sent a special Envoy to ask
him to take measures to secure the arrest of the Archbishop.† The Emperor's attitude now became so strange
as to excite suspicions in Rome that Andrea was acting
on secret instructions from him. On the 21st July he
called the Archbishop "trusty and well-beloved,' and asked
for information about his project, and, on the 23rd July,
he merely recommended the Councillors at Basle to act
with caution ‡

Andrea chose this very time to cut off all means of retreat.
On the 20th and 21st July he issued two violent and ill-
written appeals, the last of which "was no better than a
pasquinade." In the opening words of this detestable production, Sixtus IV , whom he had but a few days before
invited to attend his Council, is addressed, no longer as
Pope, but as " Francesco of Savona, Son of the Devil, thou
who hast climbed to thy high dignity through the window

* Jahrb für Schweiz Gesch , IX , 13-14.
† I found this **Brief, which, as far as I know, was up to this time
undiscovered, in the National Library, Florence
‡ BURCKHARDT, A von Krain, 34

of simony instead of entering by the door, thou art of thy father, the Devil, and seekest to do his will."*

If we remember that the Archbishop had not a single adherent among the German or French Prelates, these outrageous railings against the Head of the Church seem almost like the ravings of a maniac; but when we find that Andrea had allied himself with the enemies of the Pope in Italy, it is easier to account for his violence. This evidently took place when he went from Rome to Basle by way of Florence   He must then have received from the Florentines and other conspirators assurances without which he could scarcely have ventured on his hazardous enterprise. " A bitterly exasperated Prelate, who promised to raise the whole of the North against the Pope, was, under the circumstances, an important ally, however dubious might be his motives, and however great the peril to which he exposed the Church."† The last consideration did not certainly weigh with Lorenzo de' Medici, who already was of opinion that it would be for his advantage to have three or four Popes instead of one ‡

The experiences of Lorenzo during his first conflict with Sixtus IV, however, deterred him from again exposing himself to the risk of Excommunication.   Andrea was, there-

* HOTTINGER, 360 *seq*, 368 *seq*; BURCKHARDT, 36

† BURCKHARDT, 49.   BUSER, Lorenzo, 158, has referred to the summons to Basle addressed by Andreas to Lorenzo de' Medici. It begins in the following words. * " Spiritus sanctus qui per totum terrarum orbem dispersos in unitatem fidei congregat dignetur fovere ignem suum accensum in te, fidei et ecclesie Christi zelatore fidelissimo Agimus nempe in gaudio magno gratias ei qui te nobiscum sollicitare hoc opus sanctum et necessarium accendit; ille eciam labores tuos si perseveraveris legitime eternis gaudiis compensabit.   Age igitur pro Christo, pio fide et ecclesia illius et pro tota christianitate constanter et veni " State Archives, Florence

‡ See *supra*, p 300

fore, for the time, " only to be supported in secret, and very
cautiously. When he had been in a measure successful,
and the Pope had been thoroughly intimidated, the allies
would proceed to advocate a Council "* Not till the 14th
September did Lorenzo's confidant, Baccio Ugolini, accompanied by a Milanese Envoy, arrive in Basle.

Ugolini's Reports to his master enable us to estimate
the hostility of Lorenzo to the Papacy, and to appreciate
the reasons which induced Sixtus IV. to make the efforts
he did for his removal from Florence. " I offered him "
(Andrea of Carniola), writes Ugolini on the 20th September,
1482, " in your (Lorenzo's) name all that I could and knew
to favour this undertaking (the Schism), praising him and
flattering him as is customary. . . . It is a great thing that
he is a Friar, that is the crown of all his qualities, and he
has a fearless countenance, which awakens confidence and
knows how to keep a man in his place, and let no one
approach him. . . . The citizens (of Basle), too, could not
be better disposed . . . they would not by any means
allow their priests to observe the Interdict, and they openly
favour the Archbishop as much as they can. . . . This man
is quite fitted to serve out the Pope and the Count (Riario),
and that is enough." Ten days later this Florentine again
wrote confidentially to Lorenzo, saying, amongst other things :
" I afterwards made a long speech (to the Magistracy of
Basle) in favour of the Council, praising the lords for this
honourable enterprise, and extolling the person of Carniola,
while I drew a contemptible picture of the government of
Sixtus IV., and insisted on the necessity for a Council †
They listened thankfully to everything. . . . As regards
the matter of the Council, they declare that they are well-

---

* BURCKHARDT, *loc cit* See also BUSER, Beziehungen, 228.
† The Venetian-Papal troops were just at this time victorious.

disposed towards the Holy See, and so far as they can
have their way they will take care (they, the Councillors
of Basle!) that the Church, which they see to be in great
danger, or rather in ruins, shall be reformed to the faith
of Christ. . . . Moreover, I (Ugolini) have gained such an
ascendancy over the Carniolan (the Pope and 'Reformer'
of the future), that it rejoices him more than anything. . . .
Every hour he raises his hands to heaven and thanks God
who has sent me to him   I need not say how eagerly
the Doctors of the University read the letters which I
have communicated to the Council here.   What more can
we desire?   The Pope is more hated here than there"*

* FABRONIUS, II., 227 *seq*. In consequence, however, of the
energetic action of the Pope, who sent a great number of Nuncios
in succession to the Emperor and to Basle (see BURCKHARDT, A. von
Krain, 29 *seq*., in another place I will give supplementary extracts on
the subject from Sixtus IV.'s *Briefs, which are before me   Secret
Archives of the Vatican and National Library, Florence), and especially
because the condition of the League had completely changed, it was
in the end deemed well to leave their tool (RANKE, III., 5, 6th ed)
to his fate   Basle had at first refused either to give up or to imprison
the Archbishop, and had thus fallen under an Interdict, which, however,
was not regarded   No change took place until October, when the
Emperor openly declared against Andrea   On the 18th December,
1482, the authorities of Basle at last arrested Andrea, but still refused
to give him up   The Bishop of Suessa accordingly published a Bull
of Crusade against Basle, which occasioned great distress   The
matter was not settled when Sixtus IV. died, and was succeeded by
Innocent VIII., it was finally concluded by the suicide of Andrea,
who was found hanged in his dungeon on the 13th November, 1484.
For details I refer to BURCKHARDT, 65 *seq*, 93 *seq*. GLASSBERGLR
in Anal Francisc., II, 483, gives a full description of the danger
involved by Andrea's proceedings   In Chap XI we shall mention
that Ferdinand and Isabella of Spain also threatened to hold a
Council   Regarding the open and secret opposition to Rome in
Germany in the time of Sixtus IV, see GEBHARDT, 48 *seq*, and
DROYSEN, II, 1, 328, 341

Under these circumstances, it is not surprising that Girolamo Riario, the cause of all this trouble, became very unpopular in Rome, and a powerful party, headed by Cardinal Giuliano della Rovere, strongly urged the Pope to conclude a peace. But when the Venetian General, Roberto Malatesta, who had hitherto been fighting against Ferrara, appeared in Rome on the 23rd July, the war-party again got the upper hand *

His arrival caused great rejoicing "This is he who will redeem Israel!" shouted the people in the streets. On the 24th July Roberto was received in secret audience by the Pope, after which he at once began to make his preparations. The Proveditore, Pietro Diedo, brought money by command of the Republic to help in raising fresh troops for the Papal army ; 1000 young Romans, ready armed, were enlisted in a week   On the 15th August the Venetian auxiliaries came in, and were blessed by the Pope from a window of the Vatican.   Rome was full of warlike enthusiasm   "The banners of the Republic, together with those of the Pope, were borne through the whole City, and harmony reigned in the common camp " †

On the same 15th August the army advanced as far as Bovillae on the ancient Appian Way ‡   Castel Gandolfo, Castel Savello, and Albano surrendered.§   Alfonso retired before the superior forces of the enemy behind Velletri to the neighbourhood of Nettuno and Astura, where he expected succour by sea from Naples.

* REUMONT, III , 1, 176
† FRANTZ, 381–2 ; SCHMARSOW, 194
‡ SIGISMONDO DE' CONTI, I , 139
§ On the 19th August, 1482, Sixtus IV. wrote to Count Girolamo: * 'Gratissimum nobis fuit quod scribit nob tua de castello Gandolfo et de castello Sabello ;" the Pope hopes that all will go on well. National Library, Florence

Along this sea-shore stretches a woody morass, a desolate wilderness, the home of the buffalo and the wild boar. " In the whole of the Roman territory there is not another district so pestilential as this desert of Maremma" Its air is full of deadly fever, which has given the place the name of the Campo Morto (field of death), even down to the time of Pius IX it has been a safe refuge for murderers In the midst of these marshy thickets, at about an equal distance from Velletri and Nettuno, was a "fortified enclosure for the breeding of buffaloes and cattle, this castrum took from its Church the name of San Pietro, and from its moats the surname in Formis"* Alfonso of Calabria had here assembled his troops to await the attack His position was a strong one, for his army occupied a sort of island, covered to the south by a small swamp, and protected on the north and east by trees and brushwood. To the west, where the Papal forces made the attack, there was a meadow about 500 paces in width, which was crossed by a ditch about two feet deep to carry off the water. Behind this, Alfonso's artillery was placed, some 300 paces further back he caused a considerably deeper trench to be made for the defence of his troops †

* GREGOROVIUS, VII, 256, 3rd ed See Mél d'Archéol, V, 84 seq NOTAR GIACOMO, 148, calls the place Campo Morto, as do also Infessura and P Cyrnaus (see GREGOROVIUS, loc cit) The mistaken statement, that the name was due to the battle, occurs in PAPEN-CORDT, 490, and REUMONT, III, 1, 177

† SIGISMONDO DE' CONTI, I, 142 seq, who also gives a very good description of the battle, largely used by Sansovini in his History of the Orsini See also SANUDO, Comment., 39-40 ; a Sienese Despatch in Arch d Soc. Rom, XI, 606 seq ; the Este Reports in CAPELLI, 31-3 ; Roberto's Letter in TONINI, 390 seq., and a second Letter from him, which Valentini published, with other Reports, in Arch Veneto, 1887, fasc 65, p 72 seq ; to these we may add the **Report of Pasius, dated 24th Aug 1482, fiom the State Archives, Modena

Roberto Malatesta, to whom Riario had resigned the command, having set his troops in order of battle and exhorted them to bravery, ordered the foot soldiers to make the attack. These were mostly recruits, and were so alarmed by the appearance of the Turks, whom Alfonso opposed to them, that they fled almost immediately. The whole of the Papal army would have been cast into confusion had not Roberto, at the right moment, rushed forward with a chosen band of tried soldiers, by which means he not only repelled the onslaught of the enemy but drove him back behind the trench Sword in hand, Roberto here held his ground for a whole hour, acting at once as soldier and as leader.*

While the battle was raging at this point, Giacomo de' Conti, with six companies, attacked the camp on the right. This movement was hidden from Alfonso by the thicket. Roberto, at the same time, renewed his assault on the front. Alfonso's forces were not able to resist the two-fold onslaught of an enemy superior in numbers; they began to waver and then to fly.

Up to this moment Alfonso had "fought like a lion",† several horses had been killed under him ; now, fearing he would be surrounded and made prisoner, he also took to flight. He had some difficulty in making his way through the wood to Nettuno, where, with a few followers, he took boat for Terracina Here, under the protection of his father's galleys, he gathered together the remnant of his army.

The battle of "Campo Morto in the Pontine Marshes" thus ended in a complete victory for the Papal troops. Both sides had fought desperately. The field was strewn with wounded, and the number of dead who lay there was

* SIGISMONDO DE' CONTI, *loc. cit.*

† See the **Report of Pasius, quoted on preceding page, note †. State Archives, Modena

proportionately large ; almost all the Janissaries were among them Many flags and cannons fell into the hands of the conquerors, who also took a number of prisoners, including almost all the Chiefs and Barons.*

Roberto proceeded at once to Velletri, to attend to the wounded and rest his wearied troops. On the following day he sent his light cavalry forward to collect the baggage of the enemy.

When the news of the victory reached Rome, bonfires were lighted, the bells of the Capitol rang out, and all the Churches answered Sixtus IV, with a numerous suite, attended a Mass of Thanksgiving at Santa Maria del Popolo †

The very day after the battle, Marino surrendered to the Pope the keys of the Citadel and the captive Fabrizio Colonna; the idea of pressing on into the kingdom of Naples with the victorious army was spoken of in Rome.‡ Sixtus IV. informed the Emperor and all friendly States of the great success obtained by his General,§ and thanked the latter in a highly eulogistic Brief.||

Girolamo Riario made a splendid pageant of his entry into Rome with his prisoners The Romans were treated with the spectacle of the enemies who had but recently

---

* SIGISMONDO DE' CONTI, *loc cit.* In reference to the number of dead here given, the small strength of the army is to be borne in mind, and the fact that the warriors were clad entirely in mail

† NOTAJO DI NANTIPORTO, 1077 , SCHMARSOW, 195 , FRANTZ, 385.

‡ See the *Despatch of the 24th August from Pasius in the State Archives, Modena, cited *supra*, p 365, note †

§ See RAYNALDUS, ad an. 1482, N. 9, and the **Briefs to Genoa and Perugia of the 22nd and 24th August, 1482. National Library, Florence, and University Library, Genoa (G -IV.-1).

|| **Rob Malatestae, dated Rome, 1482, Aug 24 National Library. Florence.

threatened their very walls, now led through their streets
as captives, with heads bowed low, in the triumphal procession   Antonio Piccolomini, Duke of Amalfi, and Vicino
Orsini, son of the Grand Constable of the kingdom of
Naples, attracted the greatest attention   The Pope received the captives with kindness, and honourably entertained the Duke of Amalfi, Pius II.'s nephew, in his Palace,
before sending him back to his family *

" It is a true saying," writes Sigismondo de' Conti, " that
human happiness is never long unalloyed."   The sounds of
rejoicing were soon silenced and exchanged for lamentations
over the premature death of the victor.

Roberto Malatesta was engaged in dispersing the hostile
troops scattered about the neighbourhood of Rome, when
" the effects of his tremendous exertions in the great heat of
the unhealthy swamps overtook him   The fatal breath of
Campo Morto proved stronger than youth and courage." †

On hearing of the sickness of his General, the Pope at

* SIGISMONDO DE' CONTI, I, 144, SCHMARSOW, 195; FRANTZ,
385   Regarding the Triumphal Procession, see also NOTAR GIACOMO,
149, and the Sienese Despatches in Arch Stor Rom, XI, 608

† SCHMARSOW, 195, rejects the idea that Roberto was poisoned, and
CREIGHTON, III, 91, agrees with him, as also GREGOROVIUS, VII, 257,
3rd ed, who inclines to the same opinion   Even SIGISMONDO DE'
CONTI, I, 144, mentions the report of poison.   Count Girolamo Riario
has been suspected of the murder ; see, in his defence, TONINI, 393,
and App, 289.   Any idea that Roberto's death was due to foul play
is set aside by a Despatch given by BALAN, 230, and also by a
*Letter of Cardinal Gonzaga, dated Rome, 1482, Sept. 11, which
I found in the Gonzaga Archives, Mantua, and a passage in the
*Cronica Ferrariae of Caleffini.   Cod I -I -4, f. 156, Chigi Library,
Rome (see Appendix, N. 66)   These authorities, who are by no
means prejudiced in Girolamo's favour, may be considered as conclusive on this question   The *Diario del Corona also says . " Mori
Roberto Malatesta di febre." Barberini Library, Rome, LIV., 10,
f 410

once sent his own physician to Val Montone, where Roberto lay, and caused him to be transported in a litter to Rome He was most carefully tended in the house of the Cardinal of Milan, but he did not rally When his condition left no room for hope, the Pope, with his own hands, administered Extreme Unction.   On the 10th September the brave warrior breathed his last *

Sixtus IV. paid every possible honour to the deliverer of his capital. He personally took part in the obsequies, and afterwards caused a marble monument to be erected in St Peter's. After many vicissitudes, this monument, on which the figure of the leader, mounted on his war-horse, is carved in relief, found its way to the Louvre, where it now adorns the hall devoted to Sculpture of the Renaissance period.†

On the 11th September the Pope legitimatised the sons of Roberto and invested them with the paternal inheritance, thus refuting the imputation that he was influenced by designs upon the fief of the Malatesta; though some such hankerings, perhaps, had been cherished by Girolamo Riario ‡

The immediate consequence of Roberto's death was to nullify the good effects of the victory of Campo Morto The Venetian troops, regardless of the promises and entreaties of the Pope, withdrew. The siege of Cavi by the

* MARINI, I, 209, BALAN, 229, FRANTZ, 387. The different dates given for Roberto's death (see CIPOLLA, 617) are set at rest by Cardinal Gonzaga's Letter, which we publish in the Appendix, N. 66 Caleffini, *Cronica Ferrariae, Cod I-I-4, f 156, Chigi Library, Rome. also names the 10th September as the day Roberto's epitaph is to be found in DE ROSSI, Inscript., II, 421

† See COURAJOD in the Gaz. des Beaux-Arts, 1883, p. 233, and YRIARTE, 354 seq

‡ TONINI, 394–5

Papal forces was unsuccessful, either because of the strength of its fortifications or because the Orsini, who disliked any further extension of the power of the Pope, neglected to render assistance *

Meanwhile, Alfonso had again rallied his soldiers, and the war continued, generally to the disadvantage of the Papal troops and the detriment of the Romans, whose fields were laid waste and whose flocks were carried off   The Orsini, incensed by Girolamo's selfish proceedings, at last declared that, if no other auxiliaries arrived, they would withdraw.   Without them—as Sigismondo de' Conti justly insists—it was impossible to carry on the war against the King of Naples, and especially against the Colonna.   The Venetians, on their side, made it plain that the only thing they wanted was Ferrara, and that which might befall the Pope was nothing to them †

Meanwhile, the revived opposition in the North added to all these troubles the threat of a Council and a Schism, and Andrea of Carniola was still unchecked in his career ‡

Sixtus IV. now began to perceive " that, by his own action, he was strengthening the hands of a Power which, by its persistent efforts to acquire dominion over the cities of the Adriatic littoral, was likely soon to prove a source of serious danger to him.   Giuliano della Rovere seems to have been the person who induced the Pope to separate himself from

* SIGISMONDO DE' CONTI, I., 156.

† SIGISMONDO DE' CONTI, I , 156 ; SCHMARSOW, 196-7   Sixtus IV writes, on the 20th October, 1482, to Jordano Orsini regarding the proceedings of the enemy in the immediate neighbourhood of Rome * " Dilecte, etc , Quottidie hostes per Latium discurrunt nemine prohibente et versus S. Sebastianum et alia loca urbi vicina irrumpunt et predas abigunt." Lib brev , 15, f. 96b, Secret Archives of the Vatican.

‡ See *supra*, p 363.

the Republic, while Girolamo Riario, the soul of the war party, was probably won over by a hope of eventually obtaining the Malatesta fiefs"* On the 28th November a truce was concluded with the Duke of Calabria. On the 12th December a treaty of Peace between Rome on the one side and Naples, Milan, and Florence on the other was signed. By this treaty the possession of his States was guaranteed to the Duke of Ferrara, territories conquered during the war were mutually restored, an alliance for twenty years, which the Venetians also were free to join, was concluded, and finally, a pension was secured to Girolamo Riario.†

On the following day, the 13th December, Sixtus IV. went in procession to the newly-built Church of Sta Maria della Virtù and bestowed on it the name of Sta Maria della Pace (Our Lady of Peace). At Christmas Peace was publicly proclaimed ‡ The important point now was to obtain the adhesion of the Venetians to this alliance, which had been concluded without their knowledge. Failing this, the peace would be little more than a name.

* REUMONT, Lorenzo, II , 187, 2nd ed

† SISMONDI, XI , 242

‡ NOTAJO DI NANTIPORTO, 1080 , *Diario del Corona (Barberini Library, LIV , 10, f. 411.) See FEA, La chiesa di S. M. d p. (1809), and ARMELLINI, 433

CHAPTER X.

THIS one-sided treaty which, under the stress of circumstances, had been concluded by Sixtus IV, had a most prejudicial influence on his relations with Venice Sigismondo de' Conti, known as an historian, was sent in December, 1482, to pacify the Venetians, and to obtain the cessation of hostilities against Ferrara. The reception which awaited him was far from encouraging; no one ventured to speak to him. The Envoy, however, was not to be deterred from the accomplishment of his Mission, he delivered the letters which the Pope and the Sacred College had entrusted to him, and endeavoured, with honied words, to persuade the Doge and the Council to a truce, all his efforts, however, were ineffectual. The Signoria, after the great sacrifices which had been made, would not draw back. They believed victory to be in their hands, and were determined in any case to carry on the war Sigismondo's Mission was a complete failure.*

The irritation of the Venetians against Sixtus IV was at this time so great that they proceeded to violent menaces. They declared that, if the Pope should be led to employ his spiritual weapons, he would find himself involved in a

* See his own Report, in which (I., p. 158 *seq.*) the Briefs to Venice are inserted ; also MALIPIERO, 269 *seq.*, and Hist Jahrbuch, VII., 308 *seq.*

disastrous war in Italy, the end of which he would not live to see. They said they were in league with all the Christian Powers, and were resolved, if necessary, even to call in the Turks !*

Sixtus IV. did not allow himself to be intimidated A State Paper repelling the accusations of the Venetians was drawn up,† and it was then determined that, besides Girolamo Riario, Cardinal Gonzaga should be sent as Legate to Ferrara ‡   On the 5th February, 1483, Cesare de Varano was commanded immediately to proceed thither with all the troops he could collect §

* SIGISMONDO DE' CONTI, I , 165 seq. That these were no empty threats is evident from the Report of Sanudo (Comment., 58), who informs his Government that Melchiore Trevisan had been sent to Constantinople. See CIPOLLA, 619.

† I found in the Secret Archives of the Vatican this document, which, as far as I know, has not yet been printed, with the Title : Responsio dom nostri Sixti papae IV ad objecta sivi per venetos in causa belli Ferrariensis ; Politic varia, VII , f 309–30   The charges against Sixtus IV , which the Venetians, through their Ambassadors, had disseminated at the different Courts, are here refuted, and the ambition of Venice is sharply rebuked. The special ground of her animosity is declared to be " quod non ad eorum libitum pontificatum administramus." The importance of Ferrara as the "antimurale totius Romandiole" is asserted , were Ferrara Venetian, Forli would be imperilled   In conclusion, His Holiness still expresses the hope that Venice would perceive her error, &c   There is no date, but the document must certainly belong to the spring of 1483   See also the justificatory piece in RAYNALDUS, ad an. 1483, N. 3.

‡ *On the 13th Dec, 1482, Sixtus IV. announced to Ercole of Ferrara the Mission of Gonzaga, in order that "presentia sua consolari ac spiritualibus et temporalibus favoribus sicut necessitas exegerit promptius iuvare et reintegrationi status tui intendere possit." Copy in the State Archives, Modena   On the same 13th December the Legate's Representative at Bologna was also informed of Gonzaga's Mission The *Brief on the subject is in the State Archives, Bologna, Q 3

§ **Brief of 5th Febr., 1483, in the State Archives, Florence (Urbino).

At the end of February the Venetian Ambassador left Rome; fearing that Sixtus IV. would proclaim a Crusade against Venice, he let fly a parting threat, that in that case there should be no more peace for the Pope. If it came to the worst they would make a league with the Devil![*]

At the same time, the Congress at Cremona, which, besides the Papal Legate, the Duke of Calabria, and Lorenzo de' Medici, comprised Lodovico and Ascanio Sforza, Ercole d'Este, Federigo Gonzaga, Marquess of Mantua, and Giovanni Bentivoglio, determined to put down the Venetians by force of arms [†]

Preparations for war were hastily begun in every direction There was no time to be lost, for Ferrara could not hold out much longer. The Pope was unwearied in his exhortations.[‡] He especially insisted on the necessity of attacking Venice by sea.[§] No less than 50,000 ducats were allotted for the equipment of the fleet, the sum being raised by the creation of new offices.[||]

Early in April, Branda Castiglione, Bishop of Como, was appointed Legate of the fleet.[¶] On the 30th of the month the Pope proclaimed his alliance with Naples, Milan, Ferrara,

---

[*] CAPELLI, 37.

[†] REUMONT, Lorenzo, II., 189, 2nd ed. ; FRANTZ, 421 *seq* , 458 ; CIPOLLA, 620. Girolamo Riario was not present, as SCHMARSOW, 200, shews, in opposition to Reumont

[‡] See in Appendix, N. 67, 69, 70, 71, 72, the *Briefs of 4th March, 16th and 21st April, and 1st May, 1483, as well as Girolamo Riario's Letter of the 7th May, 1483, from the State Archives, Milan

[§] See *Brief of 3rd April, 1483, in Appendix, N. 68.

[||] CAPELLI, 37

[¶] Bonfrancesco Arlotti, Bishop of Reggio, writes from Rome on the 9th April, 1483 . *" El vescovo de Como per concistorio et da N. S^re è publicato legato suxo l'armata." (State Archives, Modena.) Regarding the operations of the fleet, see SIGISMONDO DE' CONTI, I , 181 *seq*.

and Florence, and reiterated his promises of assistance to the Ferrarese through Cardinal Gonzaga, who died soon afterwards, a victim to the fatigues of the war.* The Venetians on their side entered into negotiations with the Duke of Lorraine, " in order again to harass King Ferrante by a popular Angevine rising, while their fleet harried the coast of Apulia and took possession of the important stronghold of Gallipoli."†

By the end of May the spiritual weapons of the Pope were also launched against Venice. From the month of February the Ambassadors of Ferrara had been urging him to proclaim an Interdict ‡ Girolamo Riario exerted his influence in the same direction, and succeeded in determining Sixtus IV. to take this important step.

The Bull of Interdict was laid before the Consistory on the 24th May. All the Sacred College, with the exception of the Venetian Cardinals, declared their concurrence. Their opposition, which greatly incensed the Pope, was not calculated to alter his purpose On the same day the Bull was affixed to the Gates of St. Peter's. In the Archives of Modena the jubilant Report is still preserved in which the Ferrarese Envoy tells the Duke that he had at once hastened to St. Peter's to convince himself of the fact §

The Pope at once communicated the Bull to the Emperor, the King of France, and the other Kings

---

* RAYNALDUS, ad an 1483, N 4, 5 ; CIPOLLA, 621.

† REUMONT, Lorenzo, II , 189.

‡ See *Letter of B. Arlotti, dated Rome, 1483, Febr 21. State Archives, Modena.

§ *Letter of B. Arlotti, dated Rome, 1483, May 24, *loc cit*. The Bull (dated X Cal Junii=23rd May, *not* June, as CIPOLLA, 621, has it) is in RAYNALDUS, ad an 1483, N. 8–16 ; it was sent to Milan on the 25th May See Appendix, N. 73, *Brief from the State Archives, Milan

and Princes of Christendom for publication in their dominions[*]

As the Venetian agents in Rome refused to transmit the Bull to their native city, the Pope sent a herald to deliver it to the Patriarch of Venice, whom he charged, under pain of Excommunication and suspension, to impart it to the Doge and the Signoria "The Patriarch pleaded illness, and apprised the Doge and the Council of Ten, who enjoined strict silence, and commanded him to continue the celebration of public worship as if nothing had happened."[†]   "The indignation of the Venetians against the Pope is extreme," wrote the Ferrarese Ambassador.   "They threaten to recall all their Cardinals and Prelates from Rome, and Sixtus IV. has prepared, in anticipation of this, a new Bull against Venice."[‡] The Signoria, in the first place, appealed to a future Council,[§] and at once began to agitate at the Imperial Court,[||] as well as at those of France and of England,[¶] for its convocation, but these efforts were fruitless.   Louis XI, on the contrary, at once complied with the wishes of the Pope,[**] and had

[*] RAYNALDUS, ad an 1483, N 17 ; FRANTZ, 429. See Appendix, N 73 and 74, Cathedral Archives of St Gall

[†] FRANTZ, 426 , ROMANIN, IV , 413 *seq.*

[‡] *Report of Bonfrancesco Arlotti, dated Rome, 1483, June 16. State Archives, Modena.

[§] This appeal was affixed to the Church doors of S. Celso in Rome, in the night between the 2nd and 3rd July ; see MALIPIERO, 283   The Informatione circa l'interdetto di Sisto IV. contro Venetia in Cod LIX.–120 of the Barberini Library, Rome, is merely an extract from Malipiero The Pope already, on the 24th June, knew of the "vain and unlawful" Appeal, for the Venetians had sent a copy to their Cardinals ; see *Letter of Bonfr Arlotti, dated Rome, 1483, June 24   State Archives, Modena

[||] See in Appendix, N. 75, the *Letter of the 15th June to the Emperor   Secret Archives of the Vatican.

[¶] See Cal of State Papers, Venetian, I , 146.

[**] See *Brief to Louis XI , dated Rome, 1483, June 15, in which

the sentence against Venice published in his dominions The Venetian Ambassadors were dismissed This happy result was chiefly due to the exertions of the Archbishop of Tours and of St Francis of Paula. The latter had come to Rome in the beginning of 1483. " All the Cardinals went to see him He had three audiences from the Pope, who placed him on a seat of honour by his side, and conversed with him for three or four hours. He was so struck with admiration at the wisdom of his discourse that he granted him permission to found a new Order."* From Rome St. Francis went to the French Court, and was there when Louis XI. died (29th August) †

Sixtus IV. had never allowed himself to be alarmed by

the necessity of resorting to spiritual weapons is asserted   " De consilio igitur fratrum nostrorum sententias et censuras ecc^cas adversus prefatos Venetos pro tulimus sequuti fe. re Clementum predecessorem nostrum. . . Bullam autem censurarum huiusmodi ad Maj. tuam in praesentiarum mittimus, ut eam per totum regnum tuum si ita tibi videbitur publicari facias " Lib brev , 15, f 620-21, Secret Archives of the Vatican

* REUMONT, III., 1, 180 , SIGISMONDO DE' CONTI, 176-7 , RAYNALDUS, ad an. 1483, N. 22. See also VICTON (Vita Francisci a Paula, p 121, R 1625); FANTONI, 345 , LEGEAY, II., 503 ; and the Monographs on S Francis of Paula by SYLVAIN (P 1874), DABERI (P 1875), and ROLLAND (P 1876, 2nd ed) ; as also F. ROLLE, Documents relatifs au passage de S François à Lyon (1483), Lyon, 1864.

† Under the new monarch, Charles VIII , to whom Sixtus IV expressed his condolences on the 11th Sept, 1483 (in the *Brief Lib. brev , 16 B, f. 27, Secret Archives of the Vatican, the Mission of a Legate is also announced), the anti-Papal tendency revived again in France. The restoration of the Pragmatic Sanction was demanded, and Cardinal de La Balue, who had been sent as Legate to the French Court, could do little or nothing. See HEFELE-HERGENROTHER, VIII , 260 ; GUETTÉE , VIII , 53 seq , 59 seq. ; FIERVILLE, 147 , PICOT, I , 426 seq , HOFLER, Rom Welt, 186 , and, especially in regard to La Balue's Legation, BULAEUS, V., 763 ; FRIEDBERG, II , 503 note , BUSER, Beziehungen 240 seq , and Mèm de la Soc de l'Hist de Paris, 1884, XI , 35 seq,

the threat of a Council   He declared in Consistory that he
was quite willing that one should be held, only it must be
at Rome in the Lateran, for the right of summoning it
belonged to him ; moreover, added the Pope, the Council
will necessarily afford an opportunity for the reformation
of the ecclesiastical and temporal Princes, and also for
calling the Venetians to account for their appropriation
of portions of the States of the Church, which must be
restored.*

No decisive advantage had meanwhile been gained at
any one of the various seats of war. Not one of the
enterprises begun by the allies had been brought to a
conclusion   Contending interests threatened the League
with dissolution. But Venice also was in a deplorable
condition ; "her treasury was exhausted, her arsenals
empty."†

There seemed, indeed, to be a hope of peace in March,
1484, when, at the desire of the allies, Ascanio Sforza, a
brother of Lodovico Moro's, was raised to the purple. The
Portuguese Cardinal, Giorgio Costa, who possessed the full
confidence of the Signoria, had already made considerable
progress in this direction, when Girolamo intervened   The
selfishness of this insatiable man completely destroyed the
prospect of peace, "which, at this moment, would have been
more honourable to the Pope and more favourable to himself than it ever again could be."‡

While the Ferrarese war engrossed general attention,
internal dissensions again broke out with great violence in
Rome. The year 1483 had been a year of peace for the

* See the **Report of B. Arlotti of the 7th July, 1483. (State
Archives, Modena) Sixtus IV's Protest against the Appeal of the 15th
July is given by RAYNALDUS, ad an. 1483, N. 18–21.

† FRANTZ, 459–61

‡ SCHMARSOW, 202, from SIGISMONDO DE' CONTI, I , 185-6

Eternal City; towards its close, Cardinals Colonna and Savelli were liberated * They were joyfully welcomed by their dependents when released on the morning of the 15th November, and at once took part in the Consistory in which Sixtus created five new Cardinals.†

If the year 1483 had been one of tranquillity, the next year was stormy In January the Orsini, confident in the friendship of Girolamo Riario, began the conflict by expelling Antonio Savelli from Albano. The "factions flew to arms On the 21st February the della Valle stabbed their enemy, Francesco Santa Croce," and fortified their Palace. The Colonna now espoused the cause of the della Valle, and the Orsini that of the Santa Croce, and also barricaded their Palaces‡ The disturbances came to such a pitch that, as we learn from an Ambassador, soon no one in the City felt his life or property secure§ "Never," wrote another

---

* "Instances of brutal outrage were not wanting, the after effects of the calamity of war and of inconsiderate tyranny" SCHMARSOW, 199 Regarding the horrible scenes at d'Estouteville's funeral, see NOTAJO DI NANTIPORTO, 1081-2

† "*Questa matina son liberati li rev^{mi} cardinali Savello et Columpna de castel S Angelo, onde erano carcerati, cum omnium consensu et plausu incredibili. In questa medema hora et eodem consistorio son creati cardinali cinque." Bonfrancesco Arlotti, dated Roma, 1483, Nov 15 According to a *Report of this Ambassador, of the 1st June, the release of the Cardinals was, even at that time, expected (State Archives, Modena) See also a *Letter of Stefano Guidotto, dated Rome, 1483, Nov. 18 · * " Io gionsi qua a Roma sabbato mattina a 15 del presente e ritrovai tutta la terra in festa per esser alhora cavati di castel S. Angelo quelli dui rev^{mi} cardinali Colonna e Savello" They were present at the election the same morning (Gonzaga Archives, Mantua) GRAZIANI, 653, is mistaken in stating that the Cardinals were liberated on the 17th November

‡ GREGOROVIUS, VII, 261, 3id ed.

§ See a *Letter from B Arlotti, dated Rome, 29th May, 1484 State Archives, Modena

contemporary, "did I see such confusion. It was the 29th
of May; the whole of Rome was in arms.   It was said that
they wished to seize the Protonotary by night, he kept
watch and secured himself as well as he could.   I had two
hand-barrows full of stones set inside my doors, which I
barricaded, and I had heavy stones brought up to the
windows and into the loggia. All through the night
the cry of Bear! Bear! was heard in the Rio Ponte, and
on Monte Giordano watch-fires burned, shots were fired,
and trumpets blown "*

On the following day, May 30, the Pope made an effort
to settle the dispute in an amicable manner. He sent
messengers to the Palace of Cardinal Colonna, on what is
now called the Piazza della Pilotta, where Lorenzo Oddone,
the Protonotary, had entrenched himself, inviting him in the
most friendly terms to his presence, and promising him all
that his justice and generosity could grant   Lorenzo's
intimate friend, Cardinal Sansoni, endeavoured to persuade
him to accept the Pope's invitation   Finally, Giuliano della
Rovere himself came and offered to remain as a hostage
in the house of the Colonna until such time as Oddone
should return from the Pope, an offer, as Sigismondo de'
Conti observes, suggested rather by affection than prudence.†

Lorenzo was fully inclined to go, but his friends, fearing
for his safety, prevented him   When Sixtus IV. sent the

* See REUMONT, III, 1, 181, who is mistaken in assigning these
disturbances to the 29th March. This error is due to the omission
of the name of the month in Notajo di Nantiporto INFESSURA, 1158,
and JACOB. VOLATERRANUS, 196, are correct in mentioning the end
of May SCHMARSOW, 250, misled by Sigismondo de' Conti, speaks of
the 28th and 29th April   See, on the other hand, B Arlotti's *Letter of
the 29th May, already cited, and a **Report of Stefano Guidotto,
dated Rome, 1484, June 1   Gonzaga Archives, Mantua.

† SIGISMONDO DE' CONTI, I, 189

Conservators for the second time, and promised to forgive everything, he mounted his horse and rode away alone.   But some armed followers of his met him on the Piazza Trevi and obliged him to return.

Girolamo and the Orsini had meanwhile ascertained, through Leone Montesecco, the Prefect of the Body Guard, that Oddone had only a crowd of untrained and unwarlike retainers in his house.

All fear vanished.   After a proclamation had been made to the effect that all who should take part with the Colonna incurred the guilt of high treason, an order for the forcible arrest of the Protonotary was issued.   The attack at once began.   A panic seized the Colonna ; a great many of them left the Palace, which was soon surrounded on all sides. During the fight, which lasted but two hours, forty of the Colonna and only thirteen of their adversaries were killed. The barricades were then scaled, the Palace was relentlessly plundered, and Lorenzo Oddone taken prisoner.   On the way to the Vatican, Virginio Orsini had to defend the un-armed captive from Count Girolamo, who, in his rage, twice drew his sword against him   Sixtus IV. reproached him in violent language, and accused him of having twice sought to drive him from Rome.   "The Protonotary tried to excuse himself on the ground that his people had prevented him when he tried to go to the Vatican, but after all the terror he had undergone he could hardly utter a sound   He was given over to Virginio Orsini and confined in St Angelo"*

"It was fortunate," says Sigismondo de' Conti, "that the conflict was not protracted into the night, under cover of which shame and fear are put aside, and many more would

* SIGISMONDO DE' CONTI, I , 190 *seq* ; SCHMARSOW, 251. See Arch. d. Soc Rom, XI., 612, and Stefano Guidotto's **Reports of the 1st and 4th June, 1484 Gonzaga Archives

have taken part with the Colonna, so that the Pope and the Orsini might have been in great danger " *

The houses of the della Valle were, like the Palace of the Colonna, razed to the ground † The undisciplined soldiers billeted themselves in the houses of the Colonna quarter and wrought cruel havoc there.‡

A portion of the Roman burghers determined to beg the Pope to make peace with the Colonna Cardinal Giuliano also earnestly advocated a reconciliation, but again the Orsini and Count Girolamo prevented it. The conduct of the latter became more and more insupportable. " He extorted money from the Roman churches, and even from the College of Papal Secretaries and that of the Stradioti."§ If we may believe Infessura, whose sympathies are with the Colonna party, high words passed between Girolamo Riario and Cardinal Giuliano, even in presence of the Pope Cardinal Giuliano had granted asylum in his Palace to some fugitives from Cardinal Colonna's dwelling, and had expressed his displeasure at Riario's violence. Girolamo accused the Cardinal of protecting rebels and enemies of the Church. Giuliano replied that the men whom he protected were no rebels against the Church, but some of her most faithful servants ; that Girolamo was hunting them out of Rome,

* SIGISMONDO DE' CONTI, I , 191 Bonfr Arlotti writes on the 2nd June, 1484. *"El non si poteria dir quanto stano di bona voglia el papa et conte per questa victoria et sbatimento di Colonesi" State Archives, Modena.

† See S Guidotto's **Report of the 1st June, 1484, and the *Diario volgare del Corona in Cod LIV -10, f 413 Barberini Library, Rome.

‡ Particulars, especially with regard to the ill-treatment of P Laetus, in SCHMARSOW, 251

§ GREGOROVIUS, VII , 262-3, 3rd ed. See also SCHMARSOW, 252-3, who gives a graphic picture of Girolamo's doings in Rome, of his exactions, his usurious speculations in corn, and his insolence towards the Rota.

setting the Church of God on fire and destroying her He was the cause of all the evil deeds which were bringing ruin on the Pope and on the Cardinals. The Count, on this, flew into a rage and declared that he would drive him out of the country, burn his house over his head, and give it up to plunder, as he had done to that of the Colonna *

The attack on the Colonna still went on in the neighbourhood of Rome. The whole of Latium was soon a prey to fire and rapine. On the 27th June Marino fell, and the Colonna retired to Rocca di Papa.†

Three days later Lorenzo Oddone was beheaded in St. Angelo, after retracting the confessions torn from him on the rack. The unhappy man met death with calmness and dignity. The corpse was taken, in the first instance, to the neighbouring church of Sᵗᵃ Maria Traspontina, whence, in the evening, it was conveyed to that of the SS Apostoli Here it was received by his mother and many other women, wailing and lamenting, and was buried that same night by Infessura and a vassal of the Colonna.‡

* INFESSURA, 1168 , SCHMARSOW, 253.

† "*Marino hogi s'è dedito et accordato cum el papa," writes B. Arlotti on the 27th June, 1484 (State Archives, Modena) SCHMARSOW, 254, is, accordingly, mistaken in giving the 25th as the date

‡ NOTAJO DI NANTIPORTO, 1087, and INFESSURA, 1174-5 The former merely says of Colonna's mother, "fece gran lamento", the latter, although a partisan of the Colonna, and very hostile to Sixtus IV, is (like the Cron Rom , 37, and the above-mentioned *Diario del Corona) silent as to the words of accusation which ALLEGRETTI, 817, says she uttered at the sight of her dead son . "Questa è la testa del mio figlio e la fede di Papa Sisto che ci promesse, come lassassimo Marino, ci lassarebbe el mio figliulo" GREGOROVIUS, VII , 264, 3rd ed, and RANKE (Papste, I., 31, 6th ed) both incorporate the words in their text, but the former is fair enough in a note to call attention to the fact that they rest solely on Allegretti's authority. REUMONT, III , I, 183, does not mention them. SCHMARSOW, 254, repeats them, but, as CREIGHTON, III., 99, admits, "there is no evidence that the

On the 2nd July Girolamo and Virginio Orsini, with their troops, took the field against the Colonna.* Events soon proved that they had been very ill-advised in thwarting the efforts made to re-establish peace. Prospero and Fabrizio Colonna defended themselves bravely. " The Savelli allowed themselves to be corrupted, and thus many strongholds were indeed lost, but Paliano held out," and Girolamo found it necessary to apply to the Pope for reinforcements. He was soon compelled to own that he had little hope of subduing the Colonna.

Sixtus IV was greatly disturbed by these tidings; he had never anticipated such determined resistance † In the month of March his health,‡ which, till then, had been very

Pope made any promise to release Lorenzo." It is worthy of notice that the Mantuan Ambassador, S. Guidotto, does not even allude to the mother's words Writing on the 2nd July, 1484, he says . * " La Sta del N S el fece portare in una cassa ad una certa chiesa propinqua al castello e fu monstrato ad alcuni e poi etiam a la madre e fu sepelito la sera assai honorevolmente a Sto Apostolo" *On the 8th July he reports that Colonna's mother had died of grief, but says nothing of these words I found these two *Letters in the Gonzaga Archives, Mantua   The Sienese Report in Arch Rom, XI., 614, contains nothing in regard to the supposed exclamation. All rules of criticism require us to reject the statement of an absent writer, when all the witnesses who were on the spot are ignorant of the circumstance mentioned.

* " *Hogi a l'alba lo ill. s. conte è andato in campo, cussi el sre Virgineo." S Guidotto on the 2nd July, 1484 (Gonzaga Archives) See B. Arlotti's *Letter of the same day. (State Archives, Modena) Payments for Girolamo's troops are entered in July, 1484, in *Div Sixti IV., 1484 State Archives, Rome

† REUMONT, III, I, 184 ; SCHMARSOW, 255

‡ On the 7th January, 1483, Stef Guidotto wrote : * " La Sta de N S za tri o quatro di è stato per uno puoco di catharo col collo tuto incordato, non ge stato tempo ne honesto di chieder audientia perche etiam il feci dir a li cardinali che non ge andassimo S. Sta me fece

good, had begun to give way* Constant agitation and anxiety naturally told upon him at last In the middle of June he fell ill of a fever† Early in August his old malady, the gout, attacked him with such violence that he received the Sacraments of Penance and the Holy Eucharist.‡

Meanwhile, the rumour that peace had been concluded with the Venetians continued to gain more and more credence in Rome This was actually the case.

The warlike zeal of Milan had been gradually cooling ever since the July of 1483 The urgent demands of Sixtus IV. had failed to produce any effect.§ A year later, " Lodo-vico Moro had succeeded in severing himself from the League, of which he had been but a half-hearted member." " When the Venetians were getting the worst of it, and their finances were nearly exhausted," says Commines, " Duke Lodovico came to the aid of their honour and credit, and every one again got his own, excepting the poor Duke of Ferrara, who had been drawn into the war by himself and his father-in-law, and was now obliged to abandon the Polesina to the Venetians. It is said that the affair brought Duke Lodovico in 60,000 ducats. I know not," adds Commines, " if that is true, but I found the Duke of Ferrara, who, however, had not at that time yet given him his daughter in marriage, under this belief"‖

dire una matina che ge andassi e ritrovai che la notte gera venuto quello disturbo, non è percho gran male, anci l'è gaiardo e bello continuo comel fussi de 40 anni " Gonzaga Archives, Mantua.

* Sienese Despatch of the 17th March, 1484, in Arch Rom., XI , 610

† BURCHARD-THUASNE, I , 493.

‡ *Report of B. Arlotti, dated Rome, 1484, August 3 State Archives, Modena

§ See in Appendix, N 76, 77, 78, 79, 80, and 81, the *Briefs of July 15th, August 20th and 25th, Sept 20th, and Oct 2nd and 13th, 1483 State Archives, Milan, and Secret Archives of the Vatican

‖ REUMONT, Lorenzo, II , 190, 194, 2nd ed

Gallipoli and other places on the coast, which had been taken from him, were restored to the King of Naples. Roberto da San Severino, the Captain-General of the Venetians, became commander of the troops of the League, with a yearly salary of 20,000 florins. Riario went away empty The Peace of Bagnolo (7th August, 1484) became, as Sigismondo de' Conti justly observes, a victory for Venice, for Ercole of Ferrara was obliged to come there in person as a suppliant, and Lodovico sent his son ostensibly to take part in the festivities, but really as a hostage for the fulfilment of the conditions of the treaty.*

The Pope would not at first believe in this disgraceful Peace When, however, he could no longer doubt that his authority had been thus set at naught, his grief was extreme " Faithless Lodovico ! " he was heard to exclaim, in a voice shaken with sighs.†

His illness was no doubt aggravated by excitement. A Consistory had been summoned to meet on Wednesday, the 11th August, but as the Pope had become worse in the

---

* SIGISMONDO DE' CONTI, I , 194 ,/SCHMARSOW, 256, who draws attention to the fact that Gianfrancesco Tolentino, as Procurator and Mandatory of Sixtus IV , had the first place among those who conducted the Peace negotiations, and that, accordingly, it cannot be said that the treaty was concluded behind the Pope's back (as BROSCH, Julius II , p 27, represents it to have been), and without his knowledge or consent, but the conditions, to which the majority agreed, broke his heart

† SIGISMONDO DE' CONTI, I., 204. " Hardly five months had passed," says REUMONT, Lorenzo, II , 195, 2nd ed , " since he had conferred the Red Hat on Ascanio Maria Sforza, brother of the man who was now thwarting all his plans Ascanio began a troubled cardinalate under warlike auspices " See also SCHMARSOW, 256. The assertion that Sixtus IV took delight in wars and troubles, and, accordingly, was greatly vexed that any kind of Peace should be concluded, is a malicious invention, irreconcilable with his last authentic utterances. LAMMER in Histor Jahrbuch, I , 179

night, the assembled Cardinals were dismissed. Nevertheless, after Vespers, the Ambassadors of the League were
admitted into his presence. "When he had heard them,"
says Jacobus Volaterranus, "he complained, not, as evil-
minded and malicious persons have asserted, that Peace had
been concluded, but that its conditions were so unfavourable.
'Up to this time,' he said, 'we have carried on a dangerous
and difficult war, in order, by our victorious arms, to obtain
an honourable Peace for the security of the Apostolic See,
our own honour, and that of the League. Now, when as
you know, by the will of God, success was at hand, you
bring back conditions of Peace suited to the vanquished,
not to the victor. The Venetians had already offered our
Apostolic Legate terms much fairer and more profitable to
your Princes, terms which were honourable to the Apostolic
See, whereas these are disgraceful The cities taken in the
war were to be entrusted to our protection, the nobles were
to send us hostages and await our judgment, Ferrara was
not mentioned You propose none of these things, but, on
the contrary, shameful conditions, fraught with the seeds of
confusion and future evil rather than good. This Peace, my
beloved sons in Christ, I can neither approve nor sanction.'"*

During the night and the following day the weakness of
the Pope hourly increased ; the fever consumed his strength.
On the Feast of S Clara, 12th August, in the fourth hour of
the night, he passed peacefully away. "Four days previously," Jacobus Volaterranus informs us, "he had received
Holy Communion After his death the Penitentiaries of
the Friars-minor washed him, vested him, and laid him out
on his bier In the evening the corpse was brought to the

---

* JACOBUS VOLATERRANUS, 199, FRANTZ, 476 *seq*. See also
Donfrancesco Arlotti's **Letter of the 12th August, 1484 State
Archives, Modena.

Basilica of St. Peter, and, with all fitting honour, deposited
in the chapel which he had himself built in his lifetime, until
his monument should be ready The obsequies commenced
on the fourth day, and continued for nine days without
intermission." *

* JACOBUS VOLATERRANUS, 200; FRANTZ, 477. Regarding the
Pope's last hours, see the Despatch of Guidantonio Vespucci in
BURCHARD-THUASNE, I , 496, where the actual account of his death is,
however, wanting * " In questo punto che siamo a hore V è passato
di questa vita la santa mem. di papa Sisto " *Despatch of Vespucci
of the 12th August, Arch Medic filza 39, f. 320. (State Archives,
Florence.) With this, accord Bonfrancesco Arlotti's *Despatches of
14th and 15th August, which say that death took place between the
fifth and sixth hours. (State Archives, Modena) Stef Guidotto's
Letters of the 12th and 13th August from the Gonzaga Archives, printed
in Appendix, N 82, mention an earlier hour. The imposing bronze
monument, which Cardinal Giuliano erected to his uncle's memory,
was executed by Antonio Pollajuolo, a Florentine, in 1493, and is now
in the Chapel of the Blessed Sacrament in St. Peter's , it represents
the departed Pope in his Pontifical robes " a thick-set, almost small
figure, a bony hand with dry sinews, covered with loose leathery skin,
but with veins which seem almost throbbing with warm blood, and a
long history written in the deep furrows and angular lines of the
weather-beaten face " (SCHMARSOW, 259) , round about are ill-chosen
and, in some instances, objectionable, allegorical figures of the Sciences
See BURCKHARDT, Cicerone, 358 ; GREGOROVIUS, Grabmaler, 101 seq.
See also CROWE-CAVALCASELLE, III , 127 , BURCKHARDT, Gesch der
Renaissance, 292 , PIPER, Mythologie, I., 89 , The Ecclesiologist,
XXIX, 161 , SEMPER, Donatello, 120 (Innsbruck, 1887); Plate in
LITTA, fasc. 147.

CHAPTER XI.

IN following the course of Sixtus IV. through the mazes of
Italian politics, it is often difficult to believe that he was
once the General of a Mendicant Order ; but in the ecclesiastical sphere the case is quite different, and his action fully
corresponds to what we should naturally expect.* As early
as the year 1472 the decision of Gregory IX. regarding the
powers of the Cardinal-Protector of the Franciscans was
confirmed † A Bull of the 3rd October of that year made
the Feast of St. Francis henceforth a holiday of obligation ‡
This was followed, on the 31st August, 1474, by the Bull
known as " Mare magnum " (the Great Sea), by which the
privileges of the Franciscan-Conventuals were so greatly
augmented In it those granted by Clement IV. and
Eugenius IV , which were already very extensive, were not

---

* Regarding the abolition of the exemptions of the Mendicant
Orders from common law jurisdiction, which was contemplated by
Calixtus III , and then by Paul II , and the protest of Francesco della
Rovere against the measure, see PHILLIPS, VII , 997.

† Bull., 205-7.

‡ Bull., 209. A copy of the Bull is in the State Archives, Dresden,
D P O, No. 64.

only confirmed but considerably increased. Most ample
powers were conferred upon the Conventuals in regard to
Divine Worship during an Interdict, jurisdiction in cases
reserved to the Pope, exemption from tithes and from
episcopal jurisdiction, the administration of the Sacraments,
and the burial of the faithful in the habit and in the ceme-
teries of the Order. All who opposed them were threatened
with severe punishments * A similar Bull was also issued
in favour of the Dominicans †

Even this was not enough, for in 1479 Sixtus IV.
granted yet further favours by the "Golden Bull" ‡ To
enumerate the good things bestowed on the Mendicant
Friars, and more particularly on the Franciscans, during this
long pontificate would be an almost endless task § Highly
as we may estimate the manifold and important labours of
these Orders, there can be no doubt that the indulgence
shewn to them was excessive. Sixtus IV. also assisted the
Brothers of the Common Life, and approved the order of
the Minims and that of the discalced Augustinians.‖

* Bull, 217 *seq.* See WADDING, 1474, N. 17, Anal Francisc, II,
457 PANZER, Annal, III., 488, gives information regarding a very
ancient printed copy of the 'Mare magnum' A copy of it is in the
City Library, Frankfort, Rit Cath, 151

† Bull, 224 *seq* ; Bull praedic, 516 *seq.*

‡ Bull, 278 *seq*, Bull praedic, III., 578 *seq.*

§ See, besides Wadding, the Croniche di S. Francesco, III, 319
seq, and EUBEL, II, 223

‖ JANSSEN, I., 66, 15th ed. ; HEFELE-HERGENROTHER, VIII, 199.
Sixtus IV repeatedly came forward as the Protector of Monastic
Institutes (see his *Decree for the Dominicans at Ghent, dated
Rome, 1483, Febr. 18, Minute brevium Sixti IV., &c, f. 18, N 79,
Secret Archives of the Vatican ; and a *Bull, dated 1484, iv Cal Julii,
in reference to the Monast Trinit Milet. in the Archives of the
Greek Seminary, Rome, L II), and, especially, of ecclesiastical liberty,
see *supra*, p 314 *seq*, and the *Brief to the Doge of Venice of the 7th

The many disputes of the Religious Orders among themselves were deplorable.   Accordingly, in the " Golden Bull " Sixtus IV. expressly forbade the office of Inquisitor to be exercised by a Franciscan against a Dominican or *viceversa ;* and, to prevent the perpetual conflicts between the Secular and Regular clergy, he also issued a decree that Parish Priests were not to accuse Mendicants of heresy, and, on the other hand, prohibited the latter from telling the people that they were not bound to hear Masses of obligation in their Parish Church   Seculars and Regulars were alike forbidden to influence the faithful in regard to their place of sepulture   Sixtus IV. confirmed the rule that the Easter Confession was to be made to the Parish Priest.*

There seems to be no doubt that Sixtus IV. also desired to effect a reunion between the Franciscan Conventuals and the Observantines.   As he had himself been a Conventual, this would have meant the abolition of the Observantines. They were greatly disturbed about this scheme.   Glassberger writes in his chronicle : " During the whole course of his pontificate, Sixtus IV. did nothing that could justly be blamed, except that he wished to subject the Observantines to the Conventuals, for this reason God raised up an adversary against him in Andrea of Carniola   From all sides, even from temporal Princes like the Duke of Milan, petitions were showered upon Rome, so that the Pope exclaimed . ' The whole world is for the Observantines ! ' " St. Jacopo della Marca is said to have predicted to Sixtus IV.

Nov., 1480, in Lib brev, 13, f 160. (Secret Archives of the Vatican.) For evidence of the care of Sixtus IV. for the Greek Christians, see Bibl. de l'École des Chartes, 1877, p 269

* HERGENROTHER, VIII , 253   See REMLING, Speier, II , 172-3 , LEA, I , 293, 302. KOLDE, 205, relates the unavailing attempt of four Electors from the Rhine Provinces to induce Sixtus IV. to suppress the Mendicant Orders

that he would die suddenly if he carried out this plan. As
a fact, the Bull, which had been drafted, never appeared *

The partiality of Sixtus IV for his own Order doubtless
contributed to bring about the canonisation of St. Bona-
ventura, which was proclaimed with much solemnity in
Rome on the 14th April, 1482.† In the previous year he
had raised to the altars the Minorites martyred in Morocco
in the time of Honorius III ‡

The exertions of Sixtus IV. on behalf of the due celebration of Divine worship and chanting of the Liturgy are also
especially worthy of record.   It was by him the famous
Sistine Choir was instituted and attached to this Chapel for
the daily chanting of the Divine Office.   The reign of this
Pontiff was the beginning of a new artistic life in the Papal
Chapel ; "the most highly-gifted singers from all countries
flocked to Rome, allured by the opportunity afforded to
them of exercising their art, making their talents known,
and reaping rich rewards." §

Sixtus IV laboured assiduously to preserve the integrity

---

* GLASSBERGER in Anal Francisc., II, 455, 463 ; EUBEL, II, 278

† INFESSURA, 1148 , JACOB VOLATERRANUS, 169 *seq* , RAYNALDUS,
ad an 1482, N. 47 *seq* , Bull, 284 *seq*.; WADDING, XIV, 285 *seq* ;
Anal Franc, II, 284 , BALUZE-MANSI, Miscell, IV, 471 *seq.*, MAR-
TÈNE, II, 1672-3 ; OROLOGIO, Canonici di Padova, 157 , SCHULTE,
Quellen, II, 332 ; VALENTINELLI, Regesten, 522 (Munchen, 1865);
SUMMONTE, III, 503 *seq* ; STALIN, III., 594.

‡ RAYNALDUS, ad an 1481, N 52-3

§ HABERL, Bausteine, I, 72, and III. Die. Romische Schola Can-
torum und die papstlichen Kapellsanger bis zur mitte des 16 Jahrhunderts, Leipzig, 1887. Extract from the Vierteljahrsschrift für Musikwissenschaft, Jahrg , 3 Part II of the "Bausteine" contains the
musical catalogue of the Archives of the Papal Chapel (1888).
The well-known editor of Palestrina has in this work far surpassed
his predecessor (SCHELLE, Die papstl Sangerschule, Wien, 1872),
and has rendered valuable service by his researches in the musical
treasures of the Roman Archives

of the Faith, and, in particular, took measures against the Waldensees in Piedmont and France *

The Pope was, as the preceding history bears witness, most solicitous for the maintenance of the monarchical constitution of the Church.   In 1478 he formally annulled the Decrees of the Council of Constance.   Martin V. had already refused to recognise them, with the exception of those concerning the Faith.   In 1483 he revived the Bull of/ Pius II prohibiting appeals to a Council.†

His ardent devotion to the Blessed Virgin was an admirable trait in the character of this Pope.   Sigismondo de' Conti says that he used to pray before her statue with such

---

* LEA, II , 159, 187, 266, 416 ; BERNINO, 208 *seq.* ; Bull praedic., III , 487, 501, 577 , MARTÈNE, II , 1507, 1510; Bull , 263 *seq.* See PELAYO, I , 548, 788 , REUSCH, I., 42   Regarding Sixtus IV's ordinances against Slavery, see RAYNALDUS, ad an 1476, N. 21-2.

† RAYNALDUS, ad an. 1478, N. 46, 1483, N 18 *seq.* , GEBHARDT, 45, and *supra*, pp 326 and 377 *seq.*   That Sixtus IV was an energetic champion of Papal authority, in opposition to the false Conciliar theories, is evident from his autograph *Observations on the official Acts of the Council of Constance, which Dr. Finke has most kindly made known to me   After the words " Nos votis—conspiciebamus" in the Convocation Bull "Ad pacem" of 1413, December 8 (MANSI, XXVII , 537 *seq.*), is the remark · "Sixtus papa IIII. manu propria addidit et glosavit in originali existenti in bibliotheca : Deceptus fuit papa Johannes"   After "deinde securit civ Const," Sixtus IV. wrote " Papa habet determinare locum concilii et tempus et solus habet congregare concilium, ideo petitur ab eo, &c."   At the 5th November Sixtus IV. has added to the marginal note, "Inchoatio concilii" (see MANSI, 532) "Parvi roboris" On the Bull of Publication he wrote " Nota quod papa statuit et concilium approbat, ideo papa est super concilium, quemadmodum rex, qui statuit, est super concilium suum, quod facta per regem approbat " (Barberini Library, XVI , 63) With reference to Sixtus IV's observations on the Acts of the Council of Constance, see H FINKE, Forschungen und Quellen zur Gesch. des Konstanzer Concils , 54 (Paderborn, 1889)

fervour and recollection, that for a whole hour his eyes
never wandered from it.* The Italian shrines of our Lady,
especially those of Loreto and Genazzano, were the objects
of his particular care † In the year 1475 he instituted the
Feast of the Visitation and published an Encyclical on the
occasion ‡ He also, in many ways, promoted the devotion
of the Rosary § In Rome the Pope's veneration for the
Mother of God found expression in the erection of the celebrated churches of Sᵗᵃ Maria del Popolo and Sᵗᵃ Maria della
Pace, and of the Sistine Chapel, which was dedicated to her
Immaculate Conception ‖ In 1475 he approved of a special
Office of the Immaculate Conception for the 8th December.¶
Here also his Franciscan sympathies appear. His Order,
in opposition to that of the Dominicans, were ardent
champions of this doctrine, which was already widely diffused
in the Church. The contention between the two Orders on
this subject now broke forth anew. A Dominican, named
Vincenzo Bandelli, had asserted in public disputations and
in writing that those who declared the Conception of the
Blessed Virgin to have been Immaculate were guilty of
heresy and, accordingly, of mortal sin. The dispute became
so violent that Sixtus IV. had to interfere. Although he
did not pronounce any definite decision, the Constitution,
which he published in 1483, clearly shews to which side he
personally inclined " We," he says, "reject and condemn

* SIGISMONDO DE' CONTI, I , 204.

† TURSELLINUS, 140 seq. , DILLON, Unsere liebe Frau vom guten
Rathe, Einsiedeln, 1887.

‡ RAYNALDUS, ad an 1475, N 34 See FABRICIUS-MANSI, VI ,
491

§ Bull praedic , III , 567, 576 seq ; Bull., 268 , GIESELER, Kirchengesch , II , 4, 337.

‖ Bull , 269 seq , Bull Vatic , 205 seq. FRANTZ, 514, has misunderstood this Bull

¶ FRANTZ, 513.

the assertions of those preachers, who allow themselves to be so far carried away as to represent such as believe or maintain that the Mother of God was preserved from the stain of original sin, to be thereby tainted with heresy or guilty of mortal sin, and those who solemnly celebrate the Office of the Conception of Mary, or listen to sermons in which that doctrine is declared, as thereby committing sin—we reject and condemn, by Apostolical authority, all such statements as false, erroneous, and completely devoid of truth, together with the books which contain them We also determine and appoint that preachers of the Word of God and others, of whatever station, rank, calling, and character they may be, who shall henceforth rashly venture to maintain that the statements we have thus disapproved and condemned are true, or who shall read books containing them, holding or considering them to be true, after the pieceding constitution has been made known to them—*ipso facto*, incur the sentence of Excommunication."

In order, however, to guard against the impression that any special dogmatic decision of the doctrine in question was here involved, the Pope adds to this decree the express declaration that no such decision has yet been given by the Apostolic See, and that, accordingly, the opponents of the view of Scotus and of the Doctois of Paris cannot at present be accused of heresy.*

In the sphere of ecclesiastical policy, Sixtus IV. made considerable concessions to governments with whom he was on good terms, or from whom he expected assistance of a political nature. The influence of the secular power on

---

* Extrav commun , lib III , tit XII, c. 2   See the beautiful work, Zum Lobe der unbefleckten Empfangniss der allers. Jungfrau, 58–9 (Freibuig, 1879); DENZINGER, Die Lehre von der unbefl Empfangniss, 30 *seq* (Wuizburg, 1855, 2nd ed), FRANTZ, 513 *seq* , HERGENROTHER, VIII , 213 , Kirchenlexikon, IV , 473, 2nd ed

┇ecclesiastical affairs was thus unduly strengthened * Besides confirming the Bulls granted to the Emperor Frederick III. by Eugenius IV. and Nicholas V , regarding the exercise of patronage for the episcopal Sees of Trent, Brixen, Gurk, Trieste, Chur, Piben, Vienna, and Wiener-Neustadt, on the 8th April, 1473, he also granted him the right of presentation to 300 benefices † A Bull of 1478 also accorded to Frederick the temporary patronage of other Bishoprics ‡

Dukes Ernest and Albrecht of Saxony received from Sixtus IV., in 1476, the right of presentation to several high dignities belonging to the Chapter of Meissen, and, nine years later, that right was extended to all such posts in that city §

A Bull of the 8th July, 1479, allowed the Government of Zurich to fill up all benefices belonging to the Great Cathedral and that of our Lady and the Monastery of Embrach, even such as should fall vacant in the Papal months.‖ In consideration of the number of clerical state criminals and falsifiers of the coinage in the Republic of Venice, Sixtus

---

* An example of "the truly pertinacious energy" with which even minor States sought to impose upon the Holy See prelates devoted to their interests, may be found in the Jahrb fur Schweiz. Gesch, IX , 21 *seq.* See also, in STALIN, III , 539, the utterances of the Duke of Wurtemberg regarding his right to confer ecclesiastical fiefs. For an account of the dispute concerning the appointment to the Bishopric of Fréjus, in which Sixtus IV. carried out his purpose, see LECOY DE LA MARCHE, I , 543

† Mon Habsb , I , 316, 318.

‡ Mon Habsb , II , 386 *seq.* See Archiv fur Œsterr. Gesch , LV., 175.

§ Cod. Dipl. Sax Urkundenbuch des Hochstiftes Meissen, III , 240, 263, 272, 278 ; GESS, Klostervisitationen des Herzogs Georg von Sachsen, 2 (Leipzig, 1888)

‖ Geschichtsfreund, XXXIII , 46 *seq* , Jahrbuch fur Schweiz Gesch., IV , 9.

IV. consented that such should be tried by the secular judges in presence of the Vicar of the Patriarch.*

The control of the State over the Church in Spain had at this time assumed an immense development   Efforts to strengthen and extend this power led to important contests concerning presentations to Bishoprics.   In the autumn of 1478 Cardinal Peter Ferrici, Bishop of Tarragona, died † Sixtus IV. then conferred the Bishopric on Andreas Martinez; but King Ferdinand, who desired this preferment for Cardinal Pedro Gonzalez de Mendoza, commanded Martinez to resign at once, threatening him with exile and other severe penalties to be inflicted on himself and his relations ‡   The See of Cuença (1482) was the occasion of an, even more serious dispute   Sixtus IV had appointed his nephew, Raffaello Sansoni, to this Bishopric, while Isabella wished it to be given to her Confessor, Alfonso de Burgos The remonstrances of the Royal pair being disregarded, they broke off communication with Rome and threatened to hold ‖ a Council.   The friendship of the Spanish monarchs was of great importance to the Pope in his Italian difficulties.   In consequence, he had granted them extensive concurrent rights in episcopal nominations, and Alfonso de Burgos eventually became Bishop of Cuença   Isabella, however, it must be said, used her privilege in favour of really excellent men.§

* FRIEDBERG, 692, see 690 As to the treatment of obnoxious Bishops by Venice, see the information given by MAS-LATRIE in the Rev. des Quest Hist., 1878, April, p 571 seq.

† PANVINIUS, 325.

‡ PRESCOTT, I., 255; Archiv für Kirchenrecht, N. F., IV., 11; FRIEDBERG, 539 seq.

§ MAURENBRECHER, Studien, 13 (Leipzig, 1874), and Kath-Reformation, 378 (Nordlingen, 1880), FRIEDBERG, 540, PRESCOTT, I, 256 seq, II, 586; SENTIS, Monarchia Sicula, 102 See also HERGENROTHER in Archiv f. Kirchenrecht, N F, IV, 15, PHILLIPS-VERING, Kirchenrecht, VIII, i, 199 seq

Sixtus IV. shewed greater firmness in regard to the question of the Spanish Inquisition. This tribunal, whose office it was to punish obstinate heretics or notorious sinners who were nominally members of the Church,* was created, in the first instance, to deal with the special circumstances of the Jewish community in Spain. No other European State had suffered, to the extent that Spain was then suffering, from the unrelenting system of usury and organised extortion practised by these dangerous aliens   Persecutions were the natural consequence, and often the only alternative before the Jews was baptism or death.   Thus the number of merely nominal converts to the Christian Faith soon became very great.   The secret Jews were incomparably more dangerous than those who openly professed their religion.   "If the latter monopolised the greater part of the wealth and commerce of the country, the former threatened alike the Spanish nationality and the Christian faith.   On the one hand they contrived to insinuate themselves into a number of ecclesiastical charges, and even to become Bishops, and on the other to attain high municipal honours and to marry into all the noble families   These advantages, and their great wealth, were all covertly devoted to the gradual subjugation of the Spaniards and the undermining of their Faith in favour of the Jews and Judaism."†   Things had latterly come to such a pass that the very existence of Christian Spain was at stake‡

The Inquisition was created as a remedy for these evils

* Only such as having, through baptism, become members of the Church were viewed as rebels against her authority, and the unbaptised were not subject to the Inquisition   See GRISAR, 551, N. 1

† HEFELE, Ximenes, 277-8

‡ Such is the opinion of A HUBER, Ueber die Spanische Nationalitat und Kunst, Berlin, 1852

The necessary authorisation of the Holy See was given in a Brief of the 1st November 1478.* Ferdinand and Isabella were hereby empowered, after due examination, to nominate two or three Archbishops and Bishops, or other dignitaries of the Church, who should be secular or regular priests, commendable for their prudence and virtue, at least forty years of age, and of blameless morals, Masters or Bachelors of Theology, Doctors or Licentiates of Canon Law These Inquisitors were to proceed against relapsed Jews who had been baptised and other apostates The Pope granted them the necessary jurisdiction for proceeding, according to law and custom, against the guilty, and permitted the Spanish monarchs to dismiss them and appoint others, with the reservation that the Bull itself could not be annulled without express mention of its contents †

By the desire of Queen Isabella another effort was made to bring back those who had been led away by preaching and other peaceable means These attempts being obstinately and scornfully rejected, the Spanish monarchs, in virtue of the Papal Bull, nominated, on the 17th September, 1489, two Dominicans, Michael Morillo and Juan Martin, as Inquisitors for the city and Diocese of Seville Two secular priests were associated with them They began their work without delay. Jews who obstinately persisted in their errors were handed over to the secular power and burned.‡

Very soon vehement complaints of the harsh and irregular proceedings of the Inquisitors began to arrive in Rome Sixtus IV's Brief of the 29th January, 1482, shews that grave abuses had arisen. The Pope, in the first place, expresses

---

* Not on the 1st September, as GRISAR says, 560

† LLORENTE, I 167-8 , see IV , 410

‡ LLORENTE, I , 171 *seq*   See HEFELE, Ximenes, 282 *seq* RODRIGO, II , 71 *seq* ; GRISAR, 561.

his displeasure at the omission, without his knowledge, of certain clauses in the former Brief, which, as it appears, would have guarded more securely against abuses, brought the methods of procedure into greater harmony with the course of common law, and facilitated the concerted action which had been usual between the Inquisitors and the Bishops The result had been that these former, under pretext of the Papal Brief, had unjustly imprisoned many persons without trial, subjected them to cruel tortures, pronounced them heretics, and confiscated the possessions of those who were executed, so that numbers had fled the country in dread of a similar fate   Moved by the complaints of persons who had turned to the Holy See as "the defender of all the oppressed," after consultation with the Cardinals, he issued his commands that the Inquisitors should henceforth proceed in conformity with law and justice, and in concert with the Bishops   Sixtus IV. further declared that nothing but consideration for the King, whose Ambassadors in Rome interceded for the Inquisitors, could have induced him to continue them in their office.   Should they persist in these evil practices, and act without consulting the Bishop of the Diocese, or considering what the salvation of souls demanded, he would put others in their place   The Pope refused to grant the request of the Spanish monarchs for the appointment of Inquisitors in the other portions of their kingdom, as the Dominican Inquisition was already in force there.*

Sixtus IV., though approving of the new Inquisition in itself,† had soon fresh cause for dissatisfaction with the con-

* LLORENTE, IV, 394–7, GRISAR, 561, where, naturally, 1482 is to be read for 1492

† This is evident from the Brief of the 23rd February, 1483, in LLORENTE, IV, 402–6   No Pope has condemned the Spanish Inquisition in itself, but many for these abuses, as, especially, Sixtus V. in the Bull of the 22nd January, 1588, where he speaks of the

duct of the Inquisitors. His displeasure was directed not against the institution, but against the manner in which it was carried out. There can be little doubt that the Spanish monarchs desired to give it too worldly a character, and at times made the real danger which existed from the feigned Christians, a pretext for bringing the tribunal to bear upon their other enemies, and that the new Inquisitors were but too ready to play into their hands. Against these abuses Sixtus IV. insisted on the strict observance of the provisions of the common law. We learn something of the domineering character of Michael Morillo from a Bull of Sixtus IV., dated 21st January, 1479. From this document it appears that Morillo had removed the former Inquisitor of Valença who had been appointed by the General of the Dominicans, and had given his post to another. The Pope cancelled this act, and desired the original appointment to be maintained *

The abuses in the Spanish Inquisition, however, did not cease, consequently, when the jurisdiction of the tribunal was extended to Castille and Leon, Sixtus IV. pronounced the severest penalties against Inquisitors who should fail to exercise their office in a conscientious manner, and in accordance with the canonical prescriptions.†

It is important to note, as a significant fact bearing on the character of this institution, that " not only the ecclesiastical authorisation of the first Inquisitors, but also the first regula-

Spanish Inquisition as established by the authority of the Holy See (see RODRIGO, II , 153). An Edict of their Spanish Majesties in 1487 affirms that the introduction of the Inquisition into Spain was due to the Holy See ; see REUSS, Instructionen, 134. On the other hand, it is certain that Rome did everything to mitigate the severity of the Inquisition, and to guard against its employment for political objects ; see HEFELL, Ximenes, 315 seq.

* Bull praedic , III , 572.

† LLORENTE, IV , 410.

tions as to the mode of procedure, emanated directly from
the Pope" In order to avoid constant appeals to Rome,
often made as mere subterfuges and with a view of impeding the course of the law, he, in 1483, appointed the
Archbishop of Seville, Papal Judge of Appeals for the
Inquisition *

Notwithstanding all these precautionary measures on the
part of the Holy See, accused persons were still treated in
Spain with arbitrary cruelty and injustice. To remedy this
evil, Sixtus IV, on the 2nd August, 1483, decreed .—(1) That
decisions on appeals given in Rome were to be held valid
in Spain ; (2) that shamefaced penitents were to be absolved
in secret ; (3) that those once absolved were not again to
be molested by the Inquisitors. In conclusion, Sixtus expressly admonished the Royal pair to leave those who had
retracted, in peaceful possession of their property. "As it is
mercy alone that makes us like God, we beg and exhort
the King and the Queen, for the love of Jesus Christ, to
imitate Him, whose property it is always to have mercy and
to spare Let them have compassion on their subjects in
the city and Diocese of Seville, who are sensible of their
errors and ask for pardon."†

The appointment of a Grand Inquisitor, which took place
in this year, was another important step in the organisation
of the new tribunal The idea appears to have originated
with the Spanish monarchs. In the autumn of 1483 Sixtus
IV. entrusted the spiritual powers of this office to Thomas
Torquemada, the Dominican Prior of S. Cruz.‡ "He was

* LLORENTE, IV., 411-12 ; GRISAR, 562.

† LLORENTE, IV., 408-21 See HEFELE, Ximenes, 287 , BAUM-
STARK, Isabella von Castilien, 98 (Freiburg, 1874), ROHRBACHER-
KNOPFLER, 69.

‡ See, for further information, BARTHÉLEMY, Erreurs Hist , IV,
170 seq (Paris, 1875) Torquemada's Instruction of 1484 is in REUSS,

to direct all the business of the Inquisition, was empowered to delegate his Apostolic Mission to others, and, especially, as the Pope's representative, to hear appeals made to the Holy See, superseding the former occupant of this office."* The Grand Inquisitor's sphere of jurisdiction was, by a special Papal Brief of the 17th October, 1483, extended to the kingdom of Aragon.† A Council of Inquisition was now established, mainly with the object of assisting in the hearing of Appeals. Torquemada instituted this Council "by virtue of the plenary powers which he had received when his authority was conferred upon him by the Pope." Sixtus IV. gave his sanction to this measure.‡ The members of the Council have often been spoken of as mere State officials, this, however, is a mistake. They were State officials, and, as such, derived their temporal jurisdiction from the King, but, in their primary ecclesiastical capacity, they had no authority until it was imparted to them by the Papal Delegate. The Grand Inquisitor, nominated by the King, always received his ecclesiastical jurisdiction from an Apostolic Brief.§ He proposed, and the King nominated, the Councillors, who derived their spiritual jurisdiction from his approbation, by which he imparted to them a share in his Apostolic authority.‖

The Spanish Inquisition, accordingly, appears as a mixed, but primarily ecclesiastical, institution.¶ The fact that the

Instructionen, 1 *seq.*; the ecclesiastical character of the Inquisition is clearly manifested in the documents here printed (p. 67, form of Abjuration, and p. 70, Oath of Absolution).

* GRISAR, 563, HEFELE, Ximenes, 288.

† Bull. ord praed, III., 622. See RODRIGO, II., 101 *seq.*

‡ RODRIGO, II, 163

§ In addition to the testimonies adduced by Rodrigo, see the passages from L. a Paramo and Carena in GRISAR, 564, note 2

‖ RODRIGO, *loc cit*; GRISAR, 564

¶ Rodrigo's work, which is somewhat prolix and inaccurate, has the

condemned were handed over to the secular arm testifies to the correctness of this view.   Had the Spanish Inquisition

merit of shewing that the Spanish Inquisition cannot justly be looked upon as a purely State institution.   The Spanish scholar sums up his opinion in the following terms.   "The tribunals of the Holy Office had no essentially secular character.   They were ecclesiastical in regard to the matters of which they took cognizance, and to the authority by which they were created   But, in consideration of the Royal delegation conferred upon the judges, they may be said to have had a mixed character" (I , 276) ; "in fact the Spanish Inquisition was a spiritual court, aimed with Royal weapons "   The view which regarded it as a purely State institution was popularised in France by DE MAISTRE (Lettre à un gentilhomme Russe sur l Inquisition Espagnole, 11-12, Lyon, 1837), and in Germany by RANKE (Fursten und Volker, I , 241 *seq* , Hamburg, 1827 , and, with slight alterations, also in the 4th edition of 1877, p. 195 *seq*)   It has been recently put forward, on the Catholic side, by three other historians GAMS (Zur Gesch. der Span. Staatsinquisition, Regensburg, 1878) ; HERGENROTHER (Kirchengesch , II., 765, 3rd ed , and Staat u Kirche, p 607 *seq*) , and KNOPFLER (Rohrbacher's Kirchengesch , 68 f., and Hist -polit Bl , XC , 325 *seq* , and XCI , 165 *seq*).   In favour of the opinion we have adopted above, may be cited the old theologians of the Inquisition, such as Paramo and Carena, who must have been accurately acquainted with the matter , and, among modern writers, BALMES (Protest und Kath , II , 177, Regensburg, 1845) , PRAT (Histoire du P Ribadeneira, 347 *seq* , Paris, 1862) ; ORTI Y LARA (La Inquisicion, Madrid, 1877) , RODRIGO, GRISAR (see Innsbr Zeitschr fur Kath Theologie, 1879, p 548 *seq*) ; BAUER (*loc cit* , 1881, p 742 *seq*) ; F. X. KRAUS (Alzogs Kirchengesch , II , 106, N. 3, 10th ed) , FUNK (Lit Rundschau, 1880, p 77 *seq* , and Kirchengesch , 360) , BRUCK (Kirchengesch., p 533, 4th ed , and Kirchenlexikon, VI , 765 *seq* , 2nd ed) , and JULIO MEIGARES MARIN (Procedimientos de la Inquisicion, 2 vols , Madrid, 1886, I , 82 *seq*.)   This last, who is keeper of the Archives at Alcala, speaks with full knowledge of their contents.   On the Protestant side, see HERZOG, VI , 740 *seq* , 2nd ed (Benrath), and Allg Ztg , 1878, p 1122 Excessive regard for the authority of Ranke has prevented the general acceptance of the correct view of this question, and, in the case of Catholic publicists, it is hard to decide how far apologetic con-

been a State institution, a royal court of justice, there would
have been no necessity for this. "A court which invariably
hands over those whom it finds guilty to the secular arm
for punishment cannot itself be a secular tribunal" It was
precisely the ecclesiastical character of the new Inquisition
which made its judges decline to execute capital sentences,
and follow the custom always observed by the ecclesiastical
Inquisition of requesting that the prisoner " might be leniently dealt with," a formality prescribed by the Canon Law.*

The action of Sixtus IV, as General of his Order, would
have led to the expectation that he would prove a reforming Pope. Admonitions and exhortations on this point
were not wanting Apart from those voices which clamoured
for reform as a means for compassing other ends, many
memorials reached Rome from abroad, animated by the
purest motives, and urging the need of it on the Pope.
The abuses in the Cistercian Order, particularly that regarding *commendams*, were thus brought under his notice † In
Rome itself zealous Friars went preaching penance and

siderations may have weighed in their adoption of the theory of a State
institution Apologetic ends must not, however, be allowed to influence
the historian, whose sole aim should be truth

    * GRISAR, 572

    † I found this remarkable *Document in a collection in the University
Library at Wurzburg, M. ch q 15 (formerly belonging to the Convent
of Ebrach), f 239-43 *"Ad beatissimum in Christo patrem et
dominum nostrum dom Sixtum divina providentia papam quartum .
exhortatio de et super quibusdam gravaminibus ac injuriis per quosdam
cardinales Romanae curiae . . Cisterciensis sacri ordinis quibusdam
abbatiis ac coenobiis violenter illatis per rev. dom Johannem Cistercien.
s theol profess producta." Here, at f 240b, we read . "Commenda
est vipera matris ecclesie rumpens viscera, exterminans spiritualia et
devorans temporalia secundum ethimologiam nominis . ", f. 241b ·
"Testis est fere tota Italia, testis est ipsa Lumpardia ubi vix ordinis
sunt vestigia . . Testis est Sabaudia (where a Convent had been

amendment. Many secular priests were equally earnest, warning their hearers that God would let the Turks come to Rome as a judgment for their sins. The Pope placed no obstacle in the way of such men, but, on the contrary, gave them every encouragement, remembering how valuable the preachers of penance had been in stemming the tide of depravity during the period of the Renaissance * A secular priest, who had come to Rome in 1473 and spoken in this strain, was not only permitted by the Pope to preach everywhere, but also received material support.† Sixtus IV. sent the celebrated St Jacopo della Marca in October, 1471, to pacify Ascoli, which was torn with hatred and factions.‡

A further proof that the Pope was favourably disposed towards ecclesiastical reform is furnished by a Bull, drawn up at his command, and containing minute provisions for the amendment of the Court. Abuses which had crept in among the Cardinals were relentlessly exposed in it, and rules laid down which, had they been carried into effect, would have completely changed the aspect of the Sacred

granted *in commendam* to a boy three years of age ¹). Testis est ipsa Burgundia ubi monasteria nobilia sunt ad devorandum exposita" The author is deeply attached to his Order, whose ruin he desires to arrest, by the help of the Pope

* See, on this subject, the particulars we have given in our Vol I., p. 36 *seq*

† *Letter of J. Arcimboldus, dated Rome, 1473, Febr. 26, in the Arch Veneto, 1888, fasc 71, pp 241-2. From VOLATERRANUS, 173, we learn that Sixtus IV did not interfere when Father Paolo Toscanella preached in the strongest manner at the Papal Court against the Pope, his family, and the Cardinals

‡ Jacobo de Marchia, ord min. prof, dated Romae, 1471, Octob. 17 *"Hortamur te charitate paterna, ut ad civitatem ipsam te conferre et in eadem gratia tibi assistente divina quidquid boni poteris operari velis." Lib. brev., 14, f. 1, Secret Archives of the Vatican.

College and of the whole Court *   Unhappily, this Bull was
never published   The cause of this must be sought not in
the remissness of the Pope, but in the opposition of those
who surrounded him †   His nephews well knew what the
consequences of reform would be to them.   The Sacred
College also put obstacles in the way   A letter of Petrus
Barrocius, written in the year 1481, expressly states this,

* *Bull "Quoniam regnantium cura," s d in Cod. Vat, 3884,
f 118-132b (Vat Library   Thence in Arch d Soc. Rom , I , 479 *seq* ,
also in Cod Vat , 3883; see HABERL in the Vierteljahrsschrift für
Musikwissenschaft, III., 242), and in Cod. 422, f 239 *seq* , of the State
Library, Munich   Extracts from this Reformatio Sixti IV. are also
to be found in Cod Capponi, LXXXII , N. 26, National Library,
Florence.

† It cannot, however, be denied that Sixtus IV. ought to have done
far more than he did for the cause of reform   Even if the stormy
character of his reign be taken into account, that which was actually
accomplished in the way of remedying the sad state of things was far
too little.   It related principally to the Religious Orders ; see
GROTEFEND, I , 22 ; MOHR, Regesten, I , 98 , Jahrb f Schweiz Gesch.,
IX., 75 , MAZZUCHELLI, II., 3, 1863 , WADDING, *passim* , Bull.
praed , III , 526, 585, 588 , Chroniche di S. Francesco, III , 204 , and
*Brief to episc. Acien., dated Rome, 1480, Oct. 1 ; Lib. brev , 13, f 87,
Secret Archives of the Vatican ; *ibid.*, f 190   Abbati monasterii S
Pauli de urbe, dated Rome, 1480, Nov 22 (Reform of the Convent
at Todi); *ibid*, f 221, a Brief for Hermann elect. et confirmat
Colonien , &c , dated Rome, 1480, Dec. 6, urging the removal of abuses
Lib brev , 14, f 15b and 32 (Monastic Reform in Ireland and Sicily).
See also RAYNALDUS, ad an 1483, N 36 (Reform of the Clergy in
France)   Of even more importance than these isolated Decrees is the
Constitution of the 22nd May, 1472, against simony , see Bull , 208-9
Regarding a measure of reform attempted by Sixtus IV , in opposition
to the Election Capitulation in the Bishopric of Bamberg, see Quellen-
sammlung f Frank. Gesch , IV., LXXXXI. *seq*   The above-mentioned
Orders, confirmed by Sixtus IV., were also appointed to labour for
reform   His appointment of good Bishops is recorded by MAS-
LATRIE in the Rev des Quest. Hist , 1878, Avril, p 570 *seq*

while giving a detailed account of the corruption of the
Court "Sixtus IV," he writes, "wished to set his face
against these practices, and appointed a Commission of
reform, but the majority of the Cardinals negatived the
suggestions of the better disposed."* This could not have
happened but for the unfortunate changes which had taken
place in the members composing the Sacred College

Torquemada and Carvajal, two unflinching champions of
ecclesiastical purity, had died during the pontificate of Paul
II † In the time of Sixtus IV., many of the elder Cardinals
had gone to their reward. Bessarion, amongst others, in
1472, and, on the 21st December in the following year, at
Verona, the brave Forteguerri.‡ Three other admirable
members of the Sacred College died in 1476 · Roverella (3rd
May), Calandrini (24th July §), and Agnifilus (9th Novem-
ber). On the 11th August, 1477, Latino Orsino, and || in
1478, the austere Capranica passed away ; Eroli and Amma-

* Letter of P Barrocius to Card. Petrus Fuscarenus, dated Belluno,
1481, Aug 13, in Anecdota Veneta, ed. Contarini, p. 202. With the
description given by Barrocius, compare those of Card. AMMANATI,
Epist, 272 (820 *seq*, Frankfort ed), of B FULGOSUS, II., c 1, and
Savonarola (see VILLARI, I, 15 *seq.*, 19 *seq.*). I shall revert to this last
in the Introduction to my next Volume.

† See *supra*, p. 145. Torquemada died on the 26th Sept, 1468.

‡ These dates are taken from the *Acta Consist. of the Secret
Archives of the Vatican. Regarding Forteguerri's death, see also
N DELLA TUCCIA, 105

§ See FALEONI, 511, and SFORZA, Nicolaus V, translated by Horak,
134 (Innsbruck, 1887)

|| The important post of Camerlengo was then conferred on
d Estouteville (in a Letter of the 12th August, 1477, he announces to
the Florentines his nomination, which had taken place on that day,
see State Archives, Florence, X -II -25, f 124b), and, after his death, on
Raffaello Sansoni Riario ; see MARINI, II, 245, and *Div Sixti IV,
1482-4, f 135   State Archives, Rome.

nati in 1479 (2nd April and 10th September).* The loss
of these representatives of better days was not adequately
repaired ; during the thirteen years of Sixtus IV.'s pontificate, eight creations of Cardinals took place, and thirty-four
prelates, twenty-two of whom were Italians, were raised to the
purple ; † but, in the majority of cases, these appointments
were not made from purely ecclesiastical motives, and the ¶
worldly-minded Cardinals, such as Jouffroy (†1473), Alain
(†1474, May 3), d'Estouteville (†1483, January 22 ‡), and
Gonzaga (†1483, October 21), who died in the time of this
Pope, were but too soon succeeded by others of like character.

The first creation of Cardinals by Sixtus IV. was much
to be deplored. On this occasion his two young nephews,
one of whom was utterly unworthy of this dignity, were
raised to the purple. In the second creation, on the 7th
May, 1473,§ the wishes of temporal Princes had predominant
weight   The Archbishop of Arles, Philippe de Lévis, had
been recommended for the dignity by King René, and
Giovanni Arcimboldo, Bishop of Novara, by the Duke of
Milan. The selection of Philibert Hugonet, Bishop of Macon,
seems to have been due to the Duke of Burgundy's influ-

* For an account of Ammanati's last years, his death, and his tomb,
see PAULI'S rare monograph, 91–8.

† Of the twenty-two Italians, six were Romans   According to the
common account, Sixtus IV. nominated thirty-five Cardinals , but the
elevation of Theobald of Luxemburg (see Lettres de Louis XI., III.,
107) is very uncertain ; according to FRIZON, 523–4, Theobald was
designatus, but not *publicatus*. The *Acta Consist and other authorities say nothing about him, and I have therefore thought it right
to exclude him from the number.

‡ This date is given by the *Acta Consist., Secret Archives of the
Vatican, while BORGIA, Velletri, 382, maintains the 22nd Febr.

§ See *Acta Consist. of the Secret Archives of the Vatican, and
*Letter of Oldroandus de Bonafrugis, dated Rome, 1473, May 10
Gonzaga Archives

ence.* As to Stefano Nardini, Sixtus IV. himself said of
him that he had made him a Cardinal, in order to encourage
the members of the Court to emulate his zeal and industry.†

If Nardini, the founder of a College for poor students,‡
was worthy of a place in the Senate of the Church, the
same cannot be said of the two other Italians who received
the purple on the 7th May, 1473 Giov. Batista Cybò
had passed a frivolous youth, and the wealthy Antonio
Giacomo Venier was living in a style of princely luxury
The two Spaniards, Auxias de Podio and Pedro Gonzalez
de Mendoza, Archbishop of Toledo,§ created at this time,
were, however, excellent men.

More than three years elapsed before Sixtus IV. again
added to the numbers of the Sacred College. An Ambassador, then living in Rome, speaks of violent disputes between
the Cardinals and the Pope, who, notwithstanding all his
efforts, only succeeded in accomplishing the creation of five
new Cardinals ‖ This took place on the 18th December,
1476 ¶ Among those promoted, but one, G. B Mellini,

---

* That the nomination of Ph Hugonet was due to the Duke of
Burgundy's influence is evident from LJUBIČ, Dispacci, &c , 33

† Letter to Louis XI of the 22nd Aug, 1473. (State Archives,
Milan.) See *supra*, p 321.

‡ ARMELLINI, 645 , FORCELLA, XIII., 171

§ Details regarding the eight Cardinals created in 1473 may be
found in CIACONIUS, III., 47 *seq* , CARDELLA, III., 182 *seq* , CONTE-
LORIUS, 69 , FRIZON, 519 *seq*. See also DOMINICUS, De dignit.
Episcop , 33. The titles were, according to the *Acta Consist., conferred on the 17th May.

‖ *Letters of J. P Arrivabene, dated Rome, 1476, Dec 10, 18, and
22   Gonzaga Archives, Mantua.

¶ INFESSURA, 1145, is mistaken in saying the 17th December ; the
Cron Rom., 34, rightly gives the 18th as the date , see also *Acta
Consist , Secret Archives of the Vatican. The Cardinals were pub-
lished on the 20th, see CONTELORIUS, 71.

Bishop of Urbino, was an Italian ; two, Charles de Bourbon and Pierre de Foix, were French , one, Pedro Ferrici, was a Spaniard ; and one, Giorgio da Costa, Archbishop of Lisbon, a Portuguese.   This last died in 1503, at the age of 100, one of the wealthiest Princes of the Church of his time *

In the following March we hear of negotiations for the nomination of new Cardinals.   On the 24th of that month Sixtus IV. proposed in Consistory, John of Aragon (a son of Ferrante),† Ascanio Maria Sforza, Pietro Foscari, and his own two nephews, Cristoforo della Rovere and Girolamo Basso della Rovere.‡   The preliminary discussions lasted all through the summer,§ ending on the 10th December, 1477, in a complete victory for Sixtus IV.   On that day all those whom he had proposed were, with the exception of Ascanio Sforza, raised to the purple, and to their number were added the Minorite, Gabriel Rangone,‖ George Hesler, who had rendered important service to the house of Habsburg,¶ and, finally, a third nephew of the Pope's, Raffaello

* REUMONT, III , 1, 262; CIACONIUS, III , 55 seq ; CARDELLA, III., 192 seq. , FRIZON, 524 seq.   Concerning P de Foix, see MARTÈNE, II , 1517, 1530, and MIGNE, 921.

† Giorn. Nap., 1138 , MAZZUCHELLI, I , 2, 927.

‡ I find this fact, which has hitherto been unknown, in a *Letter of Card. Gonzaga, dated Rome, 1477, March 24   Regarding the Pope's nephews, he says : " El castellano de S. Agnolo qui el qual è arcivescovo de Tarantaso gientilhomo piamontese dicto de la Rovere buon dottore e prelato assai commendato e lo vescovo di Recanati nepote d. S. Sta ex sorore "   Gonzaga Archives, Mantua.

§ *Letter of Card Gonzaga, dated Rome, 1477, June 18, loc cit

‖ He had been recommended for elevation by the King of Hungary as early as the year 1475 ; see Mon Hung., II , 295.

¶ Frederick III. had for some years actively sought to procure Hesler's elevation (regarding this prelate's life, see WURDTWEIN, Nov subsid , XIII , 63 seq), and was expecting it in March, 1474 ; see Mon. Habsb , I , 329 seq.   Also the Brief of 1475 in MARTÈNE, II , 1497-8, and a Despatch of 1476 in GINGINS LA SARRA, I , 288   In

Sansoni Riario.* These numerous additions to the Sacred
College gave occasion for the creation of a new Title, the
first which had for several centuries taken place   Sixtus
IV gave Pietro Foscari, St Nicholas at the Colosseum
(S Nicolaus inter imagines)† as his titular Church.

If the simultaneous elevation of three Papal nephews was
in itself an extraordinary proceeding, Raffaello Sansoni's
age—he was only seventeen—did not tend to diminish its
exceptional character !   The spiritual element was no better
represented by him than by Cristoforo and Giuliano della
Rovere   " Though presenting many radical differences in
personal character, they were all great lords with essentially
worldly interests.   The fourth of the Pope's nephews on the
sisters' side, Girolamo Basso della Rovere, was a prelate of
blameless life, who never abused the favour of his uncle or
of his cousin, Pope Julius II "‡   Cristoforo della Rovere
dying on the 1st February, 1478,§ Sixtus IV , on the 10th of

February, 1477, the dignity had been promised to Hesler (see ENNEN,
III , 530), Sixtus IV then making the provision that, in the event of
his own death before Hesler's publication, the latter should be reckoned
among the Cardinals , see RAYNALDUS, ad an 1477, N. 11   Hesler
was not published until December , see *Acta Consist, f 53, Secret
Archives of the Vatican   On the 13th January, 1478, Sixtus IV. sent
him the Red Hat ; Mon. Habsb , III , 447   Hesler came, for the first
time, to Rome on the 21st January, 1480 , on the 28th January took
place the ceremony of the opening of the Mouth ; on the 1st of May he
started on his homeward journey ; see *Acta Consist, f 59, loc cit

  * See CIACONIUS, III , 63 seq , CARDELLA, III., 202 seq. , CONTE-
LORIUS, 72, who repeatedly corrects Ciaconius.

  † See ARMELLINI, Chiese, 23 ; PHILLIPS, VI , 224 ; and PAN-
VINIUS, De episc. titulis, &c., 20 , ibid , 28 and 42, concerning other
innovations made by Sixtus IV connected with this subject.   For an
account of P. Foscari, see also OROLOGIO, Canonici di Padova, 82 seq.

  ‡ REUMONT, III , i, 261.

  § *Acta Consist , Secret Archives of the Vatican   TOSI, Plate 126,
gives an engraving of Domenico's beautiful grave in S Maria del Popolo

that month, received his brother, Domenico, into the Senate
of the Church.   He "built for himself the much-admired
Palace on the Piazza Scossacavalli, and a villa in the neighbourhood of Ponte Molle, without the City, which was often
visited by Sixtus IV.   He also built the Chapel in Sᵗᵃ Maria
del Popolo, which, like his Palace, was adorned with paintings from the hand of Pinturicchio.   The little town of
Montefiascone owes to him its principal church, and his
native city, Turin, its Cathedral, which, being the work of
Meo dal Caprino, bears a striking resemblance to the churches
built by the same architect in Rome.   This member of the
Rovere family had no merit in the way of talent to recom-
mend him.   He had but little literary culture, and was not
either learned or naturally quick-witted   It was the grace
of God, his good reputation, and his true and loyal disposition which brought him to the front " *

These last nominations, together with the increasing influence of the Pope's nephews, who came in greater numbers
to Rome at this time, gave to the Court a more and more
worldly character.   The crafty Girolamo Riario, who was
made Burgher of the City and a member of the Roman
nobility in the year 1477, and, in 1480, Commander-in-Chief
of the Church, surpassed all the Cardinals in influence †
The whole demeanour of this upstart was in keeping
with his extravagant expenditure on all festal occasions.
He took pride in eclipsing all the Cardinals, even those who

* SCHMARSOW, 145 ; MUNTZ, III , 37–8 ; ADINOLFI, Portica, 144
seq , 251 *seq.*

† INFESSURA, 1147   Regarding Riario's influence, see, besides the
passages from different authorities collected by SCHMARSOW, 367,
the Florentine Ambassadorial Despatches in Appendix, N 60 and
61 , GRASSO, 332 , and the treatise of DE LA NICOLLIÈRE-TEIJEIRO,
Institution du comte palatin de Latran en faveur de Jérôme Riario,
&c., Nantes, 1886.

were of princely birth.* The purely worldly tendencies
displayed, especially by Rodrigo Borgia, Francesco Gonzaga
and d'Estouteville, among the older Cardinals, the frequent
admission of others of similar disposition into the Sacred
College, and the removal by death of so many of those who
were truly devoted to the interests of the Church, led pious
and earnest men like F. Piccolomini and Marco Barbo to
absent themselves as much as possible from Rome. Giovanni Michiel and Pietro Foscari, the kinsmen and countrymen of the latter, were essentially Venetian patricians, and
found the new order of things by no means uncongenial.†

The next creation still further promoted the worldliness
and pomp of the Sacred College. It took place on the 15th
May, 1480,‡ and was, in many respects, an important one.
With hardly an exception those raised to the purple were
of high birth : they were, Paolo Fregoso, Ferry de Clugny,§
Cosimo Orsini de' Migliorati, the "excellent Giovan Battista
Savelli, whose elevation had, up to this time, been hindered
by the Orsini party. He had given proof of his abilities in
several Legations, was endowed with an enterprising spirit
and a talent for organisation ; he had been designated for the
cardinalate by Paul II., but the sudden death of that Pope,
and the influence of Latino Orsini with Sixtus IV. had so
far kept him from that dignity. In conjunction with him,
Giovanni Colonna was also created, and the seeds of party

* See JAC VOLATERRANUS, 104 For a description of Girolamo's
Palace, see SCHMARSOW, 116, and ADINOLFI, La torre de' Sanguigni,
49 *seq* (Roma, 1863).

† See SCHMARSOW, 144 *seq*, and also KNEBEL, II , 392.

‡ Not the 5th May, as CIACONIUS, III., 77 ; CARDELLA, III , 215 ,
and CONTELORIUS have stated, but die lunae XV. Man, according to
the *Acta Consist, f 59, Secret Archives of the Vatican

§ FRIZON, 527 *seq.*, speaks of him as a distinguished man See also
Bibl de l'École des Chartes, 1881, p. 444 *seq*, and MIGNE, 688 *seq*.

strife introduced into the Sacred College, for Giuliano della Rovere was a friend of the Colonna and the Savelli, while Girolamo Riario's interests, as a temporal lord, drew him to associate himself more and more closely with the Orsini." *

The next creation, on the 15th November, 1483, did yet more to increase the influence of the great Roman families in the Sacred College, Giovanni Conti of Valmontone and Battista Orsini being then raised to the purple. The same dignity was conferred on Juan Moles, a Spaniard, on the Archbishop of Tours, Elie de Bourdeilles, and on Giovanni Giacomo Sclafenati, Bishop of Parma, who was but twenty-three years of age † The choice of this youthful Prelate gave occasion to much unfavourable comment, and completely nullified the good impression which the simultaneous elevation of the saintly Bourdeilles might have produced.‡ A yet greater error was committed in the promotion of Ascanio Maria Sforza (March, 1484) dictated as it was by worldly and political motives §

* SCHMARSOW, 147

† *Acta Consist, f 67, Secret Archives of the Vatican. CIACONIUS, III, 81 seq. CARDELLA, III, 221, is uncertain as to the date which the diligent CONTELORIUS, 76, gives correctly See also, in relation to Sixtus IV. and the Orsini Cardinals, Lett eccles di P. Sarnelli, 332 (Naples, 1686)

‡ Stefano Guidotto, in the Postscript to a *Letter, dated Rome, 1483, Nov 18, speaks of Bourdeilles as "sanctissimus et observandissimus s. religionis" (Gonzaga Archives, Mantua.) See also the statements of FRIZON, 529 seq., and MIGNE, 588

§ According to CONTELORIUS, 76, Ascanio's nomination took place on the 6th March "in secreto consistorio et die 17 fuit publicatus." The *Acta Consist of the Secret Archives of the Vatican mention only the latter event Stefano Guidotto says, in a *Letter, dated Rome, 1483, March 16, that it was believed that Ascanio would be published as a Cardinal on the following day (Gonzaga Archives) In the Lib. brev, 16 A, of the Secret Archives of the Vatican, I found, f 60, a *Brief to Ascanio, dated 1484, March 17, informing him of his nomina-

When we consider that it was this man, in conjunction with Cardinals Riario, Orsini, Colonna, Sclafenati, and Savelli (all of them admitted by Sixtus IV. into the Senate of the Church), who in 1492 carried the election of Rodrigo Borgia, we are naturally inclined to form an unfavourable opinion of this Pope, from whom so much had been hoped.*

Nevertheless, an impartial study of history must lead us to protest against the picture drawn by Infessura of Sixtus IV. Infessura was a violent partisan of his deadly enemies, the Colonna. He blesses the day when God delivered his people out of the hand of this "most profligate and unjust of Kings" Neither fear of God nor love for his people, no spark of kindness or good-will, according to this author, were to be found in him ; nothing but sensuality, avarice, love of show and vain-glory. After this tremendous general accusation he proceeds to enter into details. He cannot say a good word anywhere of Sixtus IV. It is plain from this, and from the violence of his language, that we have here a collection of everything that was reported to the Pope's disadvantage in Rome, at a time when a strong opposition to his person and to his Court prevailed there.†

tion as Cardinal, which had taken place on that day, "de unanimi consilio et consensu" of the Cardinals From a *Letter of Cardinal Arcimboldus to the Duke of Milan, dated Rome, 1476, Dec. 22, it appears that great efforts had at that time been made to procure Ascanio's elevation (State Archives, Milan) See also *supra*, p 409 Regarding A. Sforza, see also BUCHI'S work, Albrecht von Bonstetten (Frauenfeld, 1889), which has just come under my notice, especially pp 35 and 38 A request addressed by Richard III. to Sixtus IV., with regard to the appointment of a Cardinal, is mentioned in RYMER, XII , 216

* Regarding these hopes, see JORDAN, Podiebrad, 358–9. Of the twenty-three Cardinals who composed the Conclave of 1492, fourteen had been created by Sixtus IV

† This is the opinion of SCHROCKH, Kirchengesch , XXXII., 364

As regards Infessura's most serious accusation, that of gross immorality, in that corrupt age such a charge was but too frequently flung at any enemy. Later on, the austere Adrian VI was himself a victim to the slanderous tongues of the Renaissance age. Things had come to such a pass that "no one could escape calumny, and the most exemplary virtue provoked the worst detraction."* Atrocious crimes of this kind are not proved by the malignant gossip collected by a writer so open to suspicion as Infessura.† No trustworthy contemporary, not one of the

As opposed to BROSCH, who (Julius II, p 29) inclines to Infessura's view, and speaks of Sixtus IV as "a man without truth and faith, without shame and conscience," we may mention not only HEFELE-HERGENROTHER, VIII, 268, but also SCHMARSOW, 262, who express themselves in very different terms, and maintain that Sixtus was deeply penetrated with a sense of the sacredness of his priestly office. CREIGHTON, III, 115, also writes· "Infessura . has blackened his memory with accusations of the foulest crimes. These charges, made by a partisan who writes with undisguised animosity, must be dismissed as unproved "

* BURCKHARDT, Cultur, I, 187 seq, 3rd ed Even in the lifetime of Pius II an Invective appeared from the pen of an offended Humanist (probably Filelfo), making the most infamous accusations against him, many of which were quite absurd; see VOIGT, Pius II., III, 636. Here a charge similar to that made by Infessura against Sixtus IV. is not wanting, yet the moral life of Pius II. as Pope was blameless

† The passage in question, with "ut fertur vulgo, ut dicunt quidam, ut dicitur," is only in Eccard's edition, 1939. Muratori omits it, deeming it too disgraceful to place before the eyes of respectable men; referring any one who finds pleasure in such filth to Eccard (MURATORI, III, 2, 1110). Even opponents of the Papacy have protested against these accusations GREGOROVIUS, VII, 268, 2nd ed, writes. "The text of Infessura, as given in Eccard, brings terrible charges against the moral character of Sixtus, these are certainly exaggerated." SYBEL'S Zeitschr, N F, XXI, 358, admits that Gregorovius is not prepossessed in favour of Sixtus IV. In his third edition Gregorovius

numerous Ambassadors, who reported everything that took
place in Rome with scrupulous accuracy, has a word to say
on the subject, one indeed of these Envoys, immediately
after the election of Sixtus IV., extols his blameless and
pious manner of life * Whatever faults Sixtus IV. may
have committed as Pope, there was no change for the worse
in regard to morals or religion   The fact that he chose as
his confessor the blessed Amadeus of Portugal, a man of
extraordinary sanctity and mortification, is in itself a proof
of this †   We have ample evidence to prove that Sixtus IV
discharged his religious duties zealously and seriously, and
venerated his holy patrons, St. Francis and the Blessed
Virgin, with the same devotion which he had manifested
before his elevation.   Though suffering acutely from gout,
he never allowed this to prevent him from assisting at the
solemn Easter Mass.   " With touching perseverance the
feeble old man made his pilgrimages of devotion to the
Churches of Sta Maria del Popolo and della Pace, which he
had built in honour of the Blessed Virgin "‡   Sixtus IV.
must indeed have been a consummate hypocrite if his
private life was infamous while he appeared so fervent a
client of the most Pure Mother of God §

has struck out the last four words of our quotation, but he produces
no evidence in support of Infessura's statements.

  * *Despatch of Nicodemus of the 9th Aug, 1471.   Appendix, N 44
  † Regarding Amadeus, see AA SS Aug II., 572 *seq* ; Freib Kirchenlexikon, I , 669, 2nd ed
  ‡ JACOBUS VOLATERRANUS, 131 ; SCHMARSOW, 263
  § See my observations in the Hist. Jahrbuch, VIII , 729, against
SCHMARSOW, 4, 261, 327   These last passages seemed, not only to me,
but to other students, to prove that the worthy biographer of Melozzo
looked upon Infessura's charges as well-founded.   I am glad now to
be able to say that Professor Schmarsow, in writing to me (1887,
Oct. 26), protested against the idea that he adopted Infessura's
shocking view of the life of Sixtus IV.   In the further course of our

Infessura's other charges against Sixtus IV must equally be either dismissed or modified. An impartial student admits that "the historian who represents this Pope as avaricious and greedy of gain, double-faced in his policy, insatiable in his lust of conquest, passionate and tyrannical in character, without taking into account how much in his conduct is entirely, or in great measure, due to Girolamo Riario, is guilty of a serious error. History belies herself when she paints her subject in a glare of light, oblivious of the deep contrasting shadows."*

Among the darkest of these shadows is that unfortunate attachment to his nephews, in spite of his many estimable qualities, which entangled him in a labyrinth of political complications, from which at last no honourable exit was possible † The difficulties into which this deplorable weakness for his relatives led Sixtus IV. also had other most injurious effects "In order to procure the required resources, it was necessary to resort to all sorts of financial expedients, which resulted in a terrible amount of venality and corruption."‡ Even before the time of this Pope there

correspondence the Professor wrote (1887, Nov. 11). "I am willing to accept what you say against my words, only you must not make me appear to be a blind follower of Infessura," and "with the kind of documents that are before us, it would hardly be possible to prove the charge of immorality" If LEA, III, 639, still maintains the truth of Infessura's accusations, we may understand it, considering the standpoint of the author of "An Historical Sketch of Sacerdotal Celibacy."

    * SCHMARSOW, 260 See CIPOLLA, 626 An example of the manner in which Sixtus IV is made responsible for the sins of his nephews is given in WOLF, Lect, I, 952.

    † "Le népotisme," writes RIO, II., 66, "fut la grande plaie, la plaie honteuse du règne de Sixte IV."

    ‡ ROHRBACHER-KNOPFLER, 255. See BURCKHARDT, I, 150, 3rd ed. Both refer to the melancholy picture drawn by BAPT MANTUANUS, De calamitatibus temp 1 III, Op ed Paris, 1507, f 302b

existed offices which could be purchased, and to which were
attached certain sources of income. The revenues of these
offices are said to have amounted in 1471 to something like
100,000 scudi * When the danger from Turkey made the
want of money more and more pressing, Sixtus IV. further
added to this crowd of officials Four Colleges, those of the
"Stipulatori, Giannizzeri, Stradiatori, and Mamelucchi," were
revived by him.† While the expense of every Bull or Brief
went on constantly growing, as the host of officials connected
with it increased, the Annates were again raised,‡ and a
new tax (Compositio), to be paid to the Dataria in Rome §
on collation to a benefice, imposed. Besides this there was
the so-called "Quindennien," a tax to be paid every fifteen

---

* See RANKE, Papste, I , 262, 6th ed   I found also in the Ambrosian
Library, Milan, Cod A , 13 Inf, the account of *Gli uffici piu antichi,
cited above by Ranke from Cod. N , II , 50, of the Chigi Library.
REUMONT, III , 1, 283, again repeats the erroneous statement that
the creation of ecclesiastical posts in the Roman Court began with
Sixtus IV

† MORONI, VII , 186, LXVII , 172 , BANGEN, 447. The " Mamelucchi" were abolished by Innocent VIII.

‡ See KIRSCH, Die Annaten und ihre Verwaltung in der zweiten
Halfte des 15 Jahrhunderts in the Hist Jahrbuch, IX , 307. The
Manuscript of the National Library, Rome (F XLVI.–1471, MS
Sessorian, 46), here mentioned, is not so little known as Kirsch
imagines it to be, for the Anz. f. Schweiz Gesch , N F , 1887,
18, Nos. 2 and 3, gives extracts from it. Regarding a list of
Annates in the Library of S. Pietro in Vincoli, see DUDIK, I ,
66 seq

§ The extreme party of Reform looked on the Compositio as a
pretium collationis, and pronounced it simoniacal , a more moderate
party, on the other hand, considered it as a stipendium attached to the
benefice itself, see Sixti IV S P. ad Paulum III , compositionum
defensio, ed Dittrich, Braunsberg, 1883. DITTRICH, Regesten Contarini's, 279 seq. (Braunsb , 1881). See also DOLLINGER, Beitrage,
III , 218, and DITTRICH, Contarini, 381 seq (B , 1885)

years by all benefices subject to Annates, which dated from the reign of Paul II *

The venality of many of the Court officials, and the excessive exercise of the Pope's rights in the matter of taxation, occasioned, especially in Germany, a feeling of deep dissatisfaction with the Holy See, which did more than has generally been supposed to pave the way for the subsequent apostacy When the great assembly of the clergy of the Metropolitan Churches of Mayence, Trèves, and Cologne was held at Coblence, in the year 1479, numerous complaints were formulated for transmission to the Pope. Their principal subjects were the non-observance of the Concordat, unfair taxation, the great privileges of the Mendicant Orders, and the number of exemptions.†

If, notwithstanding the many imposts levied, the Papal Treasury was almost always in difficulties, this was due, not only to extravagant expenses, but also to defective financial administration Serious and growing negligence is to be observed in the manner in which the accounts of the Apostolic Treasury were kept The monthly audit had become little more than a formality The salaries of the officials were often five or eight months, or even a year or two, in arrear The deficit, which increased month by month, necessitated constant loans.‡ Under such circumstances we cannot be surprised to learn that Sixtus IV.

---

* See *supra*, p 106

† Further particulars will be found in GEBHARDT, 53 *seq* The gravamen of 1479 has been often printed ; as, for example, by LEIBNIZ, Cod. I , 439 *seq* , and GEORGI, Grav. coll., 254

‡ Everything was mortgaged, even, on one occasion, the Registrum Bullarum, upon which Petrus Mellinus lent 1000 flor. auri. It was redeemed on the 20th Aug , 1482 This fact has been kindly communicated to me by Dr Gottlob, whose book on the Cam. Ap will throw much light on these matters from authentic sources. Regarding mortgages, see also REUMONT, III , 1, 283.

at his death left behind him debts to the amount of 150,000 ducats *

This financial pressure led to a considerable augmentation of indirect taxation in the States of the Church, and also to the diversion of the revenues of the Roman University to other objects, and the imposition of taxes on the salaries of the Professors.   As Infessura, who was a member of the teaching staff of this University, speaks with peculiar bitterness of the injury inflicted on it by Sixtus IV.,† there is ground for supposing him to have been among the sufferers ‡   In this circumstance, and in Infessura's alliance

* MUNTZ, III , 64-5

† Infessura in ECCARD, 1941.

‡ See TOMMASINI, Il diario di Stef. Infessura, in Arch d. Soc Rom , XI., 494-5. In this study, the prelude to a much needed critical edition of Infessura's Diarium, the various MSS are indicated and described, and valuable information regarding the family and the life of Infessura is furnished.   Tommasini's work as critic is, however, incomplete, and coloured by partiality   Even the enumeration of critical judgments of the chronicler is, with all its apparent minuteness, very imperfect   Tommasini ignores the opinions of SCHROCKH , HERGENROTHER (see *supra*, p 416) , CHRISTOPHE, II., 295 *seq*. , BRUCK, 450 , Civ Catt., 1868, I , 147 , HAGEN, Die Papstwahlen von 1484 und 1492, p 2, &c.   He even thinks it well completely to omit the important observations of SCHMARSOW (416, note †, to which may be added Schmarsow's words, p 196, where, in speaking of the death of R. Malatesta, he says " Infessura alone directs suspicion to the Pope, on whom, without examination, he casts the chief responsibility of Girolamo's crime "), as well as the opinion expressed in REUMONT'S Lorenzo, II , 456, 2nd ed. (" Infessura exaggerates the faults of the Pope with regard to truth ")   It is even more extraordinary that the passage from REUMONT, III , 1, 367, is not given completely in this special study. Here Reumont, in the first place, points out that Infessura's special value as an authority begins with the time of Martin V and Eugenius IV , and continues during the last three pontificates of the Century down to the year 1494, and then proceeds to observe "This genuine representative of undying Roman slander has provided those who delight

with the Colonna and his Republican sentiments, may be
found the motive of the unmeasured reproaches heaped

in scandalous gossip with materials as rich as, if not richer than,
those furnished by the well-known J Burchard of Strasburg, Bishop
of Orte and Master of Ceremonies of the Papal Chapel from the
days of Innocent VIII to those of Julius II ; but a little experience
of the manner in which, even up to the present day, truth and falsehood are mingled in the history of Rome, and cartloads of fabrication
accredited by a few ounces of fact, will guard us against taking such
narrators absolutely at their word, however evil the age may be.
The Roman Liutprand of the 15th Century demands the same severely
critical examination as that of the 10th." Tommasini is also silent
regarding the manifest falsehoods of Infessura, of which Gregorovius
has given proof (L BORGIA, 11-12, Stuttgart, 1874), and the misrepresentation exposed by FRANTZ, 481 *seq*, 483 *seq* In the face
of such proceedings, Tommasini's reiterated professions of impartiality
can deceive no one , his purpose is clear Infessura must, at any
cost, be raised to the position of a thoroughly trustworthy authority
As yet he has been unsuccessful in this attempt ; it remains to be
seen whether in his edition he can adduce anything further in
support of his thesis It is unjust to say that I represent Infessura
as a "violento avversario della dominazione papale" (TOMMASINI, p
488), Infessura himself does far more to represent himself in that light
by the praises which he bestows on a murderer like Porcaro (see our
Vol II , p 233, note †), and therefore even Gregorovius describes him as
"an enemy of the Papal power" At p. 482, Tommasini himself admits
"l'amore dell' Infessura alla libertà communale di Roma," as well as
his sympathies with the Colonna and the Republican party (see pp 526,
547, 554), but he fails to draw the evident conclusion from these
admissions Infessura's position as a partisan necessarily incapaci-
tates him from forming an impartial judgment in regard to Sixtus IV
It is really time that the name of a chronicler who admits lampoons
as serious evidence in his work, should be struck out of the list of
impartial narrators of history (see TOMMASINI, 550) The writings of
such an author are only to be employed with the greatest prudence,
and after the most critical investigation. Tommasini, however, has not
thought an examination, such as we have made, of Infessura's individual
charges against Sixtus IV. necessary He has saved himself much

upon Sixtus IV., the friend of the Orsini, and the advocate of
strongly monarchical ideas   Violent personal feeling, arising from the position of the author, and perhaps from his
unpleasant experiences, is here openly expressed *   We
have a repetition of the relations which existed between
Platina and Paul II. Platina is not an impartial and
truthful authority in regard to the builder of the Palace of
S Marco, neither is Infessura to be trusted when he tells
the history of the head of the Rovere family.

trouble by not entering into the most serious accusations, or those
which some critics have proved to be absurd   On the other hand, he
brings evidence to shew that, in matters of secondary importance,
Infessura's charges are true , see p. 559.   Here, however, he is not very
fortunate, for the evidence in regard to the purchase of corn (560) by
no means proves any usurious dealing on the part of Sixtus IV   The
justice of Reumont's remarks on the mixture of truth and falsehood in
Roman slander is here exemplified   The Sienese Despatches, published
by TOMMASINI, p 606 seq , in a general way confirm Infessura's picture
of the state of things from 1482, but they do not contain a syllable
in support of his shocking accusations against the Pope   It would
certainly be an error totally to reject Infessura's testimony (as SANESI,
St. Porcaro, p. 108, Pistoja, 1887, seems to suppose me to do   I
will here observe, as a curious fact, that Sanesi himself says he has
"esaminato soltanto poche pagine" of Infessura), but it is a still greater
error to accept it unconditionally, especially when, as in regard to
Sixtus IV , it is dictated by passion, and its exaggeration is patent.
That Infessura is here as unfair as P DELLA MASTRO, whose point of
view is most narrowly Roman (Cron Rom , 37), has already been
declared by an authority like MUNTZ, III., 8. As TOMMASINI, p 577,
cites an article written by Burckhardt thirty-seven years ago, he will
be interested to hear that Burckhardt's opinion is now different.   The
worthy author of the Cultur der Renaissance, writing to me on the 12th
May, 1889, said   " I am now aware that I have set far too much value
on Eccard's Infessura, and other muddy sources, and been too much
guided by them "

    * This observation applies to the Florentine historian , see infra,
P 433

Many abuses no doubt existed in the Rome of those days,
and Girolamo Riario was certainly guilty of many unbecom-
ing actions, but Infessura is not justified in accusing Sixtus
IV. of usurious speculation in corn for his own covetous
purposes.   The Pope's great care for Rome of itself contradicts this statement, and witnesses above suspicion testify
to the relatively favourable condition of the inhabitants of
the States of the Church under Sixtus IV, excepting, of
course, in times of war   Philippe de Commines, who went
to Rome with no favourable prejudices, after he had become
personally acquainted with the state of things there, expressed
his opinion that the Popes were wise and well advised, and
that, but for the strife between the Colonna and the Orsini,
the dwellers in the States of the Church would be the
happiest people on earth, inasmuch as they paid no poll-tax
and practically hardly any other taxes *   If this last statement is to be taken with some reservation, it is still certain
that " hardly anywhere, on an average, was the taxation so
low as in the States of the Church."†

* Mém. (ed Lenglet), II , 367; KERVYN DE LETTENHOVE, I ,
184.

† REUMONT, III , 1, 279   "In his civil administration," says
SCHMARSOW, 262, "Sixtus IV. manifests extraordinary talents   No
one so well understands how to ensure the accomplishment of his
orders ; he foresees everything, directs everything, takes account of
everything beforehand. for he is well aware that quite as much
prudence and determination are necessary in dealing with the
insubordination of the starving Roman populace as in the task of
bridling the Barons.   Everything is thought out thoroughly and in
detail   If we find liberal measures restricted by conditions which
almost nullify their effect, we must recognise in this the hand of a
revising financial adviser.   Parsimony had no place in the nature of
Sixtus IV " Such is the judgment of an impartial investigator. In
his article on Infessura, where Tommasini, in addition to all this
author's other charges, also maintains those of avarice and misgovern-

The history of the speculations in corn of Sixtus IV , about
which Infessura has so much to say, is actually that the
magistrate of the Annona or Abondanza bought corn by
his orders, laid it up in granaries and distributed it to
the bakers at a settled price, according to which the value
of bread was regulated.   Abuses on the part of the subordinate officials no doubt occurred ; while men are men,
such things will arise in similar cases.   But the new system
was devised by the Pope in order to facilitate and secure the
provisioning of Rome, and affords no ground for charging
him with usurious dealing in corn.   Practically, under the
successor of Sixtus IV., the Annona protected the Roman
people from want, when, in the year 1485, the Duke of
Calabria was encamped in the Campagna and cut off
supplies *   The energetic measures adopted by Sixtus IV.,
in order to ensure public safety in Rome and other cities of
the States of the Church, as, for example, Perugia, were
appreciated by his contemporaries.†

ment, it is easy to see that he is bent on branding Sixtus IV., on any
terms, as the corrupter of Rome   Such partiality is all the more shocking in one who always seeks to call in question the fairness of other
writers   See *e g*, Arch Rom , XI , 482, 488, &c.

  * REUMONT, III , 1, 285 *seq*   See, regarding the Annona in general,
MORONI, II , 145 *seq* , RANKE, Studien, 100 (Leipzig, 1877); also
Romische Briefe, II., 170 *seq* , where evidence is given of the sacrifices
made by later Popes, in order to provide the Roman people with good
bread at the lowest possible price.   Further proof of the care taken
by Sixtus IV. for the provisioning of Rome, especially in years of
scarcity, is furnished by numerous *Briefs *e g* , to Bologna, dated
Rome, 1473, Sept 14 (State Archives, Bologna); to Perugia, dated
1474, Febr 24 (University Library, Genoa, C IV , 1); also Lib brev ,
15, f. 12, 122, 297, 696; 16 A, f. 6, 30, 45 ; 16 B, f 2, 21, 75b, 111, 139,
171b (Secret Archives of the Vatican); see MARTÈNE, II , 1540,
1541, 1542, 1548

  † THEINER, Codex, III., 484, and *Brief to Perugia, dated 1479,
May 23.   (University Library, Genoa, C. IV , 1)   A *Speech made by

The solicitude of Sixtus IV. for the welfare of his subjects is further evinced by his efforts to check the devastation of the Campagna, and to promote tillage there,* his re-
introduction of the Constitution of Albornoz,† his solicitude
about the coinage,‡ and his exertions for the regulation of
the rivers,§ and the drainage of unhealthy places in the
States of the Church. Works of this description were promoted by him in the neighbourhood of Foligno,‖ and in the
Maritima. At the latter spot there was an idea of making
an attempt to dry up the well-known Pontine Marshes In
1476 the Pope requested the Duke of Ferrara to send him

the Milanese Ambassador praises Sixtus IV for the restoration of
security in Rome and its neighbourhood. Cod Vatic , 6898, Vatican
Library

* THEINER, Codex, 491 *seq* , *ibid*, 482 *seq* , and Romische Briefe,
II , 166 *seq* , as well as REUMONT, III , 1, 284 *seq* In regard to the
promotion of agriculture by the Popes, and their relation to the
Roman Campagna, see, in general, SOMBART, Die Romische Campagna
(Schmoller's Forschungen, Vol. 8), and, to complete his account,
RATTINGER, Kirchenstaat, 42 *seq* , Hist -polit Bl , 1884, I , 24 (against
LOHER, Das neue Italien, 1883) MILELLA, I papi e l'agricoltura
nei dom temp , Roma, 1881, was not accessible to me.

† In the year 1478 ; see THEINER, Cod , 494 *seq*. ; LA MANTIA, I ,
462

‡ L'ÉPINOIS, 450 See MUNTZ, III , 244 , THEINER, Cod , 488
Sixtus IV. was, according to Friedlander, the first who had his likeness
stamped on the coins , see MUNTZ, L'atelier monét de Rome, 2 (Paris,
1884) The regard of Sixtus IV. for uniformity of coinage appears
in his *Brief to Perugia of the 21st March, 1477 University Library,
Genoa, C IV , 1

§ See the *Briefs to Perugia of the 4th Febr and 20th April, 1482
(University Library, Genoa, *loc. cit*), and THEINER, Cod , 497.

‖ See **Briefs to Cardinal Savelli, Legate in Perugia, dated Rome,
1482, May 18 (National Library, Florence), and to Barthol. archipresbyt plebis Scandiani, dated Rome, 1482, Aug. 30, Lib brev , 15,
f 17 (Secret Archives of the Vatican) Even in time of war, Sixtus
IV. found leisure for such occupations

an hydraulic architect, competent to direct these difficult works *

The accusations of greed and cruelty, which Infessura has brought against the Pope, must also be absolutely dismissed. "The most trustworthy authorities," on the contrary, bear witness to the inherent kindliness which was expressed in his countenance and speech. "He was won by the least token of attachment; the more disposed he himself was to kindness, the less worthy of further benefits did he esteem those whom he saw to have abused former ones "†

Equally unanimous is the testimony which assures us of his generosity. He could refuse nothing, " so that the pleasure he felt in satisfying people often made him grant the same appointment to several troublesome petitioners. Accordingly, for the sake of avoiding misunderstandings, he found it necessary to entrust to an experienced and firm man, like John of Montmirabile, the revision of requests, grants, and presents   Even in the Vatican, the Mendicant Friar so little understood the value of money that, if he saw any coin on the table, he could hardly refrain from at once distributing it, through his chamberlains, to friends or to the poor.   His saying, ' A stroke of the pen suffices to procure for a Pope any sum that he desires,' is an evidence of his simplicity in matters of this kind.   No Pontiff was fonder of giving, or of kinder disposition, and he was always willing to advance men and to bestow honours upon them   This amiable and benevolent temper of mind led him to adopt, in his intercourse with those around him, both high and low, a tone of affability and goodness, and even of expansive

* This appears from a **Brief of the 10th Febr, 1476, which I found in the State Archives, Modena

† SCHMARSOW, 260, see SIGISMONDO DE' CONTI, I, 204. Also TIRABOSCHI, VI, 1, 64, Tommasini has never seen the critical observations of these eminent students

confidence, which, in diplomatic negotiations, often gave cold
politicians an advantage over him.   His unpleasant experiences with the Cardinals, who had carried his election, and
with Ferrante of Naples, who was solely influenced by selfish
considerations, furnished the reasons which induced him
later on to confide practical affairs to the crafty brothers
Pietro and Girolamo Riario."*   The foregoing pages have
shewn the disastrous influence exercised especially by the
latter.   Girolamo was like the evil genius of Sixtus IV.,
bred in the cloister, and without experience of the world, the
better judgment of Francesco della Rovere succumbed but
too often to his headstrong policy.   It may truly be said,
that nothing so much tended to obscure the good, and even
brilliant, qualities, of this Pope, as his inability to shake himself free from influences which stained his honour.   It may

* SCHMARSOW, 260-61   See ARTAUD, Gesch. der Papste, IV, 164
(Augsburg, 1854)   *Sixti IV lib. Bullet, 1471-73, records, as early as the
5th Nov., 1471, alms to the amount of tria millia octingentos quinqua-
ginta duc.   From the same Register it appears that gifts were regularly
bestowed upon the poor at Christmas and Easter. (State Archives,
Rome)   Dr Gottlob will treat, in a special work, of the support accorded
to the fugitives from the East   Regarding Charlotte of Cyprus, who
again lived in Rome from the year 1482, see BELLI, 35 seq,
HERQUET, Charlotta, 205, and ADINOLFI, Portica, 99 seq, 102 seq
Generous assistance was also given to the cities of the States of the
Church   Perugia, which had suffered from the Plague and from a
year of scarcity, received in 1477 a thousand ducats as a free gift,
see *Brief to Perugia of the 18th January, 1477. (University Library,
Genoa, C IV, 1)   On the 17th October, 1471, money was sent to
assist in the restoration of the walls and bridges at Folignano near
Ascoli.   *Lib brev, 14, f 1 (Secret Archives of the Vatican); the same
volume affords many proofs of the liberality of Sixtus IV on behalf of
needy convents   See f 95b   *Abbati S Placidi ord S. Benedicti et
Henrico de Avellino canonico et decano eccl Messanen   (1472,
January 2), f 116   *Archipresbyt et Jacobo de la Fossa canonico
eccl Reginae, f 146b: *Assistance pro fabrica infirmarie conventus
ord. min. Bononien (1472, Febr 29).

be asked how such weakness can be reconciled with the
great energy often manifested in the conduct of Sixtus IV. ;
the best answer is, in the words of Melozzo's biographer,
that his was one of those peculiar characters " which are
capable at times of strong efforts of will, during which they
display really commanding ability, but which are followed
by intervals of weakness and indifference which seem
necessary to enable them to collect their forces again " [*]
The crafty Girolamo relentlessly turned these weaker
moments to account

Side by side with many excellent and praiseworthy
qualities, we see in Sixtus IV. great defects and failings ;
there are many bright points, but there are also dark
shadows

If our unbiassed researches lead us, for the most part, to
dismiss the intemperate accusations brought against Sixtus
IV. by a partisan of the Colonna like Infessura, on the other
hand, they forbid us to look upon him as an ideal Pope.
Francesco della Rovere was admirable as General of his
Order , the contemplation of his pontificate awakens
mingled feelings in our minds.   It is but too true that the
father of Christendom often disappears behind the figure of
the Italian prince ; that, in the exaltation of his own kindred,
he exceeded all due bounds, and allowed himself to be led
into worldly ways, and that great relaxation in ecclesiastical
discipline and manifold abuses prevailed in his reign,
although they were not unaccompanied by measures of
reform.   Ægidius of Viterbo may be guilty of exaggeration
in dating the period of decadence from his pontificate,[†] yet
there can be no doubt that he steered the Barque of St Peter
into dangerous and rock-strewn waters.

[*] SCHMARSOW, 260

[†] The passage is to be found in GREGOROVIUS, VII , 266, 3rd ed.
See CHRISTOPHE, 214

In his relations to learning and art Sixtus IV. appears to far greater advantage than in the sphere of ecclesiastical policy. "When we remember that this man was a poor Friar, suddenly transformed into the mightiest Pontiff of his age, we are struck with astonishment at finding nowhere in him the least trace of the straitened surroundings of his youth and early training. Instead of the narrowness and pettiness we should expect, we find him entering into the spirit of the past, and making the magnificent taste of the day his own to a degree that no other Pope had done. We see him vying with the most renowned Italian Princes in raising his capital from the dust and degradation of centuries of ruin to be a seat of splendour, a worthy and beautiful abode, endeavouring not merely to place her on an equality with the greatest cities of Italy, but to make her once more the intellectual literary and artistic centre of the world. Noting all this, we are filled with respect for a man so capable and so powerful, in spite of some violence in his temper and inequalities in his character. Notwithstanding all his faults, there is something imposing in the first of the Rovere Popes; we are constrained to admire him, and, without hesitation, place him on a level with his predecessor, Nicholas V., and his nephew and successor, Julius II."*

* SCHMARSOW, 263

CHAPTER XII.

Sixtus IV. as the Patron of Art and Learning —(a) Re-
founding and Opening of the Vatican Library —The
Secret Archives of the Vatican —Intellectual Life in
Rome —Encouragement of the Humanists.—Platina and
his "History of the Popes"—(b) Renovation and Embellishment of Rome —The Pope and the Cardinals as
Church-Builders.—The Capitoline Museum.—The Hospital of S Spirito —Artistic Versatility of Sixtus IV —
Melozzo da Forli —The Frescoes of the Sistine Chapel.

ONE title to renown, possessed by Sixtus IV, is uncontested ;
he was unwearied in his zeal for the promotion of art and
learning.   Fresh from the poverty of the Franciscan Convent in which his earlier days had been spent, and from the
arduous philosophical and theological studies which had
occupied his mind, Francesco della Rovere, on his elevation to
the Chair of St. Peter, at once set to work to adorn Rome with
the most precious and varied works of art and learning, and
to raise her to the position of the chief city of the Christian
world, and the artistic and literary centre of the Renaissance.
The prosecution of the great work of Nicholas V. was the
ideal which filled his mind, and, amid all the political and
ecclesiastical perplexities which troubled the thirteen years
of his reign, the realisation of this ideal was pursued with
a steadfast earnestness which even his opponents were constrained to admire.   In the history of Intellectual Culture
the name of Sixtus IV. must ever find an honourable place,
together with those of Nicholas V., Julius II., and Leo X.

It may safely be said that, in regard to the development of the Renaissance in Rome, Sixtus IV. occupies a position similar to that of Lorenzo de' Medici in Florence "If the Golden Age which he introduced was often the subject of exaggerated praise from the admirers of his brilliant literary Court, it is nevertheless true that he has a right to be numbered among the most popular National Popes." *

I.

Of all the works undertaken by Sixtus IV. none has a greater claim on the sympathy and interest of the historian than the re-establishment of the Vatican Library, and its opening for general use. This "most admirable of all his foundations"† occupied the Pope even in the earliest months of his pontificate.   On the 17th December, 1471, he took the first step towards rescuing the forgotten Library of Nicholas V., and providing the necessary accommodation for its preservation.‡ As time went on, "he adopted the idea of Nicholas V in its fullest extent, and made further additions to the treasures which had been saved   He endeavoured to procure valuable manuscripts, ancient codices, and modern copies from all parts, so that a book-dealer like Vespasiano da Bisticci speaks of the Pope's love of collecting as marking a new epoch, from which he occasionally dates, although, as a Florentine, he is not otherwise favourably disposed towards this Pope "§

* CROWE-CAVALCASELLE, III, 326, referring to an Eulogium in Cod, 1092, University Library, Leipzig

† CROWE-CAVALCASELLE, III, 327. See RENAZZI, I, 179–80 The Poem mentioned *supra*, p. 209, note *, in Cod, 2403, f 11b *seq* of the Court Library, Vienna, is enthusiastic in the praise of the Library of Sixtus IV

‡ MARINI, Archivi, 18 ; Arch St Ital, 3 Serie, III, 215, MUNTZ, III, 118 *seq* , and Regestum Clementis V, I, p xlv

§ SCHMARSOW, 37

The zeal with which Sixtus IV, assisted by Platina, Jacobo di Volterra, Lionardi Dati, Domizio Calderino, Mattia Palmieri, and Sigismondo de' Conti, laboured to increase the Vatican Library is evidenced by the fact that in 1475 it contained no less than 2527 volumes, 770 of which were Greek and 1757 Latin. Between 1475 and 1484, 1000 more were added, bringing the number up to more than 3500 volumes, something like three times as many as appear in Nicholas V.'s Inventory drawn up twenty years before.* In order to appreciate the importance of the collection, let us remember that ten years later the library of the wealthy Medici contained about a thousand Manuscripts.†

In the collection of Pope Sixtus IV. we observe a decided preponderance of ecclesiastical works. Theology, Philosophy, and Patristic Literature form its chief contents. The Inventory of 1475 mentions 26 volumes of St. Chrysostom's writings, 28 of St Ambrose, 31 of St. Gregory, 41 of Canon Law, 51 of Records of Councils, 51 of the works of St. Thomas, 57 of St. Jerome, and 81 of St. Augustine. The Old and New Testaments occupy 59 volumes, and Glosses on the Scripture 98 Celebrated Greek authors are represented by 109 volumes, and there are 116 on religious subjects by less-known writers of the same nation Compared with the collection of Nicholas V, the total absence of any writings in the vernacular is a defect. The classics occupy the second place, there are 14 volumes of the works of Seneca, 53 of the Latin Poets, 70 of Greek Poetry and Grammar, 125 of Roman, and 59 of Grecian History. The Latin writers on Astrology and Geometry contribute 19, and Greek Astrologers 49 volumes, Latin Philosophers 103, and

* MUNTZ, Bibliothèque, 135, 141.
† See our Vol. II., p 212. The particulars there given in regard to Nicholas's Library are supplemented by MUNTZ, Bibl, 315 seq., and Rev critique, 1886, p 282.

Greek 94   There were 55 Latin and 14 Greek works on Medicine.*

The first Librarian of the Vatican under Sixtus IV. was Giandrea Bussi, Bishop of Aleria, a man of classical culture The appointment of this ardent promoter of the art of typography in Rome renders it probable that the productions of the printing-press were not excluded from the Papal collection. An Inventory of the year 1483 distinguishes between printed books and Manuscripts †

Bussi, who died in the Jubilee Year, was succeeded by Bartolomeo Platina New and regular revenues were, at the same time, assigned by the Pope to the Library,‡ and energetic measures were taken for the recovery of books which had been borrowed and not restored.§ Platina received a yearly salary of 120 ducats (= £240 sterling) and

---

* MUNTZ, Renaissance, 121, and Biblioth., 142 and 159 *seq*   In regard to the Inventories, see also the articles of MUNTZ and DE ROSSI (355) in the Serapeum, I , 334 *seq* , VI , 301 *seq* , XII , 130 *seq*

† MUNTZ, Bibl., 141. In 1472 Bussi drew up a petition to Sixtus IV in the name of the printers, Schweynheim and Pannartz, who had fallen into great distress , to this petition is appended a most valuable list of the works which, up to that time, had issued from their press, with the number of copies of each ; see LINDE, I., 167 *seq* , LORCK, Gesch der Buchdr , 57 *seq* (Leipzig, 1882) The two printers had then printed 12,475 volumes , Bussi's letter was probably of little use to them Competition was increasing, and at length they abandoned the struggle Pannartz died after 1476, Schweynheim entirely gave up printing According to JANSSEN, I , 15 (14th ed.), Rome had, in 1475, as many as twenty printing-offices, and by the close of the Century 925 works had been produced , most of these were mainly supported by the clergy; see also FROMANN, 9 , FALK, 18 , LINDE, I , 172, III , 715

‡ **Bull of Sixtus IV , dated Romae, 1475, XVII. Cal Jul , Armar. XXXI , N 62, f. 113 Secret Archives of the Vatican

§ The Bull on the subject is printed in the Regestum Clementis V , I , p xlvi See also MARINI, Archivi, 18

apartments. Three officials, called Scriptores or Custodes,
were placed under him, and also a bookbinder. They were
paid 12 ducats a year each, and were generously supported
by Sixtus IV. in every way that he could. One of them,
Demetrius of Lucca, was a man of considerable learning.*
Platina soon died, and his place was filled by Bartolomeo
Manfredi, surnamed Aristophilo, Secretary to Cardinal
Roverella   In July, 1484, the new Librarian went, by the
Pope's desire, to Urbino and Rimini to copy Manuscripts †

The appointment of Platina, the employment of subordinate officials, and the assignment of a regular income were
the first steps towards the reorganisation of this noble Institution, which soon acquired a world-wide reputation.   On
the 1st July, 1477, Sixtus IV. published another Bull regarding the revenues of the Library and the stipend of its custodians. In the introduction to this Bull, he says that the
objects of this Institution are the exaltation of the Church
militant, the spread of the Catholic Faith, and the advancement of learning.‡

Another important work of the Pope was the separation
of the Manuscript books from the Documents and Archives.
A special place, called the Bibliotheca Secreta, was prepared,
in which the Documents arranged by Platina were to be
preserved in walnut-wood chests. "The whole room was
wainscoted, and the free space on the walls above adorned
with frescoes in chiaroscuro. This costly undertaking must
have been completed in the latter part of the Summer of
1480 " §

* MUNTZ, Bibliothèque, 137. See also VOGEL in the Serapeum,
VII , 296 seq.

† See Sixtus IV's Briefs of the 18th Oct , 1481, and 14th July, 1484,
in MUNTZ, Bibl , 300–303. Also Regestum Clementis V., I , p. xlvii

‡ MUNTZ, Bibl , 300.

§ SCHMARSOW, 206

Documents of special importance had, from the beginning of the 15th Century, been kept at St. Angelo. Having regard to the troubled state of the times, Sixtus IV caused the Charters containing the chief privileges of the Roman Church to be transferred to this place of safety, after authentic copies of them had been made by Urbino Fieschi and Platina *

The Library proper consisted, until 1480, of two halls opening into each other, one for the Latin and the other for the Greek Manuscripts. From the registers of payments it appears that, in the summer of 1480, Sixtus IV. added a third hall, which was distinguished by the name of the Great Library, and was in all probability situated on the other side of the Cortile del Papagallo, beneath the Sistine Chapel. Its walls and ceiling were painted by Melozzo, with the assistance of Antoniasso. Twenty-five years later, Albertini wrote a description of the Library, which is shorter than we could wish. He places the three portions of the Public Institution in juxtaposition, so as to separate the Library from the Secret Archives "In the Apostolic Palace at the Vatican," he writes, "is that glorious Library, built by Sixtus IV, with his portrait exquisitely painted and the epigram beneath.† There are also paintings of the Doctors, with other verses, which I give in my collection of epigrams Beside this Library is another, called the Greek one, also built by Sixtus, together with the chamber of the Custodians. There is, moreover, a third very beautiful Library, also erected by Sixtus IV., in which are the Codices

---

* BRESSLAU, Urkundenlehre, I, 129; Lowenfeld in RAUMER'S Hist. Taschenbuch, 6th Series, V, 318, DUDIK, II, 14 *seq*, Regestum Clementis V., I, p. xlix; MARINI, Archivi, 18; GACHARD, Arch. du Vatican, 7-8 (Brussels, 1874); Mél d'Archéologie, 1888, p 150, and Studi e Doc, VIII, 11.

† See *infra*, p 453

adorned with gold, silver, and silk bindings   I saw Virgil's
works in this hall, written in capital letters, besides geome-
trical, astronomical, and other instruments connected with
the liberal arts, which are also decorated with gold, silver,
and paintings." Albertini then proceeds to speak of the
Secret Library (Bibliotheca Secreta), which had been rearranged by Julius II.*

The Great Library, which contained the collection of
ancient Manuscripts, had the advantage of the two other
halls in being well-lighted by "a large glass window containing the arms of the Rovere family.   The German glass-
maker Heimann had been obliged to bring this himself
from Venice."† Here stood the long tables to which the
Manuscripts were secured by little chains—just as they
now are in the splendid Laurenziana at Florence ; but in
the 15th Century the comfort of scholars was more considered than it is in the 19th   In the cold and damp
winter days the grand Library was warmed.‡ Although
the Manuscripts were chained, they were most liberally lent
out. Platina's list of books lent is preserved,§ and shews

* SCHMARSOW, 40 seq   His researches concerning the Vatican
Library have essentially rectified and completed the earlier descriptions
of GREGOROVIUS, ZANELLI (Bibl. Vat [R 1857], p 13), and REUMONT
(Arch St Ital, N S , VIII , 1, 132 seq). Schmarsow's Monograph has
unfortunately escaped the notice of the worthy M. Muntz in his valuable
work on the Vatican Library

† SCHMARSOW, 42 ; MUNTZ, III , 119 seq.

‡ MUNTZ, Bibliothèque, 140

§ Cod. Vat , 3964, published by MUNTZ, Bibl , 269-99. In order
justly to appreciate the liberality of Sixtus IV , the extreme difficulty
of procuring Manuscripts in those days must be remembered , Lorenzo
de' Medici, in the period of his greatest magnificence, had to write an
autograph letter to Ercole d'Este, a Prince who was under great
obligations to him, for the loan of ' Dio Cassius,' and, notwithstanding
the confidential relations which existed between them, Ercole did not
send the original , see REUMONT, Lorenzo, II., 106, 2nd ed.

that several volumes were entrusted at once to the same person. Among those who availed themselves of the literary treasures of this Library, were the Pope himself, Cardinal Giuliano, numerous Bishops and Prelates, Johannes Argyropulos, Sigismondo de' Conti, Pomponius Laetus, Johannes Philippus de Lignamine, Hieronymus Balbanus, Augustinus Patritius, Jacobus Volaterranus, Francesco de Toledo, and others. The negligence of some borrowers compelled the administrators from the year 1480 to require pledges to be deposited for books lent

The reorganisation of the Vaticana, and its opening to the public, would suffice to secure for Sixtus IV. an abiding record in the history of scholars But his other efforts for the promotion of learning were by no means inconsiderable.

In the early days of his pontificate, the Humanists seem to have felt much anxiety as to the attitude the former Franciscan friar might adopt in regard to their pursuits. This feeling is evidenced by a work which Sigismondo de' Conti dedicated to the Pope, reminding him that Nicholas V, the most famous Pontiff of the age, had gained great renown by his patronage of scholars Sigismondo warned Sixtus IV not to attach too little importance to the opinion of the learned, and to what might be written of him by celebrated men. He reminded him of the words of Francesco Sforza, who said that the wound of a dagger was less to be dreaded than that of a satirical poem. In conclusion, the anxious Humanist again begged the Pope to shew honour to men who were in a position to preserve his name from oblivion and to immortalise his actions *

* "*Habeantur in pretio viri qui tuum nomen ab interitu vendicare, qui tuas res gestas immortalitati mandare possunt" Fol 603 of Sigismondo de' Conti's *Work, Ad Sixtum IV. pro secretariis, which I found in Cod. Vat, 2934, P. II, Vatican Library Sixtus IV restored the College of Abbreviators, and fixed their number at seventy-

Exhortations of this kind were not needed. Sixtus IV
perfectly understood the importance of the Renaissance ; he
was well aware that the Humanists were indispensable, and
that it was impossible, on account of some isolated excesses,
to adopt a position of antagonism towards the intellectual
life so ardently cultivated on all sides. " Full of intellect
and of taste for high culture," the ex-general of the Mendicant Order from the first resolved "to surround the Papal
Throne and his own relations with all that could give him
prestige in the eyes of the world."*   Although the attraction
which the Eternal City exercises on lovers of antiquity had
already drawn a numerous colony of learned men to Rome,
the Pope constantly sought to add to their number.   One
of his greatest acquisitions was Johannes Argyropulos of
Constantinople, the most highly gifted among the Greeks
who had migrated to Italy.   In winning him to Rome,
Sixtus IV. gained a victory over the Medici, in whose
service he had been for some time.   Argyropulos was very
successful there.   He had the satisfaction of numbering
amongst his hearers men of the greatest distinction, Bishops
and Cardinals, and even notable foreigners such as Johann
Reuchlin †   Angelo Poliziano was also his disciple.‡   The
worthy Bartholomaus Fontius was appointed to a Professorial
Chair in the Roman University under Sixtus IV.   In 1473
Martino Filetico became Professor of Rhetoric in that Insti-

two ; see CIAMPINI, 33 *seq* ; PHILLIPS, VI , 394.   In regard to the
sale of these places, see GOTTLOB, Cam Apost

   * PAPENCORDT, 517.

   † Reuchlin was among the audience of Argyropulos in the Spring
of 1482 when staying in Rome with Count Eberhard of Wurttemberg.
See MUNTZ, Renaissance, 83 , STALIN, III , 592 *seq* ; GEIGER,
Reuchlin, 25

   ‡ MUNTZ, Renaissance, 83   Concerning Argyropulos, see VOIGT,
Wiederbelebung, I., 372, 2nd ed., and LEGRAND, Bibliographie
Hellénique, Paris, 1885, 2 vols , *s v.*

tution * Even non-Italian scholars were summoned by the Pope to Rome. Among these, was, in 1475, the famous Regiomontanus (Johann Muller of Konigsberg in Franconia). Unfortunately, this great discoverer, who, by the Pope's desire, would have assisted in the work of reforming the Calendar, died in July, 1476.†

But the ambition of Sixtus IV. was not yet satisfied. He desired to win for his beloved Rome the prince of the neo-platonic philosophy, the scholar whose writings cast a halo of glory over Florence. Several of the Cardinals supported him in this project Marsilio Ficino, however, was bound to the Medici by bonds which could not be severed. He requited the Pope's gracious summons by a letter couched in the most flattering terms ‡

* Filetico had previously taught Greek there , see MARINI, II., 208 , SCHMARSOW, 55, 75 note, and 345 , and CORVISIERI in the Review, Buonarotti, Ser. II , Vol IV , 1869.

† FULGOSUS, VIII , c 13 ; ASCHBACH, Wiener Universitat, I , 556 , KALTENBRUNNER, Kalenderreform, in the Sitzungsberichten der Wiener Akad Hist Cl , LXXXII , 374 ; JANSSEN, I., 124 (14th edit), TIRABOSCHI, VI , I, 356 The statement that Regiomontanus was poisoned (BECHSTEIN, Deutsches Museum, I , 253) is a pure invention ; Aschbach supposes him to have succumbed to the summer fever raging in Rome, which was of a pestilential character ; this hypothesis, which Jovius gives as a fact, is all the more probable, inasmuch as the Plague actually prevailed in Rome at the time , see our account, supra, p 288. There is an interesting statement in the Koelhoff'schen Chronik to the effect that, after hearing Johann Cantor dispute in Rome, Sixtus IV wrote an extremely friendly Brief to his Father. Stadtechroniken, XIV., 877 In regard to the Pope's relations with Joh. Wessel, see ULLMANN, II , 353 seq., and to his encouragement of Universities, PRANTL, I., 68 , Tub. Theol. Quartalschr, p 206, 1865 See F. STALIN, Gesch Wurttembergs, I , 2, 671 seq (Gotha, 1887); PELLINI, 813 , and supra, p 260, regarding Copenhagen

‡ MUNTZ, Renaissance, 83 See the Revue des deux Mondes, 1881, Nov, p 163 Regarding the jurists whom Sixtus IV. invited to Rome, see RENAZZI, I , 185 seq

The Roman Humanists in the time of Sixtus IV. formed a very brilliant circle. While Pomponius Laetus lived almost entirely by his labours as a Professor,* " Platina wrote his History of the Popes, Campanus composed his elegies and epigrams, Aurelio Brandolini charmed even the unpoetical Pope with his verses, while a bevy of youthful writers produced Latin poems of more or less merit." † The favour shewn by Sixtus IV. to Gasparo and Francesco, the sons of Flavio Biondi, shewed his willingness to reward the services rendered by departed scholars ‡ Johannes Philippus de Lignamine, the editor of many ancient authors, was in his service. His kinsman, Philippus de Lignamine, a Dominican, continued Ricobaldo's Chronicle of the Popes down to the year 1469, and dedicated his work to Sixtus IV.§

His pontificate was very fruitful in historical works. The example of Pius II. in writing the history of his own time produced many imitators. Sigismondo de' Conti holds the first place amongst these. His " Contemporary History," in seventeen books, comprising the period from 1475 to 1510, " ensures him an honourable mention among the Cinquecento writers " Sigismondo, who is spoken of with the greatest respect by contemporaneous authors, was a Christian Humanist. These men, " the sympathetic outcome of the age of the Renaissance, had themselves experienced the antagonism between the ancient classical world and the

---

* Petrus Martyr was, from the year 1477, a disciple of P Laetus ; see HEIDENHEIMER P. M., 4 (Berlin, 1881)

† GEBHARDT, Adrian von Corneto, 4. See RENAZZI, I , 187 *seq.*; MUNTZ, Renaissance, 408-9 , and VILLENEUVE, 14, for an account of Brandolini. For the relations of D Calderino to Sixtus IV, see GIULIARI, 76 *seq.* See also MANSI-FABRICIUS, I , 297

‡ This information is furnished by Wilmanns from the Registers of the Secret Archives of the Vatican in the Gott Gel Anz., 1879, pp 1502-3.

§ FABRICIUS-MANSI, V , 279-80

mediæval point of view, but able justly to distinguish between the means and the end, were not blinded by the
splendour of the past, and held fast to the principles of Christianity" Sigismondo requited the favours of Sixtus IV and
the Rovere by a frequent and far too partial mention of them
in his work, which otherwise is both trustworthy and candid *
" Jacopo Gherardi of Volterra (Volaterranus), attracted by
Pope Sixtus IV. to the Court of Rome, followed the
example of his first patron, Cardinal Ammanati, by writing
Memoirs of his time.   Mattia Palmieri of Pisa, Papal Scrip-
tor, who died in 1482, continued the chronicle of his famous
Florentine namesake, Matteo Palmieri." †

Notwithstanding the love of literature which distinguished
Sixtus IV., the unfortunate circumstances of the time robbed
the Roman University of much of her splendour.   "The
revenues destined for the maintenance of the Institution
were often employed in the war, and taxes were imposed on
the salaries of the Professors.   Different posts connected
with the University came by purchase into unworthy
hands"‡

Sixtus IV. also encouraged literary men by appointments
to diplomatic Missions   In 1476 Georgios Hermonymos
went to England as Orator to the English§ Embassy, and in
1482 Sigismondo de' Conti, who had previously accompanied
Cardinal Giuliano to the Netherlands, was sent to Florence ||

* GOTTLOB in the Hist Jahrb, VII, 304-23   See also SYBEL'S
Hist Zeitschr, N. F, XXI, 359.   The Life of Sigismondo by Bartol.
Alpeus, preserved in the Archivio Communale of Ancona, has been
published by Faloci Pulignani, S de C. Il Topino, I., N 26

† REUMONT, III, 1, 350

‡ RENAZZI, I, 195, PAPENCORDT, 521, CHRISTOPHE, II., 295 *seq.*
See *supra*, p 422

§ OMONT, G Hermonyme in the Mém de la Soc d'Hist de Paris,
XII, 65 *seq*, and GEIGER, Vierteljahrsschrift für Renaissance, II, 197.

|| See *supra*, pp. 334 and 372

Johannes Philippus de Lignamine had, in 1475, the honour
of welcoming the King of Naples at Velletri, and was subsequently entrusted with Missions to Mantua and Sicily *

The excessive self-esteem of these favoured Humanists
often took a very offensive form.   Theodoros Gaza, considering the payment given him by the Pope for his translation of
Aristotle's Animals insufficient, is said to have scornfully cast
it into the Tiber †   The anecdote may be an invention, but
it exemplifies the insolence and greed of many Humanists,
one of whom, George of Trebizond, even went so far as to
beg money from the Sultan, to whom he wrote two fulsome
letters ‡   Francesco Filelfo, who made presents and money

* MARINI, I , 193 *seq*

† So says Jovius, while PIERIUS VALERIANUS, De infelicitate literat.,
II , 159, makes Trapezuntios die of it   Hodius doubts the whole
story , BAHR, in Ersch-Gruber, I , Section 55, p 135, refuses to reject it
altogether. See LEGRAND, I , xxxviii.

‡ Perotti (how far he received directions from Sixtus IV. remains
still uncertain , see REUMONT'S Vermuthungen, III , 1, 350, and *cf.*
Vespasiano da Bisticci [in MAI, I , 279], who, however, being a
Florentine, is not an impartial witness , Civ Catt , I , 148, 1868) accordingly made a furious attack on Trapezuntios   VOIGT, Wiederbelebung, II , 144, 2nd ed , cites· N. Perotti, Refutatio deliramentorum
Georgii Trapezuntii in Morelli , Codices ms. lat. bibl Namanaep , 51.
The last-named book was not within my reach   On the other hand,
there is in *Cod. Vat , 2934, I , f 219 *seq*, an "Invectiva Nic Perotti
in Georg Trapezunt quia Turcum omnibus quicumque fuerunt imper-
atoribus natura praestantiorem esse voluit," which is, perhaps,
identical with the " Refutatio "   Perotti here takes both the letters of
Trapezuntios to the Sultan to pieces, sentence by sentence, heaps
reproaches upon him, and calls on the Pope, the Emperor, and
all Christian Princes to punish him   " Hancine luem, hancine
pestem . . sustinere amplius poteritis? . . . Exurgite igitur, exurgite . . . et hunc sceleratissimum hominem, hanc trunculentam feram,
hoc immanissimum monstrum non ex urbe abigite, non ex Italia
exterminate . . . sed cadendum flagris et usque ad ossa dilaniandum
discerpendum dilacerandum tradite."

the chief subject of his verses, was even more covetous * If
the insolent petitions of this insatiable man were not favourably received he revenged himself by the coarsest invectives.
Each new Pope was addressed immediately upon his elevation by the " King of importunate poets," and if, like Pius
II , he failed to satisfy the immense expectations of the
petitioner, was loaded with abuse   The attacks which this
most repulsive of Humanists made on the memory of the
departed Pius II. were so horrible, that the College of
Cardinals caused him to be imprisoned at the very time
when he was striving to obtain a place at the Court †   On
the accession of Sixtus IV, Filelfo renewed his efforts in
this direction.   The Pope at first gave him no encouragement, and Filelfo's flatteries soon changed to complaints, and
finally to threats.   When he was summoned to Rome in
1474, he owed his appointment mainly to the dread of his
pen ‡   Filelfo was employed for three years as Professor
at the Roman University ; dissensions were not wanting
during this period , the most important was his quarrel with
Miliaduca Cicada, Master of the Papal Treasury.   For the
first time, however, "he was delighted with the City, its
climate, the exuberance and elegance of its life, and, above
all, with the incredible liberty which there prevailed "§

The " incredible liberty " was most strikingly displayed in

* VOIGT, Wiederbelebung, I , 531, 2nd ed , gives a detailed description of Filelfo's system of begging.

† VOIGT, Pius II , III , 637 *seq* , GASPARY, 116.

‡ This fear is manifest in the friendly manner in which Sixtus IV
caused him to be treated on his arrival in Rome ; see MUNTZ,
Renaissance, 89. BUSER, Lorenzo, 26, informs us that Filelfo begged
assistance from Lorenzo de' Medici for his journey to Rome.

§ " Et quod maximi omnium faciendum videtur mihi, incredibilis
quaedam hic libertas est." Ep. LX. in ROSMINI ; see GREGOROVIUS,
VII , 531, 3rd ed , and MUNTZ in the Rev des Deux Mondes, 1881,
Novemb , p. 168.

the permission given by the Pope to the Roman Academy to
resume their meetings, which had been suppressed. Sixtus
IV. looked upon Humanism as a purely literary movement
in no way dangerous to religion. The apprehensions which
the extravagances and the heathen tendencies of many
literary men had awakened in the mind of his predecessor
were not shared by him. "He may also have thought that
the Humanists had had their lesson and taken it to heart."
Pomponius Laetus was again perfectly free to lecture, and
the Academy held its sittings without the slightest hindrance.
The spectacle was a strange one. "While a Minorite occupied
the Papal Throne the worship of antiquity, with its excesses
as well as its good side, flourished unrebuked, and no offence
seems to have been taken at the pontificate of Pomponius
Laetus   The assemblies at his house on the Quirinal near the
Gardens of Constantine were more brilliant than ever. The
Academy was openly recognised, and this, in fact, was the
simplest way of rendering it harmless."* High dignitaries
of the Church were on friendly terms with it   On the 20th
April, 1483, when the Academicians celebrated the birthday
of Rome, a solemn High Mass, followed by a discourse from
Paulus Marsus, preceded the banquet, at which six Bishops
were present. At this Academic Feast the "Privilegium,"
by which the Emperor Frederick granted to the body the
right of conferring the title of Doctor and crowning Poets,
was publicly read †

In his treatment of Platina, one of the most violent
members of the Academy, Sixtus IV shewed great tact and
knowledge of human nature. "He managed to win this
ringleader of the opposition by treating him as an old friend,
and assigned to him successively two tasks, which removed
all danger of anti-Papal dispositions, by enlisting all his

* REUMONT, III , 1, 351   See also SCHMARSOW, 28.
† JACOB VOLATERRANUS, 185

energies and talents in the service of the very power against
which he had rebelled.   He first encouraged him to write
a History of the Popes, and then requested him to make a
collection of all the Documents regarding the rights of the
Holy See "*   By the end of the year 1474, or the beginning
of 1475,† Platina was able to offer his "History of the Popes"
to his august patron ‡   It is, in many respects, a remarkable

* SCHMARSOW, 28

† This appears from the fact that Platina's work comes down to
November, 1474   DOLLINGER, Papstfabeln, 22, is, therefore, in error
when he says that Platina's History of the Popes was written in 1460.
VAIRANI, I , 6, gives 1473 as the year in which the work was begun

‡ I found in Cod Vat 2044, of the Vatican Library the copy
presented to Sixtus IV. It is a splendid Renaissance Codex, of 236
folio pages, written on parchment. It begins, f 1: "Prohemium
Platynae in vitas pontificum ad Sixtum IIII P. M Multa quidem, &c."
The 'M' is illuminated with an exquisite miniature of the arms of the
Rovere, supported by two naked genii. Each word is written in many
colours   blue, red, green, lilac, and gold, and the effect on the fine
parchment is splendid   There is a still finer miniature at f. 2b, a
portrait of the Pope, surrounded by the inscription : "Sixtus Pont
Max," and framed in a wreath with golden acorns. The many-coloured
letters often recur, as in f 3, where the naked genii again appear, but
this time without the coat-of-arms   Here the actual history begins
"Platynae historici liber de vita Christi ac omnium pontificum qui
hactenus ducenti fuere et XX Nobilitatis maximam partem, &c"
This original copy of the History, which has become so celebrated, has
a threefold importance   (a) It contains, f 229-236b, the Life of Sixtus
IV, as found by MURATORI, III, 2, 1045-65, in a Cod Urb , that is to
say, without the addition regarding the Hospital of S Spirito   This
tends to confirm Schmarsow's view that Platina was the author of this
Vita ; see also *supra*, p 272   (b) It contains all the passages calculated to give offence, as, e g , that against John XXII., fol 177b, as well
as the violent language, of which we shall speak presently, condemning
the state of ecclesiastical affairs at that period. (c) There are many
interesting notes, probably in Platina's own handwriting, some of
which are mere corrections, and others, especially in the Biography of
Paul II , alterations of the text ; expressions are in some instances,

work for the period in which it was written. Instead of the confused and often fabulous Chronicles of the Middle Ages, we find here for the first time a clear and serviceable handbook of real history. The graphic descriptions, the elegant, perspicuous, and yet concise, style of the work have won for Platina's "Lives of the Popes" many readers even down to the present day *

In his Preface, which is addressed to Sixtus IV., Platina begins by emphasising, in the Humanistic style,† the dignity and importance of history. His declaration that he will, on principle, avoid applying expressions belonging to classical heathenism to Christian subjects, is remarkable. He begins his work with Christ, "so that, springing from the Emperor of Christians as from a living fountain, it may flow on through the Roman Bishops down to the days of Sixtus" In the lives of the earliest Popes, Platina repeatedly mentions the ancient monuments with admiration. "In the Church of Sant' Andrea near Santa Maria Maggiore," he writes, in his life of Simplicius, "as I looked at the relics of antiquity which it contains, tears often filled my eyes at the neglect of those whose duty it is to preserve it from decay."‡

toned down, and in others intensified Further particulars will be given in another place.

* See TIRABOSCHI, VI, 1, 279, VILLARI, I, 130, BISSOLATI, 73 *seq* ; MUNTZ in the Rev. des Deux Mondes, 1881, Nov, p 174. An English translation of Platina's Lives of the Popes appeared in 1888 The book was first printed by two Germans in Venice, in 1479, in 1481 another edition came out at Nuremberg (Hain, 13,047), this was followed by numerous others, some of which were mutilated ; see VAIRANI, I., 11-12 (here p 119, also the "Prohoemium Platinae ad Sixtum IV in libellum Plutarchi de ira"), and POTTHAST, Bibl , I , 495 What BISSOLATI, 165 *seq.*, adduces is unsatisfactory.

† See, in general, VOIGT, Wiederbelebung, II., 495, 2nd ed , and SIGISMONDO DE' CONTI, I., 4.

‡ His interest in antiquity is often betrayed. In opposition to the

The critical acumen repeatedly manifested by Platina is worthy of note, "though he keeps this faculty under restraint, not wishing to interrupt the flow of his narrative."* The freedom with which, in a work dedicated to Sixtus IV., he treats of the faults of both the older and the more recent Popes, is to be commended, and does equal honour to the author and to his patron It is all the more painful to find that, in dealing with the life of his former adversary, Paul II, Platina has been unable to rise to the height of an impartial historian. Death is a great peacemaker, and it might have been expected that, when Paul II was no longer on earth, Platina would have done justice to his memory. This, however, is by no means the case The labours of Paul II. are described in a very one-sided manner, and indeed often wilfully travestied and ridiculed † Even in passages in which there is no occasion for mentioning this Pope, Platina seeks one, in order to give vent to his hatred ‡ This is all the more to be deplored, inasmuch as the biographies of the Popes of the Renaissance period constitute the only original portion of his work.

Platina's language, also, in speaking of the ecclesiastical affairs of his own time, is often very intemperate. Strangely enough, these outbreaks do not occur in the lives of the 15th Century Popes, but are interpolated in those of an earlier period They are, in fact, masked attacks. When writing of Dionysius I., Platina drags in complaints of the

ignorant chroniclers of the 14th Century, he clears St Gregory the Great from the slanderous accusation of having ruthlessly destroyed the relics of the past.

* GREGOROVIUS, VII., 589, 3rd ed Platina looked with suspicion on the fable of Pope Joan, but would not omit it, as almost every one maintained it ; see DOLLINGER, Papstfabeln, p. 22.

† See SCHMARSOW, 29 See also *supra*, p. 64 *seq.*

‡ See the passages in the Life of Hadrian I. and Stephen VI

pomp and pride of the higher clergy. In the histories of Julius I, Socinus I, and Boniface III. he introduces censures, obviously aimed at the clergy of the 15th Century. The immorality of Sixtus IV's Cardinals is severely castigated in the biography of Stephen III A still more violent passage is inserted in his account of Gregory IV * There was doubtless good cause for his animadversions, but they come somewhat strangely from a man whose own life was so dissolute † Platina, however, is guilty of a worse fault, when, in dealing with the reign of John XXII, he repeats the assertion of the party of the opposition, who maintained that the Pope contradicted Scripture, in saying that Christ possessed no property. The truthfulness of this historian may be gauged by the frivolous inscriptions discovered to have been written by some of the Roman Academicians in the Catacombs of S Callisto, on the occasion on which he describes himself as having visited it out of devotion‡ with a few friends §

We cannot but be surprised that Sixtus IV. accepted the dedication of a work like Platina's Probably he was only acquainted with its contents in so far as they concerned the history of his own pontificate This portion, which comes down to November, 1474, contained nothing but what would have given him perfect satisfaction. This feeling found expression in Platina's appointment as Librarian of the Vatican in the following year. While he occupied this post, the Pope commissioned him to arrange the collection of

---

* Reflections on the danger threatened by Turkey in the 15th Century are placed in the history of Boniface V, and coupled with charges against the clergy of Platina's own time

† See the evidence from *Cod Vat , 9020, *supra*, p 64, note ‖

‡ "Invisi ego haec loca cum amicis quibusdam religionis causa" Vita Calisti I , p. 56

§ See *supra*, p. 63.

Documents containing the Privileges of the Roman Church, which are now preserved in three volumes in the Vatican Archives. This useful work, which is invaluable to the annalists of the Church,* was brought to a conclusion during the war with Florence.† Here, also, Platina proved his critical discernment in excluding the "Donation of Constantine" from his collection of Documents The Preface to the work is interesting, inasmuch as Platina not only avoids everything of an anti-Papal tendency, but also speaks with approval of the proceedings of the Popes against heretics and schismatics ‡ There appears to be no doubt that Sixtus IV. succeeded in completely winning him over to the cause of the Church. The same may also be said in regard to the proud Pomponius Laetus, who now composed poems in honour of Sixtus IV.§

Platina died in 1481 His friends, among whom were some Bishops, celebrated the anniversary of his death in the Church of Sᵗᵃ Maria Maggiore, where he was buried ‖ Mass was said by the Bishop of Ventimiglia, an Augustinian, and the tomb was sprinkled with holy water and incensed.

* RAYNALDUS, ad an 1478, N 48. Kaltenbrunner is going to publish an exact description of the Coll Platinae, together with a partial Catalogue of its rich contents ; see Mittheil des Œsterr. Instituts, VI , 208.

† This appears from the Preface, of which MARINI, Archivi, 21, and Regestum Clementis V, I , p xlix, give short passages , through the kindness of Professor Kaltenbrunner, I was able to make use of a complete copy.

‡ *" De auctoritate anathemizandi eos qui contra sedem apost moliti aliquid fuerint quique heresim et seditionem in ecclesia Dei severint tam latus in his bullis apparet campus ut fulmina quedam in prevaricatores ipsos et scismaticos e celo missa videantur " Preface to the first volume of the Coll Platinae. Secret Archives of the Vatican.

§ GREGOROVIUS, VII , 574-5, 3rd ed.

‖ See BISSOLATI, 82, and Archivio Veneto, 1887, fasc 67, p 161

Pomponius Laetus, the President of the Academy, then mounted the pulpit to pronounce an oration in memory of his departed friend. Jacobus Volaterranus informs us that it was of a thoroughly religious and serious character. A poet from Perugia, named Astreus, then, from the same pulpit, recited an elegy in verse, lamenting his loss ! That such a thing could have been done is indeed an evidence of that " incredible liberty " so triumphantly praised by Filelfo We cannot, however, suppose that serious men could fail to disapprove, when, in the very sanctuary of the Queen of Heaven, just after the Mass for the Dead, a layman, without the least token of any spiritual office, pronounced, from the pulpit, verses which, although very elegant, yet—as Volaterranus remarks—were quite alien to our religion, and out of keeping with the sacred function which had just taken place.*

The Rome of that day was indeed full of strange contrasts, against which no one protested   Christian and heathen Humanism are to be seen walking side by side in daily life, and apparently incommoding each other as little as did the reforms and abuses which prevailed together in the Church †

II.

During his long pontificate, Sixtus IV did incomparably more for the promotion of Art than for that of Literature.   It has been justly observed, that the artistic activity of

---

* JACOBUS VOLATERRANUS, 171 , SCHMARSOW, 189 , BURCKHARDT, Cultur, I., 278, 3rd ed

† See *supra*, p 406 *seq*   This may also be a fitting place to mention that Cod 14 of the Archives of the Papal Chapel contains most unseemly mythological figures, and a naked Cupid with violet stockings ; see HABERL, Bausteine, I , 72   Things of this kind cannot have come to the knowledge of the Pope, who, although an enthusiastic lover of Art, punished an obscene painter   INFESSURA, 1178

the 15th Century reached its climax in Rome in his days.*
Francesco della Rovere started with the firm determination
of carrying on the work of Nicholas V., in adorning the
capital of the Christian world with all that sheds lustre on
a secular power.   But as his individual character differed
widely from that of the first patron of Art among the Popes,
the manner in which he proceeded naturally differed also
Sixtus had, in common with Nicholas V, that love of the
ideal which was so strong in the earlier Pope, but he " confined himself to what was practical and possible, and did not
let his imagination run wild " in gigantic projects.   Accordingly, Sixtus IV. had the happiness of reigning long enough
to accomplish the greater part of what he had undertaken.†

The verses from the pen of Platina, on the opening of the
Vatican Library, which adorn the portrait of Melozzo da
Forli, tell, in a few words, what Sixtus did for Rome .—

> Templa domum expositus ; vicos, fora, mœnia, pontes .
> Virgineam Trivii quod reparans aquam
> Prisca licet nautis statuas dare commoda portus
> Et Vaticanum cingere Sixte ingum :
> Plus tamen Urbs debet   nam quæ squalore latebat
> Cernitur (sic) in celebri bibliotheca loco ‡

The approach of the Jubilee Year was, as we have shewn,
the primary occasion of the external renovation of the Eternal
City, and her transformation from the mediæval type to one
in keeping with the advancing needs of the age.   At the
present day there are but few parts of Rome that give any

* GREGOROVIUS, VII , 639, 3rd ed. See MUNTZ, III , 11, and
REUMONT, III , 1, 402

† See REUMONT in the Lit Rundschau, 1878, p 334, and MUNTZ,
III , 17

‡ See SCHMARSOW, 37   Milanesi has shewn that Baccio Pontelli
was never Sixtus IV's chief Architect , Meo del Caprino, Giovanni de'
Dolci, Giacomo da Pietrasanta, and others were employed in that
capacity.

idea of the City as it was four hundred years ago.   There was an irregular collection of narrow, crooked, and dirty streets, in which the common requirements of a great town were utterly neglected.   In many cases, projecting porticoes, stalls, and balconies seriously obstructed the ordinary traffic, not to speak of that which might be expected in the Jubilee Year.   In some places, two horsemen could not pass each other.   Pavements, with the exception of some which had been begun in the time of Nicholas V , were almost unknown, either in the middle of the streets or alongside of the houses.*

Into this gloomy and unhealthy chaos Sixtus IV., following the schemes of Nicholas V., first brought air and light.   The most important streets were paved, and it then became possible to think of cleansing them.†   We have already spoken of the difficulties encountered in the work of widening the streets, which was undertaken in preparation for the Jubilee Year.‡   The Pope, however, was not to be deterred from it.   In January, 1480, he began by the removal of the armourers' shops on the Bridge of S Angelo. " The Romans at first opposed this innovation, but soon became reconciled to what was a real benefit."§   In June of

---

* See REUMONT, III , 1, 403 *seq*

† CORIO, 264, expressly states that the measures of Sixtus IV. rendered Rome more healthy.   It is hard to realise the state of the streets in former times.   Many of the principal thoroughfares in London were not paved until the 15th or 16th Century.   Berlin was not completely paved even in the earlier half of the past Century , and its streets were not swept before the year 1600   The highly-civilised Italian cities were the first to have their streets paved ; see the dates in BURCKHARDT, Gesch der Renaissance, 212–13

‡ See *supra*, p 276 *seq*.

§ GREGOROVIUS, VII., 631, 3rd ed.   " Every one nowadays," says SCHMARSOW, 149, " takes the part of the energetic Pope who proceeded relentlessly against these abuses, although Roman chroniclers of his own time complain of his tyranny."

the same year an order was promulgated, requiring that "in all the most frequented streets projections should be cleared away, pavements laid down, at least at the sides, houses jutting out into the street wholly or partially removed, the ruined ones rebuilt, new squares laid out and those already existing widened and made more symmetrical Cardinal d'Estouteville was to superintend these improvements." *
The Pope himself came from time to time to ascertain personally how his directions were being carried out.

In the Leonine City he laid out a handsome street, originally known by his own name, extending from the moat of the Castle to the great gate of the Papal Palace (now Borgo S Angelo) ,† a third street here met the old Via de' Cavalli, which took much the same direction as the present Borgo S^{to} Spirito, and the old Via Santa, now Borgo Vecchio. The erection of the Ponte Sisto effected a complete transformation in that part of the City which lay on the right bank of the Tiber Sigismondo de' Conti says that, in consequence of the accommodation afforded by the Bridge, this dirty and uninhabited district became thickly populated ‡ Distinguished persons built houses there, and, even to the present day, the Vicolo Riario, near the Corsini Palace, remains as a memento of the villa belonging to that family which was situated there.§

Besides all that he did for the Library, Sixtus IV carried

---

* REUMONT, III , 1, 404 , MUNIZ, III , 182 , MARCELLINO DA CIVEZZA, III , 92 , P. BELLONI, La costituzione " Quae publice utilia . . ." intorno al decoro publ. e la città di Roma, 11 (Roma, 1870)

† ADINOLFI, Portica, 51 and 218 *seq* , FORCELLA, XIII., 68, 78, 85 The *Eulogy of Sixtus IV* , mentioned *supra*, p. 209, note *, expressly lays stress on the formation of the Via Sistina Cod 2403, f. 11, Court Library, Vienna

‡ SIGISMONDO DE' CONTI, I , 204

§ See BURRIEL, Caterina Sforza. I , 31

on other works of restoration in the Vatican, and built the Chapel which bears his name.   The interior of the Palace was fitted up anew, and a barrack erected for the guard   The roof of St Peter's, its Sacristy, and the Chapel of S. Petronilla were restored, and the Tabernacle of the Confession and the Chapel of the Immaculate Conception were constructed *

We have already spoken of the restoration of the churches before and during the Jubilee Year †   These works were very rapidly carried on, and Sixtus IV. also found time for building new churches.   Foremost among these we must mention Sᵗᵃ Maria del Popolo, begun in 1472, and Sᵗ Maria della Pace, both of which are worthy memorials of the Pope's devotion to the Queen of Heaven. Sᵗᵃ Maria del Popolo is a Basilica, with three naves surrounded by chapels, and with an octagonal dome supported on a drum, the first of the kind erected in Rome ; unlike the other buildings of the period, which were, for the most part, very hurriedly built, the façade of the year 1477 is a good specimen of pure Renaissance.‡

Sᵗᵃ Maria del Popolo was the favourite church of the Pope and of the Rovere family.   Sixtus IV. visited it almost every week, and the chief events of his reign were mostly celebrated there.

The Cardinals, especially his nephews, followed the Pope's

* MUNTZ, III., 111, 139, 147 ; SCHMARSOW, 229   Regarding the Tabernacle of the Confession, probably erected in 1475, see Jahrb der Preuss Kunstsammlungen, VIII , 12 seq.

† Supra, p 275

‡ SCHMARSOW, 113–14, see pp. 35, 115, 117 , REUMONT, III , 1, 408 ; FORCELLA, I., 319 seq.; FRANTZ, 167 ; PAPENCORDT, 521   "In the edifices of the time of Sixtus IV," says SPRINGER, Rafael, 103, "we observe that massive forms and grand proportions are avoided ; they have, however, the advantage of presenting in their interior ample space for sculpture and painting"   See infra, p 465 seq.

example. "Two Churches and palatial Convents, S. Pietro in Vincoli and SS Apostoli, are, in their entirety, memorials of the Rovere"* In the first-named Basilica, Cardinal Giuliano continued the work of his uncle, and in the latter, that of the nephew, Pietro Riario. This Cardinal also restored the portico of S Agnese.†

The Castles of Grottaferrata and Ostia, in the neighbourhood of Rome, are also abiding monuments of the powerful Cardinal. After the death of Bessarion, Grottaferrata was granted *in commendam* to Giuliano, who at once began to build there On account of the strategical importance of its position, the Convent was surrounded by a fortification. Those who have visited the Alban hills will remember this "incomparably picturesque group of buildings at the foot of the green hills of Tusculum, on a smooth space overshadowed by old elms and plane-trees"‡ The Castle of Ostia is of kindred character—even now, "in its decay, the most beautiful ruin of the later mediæval period in the vicinity of Rome", but the surrounding landscape is very different. Grottaferrata lies amidst rich fields and fruitful hills, about Ostia is a "melancholy, silent tract of barren, low-lying ground, formed of rubbish and sand-hills," through which the yellow, sluggish stream makes its way to the sea A long inscription on the principal tower of the Castle records that "Giuliano of Savona erected this stronghold as a refuge from

* GREGOROVIUS, VII, 635, 3rd ed. See MUNTZ, Anciennes Basiliques, 21 *seq*. Vasari has assigned to Pontelli a share in the building of SS Apostoli; this cannot however be admitted. Muntz supposes Giovanni de' Dolci to have been the Architect of this church JANITSCHEK in the Repertorium, IV, 214, concludes from its style, that it is the work of Giacomo da Pietrasanta

† FORCELLA, II, 228, X, 350

‡ REUMONT, III, 1, 409, and SCHMARSOW, 19 and 118 See also ROCCHI, 103 *seq*.

the perils of the sea, a protection to the Roman Campagna, a defence to Ostia, and to the mouth of the Tiber" He began it in the reign of Pope Sixtus IV, his uncle, and concluded the work by digging out, at his own expense, the moat which had been silted up by the river in the time of Pope Innocent VIII., in the year of Salvation 1486, the 2115th after the building of Ostia, the 2129th after Ancus, the founder of the city   The architect of the Castle at Ostia and probably also of the fortifications at Grottaferrata, was the celebrated Giuliano Giamberti, surnamed da San Gallo *

Before Cardinal Giuliano built the Castle of Ostia, the wealthy d'Estouteville, its Bishop, had provided the ruined city with walls, streets, and houses †   In 1479, d'Estouteville, who had, two years previously, succeeded Orsini as Camerlengo, began to rebuild the Church of S Agostino in Rome · this work was completed in four years ‡   He was also a great benefactor to other Roman Churches, especially to Sta Maria Maggiore and S Luigi de' Francesi.§

Mention has already been made of the buildings erected by Cardinal Domenico della Rovere.   Girolamo Basso della Rovere completed the Pilgrimage Church at Loreto, and

---

* GUGLIELMOTTI'S work, Della rocca d Ostia, &c , Roma, 1862, is admirable   See also REUMONT, III, 1, 410 *seq*, 519   For an account of Giuliano's magnificent constructions in Bologna, see Atti dell' Emilia, II , 194 *seq*, and SPRINGER, Rafael, 104

† See Anecdota Veneta, ed CONTARINI, 267 , ARMELLINI, 145

‡ SCHMARSOW, 145   See MUNTZ, III , 41 , JANITSCHEK'S Repert , IV , 76 , ARMELLINI, 107 , FORCELLA, V , 18.   Regarding the removal of the market from the Capitol to Piazza Navona by order of d'Estouteville, see CANCELLIERI, Il Mercato, 16 (1811)

§ DE ANGELIS, Basilicae S Mariae Majoris descriptio, 137 *seq.*; BARBIER DE MONTAULT, Le Card d'Estouteville bienfaiteur des Églises de Rome (Angers, 1859), and Inventaires des établ. nationaux de S Louis des Français et de S Sauveur in Thermis à Rome (Paris, 1861) , also MUNTZ, III., 285 *seq*.

caused the Cappella del Tesoro to be painted by Melozzo da Forli ; the paintings, which are in excellent preservation, are very original and striking * Another important edifice of this time was the Palace of Cardinal Stefano Nardini (Palazzo del Governo Vecchio), built in 1475 "It is the last Roman Palace which still retains something of the character of the mediæval fortress "†

It would take too long to go further into details. The relations of Sixtus IV. were undoubtedly admirable patrons of Arts , the armorial bearings of Riario Rovere and Basso on many ancient piles bear witness to their splendid achievements in this line.

Sixtus also did much in the way of restoring the bridges, walls, gates, towers, and other buildings of the City ‡ At the Capitol these works were connected with the opening of a museum of antiquities, the first public collection of the kind in Italy, and indeed in Europe § The practical Sixtus IV , by admitting the public to visit the collection, rendered it more popular than it had been in the time of its founder, Paul II Museums now began to appear everywhere in connection with and as supplementing the Libraries • The characters of distinguished men frequently present great contradictions, and we find Sixtus IV., almost simultaneously with the opening of the Capitoline Museum, dispersing many of the costly treasures of the Palace of S Marco. With similar inconsistency, he restored the equestrian statue of Marcus Aurelius and destroyed many ancient

* A detailed description is given by SCHMARSOW, 124 seq

† GREGOROVIUS, VII , 638, 3rd ed See FORCELLA, XIII , 171. An inscription on a restoration undertaken by Cardinal Gonzaga in Bologna is given in Atti dell' Emilia, II , 188

‡ MUNTZ, III , 188 seq , FORCELLA, XIII , 13.

§ MUNTZ, III , 168 seq , and Le musée du Capitole, Paris, 1882 See also MARCELLINO DA CIVEZZA, III , 91.

temples and triumphal arches.* But, however great the
injury he may have inflicted on the ancient monuments, it
was more than outweighed by his artistic embellishment of
Rome, to which he imparted a completely new aspect. In
order to encourage building in his capital, and to increase
the number of its inhabitants, he had, in 1475, conferred the
right of ownership on all who should build houses within
the City district †

One of the most beneficial works accomplished by Sixtus
IV. was the restoration of the Hospital of S^to Spirito, a
foundation of Innocent III, which had fallen into decay.‡
Pity for children deserted by unnatural mothers induced
this Pope, whom his enemies depict as another Nero, to
adopt Eugenius IV.'s undertaking. When Sixtus IV., in
his frequent visits to the dilapidated house, saw these poor,
forsaken children at play, his heart was touched, and he
decided to have the Hospital thoroughly rebuilt and richly
endowed. " He engaged the best Architects, hired a number
of labourers, and commenced operations at once. Sixtus
IV. considerably extended the original plan , he provided
portions for the girls as they grew up, so that they might
not be exposed, without resources, to the temptations of the
world." § Although the building was certainly hurried on

* See MUNTZ, III, 15 By a special Bull of 1474, Sixtus IV.
protected the old Basilicas , MUNIZ, Anc. Basil, 8

† THEINER, Cod, III , 480–81 See MARCELLINO DA CIVEZZA, II.,
725

‡ " . . Verum hoc quum longa vetustas
    Demolita foret, vix reliquiae ut remanerent,
    Sixtus id instaurat novaque omnia sumptibus illic
    Efficit immensis "

These lines are from the *Poem, cited *p. 209, note * , which is in Cod.
2403, f 12, Court Library, Vienna

§ PLATINA, Sixtus IV., 1064 , SIGISMONDO DE' CONTI, I , 205 , Bull ,
226 , FRANTZ, 165 S. Spirito was situated on the Tiber, and most

for the Jubilee Year, it was not until 1482 that the works were completed.   The Architect of the whole is unknown , he could not have been Baccio Pontelli, who, until 1482, lived at Pisa and Urbino, not in Rome.   Sixtus IV also shewed his predilection for the Order of the Holy Ghost and for the Hospital " by a grant of various privileges and an increase of its fixed revenues "* Following the example of Eugenius IV., he re-established the confraternity in the spring of 1478, and himself became a member.†   All the Cardinals and the whole Court followed him.   From that time forward, it became more and more the custom to enter this pious society.   The Confraternity-book of S^{to} Spirito has accordingly become, in its way, a unique collection of autographs ‡

of the German Hospitals of the Holy Ghost were also by the water, partly for sanitary reasons; see Zeitschr des Vereins fur Erforschung Rheinisch Gesch, II, Part 4 (Mainz, 1864)   A ground-plan of the whole institution is given by LETAROUILLY, Édifices de Rome, III., Pl 256

* BROCKHAUS, S. Spirito, 284-5, 289, 290   See also, in regard to Pontelli, REDTENBACHER, 147.

† Not 1477, as GREGOROVIUS, VII., 633, 3rd ed, and BROCKHAUS, 285, N 10, state , in Bull , 245 *seq* , for A° VI should be *read* A° VII , as RAYNALDUS, ad an. 1477, N 12, has it, and, which is conclusive, the *Confraternity-book in the Archives of S^{to} Spirito, f 65   The Bull was printed at the time (HAIN, pp. 14809-12)   Only these Latin editions were hitherto known, but a German one also exists.   In 1885 a copy of this most rare early-printed book (*s l e. a*, fol 6 sheets) was offered by the antiquary, Alb Cohn, in Berlin (Mohrenstrasse, No 53, Catalogue 164, No 429), for forty marks

‡ See DUDIK, I, 86 ; GREGOROVIUS, *loc cit* , and Mon Vat Hist Hung illust, Ser I, Tom V, Budapest, 1889   The following entry, written in a firm hand, at f 69 of the *Confraternity-book, is interesting · "Ego Rodericus de Boria episcopus Portuen card^{lis} et ep Valent S R E. vicecancellarius intravi predict sanct confraternitatem die XXI Martii, 1478, ea mente ut indulgentiam prefatam a S D N concessam consequar ideo propria manu me suscripsi." Archives of S^{to} Spirito.

The magnificent scale on which the reconstruction of this Hospital was carried out, so that even Alberti was satisfied with it, is an abiding memorial of the benevolence of Sixtus IV. Much pains were bestowed on the decoration of the interior , the spacious and airy hall for the sick was ornamented with frescoes as far as the tops of the windows, and above them with a broad frieze of pictures arranged in panels. Attention has recently been directed to these half-faded paintings, which are of the ancient Umbrian type They portray the foundation of the Hospital by Innocent III., and, in a very attractive form, the life of Sixtus IV. from his birth. The inscriptions under them are from the pen of Bartolomeo Platina *

The architectural works of Sixtus IV. extended to almost all the cities of the States of the Church, and even as far as Savona and Avignon. Assisi, Bertinoro, Bieda, Bologna, Caprarola, Cascia, Cesena, Citerna, Città di Castello, Civita Vecchia, Corneto, Fano, Foligno, Forlì, Monticelli, Nepi, Orvieto, Ronciglione, Santa Marinella, Soriano, Spoleto, Sutri, Terracina, Tivoli, Todi, Tolfa, Veroli, and Viterbo, were all, in this respect, indebted to this Pontiff †

* To BROCKHAUS belongs the merit of having first appreciated these frescoes, which are not even mentioned by Crowe-Cavalcaselle , he gives a minute description of them, 429 *seq* See also SCHMARSOW, 202 *seq* , who establishes Platina's authorship of the inscriptions A copy of the legend under each picture is given in Cod Barb , XXX, 113, *f* 80, of the Barberini Library. VILLENEUVE, 8, is mistaken in his observations regarding this MS.

† See the accounts from the Archives given by MUNTZ, 207–39 To supplement these, see also *supra*, p 427, and, with regard to what was done in Assisi, CRISTOFANI, 332 *seq* , LASPEYRES, 7, 10, 13, 14, 32 *seq*.; and REDTENBACHER, 164 , for those at Bologna, a **Brief of the 10th Nov , 1471, in the State Archives of that city. A *Brief to Savona (*s d* preceding one of the 17th April, 1483) begins with these words . * " Magno tenemur desiderio, ut capella quam in ecclesia

It is worthy of remark that Sixtus IV.'s patronage of the Arts was universal in its character.   Sculpture was encouraged in the persons of Verocchio and Pollajuolo, and he also did much for the promotion of the minor arts , medallists, engravers, glass-makers, cabinet-makers, goldsmiths, weavers, and embroiderers were all employed by him, and he also took an interest in pottery.*

In his orders for Works of Art, the Pope did not spare expense, as is evident from the fact that the Tiara made for him cost over 100,000 ducats.   In this, as in all other things, he fully realised that the duties of a Pope are very different from those of the General of a Mendicant Order †

The artistic chronicle of this pontificate is not yet exhausted   Sixtus IV. seems to have been even more active as a promoter of painting than as a builder   His practical spirit was shewn in his command, that the painters settled in Rome should form themselves into a Guild and draw up statutes ; and this was the beginning of the famous Academy of St. Luke ‡

B. Francisci istius civitatis construi facimus absolvatur et perficiatur " They were to take care that this should be speedily done   (Lib brev, 15, f 489, Secret Archives of the Vatican)   In Viterbo a palatium ad habitationem presidis provincie patrimonii was built (see the *Decree of Card Sansoni, dated Viterbo, 1484, Mai 18, Lib brev , 17, f 37, Secret Archives of the Vatican) · this building, now the Palazzo Pubblico, still bears the Pope's arms with the inscription   Sixtus IIII., Pont Max

* UGOLINI, II , 530, and REUMONT, III , 1, 520

† MUNTZ, III., 30 , REUMONT, III , 1, 426   Here is an account of the medals and coins of Sixtus IV   See also MUNTZ, Atelier monét , p 2 , Jahrb der Preuss . Kunstsammlungen, II , 105, 232–3, III , 143. The influence of the Renaissance on the leaden seals attached to the Bulls of Sixtus IV., is noticed by MAS-LATRIE in the Rev. des Quest. Hist , 1887, Avril, p 433 *seq.*

‡ MISSIRINI, Mem. p serv alla storia della Romana Accademia di S Luca, Roma, 1823 , PIAZZA, Opere pie, 621 , SCHMARSOW, 149 *seq* , MUNTZ, III , 99–111.

Sixtus IV was, in fact, for Painters what Nicholas V. had been for Architects We find, employed in his service, men whose names are held in honour by the whole civilised world Ghirlandajo, Botticelli, Signorelli, Perugino, Pinturicchio, and finally, the great Melozzo da Forli *

This last-named artist was specially in touch with the stately characteristics of the Rovere family. Every one who has visited the Vatican galleries must remember Melozzo's picture of Sixtus IV, surrounded by his kindred, appointing Platina Prefect of the Vaticana. This was originally a fresco, and was afterwards transferred to canvas. If no other work of Melozzo's had been preserved, this one, " which captivates the eye at once by its simple and reposeful presentation of clearly defined personalities," would suffice to give us a very high idea of the painter's power †

This magnificent picture was painted in 1476 and 1477. In the following year the master was working at Loreto, in 1479 he decorated the Chapel of the Choir in St Peter's, and during 1480 and 1481 he was fully occupied in painting the Vatican Library.‡ Vasari does not mention any of these works, or, indeed, any one of Melozzo's, with the exception of his picture of the Ascension in the Church of SS. Apostoli. This, the most splendid masterpiece produced in Rome during the pontificate of Sixtus IV., was unfortunately

* See MUNTZ, III , 89 seq. Pinturicchio worked, in the first instance, in the Sistine Chapel as assistant to Perugino, who was eight years his senior, and afterwards independently in the Capella Bufalini of Sta Maria in Araceli , see SCHMARSOW, B. Pinturicchio in Rom (Stuttgart, 1882), and Gott. Gel Anz , 1884, p 796 seq. Regarding Signorelli's sojourn in Rome (1482-83), see VISCHER, L Signorelli und die Ital Renaissance, 88 (Leipzig, 1879).

† SCHMARSOW, 1 seq , 42-8, 162 seq., 204, 311. The Arundel Society has brought out a very good chromo-lithograph of this picture. The wood-cut in LUTZOW, 425, is unsatisfactory.

‡ SCHMARSOW, 167.

destroyed, all but a few fragments, when the church was
rebuilt in 1711. Vasari, who saw it, speaks of it with
enthusiasm "The figure of Christ," he says, "is so skilfully
fore-shortened, that it appears to pierce the vaulting, and the
surrounding angels equally seem to be soaring or floating in
air. The Apostles, in their various attitudes, are also drawn
with such admirable adaptation to the eye of the spectator,
who views them from below, as to have won for Melozzo
the highest praise from the artists both of his own day and
of ours The buildings in the picture display a perfect
mastery of the laws of perspective."* The few remains of
this painting still extant in the Chapter-house of St. Peter's
and in the Quirinal, are just sufficient to enable us to
guess what the beauty of the whole must have been.† A
recent writer justly observes · "In boldness of conception,
in largeness and freedom of execution, the fresco in the
tribune of SS. Apostoli is a real masterpiece, and is an
unanswerable proof of the excellence which it was given to
this artist to attain."‡

The Chapel in the Vatican which bears the name of
Sixtus IV contains many splendid memorials of his artistic
tastes. This simple and noble edifice was begun in 1473 §

* VASARI, Opere, III, 52, and SCHMARSOW, 167 *seq*, and p 71
regarding Melozzo as the special inventor of the "sotto in su."

† Authentic original photographs of the figures of the four Apostles,
five Angels, and Christ, have been for the first time, published by
SCHMARSOW, Plates, 13–22 The Arundel Society has a chromo-
lithograph of two Angels

‡ SCHMARSOW, 175, who is disposed to adopt 1481 as the year in
which this painting was completed Against the earlier view, that
this great work was accomplished under the auspices of Cardinal P.
Riario, see also Gott Gel Anz, 1882, p. 1616 *seq*.

§ PLATTNER-BUNSEN, Beschreibung von Rom, II, 1, 245. In the
Vierteljahrsschrift fur Musikwissenschaft, III, 234, Haberl seems to
think that the Chapel was finished as early as 1473 In the *Eulogy

and finished in 1481 Vasari attributes the Cappella Sistina to Baccio Pontelli, but this is a mistake. It is the work of the Florentine, Giovannino de' Dolci, who must be looked upon as Sixtus IV.'s head Architect The Sistina, henceforth the special Papal Chapel for ecclesiastical ceremonies of a semi-public character, is in form a parallelogram, and measures 132 feet by 45. "For two-thirds of its height the wall on the longer sides is unbroken, then there is a cornice, and above this six round-headed windows, formerly there were two similar ones on the altar side, but these are now blocked up Their position, however, is shewn by two false ones, painted with a fac-simile of the glass that filled them, on the opposite wall adjoining the Sala Regia. Each of these latter windows has a bull's eye in the centre. In the interior, all architectural divisions are purposely avoided, with the exception of the cornice, about 3 feet in width and provided with an iron balustrade, which runs round beneath the windows. The ceiling forms a shallow circular vault resting upon brackets, and is pierced by a skylight over each of the windows. The whole was, from the first, evidently intended to be covered with paintings"*

written in 1477, which has been mentioned *supra*, p. 209, note *, the following passage occurs —

> *" Quumque intra divi sacra ipsa palatia Petri
> Nonnullas pater ille domos ornat reparatque
> Tum illic aedificat pulchrum praestansque sacellum
> Quod quum perfectum fuerit pleneque politum
> Taleque iam factum, quale ipsum destinat auctor
> Amplo et celso animo, tum demum fas erit illud
> Praesulis absque pari monumentum dicere Sixti "

Cod 2403, f 11b, Court Library, Vienna

* SCHMARSOW, 208 See BURCKHARDT, Cicerone, 99 Regarding the Architect of the Sistina, who had settled in Rome in the time of Nicholas V., and was much employed by Pius II, and appointed

A richly-sculptured balustrade of white marble, with the arms of Sixtus IV., divides the space in front intended for the Pope and the Cardinals from that of the laity. The tribune for the singers, which projects but slightly to the left, is similarly enclosed The floor is beautifully inlaid in stone.

For the decoration of this modest and unpretending building, Sixtus IV. summoned to his Court all the most distinguished painters of Umbria and Tuscany. Domenico Ghirlandajo, Sandro Botticelli, Luca Signorelli, Cosimo Roselli, Pietro Perugino, and Pinturicchio vied with each other in a noble rivalry in its embellishment.* The time taken to complete the paintings on the walls of the Sistina, which were begun in the year 1480, "greatly tried the patience of the Pope. Like Julius II. at a later period, when Michael Angelo was painting the roof, Sixtus IV. could scarcely bear to wait for the termination of the work On the anniversary of his election, the vigil of S. Lawrence," Jacobus Volaterranus tells us, "he came unannounced, and quite against his usual custom (extra ordinem), to Vespers in the Chapel to see how the frescoes were getting on. At last, on the 15th August, 1483, came the long-desired day of their completion"† On the Feast of the Assumption of our Lady, which that year fell on a Saturday, the Pope, we learn from a contemporary, came to the new Chapel and

praesidens fabricae under Paul II , see MUNTZ, Giovannino de' Dolci con docum. inediti , Roma, 1880

* LERMOLIEFF (Die Werke Italienischer Meister, 304 seq , Leipzig, 1880) infers, from the landscape, the composition, and many peculiarities, that Pinturicchio probably executed the pictures of the Baptism of Christ and the journey of Moses, which Perugino had been commissioned to paint This is not the place for a more detailed treatment of the subject, on which see SCHMARSOW, B Pinturicchio in Rom (Stuttgart, 1882), and Preuss Jahrb , XLVII , 50 seq , XLVIII., 129.

† JACOBUS VOLATERRANUS, 188, SCHMARSOW, 209-10 Volaterranus is as trustworthy in his dates as Infessura is the reverse.

there heard Mass There was no further ceremony All
the Prelates and some others assisted at the function. The
only Cardinal present was Raffaelo Sansoni. This was the
first Mass said after the completion of the Chapel, and only
the ecclesiastics belonging to it attended In commemora-
tion of the event, the Pope published an Indulgence for all
who should visit the sanctuary, including women Sixtus
IV. also attended Vespers there that same day The Prelates were placed below Cardinal Sansoni on the benches
assigned to the Sacred College. The Pope blessed the
people, both at Mass and at Vespers When it became
known that an Indulgence had been granted to those who
should visit the Chapel, the whole City was astir in a
moment The crowd in the Sistina was so great that it was
extremely difficult either to enter or to leave the Church,
and the throng continued to pass through until after mid-
night. On the Pope's coronation day, the first solemn High
Mass was celebrated in the new Chapel , Giuliano della
Rovere being celebrant and all the Cardinals assisting.*

The whole series in the Sistina consisted originally of
fifteen frescoes, twelve of which still remain on its longer
sides, the other three having given place to Michael Angelo's
colossal picture of the Last Judgment.† On the left wall,
looking to the right from the altar, are represented events
from the history of Moses. According to the custom and
taste of the period, several scenes are grouped in the same
picture around the principal subject. Moses slaying the
Egyptian, driving away the shepherds who hindered Jethro's
daughter from drawing water, going into Egypt, and, with
his sandals put away, worshipping God in the burning

* Jacobus Volaterranus, *loc. cit.*

† The series of the life of Moses and of Christ has thus been
deprived of its beginning.

bush, are thus combined, due to the pencil of Botticelli.
The whole forms "a masterpiece of vivid feeling and
expression and technical facility."*

Signorelli's farewell and death of Moses is another glorious
creation, full of dramatic power.   In contemplating it, " we
perceive at once that the artist was thoroughly aware that
the strength of his rivals lay in composition and in the
management of light and shade.   In his grouping, largeness
of conception and combination are united with great
clearness of detail.   The drawing is bold and strongly
marked, and the entire execution bears the impress of great
care and taste, as also the employment of gold on the
draperies."†

On the right wall are paintings by Pinturicchio, Botticelli,
Ghirlandajo, Roselli, and Perugino, representing scenes from
the life of our Lord.   Two of these frescoes, the Vocation
of SS Peter and Andrew, by Ghirlandajo, and St Peter
receiving the Keys, by Perugino, "stand out from among
the other mural paintings in so marked a manner, indicating
the approaching triumph of the noble ideal style in art,
that nothing but the overpowering proximity of Michael
Angelo's work could prevent the immediate recognition of
this important fact."‡   All artists agree in considering
Perugino's Institution of the Primacy "one of his most
perfect productions."   The solemn grandeur of this marvel-

* RUMOHR, II, 272.   See The Ecclesiologist, XXIX, 195   The
date of Botticelli's arrival in Rome is uncertain, according to
LIPPMANN in the Jahrb. der Preuss Kunstsammlungen, IV., 71, perhaps
it may have been in October, 1482.

† CROWE-CAVALCASELLE, IV, 8–9, who also remarks " Signorelli
unquestionably deserves a place of honour among the painters of the
Sistina", see also BURCKHARDT, Cicerone, 552.   Roselli's pictures
are the least successful, Sixtus IV.'s expression of opinion regarding
them is, however, a mere legend ; see RIO, II, 65 and 83

‡ SCHMARSOW, 227.

lous creation fully corresponds with the dignity of its subject, and this latter is enhanced to the imagination by
the situation of the picture

Ghirlandajo, however, surpassed all his companions. His
masterly genius enabled him to grasp the vocation of SS.
Peter and Andrew in its most impressive and solemn
aspect. "His picture is, so to speak, a foreshadowing of
Raphael's Miraculous draught of Fishes and Feed my
Sheep."*

The wall behind the altar was adorned by a painting of
the Assumption of our Lady, with Sixtus IV. praying
beneath it. Vasari believes this to be the work of Perugino,
but Sigismondo de' Conti remarks, in regard to this fresco,
that the Blessed Virgin seems actually to rise from the
earth towards Heaven ;† Perugino never possessed the art
of fore-shortening in its perfection "So marvellous is the
view from beneath, so real the ascent towards Heaven, that
no man then living, save Melozzo da Forli, could have
created the like," and the most recent investigations are
perhaps right in assigning the work to the great Master,
who has been called the forerunner of Raphael and
Michael Angelo.‡

As we survey this sanctuary of Italian Renaissance, we
cannot fail to acknowledge that the choice of subjects for
the frescoes in the Papal Chapel could not have been improved.§ To the chief scenes from the life of Moses on the

---

* BURCKHARDT, Cicerone, 552. See PLATTNER-BUNSEN, Beschreibung der Stadt Rom, II , 1, 252, and The Ecclesiologist, XXIX , 195
seq

† SIGISMONDO DE' CONTI, I , 205

‡ SCHMARSOW, 214 , see 317 seq   In the Repert , XI., 199, are to
be found Janitschek's remarks in support of a contrary opinion

§ See PRUDENTIUS ROMANUS, Romisches Leben, in the Wiener
"Vaterland," 1888, May 20, and REUMONT'S Romische Briefe, I , 75
seq.

one side, correspond on the other those from the life of our Lord, as the fulfilment of their typical signification What Moses, the leader of the chosen people, foreshadowed, has been perfected by Christ for all time   Peter, who lives in his successors here, reigns as the Vicar of Christ.   Through him the human race is brought to the Saviour, as the Jewish nation, the type of Christendom, was led by Moses to the feet of the Christ.   The development of the whole plan of Salvation is concentrated in the three names : Moses, Christ, Peter   Thus, the magnificent drama of the Story of the Church is presented to the spectator as the Life and the Truth in the frescoes of this Chapel, which, in its historical aspect, is the most remarkable in the world, and thus worthily was the building fitly inaugurated, which after-wards, under another Pope of the house of Rovere, was to be enriched with the marvellous productions of the giant genius of Michael Angelo.

APPENDIX

OF

UNPUBLISHED DOCUMENTS

AND

EXTRACTS FROM ARCHIVES.

APPENDIX.

I. CARDINAL AMMANATI TO FRANCESCO SFORZA, DUKE
OF MILAN *

1464, Sept 1, Rome

La Ex V. havera inteso la nova creatione del pontefice et forse
in se medesma pensera quanto sia da stimarla   Signore, primum
et ante omnia, questi r^{mi} cardinali antichi, creati da altri papi che
Pio deliberorno unanimiter fra loro de non eleggere se non de loro
medesmi parendoli che N S. defuncto per esser stato pocho nel
cardinalato non li havesse charezati ne stimati tanto quanto
haveriano voluto, che imputavano allo haver poco provato ch' è
esser cardinale.   Ne da questo proposito se potiano revocare.
Alchuni de novi, non essendo dacordo, ne vedendo haverli a
riescire il fatto loro proprio per gratificarsi se ne andorono con li
prefati antichi.   Onde che ancora io vedendo la necessita della
cosa per non esser scluso dalla gratia sua et perche sempre me
haveva mostrata optima voluntà verso de V Ex. ne andai con li
altri.   A Dio se vole referire tutto che in tal loco et tempo mirab-
iliter opera.   Io sono de opinione ch' ogni giorno piu V Ex sara
satisfacta et che le demonstrationi et opere de questo pontifice ve
saranno accepte et grate et il parlare suo quotidiano assai efficace-
mente lo demonstra . . . .

[Original in Ambrosian Library, Milan.   Cod Z -219, Supp]

* The above letter is entirely in his own handwriting , see *supra*, p 13

2. JOHANNES PETRUS ARRIVABENUS TO MARCHIONESS BARBARA
OF MANTUA.*

1464, Sept 2, Rome.

The Archbishop of Spalatro (L. Zane), che foe nepote del
vicecancelliere vechio è facto thesaurere.† El rev. monsignor
vicecancelliere secondo el iudicio havera gran conditione et
merito chè s'è fatigato a la real.‡

[Original in Gonzaga Archives, Mantua.]

3 CARDINAL GONZAGA TO HIS FATHER, LODOVICO DE
GONZAGA §

1464, Sept. 4, Rome.

. Costui comincia a far del altiero e molto stima suoa
dignitate; puoria accadere chel concilio che è statuito de far in
termino de tre anni lo faria puoi humiliare

[Original in Gonzaga Archives, Mantua]

4 JOHANNES PETRUS ARRIVABENUS TO MARCHIONESS BARBARA
OF MANTUA.

1464, Oct. 3, Rome

The Plague is raging in Rome.‖ Questo papa ha mutato la
stampa del piombo de le bolle, da un canto fa S. Paulo e S. Petro
che sedeno; da l' altro lui è in cattedra e doi cardinali presso cum
alcune persone denanti in ginochione ¶

Discontent on the part of the Secretaries, because most of them
had not yet had audience.** The influence of the Bishop of
Vicenza with Paul II ††

[Original in the Gonzaga Archives, Mantua]

---

* See *supra*, p 124   † See GOTTLOB, Cam. Apost.
‡ This account of Card Borgia is repeated by J. P. Arrivabenus in a
*Despatch of 4th Sept , 1464 * "El rev mons vicecancelliere ha gran credito
et certo l'ha meritato cum costui " (Gonzaga Archives.) Regarding Borgia's
part in the Conclave, which is here alluded to, see also *supra*, p. 12.
§ See *supra*, p 25   ‖ See *supra*, p 29, note §.
¶ See *supra*, p. 108   All Paul II 's leaden Bulls are distinguished by their
tasteful and delicate execution , see Arch St Ital (3rd series), IX , 2, 195 ; and
Mél d'Archéologie, 1888, p. 454   The Medals of this Pope are equally fine ;
see Jahrbuch der Preuss Kunstsammlungen, II , 92 f
** See *supra*, p 26.   †† See *supra*, p 111 *seq*.

5 JACOPO DE ARETIO TO MARCHIONESS BARBARA OF MANTUA.*

1464, Oct 9, Rome

. . . Lo r^{mo} mons vicecancelliere ne ha hauta una pesta de questa sua malattia insino al presente, pur heri comenzo ad usir fora, non è perho ancor salda la cicatrice de la peste, molto gia giovato l'alegreza che ha hauta de la restitution sua al pristino officio, che papa Pio glavia interdetto; † cum detrimento perho è facta questa restitutione de molti poveretti che haviano compero l'officio et io so uno di quelli, è perho dato ordine che sieno restituiti li denari che difficil cosa sira perche non è picciola somma onde forse per questa casone qualche sancto ce aiutera   .

[Original in Gonzaga Archives, Mantua]

6. TRISTANO SFORZA TO FRANCESCO SFORZA, DUKE OF MILAN ‡

1464, Oct 21, Rome.

. . . Disse§ poy come con Veneciani non credeva poter mantener amicitia perche erano molti in quel regimento li quali gli erano inimici, item di sua natura erano tanto insolenti che non li potria comportare et diceva che se rendeva certo venendo qua la loro ambasciata, non li stariano XV. di, che seriano in discordia con S Sta .   .

[Original in the Ambrosian Library, Milan   Cod Z-219, Supp]

7 CARDINAL GONZAGA TO HIS MOTHER, MARCHIONESS BARBARA OF MANTUA ||

1464, Dec 28, Rome.

Hoggi havendo terminato la Sta di N S. che li cardinali portino di continuo berette rosse parendo essere colore conveniente a la dignitate, ne donoe una per ciascuno et ha inhibito che in corte niuno altro le posse portare rosse su la fogia da preti et la S Sta portara la beretta e capuzino de cremesino. El di de natale celebroe esso nostro S^{re} et io cantai l'evangelio nel quale me feci grande honore   .

[Original in the Gonzaga Archives, Mantua]

---

* See *supra*, p 38   † See VOIGI, III., 553, N 1.
‡ See *supra*, p 95   § Paul II || See *supra*, p. 25

8. POPE PAUL II TO THE DOGE CRISTOFORO MORO, AND THE
SENATE OF VENICE.*

s. d [1464/5].†

Paulus II . . . . Christoforo Moro duci universoque senatui
Veneto salutem. "Vas electionis, etc." The Pope draws the
attention of the Venetians to the many misfortunes which they
endured, to the calamities in the East, Plague, &c. These are
judgments from God for their cupido dominandi. Intermissa
fidei causa Tergestum ‡ imperialem urbem oppugnare aggressi
quantum eris et temporis perdideritis et quod iacturis affecti
fueritis, ipsa rebus infectis soluta obsidio patefecit Serious charges
are then made against the Venetians ·—(1) You despise the priests
and Bishops, (2) you have occupied lands belonging to the Church,
(3) you have, without permission, imposed tithes on benefices, but
prohibited the Papal tithes, (4) you exclude the clergy from public
offices "ut iam quicunque apost. sedis gratiam promeruerit in
propinquo ab omnibus publicis rebus se cognoscat extorrem."
Warning and admonition to turn from this course.

[Cop s d. Cod. Ottob, 1938, f. 9–16. Vatican Library.]

9. METRICAL INSCRIPTION ON THE CHURCH AND PALACE
OF S MARCO §

Patritius Veneta Paulus de gente secundus
Barbo genus magni princeps vicerector Olympi
Hec patribus monumenta dedit decora alta . . . ‖
Marmoribus templum Marci reparavit et arte
Et posuit latis miranda palatia muris
Cesareae quales fuerant sub collibus aedes
Hinc hortos dryadumque domos et amena vireta
Porticibus circum et niveis lustrata columnis

[Secret Archives of the Vatican, Armar., XXXIX., T. X, f 83b ¶]

---

* See *supra*, p. 96.

† As the contest about tithes lasted until 1468, this very ample letter
(rather a treatise than a letter) may be assigned to a later date I have selected
an earlier one on account of the mention of the war with Trieste.

‡ Manuscript. *Trigrestum.*

§ See *supra*, p. 78.

‖ An illegible word, perhaps meaning "reformans"

¶ These verses are preceded by others, which also occur "in frontispicio

10. Jacopo de Aretio to Marchioness Barbara of Mantua *

1465, Jan. 31, Rome.

. . . La Sta de N. S. sta anchor bene et attende a far una mirabil mitra la qual chiamano el regno, perche se fa al exemplo de quella de S Silvestro cum li tri corone, chiamata el regno, vole anchora come per altra ho scripto che questi r^{mi} s. cardinali usino insegni cioè ornamenti differenti da li altri prelati † et perche similmente è honesto che Sua B^{ne} sia differentiata da li cardinali comenza a usare lo scapuccino de cremesi, non so quello usaranno li cardinali, ditto messer Johanni porra referire. Questo so che S. Sta è molto tenace et strecta a concedere gratie exorbitanti da rasgione come sono dispense et altre gratie difficili et per tanto tutti li officiali se lamentono perho che simili gratie son quelle che mettono dinari in corte per rispecto de le taxe et nel dare audientia S. B. fa a modo usato cioè che pena usa a darla, ma ristora in una cosa che quando la da ascolta volontieri et non fa caso che nel dire l' homo. sia longo . . . .

[Original in the Gonzaga Archives, Mantua.]

11. Augustinus de Rubeis ‡ to Francesco Sforza, Duke of Milan §

1465, April 21, Rome

. . De le altre cerimonie facte per la Sta del N S^{re} a questa pasqua et de una mitria in tre corone papale de precio forsi de piu de LX^m ducati, quale ha facta fare il papa nova, portatola il di de pasqua et con essa celebrata la messa informarà a piena la V Sta praedict Francesco de Varese che ha veduto ogni cosa.‖

[Original in the Ambrosian Library, Milan]

hortorum divi Marci"; Marini, II, 199, has published them without more exactly mentioning their source. Some verses on Paul II's palace, composed by Porcello de' Pandoni, are in Muntz, II., 54 Verses " in laquearibus templi S. Marci" in de Rossi, Inscript., II., 439; see also Mél. d'Archéol, 1888, p 455, N. 3.

* See *supra*, p 26   † See *supra*, p. 477, No 7
‡ Regarding this Ambassador, see also Portioli, 23
§ See *supra*, p 107
‖ I have sought in vain for this Report In the Gonzaga Archives, Mantua, I found a *Letter of Bald Suardo to Marchioness Barbara, which speaks of

12 INSTRUCTION FOR THE MILANESE AMBASSADOR, EMANUEL
DE JACOPO* TO LOUIS XI †

1466, March 3, Milan.

Cose che sono da dire per Emanuele a la M^{ta} del re de Franza
The Venetians are always spreading injurious reports regarding
France.

Item diray a la M^{ta} sua chel ne pare per bene de la M^{ta} Sua che
sopraseda ad dare l' obedientia al papa perche, soprasedendo, el
papa se sforzarà sempre ad compiacergli et fargli cosa grata per
indurlo ad questa obedientia et questo finche la M^{ta} Sua havera
assetato ad suo modo le cose de suo regno, perche dapoy sempre
pora fare quello sera de suo piacere . .

[Copy in National Library, Paris. Fonds Ital., Cod 1611]

13. POPE PAUL II TO BOLOGNA ‡

1466, April 29, Rome

Intelleximus quod Rhenus fluvius qui iam pridem proprium
alveum egressus fuit magnam partem agri nostri Bononiensis
inundat maximumque damnum ex huiusmodi inundatione resultat
tam civibus civitatis nostre Bononie quam incolis comitatus territorii
eiusdem . . .

Yet greater damage is to be feared for the future. Therefore
they are to take measures to have the river led back to its bed
Dat Romae apud S Marcum sub annulo piscatoris die XXIX.
Aprilis 1466 pont. nostri a° 2°

[Original in the State Archives, Bologna, lib. Q.–3]

14 TIMOTEO MAFFEI TO PIERO DE' MEDICI.§

1466, June 15, Rome

The Pope will again take measures to promote peace in Italy,
although he found the Venetians disinclined for it. Tuum dolorem

_____

the new mitre made by order of Paul II   The cost is here estimated at 30,000
ducats; much higher sums are named by CANENSIUS, 43–4, and AMMANATI,
Comment., p 371 (Frankfort ed of 1614).

   * See REUMONT, Diplomazia, 367, and Lettres de Louis XI , III , 10, 55,
145, 327.

   † See *supra*, p. 100   ‡ See *supra*, p 34.
   § See *supra*, pp 86 and 154

tuasque lachrymas, quas pro irruptione Turcorum in Albaniam emisisti, gratas habuit: sed gratiorem oblationem quam illi tuo nomine tuoque iussu feci . . .

[State Archives, Florence Av il princ, f. 17, N. 506]

15 CARDINAL GONZAGA TO MARQUESS LODOVICO OF MANTUA.*

1466, July 5, Rome

Illmo S^r mio patre Veneri proximo † in consistorio la Sta de N. S. molto turbato et alteramente propose che de novo la S. de Vinesia ha fatto publicare ne le terre suoe de vuolere riscuotere da preti sei decime, per la qual graveza pare chel clero se ne sia dogliuto et ha havuto ricorso a la sede apost^{ca}. Parse che la S B^{ne} ne fosse grandemente sdignata e che chi li havesse consentito de facto haveria mandato de la excommunicatione et interdicti cominciando a rumpere cum lor con larme spirituali. Pur essendo iudicata la cosa de grande importantia e digna de molto contrapeso foe determinato che se gli facesse pensiere sopra e puoi nel primo consistorio se pigliasse el partito de quanto se havesse a fare pro honore sedis apostolice Qui è opinione dalcuni che essendo Venetiani secretamente in acordio col Turcho vogliano cum questo riscuotere fare doe cose: restaurarsi de le spese fatte per el passato et occultare tanto piu la intelligentia de la pace col Turcho credendo che quando la brigata veda fare queste aspere exactioni debba stare in opinione che pur siano in guerra dal canto de là . Romae v. Julii, 1466

Ill. D V. filius observ^{mus}.

F. CARD^{LIS} DE GONZAGA

[Original in the Gonzaga Archives, Mantua]

16 CARDINAL GONZAGA TO MARQUESS LODOVICO OF MANTUA ‡

1466, July 19, Marino

. . . Circa quelle decime da Vinesia foe pur concluso doppo molti ragionamenti de mandarli un messo ea de causa ut desisterent da metterle e casu che nol facessero mettere man a l' arme spirituali e mandare excommunicatione et interdicti. Tamen el messo fu

fatto soprastare de qua per alcuni dì che penso sia o per vedere se
interim cum littere et altre trame se puotesse assettare o che el
papa * voglia prima vedere de havere qualche intelligentia o cum
el re Ferando * o cum *qualche potencia* per non rimanere solo a la
pugna . . . Marini, xix Julii, 1466.

[Original in the Gonzaga Archives, Mantua]

17. Bartholomaeus de Maraschis to Marchioness
Barbara of Mantua.†

1466, Sept 1, Rome

A questi di scrissi como in Alemagna era scoperta una setta de
heretici quasi simili a questi fratizelli de la opinione ‡   Qua a la
corte erano mandate littere sopra ciò dal vescovo Laventino al
quale daria pocha fede cum sit chel ne habia puocha se non se
havesse per altre vie questo esser vero, pur ho cercato havere
copia de una littera mandata da esso Laventino al vescovo de
Ratisbona § che in vero è una brutta cossa et questa copia mando
a la Ex. V.   El papa pur ha habuti tri termini de febre terzana,
non grande, credese presto guarirà . . .

[Original in the Gonzaga Archives, Mantua]

18 Cardinal Gonzaga to his Father, Marquess Lodovico
of Mantua ‖

1467, Jan 7, Rome

. . . Questa matina in consistorio secreto fossemo sopra la
materia del soccorso che dimanda el Scandarbec et in summa el
papa disse che li daria cinque milia duc^n ne piu voleva dargene
allegando che anche lui bisognava provedere a li fatti suoi,

---

* These words are in cipher with the key annexed
† See *supra*, pp 116 and 189
‡ Regarding these heretics, see *supra*, p 113 *seq*
§ I found this letter, dated Breslau, 1466, June 11 (which Janner, III., 565,
cites from Cod. 716 of the Konigl Kreissbibl , Ratisbon), also in Cod 4764,
N. 14, of the Court Library, Vienna , it is printed in the Anal Francisc , 422,
now also by Dollinger, Beitr. z. Sectengesch. d. M.-A., II , 625-6 (Munchen,
1890), from Cod. Paris Library, 5178, with the wrong date, 11 Jan , 1466, and
other variations
‖ See *supra*, pp. 89 and 155.

monstrando pur de temere de qualche novitate. Qui el card^le de li Ursini comincioe a dire che la S Sta non haveva a temere da niuno lucco, allegando le ragione perche non, el papa se ne scaldoe e corruciato usci a campo dicendo che sapeva del certo chel re haveva consultato cum cinque soli, di quali uno ge ne haveva dato adviso, se doveva assaltare el stato de la chiesia o non, e che questi cinque gli havevano persuaso che lo facesse e cussi anche lo re se li monstrava molto animato .

[Original in the Gonzaga Archives, Mantua]

19. JOH. BLANCHUS* TO GALEAZZO MARIA SFORZA, DUKE OF MILAN.†

1468, Febr 28, Rome

. . . Haveano bene essi ambasciatori ‡ tutti insieme pensato de andare hozi tutti al papa ad visitarlo e dolersi de questi tractati che gli sono stati facti contra et ad offerirli voy sig principali de la liga molto largamente per consolarlo alquanto, etc , ma havendo loro mandato da S Sta ad richiederlo de audientia per potere exequire dicto loro pensiero senza farli assapere alcuna cosa de quello gli volessero dire et essendoli facta lambassata venne de fuori el suo cubiculario et dixe al misso che l' haveva per doe volte facta lambassata, ma che S. Sta non havea resposto ne si ne non, el che se iudica sii per grande affanno che ha S Sta de questi tractati come e da credere debba havere Credo starano mo ad expectare che S Sta mandi per loro.

Questi tractati hano molto diminuita la reputatione del papa appresso quelli che intendeno qualche cosa. S. Sta se partite da le habitatione de S Petro et venne ad habitare ad S Marco § per levarse de le mano de Orsini et stare fra Colonesi. Ma ad quello se vede l' è || periculo per tutto Credo che S Sta sii in grande affanno et como el tractato se andara scoprendo maiore tanto maioremente gli crescera l' affanno et cosi e converso sel tractato ser de poca stima.

[Original in the State Archives, Milan, Cart. gen ad an]

---

* See, regarding this Ambassador, GINGINS, Dép. Mil , L., xvi , II , 37, 308, 368

† See *supra*, pp 46 *seq* and 58   ‡ Of the League

§ In MS · *Maro* || In MS : *le*

20. Augustinus de Rubeis to Galeazzo Maria Sforza,
       Duke of Milan *

1468, Febr 29, Rome

Illustr , etc.   El me occorre de presente de scrivervi una nova
hystoria accaduta qua acio V. Ex. sapia la cossa como passa,
perche so bene se ne dira variamente   Nam in questa corte erano
alcuni docti, gioveni, poeti e philosofi tra li quali se domandaveno
li principali uno Calimacho Venetiano, secretario del rev^{mo} cardinale
de Ravenna,† uno Glaucho Coldelmero pur de Venesia, Petreo
secretario del rev^{mo} cardinale de Pavia,‡ non so di che payse
fusse , uno altro Platano Mantovano, secietario del rev^{mo} cardinale
de Mantua § et uno familiaro del rev^{mo} vescovo de Feltro,‖
thexaurero apostolico con molti altri scriptori et cortesani de
diversi lochi, sed del dominio vostro non ce ne era veruno.   Quali
havevano facti una certa secta za piu di de persone asay et tuta
volta multiplicava de gente de ogni condicione, la piu parte
famigli de cardinali et de prelati.   Et costoro tenevano opinione
chel non fusse altro mondo che questo et morto il corpo morisse
la anima et demium che ogni cossa fusse nulla se non attendere a
tuti piaceri e volupta, sectatori del Epicuro et de Aristippo dummodo potessero far senza scandalo, non za per tema de Dio, sed
de la iusticia del mondo, havendo in omnibus respecto al corpo,
perche l' anima tenevano per niente.   Et ita non facevano altro che
goldere manzando carne la quadragesima, non andar may a la
messa, non se curai de vigilie ne de santi et al tutto contempnendo
papa, cardinali et la giesia catholica universale.   Dicevano che
santo Francesco era stato uno ypocrita et demum se facevano beffe
de dio e de li santi, vivando al suo modo usaveno maschii e femene
promiscue et indifferenter cum singulis similibus, etc.   Se vergog-
naveno esser domandati per nome christiani   Piopterea se li
havevano facti mutare et se chiamaveno li soprascripti nomi
stranei et de simile   Dicevano che Moyses era stato un grande
inganator de homini con sue leze et Christo un seductore de
popoli e Machometo homo de grande ingegno, che se tirava dreto
tuta gente per industria e malitia sua, siche era grande mancha-
mento alli moderni docti sequir tal leze e norme se non viver al

* See *supra*, p 50 *seq*   † B Roverella   ‡ Ammanati
§ F. Gonzaga   ‖ A Faseolus ; see *supra*, p. 112

suo modo, etc   Gli era ancora uno de li principalissimi chiamato
Julio Pomponio doctissimo homo, Romano, qual circha uno anno
ando a Venesia et li par legesse et modo sia destenuto pur per tal
cason.   Tandem devenerant isti ad tantam insolentiam ultra laltre
pacie che tutoldi andaveno vociferando et digando che certa-
mente il papa morirà presto inante passasse il mese de marzo
proximo mo luno mo laltro et in diversi lochi et modi siche se ne
faria un altro et che le cosse andariano per altra via   Intanto ch'
essendone piu fiate avisata S Sᵗᵃ se ne faceva beffe credando fusse
per vaticinii o per astrologia, etc.   Et tra laltri lo nostro revᵐᵒ cardinale de Thyano * sentendone pur qualche cossa ghe ne dedi
notitia per scaricho suo et anche non lo extimo Sua Bⁿᵉ ni may
monstrò farni caso fin ch' un Juliano de l' Aquila, altre fiate factor
de monsigʳᵉ de Pavia† la in quele parte et nunc fora de casa sua
cum pocha gratia et qual era molto mal contento, fu temptato da
alcuni de questi ita superficialiter de la morte del papa maxime dal
dicto Petreo per esser stati piu domestici in una casa medesima, al
qual dando parole generale subito pensò retornare in gratia del
patrono col scoprir questa cossa.   Et ita fecit et immediate esso
monsignore feci chiamare dicto Petreo interrogandolo de questa
materia ac etiam examinandolo suptilmente.   Qui confessus fuit
et non negavit qualiter erano una brigata che havevano determinato
amazar lo papa et mettere sotto c sopra tuta la corte e nominò
Calimacho dicto de sopra per lo capo de la brigata et che questo
facto havevano ordinato far il di primo de quaresma ala messa
papale in dacione cinerum.   Dil che replicandoli lo cardinale como
haveva potuto consentir saltem a la pernicie sua chel sapeva pur li
voleva ben, gli rispose haveva pensato dirli quello giorno et confor-
tarlo che non andasse a la messa per bene de la persona sua et
camparlo a quelo modo   His autem intellectis immaginò S Rᵐᵃ
S. scrutari hanc rem medulitus per poterne meglio chiarire la Sᵗᵃ
del papa et dixit isti chel dovesse andar a veder da quelo Calimacho et informarse bene de la cossa, postea ritornar con intentione sel se ne trovava fondamento de poterne certificare lo papa
et darli ne le mane luno et laltro.   Sed fo tristo et fece notitia ad
esso Calimacho, a Glaucho, et luy insemo, quali erano capita istius
factionis, et se ne fugireno senza altro indusio ni retornar dal
cardinale.   Tamen incontinenti fece sapere il tuto al papa, sed non

* N Forteguerri.   † Ammanati

se potereno havere costoro ; ma alchuni altri seguaci foreno pigliati, che non sano lo trattato formaliter   Nientedemeno son stati examinati e cosi se recitava questa hystoria multifariam et multis modis   Alchuni dicevano che havevano tractato de amazare lo papa et mettere a carne e sacho tuti li preti et altri quando gli fosse stato possibile menando le mano a tuti, etc.   E per fornir meglio tal pensere havevano trama etiamdio con uno d. Lucha de Tocio,* citadino Romano, bandito za piu anni passati , ma perche è doctore e valente homo stava presso la M^{ta} del sig^{re} re Ferando con bona reputatione e nome de regio consiglero, il qual haveva luy anchora intelligentia de molto altro numero de banditi e sfidati da Roma bene piu de quatro o cinque cento persone, le qual tute dovevano entrar in questa terra secretamente cum ordine dato al primo di de quaresima nel hora de la messa papalle quando zetasse la cenere in capo lo papa, retrovarsse insemo nascosti per le ruine sono a canto al palazo de le case zetate a terra per ampliarlo e tarlo mazor, qual e grandissimo spatio dascondere nedum tanti homini, ma uno exercito, etc.   Da laltra parte dovevano venir circha L. o LX persone cum quili altri cortesani soprascripti su la piaza de dicto palazo et incomenzare questione con li famigli di cardinali e prelati, che stano expectando li patroni li, per occupare alcuni pochi fanti che stano a la guarda del papa, perche a dire lo vero viveva molto liberamente e cum pocha custodia.   E cossi quisti altri nascosti, atachato lo rumore dal canto di qua, subito dovivano entrar la giesia, amazar lo papa et quanti ne havessero voluto de nuy altri   Postea sachezar, rubar e far al suo modo con intentione esso d. Lucha de Tocio de introdur uno novo stato di populo e farsi luy patrono de li altri se la fantasia li sequeva   Alcuni altri dicono questo facto se doveva far hogi, che è la dominica de carneval e tuto lo populo va a festo in Testazo e li fanti de la guarda e li altri officiali, ita che restano poche persone per Roma e ne le case et nel hora de la festa far lo insulto al palazo, zetar a terra le porte et amazar lo papa ; il che seria stato fornito in ante se fusse sentuto la cossa e potuto gionger lo succorso, deinde andare de casa in casa a li cardinali et altri e far lo medesimo.   Et alcuni

---

* Compare our Vol. III., p. 107 *seq.* and *supra*, pp. 49, 52, 58   In a *Brief of Sixtus IV (without address), dat Rome, 1483, Sept. 23, "Lucas Tozolus eques Romanus car^{mi} in Christo filii nostri Ferdinandi Sicilie regis ill orator," is mentioned.   Secret Archives of the Vatican

dicevano se doveva far lo dì de le palme per lo soprascripto modo, etc. Il perchè non se potendo sapere ben el vero, deliberassemo nuy oratori de la liga andar al papa per sapere avisar li nostri principali de la verità intesa de Sua B^{ne} e per offerirse li in tal caso, etc. Fu contenta haverci auditi et ce ringratiò Postmodum ce narrò tuto il facto de le heresie ut supradictum est nominando li sopradicti principali tuti et su questa parte monstrò far un gran caso de voler extirpar tal heresia dolendose non haver havuta prima notitia, etc. De questa altra conspiracione in la persona sua ce disse haver inteso tuto quanto e scripto de sopra, sed che anche non trovava lo fundamento, perchè non se erano potuti haver li principali, quali cerchava tuta via de trovare e credeva li haveria Et lo piu havesse potuto intervenir fin a mo era la confessione de uno di presi chi diceva del certo lo predicto d Lucha de Tocio esser dentro de Roma per questa cason et che li haveva parlato luy ben che non se ne sia potuto trovare indicio ne certeza alcuna, imo a mandato il papa fin a Napoli a sapere sel se absentato niuno dì de là et anche non è venuto la risposta; adjungendo costuy ultra de cio che esso d Lucha haveva etiamdio tractato in castello S. Angelo et haveva mandato mille ducati a certi fanti de la guardia per dover pigliar lo castello a sua richesta, etc A facto fare inquisitione grande il papa per cavarne la verità et non ha trovato altro fundamento Se crede che quisto tal confesso simile cosse lo habia * facto per intrichar et alongar la iusticia de la persona sua. E questo è usque nunc cio che se trova Non se cessa de fare ogne diligentia per haver li principali, et ha lo papa facto bandir che li da uno de li tri caporali in le mane videlicet Calimacho, Glaucho e Petreo o che li acusa in modo che li se possano haver li sera donato CCC ducati per chiaschuno e de d. Lucha de Tocio V^e ducati. Cum questo poteria forte essere se sentirea piu ultra et non dubita il papa de haverne qualche uno o tuti, confidandosi non se debiano reducere in diminio alcuno che li siano mandati fin qua, e dice del tuto ne avisarà nuy altri et io a V. Ex. scrivaro quanto succederà, a la qual me recommando

Romae die xxviii Februarii, 1468

Eiusdem i et ex D. servulus Augustinus de Rubeis.

[Original in the State Archives, Milan, Cart. gen. *Placed by mistake in the fasciculus,* "Florence, 1478."]

* In MS.: *habiano.*

21. Joh Blanchus to Galeazzo Maria Sforza, Duke
of Milan.*

1468, Feb 29, Rome.

Ill^{me}, etc Per la alligata de XXVII. del presente ho scripto a
V. Ex. quello se diceva per Roma et per alcuni di principali de
questa corte circa questa coniuratione et tractati. Dapoy heri sera
la Sta de N S^{re} mando ad dire ad questi rev^{di} et mag^{ci} ambaxatori
de la liga che potevano andare da Sua B^{ne} et cosi gli anday ancora
io con loro et doppo condolutose essi ambaxatori in nome de voy
signori principali de la liga de questa coniuratione et offerto le
persone e stati et gente vostre ad soe deffese e favori et demum
domandato come passavano queste cose, S. Sta respose et dixe che
uno signore del mundo l' haveria avisato che la se guardesse perche
lera certificato che per alcuni in Roma se tractava de stranie cose
etiam contra la persona soa et che deinde vennero alcuni cardinali
da se et nomino solamente el cardinale de Mantoa † ad dirli de
certa mala vita et heresia che seguivano alcuni scellerati scolari
nominandone quatro per principali, cioe Calimaco, Petreo, Glaucho
et un altro extraneo nome dicendo che costoro se havevano electo
una vita achademica et epicurea perche ultra che haveano manzato
la quaresima passata et tutta via manzavano li venerdi et sabbati
carne et non servavano vigilia alcuna et seguivano li appetiti
carnali con maribus et feminis et facevano mille altre scelleragine
quod abhominabilius est negavano la divinità cioè non esser Dio
et negavano che fosse l' anima dicendo che morto el corpo era
morta l' anima et subjungevano che Moyses fo seductore del
popolo et che Christo fo falso propheta et ultra questo non se
volevano per niente chiamare ne lassare chiamare per li proprii
nomi, ma se havevano posti li nomi predicti che forono nomi de
achademici et epicuri dicendo S Sta che non gli bastava esser loro
cativi ma che andavano seducendo questo et quello altro et che
ne havevano seducto alcuni et maxime uno Lucido che stava
con suo parente che è qua suo depositario, subjungendo S. Sta che
non solamente se andavano gloriando de questa loro scellerata
vita et heresia, ma andavano detrahendo al honore de Dio et de
la chiesa dicendo male de S Sta et delo clero del mondo et
dicendo. guarda se questi preti sono inimici de layci che hano
facta la quaresma et voleno che nuy la jeiuniamo et piu ce hano

* See *supra*, p. 59, *seq* †   † F Gonzaga

ligati che non possiamo pigliare piu che una mogliere et multa
huiusmodi, dicendo ancora S Sta che non gli bastava questo ma
che piu ultra dicevano che presto se vederia de nove cose et
maxime verso uno certo prete dixero date de bona voglia che fra
pochi di non te bisognera fare piu tante supplicatione perche
havemo uno iudicio chel papa ha ad morire presto et sapemo che
ad ogni modo el morirà presto et seguirano de le altre cose relevate
et similia et dice S Sta che per questo loro avantarse de simile
cose li dicti cardinali hano voluto intendere la facenda et poy gli
lo sono venuti ad dire ut s

Ma dice S Sta che per alhora non pote haver gratia de fare
prendere dicti quattro scellerati perche fugirono, ma spera haverli
perche vano latitando qui dintorno et che è su la via de haver
almanco Calimaco ch' è el principale et dice S. S. non potendo
havere loro ha facto prendere le loro cose et hagli trovati soy
epygrammata et versi et soneti intitulati ad pueros in genere turpe
dove demonstravano molte loro ribaldarie et dice che havendo
facto pigliare alcuni che practicavano con loro per questo et per
la fuga de loro se comenzò ad credere che la conjuratione fosse
de grande importantia et questo . . * mercordi proxime passato
et che quello di medesmo che se corse el palio de le giovenì †
venire uno Roma [no] ad dire ad S. Sta che se guardasse intorno
perche l' haveva veduto alcuni banditi che erano venuti in Ro[ma]
et che non gli degono esser venuti se non per fare male, etc , et
gli ne mostrò uno addito che era   . * alla festa del palio   Et
dice S Sta che alhora fece demandare el vicecamerlengo et reprehendendolo che [non §] havesse mandato bando che li banditi
non potessero venire in Roma ad queste feste de carnevale . . .*
commise che dovesse andare ad fare prendere dicto bandito et
cosi fu preso luy et uno suo [compagno ‡] et dice che interrogandolo el vicecamerlengo et reprehendendolo chel fosse venuto
in Roma essendo bandito per la vita come era, el repose et
confessoe che l' era venuto ad videre le feste, ma dice S Sta che
como cativo che le fece una inventione dicendo che l' era venuto
in Roma con uno factore de d Luca Tozolo § Romano bandito
che sta ad Napoli con la M^ta del re et che esso d. Luca doveva

---

* What follows is destroyed by damp   † See *supra*, p. 31 *seq.*
‡ Destroyed in original
§ Regarding this matter see CANENSIUS, 80, and PLATINA, 779

anche luy essere gionto in Roma perche el l' haviva lassato in la
silva de Velitri et piu ultra accusò dicto d Luca dicendo che esso
d Luca haveva mandato in Roma mille ducati in mano de li suoi
parenti per dispensarli in certi suoy pensieri che l' haveva facto
Et dice S. Sᵗᵃ che intendendo questo gli crescette el suspetto e
che ha mandato ad cercare per tuta Roma esso d. Luca et postoli
la taglia adosso como per l' altra littera io scrivo et che interim
che lo faceva cercare è venuto S S un cittadino Romano
cognato desso d. Luca ad pregare S Sᵗᵃ che non se fatichi piu
in cercarlo perche el non era venuto et che sel fosse venuto l' haveria
facto capo ad casa soa et che luy voleva obligare la vita chel non
era partito da Napoli et diceloli S Sᵗᵃ come nuy intendiamo che
l' ha mandato qua mille ducati da farne certi suoy designi, etc.   el
gli respose che l' e vero che per littera di cambio l' ha mandato
mille ducati per la dote de una soa figliola la quale S Sᵗᵃ sa che
l' hano voluta maritare al suo medico et che non li [ha] mandati
per altra casone.   Et dice S. Sᵗᵃ che l' e vero chel suo medico li
di passati gli richiese licenza de prendere dicta soa figliola per
mogliere, ma che el gli dissuase questa cosa con dirgli che may
ad sua instantia ne de homo del mondo el non faria gratia al dicto
d. Luca de retornare ad Roma perche l' era bandito che havendo
facta pace con un altro Romano et havendoli data sicurta de non
lo offendere, lo fece poy amazare et che la seria cosa de troppo
male exempio et che facendo quella gratia bisognaria poy farne
molte altre simile et che non voleva tiarse questo carico ad le
spalle et per questo pare quasi che S. Sᵗᵃ sii fuori d' ogni suspecto
de d Luca et dice che l' expecta per tutto hozi la certeza da
Napoli.   Nientedimeno S. Sᵗᵃ non abandona la impresa de in-
vestigare meglio la cosa et dice S Sᵗᵃ che per questo ha cognosciuto che dicto bandito che ha accusato d. Luca ut supra lo
ha facto per dare favore et dilatione alla pena che l' ha ad patire
luy et piu ultra dice che gli ha accusato uno signore ben grande
et grande et che crede chel dica le boxie dechiarando S. Sᵗᵃ che
pro certo el non gli ha accusato el re Ferrando   Dice S Sᵗᵃ che
da principio che gli fo dicto che questi conjuratori havevano intelligentia con uno gran signore gli andò l' animo sopra el re de Boemia
dicendo chel credeva che l' uno heretico se intendesse con l' altro.
Item dice che questi ribaldi hano qualche volta dicto de volere
andare ad trovare el Turco et ch' unaltro de questi scolari che al

presente e a Venetia fin l' anno passato andò ad Venetia per volere deinde andare ad trovare el Turcho et qui comenzò S. S.ta ad damnare molto questi studii de humanità dicendo che se Dio gli prestava vita, voleva providere ad due cose . l' una che non fosse licito studiare in queste vane historie et poesie perche sono piene de heresie et maledictione , l' altra che non fosse licito imparare ne exercire astrologia perche da essa nascono molti errori dicendo li putti non hano ad pena dece anni che senza che vadano ad scola sano mille ribaldarie, pensate come se degono poy impire de mille altri vicii quando iegeno Juvenale, Terentio, Plauto, Ovidio et questi altri libri, dicendo Juvenale monstra de reprendere li vicii, ma el ne fa docto et li insigna ad chi lo lege, come fano anche questi nostri predicatori quali qualche volta havemo reprehesi che predicando insignano fare de le cose lascive che l' homo non le intese may piu et questo quando se mettono ad volere dire : in questi modi se po fare uno peccato , dicendo S S.ta che gli sono tanti altri libri che se possono legere et che legendoli l' homo se farà tanto docto quanto bastarà et che le meglio dire una cosa per li proprii vocabuli cha per queste circuitione che usano poeti Retornando ad damnare molto li dicti 4 coniuratori che ex toto negano Dio dicendo che li pagani et gentili et li altri antichi servavano qualche religione et costoro negano el tucto Et qui el mag°° d. Lorenzo da Pesaro* allegò molte cose et de Romani et de altri antichi in le quale servarono grandissima religione et tante cose allegò ad questi propositi esso d Lorenzo chel papa ne prese piacere assay et lo stava volunteri ad audire. Fo etiamdio allegato et testamento vechio et testamento nuovo et rasone civile et rasone canonica per esso d. Lorenzo et per li altri ambaxatori de la liga perche tutti sono doctori chi in utroque et chi in jure civili tantum Fo etiamdio recordato che como è prohibito alli preti de seguire le lege civile per le conditione differente che sono dal temporale al spirituale così se po prohibere el studio de le poesie et astrologie perche da esso se cava mille heresie, etc Ad un altra cosa dixe S. S.ta che la voleva provedere cioè alle zanze et bosie che se dicono qua in campa de Fiore et che ordinarà uno decreto opportuno ad questo et che farà fare de li schizzi ad questi zanzatori che se fano ad Venetia dicendo che quando Pier

* In reference to this Ambassador, see *supra*, p 60, and Lettres de Louis XI , Vol. III., 278-9, 343

Brunoro fo mandato in la Morea uno Venetiano gli dixe va pur
che tu non ne tornaray may et che essendosene doluto Piero
Brunoro così la S^ra fo statim preso dicto Venetiano et dattoli
XXV squassi de corda et poy bandito et molte altre cose dixe ad
questo proposito dicendo maxime che tutto quello fo dicto in
campo de Fiore o vero o boxia, o ben o male che sia fu scripto per
tutto el mondo et che del vero et bene se po havere l' homo per
excusato, ma che de la bosia et male el se voria castigare cioè
castigare quelli che lo andasseno fingendo et seminando.

Demum la S Sta dixe che ad ogni modo l' haveria deliberato
communicare questa cosa con li prefati ambaxatori et con li
cardinali, ma che l' era stato fin hora ad non dirne altro perche
el non sapeva ancora dire alcuna verità de tradimento se non le
bestialitate suprascripte et così li cardinali sono andati questa
matina ad palazo per questa casone le quale tutte cose me è
parso significare a V Ex alla quale humilmente me recommando.
Datum Romae ult. Februarii, 1468.

[Original in the State Archives of Milan Cart gen. *Wrongly
placed under February*, 1463]

22. Aug. de Rubeis to Galeazzo Maria Sforza, Duke of Milan.[*]

1468, March 4, Rome

Circha li tractati contra la persona del papa de li quali ve
scripsi per altre mie, se facta ogni diligencia et inquisicione per
sentir piu oltra et tandem non se trovato fin a qui altro che
parole paze e vane de coloro che zanzaveno [†] chel se voria amazare
lo papa et chel se poteria bene far per quello modo che io scripsi
et ch' essendo questo popolo et tuta la corte mal contenta [‡] et
disposta non manchava se non che qualch' uno incomenzasse che
tutol mondo poy gli tirarey dreto, &c. L' è[§] vero che quelli
principalli per anchora non se suni potuti havere. Se cercha per
ogni modo haverli ne le mano et crede prefata Sta da loro se
saperia piu inanti De d Luca Tozo s' è [||] trovato non essere
vero se sia ullo tempore partito da Napoli ni sia intervenuto ni

---

[*] See *supra*, p 59   [†] =cianciavano, dicevano ciance.
[‡] See our account, *supra*, p 27 *seq.*   [§] Manuscript: *Le*
[||] Manuscript *se.*

conspirato a la cosa   Lo papa ha molto piu che prima ordinate le guarde de palazo et sta con pur asay major respecto chel non soleva.   Le feste de carnevale, corsi de palii, convito al popolo la domenica pasata et laltre tute se sonno facte al modo usato como laltri anni ho scripto et nulla è inmutato ni manchato.

P.S—Del resto de quella heresia se ne trova pur molti intricati et tutavolta se va cercando de laltri et lo papa ha intentione de stirpare questa secta.

[Original in the State Archives, Milan, Cart gen]

23 POPE PAUL II TO FLORENCE.
1468, May 16

The Pope expresses his affection for Florence (see *supra*, p. 14) and praises the Florentines for having accepted the peace Paul II. then speaks of his constant zeal from the beginning * of his reign for war with the Turks   Hactenus enim ducenta milia florenor in huiusmodi christianorum subsidia erogavimus † . . .

Datum Romae apud S Marcum, xvi Maii, 1468

[Copy in the State Archives, Florence X –II –23, f 172]

24. GIACOMO TROTTI ‡ TO BORSO, DUKE OF MODENA §
1468, July 8, Rome.

The Pope is going to leave Rome because the Plague is raging there ∥ Persona non rimane qui,¶ chi va de qua chi de la, ne mor[ono] 40 e 50 el di   All are fleeing from the Plague-stricken

---

* The Milanese Ambassadors, Laurentius de Pesaro and Joh. Blanchus, writing home from Rome, on the 24th April, 1468, speak in the following words of the Pope's disposition on this subject   " * El papa monstra secundo ha dicto questa sera chel voglia che se attendi omnino ad fare expeditione contra el Turco." State Archives, Milan

† See *supra*, p 158   The statement of Paul II is corroborated by the testimony of Sixtus IV ; see RAYNALDUS ad an 1471, N 71

‡ This diplomatist was still with Paul II. in the autumn of 1470 , see WURDTWEIN, Nov Subsid , XIII , 69.

§ See *supra*, p 190.

∥ The Plague had reached Rome in the beginning of April , see *Despatch of Augustinus de Rubeis, dated Rome, 1468, April 2 (State Archives, Milan) By the end of the month it was making great ravages , see *Letter of A Patritius, dated Rome, 1468, April 27, Angelica Library, S 1, 1, f. 117.

¶ Laurentius de Pesaro writes from Rome on the 3rd June, 1468   " *omne persona fugge " State Archives, Milan

city where are only to be seen sick people being carried. Three Cardinals have remained in Rome, but with closed doors, so that no one of their household may go out

[Original in the State Archives, Modena]

25 TOMMASO SODERINI* TO FLORENCE †

1468, Nov 29, Venice

News reached Venice that the Emperor had arrived in Porde none ‡ Questa S per honorare la M^{ta} Sua ha electi sedici imbasciadori Quattro gli sono iti incontro insino a Frigoli et domattina si partono gli altri dodici per riceverlo a Padova Haveano apparechiato qui splendissimamente la casa del marchese di Ferrara per la stanza sua, ma dicono ha mandato a dire non vuole passore per Vinegia, ma che fa la via di Padova a Ferrara. Manda questo dominio due oratori che anno a compagnare la persona sua insino a Roma e quali sono M Piero Mozanigho et M. Triadono Gritti . . .

[State Archives, Florence, X –II –24, f. 81b–82]

26 JOH PETRUS ARRIVABFNUS TO MARCHIONESS BARBARA OF MANTUA §

1468, Dec 26, Rome

Illma madonna mia L' ordine dato de mandare incontra a limperatore prima quatro prelati e insieme doi auditori de rota e doi advocati consistoriali come scrissi a V. Ex vene servato e cussi subsequenter li doi card^{li} ‖ e Suoa M^{te} ad una terra chiamata Otriculi lontana de qua quaranta miglia entroe in barcha nel Tevere e vennesene fin presso a Roma a sette miglia ad un luoco che se dice la Valcha dove smontoe in terra, e qui da quelli doi card^{li} etprelati mandati, li qualilhavevano per terra seguitato eia aspettato e da molte altre persone che li erano andate in contra

---

* Florentine Ambassador in Venice

† See *supra*, p 161

‡ See TODERINI, 13 and 113 The Oration pronounced at Pordenone in presence of the Emperor, by Petrus Molinus, one of the Venetian Ambassadors, is in the British Museum (MS 15906, f 14b)

§ See *supra*, p 162 *seq*

‖ d'Estouteville and F Piccolomini

Quello dı che foe la vigilia de natale stimandose che havesse ad giongere de dı, el collegio dı cardʰ se congregoe a la porta de S Maria del populo, e cussi tuta la corte e la citade col baldachıno fatto cum larme del papa e suoe de damaschıno bıancho brochato doro, ma retardoe ınfina a le tre hore de notte ad intrare, che dicono alcunı foe per la gıornata longa, alcunı per esserlı data quella hora da astrologı * Sentendo la suoa venuta lı cardʰ se lı fecerono ıncontro un puocho fuora de la porta, et a la porta Suoa Mᵗᵉ entroe sottol baldachıno vestita dun vestitello de panno negro e col suo capuzıno et capello, de nantı lı andavano el S. de Camarıno . . . et questı altrı sıgnorı e baronı ecclesıastıcı cum le torze ın man, la terra era apparata de pannı et altrı ornamentı dove haveva a passare et feceronolı fare un longo cırcuıto et passaıono da S Marco, passate le cınque hore gıonse a S Petro dove la Sᵗᵉ de N. S laspettava ın la capella magıore e quı se ıngınochıoe a basarlı el pede e puoı la mane dı puoı levandose a basare el volto el papa se levoe un puocho da la sede suoa Era presso la cathedra del papa per spacıo de doı homını al lato dextro apparıchıata una sede per lımperatore ma pıu bassa dun brazo e pıu emınente che el luoco dı cardʰ un grado; quı fatte alcune oratıone e cerimonıe ascesero ın palatıo tutı doı al pare e N S. teneva lımperatore per mane allato mancho e cussı se andarono fin a la camera del papa e dı puoı el collegio compagnoe lımperatore a la camera suoa, che è pıu bassa ın palatıo dove allogıoe anche altra fiata, puoı la messa de la nocte che foe perho cantata presso al gıorno, N. S. lı dede la beretta e la spatha et al ma† . . tore levangelıo exııt edıctum a cesare augusto et mons mıo ‡ dısse la omelıa, herı a † . . andoe gıuso col papa sottol baldachıno pur a mane ın S. Petro et communıcosse ın la messa† . . N S ascese nel trıbunal alto avantı le scale de S Petro dove deda la benedıc-tıone e † . . sotol baldachıno e vedevase lo ımperatore che certo monstro una gran ıeverentıa col capo scoperto, e Sᵗᵉ Suoa lo faceva coprıre, nel tornare suso N. S compagnoe lımperatore ınsına a la camara suoa e lı voleva lascıarlo, ma Suoa Mᵗᵉ fece resıstentıa et volse venıre cum N S bene doe sale fin a pıede de una scala per la qual puoı se ascende a le sale de sopıa e quı

---

* Frederıck III. was greatly gıven to Astrology, see FʀɪEDRICH, Astrologıe und Ref, 29 *seq*

† What follows ıs completelɣ destroyed   ‡ Card Gonzagn

se lasciarono che erano passate le xxiii. hore, portoe indosso
limperatore una turcha de veluto negro senza altro ornamento,
questa matina credo uscira anche fuori a la messa.   In palatio è
dato logiamento a S M^{te} e parichii di suoi, li altri che se dice ha
di cavalli 600 sono divisi per le hostarie* e sento che N S. a li
hosti ha fatto gia el pagamento per octo di, che tanto se ragiona
habbia a stare qui, et ha ordinato li sia facto honore.   Sono fatti
venire in la terra giente darme assai et di fanti e balestrieri quatro
milia   Finqui cussi è stato el progresso suo, cum S M^{te} è uno
abbate de Casanova Savoino el qual è tanto inimico al duca de
Milano, e sento ha buona condicione seco in modo che essendo
mal dispuosto el papa e lo collegio a la promotione del vescovo
de Bressa è opinione dalcuni che forsi questo abbate se habia a
fare card^{le} a petitione de limperatore el qual non pare voglia
domandare todescho alcuno   Doi ambasciatori Venetiani sono
venuti col imperatore, messer Paulo Moresini e messer Antonio
Preoli   .   Rome xxvi Decem^{bs}, 1468
                        Ser^{or} Jo PETRUS ARRIVABENUS
[Original in the Gonzaga Archives, Mantua]

27 POPE PAUL II. TO BOLOGNA †

1469, March 6, Rome

Concerning the overflow of the Reno ‡   The Pope expresses
his astonishment that nothing had yet been done to prevent it, and
desires that measures should at once be taken against this calamity.
He gives this command because he (the Pope) is bound to watch
over the general welfare.   Dat Romae vi Martii, 1469, Pont nostri
A° 5°.

[Original in the State Archives, Bologna   Lib Q, 3.]

28. POPE PAUL II TO CARDINAL STEPHAN DE VARDA.§

1471, Jan 14, Rome.

Stephano tit sanctor Nerei et Achillei presbyt card^{li} et archiep
Colocensi   Dudum siquidem, etc.   .   The King has often

---

* See GOTTLOB, Cam. Apost.   † See supra, p 34.
‡ See supra, p 34.   § See supra, p. 123.

requested him to send him the Cardinal's Hat as he has long since
raised him to the purple. He had expected him to come in
person to Rome; now, however, he sends him the hat by Gabriel
de Verona, ordin minor. nuntium nostrum.

[Lib brev, 12, f. 77b. Secret Archives of the Vatican.]*

29 CARDINAL FR GONZAGA TO HIS FATHER †

1471, Jan. 17, Rome

He gives an account of the deliberations of the Commission of
Cardinals appointed to consider the Turkish business This
Commission held its sittings in the house of Cardinal Bessarion
and resolved. che per quest' anno non se havesse ad fare provisione
de offendere, ma solum che bastasse a defendre et per mare
tantummodo, ad che pareva bastariano cento quaranta galee e xx
nave grosse, ma che ben se disponesse come per li anni seguenti
se havesse e per terra e per mare tendere a la ruina del Turco, ma
tre cose concorrevano qui chel se intendesse la celeritate de le
provisione, la perseverantia desse che pareva se dovesse promettere
per xxv anni aut ad minus per x. e la rata che ciascuno volesse
contribuire a questa impresa. Non li fue de ambasciatori chi
facesse offerta alcuna speciale, quelli del re e de Venetiani assai
dissero in persuadere le provisione opportune se facessero, Fiorentini temporezano cum parole generale, quelli del duca dissero
non havere commissione a questo, ma chel suo signore è cussi
ben dispuosto a fare tutto quello che li metta bene et honore che
volendo N Ste da lui cosa alcuna ge lo puo scrivere et trovarallo
per la observantia chel ge ha obedientissimo a fare ciò che sia
dovere suo, e tuti insieme conclusero che essendo el papa capo
e pastore dugniuno li parera che S Sta havesse prima a specificare
la rata suoa per dare exemplo a li altri et che anche quella che
sa e conosce la potentia de ciascuno puoria taxare quanto li paresse
che ugniuno havesse a conferire Questa fue la relatione de le
cose agitate apud deputatos The Cardinals were summoned to
treat further on the subject dominica proxima in furia. The
deliberations lasted from the 22nd hour fin presso le sei hore de
nocte: ne la qual consultatione furono varie sententie e parole
assai che non accade de extendere; demum fatta la conclusione

secundo lo comune parere furono chiamati dentro li ambasciatori
a li quali N. S. se duolse che in omnibus li facessero cussi puocha
demonstratione de reverentia che havendoli fatto richiedere non
hanno voluto fare dechiaratione alcuna de suoa voluntate. . . .
The Pope then informs the Ambassadors· che communicata re
cum cardinalibus et examinate le facultate suoe li offereva de darli
lo quarto de le intrate suoe che pigliava L^m duc^ti l' anno, perche
dice l' intrate suoe tanto del temporal quanto del spiritual senza
lalumiera, la qual gia è dedicata a la crociata,* non essere piu che
cc^m ducati † e per suoa iustificatione offerse de fare monstrare li
libri daltri pontifichi e suoi, e de ciò ne fue data commissione al
card^le de Theano ‡ chi fue thesauriere a tempo di Pio et al
card^le de S. Marco,§ el qua ha fatto un gran tempo lofficio del
camarlengo, che insieme havessero ad examinare li conti et intrate
suoe. . . . Non parse che la offerta satisfacesse a la brigata et
maxime a Venetiani ‖ li quali hanno havuto a dire che N. S.
deveria vendere le suoe zoie, darli el tuto de le intrate suoe reser-
vato solamente quanto bisogna per lo vivere etiam extenuato et
che nui cardinali li doveressimo mettere la metade de le intrate
nostre et in summa metteno la taglia come se ce havesserono in
presone. Replicorono che la S B^ne specificasse quante galee
voleva mantenere alimpresa dicendo che non volevano questa
offerta de denari ne del quarto, perche lhora era tarda la cosa fu
remessa ad un altro consistorio . .

[Original in the Gonzaga Archives, Mantua]

30. POPE PAUL II. TO THE INHABITANTS OF RHODES ¶

1471, Jan 20, Rome

In view of the common danger all must render assistance.**
The Pope exhorts them to courage. Aderit et Deus ipse nosque
quoad poterimus nihil in tanta re pretermittemus In conclusion,
he urges them speedily to repair the ruinous walls of Rhodes.

[Lib. brev, 12, f. 86b. Secret Archives of the Vatican.]

* See *supra*, p. 80.   † See GOTTLOB, Cam Apost.
‡ N Forteguerri.   § M. Barbo.
‖ See ROMANIN, IV, 353, note 1.   ¶ See *supra*, p 183
** Regarding the sufferings of the people at Rhodes, see also BOSIO, 253 *seq*,
257 *seq*.

31 Pope Paul II to the Grand Master of Rhodes, Giambatista Orsini.*

1471, Jan 20, Rome

He had received their letters, from which he perceived their fear of the Turks. Timendum quippe est, sed non ita ut ab auxiliis ac remediis desistatur, quinimo est eo melius et celerius providendum Itaque nolite vobis ipsis deesse, sed bono animo sitis. He promises help, and urges them to lose no time in improving the fortifications and moats of the island.

[Lib. brev, 12, f 87b, *loc cit.* Secret Archives of the Vatican.]

32 Pope Paul II to Duke Borso of Modena †

1471, March 3, Rome

The Pope in a few words informs the Duke, who intended to visit Rome, that he was sending the Archbishop of Spalatro [Lor. Zane], who is "thesaurarius ac provinciae nostrae marchiae Anconitanae gubernator," to greet him He will inform the Duke that his arrival is very agreeable to him (the Pope)

[Original in the State Archives, Modena.]

33 Pope Paul II to the Grand Master of Rhodes, Giambatista Orsini ‡

1471, March 12, Rome

An exhortation to courageous constancy against the attacks of the Turks, *as above*, No 31.

[Lib brev., 12, f 112 Secret Archives of the Vatican]

34. Pope Paul II. to the Governor of Spoleto §

1471, April 5, Rome.

Habes bullam de non recipiendis muneribus alias per nos editam.|| This is to be observed exactly (ad unguem). Prohibe-

---

* See *supra*, p 183 G Orsini had been appointed Grand Master of Rhodes by Paul II., in 1467, on the death of Zacosta (see Cron Rom , 32), and died in 1476; see Reumont, III , 1, 521

† See *supra*, p 184.   ‡ See *supra*, p 183.

§ See *supra*, p. 35. || Printed in Bull , V , 184 *seq*

mus ne aliquo pacto in causis vertentibus in prima instancia
sportule alique recipiantur preterea ne gratis paleas nec ligna
deferri tibi facias

Simile rectori Patrimonii

    ,,   ,,   Campanie

    ,, gubernatori Fulginei, Fani, Cesene, Asculi, Reatis et
Interamni, Urbis veteris, Vetralle

    [Lib brev, 12, f 142   Secret Archives of the Vatican.]

35 CARDINAL FR GONZAGA TO HIS FATHER *

1471, April 10, Rome

.   Che parlamenti siano stati fati fra lor † non posso altramente de certo sapere, bene uso ugni industria possibile per
cavarlo per indirecto e quando el S^r fue qui a visitarme sabbato
passato ‡ cussi inter loquendo me li acostai e dissi che queste suoe
visitatione davano molto da dire a la brigata la qual pensava che
fusserono per conduie el papa a Ferrara, il che a me piaceria
grandemente perche essendo io cupido del bene de N. S. e de la
sede apostolica lo comprobaria parendomi che seria molto expe-
diente e proficuo considerato come sta tuta la Germania verso di
nui et che la Franza piu volte ha domandato el concilio e questo
io lhaveria piu caro ad Ferrara perche seressemo in una terra libera
et buona e ne la qual per la mia particularitate essendo non manco
fiolo a Suoa S^ra che al marchese de Mantuoa seria bene visto
Rispuoseme che parlava prudentemente e Dio volesse che tuti li
altri fussero de questo parere le qual parole me fecerono credere
che qualche cosa ne fusse.   Io mandai puo per Jacomo Trotto §
cum monstrare de voler per lo mezo suo fare intendere al S. el
fatto de quella bolla,‖ a la qual non era stato presente lui e puoi
entrai a dirli de questa andata a Ferrara commendandola et infer-
endo che lo fusse quodamodo necessaria et chel S faria una

---

* See *supra*, p 188
† Paul II. and Borso d' Este
‡ 6th April
§ The Ambassador of Modena to Rome, of whom in the *Report from the
Chigi Library, cited *supra* p 186, Fr Ariostus speaks in most favourable
terms
‖ Concerning a " fraternitate o compagnia che se chiamasse de la pace "

sancta opera a usarli ugni industria   Rispuoseme tacete monsignor
che ad ugni modo la conduremo. Lo rev^{mo} monsignor cardinale
de S Maria in Portico * el qual è nepote del papa me disse questi
dì, el seria pur bene fatto de celebrare una dieta in qualche buon
luoco in Italia et anticipare avanti che per necessitate fussemo
costretti da altri a farla e forsi puoi dove nui non voressimo   Tute
queste parole e coniecture me fanno presumere che qualche cosa
ne sia , andaro investigando piu che puotrò per darne aviso a V S
et maxime passati che siano questi di sancti ne li quali se attende
a lanima   . †

[Original in the Gonzaga Archives, Mantua.]

36. POPE PAUL II TO JOHN II, MARGRAVE OF BADEN AND ARCHBISHOP OF TRÈVES.‡

1471, April 19 ——

The Pope returns thanks for the iocale addamantibus ac rubinis
ornatum sent to him through Hermann Frank, and praises the
Archbishop sed ne te lateat nos munera recipere non consuevimus
He accepts the present, however, in order that the Archbishop may
have no doubt of the favour he bears him, and sends him in return
crucem etiam addamantibus atque rubinis et unionibus redimitam
que multas sacras reliquias   . tetigit §

[State Archives, Venice.] ‖

37. POPE PAUL II. TO CARDINAL FR. PICCOLOMINI ¶

1471, June 26, Rome

Card^h Senensi legato.   Accepimus plures litteras tue circ^{nis} ex

* Bat Zeno

† Further particulars of the negotiations, which undoubtedly took place in
1471, concerning a fresh Congress or Council, are wanting   The sudden death
of the Pope afterwards turned the thoughts of all in another direction , but this
question soon came again to the front ; see *supra*, p 217.

‡ See *supra*, p 110

§ See also the Brief to the King of Portugal (MARINI, II., 201), and that to the
King of Hungary in TELEKI, XI , 122-3

‖ I am indebted to the kindness of Canon Fraknói, Vice-President of the
Hungarian Academy, for a copy of this Brief

¶ See *supra*, p 181

Ratispona, ex quibus intelleximus, quid usque in eam diem a te factum sit circa ea quae tibi a nobis sunt demandata in causa expeditionis in Turchos, et quomodo ad illos principes qui Ratispone aderant concionem habueris mentemque nostram spem et rei necessitatem aperueris illorumque responsionem.   Commendamus plurimum prudentiam et diligentiam tuam   Ita enim est faciendum . . . Quare non cessabis similiter in futurum ab ipso bono opere, sed instabis et perseverabis industria et diligentia, ut nichil boni quod fieri in hanc rem possit postponatur praesertim autem nunc, quum Turchus . illam (scl. religionem christianam) extinguere contendit.   Super his et aliis etiam lator praesentium, qui ad te revertitur, poterit coram latius referre, quae a nobis audivit , de occurrentibus successu temporis Nos tuis literis facies certiores

[Lib. brev , 12, f. 162   Secret Archives of the Vatican.]

38 POPE PAUL II. TO BORSO, DUKE OF FERRARA *

1471, July 10, Rome.

A melancholy report had lately been circulated in Rome regarding a danger which threatened the Duke.† He now hears that this danger has happily been overcome. The Pope exhorts the Duke to strengthen his health, and thanks him for his beautiful present.

[Lib. brev., 12, f. 175b.   Secret Archives of the Vatican.]

39 POPE PAUL II. TO CARDINAL FR PICCOLOMINI ‡

1471, July 13, Rome.

Cardinali Senensi legato.   Sollicitabat nos antea cura non mediocris, quod car^m in Christo filii nostri Friderici imperatoris tardior ad istam Ratisponensem dietam adventus de die in diem videbatur diferri, cum ad praescriptum diem multi iam convenissent.   Vere-

---

* See *supra*, p. 190   Among the Briefs of Paul II in the State Archives of Modena I saw neither this nor the Brief of 20th July.

† According to the Diario Ferrar., 229, Borso had been suffering since the 27th May from "febri continue fiemmatiche che mai non lo abbandonorno insino a ia morte" [20th August]   The Duke had probably contracted this sickness in Rome ; see also Atti e mem. d. deput. di storia patria Moden , V. (1870), 418 *seq*

‡ See *supra*, p.181.

bamur namque, ne si ejus optata presentia deesset, dissolveretur quicquid tam necessario tempore principum consiliis et subsidiis iuste desiderabamus fieri in Turchum   Sed tu, dilecte fili, qua soles diligentia progressum omnem et quae ad eam diem sequuta sunt, tuis literis datis Ratispone *duodecima iunii* plene significans nos admodum recreasti . .   Speramus namque et ita optamus, quod et ipsius car^m^ filii nostri pium studium et sincere principum voluntates te maxime operam dante accendentur ad tam sanctum opus magis ac communi periculo consulent .   . Confidimus enim devotionem tuam cunctos principes in ipsa dieta presentes efficaciter cohortari et inducere ad prosecutionem hujus rei posse

[Lib. brev , 12, f. 174b   Secret Archives of the Vatican.]

40 POPE PAUL II TO BORSO, DUKE OF FERRARA.*

1471, July 20, Rome

Up to this time he had no tidings regarding the Duke's state of health; he exhorts him to thank God for his recovery. The Pope in conclusion assures Borso of his prayers

[Lib. brev., 12, f 176b   Secret Archives of the Vatican]

41. POPE PAUL II TO ALBRECHT, MARQUESS OF BRANDENBURG †

1471, July 20, Rome

Marchioni Brandeburgensi principi electori   Intelleximus, dil° filio nostro tit. sancti Eustachii diacono card^li^ Senensi isthic in Ratisponen conventu sedis apost. legato per suas maxime significante, nobilitatem tuam absolutionis beneficium devote suscepisse, quod ipse tibi auctoritate nostra impendit et te sancte matris ecclesie mandatis ac nostris etiam reverenter parere velle accepimus , placet hoc nobis quam maxime . . . Here follow words of praise .   . Cuius (scil Dei) quoque gratiam maiorem ut denique assequaris, nunc potissimum assurgere debes et totus pio operi intendere atque accingi ut scilicet pro fidei puritate

---

* See *supra*, p. 190.

† See *supra*, p 128   Albrecht had been excommunicated, 1446, Oct. 15, because he persisted in marrying his daughter, Ursula, to the son of the excommunicated G Podiebrad, in spite of all warnings to the contrary

servanda atque eius tutela in hac contra Turchos expeditione penitus studeas et alios principes adesse diligentissime horteris, ingenium tibi ut praediximus perspicacissimum est atque ad omnia mature cogitanda et aggredienda prudentissimus haberis et nos scimus te gratia multum valere et auctoritate . . .

[Lib brev , 12, f 176b   Secret Archives of the Vatican]

42. Nicodemus de Pontremoli to Galeazzo Maria Sforza, Duke of Milan *

1471, Aug 2, Rome

. . . Per altre mie havera inteso V. Cels che la morte del papa fo in un subito in questo modo che essendo lui stato la matina in consistoiio cioè el venerdi a vintisei del passato da le dodece hore fino a le deceocto de la megliore voglia del mondo, cenò a le vintidoe hore, mangiò tre poponi† non molto grandi cossi alcune altre cose di trista substantia come si era assuefacto mangiare da alcuni mesi in qua.   Poi ad una hora de nocte disse ad un M Petro Franzoso suo cubiculario chel se sentiva tutto grave. Esso M. Petro gli recordò non desse audientia per quella sera, ma andasse un poco a posare.   Giettosse in suso un letuzo dove gli pigliò grande ambascie e tale che essendo uscito esso M Petro de la camera per licentiare la brigata et lassarlo dormire un poco, senti passate de poco le doe hore bussare lusso‡ de la camera dove el papa se era a pena possuto condure et aprendo lusso trovò el papa presso de morto cum molta bava a la bocca et atacandossegli el papa al colo hebero a cadere ambe doi in modo se abandonò.   Essendo li presso una cadrega M Petro cum molta difficulta ce l' assectò suso et tornò al usso a domandare M. Doymo suo compagno.   Quando tornarono dentro el papa havia posate le mane in suso li pomeli de nanti de la cadrega et appozato el capo al muro et vedendolo cum molta bava ala bocca volendolo aiutare el trovarono morto passate de poco le doe hore,§ adeo che dal principio del dolorse

---

* See *supra*, p 190.

† The death of Frederick III. is also said to have been caused by too liberal an indulgence in melons ; MAILATH, I., 319.

‡ =l' uscio

§ According to our reckoning eleven at night.   Our statement is confirmed by the best authorities ; see *Acta Consist (26 July, 2nd hour of the night,)

et morire non fo una hora   Cardinal Barbo was at once summoned. Disturbances had, up to this time, occurred only in Todi Qui sono concorsi molti sbanditi et facte alcune picole vendete et robarie, tamen el popolo se deporta fin mo assai bene

[Original in the State Archives, Milan.   P. E Roma]

43. VOTING LIST OF THE CONCLAVE OF THE YEAR 1471 *

[I] *Voce pate ne la creatione del Papa successore ad Papa Paulo.*

Niceno[1] ad Rohano,[2] Bologna,[3] Sanct †,[4] Pavia,[5] S. Petro in vinc[6]

Rohano[2] ad Niceno,[1] Bologna,[3] Sanct.†,[4] Mantoa.[7-8]

Orsino ad Thiano,[9] Ravenna[10] et S. Petro in vinc[6]

Bologna[3] ad Niceno,[1] Rhoano,[2] Sanct.†,[4] Ravenna[10] et Pavia[5]

S. Croce[4] ad Niceno,[1] Rhoano[2] et Bologna.[8]

Secret Archives of the Vatican N d TUCCIA, 100, LANDUCCI, 11, GRAZIANI, 643 , Cron Rom., 34 , NOTAR GIACOMO, 108   *Letter from the Archbishop of Milan to Galeazzo Maria Sforza, dated Rome, 1471, July 27 (11 hore di nocte ad xxvi) , State Archives, Milan (P E Roma) ; *Letter of Cichus by order of the Duke of Milan, dated Gonzaghe ult Julii, 1471 (venerdi di piox passato la nocte sequente fra 11 et tre hore). *Loc cit* Infessura is wrong in giving the 25th July as the date ; the Cronica di Bologna, 788, has the 27th   PALACKY, V , 1, 61, and CARO, V., 1, 360 *seq* , follow the last statement. This is adopted by CHEVALIER, 1740, and KRAUS, 802 ; PLATINA also falls into the same error REUMONT, Lorenzo, I , 223, 2nd ed., is also in error in asserting that the Pope died in the night between the 25th and 26th of July. TROLLOPE, The Papal Conclaves (London, 1876), even gives the 18th July as the date. Regarding the foolish reports which at once arose concerning the death of Paul, see CIPOLLA, 558

* See *supra*, p. 202   The above list is certainly the oldest extant. AMMANATI's statements are somewhat different, Epist , f. 209 (Frankfort ed., N 395) , but little weight can be attached to them because the letter in question is an apology   *Cichus Simoneta had, on the 31st July, 1471, by desire of the Duke, informed the Roman Ambassadors in writing that the Duke wished one of the following Cardinals to become Pope   Rhotomag. (d'Estouteville), S. Crucis Reatinus (Capranica), Gonzaga, S Pietro in vinc. (Fr. della Rovere), S Crisogoni Papien. (Ammanati), Card. Aquilan. (Agnifilus)   State Archives, Milan

[1] Bessarion	[2] d'Estouteville	[3] Calandini
[4] A. Capranica	[5] Ammanati	[6] Francesco della Rovere
[7 8] Fr. Gonzaga.	[9] Forteguerri	[10] Roverella

Spoleti [11] ad Thiano [9] et Ravenna [10]

Thiano [9] ad Spoleti [11] et S Petro in vinc [6]

Ravenna [10] ad Bologna,[3] Thiano,[9] Napoli [12] et S Petri [6]

Pavia [5] ad Niceno,[1] Rhoano [2] et Bologna [3]

Napoli [12] ad Niceno,[1] Spoleto [11] et Ravenna [10]

Aquila [13] ad Thiano,[9] S Marco [14] et S. Petri [6]

S Marco [14] ad Niceno [1] et Spoleti [11]

S. Piero [6] ad Orsino, Bologna,[3] S †,[4] Thexno,[9] Aquila.[13]

Vicecanc [15-16] ad Ravenna.[10]

Mantoa [7-8] ad Rhoano [2] e Vicecancell.[15-16]

Monferrato [17] ad Rhoano,[2] Bologna,[3] Theano,[9] Pavia,[5] Aquila,[13] S Petro [6] e Mantova [7-8]

S Maria in portico [18] ad Ravenna,[10] Aquilla,[13] S. Petro in vinc.[6]

S Lutia [19] ad Orsino, Aquilla,[13] S Petro in vinc [6]

[II] *Voce havute*

Niceno da S. Marco, Napoli, Rohano, Bologna, S.†, Pavia.

Rohano da Mantoa, Monferrato, Niceno, Bologna, S †, Pavia

Orsino da S Lutia S Piero in vinc.

Bologna da Monferrato, Ravenna, Niceno, Rohano, Pavia, S.†, S. Petro

S † da Niceno, Rohano, Bologna, S Pietro.

Spoleti da Thiano, S Marco, Napoli.

Thiano da Monferrato, Ravenna, Aquila, Orsino, Spoleti, S Pietro.

Ravenna da S Maria in port, Napoli, Vicecanc., Bologna, Orsino, Spoleto et S. Pietro *

Pavia da Monferrato, Niceno, Bologna

Napoli da Ravenna

Aquila da S. Lucia, S. Maria in port, Monferrato, S Petro

S Marco da Aquila.

S Pietro ad vinc da S Lutia, Monferrato, S. Maria in port., Ravenna, Thiano, Aquilla, Niceno, Bologna † et Orsino.

---

[11] Eroli   [12] Carafa.   [13] A Agnifilus

[14] Barbo   [15-16] R Borgia   [17] Theodore of Montferrat

[18] B. Zeno   [19] G Michiel.

* This is a variation from List I. where the name of Roverella does not occur among those who voted for F. della Rovere

† In List I it is not stated that Calandrini gave his vote to F della Rovere.

Vicecancell da Mantoa

Mantoa da Monferrato, Rohano

Monferrato : *niente.*

S Maria in port. · *niente*

S Lucia *niente*

Voce agiunte al papa altra le prime nove · Vicecanc , Rohanno, S Marco

[Contemporary Copy in the State Archives, Milan,

Roma ad an]

44 NICODEMUS OF PONTREMOLI TO GALEAZZO MARIA SFORZA, DUKE OF MILAN *

[1471, Aug 9, Rome †]

The Cardinal of S. Pietro in Vincoli had that very hour been elected Pope All Rome rejoices · essendo stato cognosciuto relligioso et sanct^{mo} homo etiam in minori gradu et perho e anche opinione de ognuno che debia essere optimo pastore per s. chiesa et per tutta la fede christiana

[Original in the State Archives, Milan]

45. SIXTUS IV. TO GALEAZZO MARIA SFORZA, DUKE OF MILAN.‡

1471, Aug 16, Rome.

He returns thanks for the Duke's congratulations on the Papal dignity, quam Dei clementia non meritis nostris adepti sumus. The Duke had loved him when he was yet in minoribus ; he, on his part, had continually loved the Duke Erit igitur noster hic pontificatus ad omnem honorem et dignitatem tuam facillimus. He knows him to be one of the Princes most devoted to the Apostolic See, quod clarissimis argumentis nuper vacante sede in Romandiola demonstrasti § " Dat. Romae apud S. Petrum sub

* See *supra*, p 204

† The original bears as date vii Aug., wrongly written instead of ix Aug , and the superscription "cito, cito "

‡ See *supra*, p. 215

§ See the **Brief of Sixtus IV to the Duke of Milan of 31st August, 1471. State Archives, Milan

annulo piscatoris xvi Aug, 1471 ante coronationem." His autograph signature follows.

" F[ranciscus]* vester ex optimo corde manu p pª."

[Original in the State Archives, Milan.   Autograph]

46 NICODEMUS OF PONTREMOLI TO GALEAZZO MARIA SFORZA, DUKE OF MILAN.†

1471, Aug 28, Rome.

Cum questa sera la lista ‡ de li voti dati in conclave in la
assumptione de questo novo pontefice, qual me è stato difficile
havere respecto al juramento, hanno ex consuetudine nedum de
darla, ma de non participarla cum persona   Recordomi haver
scripto per altra mia a § V. Cels quello havete ad extimare et
persuadervi di questi voti. Rimettomi a quel medesimo et a
V. C. me rec   Ex Roma, xxviii. Aug, 1471.

[Original in the State Archives, Milan]

47. POPE SIXTUS IV. TO GALEAZZO MARIA SFORZA, DUKE OF MILAN ‖

1472, June 22, Rome

Ad veterem benevolentiam quae tibi nobiscum semper inter-
cessit¶ nova accessit necessitudo by the betrothal of Girolamo
Riario to Caterina Sforza, he sends Girolamo to Milan as the
Duke wished   Sit super hec sponsalia benedictio nostra, super te
et filios tuos et filios eorum   . .

[Original in the State Archives, Milan   Autograph.]

48 POPE SIXTUS IV. TO GALEAZZO MARIA SFORZA, DUKE OF MILAN **

1472, June 22, Rome.

He earnestly exhorts the Duke, carissimum in Christo filium

---

* The Brief is not signed "Sixtus IV ," because it was written before the
Coronation   Only the baptismal name is therefore used.

† See *supra*, p 202.

‡ See No. 43 of this Appendix

§ Of the 20th Aug., 1471 , see *supra*, p 202.

‖ See *supra*, p 248   ¶ See *supra*, p 215   ** See *supra*, p 248.

Ferdinandum, Sicilie regem illustrem, affinem tuum eo amore
prosequi qui esse debet inter amantissimos affines   He could do
nothing more pleasing to him than this

[Original in the State Archives, Milan   Autograph]

49. POPE SIXTUS IV. TO GALEAZZO MARIA SFORZA, DUKE OF MILAN *

1473, Febr. 24, Rome

He thanks him for his good reception of Girolamo Riario
His pauculis diebus laboravimus aliquantulum eodem morbo
pedum qui et superiore anno nos invasit licet minus doloris et
molestie nunc nobis attulerit .   .

[Original in the State Archives, Milan.   Autograph]

50 POPE SIXTUS IV TO GALEAZZO MARIA SFORZA, DUKE OF MILAN †

1473, Nov 2, Rome.

Rediit ad nos dil filius noster Petrus tit S Sixti presbyter
cardinalis, patriarcha Constantinopolitanus, noster secundum
carnem nepos, qui quanta cum humanitate, quo apparatu, qua
liberalitate, qua iocunditate animi eum exceperis abunde nobis
explicavit   The Pope thanks the Duke for this, and confirms
all that the said Cardinal has settled with the Duke

[Original in the State Archives, Milan   Autograph.]

51. POPE SIXTUS IV TO GALEAZZO MARIA SFORZA, DUKE OF MILAN ‡

1474, June 1, Rome

The Pope declares his intention of taking care for the peace of
his subjects , he will, in particular, take measures against the rebellion in Todi , he therefore requests the Duke to send troops iuxta
requisitionem Hieronymi generis tui Imole in temp. vicarii .

[Original in the State Archives, Milan   Autograph]

---

* See *supra*, p 249   † See *supra*, p 252
‡ See the Brief to Perugia in Arch. St Ital , XVI , 588, and *supra*, p 263

52. POPE SIXTUS IV. TO GALEAZZO MARIA SFORZA, DUKE OF MILAN *

1474, June 25, Rome.

The Papal Legate is advancing with an army against Città di Castello nihil tamen aliud quam obedientiam exacturus et res civitatis illius pro omnium quiete compositurus Eam si Nic Vitellius prestare voluerit clementiam et pietatem inveniet, nam et natura ipsius nepotis et legati nostri mitissima est et nos obedientiam quaerimus non vindictam . . . †

[Original in the State Archives, Milan. Autograph.]

53 POPE SIXTUS IV TO GALEAZZO MARIA SFORZA, DUKE OF MILAN ‡

1474, July 5, Rome.

The Pope expresses his astonishment at a letter of the Duke's concerning the affair of Città di Castello Sixtus IV justifies his action in the matter, A Nic Vitello nihil aliud quam obedientiam exegimus, deponat dominatum, vivat ut privatus et clementiam in nobis inveniet, exititios introducere non est nobis consilium . . . Quis est regum aut principum qui in dominio suo populum inobedientem aut rebellem aut tyrannum possit tolerare? Quare miramur quod nobis hoc persuadeas cum potius presidium a te speremus The Florentines say they fear on account of Borgo S. Sepolcro · vana est ista suspicio, for he had assured them on his Papal word that his troops should undertake nothing against Florence §

[Original in the State Archives, Milan. Autograph]

---

* See *supra*, p. 265.

† Sixtus IV expressed himself in similar language in his *Brief to Florence, dated 1474, June 28 (a Copy is in the State Archives, Florence), and in that to Ercole d'Este, dated 1474, July 14 (the Original is in the State Archives, Modena).

‡ See *supra*, p. 266

§ The principal passage of this Brief of the 28th June, 1474, is printed *supra*, p 265, note ‡, from the State Archives, Florence Sixtus IV also communicated the document on the same 28th June, 1474, to the Duke of Milan, see *Brief of this date in the State Archives, Milan. Autograph.

54 Pope Sixtus IV. to Galeazzo Maria Sforza, Duke
of Milan *

1474, July 28, Rome.

Yhs

Sixtus papa IIII

Carissime fili salutem et apost benedict

Ve habiamo scripto molti brevi per li quali asai amplamente
avete potuto intendere la iustitia nostra in li fati de cita di Castello
E per questo si maravigemo asai e non possiam credere quillo ne †
scripto de Fiorense cioche voi non solo incitati Fiorentini contra
di noi, ma anco prometete a loro ogni subsidio contra ‡ di noi
A fili carissime quid tibi fecimus ? Non se ricordiamo averve
offeso mai nec verbo neque opere, anco per lo singulare amore
vi portiamo tuto quello abiamo potuto fare per voi habiamo fato
e faremo sempre. A a numquid redditur pro bono malum ?
quare § foderunt foveam anime mee ‖ A fili carissime consciderate
la iustitia de le mie petitione. Considerate contra quem agitur,
quod contra dominum, cui illa civitas subiecta est, contra ecclesiam
suam, contra vicarium suum, contra patrem te cordialiter amantem,
contra affinem, contra illum qui ortum habuit ex civitate tibi
subiecta. Velis ergo fili mi desistere ab inceptis ut ira Dei non
veniat super te, quod absit et velis bene consciderare petitiones
meas iustas et faveas Deo pro debito ac honore tuo, cuius con
servationem semper quesivi. Speramus pro nobilitate animi tui
quod sicut ego sum tibi bonus pater, ita eris nobis bonus filius
Fomo riquiesti pro parte vostra se volemo v' intromitesti in acordare questa cossa Dicemmo quello habiam risposto ad ogni altro
chi na ¶ fato simile domanda che non ne pare via honesta dovere
mendicare acordio con nostri subditi, ma quando voi o altro
lo facesse come da si ch' eravamo contento quod non petebamus
a subditis nisi obedientiam veram e de questa mia risposta
non credo vi dovesti scandalisare. Precamur igitur vos ut pro

---

* See *supra*, p. 267 The letter is all written by his own hand Regarding
the rarity of such Papal autographs, see CAMPORI, Lettere ined di sommi
pontefici, p. vii. (Modena, 1878).

† = n'l   ‡ Manuscript: c.
§ Manuscript qr.   ‖ JEREM., 18, 20.
¶ = n'ha

conscientia vestra ac honore vestro non velitis esse contra * eccle
siam domini prout vos facturos speramus.   Bene valete

Ex urbe 28 Iulii, 1474.

[A tergo:]

Cariss in Christo filio Galeaz Marie duci Mediolani ill
dentur in propriis manibus.

[Original in the State Archives, Milan.   Autograph]

55   POPE SIXTUS IV. TO GALEAZZO MARIA SFORZA, DUKE OF MILAN †

1474, Oct 10, Rome.

Hodie conclusum est Deo auctore et publicatum inter dil.
filium Johannem nostrum secundum carnem nepotem et natam
dil. filii nobilis viri Friderici ducis Urbini matrimonium . . .‡

[Original in the State Archives, Milan]

56   POPE SIXTUS IV. TO FLORENCE §

1475, Oct 21, Rome

He can hardly believe that they shew favour to N Vitelli, who
is fighting against the Church.   They must not do this   Secus
autem quod absit et quod non credimus iniurie resistere lacessiti
cogeremur

[Copy in the State Archives, Florence, X –II –25, f. 92–92b.]

57   REPORT OF THE MILANESE AMBASSADORS IN FLORENCE REGARDING THE CONSPIRACY OF THE PAZZI.‖

1478, April 28, Florence

Il cardinale nipote del conte Girolamo per la peste de Pisa

---

* Manuscript c.   † See *supra*, p 270
‡ On the 14th October, 1474, Sixtus IV wrote to Florence *"Nuperrime
cum dil fil nob. viro Federico Urbini duce de nata eius dilecto filio Jo. de
Ruere nostro secundum carnem nepoti in matrimonio locando transegimus,
quod gratum vobis esse non dubitamus " (State Archives, Florence, X –II –25,
f. 69b)   See the Brief to the Duke of Ferrara, dated 1474, Oct 14, in MARTÈNE,
II , 1670

§ See *supra*, p 296   Lorenzo's letter of apology, dated Florence, 1475,
Dec 25, is published in MORENI, Lettere di Lorenzo il M al S. P. Innocenzo
VIII , 1 *seq* (Florence, 1830), but—as REUMONT, Lorenzo, I., 258 2nd ed ,
observes—assigned in an incomprehensible manner to the successor of Sixtus IV.

‖ See *supra*, p 304 *seq*.   Eine Munze auf die Pazzi-Verschworung in RICHA,
VI , 142

stavasi ad un palazzo di M Jacopo de Pazzi non molto discosto
da Firenze ed aveva molte volte detto a Lorenzo de Medici
trovandosi con lui che voleva un giorno venire a Firenze per vedere
il suo palazzo e chiesa maggiore per cui Lorenzo lo aveva invitato
a venire ed a disinare in casa sua domenica scorsa che fu ai 26 di
Aprile e col cardinale aveva pure invitato l' arcivescovo de Pisa
governatore suo e da Firenze M. Jacopo de Pazzi e moltri altri
cavalieri e cittadini per onorare il cardinale ed erasi disposto un
solennissimo apparato, el cardinale col arcivescovo venne la
domenica mattina e smontato si pose nel duomo alla messa grande
che era cantata solennemente e circa il momento che si intonava
l'agnus Dei,* etc, quando Giuliano e Lorenzo ambedue se trovarono
in duomo che secundo l' usanza passegiavano pero ben separati
l' uno dall altro Lorenzo fu assaltato da alcuni, tutti forastieri e per
la piu parte Spagnuoli della famiglia del cardinale o forse dell'
arcivescovo, ma che se seppe presto reparare, mentre dal famiglio
ed alcuni giovani fu ajutato essendosi essi interposti ripararono i
colpi coi loro mantelli che ancora si vedono traorati   Lorenzo
scappò il pericolo e fu soltanto leggermente ferito alla gola e tosto
ritirato in sacrestia; certo Francesco Neri suo compagno nel
ripararlo fu ammazzato.   Mentre che Lorenzo fu così assaltato ed
in un punto medesimo da un altra parte del duomo a Giuliano fu
facto simile assalto da costoro insieme con uno Franceschino de
Pazzi e Bernardo Barunzelli che ambedue proditoriamente quella
matina si erano accompagnati con Giuliano e loro due furoni i
primi a dargli delle ferite e così il povero Giuliano rimase morto
con innumerevoli ferite che doveva essere pietà a vederlo   Dio
non volle la morte de Lorenzo per evitare maggiore male. .   .
Non si potrebbe esprimere quanta dimonstrazione abbia fatto
questo popolo a Lorenzo e casa de Medici   The people shout
Palle, palle ! Execution of the guilty : L' arcivescovo dopo gli vene
concesso di potersi confessarse e comunicare fu appicato per la
gola lui ed il fratello con Jacopo Salviati suo nipote, Jacopo de M
Poggio con tutti quelli che erano presi in palazzo ed erano gettati
fuori dalle finestre del palazzo de Sⁿ col capestro appicato al
colonello delle finestre e di la un pezzo tagliavasi i capestri e
cadevano in piazza, in piazza che erano caduti straziavansi dal

* NOTAR GIACOMO, 133, gives the same account.

popolo e dalla moltitudine in pezzi. . . El numero delle persone impiccate, tagliate a pezzi e morte in questo facto forse ascende ad un centinajo di persone.   .

[State Archives, Milan, Cart. gen]

58 ALBERTINUS, PRIOR OF S MARTINO, TO MARCHIONESS BARBARA OF MANTUA.*

1478, April 28, Florence.

He arrived in Florence on the 27th.   Nui habiamo trovato Firenza in grande travaio cum credo sapia la prefata V. S.   Lordine de la cosa sicondo posso intendere è questo · zoè essendo venuto il card^le nepote del conte Jeronimo a Fiorenza non si dice perche se non che mal per lui et per altri, ditto card^le non volse intrar in Fiorenza, ma si redusse di fora a uno zardino de quelli de Pazi e de li a certi di questi Pazi fezeno uno convido a Fesole dove fu invitado Lorenzo de Cosimo e Zuliano de Cosimo, ma Zuliano no possette andarli cha haveva due anguinalie, sichel disegno de Pazi non potete haver effetto, ma non pentiti fezeno che Lorenzo convidoe il card^le a casa sua a pasto per haver ditto Lorenzo e Zuliano a suo a piacere, siche aparichiatto il convido amplo e magnifico venuta lora de la messa andono in S. Liberata e tardono la messa piu che fu possibile per far fastidio al popolo azio se havesse a partire, ma pur seguendo la messa quando il prete fui a la levatione† se levò Franceschino de Pazi e amaza de fatto cum certe sui compagni Zuliano de Medici ; da po volse e menò per dar a Lorenzo e uno suo compagno li volse pihar il colpo e piliò la morte de fatto per modo che ditto Franceschino tahò la testa cum una spala a ditto compagno de Lorenzo e cum quello medesmo colpo ferì Lorenzo in de la gola, ma non ha grande male   Il card^le fuzi e larcivescovo de Pisa corse al palazo‡ cum certi fanti . . . e funo a li mane, il popolo corse e non potendo intrare andono a una altra porta e brusola e introno dentro e preseno larcivescovo e de fatto lo inpicono lui e il fratello, possa preseno il card^le cum tuti quelli de li sui che poteno havere e furono inpicati e similiter il prete che havea cantato la messa e dui garzoneti che erano ragazi del card^le per modo che quello di

<hr>

* See supra, p 304 seq.   † See supra, p 309, note *.
‡ For what follows, see REUMONT, Lorenzo, I., 289 seq., 2nd ed

fui la domenica ne forono inpichati 36 ; il luni seguente* ne fono
inpichati 16, ozi che martidi ancho non e fatto altro, ma questa
notte è sta menato Ser Jacomo de Pazi cum circha 18 altri e tuta
via ne sono menati e tuti secondo se dice siranno inpichati, il
card⁰ e pur vivo, ma in presone in del palazo de li Sⁿ cum grande
guarda, se tene perho che non morirà, altro non ho presentuto
fin a questa hora presente e che hore nove et di 28 del presente . . . Dopo questa hora siamo a messa a l' Anunciata et
havemo fatto oratione speciale per V S e tornati a lozamenti ne
stato ditto alcuni soldati del conte Jeronimo sono stati taliati a
pezi venendo lor a Fiorenza   Non ho potuto intendere altro mi
ric⁰ᵒ a V M S   Florentie die 28 Aprilis, 1478

E. D V serᵒʳ fidᵐᵘˢ don Albertinus prior S Martini.

[Original in the Gonzaga Archives, Mantua.]

59 Instruction from Sixtus IV. for Ludovico de Agnellis
   and Antonio de Grassis Nuncios to Emperor Frederick
   III †

1478, Dec. 1

Instructiones datae r patrib dom. Ludovico de Agnellis
protonot apost et Antonio de Grassis ‡ s. palati causar auditori
ad Mᵗᵉᵐ Imp S. D. N. oratoribus.   Primo salutabunt serᵐᵘᵐ
Imperatorem . . . Complaints against Lorenzo de Medici   Item
audivimus Venetos misisse ad suam Mᵗᵉᵐ Jacobum de Medio,§
qui diu in curia nostra ista versatus est et cognitus, cuius dicta
bene advertat, est enim magnus fabricator et Cretensis, qui iuxta
apostolum consueverunt esse mendaces‖ . . . Insuper sciat
Serenitas S, quod Veneti convenerunt cum rege Franciae, ad

---

* 27th April.   † See *supra*, p 326.
‡ Some Manuscripts have Frassis, a mistake which Ranke, Papste, III , 4*,
has not noticed   It is hard to understand how Ranke, *loc cit* , can speak of
this Instruction as "the oldest" which came before him among the Manuscripts
which he saw.   The Berlin Historian made use of Cod. VII , G. 1, 99, of the
Altieri Library in Rome, which contains the well-known Instruction of 1472
for Card Barbo, cited *supra*, p 224, and frequently to be met with among the
Manuscripts in the Roman Libraries   The texts communicated by Ranke are
not correct.
§ See, regarding him, Gott Gel. Anz , 1879, p 282
‖ Tit , 1, 12

quem cum istis de liga miserunt oratorem, ut fiat scandalum in
ecclesia, obliti quot quantasque pecunias exposuerimus contra
Turcum in eorum et caeterorum defensione Christianorum.
Miramur certe, quod ipsi qui se profitentur Christianos velint
maiorem fidem servare erga Laurentium de Medicis quam erga
Deum et sedem apost . . miramur potissimum, quia anno
superiori, ut per coniecturas satis per omnes cognitum est, Carolus
de Montone instigatione ligae venisset ad damna ecclesiae, nam
habebat in Perusia tractatum civitate ecclesiae, qua habita omnes
aliae civitates et tota ecclesia fuisset perturbata, cum etiam
detecta proditione publice aggressus fuisset Senenses et pax
Italiae fluctuaret cum tamen Turcus esset prope Forum Julii
et iam abduxisset magnam praedam, ipsi nihil dicebant, Carolum
non reprimebant, nec per ligam quidquam dicebatur de Turco, sed
potius de iuvando eundem Carolum, contra cuius oppidum
misimus exercitum nostrum, ne amplius perturbaret pacem Italicam
Juvabatur iste ab omnibus, prout per nostros suae Ser[ti] iam scripsimus, et cum reverteret Florentiam colebatur ab omnibus ac si
Deus esset Scripseramus tum primo ad Venetos, ut vellent eum
revocare . . . et nunquam nobis responderunt Nunc autem
ecclesia juste contra ipsum Laurentium mota, clamant Veneti,
clamat tota ista liga, petunt cum rege Franciae concilium in Gallis
in dedecus nostrum . . parum advertentes, ad quos spectat congregare concilium . . . eapropter hortamur M[tem] suam, ut non
praestet eis aures . sed rogamus M[tem] Suam, ut pro debito
suae protectionis quod habet ad ecclesiam et pro honore
suo . . velit scribere regi Franciae similiter et isti ligae osten-
dendo, quod non recte faciunt et . . . quod debent magis favere
ecclesiae iustitiam habenti, quam uno mercatori, qui semper magna
causa fuit, quod non potuerunt omnia confici contra Turcum, quae
intendebamus parare et fuit semper petra scandali in ecclesia Dei
et tota Italia.

His age and infirmities make it impossible for him to leave
Rome, but he hopes to see the Emperor in Rome, and there to
take counsel with him regarding the affairs of Christendom.

Reddat igitur nos certos et de tempore et de via, per quam
venturus erit . . . Item dicat suae Ser[ti], quod rex Franciae et alii
complures principes querunt se intromittere, ut fiat ista concordia
inter nos, Laurentium et alios, quibus respondimus, quod semper

parati sumus ad pacem, dummodo fiat cum honore Dei et ecclesiae
Tamen cum ipse sit primus inter principes temporales . . optare-
mus, ut ipse, qui est ecclesiae protector, haberet istum honorem
He should do this.

[Cop in the Secret Archives of the Vatican, Instruct. divers,
II., 30, f 55b–57 et LV, f 43b *seq.*; Vatican Library, Cod
Ottob, 2726, f 40b–43, Altieri Library (see *supra*, p 515,
note †), Barberini Library, XXVII, 4, f 81, Borghese Library,
I –34b.; Chigi Library, Q 7, 6, Corsini Library, 33, F. 1,
f. 68–70.]

60. Pier Filippo Pandolfini to Florence.*

1479, March 20, Rome

Tutta questa corte generalmente desidera et vorrebbe pace et ne
parlono publicamente, in questa medesima sententia è la maggior
parte de cardinali, ma sono in luogo che non ardiscono parlare
quello intendono et alcuni che lanno fatto ne sono stato molto
represi et con parole non conveniente dal conte Je[ronimo] et da
M Aniello imb[re] del re in modo che qui ogni cosa si fa secondo
la voglia del conte Je[ronimo] il qual in omnibus dipende dal
re . . . .

[State Archives, Florence, X –II –24.]

61 Pier Filippo Pandolfini to Florence.†

1479, March 25, Rome

The Cardinals wish that the negotiations for peace should not
be broken off. ma il conte ‡ puo piu lui solo che tutto il collegio
et pero sanza lui nulla e da sperare si possi fare.

[State Archives, Florence, X.–II –24]

62 Pope Sixtus IV. to Louis XI., King of France §

1479, April 6, Rome.

He announces the suspension of the censures and the cessation
of hostilities with the Florentines : Quod significamus tue M[ti] ut
optimum animum nostrum et dispositionem cognoscat ad com-

---

* See *supra*, pp 327, 413   † See *supra*, pp 327, 413
‡ Girolamo Riario.   § See *supra*, p 328

placendum tue M^u et ad pacem ipsam dummodo fiat cum honore apost sedis.

[Contemporary Copy in the State Archives, Milan.]

63 CARDINAL GIULIANO DELLA ROVERE TO LOUIS XI , KING OF FRANCE *

1479, April 7, Rome

He has been silent because there was nothing important to tell, et fere nulla spes pacis erat.   Now, however, the Pope has yielded to his Majesty's request   arma deposuit censurasque et interdicta suspendit .   .

[Contemporary Copy in the State Archives, Milan]

64 POPE SIXTUS IV TO DUKE PHILIBERT I OF SAVOY.†

1481, Sept 18, Bracciano.

Quod toto nostro desiderio expectabamus et iocundissimum nobis fuit, hodie intelleximus a nostris   the reconquest of Otranto This opportunity must be seized to resist the Turks   it will never return if now allowed to escape   Ecce tempus salutis, tempus glorie, tempus victorie quod si negligatur nullum tale unquam recuperare poterimus   Parvo negocio bellum nunc confici potest quod non sine maximo dispendio maximis calamitatibus nostris . . postea conficietur   He has done everything, and ought now to be supported.

Simile imperatori.

Regi Francie, Anglie, Scocie, Polonie, Dacie, Hungarie, His-panie, Portugallie.

Duci Maximiliano, Britanie, Mediolani.

Electoribus imperii.

Duci Ferrarie, Sabaudie

March Montisferrati, Mantue.

Florent Lucens Senensib ‡

[National Library, Florence   Cod Magliab , II –III –256, f 52b]

---

* See *supra*, p 328   † See *supra*, p. 344
‡ Of these Briefs I found that addressed to the Duke of Milan in the State Archives, Milan, and that to the Florentines in the State Archives, Florence (X –II –25, f 168b)   Both are dated Bracciano, 1481, Sept 18, and agree with each other ; the text, however, differs from the one given above

65. Pope Sixtus IV to Cardinal Fregoso, Legate of the Crusader Fleet.*

1481, Sept 18, Bracciano

He has received the Legate's letter of the 11th of September concerning the conquest of Otranto. Great joy at this success, which will confer everlasting glory on the Legate and the Duke of Calabria

Reliquum est ut quod prospere inceptum est felicibus incrementis perficiatur hostesque ipsos omni conatu persequamur ut hac cura et periculo Italiam perpetuo liberemus, ad quam rem intrepide capessendam omnes christianos principes exhortati sumus † Quare quod in te est cum classe nostra reliquias belli prosequere et hostes quam maximis potes damnis contere ne oblate divinitus occasioni desimus. . . Quod prestare ipsi possumus libenter facimus utinamque soli possemus neminem certe requireremus The Pope is surprised that the patroni triremium complain without cause.

[National Library at Florence. Cod. Maghab., II.–III –256, f 38]

66. Cardinal F Gonzaga to Federigo I of Gonzaga ‡

1482, Sept 11, Rome

. Essendo accaduta questa accelerata et immatura morte de la bo me. del Sr Roberto Malatesta causata da una febre continua terzana dopia cum fluxo vehementissimo per il che tandem heri tra la prima e seconda hora de nocte expiravit § The Pope has to-day legitimatised Roberto's sons per la successione

[Original in the Gonzaga Archives, Mantua]

67 Pope Sixtus IV. to the Duke of Milan.‖

1483, March 4, Rome

Dispensatio duci Mediol. pro impositione novae gabellae seu

---

* See *supra*, p 345   † See No 64 of this Appendix
‡ See *supra*, p. 369
§ Caleffini, in his *Cronica Ferrariae, writes, Roberto died yesterday * "de una ferita che l' have adi passati in lo facta d' arme fra lui, conte Hieronymo, duca de Calabria et Romani ; " a "fluxo" having supervened Nothing is here said of poison. Cod I –I –4 of the Chigi Library, Rome.
‖ See *supra*, p 374.

datu ad succurrendum eius gravissimis impensis presertim pro defensione Ferrariae.*

[Original in the State Archives, Milan.   Autograph.]

68   Pope Sixtus IV. to the Duke of Milan †

1483, April 3, Rome

A long letter urging the importance of naval warfare against Venice   Verum quia et a principio et semper expedire ac necessarium esse diximus ut valida classis maritima instrueretur sine qua ullus bonus rerum successus vix sperari posset huiusmodi rem tanti momenti esse ut in ea certissima victoriae spes collocata sit, commemoramus

[Original in the State Archives, Milan.]

69. Pope Sixtus IV to the Duke of Milan ‡

1483, April 16, Rome

Instat apud ducem ut contribuere velit quam citius pecunias per eum solvendas pro armanda classe   .

[Original in the State Archives, Milan]

70. Pope Sixtus IV to the Duke of Milan.§

1483, April 21, Rome

Sixtus IV. hortatur ducem ad solvendum stipendia promissa pro armanda classe contra Venetos.

[Original in the State Archives, Milan]

71. Pope Sixtus IV to the Duke of Milan ‖

1483, May 1, Rome

An exhortation to send aid to Parma for the rescue of Ferrara.

[Original in the State Archives, Milan.   Autograph.]

---

* Thus in a contemporary statement of contents.

† See *supra*, p 374   ‡ See *supra*, p. 374.

§ See *supra*, p. 374   ‖ See *supra*, p. 374.

72 GIROLAMO RIARIO TO THE DUKE OF MILAN *

1483, May 7, Rome

As Ferrara is in the greatest danger, the Duke is urged to send help as soon as possible

[Original in the State Archives, Milan. P E. Milano]

73 POPE SIXTUS IV TO THE DUKE OF MILAN.†

1483, May 25, Rome

Dilecte fili, etc Mittimus nobilitati tue bullam censurarum adversus Venetos quam publicari hic fecimus He is to allow this Bull to be published in his domains

[Original in the State Archives, Milan. Autograph]

74 POPE SIXTUS IV. TO ULRICH VIII ,‡ ABBOT OF ST. GALL §

1483 June 5, Rome

. Cum superioribus diebus decrevimus bullam censurarum adversus Venetos, qui ab oppugnatione civitatis nostrae Ferrariensis . . desistere noluerunt, mittimus ad te bullam . allegatam, te quoque hortamur ut personaliter ad confoederatos omnes tamquam orator noster accedas et . opereris ut bulla ipsa publicari possit. . .

[Original in Cathedral Chapter Archives, St Gall ‖]

75 POPE SIXTUS IV TO EMPEROR FREDERICK III ¶

1483, June 15, Rome

He sends him the Bull against Venice, and exhorts him to let it be published in the Empire et cum effectu observari. Describes the ambition and thirst for conquest of the Venetians The Pope hopes that the Emperor will proceed against these enemies qui

---

* See *supra*, p 374   † See *supra*, p 376

‡ Rosch aus Wangen, Abbot from 1463-91 ; see MOOYER, Onomasticon Hierarchiae Germ., 138 (Minden, 1854).

§ See *supra*, p 376

‖ This Brief is also in Lib brev , 15, f 601, Secret Archives of the Vatican, and there is a contemporary Copy in the State Archives, Milan

¶ See *supra*, p 376

scisma in ecclesia Dei querunt.   The Emperor must shew himself
a Catholic Prince

[Lib. brev., 15, f 623.   Secret Archives of the Vatican.]

76 Pope Sixtus IV. to the Duke of Milan *

1483, July 15, Rome

The Pope again most urgently begs him to begin the war against
Venice in Lombardy

[Original in the State Archives, Milan   Autograph.]

77 Pope Sixtus IV to the Duke of Milan

1483, Aug 20, Rome

Exhorts him to send assistance to Ferrara, for this is the most
important point

[Original in the State Archives, Milan   Autograph]

78 Pope Sixtus IV. to the Duke of Milan

1483, Aug. 25, Rome

The necessity of still maintaining the fleet is urgently insisted
on.

[Original in the State Archives, Milan   Autograph]

79 Pope Sixtus IV. to the Duke of Milan

1483, Sept 20, Rome

The fleet must still be kept up for some time   The Duke
ought to lend his aid

[Original in the State Archives, Milan   Autograph]

80 Pope Sixtus IV to the Duke of Milan

1483, Oct 2, Rome.

Urgent exhortations to send support, especially for the fleet,
whose maintenance is very necessary.

[Original in the State Archives, Milan.   Autograph]

* For Nos. 76 to 80, see *supra*, p 385

81. Pope Sixtus IV to the Duke of Milan *

1483, Oct 13, Rome

Non possumus satis mirari quod res Ferrariensis ita negligatur . Nihil factum est eorum quae in dieta et post dietam ordinata sunt   The Duke must send help most speedily.   He (the Pope) is not to blame if Ferrara be lost   Similia Regi et Florent.

[Lib. brev., 16 B, f. 98   Secret Archives of the Vatican.]

82. Stefano Guidotti to Mantua †

1484, Aug 12, Rome

A quest' hora che sono quattro de notte ‡ le passato di questa vita el papa   The Cardinals assemble in the Palace during the night.   The beginning of disturbances is already to be seen

[Original in the Gonzaga Archives, Mantua]

---

* See *supra*, p. 385   † See *supra*, p 388
‡ The same *Stefano Guidotti writes still more precisely on the 13th Aug ·
" Ale 4 hora e ¼ el passò di questa vita, benissimo disposto e recevuti tuti i sacramenti ecclesiastici resi il spirito a Dio." (Gonzaga Archives)   The Lib confrat Sta M. del Anima also says that the Pope died between the 4th and 5th hour of the night, as does the record from the Library at Munich in SCHMARSOW, 377   A Sienese Despatch mentions the 3rd hour , see Arch d Soc. Rom., XI , 618.

PRINTED BY NEILL AND CO , LIMITED, EDINBURGH

CPSIA information can be obtained
at www.ICGtesting.com
Printed in the USA
LVHW061313020623
748644LV00044B/621

fs

The quality of your thinking depends on the models in your head.

Mental models help you see the world as it is, not as you want it to be. When you see the world as it is, you can more easily align yourself with it. Suddenly you have a tailwind instead of a headwind.

When I started FS, one of my goals was to share the tools that have changed my life with the world. Accomplishing that is what led us to create the Great Mental Models project. This book series aims to help equalize opportunity in the world by making a high-quality, multidisciplinary, interconnected education free and available to everyone.

We know it's a big ambition, and we're glad we have a partner who shares our vision. The physical books wouldn't be possible without Automattic, an amazing company dedicated to giving great ideas a voice and a global platform. Like us, they believe knowledge is meant to be shared as widely as possible, and we're grateful for their support. (Check out their Afterthoughts on page 369.)

To each and every reader, I want to thank you for your curiosity. I'm so excited that you are on this journey with us. To learn more about the Great Mental Models project, visit fs.blog/tgmm.

Shane Parrish
Founder of FS

Published in 2021 by Latticework Publishing
201-854 Bank Street, Ottawa, K1S 3W3
Copyright © Farnam Street Media Inc.
Creative direction by Garvin Hirt and Morgwn Rimel
Designed and typeset by FLOK, Berlin
Illustrations by Marcia Mihotich, London
Printed in Latvia by Livonia Print

A portion of this work has appeared online at fs.blog.

www.fs.blog

Book ISBN: 978-1-9994490-6-3
Ebook ISBN: 978-1-9994490-7-0

The Great
Mental Models
Vol.3

Systems and Mathematics

Contents

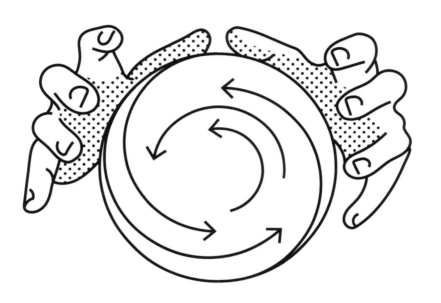

Introduction

In Volume I of *The Great Mental Models*, we introduced nine general thinking concepts to get you started on the journey of building a latticework of timeless knowledge. Time and again those models have proven indispensable in both solving problems and preventing them in the first place.

In Volume II of *The Great Mental Models*, we continued the journey and explored fundamental ideas from physics, chemistry, and biology. The truths about the physical world, from the forces that allow us to manipulate energy to the behaviors that drive the actions of all organisms, are constants that can guide our decisions so that our actions are aligned with how the world works.

« How much you know in the broad sense determines what you understand of the new things you learn. »

Hilde Østby and Ylva Østby[1]

In this book, Volume III, we will consider some of the basics of systems thinking and mathematics. Although these subjects can appear abstract, as soon as we start taking them apart, we quickly see that they describe so many of the behaviors and interactions that govern our lives. We hope you are excited about embarking on this next step of the journey.

« The more moving parts you have in something, the more possibilities there are. »

Adam Frank[2]

[1]
Hilde Østby and Ylva Østby, *Adventures in Memory* (Vancouver, Canada: Greystone Books, 2018).

[2]
Marc N. Kleinhenz, "Doctor Strange Advisor Explains the Science Behind Marvel's Multiverse," ScreenRant, March 2, 2017, https://screenrant.com/doctor-strange-multiverse-science/.

About the series

The Great Mental Models series is designed to inspire and challenge you. We want to give you both knowledge and a framework for making it useful.

One of our goals for the series is to provide you with a set of tools built on timeless knowledge that you can use again and again to make better decisions. It is a guide to dozens of mental models, spread across multiple volumes, that define and explore the foundational concepts from a variety of disciplines. We then take the concept out of its original discipline and show you how you can apply it in less obvious situations. We encourage you to dive into new ideas to augment your knowledge toolbox but also to leverage what you already know by applying it in new ways to give yourself a different perspective on the challenges you face.

In the first book, we explained that a mental model is simply a representation of how something works. We use models to retain knowledge and simplify how we understand the world. We can't relearn everything every day, so we construct models to help us chunk patterns and navigate our world more efficiently. Farnam Street's mental models are reliable principles that you can see at work in the world time and again. Using them means synthesizing across disciplines and not being afraid to apply knowledge from different areas far outside the milieu they usually cover.

Not every model applies to all situations. Part of building a latticework of mental models is educating yourself regarding which situations are best addressed by which models. This takes some work, and you're likely to make some mistakes. It's important to constantly reflect on your use of models. If something didn't work, you need to try to discover why. Over time, by reflecting on your use of individual models, you will learn which models will best help you tackle which situations. Knowing why a model works will help you know when to use it again.

3
Peter M. Senge, *The Fifth Discipline*
(London: Random House Business,
2006).

« Systems thinking is a discipline for
seeing wholes. It is a framework for seeing
interrelationships rather than things, for
seeing patterns of change rather than static
"snapshots." »

Peter Senge[3]

About this book

This book examines some of the core mental models from systems and mathematics. Systems are everywhere, and we live our lives as part of many of them. Mathematics, too, explains the dynamics of how much of our world works. We start each chapter by explaining the theory behind the concept and then situate it in real-world examples. We want you to see each concept in action and be inspired to find analogous uses in your own life. In order to achieve this goal, we show how using the model as a lens will help you see stories and themes in history in a new way.

As you go through this book, you will begin to see just how interconnected systems and mathematics are. Although we have broken the components apart to consider them separately, by the end we guarantee you will be making connections between the models. You will start to see how bottlenecks connect to surface area and how feedback loops underpin the behavior of so many system interactions. Often the lessons and insights are relevant both at an individual and organizational level. As you learn the models, you will start to see the principles they cover in almost any situation where you find yourself. You'll see things others don't and avoid costly mistakes.

Some of the models in this book function like metaphors, especially in the mathematics section. We aim to show you how to use these models to uncover the dynamics in a variety of challenging situations you may face and give you insight on how to harness the ideas they suggest to positively influence your outcomes. The more you know, the easier it is to design solutions that will work.

Other models, especially from systems, have a more literal application. Because systems are so ubiquitous, it's not useful to try to apply these models outside of systems. Rather, we try to give you ideas for considering just how much of life is part of a system so you can expand your application of systems thinking.

When looking at historical examples through the lens of a model, it's important to remember that we are not attempting to demonstrate causation. We are not saying that what happened in a particular moment in history can be explained by, for example, a mathematical formula or that a particular historical figure used the described model to guide their decisions. We are simply showing you how you might understand that bit of history differently when you use a particular model as a lens or giving you a different perspective on why a particular person's decisions led to the outcomes they did. You therefore will get inspiration for applying the same model to non-intuitive situations in your own life.

Finally, all these models, as with those covered in the previous books, are value neutral. They can be used to illuminate both the positive and negative aspects of any situation. They might work well in one situation but not in another. We try to balance use of the models with noting some of their limitations so you have ideas for when you might want to take an alternate approach.

You will learn the differences in how to apply each model through the stories we have chosen to explain them. Each example is crafted to give you insight into where the model can apply. You can take the elements of each story as a signpost directing you to find similar situations in your life where the lens of a particular model will be most useful.

The most important thing to remember is that all of these models are tools. You are meant to try them out, play with them, and learn what you can use each of them to fix. Not all tools are useful for all problems, and just as a traditional toolbox has a hammer when you need to pound a nail but a wrench for when you need to turn a bolt, you'll learn through practice which tools are useful in which situations. The best way to do that is to start by being curious. As you begin each chapter, be open to learning and updating your knowledge. Then, practice. Pick a new model every day, apply it to a situation you are in, and see if you can improve your understanding and decision-making. Finally, reflect. Take some time to evaluate your success and failures. In doing so, you will begin to learn the full potential of the toolkit you are building.

Time to get started.

Systems

In spite of what you majored in, or what the textbooks say, or what you think you're an expert at, follow a system wherever it leads. It will be sure to lead across traditional disciplinary lines.

Donella H. Meadows[1]

Systems

1
Donella H. Meadows, *Thinking in Systems* (Vermont: Chelsea Green Publishing, 2008).

Feedback Loops

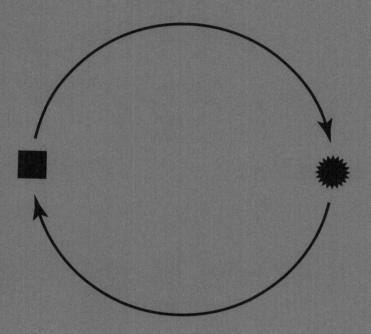

—
Listen and incorporate

Feedback Loops

Feedback loops are everywhere in systems, making them a useful mental model.

Think of "feedback" as the information communicated in response to an action. Whether we realize it or not, we give and receive different forms of feedback every day. Sometimes feedback is more formal, as is the case with performance reviews. Other times, it is less so. Our body language is a form of feedback for people interacting with us. The tone you use with your kids is feedback for them.

Feedback loops are so important. One of the reasons we say at FS the five people closest to you matter most to your outcomes and happiness is because of the quality of feedback they offer you. The people you spend the most time with are the ones who give you the most feedback on your behavior and thus have the most impact on the choices you make and the ways you change.

Once you start looking for feedback loops, you see them all over the place, giving you insight into why people and systems react the way they do. For example, much of human behavior is driven by incentives. We want to take actions that lead to us getting something good or avoiding something bad on a range of timescales. The incentives we create for ourselves and other people are a form of feedback, leading to loops that reinforce or discourage certain behaviors. If you get visibly upset whenever someone at work offers you constructive criticism, you'll incentivize your colleagues to only tell you when you're doing something well—thereby missing out on chances to improve.

The challenge in using this mental model is that the ubiquity of feedback loops can become overwhelming. How do you know which ones to pay attention to? Or which ones to adjust to improve your outcomes?

We are constantly offering feedback about our feelings,

preferences, and values. Others are communicating feedback, but we don't necessarily receive it or interpret it correctly. A critical requirement is learning how to filter feedback. Not all of it is useful. The more quickly you learn to identify good feedback and accept and incorporate it, the more progress you will make toward what you want to achieve.

Learning to communicate your feedback in a way that makes it easy for others to receive is a valuable skill to develop.

There is a larger implication here about working with the world. The world offers us feedback, but do we listen and incorporate, or do we just keep wanting it to work differently than it does?

The technical definition of feedback loops comes from systems theory. A feedback loop is when the outputs (information) of a system affect its own behaviors. Depending on the complexity of a system, there may be a single source of feedback or multiple, possibly interconnected, sources. While it helps to first consider feedback in a simple system as we will do below, we are all part of many large systems that contain many interconnected feedback loops.

Feedback loops are a critical model because they are a part of your life, whether you are aware of them or not. Understanding how they work helps you be more flexible with the variety of feedback you receive and incorporate, and you can offer better feedback to others.

There are two basic types of feedback loops: balancing and reinforcing, which are also called negative and positive. Balancing feedback loops tend toward an equilibrium, while reinforcing feedback loops amplify a particular process. Your thermostat and heating system run on a balancing feedback loop. Information about the temperature of the house is communicated to the thermostat, which then adjusts the output of the furnace to maintain your desired temperature. Reinforcing feedback loops don't counter change, like your thermostat does. Instead they keep the change going, as with the popularity of trends in fashion or the loops usually involved in poverty. Breaking out of reinforcing loops often requires outside intervention or a new change in conditions. Or they burn themselves out.

Within complex systems, feedback is rarely immediate. It can take a long time for changes in flows to have a measurable impact on how the system works. This delay can complicate establishing cause and effect. In our lives, problems arise when the feedback for our actions is delayed or indirect, as is often the case.

A challenge to improving our decision-making is getting accurate feedback on past decisions. On one hand, consequences may take a long time to become apparent or be hard to directly attribute to a particular decision. On the other, we may trap ourselves in maladaptive behaviors when something we do receives positive short-term feedback but has negative long-term consequences. Thus it's important to remember immediate feedback isn't the only feedback. When you eat junk food, there is an instant hit of pleasure as your body responds to fat and sugar. After a little while though, you receive other feedback from your body that indicates your choice of junk food had negative consequences. And over longer periods, conditions such as type 2 diabetes or high blood pressure provide more feedback from your body about the effects of your eating habits.

The faster you get accurate feedback, the more quickly you can iterate to improve. Feedback can cause problems, however, if it is too fast and too strong, as the system can surge. It's like when you press the gas or brake too heavily when first learning how to drive. Balancing feedback is usually more useful in quantities that don't cause extreme oscillation.

Feedback loops are a useful mental model because all systems have them, and we are surrounded by systems.

— Sidebar: Adam Smith and the Feedback Loop of Reactions

Adam Smith and the Feedback Loop of Reactions

You probably know Adam Smith as one of the most influential economists of all time, notable for his notion of the "invisible hand" of the market. But Smith's first book, *The Theory of Moral Sentiments*, is a work of philosophy.[1] In it, he describes a different sort of invisible force that guides us: how the approval and disapproval of others, real or imagined, influences our behavior.

We are, by nature, selfish. We value ourselves above all other humans. Smith illustrates his point by suggesting that the news that your little finger must be amputated would likely be more stressing than the news of the deaths of a huge number of strangers overseas. Yet despite our inherent selfishness, the majority of people the majority of the time are cooperative and kind to each other. Smith believed our interactions with others are responsible for our well-established reciprocity. He saw their responses to our behavior as feedback guiding how we act in the future. To do something selfish usually warrants a disapproving reaction. To do something selfless usually merits an approving one.

The feedback loop of others' reactions to our actions is the basis of civilization. Russ Roberts writes in *How Adam Smith Can Change Your Life*, "Smith's vision of civilization is the stream of approval and disapproval we all provide when we respond to the conduct of those around us. That stream of approval and disapproval creates feedback loops to encourage good behavior and discourage bad behavior."[2]

This type of feedback doesn't just cover formal punishments and prohibitions according to the law where we live. It also covers the ways people respond to behavior that is just considered the norm. If a friend says hello to you in the street and you fail to acknowledge them, you haven't broken any laws, but they're likely to respond in a negative fashion. So you adhere to the norm. Smith writes:

When Nature formed man for society, she endowed him with a basic desire to please his brethren and a basic aversion to offending them. She taught him to feel pleasure in their favorable regard and pain in their unfavorable

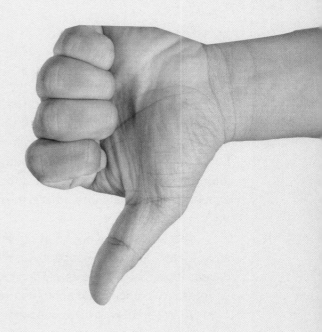

regard. She made their approval most flattering and most agreeable to him for its own sake, and their disapproval most humiliating and most offensive.[3]

Smith asked readers to imagine a person who grows to adulthood without any interactions with other people. He believed such a person would have no awareness of their character and no notion of the right or wrong way to act.[4] Our desire to be loved and accepted prompts moral behavior relative to the standards of our society. We in turn respond with approval of the same behavior on the part of others.[5]

But Smith also recognized that morality is not fixed and changes over time. Ideas that are now unthinkable were once considered moral or at least neutral. Then the feedback loop changed as people began to respond in less positive ways. Smith gives the example of infanticide, unthinkable in most countries today. But before the advent of accessible birth control, it was an accepted part of life in many countries. The ancient Greeks had no qualms about leaving sickly or otherwise unwanted babies to face the elements, lest they be a burden on their families. It still occurs in cultures without access to birth control or abortion.[6] Smith writes, "We constantly hear men saying, 'It's commonly done,' apparently thinking that this a sufficient excuse for something that is in itself the most unjust and unreasonable conduct."[7]

1
Jack Russell Weinstein, Internet Encyclopedia of Philosophy, accessed August 14, 2019, https://www.iep.utm.edu/smith/.
2
Russell D. Roberts, *How Adam Smith Can Change Your Life: An Unexpected Guide to Human Nature and Happiness* (New York: Portfolio/Penguin, 2015).
3
Smith, ibid.
4
Adam Smith, *The Theory of Moral Sentiments by Adam Smith* (London: Printed for A. Millar, A. Kincaid, and J. Bell in Edinburgh, 1761).
5
Smith, ibid.
6
Sandra Newman, "The Roots of Infanticide Run Deep, and Begin with Poverty," Aeon, November 27, 2017, https://aeon.co/essays/the-roots-of-infanticide-run-deep-and-begin-with-poverty.
7
Smith, ibid.

Everyday loops

We can address many of the challenges we face every day by adjusting feedback loops. Figuring out how to change behavior (ours and others'), dealing with inaccurate information, and building trust are ongoing challenges. How to get customers to buy your product and not the competitors'; how to sort through information to find what is relevant to your decision; how to cooperate effectively with others: these are all common situations that we face.

All of these dynamics play out on the larger social scale as well. How do societies incentivize the behavior they want and disincentivize the behavior they don't want? How do they get people to trust each other enough to keep society functioning?

Any system with an unchecked reinforcing feedback loop is ultimately unsustainable and destructive. Balancing feedback loops are more common in systems because they are sustainable. In many societies, a legal system has historically served to stop reinforcing feedback loops from crumbling the social infrastructure and to promote balancing feedback loops that support desired dynamics. How they do it suggests options for addressing similar issues with feedback loops in our own lives.

Let's explore four aspects of social systems through the lens of feedback loops.

1. Creating the right future incentives
2. Influencing behavior at the margins
3. Dealing with information cascades
4. Building trust

1. Creating the right future incentives

We want to minimize, as much as possible, making a choice today that creates a negative reinforcing feedback loop down the road. Thus it is very important to consider the future incentives a decision will create.

1
Ward Farnsworth, *The Legal Analyst* (Chicago: University of Chicago Press, 2007).

2
Farnsworth, ibid.

A classic example of today's solution inadvertently creating a reinforcing feedback loop of future problems is paying off kidnappers. The immediate problems are someone being kidnapped and the demand for money to release that person. If you have the resources to meet the kidnappers' demands, you might want to pay the money right away. You save a life and solve the problem.

However, your response communicates to the kidnappers that you will meet their demands. You thus create an incentive for them to kidnap again, as well as signal to other would-be kidnappers that there is money to be made. By paying a ransom, you create a powerful reinforcing feedback loop that causes more problems in the future.

In many legal systems, each decision by a court is a bit of information that moves via a feedback loop into the stock of legal options to influence both how the system responds to future cases and how judges form future decisions. In *The Legal Analyst*, Ward Farnsworth explains that in making decisions courts will consider "what incentives people will have after the case is over."[1] Courts need to be careful. If they compensate for a wrong now, they could create a climate that increases the chances of that wrong happening again.

One set of issues courts often face are questions of liability. If something bad happens to me, then does someone else need to pay to compensate? Sometimes the answer is yes, but not indiscriminately so. If we go back to the kidnapping, let's say I work for the government. Am I liable to compensate the victim's family for the loss of life if I choose not to pay the ransom? Most courts will answer no. If I am held liable, it incentivizes me to pay in the future, and we are back in the same reinforcing feedback loop. When considering certain instances of liability, Farnsworth states that "instead of looking back and deciding who should bear the suffering, [a court] can look ahead and decide what ruling will make the suffering less likely to occur later."[2]

3
Farnsworth, ibid.

There are other situations in which choosing an immediate benefit creates reinforcing feedback loops that remove the possibility of future benefits. Therefore there are other areas where there are laws designed to support balancing feedback loops, such as protecting attorney-client privilege, or copyright and patent laws. Although one could argue for the immediate benefit of, say, forcing a defense attorney to testify about what their client disclosed, the feedback loop created would incentivize undesirable behavior. As Farnsworth summarizes concerning copyright protection, "Once books and music exist, there's a great case for free distribution of them. But then they are less likely to exist at all next time."[3]

People look around and often see what they view as unfairness—but they don't realize that the unfairness has a purpose. Unfairness in specific cases creates fairness on the whole, for the reasons laid out here. Often things happen that look like an injustice to the individual, and may be so. But those things may create greater justice for the collective. Think of someone being "overly" punished; that may seem unfair to them, but if it is successful in deterring others, it's not always such a bad idea.

2. Influencing behavior at the margins

Not everyone is likely to change their behavior in response to pressures, such as social or economic changes, at the same intensity and rate. Some people need more convincing; others need more time.

A good customer retention strategy doesn't lump all customers into one group. It might, for example, have a different course of action to retain people who have been customers for six months versus ten years. Or it won't focus on getting people to buy during this transaction but will factor in how much they might buy over their lifetime. These are examples of considering margins. Farnsworth explains that "thinking at the margin, most importantly, means looking at problems not in a total,

4
Farnsworth, ibid.

5
Farnsworth, ibid.

all-or-nothing way, but in incremental terms: seeing behavior as a bunch of choices about when to do a little less along one dimension and a little more along another."[4]

Let's consider the consumption of sugary drinks. Influencing behavior at the margins means that you won't see the problem as a binary of consumption or no consumption. You will look at how you can influence behavior in different areas. Maybe you want people to consume fewer drinks. Maybe you want them to substitute sugar-free drinks as a healthier option. If we were thinking about putting in rules to reduce the consumption of sugary drinks, we could tax them, or limit where they could be consumed or sold, or limit the age of people who can buy them. Farnsworth writes that "the activities of individual people have margins...and then groups of people have marginal members," and that often a legal rule is created with "the hope, realistic or not, is just that it cuts down on the practice at the margins."[5]

Using feedback loops as a lens, we can understand influencing behavior at the margins as instituting a series of incentives that create loops. Over time this feedback changes the system to produce the desired outcomes. We can tailor our feedback to adjust to nuances in behavior that, when combined across a large population, can have significant positive impacts on our system.

Another reason to pay attention to the margins is that they are often the place where reinforcing feedback loops start. A loyal customer of twenty years is not likely going to be the first to leave after a price hike. It's probably going to be the person who just purchased recently. However, when they leave to go to a competitor or even just buy less, there is a danger of setting off a negative reaction that sees sales plummet. Better to have in place a series of balancing feedback loops at the margins, such as loyalty programs, that encourage customer retention.

Criminal law has to work at the margins in terms of deterring unwanted behavior. For example, if a criminal "faces

Though they usually have little to no nutritional value and have been blamed for rising obesity rates, soft drinks are part of the everyday lives of millions of people all over the world. They were first introduced in the 17th century as a mixture of water and lemon juice sweetened with honey.

6
Farnsworth, ibid.

7
Farnsworth, ibid.

8
Farnsworth, ibid.

9
Donella H. Meadows, *Thinking in Systems* (Vermont: Chelsea Green Publishing, 2008).

execution for the crime he has already committed, he pays no additional price for adding murder to it."[6] Thus we don't want thieves to get a death sentence. Then there is no incentive for them not to kill people in the course of their thievery. Farnsworth explains, "The designers of criminal penalties have to worry about preserving *marginal deterrence*, scaling penalties so that there is something more to fear by doing a little worse."[7] In essence, creating a balancing feedback loop that responds with appropriate consequences depending on the severity of the crime.

One of the issues as systems get larger is that there are more margins on which to adjust behavior. If you "try to force substitutions, you may create unwanted ones."[8] Adjusting a feedback loop in the attempt to balance it may create an undesirable reinforcing feedback loop somewhere else. For example, if you make it more difficult for people to consume sugary drinks in public, do you then force them into consuming in private indoor spaces? If you do, there is the danger that consuming sugary drinks in the home could lead to increased consumption with fewer judgmental eyes around. It could also normalize the behavior for children in the household, leading to another generation of sugary drink consumers.

« The concept of feedback opens up the idea that a system can cause its own behavior. »
Donella H. Meadows[9]

3. Dealing with information cascades
Information cascades are a reinforcing feedback loop. They can be evaluated as either positive or negative, depending on the information they communicate. Information cascades occur because we rarely have perfect information, and in many situations we look to others to determine what we ought to do. Farnsworth gives an excellent and common example of an information cascade:

Street performers often rely on making their acts as eye-catching and instantly captivating as possible in order to attract a crowd. Seeing as people do not have to pay to watch, a core skill is drumming up the goodwill necessary for spectators to donate.

Anthony Bourdain - (1956-2018).
A much-loved culinary rock star,
Bourdain inspired readers of his
books and watchers of his TV
shows to view food as a means
of better connecting with other
people, other cultures, and
themselves. His memoir, *Kitchen
Confidential*, revealed the secret
world of professional kitchens and
led to several travel cooking shows.

10
Farnsworth, ibid.

11
Anthony Bourdain, *Kitchen
Confidential* (New York: Bloomsbury
Publishing, 2000).

12
Farnsworth, ibid.

A street performer attracts a small gathering. The group gets larger as people with low curiosity thresholds come to see what's going on. Then the crowd really grows as people with normal thresholds see a mass of spectators converging on the sidewalk and can't resist investigating what the fuss is about.[10]

In the book *Kitchen Confidential*, Anthony Bourdain* offers a lot of advice to would-be restaurant-goers based on his years working in the industry—useful tips such as try the local food and never ask for your steak well done. One other insight he suggests is that when choosing which restaurant to go to, pick the one that looks the busiest. If lots of people are eating there, the food must be fairly good.[11] Restaurateurs are aware of the effects of signaling.

Restaurateurs know that the more customers you seat, the more will come in the door. This is why they will seat the first patrons of the evening close to the window and why they don't mind a line of people waiting to be seated. They understand that the more people there are signaling their interest in the restaurant, the greater the reinforcing feedback loop communicating how great their restaurant is. Farnsworth explains, "People draw inferences from what they see others doing and do the same; now even more people are doing it, and they create a still stronger impression on the next."[12] People who were on the fence about the restaurant will be drawn in by the apparent interest. As they join the queue, the interest of the next threshold level gets piqued.

There are other information cascades, some of which can be damaging if left to grow unchecked. Many legal systems have rules designed to interrupt reinforcing feedback loops of illegal activity. Most of us think we are fairly law-abiding citizens. But we break the law more often than we realize. Just think of speeding. When was the last time you drove under the speed limit for your entire car journey? When it comes to things like speeding—or consuming pirated media, insider trading, or paying someone under the table—we often draw inferences about acceptable behavior from the people around us. However, a legal system cannot prosecute everyone who speeds. So how does it interrupt the loop?

Farnsworth writes, "Ignorance and uncertainty are the best soil for a cascade; people rely on what others think when they have no strong knowledge of their own, and the fragility of the consensus makes it easily vulnerable to shocks."[13] Thus two common legal solutions for dealing with a negative information cascade are laws that require public disclosure of information and prosecuting in certain high-profile situations to make a visible example.

Sometimes having more easily available and accurate information can interrupt a cascade. Think of the disclosure of financial information for publicly traded companies. And the prosecution of high-profile cases not only acts as a deterrent, but the publicity involved often provides more information about the legal territory. The prosecution of Al Capone for tax evasion probably did a lot to educate people about their basic tax responsibilities.

Ultimately these types of actions by the courts are "meant to send signals, stronger than the ones people get by watching each other."[14] And it is those signals that interrupt the reinforcing feedback loop of an information cascade.

4. Building trust

Complex societies require a fair amount of trust between members to function. Look at how much trust we place in the other drivers on the road every time we get into a car. We trust that they will stop at red lights and stay in their lane. We are vigilant for the occasional mistake, but we drive as if other drivers will obey the same rules and quickly notice when they don't. Trust is everywhere, from the trust we place in the people of our children's school system to those who work in our food

13
Farnsworth, ibid.

14
Farnsworth, ibid.

15
Farnsworth, ibid.

and safety systems. For these types of relationships that lack direct interaction, the processes we go through—and the legal enforcement of those processes—facilitate a lot of this trust. Farnsworth writes, "Law often amounts to a substitute for trust in situations too complex or dispersed for trust to arise."[15]

There is an experimental game that is widely performed and cited that explores the building of trust in social interactions: The Prisoner's Dilemma. To understand some of the dynamics of the feedback loops involved in trust, it's helpful to look at that game, as well as one of the strategies for playing it, tit-for-tat.

The thought experiment goes as such: Two criminals are in separate cells, unable to communicate. They've been accused of a crime they both participated in. The police do not have enough evidence to sentence both, though they are certain enough of their case to wish to ensure both suspects spend time in prison. So they offer the prisoners a deal. They can accuse each other of the crime, with the following conditions:

- If both prisoners say the other did it, each will serve two years in prison.
- If prisoner A says the other did it and prisoner B stays silent, prisoner B will serve five years and prisoner A zero (and vice versa).
- If both prisoners stay silent, each will serve one year in prison.

In game theory, the altruistic behavior (staying silent) is called "cooperating," while accusing the other is called "defecting."

What should they do? If they were able to communicate and they trusted each other, the rational choice is to stay silent; that way, each serves less time in prison than they would otherwise. But how can each know the other won't accuse them? After all, people tend to act out of self-interest. The cost of being the one to stay silent is too high.

A \ B		Prisoner B	
		Cooperation	Defection
Prisoner A	Cooperation	A: 1 year B: 1 year	A: 5 year B: 0 year
	Defection	A: 0 year B: 5 year	A: 2 year B: 2 year

Numerous tournaments have been held in which participants use different strategies to compete to win the most points in the iterated Prisoners' Dilemma. The results show how repeated interactions between self-interested agents can lead to cooperative behavior.

Robert Axelrod - (b. 1943). Axelrod
has been a professor of political
science and public policy at the
University of Michigan since 1974.
His interdisciplinary work on
the Iterated Prisoner's Dilemma
revealed the most effective
strategy to be "tit-for-tat," wherein
a player begins by cooperating,
then reciprocates their opponent's
choices. Axelrod's research into
the evolution of cooperation has
had significant implications for
policymakers, particularly with
regard to international conflicts.

16
Some of the material on the
Prisoner's Dilemma appeared
at https://fs.blog/2020/02/
prisoners-dilemma/.

17
Farnsworth, ibid.

The equilibrium outcome when the game is played is that
both accuse the other and serve two years. In the Prisoner's
Dilemma, you are always better off defecting, which means not
trusting the other player. Your outcomes are not usually great,
but defecting prevents them from being horrible.[16]

We can imagine, however, in iterated versions of the
game, that defecting might not always be the best choice. If
you have to face the same situation over and over, figuring out
ways to trust is worth the investment.

Feedback loops are one of the key mechanisms that
provide the information we use to make trust-based decisions.
What happened before in your interaction with a person provides feedback that may cause you to modify your behavior.

The loop of information is the basis for the classic
strategy of the Prisoner's Dilemma, tit-for-tat. In a repeated
Prisoner's Dilemma, the best solution, based on experiments
conducted by Robert Axelrod*, is to cooperate first, and then
in subsequent rounds, to do what the other player did in the
previous round. You start off trusting, and more importantly,
you create a feedback loop that says you are capable of and
willing to trust.

The law has a couple of mechanisms that help in encouraging a basic level of trust. The first is that legal systems often
enforce contracts. Knowing that there are repercussions to
defecting on our agreement might dissuade me from defecting
the first time we work together. Consequences also increase
the costs of defecting, even if we will never work together
again. In addition to protecting individuals in the one-off,
contract enforcement also helps to create feedback loops
that promote and incentivize trust. Farnsworth explains that
"contracts give everyone a convenient way to beat prisoner's
dilemmas and enjoy the gains that come from cooperation."[17]
The point here is that we can trust the feedback loops of the
system to enforce micro-interactions so we can establish
trust. We can imagine that after a few interactions, those gains

that come from cooperation contribute to a feedback loop that encourages people to prioritize cooperation in those situations.

The law can also impose rules and associated penalties for noncompliance in situations where contracts are not possible. Paying your taxes is a way of participating in a sort of contract with your fellow citizens, and most countries have laws that penalize people for not paying. Rules can also govern the use of common or public stocks to incentivize people to cooperate for the common good.

This is often the intent with rules governing fishing quotas. To prevent all of those who fish for a living from acting in their self-interest and depleting the stock beyond sustainable levels, laws regulate how much each can fish. Enforcing quotas is a way of forcing a level of cooperation to maintain a common good.

As we can easily imagine, no one cooperating can quickly become a reinforcing feedback loop with negative consequences in many situations. The less people cooperate, the less incentive there is for future cooperation. To prevent that loop from beginning, the law can impose rules that discourage the initial defection.

— Sidebar: Kandinsky's Iterations

Conclusion

Feedback loops are a common component of many systems. They carry the information that a system responds to. Complex systems often have many feedback loops, and it can be hard to appreciate how adjusting to feedback in one part of the system will affect the rest. Using feedback loops as a mental model begins with noticing the feedback you give and respond to every day. The model also gives insight into the value of iterations in helping adjust based on the feedback you receive. With this lens, you gain insight into where to direct system changes based on feedback and the pace you need to go at to monitor the impacts.

Kandinsky's Iterations

We learn from our efforts. Our first try at anything is rarely any good, but the experience of trying gives us feedback. If we pay attention to it, this feedback can help us improve in our next effort. Through many iterations, by paying attention to and incorporating feedback, we end up becoming more capable. Too often we remove the learning process, including the inevitable failures and disappointments, in success stories. In particular, when it comes to artistic creation, we look at the final product of a painting or piece of music without seeing all of the iterations that came before.

In *How to Fly a Horse*, Kevin Ashton tells the story of how Wassily Kandinsky created one of his most famous works, *Painting with White Border*. The piece was not the single output of a flash of inspiration; rather, it was a monthslong process in which Kandinsky used the feedback from small changes to get to his vision for the final product.

Kandinsky started with what would be called *Sketch 1 for Painting with White Border*. Based on the feedback he received from looking at the effort, he continued to iterate. As Ashton describes it: "His second sketch, barely different, diffused the lines until they were more stain than stroke....More sketches followed. He made twenty sketches, each no more than one or two steps different from the last. The process took five months."[1] The finished work is Kandinsky's 21st picture.

Ashton describes Kandinsky as trying to solve certain problems in his painting (these can also be understood as artistic goals). Each iteration Kandinsky produced gave him feedback on whether he was closer to solving his problems. Eventually he had enough information from the feedback on multiple iterations to produce the painting he wanted.

1
Kevin Ashton, *How to Fly a Horse* (New York: Anchor Books, 2015).

Equilibrium

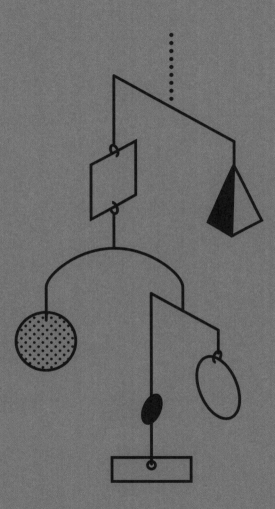

—
Dynamic balance

Equilibrium

Usually when systems stray too far from their equilibrium, they fall apart. When we consider just the pure functioning of a system, equilibrium is a good thing. Using this model as a lens helps us understand where we might intervene to promote equilibrium, but it also cautions us that in complex systems, anticipating what is needed for equilibrium is exceptionally difficult.

A system can be said to be at equilibrium when it is in a stable state. All the forces acting upon it and within it are in balance. When we use the term *equilibrium*, we're typically referring to a state where things within a system are consistent and not changing, known as *static equilibrium*. But most real-world systems are more apt to experience *dynamic equilibrium*, meaning things fluctuate within a particular range. They achieve this using balancing feedback loops. If a variable becomes higher or lower than the desirable range, feedback loops kick in to bring it back.

One way to conceptualize the idea of equilibrium is to imagine a hypothetical family whose overall household forms a system. For the household to run in the way that's best for everyone on average, many variables need to stay within the desired range. If they get out of that range, the family makes adjustments to restore balance. If they can't bring a variable back to the ideal range, the household may need to shift to a new equilibrium. For instance, to cover their living costs, the family needs a certain amount of money to flow into the household each month as well as to keep their stock of money for emergencies at a comfortable level. When they decide to start paying for piano lessons for one of the children, they may cut down on meals out to maintain an equilibrium. The family also needs their home to remain within a certain cleanliness range for them to remain happy and healthy. When they decide to get a dog, remaining at equilibrium means they have to spend more

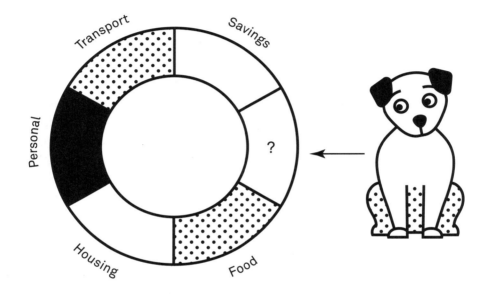

Transport

Savings

Personal

?

Housing

Food

There are only so many hours in a day and so much money available to spend.
Adding in new commitments means adjusting our current equilibrium.

Walter Cannon - (1871-1945). A key figure in the field of physiology, Cannon is the originator of the terms *fight-or-flight* and *homeostasis*. He was chair of the Harvard Medical School Department of Physiology for 36 years. During World War I, Cannon performed fieldwork studying the effects of shock in order to develop better emergency wound treatments.

1
Kevin Rodolfo, "What Is Homeostasis?" *Scientific American*, January 3, 2000, https://www. scientificamerican.com/article/what-is-homeostasis/.

time cleaning to compensate for the mess it makes. When one family member is away for the week, the others reduce how much they clean. If you imagine your household—even if it's just you—you can think of innumerable variables you're always tweaking to keep things as you like them.

Homeostasis is the process through which organisms make continual adjustments to bring them as close as possible to their ideal conditions. Changes in external conditions lead to changes in internal conditions, which may shift a system away from what it needs to work well.

Physician Walter Cannon* coined the term *homeostasis* in his iconic 1932 book *The Wisdom of the Body*. Cannon marveled at the many variables our bodies manage to keep within narrow parameters, including blood glucose, body temperature, and sodium levels. Although systems theory did not exist as a field of study at the time, Cannon was espousing a view of the human body as a whole system that needed to maintain a stable internal state in response to its ever-changing environment.[1]

An important point is that systems can have multiple different equilibria. Just because a system is at equilibrium, that doesn't mean it's functioning as well as it can. It just means things are stable. Sometimes systems achieve equilibrium in inefficient ways. If you're feeling ill one week and struggling to focus on work, you might work extra hours each day to get your usual work done. You've maintained equilibrium, but you would have probably been better off overall if you did less. Short-term deviations from equilibrium are often what is needed to maintain it in the long term. An argument with a sibling that takes work to resolve might shift your relationship with that sibling away from its equilibrium for a few weeks, but in the long run, it could make things more stable between you by resolving tension.

— Sidebar: A Different Look at Homeostasis

A Different Look at Homeostasis

In his book *The Strange Order of Things*, Antonio Damasio explores the role of homeostasis in evolution. He explains that homeostasis "ensures that life is regulated within a range that is not just compatible with survival but also conducive to flourishing, a projection of life." He further clarifies the concept by saying, "Homeostasis refers to the process by which the tendency of matter to drift into disorder is countered so as to maintain order but at a new level, the one allowed by the most efficient steady state."[1]

Organizations, communities, and countries—all are systems that must respond to environmental changes with modifications intended to bring them closer to a desired state. When we go through external challenges, whether it be war, competition, or extreme weather, homeostasis kicks in to help us return to a point where the surrounding system functions at its best. Sometimes that can simply be a matter of what feels good rather than a precisely definable set of conditions. Unlike biological systems, we as humans can change the state we aim for, such as when we realize something else would work better.

Damasio argues that feelings act as the key to understanding the biological role of homeostasis. Our feelings are a feedback loop that provides information to our body system about how we are doing. You have to be able to monitor the adjustments and responses to make changes that put you back on track. We do this through the value judgment of feelings. After a disaster, for instance, homeostasis does not need to (and frequently doesn't) return the system to its previous state. Instead, it's more useful to think of homeostasis returning a system to a place where it "feels good" under new conditions.

Therein lies the potential of homeostasis. How systems define themselves as "feeling good" will have a huge impact on their ability to adapt to stress and change. In biological systems, feelings are a critical component of how we assess problems. When your blood glucose drops, you feel terrible, which causes behavior that seeks to bring you back to where you feel okay. But that level of okay is a range, and Damasio's idea is that homeostasis normally keeps us at the end of the range that allows us to develop. As variables under- and overshoot and external conditions change, systems can never stop making adjustments. Homeostasis is never a static state.

1

Antonio Damasio, *The Strange Order of Things* (New York: Vintage Books, 2018).

2
Arabella L. Simpkin and Richard M. Schwartzstein, "Tolerating Uncertainty: The Next Medical Revolution?," *New England Journal of Medicine* 375, no. 18 (2016): 1713–15.

When information can help

When we look at biological systems, we can easily see that information is required to maintain homeostasis, or dynamic equilibrium. In our bodies, various components are constantly communicating an incredible amount of information about everything from the sensations on our skin from the external temperature to the potassium levels in our blood. Without accurate information, our bodies cannot work properly. Using this model as a lens, we can understand which situations might benefit from information to maintain an equilibrium. One such situation is the modern approach to doctor-patient communication in many medical systems.

The doctor-patient relationship is universally unbalanced in terms of power and knowledge. Doctors have more knowledge about both medicine and the system used to treat patients. This dynamic has led to patients being passive participants in their health care, given neither the knowledge nor the opportunity to make decisions regarding their treatment. Now, in some places, the relationship has started to change, with patients becoming more active participants. There is growing recognition in some medical systems that the experience of treatment (and consequently sometimes health outcomes) improves when patients are more active participants in making treatment-related decisions. To facilitate this participation, in some medical systems patients are now given much more extensive information about their condition and the various treatment options, including associated risk.

Part of the reason for the change to more patient participation is the acknowledgment that diagnostics and treatments are rarely black and white. In a paper called "Tolerating Uncertainty," the authors write that "doctors have to make decisions on the basis of imperfect knowledge, which leads to diagnostic uncertainty, coupled with the uncertainty that arises from unpredictable patient response to treatment and from health care outcomes that are far from binary."[2] It doesn't make sense

People who are actively supported in making decisions about their health care often experience more favorable health outcomes, including less anxiety and a quicker recovery.

3
Cathy Charles, Amiram Gafni, and Tim Whelan, "Shared Decision-Making in the Medical Encounter: What Does It Mean?," *Social Science & Medicine* 44, no. 5 (1997): 681–92.

4
David S. Walonick, "General Systems Theory," accessed October 2020, https://www.statpac.org/walonick/systems-theory.htm.

for a doctor to make treatment decisions for a patient in isolation, because any treatment is going to have consequences that the patient will disproportionately bear. Involving a patient in the discussion of their care options also serves to minimize blind spots and bias. Explaining options to a patient means that a doctor has to at least acknowledge the options that exist, and coming to a solution through dialogue with a patient helps to make the solution situation specific.

One of the methods for increasing the information available about treatment options in the doctor-patient relationship is through a process called shared decision-making (SDM). SDM does not put the responsibility for a decision on one party or the other but instead provides the resources necessary for the doctor and patient to come to an acceptable decision together. In a 1997 paper, the authors explain that "SDM is seen as a mechanism to decrease the informational and power asymmetry between doctors and patients by increasing patients' information, sense of autonomy and/or control over treatment decisions that affect their well-being."[3]

For patients to make an informed choice about their care, they need to understand the benefits and harms of the various treatment options. They might also require the support of a loved one, multiple opportunities to hear and assess the information, the ability to ask questions, and some time to process the information. One definition of dynamic equilibrium is "when the system components are in a state of change, but at least one variable stays within a specified range."[4] A medical situation is just such a system because many parts are usually in a state of change, specifically the exact parameters of the health issue itself. Usually, too, in more complicated health situations, there are many doctors and specialists involved. In addition, the needs and desires of the patients are not always static. SDM tries to keep the information variable within a range that allows for both the doctor and patient to navigate the situation in an informed way.

Exploiting Assumptions

If you become too dependent on a particular equilibrium to perform well, you make yourself vulnerable to being thrown off by changing circumstances. Being able to function in a wider range of conditions makes you more versatile and flexible. It's also useful to have homeostatic processes in place to enable you to get back to what you find optimal after any sort of disruption. In competitive situations, those who flounder when they're thrown off their equilibrium by something unexpected without having the mechanisms to reorient often suffer. Sometimes you can transcend your abilities by thinking about what an opponent expects or considers normal. You can also achieve more by rethinking what the equilibrium is in your field.

Take the case of card tricks. When an audience watches a magician perform a trick, they start with certain assumptions and expectations. The same is true for professional magicians watching other magicians perform a trick. Their equilibrium consists of a set of assumptions that enable them to identify how a trick works by watching it or to reverse engineer it from the end point. Professional magic includes all sorts of conventions and assumptions. One unspoken assumption is that a magician performing a particular named trick does it the same way every time, using the same technique. To figure out how the trick works, you need to identify that technique.

One American magician, Ralph Hull, managed to invent a card trick no one—not even the smartest expert magicians—could fathom by rethinking the equilibrium of card magic. He called it "The Tuned Deck."[1] Hull would show the audience a pack of cards, claiming he could sense the location of any of the cards by detecting minute vibrations. He would then allow an audience member to pick a card, look at it, then put it back into the pack. Hull moved the cards around, shuffling them one way and another, then pulled out the correct card. Its unique vibrations revealed its location, or so he said.[2]

No one managed to figure out how he did the trick, despite expert magicians watching him perform it again and again. Only at the end of his life did Hull reveal the secret: The Tuned Deck didn't have one single secret. Hull would use a mixture of different techniques, moving between them depending on whether an audience seemed to be twigging onto what he was doing. If a professional magician were watching, he might use a few different consecutive methods until he threw them off the scent.[3] The real trick was that Hull shifted away from the equilibrium assumption that a trick with a name had to be done the same way every time.

1
Daniel C. Dennett, *Intuition Pumps and Other Tools for Thinking* (New York: W. W. Norton, 2014).
2
John Northern, Hilliard, Carl Waring Jones, Jean Hugard, and Harlan Tarbell, *Greater Magic: A Practical Treatise on Modern Magic* (Silver Spring: Kaufman and Greenburg, 1994).
3
Dennett, ibid.

5
Annie Janvier, and John Lantos,
"Ethics and Etiquette in Neonatal
Intensive Care," *JAMA Pediatrics*
168, no. 9 (2014).

In order for information to be closer to equilibrium for both patient and doctor in medical treatment situations, it's important to recognize the elements that might affect the flow of information. It's not enough to share raw information. Doctors and patients also have to build trust that will allow that information to be accepted and processed. In a 2014 analysis of parent experiences in neonatal intensive care units (NICUs), the authors explain, "When families voice their dissatisfaction with the NICU, it is often not because they think their baby has not received good medical care. Instead, it is because the parents' needs have not been acknowledged and addressed."[5] Actions like saying a baby's name and acknowledging the parents' caregiving role help create a communication environment where the information needed for good decision-making can be heard and understood.

Medical situations are often complex. They can involve a lot of people and a lot of uncertainty. In addition, they almost always include very powerful emotions. To allow information to come as close as possible to equilibrium in these types of situations can provide enough structure to support positive functioning in a changing environment.

— Sidebar: Exploiting Assumptions

The complexity of equilibrium

Beginning in the 1960s, scientists began to ask questions such as: How could humans survive for a long time in space—or even form permanent settlements on other planets? What does it take to sustain life within a sealed environment, like a spaceship or underground bunker on Mars? How can we create an ecosystem in a closed environment, capable of reaching an equilibrium necessary to keep people alive?

In asking these questions, scientists recognized that our planet is itself a closed system. Innumerable complex processes come together to enable humans to survive. Beginning with experiments in which samples of microbial life were sealed permanently into flasks (some of which are still alive today),[6] researchers began to demonstrate ways in which closed systems could sustain themselves. Such experiments, on a modest scale, formed an important part of the Russian and US space programs. But the project known as "Biosphere 2" (with planet Earth being Biosphere 1) was on a scale unlike anything that came before it, and few experiments since have matched its sheer scale, audacity, and ambition.

Biosphere 2 consists of a 180,000-square-meter structure located in the desert near Tucson, Arizona. Its above-ground structure is made of almost 204,000 cubic meters of glass supported by a steel framework with a maximum height of 27.7 meters.[7] Parts of the building are rectangular, parts are pyramid-shaped, and parts are domed. Inside, Biosphere 2 contains the following five separate ecosystems mimicking key environments in the outside world:

1. Coastal fog desert
2. Tropical rainforest
3. Savanna grassland
4. Mangrove wetland
5. Ocean

Biosphere 2 also includes areas for agriculture and underground areas for housing the equipment necessary to keep the whole thing functioning. It was the brainchild of John Allen and Ed Bass. Allen was a metallurgist and Harvard MBA who, following a psychedelic trip in the 1960s, founded a commune called Synergia Ranch in Santa Fe, New Mexico.[8] Successful relative to other similar projects at the time, Synergia attracted the attention of Ed Bass, a young billionaire heir to an oil fortune.[9] Together they launched several ambitious projects before deciding in 1984 to set out and discover what it would take to form a Mars colony that humans could live in. With Bass's fortune and Allen's ambition at hand, they assembled

6
William F. Dempster, "Biosphere 2 Engineering Design," *Ecological Engineering* 13 (1999): 31–42, https://ecotechnics.edu/wp-content/uploads/backup/2011/08/Ecol-Eng-1999-Bio-2-Engineering-Design-Dempster.pdf.

7
"Biosphere 2," Britannica.com, accessed November 5, 2020, https://www.britannica.com/topic/Biosphere-2.

8
Jordan Fisher Smith, "Life Under the Bubble," *Discover*, December 19, 2010, https://www.discovermagazine.com/environment/life-under-the-bubble.

9
Smith, ibid.

a team of experts and began the monumental task of making Biosphere 2 happen.

In 1991, the "Biospherians"—a team of eight individuals who'd spent years preparing—were sealed inside Biosphere 2 for two years. The aim was for them to maintain a functioning ecosystem with nothing (not even air) coming in from the outside. They would farm all of their food, growing plants and raising animals, and strive to maintain all conditions necessary for their survival. By the time they emerged, the Biospherians had endured a great deal. Oxygen levels had sunk drastically, to the point where it proved necessary to bring in outside oxygen to keep them alive. They struggled to meet their caloric requirements while engaging in so much physical work, though this lifestyle left them healthier than before and they suffered no major health problems during the experiment. The Biospherians frequently fell out with each other and with those controlling the experiment.

Much of the contemporary media coverage of Biosphere 2, as well as its representations in popular culture, depicts the whole thing as a failed experiment replete with fraud and trickery. But this is the result of a gross misunderstanding of both the aims of the project and indeed the nature of science. Experiments aren't meant to "succeed." They're meant to provide us with informative data about the world that we can use as the basis for future experiments. None of the people who worked on Biosphere 2 expected everything to run perfectly from the first day. They understood that for a system—in this case, the biosphere within the dome consisting of plants, animals, and people as well as air, water, and more—to achieve an equilibrium, a lot of variables need to be right. Only by trying out the experiment could they discover what all of those variables were. They couldn't preempt everything, and it would have been hubris to think they knew everything an ecosystem needs to function well.

As a voyage of discovery, Biosphere 2 excelled. It showed

us that maintaining life in a sealed environment is almost infinitely complex because ecosystems are complex adaptive systems. Under natural conditions, they have countless feedback loops in place to maintain an equilibrium. An artificially created ecosystem requires humans to maintain those feedback loops, in part by preempting what they'll need to control but also in part by learning to sense when something is going wrong so they can create a new feedback loop.

When left alone in their typical conditions, systems are pretty good at reaching an equilibrium. But when we try to control them or we disrupt their conditions, it takes a lot of effort to bring them to a desirable balance. Despite the early stage of the project, the achievements of the Biospherians were remarkable. They did manage to produce almost all of their food, get enough clean water, and keep hundreds of plant and animal species alive. Anyone who has ever tried to grow vegetables at home or even keep a few houseplants alive can appreciate the scale of the experiment. Those who view the project as a comical failure have arguably failed to think about the sheer complexity of getting a system like that to an equilibrium. Just maintaining the level of balance the Biospherians achieved was a monumental act deserving of acclaim.

Not only that, but Biosphere 2 is an important reminder of the effect of human activity on ecosystems. It highlights how small, misguided interventions can have catastrophic knock-on effects and just how much damage we can do anytime we interfere with nature. Everything that went into Biosphere 2 required careful examination for ways in which it might both be unable to maintain its equilibrium and also disrupt the overall balance of the ecosystem. Linda Leigh, who helped develop Biosphere 2 and was one of the participants sealed inside, described the complexity of choosing which animal species to include.[10] Every animal needed to be evaluated for how it might interact with everything else. For example, they consulted a bat specialist to choose a bat species that

10
Lisa Ruth Rand, Peder Anker, Dana Fritz, Linda Leigh, and Shawn Rosenheim, "Biosphere 2: Why an Eccentric Ecological Experiment Still Matters 25 Years Later," *Edge Effects*, updated February 12, 2020, https://edgeeffects.net/biosphere-2/.

Many of the original biospherians continued to live together in New Mexico decades after the experiment. Though the experience created terse divisions, it also created powerful bonds. A couple would have even volunteered to go back in.

could pollinate some of the plants. Yet when they looked at the knock-on consequences of including that species, they were huge:

> One of those bats would nightly have needed to eat twenty two-centimeter-long night-flying moths, and would have had to have encounters with over a hundred per night in order to catch the twenty. Where would all of the moths come from? What would their larvae eat, and could we have enough and the correct habitat for the moths' eggs? In addition, the air handlers, as designed, would have sucked the moths in and killed them. Engineers suggested a fine screen over the opening to the fans in order to give the moths a chance to survive the pull. That screen would increase the electricity needed to pull the air through, a budget increase that was not supported.[11]

In another example, an expert tried to find a hummingbird species that could live inside Biosphere 2.[12] They had to ask lots of questions about each option a casual observer might not think to consider. What shape is this type of hummingbird's bill? Will it be the right size to pollinate enough plants? What kind of mating display does this type of hummingbird exhibit? Will it be at risk of colliding with the glass during this display? And so on. The considerations were endless.

Even the most seemingly inconsequential things had the potential to compound and endanger the lives of everything in the ecosystem. As Shawn Rosenheim explained, "Part of the point in building a self-sustaining world was to make the unimaginably rich interconnections of the actual Earth newly vivid."[13] The initial two-year closure experiment was meant to be the first of 50 such experiments, with the aim of improving incrementally each time. As a starting point, the first closure went better than expected. For instance, 30% of the species

11
Smith, ibid.

12
Smith, ibid.

13
Rand et al., ibid.

inside "went extinct," but researchers had predicted anywhere up to 70%.

At the time of writing, Biosphere 2 still stands, having been donated to the University of Arizona in 2011. From the outside, it looks like a shadow of its former self. The windows are murky without sufficient funds to employ a full-time crew to keep them clean, and rust accumulates on the structure. But inside, Biosphere 2 remains full of life. Many of the microcosms within it are thriving, having found the equilibrium they need to function as they would in the outside world. Researchers still utilize it as a unique place for valuable controlled experiments they can't easily do anywhere else.

Conclusion

Systems are rarely static. They are continuously adjusting toward equilibrium, but they rarely stay in balance for long. In our lives we often act like we can reach an equilibrium: once we get into a relationship, we'll be happy; once we move, we'll be productive; once X thing happens, we'll be in Y state. But things are always in flux. We don't reach a certain steady state and then stay there forever. The endless adjustments are our lives.

Bottlenecks

—
The limiting factor

Bottlenecks

All systems have parts that are slower than others. The slowest part of a system is called the "bottleneck" because, as the neck of a bottle limits the amount of liquid that can flow through, bottlenecks in systems limit the amount of outputs they can produce. Using bottlenecks as a model gives us insight into how a limiting factor can hurt or help us.

No one wants to be a bottleneck, which is easily conceptualized as that person who makes everyone else wait. We see this behavior in people who can't delegate. If you have to make every decision yourself, there's likely a long line of people twiddling their thumbs while waiting for you to move their projects forward.

Bottlenecks tend to create waste as resources pile up behind them. In manufacturing, they limit how much you can produce and sell. If you work in an industry that depends on timely information, then you risk inputs becoming irrelevant before they make it through the bottleneck.

A bottleneck is also the point that is most under strain. It can be the part that is most likely to break down or has the most impact if it does. In trying to improve the flow of your system, focusing on anything besides the bottleneck is a waste of time. You will just create more pressure on the bottleneck, further increasing how much it holds you back by generating more buildup.

Every system has a bottleneck. You cannot completely eliminate them because once you do, another part of the system will become the new limiting factor. You can, however, anticipate bottlenecks and plan accordingly. Or you can leverage the need to overcome them as an impetus for finding new ways of making a system work. Sometimes you can overcome bottlenecks by adding more of the same, such as dedicating more resources to ease the pressure on a bottleneck. But sometimes the sole solution is to rethink that part of the system.

What you want to avoid is opening up one bottleneck only to create additional, worse ones for yourself later on. If bottlenecks are unavoidable, we at least want them to be in a less disruptive place.

Although the terms are sometimes used interchangeably, a bottleneck is different from a constraint. A bottleneck is something we can alleviate; a constraint is a fundamental limitation of the system. So a machine that keeps breaking down is a bottleneck, but the fact there are twenty-four hours in the day is a constraint.

You also need to be aware of false dependencies disguised as bottlenecks. We often hear explanations in the form of "I won't do X before Y." Most statements of this type are only in place to make you feel good about procrastinating when you are the bottleneck. For example, you might say you will start writing every day once you move house and have a dedicated desk for it. If the bottleneck is a lack of a suitable workspace, then moving will alleviate it. But if the bottleneck is something else, like time or ideas, you're setting up a false dependency. The bottleneck will still be there once you move. Even if the problem is your workspace, you could still find ways to make progress, such as by going to the library or a coffee shop. Anything you do now will make it easier to get into the habit of daily writing.

If you think you've identified a bottleneck, it's a good idea to do what you can to validate that this factor is indeed the limiting factor. Otherwise you might end up solving the wrong problem.

The Trans-Siberian Railway

How you deal with your bottleneck can have huge impacts on the overall quality of your system. Often we tend to just deal with our bottleneck whatever the cost. But since there is always one in every system, anticipating the consequences of how we deal with our bottleneck is important. Some

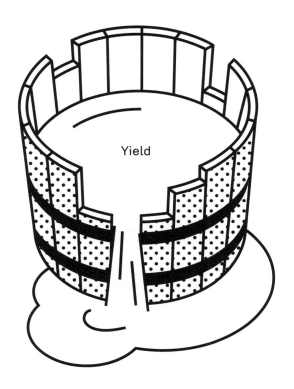

Yield

Liebig's law of the minimum refers to the idea that a plant's growth will be limited by the nutrient that is least available. Yield is thus constrained by resource limitation.

bottlenecks are better to have than others because they are easier to organize the rest of our system around.

The building of the Trans-Siberian Railway (TSR) was a complicated project with many moving parts that borrowed from future resources to address its bottleneck. It is both an inspiring and cautionary tale, as sometimes dealing with bottlenecks in the most expedient way possible can cause significant issues later on.

The TSR was a massive undertaking. Not only is it the longest railway in the world, but the challenges faced in building over that distance were unmatched at the time. The railway spans the entirety of Russia from St. Petersburg in the west, close to Finland, to Vladivostok on the Pacific Ocean just east of North Korea.

As W. Bruce Lincoln describes in *The Conquest of a Continent*, there were multiple sources of challenge to building the TSR:

> Construction crews would have to work thousands of miles away from their bases of supply. Rails and bridge iron would have to be brought to Siberia from foundries as far away as St. Petersburg and Warsaw, ties would have to be cut in European Russia and shipped across the Urals because almost no hardwoods grew in the steppe or the taiga, and stone for bridge piers and abutments would have to be transported from quarries on the western frontier of Mongolia. Then, as the tracklayers moved deeper into Siberia, terrain and climate would magnify the obstacles. Then endless forest, the gorges cut from solid rock, the mountains of the Transbaikal, the treacherous permafrost, the short winter days, and the deep, deep Siberian cold all presented obstacles on a scale that the world's builders had yet to face.[1]

1
Bruce W. Lincoln, *The Conquest of a Continent* (New York: Random House, 1994).

This poster was produced by Intourist, the only travel agency in Russia during the Soviet era as well as the first Russian company to acquire an American firm.

2
T. R. Reid, *The Chip* (New York:
Random House, 2001).

Given the scope of the undertaking—9,458 kilometers, two to three times longer than the transcontinental railways that had been built in North America at the time—it's not surprising that addressing a bottleneck could have far-reaching consequences.

One critical point about bottlenecks is they can move around systems. You fix one only to introduce another. In *The Chip*, T. R. Reid gives an example of shifting a bottleneck that threatened an entire system. He describes a textile factory that started falling far behind its normal production rate. To figure out what was going on, the factory manager followed the output process on the production floor. They found the employees constantly had to rethread their sewing machines because a cheaper thread they'd bought kept breaking. To save 15¢ per spool, they were losing $150 per hour in production output.[2]

The TSR was a complex undertaking, so attempts to alleviate a bottleneck could easily cause unanticipated consequences. Problems beset the project. There was a continual shortage of local supplies. There were limits to construction schedules caused by the seasonal weather. The fact that all decisions about the railway had to go through a central committee in St. Petersburg with a weeks-long communication delay created uncoordinated short-term solutions to problems.

In addition, the deepest lake in the world sits in the middle of the route. Originally the main line stopped on one side of the lake and goods were ferried across to the rail continuation on the other shore. This situation created a huge physical bottleneck in terms of the movement of goods and people until a track was completed around its southern shore decades after the main line was built.

Finally, and perhaps most critically for the actual construction, was the bottleneck created by the extreme shortage of labor, which had significant impacts on the functioning of the other parts of the system.

The picture was taken by Sergey Prokudin-Gorsky, a chemist and photographer who documented early 20th-century Russia through photos he developed in his railroad car darkroom.

The railway was built as five separate projects that were worked on simultaneously. One of the consequences of deciding to work this way was that the railroad wasn't treated as one project when it came to labor. Each of the five projects competed with the others for part of the same pool of resources.

The desire to shorten the total building time resulted in a trade-off that augmented the labor bottleneck. As Christian Wolmar explains in *To the Edge of the World*, this construction approach created a competition for resources that, combined with a low local population density, meant that there weren't enough locally available workers. They had to be imported.[3] In order to ease the pressure on the labor bottleneck, skilled workers were imported from all over Europe to work along the length of the TSR. For the eastern section, thousands of workers were brought in from China, Japan, and Korea. And on all parts, but in particular the middle section that ran through the Siberian prison camp area, convicts were used in the construction of the track.

The enormous time pressures placed on the men charged with building the railway meant that the labor bottlenecks were often addressed with excessive sums paid to contractors. Thus labor absorbed most of the money available for the project. As Wolmar describes, local peasant contractors were unsupervised, and there was no competitive tendering process. Contractors "often asked for extra payment, once work had begun, as they knew that there was no alternative supplier because the imperative was to get the job done quickly."[4]

The problem with easing the pressure on the labor bottleneck by subcontracting the work to those without sufficient experience manifested on the train track itself. The incentive for the contractors was to pocket money in the short term. The labor shortage could be solved with money, yet there was only so much funding available. Something had to give. What got sacrificed was safety. "With very little supervision of the work,

3
Christian Wolmar, *To the Edge of the World* (New York: Public Affairs, 2013).

4
Wolmar, ibid.

5
Wolmar, ibid.

6
Wolmar, ibid.

contractors boosted their profits by skimping on material or building to below the required standard, resulting in embankments that were too narrow, insufficient ballast, inadequate drainage, and a host of other failings."[5] To save money on building materials because the labor was so expensive (and the cut directly pocketed by the subcontractor so high), the inclines in many places were too steep and the curves too tight. It was a dangerous railway.

For the TSR, solving the labor shortage created a materials bottleneck because the money used to solve the labor problem meant there wasn't enough left over to purchase quality materials. Accordingly, the central committee thousands of miles away could not keep up with the demands to solve workmanship and safety issues. They were unable to react fast enough, so the integrity of the track was compromised.

Despite the remarkable achievement of building the TSR, the cost-cutting on materials and the shortening of the route through unsuitable terrain with steep grades and tight corners meant it had problems from the start. Wolmar explains that "almost as soon as each section of the line was completed, improvements had to be made to ensure it was functioning properly."[6] Even with the sustained effort, the locomotives wore out quickly, goods were shipped painfully slowly, and accidents and deaths occurred all the time.

Spending money without quality assurance only moves problems into the future. Russia effectively had to build the same railroad multiple times because the first track was almost unusable.

On a project with the scope of the TSR, bottlenecks are inevitable. Identifying them and planning how to manage them is part of the process of construction. The lesson here is to be careful how we address bottlenecks so that we don't create huge problems for ourselves later on.

Often when we encounter a bottleneck, we keep patching over it so it bounces back to being the bottleneck again. On

The first nylon stockings were sold in October 1939. Although the stockings were instantly popular, developments continued to make them less fragile and more comfortable to wear. Along with coffee and chocolate, they became symbolic of the kind of small luxuries that were hard to obtain in wartime.

7
Peter J. Andrews, "The Invention
of Nylon," Encyclopedia.com,
accessed January 31, 2020, www.
encyclopedia.com/science/
encyclopedias-almanacs-
transcripts-and-maps/
invention-nylon.

the TSR, the money used to solve the labor shortage also created incentives to keep that shortage going. Throwing money at the problem without understanding the system is unlikely to yield the intended benefits.

Instead of addressing bottlenecks as they appear, your time might be better spent on a root-cause fix that makes a foundational improvement that leads many bottlenecks to disappear indefinitely. One way to achieve foundational improvement is to simulate conditions you are likely to face to try to find bottlenecks ahead of time. Instead of merely fixing the problem, we can solve a bottleneck by asking how the system could be designed to not have that problem exist in the first place. Addressing bottlenecks is a never-ending job and must always be factored into your planning.

Bottlenecks and innovation

Bottlenecks inspire innovation. When a limit emerges, we're often forced to try something new to alleviate it. Many inventions come about as the result of shortages of resources that prompt people to find alternatives. Innovating as a response to bottlenecks is common during wars when necessary materials may be unobtainable. Looking at the past century, many things we now use regularly were invented at times of conflict to alleviate bottlenecks in supply.

Nylon was the first synthetic fiber, and today we use it in everything from swimwear and fishing nets to seat belts and tents. Being light, strong, and waterproof, it is versatile and practical.[7] Nylon was invented in the early 1930s as an alternative to silk and began commercial production toward the end of the decade. The United States obtained most of its silk from Japan at the time but found itself risking losing access due to rising tensions between the nations. Nylon eliminated that bottleneck by providing an alternative material manufactured in the United States.

While it was invented in response to a shortage, it

proved to have advantages over silk in common products as well as new uses. In particular, nylon stockings were popular during the early 1940s, before nylon's production was diverted for military purposes. It served an essential wartime role as parachute and tent material. DuPont, the inventors of nylon, decided not to trademark it so it would seem like a material in itself, not a brand.[8] By being available for experimentation and development, nylon continues to find many uses.

Similarly, the United States had difficulties obtaining rubber during World War II due to conflict with Japan. Ameripol, a synthetic rubber that didn't rely on access to Asian natural resources, was invented by chemist Waldo Semon[*] as an alternative.[9] Not having any rubber would have been disastrous for the war, as it was integral for practically every item and device used in the fighting, in particular as a material for tires. Without rubber, as innocuous as it seems, vehicles like planes and tanks wouldn't have been able to operate. It's very possible that without the rapid effort to invent a viable form of synthetic rubber and develop the capacity to produce almost a million tons of it, the Allies would have lost the war.[10] Now most rubber is synthetic.

Medical science tends to advance the fastest during wars. Facing new demands and shortages of essential supplies, people find creative ways to deal with injuries and diseases. During the American Civil War, dozens of new types of prosthetic limbs were invented, and surgeons became more adept at using ligatures. At the start of the war, the mortality rate from infections was 60%. By the end, it was 3%.[11] During World War II, production capabilities for penicillin skyrocketed.[12]

During World War I, many people became malnourished or undernourished due to food rationing. Nutrients became a bottleneck. Lack of adequate food was problematic for children, many of whom developed rickets (soft bones due to vitamin D deficiency). Many soldiers suffered serious bone

[*] Waldo Semon - (1898-1999). Semon's work as a chemist at the Goodrich Corporation is sometimes credited with having been central to the Allied forces winning World War II. He invented over 5,000 synthetic rubber compounds, most notably Ameripol and vinyl, and held 116 US patents.

8 Audra J. Wolfe, "Nylon: A Revolution in Textiles," *Science History Institute*, October 2, 2008, www.sciencehistory.org/distillations/nylon-a-revolution-in-textiles.

9 Jon Marmor, "Waldo Semon: He Helped Save the World," *Columns, the University of Washington Alumni Magazine*, September 1999, www.washington.edu/alumni/columns/sept99/semon.html.

10 "US Synthetic Rubber Program: National Historic Chemical Landmark," American Chemical Society, ACS Office of Communications, 1998.

11 Edward Tenner, *Why Things Bite Back: Technology and the Revenge of Unintended Consequences* (New York: Vintage Books, 1997).

12 Tenner, ibid.

Kurt Huldschinsky - (1883-1940).
Working as a pediatrician in
Berlin in 1918, Huldschinsky
experimented with treatments
for rickets, a condition related
to wartime malnourishment. He
ultimately discovered exposure to
UV light is an effective cure. During
World War II, Huldschinsky and his
family were forced to flee to Egypt,
where he remained for the rest of
his life.

13
Neetha Mahadevan, "World War I
Centenary: Sun Lamps." *Wall Street
Journal*, updated October 31, 2018,
https://graphics.wsj.com/100-
legacies-from-world-war-1/
sun-lamps.

breakages. Kurt Huldschinsky[*], a doctor working in Berlin, discovered he could cure rickets by seating children in front of an ultraviolet lamp. Research after the war identified why this worked: a sun lamp simulates sunlight and prompts the body to produce vitamin D, thereby helping to alleviate the bottleneck in access to nutritious food caused by the war. Today sun lamps are a common medical tool for everything from skin conditions to seasonal affective disorder.[13]

The need to overcome the effects of a lack of nutritious food led to the invention of an alternative way of meeting people's nutritional needs. Wartime medical innovations developed as a response to bottlenecks have, in many cases, ended up benefiting everyone.

Conclusion

Although we tend to view bottlenecks as something negative, they can nudge us toward new ideas and better ways of solving the same problems. Using bottlenecks as a mental model not only helps us conceptualize them in the literal sense when looking at a system but also teaches us that they are not something to fear. When there are no severe bottlenecks, we may not think to improve things. After they emerge, we're forced to be more creative and watch that we don't transfer the pain somewhere worse. In the long run, they can make us better off.

Scale

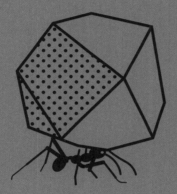

—

Bigger or smaller = different

Scale

Systems come in a variety of sizes, and they change as they scale up or down. Sometimes it is more effective to stay small because you anticipate that the changes growth will require of your system are not ones you want to make. When scaling up, it's important to be aware that growth in systems is often non-linear, which means that changing a single component might have effects that fundamentally alter your system and create both new opportunities and new dependencies. In baking, for example, it's common that doubling a recipe doesn't always work. You often need less yeast; because of the geometry of the bread you're baking, double the yeast might cause the fermentation to be too fast. Scale as a model gives us insight into how size might impact our system choices.

When we study a complex system, it's beneficial to consider how its functioning behaves differently at different scales. Looking at the micro level may mislead us about the macro, and vice versa. In general, systems become more complex as they scale up. Greater size means more connections and interdependencies between parts. Thus, it's important to combine scale with bottlenecks. As systems become larger, different parts might struggle to keep up. Imagining your business scaling up in some areas faster than others lets you anticipate breakages and bottlenecks.

« If you do not look at things on a large scale, it will be difficult to master strategy. »

Miyamoto Musashi[1]

1
Miyamoto Musashi, *Honor: Samurai Philosophy of Life: The Essential Samurai Collection* (Somerville: Bottom of the Hill Publishing, 2010).

To give an example of how things change as they scale, consider a company at two different sizes. As a small company with a handful of people with close personal relationships working together in a garage, there's no need for an HR department or management consultants. They can work together and solve problems face-to-face. Proximity can discourage them from letting too much tension build up. No one is going to steal a coworker's lunch from the fridge because it's a tight-knit group and the culprit would be obvious.

Fast-forward a few years when the company is larger, with 600 employees in several offices. Many have never met, and few are friends. Scaling up means the system has completely changed. It's now necessary to hire people whose entire job is to organize and make sure everyone gets along. To avoid communication bottlenecks, the company divides into teams, meaning they are better able to manage social dynamics. Provided links remain between parts, systems can safely scale in this fashion: by dividing into parts. But things will always be different as a system scales, and a collection of teams within a company will never be able to communicate like a small company. The larger the company grows, the more work it takes to ensure information flows to the right places.

As companies increase in scale, parts of the system break because what works for ten people doesn't typically work for a thousand. As changes to the system are implemented in response to growth, the question always is: How will this system fare in the next year? Ten years? A hundred years? In other words, how well will it age?

As growth occurs, resilience can be increased by keeping a measure of independence between parts of a system. Dependencies tend to age poorly because they rely on every one of their dependencies aging well.

— Sidebar: Economies of Scale

Long-lived Japanese family-run companies

Success often sows the seeds of its destruction. Sometimes getting bigger means becoming more vulnerable, and some things are most apt to survive if they stay small. After all, the majority of species on this planet are insects—tiny, simple creatures.

Economies of Scale

In economics, production processes change as they scale. The more of something that is produced, the more the marginal cost of each additional unit tends to shrink. As more people can afford a product, demand tends to increase. Owning it may become a norm or habit. Economies of scale work because they enable cost-cutting measures, such as purchasing materials in bulk. Systems do not scale indefinitely; economies of scale begin to break after a certain point. Eventually saving any more money becomes impossible, or there may be no more possible customers. In addition, limitations exist when there are dependencies on finite resources, such as energy, raw material, or computing power.

In business, scaling is often seen as inherently good. The bigger a company gets, the more successful we consider it. We hear laudatory stories of how fast new companies grow— hiring more people, opening new offices, and spreading their products or services to vast new audiences. But getting bigger can make companies more fragile. During difficult economic times, companies that scaled too fast can struggle to sustain themselves. Sometimes, when longevity is the goal, staying small and simple can be a superpower.

Most businesses fail in the first few years. The largest companies around at any given point in time, however mighty they may seem in the moment, don't last long. The average life span of an S&P 500 company is 24 years, and this number is decreasing over time.[2] In most parts of the world, a company lasting a few decades is remarkable. Yet in Japan, that's not the case. The country is home to an astonishing number of incredibly old companies, known as *shinise*.[3] Over 50,000 Japanese companies are more than a century old, with nearly 4,000 dating back over 200 years.[4]

Why are long-lived companies more common in Japan than the rest of the world? It's impossible to know for certain. But most of the oldest companies have something in common: the way they scale. Or rather, the way they *don't* scale.

Long-lived Japanese companies tend to be small. They're owned and run by relatives and people with close relationships. They usually have fewer than a hundred employees and trade within a small area inside Japan. Durable, loyal customer relationships are integral to their business models. Also, they are driven by a strong internal philosophy that goes beyond their products and services, enabling them to adapt to changing times.

By staying small, long-lived Japanese companies can hold on to their traditional values. Being no larger than necessary benefits them during less favorable economic conditions. In a small team where a job may last a lifetime, diffusion of

2
Scott D. Anthony, S. Patrick Viguerie, Evan I. Schwartz, and John Van Landeghem, "Corporate Longevity Forecast: Creative Destruction Is Accelerating," Innosight, 2018, https://www.innosight.com/insight/creative-destruction/.

3
Kim Gittleson, "Can a Company Live Forever?" BBC News, January 19, 2012, https://www.bbc.co.uk/news/business-16611040.

4
Joe Pinsker, "These Japanese Companies Have Stayed in Business for Over 1,000 Years," *Atlantic*, February 13, 2015, https://www.theatlantic.com/business/archive/2015/02/japans-oldest-businesses-have-lasted-more-than-a-thousand-years/385396/.

5

"Kongo-Gumi Co., Ltd.," Takamatsu Construction Group, accessed August 15, 2019, https://www.takamatsu-cg.co.jp/eng/about/group/takamatsu/kongogumi.html.

6

Mariko Oi, "Adult Adoptions: Keeping Japan's Family Firms Alive," BBC News, September 19, 2012, https://www.bbc.co.uk/news/magazine-19505088.

7

Joanna Gillan, "Kongo Gumi: Oldest Continuously Operating Company Survives 1,400 Years before Crash," Ancient Origins, September 5, 2015, https://www.ancient-origins.net/history/kongo-gumi-oldest-continuously-operating-company-survives-1400-years-crash-003765.

8

Irene Herrera, "Building on Tradition: 1,400 Years of a Family Business," Works That Work, accessed August 15, 2019, https://worksthatwork.com/3/kongo-gumi.

responsibility is less of a problem as there's nowhere to hide. Employees may be more invested and take their work as a point of pride.

Take the case of perhaps the most famous long-lived Japanese company, Kongo Gumi. A construction company specializing in high-quality Buddhist temples, it operated independently from 578 AD to 2006. Today it exists as a subsidiary of a larger company. At the time of Kongo Gumi's liquidation, it was the oldest company in the world, having built Japan's first-ever Buddhist temple. Throughout the entirety of that time, it remained in the hands of the same family—40 generations of them. Each owner passed the company on to his oldest son.[5] However, to ensure this close-knit succession system worked no matter what, it had some flexibility. If the oldest son didn't have the right leadership potential, a younger son would take over. If none of the sons were suitable or an owner had no male children, they would select a suitable husband for a daughter, then adopt him. Adult adoption for business purposes is a common practice in Japan even today, enabling companies to stay within a single family for many generations.[6] At one point, the widowed wife of an owner took charge of Kongo Gumi.[7]

To give context for the length of time Kongo Gumi remained in operation building iconic temples, at the time of its founding, the Roman Empire had just collapsed. The prophet Muhammad was not yet a decade old.[8] The world changed a great deal between then and 2006. Kongo Gumi survived numerous wars, periods of immense political upheaval, economic crises, and other disasters. It managed this by adapting to the times. For instance, during World War II, demand for Buddhist temples was low. The company switched to making coffins.

Other notable long-lived Japanese companies likewise keep things small and within a single family. The same family has owned the Tsuen Tea shop for 24 generations and the Nishiyama Onsen Keiunkan inn for 52. In some cases, even the

Seiganto-ji, a Tendai Buddhist temple and UNESCO World Heritage site
was built by Kongo Gumi using techniques developed 1,400 years ago.

9
Geoffrey West, *Scale* (New York:
Penguin, 2017).

staff pass their jobs on to their children. Other companies of comparable ages may not have remained in the possession of their founders' descendants but were under the ownership of the same families for long periods.

Scaling up is not always advantageous. Systems change as they get bigger or smaller, and so, depending on your goals and desires, staying small and flexible might be the ideal choice to realize them.

— Sidebar: On Being the Right Size

« Scaling up from the small to the large is often accompanied by an evolution from simplicity to complexity while maintaining basic elements or building blocks of the system unchanged or conserved. »

Geoffrey West[9]

The story of illumination

Humans often think linearly. If we double our inputs, we'll get double the outputs. It's hard for us to imagine that double our inputs will give us half the amount of outputs, or four times the amount. Understanding that systems can scale nonlinearly is useful because it helps us appreciate how much a system can change as it grows.

Since the dawn of time, humans have had to contend with one of our greatest foes: the dark. Without any source of artificial light, once the sun goes down, our eyes are ill-equipped to see our surroundings, and we cannot keep watch for danger. Nor can we carry out useful daytime activities like making tools or foraging for food. For this reason, throughout history people have been willing to put a remarkable amount of effort and ingenuity into developing artificial light and making it better, safer, cheaper, and accessible to more people.

On Being the Right Size

In 1926, British-Indian scientist J. B. S. Haldane published an essay entitled "On Being the Right Size," which explores the role of scale in biology. Different animals are of different sizes. What's less obvious is the link between an animal's size and its appearance. In general, it would be impossible for a species to become much bigger or larger without changing its appearance.

For instance, Haldane imagines what would happen if a gazelle became much larger. The only way its long legs would be able to support its weight would be by becoming either short and thick or long and spindly but with a smaller body. Incidentally this is how rhinoceroses and giraffes manage.

Not only does changing an animal's scale require it to look different, but it also transforms the impact of gravity upon it. "You can drop a mouse down a thousand-yard mine shaft," Haldane writes, "and, on arriving at the bottom, it gets a slight shock and walks away, provided the ground is fairly soft. A rat is killed, a man is broken, a horse splashes." The reason is air resistance, which prevents a mouse from falling too fast due to the ratio between its weight and surface area.

10
Jane Brox, *Brilliant: The Evolution of Artificial Light* (London: Souvenir, 2012).

11
Brox, ibid.

12
Brox, ibid.

Each time the technology available to supply us with light has improved, there have been two interesting results. We've had to scale up the infrastructure necessary to fuel it, and we've changed our productivity scale.

The first attempts humans made at illumination, around 40,000 years ago, were simple unworked pieces of limestone with a smidgeon of burning animal fat, held in cupped hands. As time progressed, people used shells, then fashioned lamps out of pottery, making incremental improvements to the design.[10] Early lamps took little work to power, but their light had a tiny range and went out easily. They extended the range of human activity only a little, though it was enough to allow us to make art on the walls of caves.

While the Romans likely made the first beeswax candles, cost considerations meant that for many more centuries, most people used any available form of oil for lighting.[11] There were no elaborate systems behind this activity; people made their own fuel. It was labor-intensive to make and maintain, and still only brightened the night a fraction, but it was enough that the value of artificial light was evident.

It can be hard for us to imagine how lacking an effective means of artificial light limited the scale of human activity. Artificial light allowed productive time to scale. People could work longer and produce more.

There was a time when all the women in a village would cluster in one cottage at night, sit in a tiered circle around a single lamp, and share its rays as they sewed, made lace, and the like.[12] They were limited to whatever work they could manage by their share of the light. Outside, the streets would remain dark until the 17th century. Most activities outside the home were restricted to daylight hours, which kept the world small. Unless you were rich, brave (or foolhardy), or doing something illegal, the night was off-limits for most activities. In cities throughout Europe in the Middle Ages, night meant a total shutdown. The city gates closed, chains ran across roads to prevent movement, and a night watch patrolled the streets to ensure no one was out.[13]

Moving into the 18th century, whale oil became a widespread choice for lamp fuel. This led to a drastic change. For the first time, people fueled their lights with something they didn't make themselves. Whale oil came from far away and was purchased in its prepared form. The system required to make whale oil was a huge increase in scale from people producing their own forms of fuel. It took elaborate, dangerous operations aboard ships to find, kill, and extract oil from whales, each of which could yield up to 1,800 gallons of oil.[14] Light was an industry for the first time. For individuals, purchasing fuel was more efficient than making it themselves.

However, the light produced by burning whale oil was still no brighter than older forms of oil. The next change in artificial lighting would require a giant change in the scale of the surrounding systems. The transition from candles and oil lamps to gas also enabled human affairs to scale up, transforming areas such as factory work.[15]

Burnt gas, a by-product of coke production, produced a much clearer, stronger flame than anything to come before it.[16] Factories embraced it first, for it offered a way to approximate the kinds of precise work previously only possible in daylight. In *Disenchanted Night*, Wolfgang Schivelbusch says that "modern gas lighting began as industrial lighting." The new artificial light, he explains, "emancipated the working day from its dependence on natural daylight....Work processes were no longer regulated by the individual worker....In the factories, night was turned to day more consistently than anywhere else."[17] Factories could scale up production and run at any time of day, all year round.

Though the first gas systems were built for individual factories and dwellings, inventor Frederick Albert Winsor* came up with the idea of a centralized supply connected via underground pipes to all of the buildings in an area.[18] This

* Frederick Albert Winsor (Friedrich Albrecht Winzer) - (1763-1830). The inscription of Winsor's memorial in London, "At evening time it shall be light," is a good reflection of his contributions. As an inventor, he pioneered the idea of supplying gas to buildings through underground pipes and founded the first gas company.

13
Brox, ibid.

14
Brox, ibid.

15
Wolfgang Schivelbusch, *Disenchanted Night* (Oakland: University of California Press, 1988).

16
Brox, ibid.

17
Schivelbusch, ibid.

18
"Frederick Albert Winsor (Winzer) Biography (1763–1830)," How Products Are Made, accessed August 11, 2020, http://www.madehow.com/inventorbios/79/Frederick-Albert-Winsor-Winzer.html.

19
Brox, ibid.

20
Schivelbusch, ibid.

21
Brox, ibid.

22
Brox, ibid.

would be cheaper, decreasing the marginal price of adding additional users—as well as cementing gas's place as an essential utility for the modern home.

Here we see another increase in the scale of the systems surrounding lighting. Not only did gas have its own production system outside of the home, it also had its own distribution system, further removing people from the process of making their light. They didn't even have to tend gas lamps to keep them working; they just turned them on and off. Jane Brox writes in *Brilliant* that "gaslight divided light—and life—from its singular, self-reliant past. All was now interconnected, contingent, and intricate."[19] People's homes became part of a larger system.

Two consequences of this increased scale were, as Schivelbusch argues, the loss of autonomy for individual house-holds and the regulation of utilities in geographical areas.[20] Houses became part of an infrastructure that increased the scale of the city. Gas lighting provided for households many of the same benefits it gave to industries—activities were no longer bound by the availability of daylight or constrained by the cost and coverage of a candle. But households became depen-dent on infrastructure they had very little say in.

Gas also scaled up what people could do during the night out on the city streets. Gas streetlamps soon became wide-spread in cities in England and the United States. No longer did people have to hide away at night while armed watchmen prowled the streets. Now "nightlife" came into existence as a concept.[21] New activities or better versions of old ones became possible: coffeehouses and taverns stayed open late as patrons socialized, shops lit up their windows so people could window-shop their wares, areas of cities grew famous for their beautiful appearance at night, and theaters could create visual effects and better distinguish the stage from the audience.[22]

Artificial light increased the scale of what we could see at night and thus opened up new businesses and new ways of conducting one's day. Festivities and holiday celebrations began to move later and later into the evening.

With the advent of electricity—a means of making light without fire—human activities during the night were able to further scale up by an order of magnitude. It was much cheaper, safer, and easier to use for the end consumer once electric technology progressed, and it could evenly light a whole space as well as the sun could. Electric light would also require surrounding systems on a scale never seen before, taking gas as its model.

Electric light was at first an oddity that seemed to possess no practical value. Humphry Davy discovered the arc light, which used carbon sticks, but it faced the problem of being too bright and short-lived to be practical. Inventing the incandescent bulb would take several more decades of problem-solving, with Thomas Edison and his lab finding the right filament material for bulbs that could scale.[23]

Having solved that problem, Edison needed a way to supply electricity to homes. As Jane Brox explains it, gas was both a rival and an inspiration. Edison copied the concept of a central supply with a grid connecting houses. As with gas, factories proved eager customers, especially those that used flammable materials.[24] Although gas had already enabled factories to run through the night, electrical lighting was cheaper, easier to see by, and less likely to cause fires.

Achieving the ambition of supplying as many people as possible with electric light required creating supporting systems on a whole new scale. It meant digging tunnels for cables and building power stations. Generating electricity meant massive-scale engineering undertakings, like utilizing the power of Niagara Falls.[25] The electric grid, which continues to connect ever more people around the world by transmitting electricity from power plants via power lines, would end up being one of humanity's greatest ideas.[26]

23
Jennifer Latson, "Thomas Edison Invents Light Bulb and Myths about Himself," *Time*, October 21, 2014, https://time.com/3517011/thomas-edison/.

24
Brox, ibid.

25
Brox, ibid.

26
J. M. K. C. Donev et al., "Electrical Grid," Energy Education, University of Calgary, 2020, https://energyeducation.ca/encyclopedia/Electrical_grid.

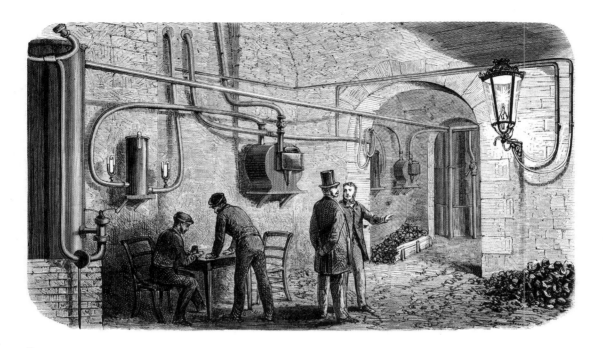

Today, the term *gaslighting* has a less positive association; it refers to a form of psychological manipulation intended to make the victim doubt their own ability to deduce the truth. The term comes from a 1938 stage play in which a husband searches for jewels in the apartment above theirs, which previously belonged to a rich woman who was murdered. Each time he lights the gas lamps up there, it reduces the supply to the rest of the building and causes the lights to dim.

27
Schivelbusch, ibid.

As light coverage increased, new concerns emerged. As Schivelbusch notes, "The twentieth century was to experience this relentless light to the full. The glaring and shadowless light that illuminates H. G. Wells's negative Utopias no longer guarantees the security of the individual. It permits total surveillance by the state." As the coverage of artificial light has scaled up, the opportunities for and constraints on individuals have changed. As wonderful as artificial light is for navigation and safety, most of us realize it has limits. To banish completely darkness suggests "a nightmare of a light from which there is no escape."[27]

Artificial light changed the scale at which human activities can happen. In many ways, the limits of our lights are the limits of our world. There are still places where we lack the means to eradicate darkness, such as outer space and the deepest parts of the oceans.

When you scale up a system, the problems you solved at the smaller scale often need solving again at a larger scale. In addition, you end up with unanticipated possibilities and outcomes. As the scale increases, so does its impact on other systems. Increasing the size of a system does not result in just more of the same; there are often new impacts and requirements as the system develops new capabilities.

Looking at the development of artificial light through the lens of scale, we see how important it is to be aware of how scale changes might impact the system as a whole. A more interconnected, larger system may be able to handle variations better, but it may also be vulnerable to widespread failures. Increasing the scale of a system might mean using new materials or incorporating methods like the ones that worked on a smaller scale. It might mean rethinking your whole approach.

Conclusion

Systems change as they scale up or down, and neither is intrinsically better or worse. The right scale depends on your goals and the context. If you want to scale something up, you need to anticipate that new problems will keep arising—problems that didn't exist at a smaller scale. Or you might need to keep solving the same problems in different ways.

Using this model as a lens suggests that as systems scale up, you increase the impact of failures, but you also increase the size of successes. Although it might seem easiest to just do safe, small-scale things that can't go too wrong, staying small isn't always the right answer. Sometimes being small is what it takes to survive, but if it's all you ever do, then you miss out on the larger potential upsides.

Margin of Safety

—
Expect the unexpected

Margin of Safety

When we interact with complex systems, we need to expect the unexpected. Systems do not always function as anticipated. They are subject to variable conditions and can respond to inputs in nonlinear ways.

A margin of safety is often necessary to ensure systems can handle stressors and unpredictable circumstances. This means there is a meaningful gap between what a system is capable of handling and what it is required to handle. A margin of safety is a buffer between safety and danger, order and chaos, success and failure. It ensures a system does not swing from one to the other too easily, causing damage.

« This world of ours appears to be separated by a slight and precarious margin of safety from a most singular and unexpected danger. »

Arthur Conan Doyle[1]

For example, engineers know to design for extremes, not averages. In engineering, it's necessary to consider the most something might need to handle—then add on an extra buffer. If 5,000 cars are going to drive across a bridge on an average day, it would be unwise to construct it to be capable of handling precisely that number. What if there were an unusual number of buses or trucks on a particular day? What if there were strong winds? What if there were a big sports match in the area, and twice as many people want to cross the bridge? What if the population of the area is much higher in a decade? Whoever designs the bridge needs to add on a big margin of safety so it stays strong even when many more than 5,000 cars cross it in a day. A large margin of safety doesn't eliminate the possibility of failure, but it reduces it.

1
Arthur Conan Doyle, *Tales of Terror and Mystery* (London: Pan Books, 1978).

For investors, a margin of safety is the gap between an investment vehicle's intrinsic value and its price. The higher the margin of safety, the safer the investment and the greater the potential profit. Since intrinsic value is subjective, it's best this buffer be as large as possible to account for uncertainty.[2]

When calculating the ideal margin of safety, we always need to consider how high the stakes are. The greater the cost of failure, the bigger the buffer should be.

To create a margin of safety, complex systems can utilize backups—in the form of spare components, capacities, or subsystems—to function when things go wrong. Backups make the system resilient. If an error occurs or something gets broken, the system can keep functioning. One way to think of backups is as an alternate path, like how you might have multiple routes to your office in mind so you can still get there if there's a car accident blocking one road. A system can't keep working indefinitely without anything breaking down. A system without backups is unlikely to function for long.

As with margins of safety, the higher the stakes, the greater the need for backups. If a part in your pen breaks, it's not a big deal. It's a different story if a critical part in an airplane breaks. If you're going to the local shops, taking your phone in case you need to communicate with anyone is sufficient. If you're going hiking in the wilderness alone, you might want more than one communication method. You're safer in an airplane than a car, in part because it has so much backup; after all, the cost of failure is higher.

We have to be careful with margins of safety, as they can make us overconfident. If we get too reckless, we cancel out the benefits. When humans are involved in a system, too much margin of safety or backup can lead to risk compensation. For instance, we all know we should wear a seat belt in a car, but do they make us safer? Some research suggests they might not reduce car accident fatalities because people drive with less care, feeling there is a margin of safety between them and

2
Benjamin Graham, *The Intelligent Investor* (New York: Harper, 2006).

3

David Bjerklie, "The Hidden
Danger of Seat Belts," *Time*,
November 30, 2006, http://
content.time.com/time/nation/
article/0,8599,1564465,00.html.

injury. This puts pedestrians and passengers at a higher risk
even if drivers are safer.[3]

The risk of a system failure is not fixed. Failure rates can
remain consistent when humans are involved because margins
of safety sometimes create perverse incentives. If we change
our behavior in response to the knowledge that we have a margin of safety in place, we may end up reducing or negating its
benefits. Setting your watch to be 15 minutes fast could help
you be on time more often. If you follow the time it displays,
you'll have a buffer in case of delays. But if you remember the
time is wrong and amend it in your head, it won't make any
difference to your punctuality.

Conversely, margins of safety and backups can also
make us too cautious. Not all situations we face are like building a bridge, where it either stands or it doesn't and collapsing
results in death. There is a difference between what's uncom-
fortable and what ruins you. Most systems can be down for an
hour. Our bodies can go without food or water for days. Most
businesses can do without revenue for a little while. Too much
margin of safety could be a waste of resources and can sow the
seeds of becoming uncompetitive. If you know it's impossible
to fail, you get complacent. But too little margin of safety can
lead to destruction. You can't weather inevitable shocks.

— Sidebar: Minimum Effective Dose

Learning as a margin of safety

How can we develop a margin of safety in our lives? Things go
wrong, at least once in a while, and it would be ideal to have a
way of increasing our resilience in the face of dramatic change
by having a built-in margin of safety. Learning is one way of
applying this model on an individual level.

The more we learn, the fewer blind spots we have. And
blind spots are the source of all mistakes. While learning more
than we need to get the job done can appear inefficient, the
corresponding reduction in blind spots offers a margin of

Minimum Effective Dose

The difference between medicine and poison is in the dose. Too much of a beneficial substance can be harmful or lethal, and a tiny amount of a harmful substance can have beneficial effects. It's necessary for doctors to give patients doses of medication that are big enough to be effective but not so big as to be dangerous. Prescribing a bit less than the harmful amount isn't much good. A patient could take too much or take their doses too close together.

So pharmacologists calculate the minimum effective dose: the lowest possible amount of a medication to achieve a meaningful benefit in the average patient. Then they calculate the maximum tolerated dose: the largest amount an average patient could take without suffering harm. For example, a vaccine contains the minimal possible dose of a virus necessary to get the body to produce an immune response. Too much could cause actual illness; too little would not be protective. Knowing this window means doctors can ensure a margin of safety by starting with a low dose they still know is likely to work.

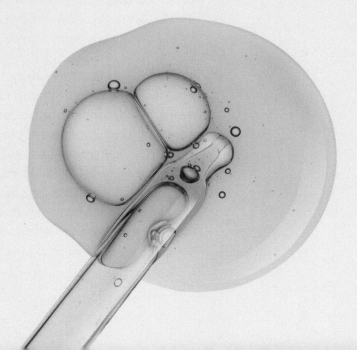

Chris Hadfield - (b. 1959). Like
many children, Hadfield dreamed
of becoming an astronaut while
growing up in Ontario. Against all
the odds—Canada didn't even have
a space program at the time—he
worked his way up through the
Air Force, gaining the experience
necessary to realize his dream
once the Canadian Space Agency
launched. Since his retirement
in 2013, Hadfield has spoken
and written widely about his
experiences.

4
Chris Hadfield, *An Astronaut's
Guide to Life on Earth* (Toronto:
Vintage Canada, Penguin Random
House, 2013).

5
Hadfield, ibid.

safety. Knowledge allows us to adapt to changing situations.

One profession that demands that an individual have far more knowledge than they will ever use is astronaut. Carrying out your job in the hostile environment of space means that you have to prepare for as many variables as possible in order to have the best possible response to any challenge. Learning is a way for an astronaut to develop a large margin of safety, giving them the chance to deal with the unexpected in space. The human capacity for not only learning but also the ability to flexibly apply knowledge in novel situations is one of the main reasons we need astronauts in space. They respond to new information, use creativity, and make assessments in a way that only humans can.

In his book *An Astronaut's Guide to Life on Earth*, Chris Hadfield[*] explains how and why astronauts learn as much as they can. They don't stop at what they need to know but continue lifelong learning to prepare for any eventuality they can think of. They reduce blind spots. He says of astronauts that "no matter how competent or seasoned, every astronaut is a perpetual student."[4] They are "trained to look on the dark side and imagine the worst things that could possibly happen."[5] And then they train for them. Hadfield describes hours in simulators and classrooms, constantly training and preparing for an incredibly vast array of potential scenarios.

The culture of the space program is one of constant debriefs about every detail. The point of these is not to be pedantic or shame anyone but to get the information necessary to learn and to improve the program. Thus for both the individual astronaut and the space organization they are a part of, there is a recognition that ongoing learning is the key element in creating a margin of safety in space operations.

Although astronauts are well educated and experienced, they come into the space program with an incredible amount to learn. Hadfield says of his early career, "Training in Houston, I hadn't been able to separate out the vital from the trivial,

The International Space Station is a collaborative project between five space agencies: NASA (USA), Roscosmos (Russia), CSA (Canada), ESA (Europe), and JAXA (Japan). The first ISS component was launched in 1998, and at the time of writing, the station has been continuously inhabited since November 2, 2000.

6
Hadfield, ibid.

7
Hadfield, ibid.

8
Hadfield, ibid.

to differentiate between what was going to keep me alive in an emergency and what was esoteric and interesting but not crucial." Throughout the program, working both in space and on the ground, he says of his development that "over time, I learned how to anticipate problems in order to prevent them, and how to respond effectively in critical situations."[6] Hadfield's experience demonstrates why it's important for them to learn meta skills: astronauts always need to know something; they just don't know ahead of time what knowledge they will have to utilize in the variety of life-or-death situations they will face on a space mission.

In the space program, learning is critical to success. "Our core skill," Hadfield writes, "the one that made us astronauts— the ability to parse and solve complex problems rapidly, with incomplete information in a hostile environment—was not something any of us had been born with. But by this point we all had it. We'd developed it on the job."[7]

While the space missions get all the attention, the job of an astronaut is so much more. If all someone wants to do is be in space, they aren't a good fit for the program, because there is no guarantee of any one individual getting the go-ahead for a mission. Rather, most of the job of an astronaut is performed on Earth, doing things like learning Russian and practicing mechanics in a space suit submerged in a pool. The training is ongoing, with a mission to space only a possibility.

Hadfield spent six months commanding the International Space Station (ISS). There are three to six people on the ISS at any given time, and when things go wrong, at least one, but preferably two, of them can deal with it. There isn't any time for someone to be flown in to solve a problem.

Although astronauts can communicate with the ground to get insight and advice, they have to rely on the group up in space to fix any problem. That is why, Hadfield says, that "having 'overqualified' crewmates is a safety net for everyone."[8]

Astronauts need to be good at everything. That

redundancy is necessary in case one of them is incapacitated or in need of help. This means that time on Earth is best spent learning things like how to pull a tooth or fix a toilet in space. "The more you know and the keener your sense of operational awareness, the better equipped you are to fight against a bad outcome, right to the very end."[9]

Our ego gets in the way of capitalizing on the margin of safety that is produced by knowing more than you need to. Often we learn enough to solve today's problem but not enough to solve tomorrow's. There is no margin of safety in what we know. Another way our ego gets in the way is that we tend to coast on our natural strengths, too afraid or intimidated to dive into being the worst at something. But as Hadfield explains, "Early success is a terrible teacher. You're essentially being rewarded for a lack of preparation, so when you find yourself in a situation where you *must* prepare, you can't do it. You don't know how."[10] And life will throw at you challenges that require capabilities outside your natural strengths. The only way to be ready is to first build as vast a repertoire of knowledge as you can in anticipation of the possibilities you might face, and second to cultivate the ability to know what is relevant and useful.

Hadfield concludes that in space and on Earth, "truly being ready means understanding what could go wrong and having a plan to deal with it."[11] Even if the plan is just knowing how you deal with uncertainty, these plans, based on learning, are your margin of safety. Astronauts train in simulators all the time for all sorts of disasters that may come to pass on a mission. Instead of being disheartening, Hadfield suggests ongoing simulations have incredible value because they teach the astronaut how to think clearly in real-life situations.

After decades in the space program, Hadfield offers this perspective on life: "If you've got the time, use it to get ready....Yes, maybe you'll learn how to do a few things you'll never wind up actually needing to do, but that's a much better problem to have than needing to do something and having no clue where to start."[12]

9
Hadfield, ibid.

10
Hadfield, ibid.

11
Hadfield, ibid.

12
Hadfield, ibid.

Jacques Jaujard - (1895-1967). As director of the French National Museums during World War II, Jaujard risked his life innumerable times to help protect France's public and private art collections. His passion for protecting the country's cultural heart continued after the war when he helped found the French Commission on Art Recovery, dedicated to bringing works of art home. For his courageous work, Jaujard was awarded the Medal of the Résistance and made a commander of the Legion of Honor, the highest French order of merit.

13
Hadfield, ibid.

14
"The Monuments Men," Monuments Men Foundation, accessed August 19, 2019, https://www. monumentsmenfoundation.org/ the-heroes/the-monuments-men/ jaujard-jacques.

After all, "when the stakes are high, preparation is everything."[13] The more you know, the more you will be able to anticipate and avoid problems. Knowledge then can be conceptualized as a margin of safety, a buffer against the inevitable unexpected challenges that you will have to face.

« The professionals plan for "mild randomness" and misunderstand "wild randomness." They learn from the averages and overlook the outliers. Thus they consistently, predictably, underestimate catastrophic risk. »

Benoit Mandelbrot

Anticipating the worst

We cannot have a backup plan for everything. We do too much in a day or a year to devote the resources necessary to plan for dealing with disaster in all of our endeavors. However, when the stakes are high, it is worth investing in a comprehensive margin of safety. Extreme events require extreme preparation.

"To lead is to anticipate" was the motto of Jacques Jaujard*, director of the French National Museums during World War II.[14] If this is true, Jaujard was a perfect leader.

Before the war started, many French people refused to believe the Nazis would target Paris and disturb the cultural treasures contained within its museums and galleries. But Jaujard was less optimistic. Considering the irreplaceable work in his care, he wanted to err on the side of caution. Jaujard had seen things most French people hadn't that impressed upon him the role of art in conflict. During the Spanish Civil War of the 1930s, he assisted with the transportation of artwork from the Museo del Prado in Madrid, Spain, to Switzerland. Artworks are vulnerable to destruction from bombing, fire, and so on during wars. They're also vulnerable to seizure by a

The Monuments Men Foundation for the Preservation of Art was set up to celebrate the legacy of people who helped guard cultural property during World War II. The nonprofit continues to work on returning looted artworks—many of which never made it home—something that has been the subject of several books and a George Clooney film.

15
Agnès Poirier, "Saviour of France's
Art: How the Mona Lisa Was
Spirited Away from the Nazis,"
Guardian, November 22, 2014,
https://www.theguardian.com/
world/2014/nov/22/mona-lisa-
spirited-away-from-nazis-
jacques-jaujard-louvre.

16
Agnès Poirier, *Left Bank: Art,
Passion, and the Rebirth of Paris
1940–1950* (London: Bloomsbury
Publishing, 2016).

17
Poirier, ibid.

18
Noah Charney, "Did the Nazis
Steal the Mona Lisa?," *Guardian*,
November 12, 2013, https://
www.theguardian.com/
artanddesign/2013/nov/12/
nazis-steal-mona-lisa-louvre.

19
Aurelien Breeden, "Art Looted by
Nazis Gets a New Space at the
Louvre. But Is It Really Home?,"
February 8, 2018, https://www.
nytimes.com/2018/02/08/world/
europe/louvre-nazi-looted-art.
html.

20
Poirier, ibid.

country's enemy—for profit, as a means of subjugation, and to erode culture. Jaujard's experiences taught him it was best to move Paris's treasures away if there was any risk whatsoever of attack.[15] That way, no matter what, France could hold on to a piece of its pride knowing part of its culture was safe.

Anticipating that invasion by the Germans was inevitable, Jaujard developed a plan. What turned out to be mere days before the war reached France, Jaujard announced that the Louvre would close for three days for maintenance. But once the doors opened again, it was empty. Where had the thousands of pieces of artwork gone?

While the Louvre was closed, a team of hundreds of Louvre staff, art students, and other volunteers packed up every piece for transportation.[16] Some paintings could be rolled into tubes; others were large enough to need transporting in trucks intended for theatrical sets.[17] Then a crew of vehicles, including everything from taxis to ambulances, slipped through the night and left Paris for the countryside. Before the war even began, the artwork was installed in the basements and other safe storage spaces of castles around France.

By starting before the threat was imminent, Jaujard and his team ensured a margin of safety for the Louvre's treasures. His forethought was wise. The Nazis stole an estimated five million works of art,[18] around 100,000 of which came from France.[19] One of Hitler's ambitions was to build the Führermuseum in Austria featuring artwork plundered from other nations.

In 1940, Count Franz Wolff-Metternich, appointed by the Nazis to secure artworks for them, visited Jaujard. When he saw the Louvre was empty, the count looked relieved.[20] He was not a Nazi in his beliefs, and he became an unexpected ally for Jaujard until his lack of loyalty cost him his job. After that, Jaujard was at an even greater risk than before, lacking any support from within the Nazi regime.

To reduce the risk of the Nazis discovering the hidden artwork, Jaujard and his team had dispersed it across multiple locations. If the Nazis found any of these stashes, it would only be a small portion of the total. Jaujard built in extra safety mechanisms at every point, supplying equipment to maintain the right temperature and humidity conditions and relocating pieces any time he doubted their safety. Should some disaster compel someone to choose the most important pieces to save, Jaujard labeled the cases with colored circles denoting levels of importance.[21]

For years, the collection remained in hiding. The Louvre's treasures were moved repeatedly. As the Nazi occupation progressed, Louvre curators sometimes resorted to sleeping next to the most important pieces.

One notable figure among the hundreds involved in the Louvre operation was Rose Valland*. She worked in the Nazi's art theft division recording the whereabouts of the thousands of stolen paintings that left France. But she was not loyal to the Nazis, and she used her position to make copies of the information on French artwork. Her being unassuming allowed her to spy on the Nazis without them suspecting her of anything. They didn't even know that she could speak German and was able to eavesdrop on their conversations.

After the war her records helped with the repatriation of many works that might otherwise have been lost, including more than 20,000 items hidden in Neuschwanstein Castle in the Bavarian Alps. Up until her death, Valland continued to work to help bring home French art and cultural items.[22]

Due to the extreme prudence of Jaujard and his team, by the end of the war, not one item from the Louvre's collection was lost or damaged. The collection stayed safe from the Nazis, as well as avoiding damage by fire or water, or even theft. Acting early and being cautious worked.[23]

After the war ended, the Louvre opened its doors again at last. The survival of the Louvre's collection symbolized the resistance of many French citizens to Nazi occupation.[24] We could say what Jaujard did was a waste of effort and irrelevant

*
Rose Valland - (1898-1980). A fearless guardian of French culture, Valland was one of the unsung heroes of World War II. Working alongside Jacques Jaujard, she played a central role in protecting the Louvre's collection. By working in the Nazi's art theft division, Valland was able to covertly record the whereabouts of tens of thousands of pieces. After the war, the information she risked execution to collect proved invaluable for restitution efforts. Valland continued to fight for the safe return of French artwork for the rest of her life, ultimately becoming one of the most decorated women in French history.

21
Gerri Chanel, *Saving Mona Lisa: The Battle to Protect the Louvre and Its Treasures from the Nazis* (London: Icon Books, 2018).

22
"Valland, Capt. Rose: Monuments Men Foundation," Monuments Men Foundation, accessed May 26, 2020, https://www.monumentsmenfoundation.org/valland-capt-rose.

23
Chanel, ibid.

24
Poirier, ibid.

25
Eleanor Beardsley, "France
Hopes Exhibit of Nazi-Stolen
Art Can Aid Stalled Search for
Owners," NPR, February 23, 2018,
https://www.npr.org/sections/
parallels/2018/02/23/588374670/
france-hopes-exhibit-
of-nazi-stolen-art-can-
aid-stalled-search-for-
owners?t=1561971635984.

to the outcome of the war for the French. But Jaujard was simply doing his job as the director of the French National Museums: helping to preserve the country's soul, the heritage and
history that made it worth fighting for and part of what made
France special.

Of course, the Nazis lost in the end. But many of the
artworks they took from other museums were never returned
or were damaged beyond repair. The Louvre itself still hosts
around 800 artworks that never made it back to their original
owners.[25] We can learn from Jaujard's removal of artwork from
Paris during the war the importance of building in a significant
margin of safety when the risk of failure is high. The future is
seldom predictable, and so the greater the threat, the more it's
important to plan for the worst.

Conclusion

Looking at our world through the lens of margin of safety
suggests that redundancy is sometimes useful. Broad compe-
tence seems very costly compared to specialization, but it is
more likely to save us in the outlier situations of life. Efficiency
is good for small tasks where failure has little consequence,
but life is not exclusively filled with minor challenges and minimal consequences. We are all going to face extreme events
where failure is disastrous.

Using margin of safety as a model suggests that we
should not give in to the temptation of improving our current
efficiency while making our future selves vulnerable to calamity. A margin of safety can be an excellent buffer against the
unexpected, giving us time to effectively adapt.

Churn

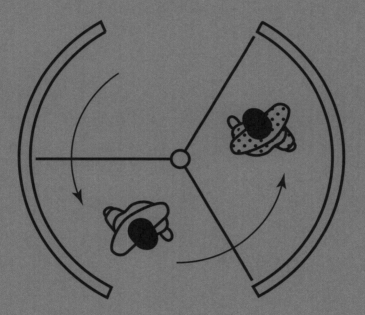

—
There's always movement

Churn

Within systems, components are constantly wearing out and getting used up. This includes both the material and information (the stocks) within a system and the parts of the system itself. Keeping a system functioning requires ongoing replenishing of both the stocks and the parts used to maintain them. We call this process of attrition "churn."

There are examples of churn everywhere. The skin cells on your body are constantly being replaced. Trees in a forest die, and new ones grow. The parts in a car deteriorate with time; some need replacing, and some render the car unfixable once they break. People move in and out of cities. System components are never static, and understanding how and why the stocks change or the parts wear out is important. The churn model is a lens through which you can look at that kind of system change and learn how to work with it.

In business, churn refers to losing a customer, whether that's because they canceled a subscription, stopped buying a product, moved away from a store, or something else. No business can retain every customer forever. However, the rate of churn varies depending on factors like the availability of alternatives, ease of switching, and overall satisfaction. Often given as a percentage, churn is a good metric for whether a product fits its market.

Growth may be good in business, but churn is also important to consider. It doesn't matter how many new customers a company gets through the door if they don't stick around long enough to earn back their cost of acquisition. If churn is high, a company may run out of money to acquire new customers.

Churn can also refer to the turnover of employees, something that varies between industries because of the varying costs for both employees and employers. If hiring and training new employees is costly, a company has an incentive to keep churn low, and vice versa. Fast-food restaurants, for instance, have a higher churn rate than governments. A certain level of churn, even just from people retiring, helps bring in new perspectives and experiences. Too much churn prevents expertise from accumulating.

When churn is too high in a system, replacing what is lost or used up becomes a process of running to stay in the same place. Once we get stuck in the trap of keeping up with churn, it's time to step back and reassess if it's worthwhile or if there's another way.

Since churn of some sort is inevitable in all systems, it's useful to ask how we can use it to our benefit. Is it worth going through contortions to keep every customer, or should we let a certain percentage go and focus on the core customers who keep our business going? Is it worth trying to retain employees who have lost interest in the job or who would experience more professional growth elsewhere? Understanding your situation through the lens of churn can help you figure out how to harness the dynamics that drive it.

Cults

We can never eliminate churn in groups of people. When the purpose of an organization becomes preventing members from leaving, it turns into a cult. A cult is a group doing everything possible to control its members. Avoiding churn becomes the whole purpose, as opposed to whatever the initial aim was. Every detail is intended to entrap members tighter. Even if the initial purpose was positive, this process can only ever end up harming members.

"Today is the first day of the rest of your life." You might have heard these words as a motivational quote, but their origins are somewhat more sinister. Charles Dederich[*], founder of the cult Synanon, is the originator of this quote. Synanon is one of the most notable cults in US history for several reasons. Its success in attracting members lent it a place in popular

Charles Dederich - (1913-1997). After having his life repeatedly derailed by alcoholism, Dederich joined AA and was inspired to start his own drug and alcohol rehabilitation program. At its peak, the cult Synanon had assets of up to $50 million and thousands of members.

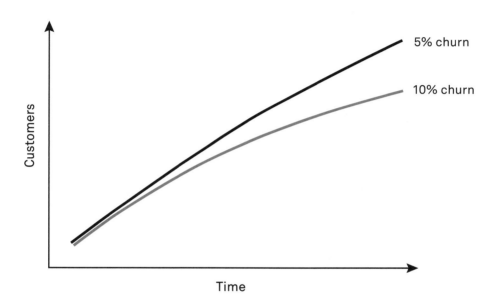

When we have a customer retention rate of 90%, we may think we're doing great. But over time, the 5% difference between us and our competitor means we have less growth and have to work a lot harder to keep up.

culture, earning mentions in well-known songs and books between the 1950s and 1990s. It gained support from political figures like Senator Thomas J. Dodd and Nancy Reagan[*]. Synanon was also practically unrivaled in the intensity of its efforts to prevent members from leaving or the outside world from impeding its activities. It was an efficient churn-minimizing machine. Though the organization began with positive intentions, the goal of holding on to members became all-encompassing.

Synanon began in 1958 as a drug addiction rehabilitation program. Dederich, a former alcoholic, started the group in his small flat, using a $33 (about $300 today) unemployment check.[1] By its demise in 1991, Synanon had progressed to an incomprehensible level considering its inauspicious origins; it had morphed into a full-blown cult with thousands of indoctrinated members.[2]

When Dederich founded Synanon, treatment options for people with addictions were limited in the United States. Having dropped out of university and failing to hold down a job or make relationships work due to his own out-of-control drinking, he knew the cost of uncontrolled addiction for individuals and their families. Although Alcoholics Anonymous existed at the time, rehabilitation facilities were not widespread, and the belief that addiction is a personal failure was prevalent. Based on his own experiences, Dederich initially believed addiction was curable, provided an individual changed their social context and helped others.[3] Although we now know that environment and relationships do play a significant role in addiction, his belief ended up justifying control at the expense of treatment.

A decade after Synanon's founding, Dederich changed his mind about the nature of drug addiction. He decided it was impossible for people with addictions to ever make a full recovery and go on to live regular lives. Synanon members were now expected to stay in the group. Forever.

[*] Nancy Reagan - (1921-2016). Beginning her career as a Hollywood actress, Reagan is best known for the anti-drug campaigns she launched as First Lady of the United States.

[1] Lawrence Van Gelder, "Charles Dederich, 83, Synanon Founder, Dies," *New York Times*, March 4, 1997, https://www.nytimes.com/1997/03/04/us/charles-dederich-83-synanon-founder-dies.html.

[2] Jyotsna Sreenivasan, *Utopias in American History* (Santa Barbara: ABC-CLIO, 2008).

[3] Hillel Aron, "The Story of This Drug Rehab-Turned-Violent Cult Is *Wild, Wild Country*-Caliber Bizarre," *Los Angeles Magazine*, April 23, 2018, accessed August 16, 2019, https://www.lamag.com/citythinkblog/synanon-cult/.

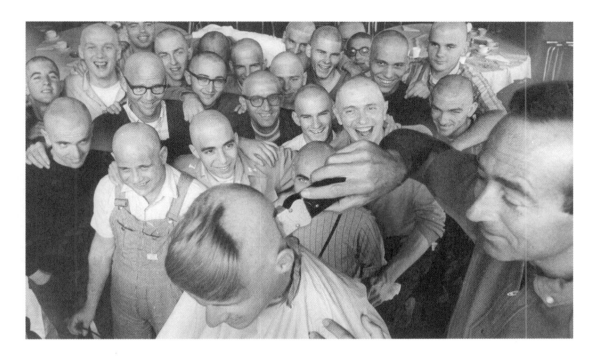

Members of Synanon have gone on to establish numerous drug treatment centers and therapeutic communities all over the United States. Developing safe, effective treatments for addiction remains a work in progress, with social stigma and legal restrictions on proven harm-reduction methods serving as major barriers in many countries.

4
Sreenivasan, ibid.

Dederich began using brainwashing techniques to eliminate churn while using the threat of force to deter potential defectors. To grow Synanon further, he started accepting new types of members, including middle-class people in search of personal growth and young people sent to him by court order—showing that the organization had mainstream approval at the time.

Synanon's control over members to prevent them from churning was total, using a combination of brainwashing, denial of autonomy, and threats of violence. Synanon members shaved their heads, wore overalls, and quit smoking and drugs cold turkey. As they went about their day in dedicated Synanon buildings, they listened to Dederich repeating his views over radio stations for hours on end. Married couples who joined together had to divorce. Members were not permitted to have children.

Perhaps the most extreme mind-control technique was "The Game." During lengthy sessions, members were encouraged to criticize each other and air grievances with anyone in the group. In theory, the purpose was to ensure no secrets were held and no hierarchies emerged. In reality, it served to break members down emotionally before rebuilding them with support from others.[4] The Game is best viewed as a deliberate form of traumatic bonding in which cycles of abuse appear to strengthen relationships. Synanon also had a paramilitary group equipped with hundreds of guns and capable of attacking anyone who opposed Dederich or left. A lawyer who sued Synanon found a live rattlesnake in his mailbox, its rattle removed.

When Synanon came under legal scrutiny for operating without medical licensing, Dederich declared it was no longer an addiction treatment program and was now a religion. Once again this move allowed more control over members. A rehabilitation or personal development program has an end point. A religion does not. Dederich had a stronger justification for

5
Sreenivasan, ibid.

6
"Bourbaki, Nicolas," Complete
Dictionary of Scientific Biography,
accessed August 19, 2019,
https://www.encyclopedia.com/
people/science-and-technology/
mathematics-biographies/
nicolas-bourbaki.

preventing the churn of members.

Synanon met its end when the IRS revoked its tax-exempt status and ordered it to pay millions in back taxes.[5] Its story teaches us that churn is inevitable within any system and seeking to eliminate it perverts the goals of a system. Regardless of initial intentions, a group that tries to stop *anyone* from leaving can only end up violent and coercive. People being able to leave as they wish places checks on abuses of power. The same is true for countries or companies. People need the freedom to vote with their feet if things get too bad. In this sense, lack of churn can be a powerful indicator that something is not right.

Using churn to innovate

Churn, at the right level, is a healthy part of systems. Components need to change and be refreshed. In some cases, when churn isn't naturally high enough, it can be necessary to build it into a system as a deliberate process. People leaving a business can be good. New people bring in fresh ideas. And if you mandate a degree of churn, you can make it less likely that people stay for the wrong reasons or that you do harmful things to prevent them from leaving.

The value of churn varies with the kind of group you are trying to create, but for organizations wanting to invent and innovate, having a fixed tenure with no bonuses or promotions can keep the focus where it needs to be. This is what a group called Bourbaki did with its members: it ensured a regular turnover to allow for the flow of ideas and inspiration.

In 1935 a group of eminent young French mathematicians met in a Paris café.[6] Among them were André Weil (a foundational figure in number theory and algebraic geometry), Henri Cartan (a major advancer of the theory of analytic functions), Claude Chevalley (a significant figure in many mathematical theories), Charles Ehresmann (best known for the concept of the Ehresmann connection), and Szolem Mandelbrojt (who received recognition for his mathematical analysis work). As a collective, they had an ambitious goal—though it was a realistic one, considering their credentials. They wanted to compile all existing mathematical knowledge into a single overarching theory, then produce comprehensive textbooks covering it.[7]

They decided that everything they produced should be a group effort and not the work of any particular individual. How else could it be a unified theory reflecting the best of mathematical knowledge at the time and not the opinions of one person? So the mathematicians created a fictional persona to whom they attributed their work: Nicolas Bourbaki* of Poldevia. They took pains to make him seem like a real person.[8] Many of the students who used their textbook never had any idea that Bourbaki was a group.

Aside from a break during World War II, the members of Bourbaki met for a week two or three times each year to work on their textbook series. It was a truly collaborative effort. The mathematicians argued over and debated every single sentence until everyone was at least reasonably satisfied. Each textbook took years of criticism and rewriting to complete. To a casual observer, the approach looked chaotic. There was no discernible system to it. But it meant their work was rigorous. Sometimes, amid a heated disagreement, they would come up with a new way of doing things. The resulting textbooks did indeed have a significant impact on mathematics. By some accounts, the approach they took to conveying knowledge has become the standard.[9]

To understand why Bourbaki is relevant to the mental model of churn, we need to consider the context in which the group began. Unlike other countries, France did not exempt certain professions, including academics, from military service during World War I. This meant that distinguished mathematicians were as much at risk of dying on the front lines as anyone else.[10] Those who survived that war tended to have been over 45 years at the time—old enough to be excused

*
Nicolas Bourbaki - (b.1934). Little is known about the biography of the mysterious Nicolas Bourbaki of Poldevia, despite him being widely considered one of the most important mathematicians of the 20th century. Bourbaki's mastery of almost every area of the field makes his reputation as a genius well earned. In 1913, he was appointed as Privatdozent at the University of Dorpat. Bourbaki had a daughter, Betti, who married the famed lion hunter Hector Pétard in 1938. It's unlikely we'll ever see another mathematician as great as Bourbaki.

7
Marjorie Senechal, "The Continuing Silence of Bourbaki," *The Mathematical Intelligencer*, accessed August 19, 2019, http://ega-math.narod.ru/Bbaki/Cartier.htm.

8
Amir D. Aczel, *The Artist and the Mathematician: The Story of Nicolas Bourbaki, the Genius Mathematician Who Never Existed* (London: High Stakes Publishing, 2007).

9
Aczel, ibid.

10
Maurice Mashaal, *Bourbaki: A Secret Society of Mathematicians* (Providence: American Mathematical Society, 2006).

from service in the next world war. With the deaths of so many young mathematicians, many of those teaching and writing textbooks in 1935 tended to be reasonably elderly. Though experienced, they were not always entirely up to date with the latest research. The field missed out on the usual regular influx of new figures with new ideas. Having lost a generation of mathematicians, no doubt with many potential geniuses among them, the field stopped progressing at its usual speed in France.[11]

11
J. J. O'Connor and E. F. Robertson, "Bourbaki: The Pre-War Years," Bourbaki 1, accessed August 19, 2019, http://www-history.mcs.st-and.ac.uk/HistTopics/Bourbaki_1.html.

« [Our aim is] to define for twenty-five years the syllabus for the certificate in differential and integral calculus by writing, collectively, a treatise on analysis. Of course, this treatise will be as modern as possible. »

André Weil's original proposal

Part of what made Bourbaki such a revolutionary collective was its insistence that members churn at regular intervals. This ensured an inflow of new perspectives and knowledge. Bourbaki members were asked to retire at the age of 50 and invite new, younger mathematicians to join in their place. While we may decry this as ageist today, it was not a critique of their expertise. The intention was to keep bringing people who had studied the latest theories into the fold. Anyone who wanted to leave the group at any point for any reason could without impediment. If a mathematician lost interest, they didn't stay. Only those who wanted to remain part of Bourbaki stayed. Its membership was never static.

Bourbaki still exists in name and runs seminars, although the group no longer publishes anything. But this vibrant, ever-shifting group played an important role in mathematical history in the 20th century. There may be a time one day that calls for it to rise and once again revitalize the field.

Using the lens of churn on the story of Bourbaki demonstrates there can be value in constant change. Harnessed and directed appropriately, churn brings in new ideas and increases our adaptability. It's what allows for evolution by selecting for beneficial traits. Within Bourbaki, the churn of members selected for those people with up-to-date knowledge of mathematics and enthusiasm for the project. Within any system, parts need replacing from time to time in order to keep the whole functioning well and to remove anything that proves a hindrance. Churn helps systems improve over time, and it is both undesirable and unrealistic for all the parts to stay the same. However, no matter how often the parts are replaced, no system can function forever. Bourbaki no longer exists in its original form as a producer of textbooks. Its environment changed, and it ceased to be the thing best suited to that task. But while it pursued its original goal, churn helped Bourbaki stay relevant and useful.

Conclusion

Churn is not something to fear. Replacing components of a system is an inevitable part of keeping a system healthy. New parts can improve functionality. When we use this model as a lens, we see that new people bring new ideas, and counterintuitively, some turnover allows us to maintain stability. Replacing what is worn out also gives us a chance to upgrade and expand our capabilities, creating new opportunities.

Algorithms

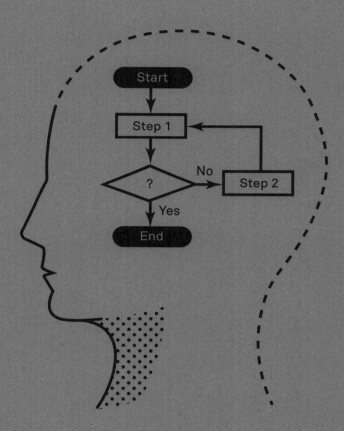

—
Recipes for success

Algorithms

Algorithms turn inputs into outputs. One reason they are worth understanding is because many systems adjust and respond based on the information provided by algorithms. Another reason is that they can help systems scale. Once you identify a set of steps that solve a particular problem, you don't need to start from scratch every time. An algorithm as a model does not need to be about turning your life into processes with end-to-end automation. In this chapter we will explore how algorithmic thinking can help you prevent problems and discover answers.

« "Algorithm" is arguably the single most important concept in our world. If we want to understand our life and our future, we should make every effort to understand what an algorithm is, and how algorithms are connected with emotions. An algorithm is a methodical set of steps that can be used to make calculations, resolve problems, and reach decisions. An algorithm isn't a particular calculation, but the method followed when making the calculation. »

Yuval Noah Harari[1]

*
Daniel Dennett - (b. 1942). Dennett is a philosopher and cognitive scientist, notable for his work on free will, consciousness, evolution, and atheism. He is currently a professor of philosophy and director of the Center for Cognitive Studies at Tufts University. Dennett has published over 400 journal articles on the mind, as well as a number of acclaimed books.

1
Yuval Noah Harari, *Homo Deus: A Brief History of Tomorrow* (New York: Harper Perennial, 2018).

2
Daniel Dennett, *Intuition Pumps and Other Tools for Thinking* (New York: W. W. Norton, 2013).

Algorithms are useful partly because of the inherent predictability of their process. That's why we like them. We can think of algorithms as a series of if–then statements that are completely unambiguous. In *Intuition Pumps and Other Tools for Thinking*, Daniel Dennett* defines an algorithm as "a certain sort of formal process that can be counted on—logically—to yield a certain sort of result whenever it is 'run' or instantiated."[2] The reliability of a well-designed algorithm in terms of producing consistently logical results is its most attractive feature. Mix flour, water, eggs, and other ingredients in a certain way, and voila! A scrumptious cake results.

Dennett includes the three defining characteristics of algorithms:

1. Substrate neutrality: "The power of the procedure is due to its logical structure, not the causal powers of the materials used in the instantiation."[3] It doesn't matter whether you read your recipe on a phone or a book; neither has impact on the logic of the algorithm.

2. Underlying mindlessness: "Each constituent step, and the transition between steps, is utterly simple."[4] For a recipe to be an algorithm, it must tell you the amounts of each ingredient you need as well as walk you through the process in steps so clear that there is no room for interpretation or misunderstanding.

3. Guaranteed results: "Whatever it is that an algorithm does, it always does it if it is executed without misstep. An algorithm is a foolproof recipe."[5] Using a good algorithm, the cake will look and taste the same every time.

Algorithms can be simple, like a recipe containing a clear set of instructions that do not vary over time. They can also be complicated, like computer algorithms that try to predict future locations of crime. Furthermore, if we extrapolate our ideas about algorithms beyond humans and our technology, it's possible to consider something like the execution of DNA code as an algorithm, or human learning as being the product of biological algorithms.

Some algorithms can evolve and learn over time. Others stay static. Depending on the requirements of a system, different types of algorithms are more useful for obtaining the information necessary to maintain resiliency and proper functioning.

3
Dennett, ibid.

4
Dennett, ibid.

5
Dennett, ibid.

6
"What Is a Constitution?,"
Constitution Unit, University
College London, June 7,
2019, https://www.ucl.
ac.uk/constitution-unit/
what-uk-constitution/
what-constitution.

Moving beyond computers, all systems need algorithms to function: sets of instructions for adapting to and solving problems. Increasingly, algorithms are designed to be directionally correct over perfect. They often evolve—or are designed—to get useful and relevant enough outputs to keep the system functioning properly. Neither nature nor humans worry about producing algorithms that produce the most optimal outputs 100% of the time. When we look at a system, it's useful to consider the underlying instructions dictating its behavior in order to determine how to intervene to improve it.

Pirate constitutions

When groups of people work together with a shared goal, they need coherent algorithms for turning their inputs into their desired outputs in a repeatable fashion. For many people to move toward the same aim, they must know how to act, how to resolve problems, and how to make decisions in a consistent and reliable manner.

For people to follow systems of rules, the right incentives need to be in place. Often the threat of force is relied upon for compliance, especially when people have not chosen to be part of a system or cannot leave it. But when people choose to work together, it's possible for them to evolve systems of rules that benefit them and that avoid pitfalls such as unjust leadership.

A constitution is one means of making that happen. It can be thought of as a high-level algorithm to limit the power and define the responsibilities of those charged with governance.[6] It is a means of increasing the chance that leaders work for the benefit of the people, not for their own enrichment. It exists on a level higher than law; it determines how the law itself works. Welding politics, literature, and law, a constitution is something to turn to for guidance when leaders face problems, as well as a source of reassurance for the people. For countries, designing a constitution tends to be a meticulous process that takes into account political ideals. However,

Many pirates had articles that were surprisingly egalitarian. As recorded by Captain Charles Johnson, the first article of the 11 issued by the infamous Welsh pirate Black Bart, born John Roberts, to his crew stated: "Every Man has a Vote in Affairs of Moment; has equal Title to the fresh Provisions, or strong Liquors, at any Time seized, and may use them at Pleasure, unless a Scarcity make it necessary, for the Good of all, to vote a Retrenchment." Johnson's identity is unknown, with some scholars believing he was actually *Robinson Crusoe* author Daniel Defoe.

7
Peter T. Leeson, *The Invisible Hook:
The Hidden Economics of Pirates*
(Princeton: Princeton University
Press, 2011).

it's not just countries that have constitutions. The concept can make sense for any group of people with rules to follow and leaders to keep in check. Nor does a constitution need to be about lofty ideals; it can evolve without planning to achieve quite different aims. All it takes is for a group of people to aim for the same outcome and look for the best, most consistent way of achieving it. A constitution will never be perfect, but clear goals and consistent application with the ability to make amendments can increase the chance it achieves its intendend outcomes.

In popular culture, pirates of the past are often portrayed as lawless, wild rebels. They roamed the high seas, answering to no one and plundering treasure from whatever hapless ships happened to sail into their paths. In reality, this wasn't the case. To be a successful pirate, it has always been necessary to operate like a controlled business. The pirates who survived the longest and became the richest during the heyday of piracy did so by following rigid rules underscored in many cases by something a lot like a constitution, known as articles, as Peter T. Leeson explains in *The Invisible Hook*.[7]

We can think of pirate articles as an algorithm that helped turn physical labor and resources, such as gunpowder, into valuable plundered goods and money. Every detail that went into a ship's articles needed to have a positive contribution to its profits. Pirates opted for whatever rules helped their bottom line without considering factors that were relevant for landed people.

Looking at the way they formed their articles during the golden age of piracy in the early 18th century can teach us a great deal about how groups of people use algorithms to ensure collaboration toward shared goals. They also show us that algorithms need room for adaptation and change if they cease to work for the people involved as well as mechanisms for modification if something breaks. By seeking profit above all else, pirates ended up designing a legal system that was far ahead of its time and arguably fairer than that of mainstream society in that era.[8]

When a person joined a pirate fleet, they renounced their connection to mainstream society and became part of a floating society. That meant they could no longer rely on mainstream law to protect and govern them. As Leeson writes, "Pirates had no government....Pirates had no prisons, no police, and no parliament. They had no barristers, no bailiffs, and no royal bench." With an average crew comprising 80 members,[9] usually from different countries, they couldn't rely on standard social bonds.[10] At the same time, pirates needed to be able to cooperate seamlessly, to ensure everyone put in their full effort, and to ensure adequate leadership without abuse of power. If they could overcome all of these hurdles, the rewards could be enormous. A pirate could earn a hundred or even a thousand times as much per year as a merchant seaman.[11] As a result they had a strong incentive to come up with articles that helped them attain the level of organization needed for dangerous attacks.[12] Articles were designed to pro-duce a set of repeatable behaviors in the pirates who followed them and thereby tame uncertainty in the high-stakes situa-tion of raiding another ship. They couldn't control external fac-tors, like the weather or the behavior of the crew of a captured ship, but they could ensure their fellow crew members behaved in predictable ways best suited to profiting.

A typical set of articles required a crew to keep their weapons in good shape, not gamble with each other aboard the ship, not drink below deck after eight p.m., and resolve any dis-agreements on the shore.[13] All had obvious benefits. A pirate with poorly maintained weapons would not be able to fight as well when taking control of another ship. Gambling could lead to conflict and reduce cooperation. Drinking below deck would disrupt the sleep of other pirates. Resolving disagreements on the shore meant that fights couldn't injure bystanders or harm the ship. Articles covered the allocation of plunder (which

8
Leeson, ibid.

9
Leeson, ibid.

10
James Surowiecki, "The Pirates' Code," *New Yorker*, July 2, 2007, https://www.newyorker.com/magazine/2007/07/09/the-pirates-code.

11
Leeson, ibid.

12
David D. Friedman, Peter T. Leeson, and David Skarbek, *Legal Systems Very Different from Ours* (independently published, 2019).

13
Friedman, Leeson, and Skarbeck, ibid.

Ching Shih - (1775-1844). One of
the most successful pirates in
history, Shih was also one of the
only female ones. She initially ran
her fleet with her husband Zheng
Yi, before taking control after his
death. Shih is notable for three
reasons: the enormous size of her
fleet, the system of governance
she enforced, and the fact that
she ultimately negotiated a peace
agreement with the Chinese
government that allowed her a
peaceful retirement.

14

"Pirate Code of Conduct and Pirate
Rules," The Way of the Pirates,
accessed February 17, 2020, http://
www.thewayofthepirates.com/
pirate-life/pirate-code/.

15

Peter T. Leeson, "An-Arrgh-Chy:
The Law and Economics of Pirate
Organization," Journal of Political
Economy 115, no. 6 (2007):
1049–94.

16

Leeson, ibid.

17

Leeson, ibid.

18

Surowiecki, ibid.

19

Anita Sarkeesian and Ebony
Adams, History vs. Women: The
Defiant Lives That They Don't Want
You to Know (London: Faber and
Faber, 2020).

20

This is based on the estimates of
Richard Glasspoole, a hostage on
one of her ships for two months.

21

"Queen Anne's Revenge
Conservation Lab," QAR Project,
accessed January 13, 2020,
https://www.qaronline.org/
history/blackbeard-facts.

was equal, aside from leaders receiving a bit more), bonuses for anyone who showed unusual bravery (to compensate the added risk involved), and what we could consider a prototype of disability benefits for anyone injured in battles.[14] Plus they stipulated punishments for wrongdoing, what leaders could and couldn't do, and requirements for any new rules.[15]

All very impressive, but why would a bunch of violent criminals want to follow a set of rules imposed upon them? Because pirate society was democratic at a time when mainstream society was not.[16] Implementing a set of articles required unanimous agreement from everyone on board. This ensured pirates only joined a ship if they were willing to follow its rules.

What if a tyrannical captain decided to abuse his power? Pirates had a solution for that too. They voted their captains and quartermasters into power by majority and could remove them from office at any time, for any reason.[17] Everyone had weapons, and if a captain didn't want to respect the results of a vote, they didn't have much choice once the crew turned on them. Dividing leadership between two people provided an additional check. Captains led during battles, and quartermasters handled the day-to-day matters.[18]

Ching Shih* is a pertinent example of how tight systems of rules helped pirates succeed. Born in China in 1775, Ching Shih may have been the most successful pirate to ever live. She began her career as a sex worker in Canton, where she met the pirate Zheng Yi. He proposed to her, and she agreed— provided she had an equal share of his wealth and power aboard his Red Flag fleet. When her husband died, she took full control, becoming one of few female pirates.[19] At one point, she oversaw 70,000 to 80,000 pirates and up to 2,000 ships, a fleet of unusual size.[20] To give context, the most famous pirate of all, Blackbeard, probably never led more than 700 individuals, with his crew typically numbering a few hundred.[21] Ching Shih was essentially leading a floating city that needed to be able

A classic Chinese junk boat. Junks fitted with weapons were often used by Chinese pirates.

22
Urvija Banerji, "The Chinese
Female Pirate Who Commanded
80,000 Outlaws," Atlas Obscura,
April 6, 2016, https://www.
atlasobscura.com/articles/
the-chinese-female-pirate-who-
commanded-80000-outlaws.

to control itself without the help of the standard legal system. After all, a pirate who discovered that a crewmate had stolen his already-stolen plunder couldn't report them to the police.

Ching Shih laid out a strict set of rules for all of her pirates that was designed to ensure both her power and their success. When they attacked other ships, she ordered her crew only to harm anyone if they failed to surrender. They could not step onto land without permission—the penalty for doing so twice was death. After the looting of a ship, they had to report all goods and not keep more than a fifth. Deserters were mutilated. It was the death penalty for anyone who gave unsanctioned orders, harmed land people without provocation, or raped a female captive.

Ching Shih's might was so great that, unlike most pirates, she was able to peacefully retire in great wealth, having negotiated terms with the Chinese government.[22]

The existence of pirate laws might be surprising at first glance, but when we consider the context in which pirates worked, they were necessary for success and survival. Looking at how pirate leaders like Ching Shih managed to lead large numbers of pirates in high-stakes situations teaches us how algorithms can ensure cohesion within systems. For a system to produce its intended output, the goals of its parts need to be aligned in the same direction. This increases the chances of consistently achieving a predictable outcome.

Controlling so many pirates was a major challenge, but Ching Shih managed it by enforcing a strict system of rules. Her enforcement is the critical component for understanding her actions through the lens of algorithms. Part of the definition of an algorithm is that it uses the same input every time and produces the same output every time. By all accounts, Ching Shih was invariant in her application of the rules. There were no exceptions. Of course, pirates operated in a complex world where conditions were always changing, and even the tightest system of rules couldn't ensure the same outcomes each time they raided a ship. But her strict enforcement gave Ching Shih the best opportunity to produce consistent and reliable outputs.

— Sidebar: New Numbers

Finding quality inputs

Algorithms are developed to get a certain output. As we've discussed, you start with inputs, you follow a process, and you end up with expected outputs. However, sometimes it's not obvious which inputs will result in the desired outputs. So one way to use this model is to help you determine and refine what kind of inputs to feed into it in the first place. You can consider it "algorithmic thinking." You may not have the luxury of a completely closed system where you can implement complete end-to-end automation, but the lens of algorithms can show you how to organize your system to leave as little to chance as possible.

In the late 1920s, one company developed a repeatable process to try to create the world's first broad-spectrum antibiotic. After World War I, scientists had a good understanding of bacterial infection. They were able to identify some of the primary bacteria, such as *Streptococcus*, that caused incurable infections. They also understood how and why bacterial infection often occurred, such as from exposure to contaminated tools and instruments. But once infection took hold in the body, there was no way to stop it. What was missing was an understanding of bacteria—how it worked and where it was vulnerable.

Bayer, a giant German pharmaceutical company whose origins lie in dye-making, decided there was money to be made if they could find a cure for bacterial infections inside the body. There was some indication that a substance with bacteria-fighting properties could be created; earlier research had produced a treatment for syphilis called Salvarsan, but nothing else had been found in the subsequent 15 years.[23]

23
Thomas Hager, *The Demon Under the Microscope* (New York: Harmony Books, 2006).

New Numbers

Where algorithms can become really interesting is when seemingly innocuous, standard inputs create entirely brand-new outputs.

Algorithms seem to be a natural consequence of repetitive actions. For most humans, doing the same thing in the same way over and over gets boring. We thus wonder if there is a way to codify those repetitive actions to streamline the process. A lot of modern math seems to be a result of the codification of the processes used to manipulate numbers. When you multiply 157×2,693, you probably don't count the individual units in each group in sequence. You likely use a calculator (programmed with algorithms) or a pencil-and-paper method that has you starting with 7×3.

One way to interpret the history of numbers is that certain numbers didn't exist until they were produced by an algorithm. Think of negative numbers. They are common enough now, especially for those of us who live in cold climates, but if you think about it, they aren't intuitive. It's hard to imagine ancient humans looking at a bunch of mammoths and thinking there might one day be a negative amount of them. There could be ten mammoths on the plain, two mammoths, or no mammoths, but negative five mammoths? Not likely.

In the book *Arithmetic*, Paul Lockhart suggests that negative numbers are the result of subtraction. Imagine you are in agriculture 3,000 years ago. The addition algorithm says that when you have three bags of grain, and you trade for two more, you will have five bags of grain. But then you decide to give one to your poor cousin. Now you have to "un-add," or subtract. The act of subtracting is really the acknowledgment of the negative. You have five bags of grain and negative one bag of grain. And if you are interested in the processes you've just exposed your numbers to, you've got an interesting problem.

Lockhart says, "The issue here is symmetry—or rather, the lack thereof. With addition, no matter what number I have and no matter what number I add to it, their sum is a perfectly valid entity, already extant in the realm of numbers. With the subtraction operation, however, we have an unpleasant restriction: the number we are taking away cannot exceed the number we have. There definitely already is a number that when added to three makes five, but (at the moment) none of our numbers play the role of 'the thing that when added to five makes three.'"[1] Use of subtraction quite likely prompted the idea of negative numbers, which aren't obvious in the physical representations of amounts we would have encountered in everyday life.

Essentially our process might have gone something like this: Let's say our ancient subtraction algorithm for two values is something along the lines of *input two distinct, countable whole quantities. Remove the quantity of the second value from the quantity of the first value.* So five bags of grain minus one bag of grain becomes four bags of grain. But because our algorithm didn't say anything about the minimum value of the quantities, we could easily input six and then nine. Which leaves us with what? The non-intuitive concept of a number representing negative three.

The same thinking gives us an understanding of how we got irrational numbers. After some playing around with numbers and their properties, a process was invented called "square root." The square root of a number is another number that, when multiplied by itself, gives you the original number. So the square root of 9 is 3, and the square root of 64 is 8. We can have a lot of fun plugging various number inputs into the algorithm that calculates a square root. Some numbers don't get such pretty results, and their square root is a fraction. But they are still rational numbers. However, plug 2 into the algorithm for calculating square root (and why wouldn't you? It's such an accessible little number) and you get something entirely different. The world's first irrational number.

1

Paul Lockhart, *Arithmetic* (Cambridge: Belknap Press, 2017).

Streptococcus pyogenes is a type of bacteria that can cause multiple ailments in humans ranging from skin infections to scarlet fever and streptococcal toxic shock syndrome.

Heinrich Hörlein - (1882-1954).
German scientist Hörlein became
head of pharmaceutical research
at IG Farben, a conglomerate of
chemical companies including
Bayer, in 1926. Hörlein collaborated
with the Nazi party during World
War II, aiding in the development
and dissemination of toxic nerve
gases used to murder millions of
people in death camps. Although
he was eventually acquitted of war
crimes in one of the Nuremberg
trials, the sheer scale of IG
Farben's contribution to genocide
makes it dubious that he was
entirely oblivious.

*

Gerhard Domagk - (1895-1964).
A pathologist and bacteriologist,
Domagk received the Nobel Prize
for Physiology and Medicine for
discovering the antibiotic Prontosil,
one of the first antimicrobial
drugs ever. It proved revolutionary
for treating conditions such
as meningitis and pneumonia.
Domagk also helped develop the
skin disinfectant Zephiran, still in
widespread use today.

24
Hager, ibid.

25
Hager, ibid.

26
Hager, ibid.

In charge of pharmaceutical research for Bayer was Heinrich Hörlein[*]. He thought the research to find bacteria-killing drugs was lacking scale and therefore too much was dependent on individual scientists. So at Bayer, he created an industrial system to identify possible antibacterial compounds and hired dozens of people to put each antibiotic candidate through the same algorithmic-like process.

In *The Demon Under the Microscope*, Thomas Hager explains Hörlein knew the search would take years but also knew that success would result in enormous profits. Thus he aimed "to expand drug research from the lab of a single scientist to an efficiently organized industrial process with carefully chosen specialists guided by a coordinated strategy." Hörlein hired Gerhard Domagk[*] to run the "recipe," putting each compound created by the chemists through an identical testing and evaluation process to see if the result would be an antibiotic that was safe for humans.[24]

Domagk and his team tested the chemicals given to them by Bayer's chemists. One of the most prolific chemists was Josef Klarer. He produced hundreds of new chemicals that were systematically tested by Domagk and his assistants. Each chemical compound was tested against a panel of "the most common and deadly bacteria: tuberculosis, pneumonia, *Staphylococcus*, *E. coli*, and *Streptococcus pyogenes*." After a bit of initial refining, Hörlein and Domagk created "a smooth-functioning, reliable machine for discovery." The chemicals were tested both in test tubes and in living animals. In the animals, each chemical was "delivered three different ways (intravenously, subcutaneously, and by mouth)." Every chemical was tested the same way in mice, and meticulous records were kept of each test.[25]

Time went by. Thousands of mice died. But they did not give up on their process. As the years went on, "despite the repeated negative results, Domagk changed neither his methods nor his approach."[26] The team knew their recipe for testing was correct, and one day it would produce a result that would allow them to refine their inputs.

In the fall of 1932, the methodology and patience paid off. Klarer decided to attach sulfur to an azo compound. Chemical Kl-695 was put through the testing process that thousands of other chemicals had been put through in the previous years. For the first time, the process produced the desired result: mice that recovered from bacterial infection with no apparent toxicity. Domagk didn't yet know how it worked, only that it did. "Strangely, it did not kill strep in a test tube, only in living animals. And it worked only on strep, none of the other disease-causing bacteria. But given the number and deadliness of strep diseases, it worked where it counted." Funny enough, Domagk was on vacation during the first round of testing of Kl-695 and so missed witnessing the initial breakthrough.[27] But the process by then was so entrenched, any one of the dozens of people on the team could run it.

The discovery of chemical Kl-695 allowed the team at Bayer to refine the inputs they put into their testing algorithm. "Klarer now made variations on Kl-695, finding that as long as sulfa was attached to the azo-dye frame in the correct position, the drug worked against strep. Attaching sulfa to an azo dye—any azo dye—somehow transformed it from an erratic, ineffective chemical into an efficient anti-strep medication."[28] They kept refining their inputs so that more effective azo-sulfa compounds were discovered, including Kl-730.

What the Bayer scientists didn't realize was that it wasn't the azo-sulfa combination that was the key, but rather the sulfa itself. Later research demonstrated the efficacy of the sulfa in treating strep infections. Structurally sulfa looks a lot like PABA, a key nutrient for some disease-causing bacteria like strep. The bacteria bind to sulfa, mistaking it for PABA, but cannot metabolize it, effectively killing them. Sulfa is cheap and widely available, so once Bayer's sulfa antibiotic was on the market, many companies began to make their own.[29]

27
Hager, ibid.

28
Hager, ibid.

29
Hager, ibid.

30
Hager, ibid.

Bayer's algorithmic-like approach that led to the discovery of the antibiotic properties of sulfa had wide-reaching effects. "Sulfa also changed the way drug research was done. Before sulfa, small laboratories followed investigators' hunches, and patent-medicine makers cobbled together remedies without testing the results. After sulfa, industrial-scale chemical investigation guided by specific therapeutic goals—the system for finding new medicines pioneered by Hörlein and his Bayer team—became the standard. Successful drugmakers were those who followed the Bayer model."[30] Bayer continued to discover many useful antibiotics using a system that codified the process as much as possible.

Having the correct algorithm can help you even if you aren't sure about the best inputs to get you the results you want. By testing various inputs in a repeatable process, you can use the results to refine what you feed into the algorithm. You don't always need to be good at knowing the answers, you just need to have a good algorithm for finding them.

Conclusion

At their core, algorithms are a clear set of rules that provide instruction on what to do. We can also conceptualize them as if–then processes that are useful because they can help us ignore variables that don't matter and focus on requirements. Algorithms as a model suggest a way of thinking that explores what processes can be put in place to get us the results we want.

Complex Adaptive Systems

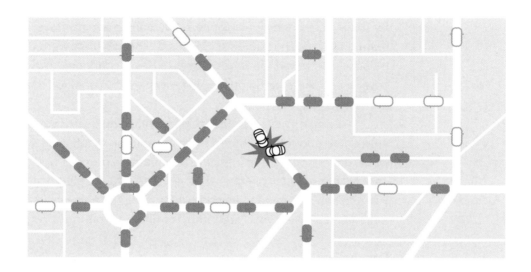

« Often, scholars distinguish between complex systems—systems in which the entities follow fixed rules—and complex adaptive systems—systems in which the entities adapt. If the entities adapt, then the system has a greater capacity to respond to changes in the environment. »

Scott E. Page[1]

Some systems are simple and nonadaptive. You can learn how they work by learning about their parts. They don't change based on their environments. For instance, imagine a basic pocket watch. You can take it apart to figure out how it works, and it keeps working the same regardless of what goes on around it—within limits.

Complex adaptive systems have properties that are greater than the sum of their parts. You cannot understand them from studying their individual components, which may be simple but which interact in unpredictable, nonlinear ways. A few, often basic rules enable the parts to self-organize without centralized control. The way the various components interact and pass information between themselves creates complexity. A system's ability to change in response to its environment and in pursuit of a goal makes it adaptive.[2] Complex adaptive systems have "memories"—they are impacted by what has happened to them before.

One example of a complex adaptive system is the traffic within a city. While cars are simple systems in the sense that the way they work is a logical outcome of all of their parts working together, when we look at the combined interactions of cars, we see remarkable self-organization. Traffic changes its behavior based on information from its environment. Focusing on one car won't teach you about the entire system because what matters is the interactions between them.

In *Complexity: A Guided Tour*, Melanie Mitchell defines a complex system as one "in which large networks of components with no central control and simple rules of operation give rise to complex collective behavior, sophisticated information processing, and adaptation via learning or evolution."[3]

Within complex adaptive systems, components are all interdependent. They can directly or indirectly influence the behavior of the entire system. If one car breaks down on a main street, it can have knock-on effects for the traffic in the rest of the city. Interactions between parts amplify the impact of tiny changes.

In a complex adaptive system, we can never do just one thing.[4] Any time we intervene, unintended consequences are almost inevitable. Often when we try to improve a complex adaptive system, we end up making things worse because we overestimate our degree of control.

To work with complex adaptive systems, we cannot expect them to be governed by predictable rules. Nor can we expect to understand the macro by examining the micro. To handle complex adaptive systems, we need to be comfortable with the nonlinear and the unexpected.

Another aspect of complex adaptive systems that can derail us is their ability to learn and change in response to new information. Consider a model that predicts the spread of the flu among a population. It will need to anticipate that people can change their behavior. If people hear warnings of an epidemic or see others getting sick, they may be much more likely to get vaccinated.[5]

We can still learn from complex systems; we just need to be humble and use the scientific method. We must not mistake correlation for causation, and we should always be open to learning more about the system and accepting that it will change. What we learned

yesterday may guide us, but it can change tomorrow. We shouldn't give up just because a system is complex.

From the outside, complex adaptive systems can look chaotic, but they tend to work best when slightly disorganized, as this allows for mutations and experimentation. In the long run, deviations tend to cancel out into more coherent patterns of functioning.

« No gluing together of partial studies of a complex nonlinear system can give a good idea of the behavior of the whole. »
Murray Gell-Mann[6]

1
Scott E. Page, *Diversity and Complexity* (Princeton: Princeton University Press, 2011).
2
Serena Chan, "Complex Adaptive Systems," MIT, November 6, 2001, http://web.mit.edu/esd.83/www/notebook/Complex%20Adaptive%20Systems.pdf.
3
Melanie Mitchell, *Complexity: A Guided Tour* (New York: Oxford University Press, 2011).
4
Garrett Hardin attribution from *Living Within Limits*.
5
Nate Silver, *The Signal and the Noise: The Art and Science of Prediction* (London: Penguin, 2013).
6
Joachim P. Sturmberg and Carmel M. Martin, *Handbook of Systems and Complexity in Health* (New York: Springer, 2013).

Critical Mass

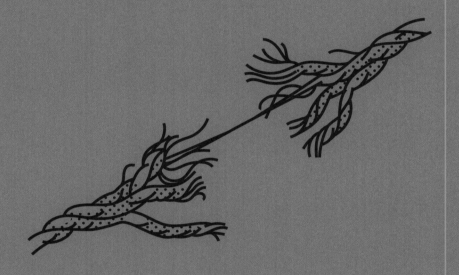

Critical Mass

A system becomes "critical" when it is on the verge of changing from one state to another. The final unit of input before the change has a disproportionate impact. It is the proverbial straw to break the camel's back. Before a critical mass is reached, the camel can support the amount of weight it's required to carry. Then the weight passes a threshold where any additional amount is disastrous, and the final straw tips the camel into another state. Once a system passes a certain threshold and enters a critical state, it only takes a tiny nudge to change it.

When a system changes from one state to another, we say it has achieved critical mass, also known as reaching the tipping point. In social systems, critical mass tends to mean when enough people have adopted something, such as a belief or product, that its growth can sustain itself. In his 1978 book *Micromotives and Macrobehavior*, game theorist Thomas Schelling* wrote, "The generic name for behaviors of this sort is critical mass. Social scientists have adopted the term from nuclear engineering, where it is common currency in connection with atomic bombs."[1]

The amount of energy required for a system to achieve critical mass is variable. Different systems have different properties and thus require varying amounts of inputs to tip from one state to another.

Heated water is at critical mass when it is hot enough to change from liquid to gas. There is a massive difference between 211 and 212 degrees Fahrenheit. One is the boiling point; the other is not. In business, critical mass is the point where a business makes enough money to no longer need outside investment or the point where the financial growth of a company becomes self-perpetuating. In epidemiology, critical mass can refer to the point where enough people are vaccinated in a population to prevent an infectious disease from

*
Thomas Schelling - (1921-2016).
Economist Schelling co-won the
2005 Nobel Prize in Economic
Sciences along with Robert J.
Aumann for research applying
game theory to social, political, and
economic problems. Their insights
into conflict and cooperation have
proved relevant for international
peacekeeping efforts.

1
Morton Grodzins, "50 Years Ago in
Scientific American: 'Metropolitan
Segregation,'" *Scientific American*,
September 18, 2007, https://
www.scientificamerican.com/
article/50-years-ago-in-scientific-
american-white-flight-1/.

spreading to vulnerable people who cannot be immunized.

Using critical mass as a model helps us understand the effort required to achieve sustained change. Systems have certain inflection points where they change from one state to another. It doesn't help us to focus solely on the tipping point and ignore the work required to bring a system there. Because the inputs that tip a system into a new state tend not to have a linear effect—the final unit of input that leads to the change in state has an outsized marginal impact—we are disproportionately impressed by them. We are also disproportionately affected by them. But the straw only breaks the camel's back when there is already a lot of weight on it. Putting one piece of straw on a camel isn't always going to have the same effect.

The critical mass lens also helps us identify the parts of a system we can target to advance change. In social systems, for example, we don't need to spend equal effort changing everyone's mind. We can instead focus our efforts on changing the minds of opinion leaders to more quickly progress change.

Systems in a critical state tend to be precarious, but they don't stay that way for long because they're so easily tipped.[2] Getting insight into what could be the straw is valuable, as is recognizing when a system is poised on the edge of instability. A pencil balanced on its end may appear at equilibrium as it remains upright. But it could topple at the slightest disruption, so it is not stable.[3]

— Sidebar: The Overton Window

The work required for change

We like to tell stories about the tipping points. We look at the landmark cases or individual actions that sparked a cascade of change in the past and wonder how we can re-create them to push our current system into a new state. Using the mental model of critical mass, however, reminds us that it is equally important to pay attention to the effort involved in the buildup.

In September 1893, New Zealand became the first

2
Allen Downey, "Self-Organized Criticality and Holistic Models," February 24, 2012, http://allendowney.blogspot.com/2012/02/self-organized-criticality-and-holistic.html.

3
Steven H. Strogatz, *Sync: How Order Emerges from the Chaos in the Universe, Nature, and Daily Life* (New York: Hyperion, 2003).

The Overton Window

Day by day, people's minds don't change that much. It's unusual for someone to wake up one day and decide to completely change their tack on a pertinent issue. But in the long run, over decades, the ideas in the mainstream alter drastically. Fringe ideas become mainstream, and mainstream ideas become fringe. One way to understand this phenomenon is by considering the Overton Window, a concept developed by Joseph P. Overton in the 1990s as part of his work for the Mackinac Center for Public Policy.

The Overton Window refers to the range of ideas considered acceptable for politicians to propose as policy. Ideas outside of that, no matter how good, cannot gain widespread support. They're too extreme for the current climate and are best avoided lest they harm one's chances of re-election. Over time, the Overton Window shifts. Some politicians may advance far-out ideas in a deliberate attempt to move the Window further from the norm and make more moderate ideas more palatable.

Ideas move in a progression: unthinkable → radical → acceptable → sensible → popular → policy.[1] For instance, the suffrage movement shifted the Overton Window to make the idea of women being able to vote move from unthinkable to policy. Now to suggest otherwise would be unthinkable.

Politicians must prioritize the Overton Window over their personal beliefs.[2] It's important to recognize that the Overton Window isn't universal. The conservative political positions of one country may be considered liberal in another.

The value of the Overton Window as a concept is that it encourages us to recognize that attitudes and opinions are not static. What we consider acceptable today may one day be unacceptable. Ideas that are fringe and wacky now may one day be mainstream.

1
Rutger Bregman and Elizabeth Manton, *Utopia for Realists and How We Can Get There* (London: Bloomsbury, 2018).
2
Nathan J. Russell, "An Introduction to the Overton Window of Political Possibilities," Mackinac Center for Public Policy, January 4, 2006, https://www.mackinac.org/7504.

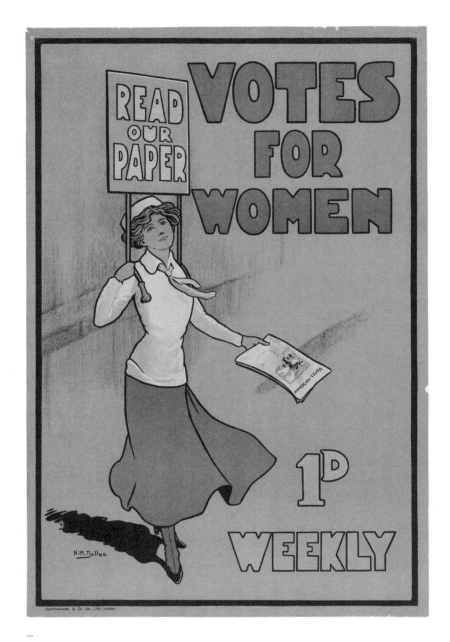

Of the 198 countries and territories that hold national elections, none actively ban women from voting, although complex barriers remain in some. In many countries, women turn out to vote at higher rates than men, though they remain underrepresented in positions of political power.

Learmonth Dalrymple - (1827-1906). Dalrymple campaigned extensively for better educational opportunities for women in New Zealand. Her work led to the opening of Otago Girls' High School and the admission of women to the University of New Zealand. Dalrymple was also an active suffragette and temperance campaigner.

4

"Women and the Vote," NZ History, Ministry for Culture and Heritage, December 20, 2018, https://nzhistory.govt.nz/politics/womens-suffrage.

5

Katie Pickles, "Why New Zealand Was the First Country Where Women Won the Right to Vote," *The Conversation,* The Conversation Trust UK, September 19, 2018, https://theconversation.com/why-new-zealand-was-the-first-country-where-women-won-the-right-to-vote-103219.

6

"NZ in the 19th Century," New Zealand History, New Zealand Government, December 11, 2019, https://nzhistory.govt.nz/classroom/ncea3/19th-century-history-1870-1900.

7

"Dalrymple, Learmonth White," Te Ara—The Encyclopedia of New Zealand, Ministry for Culture and Heritage Te Manatu Taonga, accessed May 26, 2020, https://teara.govt.nz/en/biographies/1d2/dalrymple-learmonth-white.

8

Patricia Grimshaw, *Women's Suffrage in New Zealand* (Auckland: Auckland University Press, 2013).

9

Grimshaw, ibid.

10

Grimshaw, ibid.

self-governing country to give most adult women the right to vote in parliamentary elections. American women would not earn this right for another 27 years and British women for 25. An important thing to understand about women's suffrage in New Zealand is that it was far from a sudden change, even if it may have appeared as such from afar. Through the efforts of many people over many years, there was a slow shifting of the Overton Window to the point where women being able to vote became reasonable in the minds of enough people to shift the voting system into a new state.

Certain unusual aspects of New Zealand's society and events in its history helped lay the groundwork for changes in the voting system even before the official suffrage movement began.[4] Many of the people living in New Zealand had settled there in recent decades and desired to create a fairer society than the European one they had left behind.[5] Seeing as the population was small (under 750,000 in 1893, including 40,000 Maori),[6] fewer minds needed changing to create a critical mass. The movement received support from prominent male politicians early on, which aided in getting a foothold in Parliament.

Women receiving equal access to education in New Zealand was another key factor in the buildup of opinion change to critical mass. Due to the campaigning of educationalist Learmonth Dalrymple[*], girls received the same secondary education as boys, with the first school for girls opening in 1871.[7] Dalrymple also successfully ensured women were able to attend university, where they made up half the student body by 1893.[8] Greater education led to improved employment prospects outside of the home, beyond the customary option of domestic labor. More and more women entered the workforce once they had better education, gaining social influence in areas such as teaching, journalism, medicine, and the arts.[9] When they faced worse working conditions than men, New Zealander women began to unionize.[10]

In many ways, the New Zealand suffrage movement was entwined with the temperance movement, which sought to restrict or prohibit the consumption of alcohol. Throughout the 19th century, alcohol became a growing problem in many countries, leading to poverty, violence, crime, and harm to family life. For New Zealanders, it was particularly harmful among men working in the agricultural, maritime, and industrial industries.[11] As in many other countries, it was reported that many men drank away their wages before even making it home on the weekend, leaving their wives and children bereft. Seeing as women tended to suffer the most as a result of widespread heavy drinking, they were influential in the movement.

Although the temperance movement never achieved the aim of total prohibition in New Zealand, it constructed a framework for women to politically organize. Alongside unionization, it gave women the confidence that they could have influence if they worked together in sufficient numbers with clear goals and a sense of focus. As Patricia Grimshaw writes in *Women's Suffrage in New Zealand*, "Women, on the practical side, learned the arts of organization, administration, and leadership which could be turned to use in later years in their own cause. Women, on the ideological side, entered a sphere in which a new outlook on their basic rights developed rapidly, spurring them to aim at the realization of their full rights as women."[12]

All of this work culminated in the suffrage movement, led by Kate Sheppard*, which built upon the social change that had been growing since the country's founding. In the early 1890s, Sheppard organized several petitions in favor of women being able to vote, which she presented to Parliament. Despite initial failures, the movement kept trying, gaining more and more support each year. By 1893, her petition amassed 32,000 signatures, a number all the more impressive considering the tiny population of the country at the time. After numerous attempts, the bill passed by a whisker. The changes in opinion had reached critical mass.

* Kate Sheppard - (1848-1934). A leader of the New Zealand women's suffrage movement and lifelong activist who believed no area of society should be off-limits to women. Sheppard went on to aid in suffrage movements elsewhere in the world. To honor her legacy, her image has appeared on the New Zealand $10 bill since 1993.

11 "Temperance Movement," NZ History, Ministry for Culture and Heritage, March 13, 2018, https://nzhistory.govt.nz/politics/temperance-movement/beginnings.

12 Grimshaw, ibid.

13
Grimshaw, ibid.

In turn, women earning the right to vote in New Zealand helped motivate and inspire similar movements elsewhere because it showed wider suffrage was possible. After World War II, women's political emancipation spread around the globe, a visible symbol of wider improvements.[13] Once you pass a tipping point, the whole nature of a system changes. It develops new properties, and new things are possible. New Zealand was that tipping point for women's suffrage in many other countries.

When we look back at significant social changes, it's important to recognize the work involved in building a critical mass. Women getting the vote in New Zealand was the result of years of effort on many different fronts to build the capabilities needed to change opinions. As social norms regarding women voting started to change, the movement gained the critical mass necessary for petitions in Parliament to be the final straw that resulted in a new state.

We can learn from the mental model of critical mass that changing a system doesn't require changing everything about it. Changing a small percentage of its parts can shift the whole thing into a new state. Getting people to alter their beliefs doesn't mean convincing everyone; once you pass a threshold, the change perpetuates itself.

— Sidebar: Minority Opinions

— Sidebar: Madeline Pollard

Organic cities

In nuclear physics, critical mass refers to the minimum amount of fissile material needed to start a self-sustaining reaction. You can pile up the uranium, and nothing will happen until a high enough density is reached. To focus on what prompted the change from inert to active in a nuclear reaction isn't all that interesting. It's just one more bit of uranium. The more interesting question is, how much is needed to kickstart the reaction to continue without further inputs? The lens of critical

Minority Opinions

Sometimes, people change their minds a lot in a short time. Although it can seem as though this shift occurs overnight, what really happens is that things change slowly until a critical mass of people hold a viewpoint. Interestingly, a majority is not required for things to tip and result in almost everyone changing their minds. Once opinion leaders hold a viewpoint, it spreads easier because people who don't hold this same viewpoint face negative consequences. Targeting opinion leaders can accelerate getting to the tipping point.

Researchers at Rensselaer Polytechnic Institute identified the percentage of a population necessary for social change as 10%. They stated that this holds true regardless of the type of network.[1] However, other research suggests the number is much higher, with around 25% of a population being the tipping point. Past this point, a minority view can replace the prevalent status quo. The researchers attribute this to most people not being as committed to their opinions as they imagine, meaning they're liable to change their mind as those around them do. The 25% figure is likely to vary depending on the extent of the stake people have in their viewpoints and the social clout of the minority seeking to change things.[2]

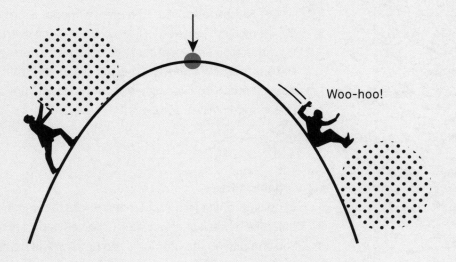

Woo-hoo!

1
"Minority Rules: Scientists Discover Tipping Point for the Spread of Ideas," ScienceDaily, July 26, 2011, https://www.sciencedaily.com/releases/2011/07/110725190044.htm.

2
Ed Yong, "The Tipping Point when Minority Views Take Over," *Atlantic*, June 7, 2018, https://www.theatlantic.com/science/archive/2018/06/the-tipping-point-when-minority-views-take-over/562307/.

Madeline Pollard

Unprecedented legal decisions are often the most visible sign of significant social change. They can appear sudden and dramatic, but they are usually the result of a slow build of changing opinions that becomes impossible to ignore at a certain point. One such case that stands out is that of Madeline Pollard and her legal battle with a congressman William C. P. Breckinridge.

In 1894, the attention of Americans was ensnared by Pollard's suing Breckinridge for breach of promise, seeking compensation of $50,000. The story went far beyond the two of them and was symptomatic of the wider social changes that would soon earn women the right to vote.

The pair met when Pollard was a struggling seventeen-year-old student with no parents and he was a successful politician three decades older. They began a lengthy affair, during which he financially supported her and she gave birth to, then gave up, two of his children. Pollard believed Breckinridge intended to marry her only to discover he had lied.[1] She decided to sue, even though women had been laughed out of court for similar cases only a few years earlier.[2] The trial was vicious, and the media lapped it up.[3] But Pollard ended up winning, a victory that set an important precedent. It helped highlight the double standards of the time. While we could look at the case as a turning point, it was really the result of changing opinions building up until a critical mass was reached.[4]

1
Patricia Miller, "How to Arrange an 1890s-Style Shotgun Wedding," Literary Hub, November 15, 2018, https://lithub.com/how-to-arrange-an-1890s-style-shotgun-wedding/.
2
Melba Porter Hay, *Madeline McDowell Breckinridge and the Battle for a New South* (Lexington: University Press of Kentucky, 2009).
3
Anna Diamond, "The Court Case That Inspired the Gilded Age's #MeToo Moment," Smithsonian.com, November 1, 2018, https://www.smithsonianmag.com/arts-culture/court-case-inspired-gilded-age-me-too-movement-180970538/.
4
Gail Collins, "A Predatory Congressman, His Jilted Lover and a Gilded Age Lawsuit That Foreshadowed #MeToo," *New York Times*, December 19, 2018, https://www.nytimes.com/2018/12/19/books/review/patricia-miller-bringing-down-the-colonel.html.

mass is thus a useful one to apply to other situations where we'd like to produce self-sustaining reactions, such as cities.

Cities are complex systems where planners have often misidentified the elements required to create enough density to produce self-sustaining interactions.[14] In cities, it's not the amount of infrastructure that produces interactions, it's how that infrastructure is laid out. A certain number of interactions are required for a city to function well and adapt to meet the needs of those living in it. What makes a city safe, interesting, prosperous, and creative isn't the buildings or streets. It's how the infrastructure fosters interactions and relationships between people.

Jane Jacobs[*] wrote extensively in *The Death and Life of Great American Cities* about how to achieve self-sustaining interactions in cities and why they are important. She argued that when we isolate parts of cities, we miss the many interconnected functions that they perform. For example, "A city sidewalk by itself is nothing. It is an abstraction. It means something only in conjunction with the buildings and other uses that border it, or border other sidewalks very near it."[15]

The system formed by a sidewalk and its users is what makes an area both safe and interesting. When the area around a sidewalk is subject to active mixed uses—homes, cafés, shops, and so on—there are always eyes upon it and people passing through. These people do not need to know each other or even talk to each other. It is enough that they see each other, are aware they are watching and being watched, and observe each other's behavior. Jacobs writes, "The basic requisite for such surveillance is a substantial quantity of stores and other public places sprinkled along the sidewalks of a district; enterprises and public places that are used by evening and night must be among them especially."[16]

It is the interplay of people that ensures a sidewalk is safe and places limits on antisocial behavior. People moderate how they act knowing someone is or might be watching. Any

[*] Jane Jacobs - (1916-2006). Jacobs was a luminous, radical figure in the field of urban planning. Her first book, *The Death and Life of Great American Cities*, argued against orthodox planning in favor of versatile, mixed-use development. Jacobs campaigned against the destruction of thriving neighborhoods under the guise of "slum clearance."

14
Christopher Alexander, *A City Is Not a Tree* (Portland: Sustasis Foundation, 2015).

15
Jane Jacobs, *The Death and Life of Great American Cities* (New York: Random House, 1961).

16
Jacobs, ibid.

17
Jacobs, ibid.

18
Jacobs, ibid.

19
Jacobs, ibid.

20
Jacobs, ibid.

antisocial behavior that does break out is likely to be swiftly halted by the interventions of bystanders. An organic, unorganized system of control enforced by social norms is more immediate and effective than the use of police, although the threat of them being called plays a role.[17]

To understand why neighborhood safety breaks down in certain situations, we need to consider a sidewalk as needing a minimum number of interactions in order to function as part of a city system instead of just a piece of concrete. You'd feel safer at night walking along a street lined with bars open late than one with stores that close at 5:00 p.m. You'd feel safer walking along a main street passing the fronts of houses than an alleyway only visible from a couple of windows. You would feel safer on a crowded street than an empty one with a police officer present. You feel safer on a sidewalk that is part of a whole system of self-sustaining interactions.[18] The more people that are using a sidewalk, at different times and for varied purposes, the better it functions as a safe space. This is true outside of cities, but other factors are likely to be relevant for safety in towns or rural areas.

It is this "intricacy of sidewalk use, bringing with it a constant succession of eyes" that also makes an area lively and interesting, and therefore a desirable destination.[19] Activity attracts more activity. Many people using an area brings economic benefits, which further attracts more businesses, especially more unusual and specialized ones, which in turn attract more people.

Visual activity is appealing to the eye. We like to watch things happening and other people going about their days, so crowds attract more crowds. People who *watch* attract more people who *do* by making an area safer, and people who *do* attract more people who *watch* by making an area interesting.[20] It is a feedback loop that is dependent on a myriad of uses and interactions.

Our experience of a city also has to do with the

21
Charles Montgomery, *Happy City: Transforming Our Lives through Urban Design* (London: Penguin, 2015).

relationships it fosters with other people. Again, interactions are paramount. Both social isolation and a lack of privacy are risks in cities. An individual may contend with both throughout the course of a day in a poorly designed city. Ideally we gravitate toward spaces where we can have controllable levels of interaction with others. In *Happy City*, Charles Montgomery says, "The richest social environments are those in which we feel free to edge closer together or move apart as we wish. They scale not abruptly but gradually, from private realm to semi-private, to public; from boardroom to living room to porch to neighborhood to city."[21]

One instance of an environment that allows individuals to regulate their level of interaction but also accommodates a wide variety of users is a plaza or square. Present at varying scales as a standard feature of the city, squares are mixed-use areas in which one could, among other things, meet a friend or date, enjoy a coffee at a sidewalk café, watch a street performer, exercise a dog or child, attend a protest, or strike up a conversation with a stranger. The surrounding bustle allows for both safety and interest. You feel safe meeting a date or talking to a stranger because there are enough people around to take note if something goes wrong. But you also feel comfortable having a private conversation with a friend or writing in a notebook because no one is likely to pay much attention to you in particular with so much going on.

Space alone does not create this environment. An overly large square can actively repel people as it feels overexposed and empty. A popular one must have enough activity and reasons to visit in a small enough space to create the density needed for spontaneous and ongoing interactions to occur.

Strøget is a network of pedestrianized streets in Copenhagen created in the 1960s as part of an effort to switch the city's focus from cars to pedestrians and cyclists. Closing off the area to cars was a controversial move. People didn't believe Danes would simply want to mingle in a public space,

Since 1950 it has been a tradition that newly graduated midwives dance around the Stork Fountain in Amagertorv square, which also served as a meeting point for protest leaders in the 1960s.

considering the country's typically cold weather and lack of a preexisting café culture.

But today, Strøget is a lively area with an annual peak of 120,000 visitors braving the icy Danish winter on the last Sunday before Christmas.

Strøget works because it manages to combine many possible uses in one area, making it a busy and engaging place to visit. It facilitates the interactions needed for a city to function in a way that promotes needs like psychological safety and controllable social engagement. Pedestrians and cyclists pass through on their way to somewhere else. Shoppers visit both luxury boutiques and chain stores. Others visit the theater or church. Street performers attract audiences, as do peaceful demonstrations. People sit at pavement cafés or wander along eating inexpensive street food. Tourists visit museums and art galleries.[22] People are willing to brave the cold because the area has so much to offer.

Architect Jan Gehl* has since applied the principles of Strøget to other parts of Copenhagen and cities around the world. The city was able to promote a new sort of street culture by recognizing that a bustling public space is the product of a number of factors coming together at a certain density.[23] Street culture is not specific to certain cultures; it is about having the right kind of spaces for it. These spaces recognize that a minimum of interactions must be maintained in order for them to function in a self-sustained way. The actual architecture should be invisible because the focus is on the people and on bringing out their best qualities.

The idea that infrastructure needs to promote and facilitate a certain number of interactions and not just look good explains why some attempts to design and build cities from scratch have been riddled with problems. If you focus on the infrastructure first and just build a list of requirements—like houses, stores, and streets—you increase the chance that your city won't function well. Rather, the infrastructure needs

*
Jan Gehl - (b. 1936). While cities have long been built with cars in mind, architect and consultant Gehl focuses on building for people. He is the founder of Gehl Architects, and his work reimagines the potential of public spaces. One of his most significant contributions is the development of Strøget, as detailed in his book *Public Spaces, Public Life*. Gehl has also worked on urban design projects in London and New York.

22
"Strøget - The World's Longest Pedestrian Street - Copenhagen - Copenhagen Visitors," Copenhagen, accessed February 3, 2020, https://www.copenhagenet.dk/cph-map/CPH-Pedestrian.asp.

23
Montgomery, ibid.

24
Alexander, ibid.

to be designed to facilitate a critical mass of interactions—
something that planned cities often miss. Planned cities may
try to design out those interactions because designers see
them as a waste of time, or they may even want to discourage
any type of organized action.

Planned cities often segregate different functions, like
workplaces and homes, ignoring the benefits of mixed-use
areas, which are the standard in natural cities. Visually this
looks ordered and pleasing, but it doesn't promote the interactions cities require. It's useful for people to be able to access
resources close to where they live. It cuts down on commuting
and increases time people can spend on relationships.

Mixed-use areas combining residential and commercial
elements create more interactions than those segregated for
one function. Planned cities may segregate roads and sidewalks for pedestrians, viewing driving and walking as distinct
activities. But this prevents people from being able to hail a
taxi and combine the two functions.[24]

Brasília, the federal capital of Brazil, was designed in the
1950s and '60s to replace Rio de Janeiro as the capital. Architect Oscar Niemeyer and urban planner Lucio Costa crafted
a vision of a utopian city from scratch. In the visual sense,
Brasília is a stunning World Heritage site. From the air, it has a
beautiful birdlike form. As a place to live, it functions less well.

Areas of Brasília have specific uses: people live in one
part, work in another, and shop in another. Without mixed-use
areas or much catering to pedestrians, the city cannot form
a street culture. Communities cannot cohere due to a lack of
areas where people can mingle. Visual order—Brasília is laid
out in a grid—does not translate into good function.

Everything in Brasília was built new and modern to
similar specifications. Yet cities need buildings of varying age
and quality to allow for people at different income levels. The
architects and designers never planned for low-income housing, despite Brasília needing inexpensive labor as much as any

The architecture of many of Brasília's buildings led to the city being declared a UNESCO World Heritage site in 1987. The planned city is just one part of the larger Federal District that is generally referred to by the same name and has evolved a great deal since its construction.

25
Jordi Sanchez-Cuenca, "Uneven
Development of Planned
Cities: Brasília," Smart Cities
Dive, Industry Dive, accessed
February 3, 2020, https://
www.smartcitiesdive.com/ex/
sustainablecitiescollective/
uneven-development-planned-
cities-brasilia/121571/.

26
James C. Scott, Seeing Like a State
(New Haven: Yale University Press,
1998).

other city.[25] As a result, unofficial areas have sprung up around the city that house its poorer residents. Only by deviating from the plan can it function at all.[26]

So although Brasília contains the same parts as a typical city, those parts do not facilitate much interaction. It seems as if its designers believed that the arrangement of the infrastructure is irrelevant to city functioning. But how the infrastructure is laid out is critical because it facilitates the critical mass of interactions cities need to be able to adapt and grow to meet the needs of those living in them.

Conclusion

The mental model of critical mass gives us insight into the amount of material needed for a system to change states. We can categorize material as interactions, connections, or efforts. When enough material builds up, systems reach their tipping point. When we keep going, we get sustainable change. Using critical mass as a lens on situations where you want different outcomes helps you identify both the design elements you need to change and the work you need to put in.

Emergence

Organization without an organizer

Emergence

When we look at systems on the macro scale, they sometimes exhibit capabilities that aren't present on the micro scale. This is known as emergence: when systems as a whole function in ways we can't predict by looking at their parts. As Aristotle put it thousands of years ago, "The whole is something over and above its parts, and not just the sum of them all."[1] The mental model of emergence reminds us that new capabilities are often produced from seemingly innocuous elements.

« You look at where you're going and where you are and it never makes much sense, but then you look back at where you've been and a pattern seems to emerge. And if you project forward from that pattern, then sometimes you can come up with something. »

Robert M. Pirsig[2]

1
Ratcliffe, *Oxford Essential Quotations* (Oxford: Oxford University Press, 2018).

2
Robert M. Pirsig, *Zen and the Art of Motorcycle Maintenance: An Inquiry into Values* (London: Vintage Books, 1974).

3
Lisa Margonelli, "Collective Mind in the Mound: How Do Termites Build Their Huge Structures?," *National Geographic*, August 1, 2014, https://www.nationalgeographic.com/news/2014/8/140731-termites-mounds-insects-entomology-science/.

4
"The Animal House," PBS, October 28, 2011, http://www.pbs.org/wnet/nature/the-animal-house-the-incredible-termite-mound/7222/.

We cannot understand systems with emergent properties by reducing them to their components. Termite mounds exhibit emergent properties. A single termite is powerless, but a million or two working together can build a complex mound up to 17 feet tall, requiring the movement of a ton of soil and several tons of water each year.[3] Without a leader orchestrating their movements, termites build ventilation and cooling systems, storage chambers, fungal gardens, and specialized housing for the queen.[4]

Emergence is either strong or weak. Weak emergence occurs in systems in which functions are based on identifiable rules. We can model weak emergence by identifying the underlying rules. Strong emergence does not have identifiable rules behind it, so we cannot model it. So it's possible to construct

Termite social structures share similarities with those of ants, wasps, and bees, in an example of convergent evolution. Queen termites are the subject of study by researchers looking at aging as some species have been known to live for over a decade after establishing colonies in laboratory settings.

5
Mark A. Bedau, "Weak Emergence,"
Noûs 31 (1997): 375–99, https://doi.
org/10.1111/0029-4624.31.s11.17.

6
Diana Taylor, *Disappearing
Acts: Spectacles of Gender and
Nationalism in Argentina's "Dirty
War"* (Durham: Duke University
Press, 2005).

a computer simulation of the flocking behavior of a group of
birds (weak emergence) but not of the interplay of cells in our
brains that creates consciousness (strong emergence).[5]

One of the primary features of emergence is self-
organization. The parts of a system may appear to interact
in chaotic ways, but the whole can seem orderly. This occurs
without centralized control—the parts organize themselves
from the bottom up. For instance, flocks of birds tend to fly
in a coherent shape. They don't manage this by following
the instructions of a leader; instead, each bird instinctively
follows certain rules, like keeping an even distance between
themselves and their neighbors.

— Sidebar: Emergence and Complexity

The Mothers of the Plaza de Mayo

Emergence is all about understanding that sometimes systems
can exhibit capabilities that are beyond the additive properties
of their components. Using it as a lens suggests that groupings
of people can produce results that are non-intuitive when you
consider how the capabilities of any one person should scale.
The cumulative actions of groups of people can also result
in novel outcomes different to their initial intentions. We can
see emergence in protests, where groups of people with little
power can end up having a tremendous influence. Protests can
also have unexpected results that organizers and participants
never planned.

Every Thursday evening between 1977 and 2006, a
group of women, many quite elderly, met in the Plaza de Mayo
in Buenos Aires, Argentina. Mostly wearing matching white
headscarves, they walked across the square while chanting
and holding banners. Though their methods were humble, what
they peacefully achieved over the decades is remarkable.[6]

Periods of history form a coherent narrative under a
name only in retrospect. We know the period of state terror-
ism in Argentina between 1976 and 1983 as the Dirty War. The

Emergence and Complexity

Emergence is not synonymous with complexity. Some complex systems exhibit emergent properties, some only resultant properties. Some simple systems have complex emergent properties.

For example, a nuclear power plant is a complex system with numerous parts all working together. But it does not display emergence: the parts work together as expected. Meanwhile, a much simpler game of chess can show emergence, as there are novel outcomes originating from simple rules. The rules governing how pieces can move are basic, but they lead to complex, high-level strategies, and the outcomes of games are unpredictable. The rules don't tell you how a game will end.

7
Uki Goñi, "Forty Years Later, the Mothers of Argentina's 'Disappeared' Refuse to Be Silent," *Guardian*, April 28, 2017, https://www.theguardian.com/world/2017/apr/28/mothers-plaza-de-mayo-argentina-anniversary.

8
Lester Kurtz, "The Mothers of the Disappeared: Challenging the Junta in Argentina (1977–1983)," International Center for Nonviolent Conflict, July 2010, https://www.nonviolent-conflict.org/mothers-disappeared-challenging-junta-argentina-1977-1983/.

9
Lyn Reese, "Speaking Truth to Power Madres of the Plaza De Mayo," Madres of the Plaza De Mayo, Women in World History Curriculum, accessed August 23, 2019, http://www.womeninworldhistory.com/contemporary-07.html.

average Argentinian person simply experienced it as a period of extreme, random violence. Due to media censorship, many people didn't even know much about the events at the time if no one they knew personally was targeted.

After the Argentinian military performed a successful coup against President Juan Domingo Perón, it declared anyone who opposed its policies an enemy of the state. Anyone who came under suspicion, even if they were not an actual threat, risked going missing. Argentinians referred to these people as *los desaparecidos*, meaning "the disappeared." The government did everything possible to erase any proof they ever existed or to obscure their whereabouts. Many were drugged and thrown from airplanes to prevent their bodies from being found. The total death toll is estimated at 30,000.[7] In addition, the children of pregnant desaparecidos were put up for adoption or sold, with many never learning their true backgrounds. Even to attempt to trace the whereabouts of a missing friend or family member could be fatal.

Despite the fierce censorship and punishment of dissenters, one group retained power—by virtue of their powerlessness and vulnerability. For the mothers of the many people who disappeared, the grief was unbearable. A handful couldn't contain it any longer, and despite the extreme risk, they decided to challenge the regime. On April 30, 1977, a group of 14 mothers met in the Plaza de Mayo and marched, demanding to know what had happened to their children. Soon their numbers grew to the hundreds.[8] The Mothers wore white headscarves embroidered with the names and dates of birth of their children, which became a symbol of their movement.[9] As the disappearances continued, their tactics grew bolder.

The Argentinian government didn't know how to respond. Murdering a visible group of mothers and grandmothers would risk a major backlash. In any case, annoying as they were, a handful of women seemed harmless. They had no power to oppose the government. Officials called them crazy and left it at that.

Groups associated with the Mothers of the Plaza de Mayo
continue to work for justice and have received awards for their
contributions to human rights protection.

10
Goñi, ibid.

11
Taylor, ibid.

12
Erin Blakemore, "30,000 People Were 'Disappeared' in Argentina's Dirty War. These Women Never Stopped Looking," History.com, March 07, 2019, accessed August 23, 2019, https://www.history.com/news/mothers-plaza-de-mayo-disappeared-children-dirty-war-argentina.

13
Blakemore, ibid.

But they misunderstood the potential for and impact of emergence. As individuals, the Mothers of the Plaza de Mayo had no power or influence over the government. At first they had little support because most people didn't even know about the disappearances.[10] When they worked as a group, repeating the same actions each week for years, the total effect was greater than the sum of its parts. They had a power that was the result of them coming together. Seeing as the regime relied on scaring people into silence, speaking out was the most impactful thing they could do.

As Diana Taylor writes in *Disappearing Acts,* "Only by being visible could they be politically effective. Only by being visible could they stay alive. Visibility was both a refuge and a trap—a trap because the military knew who their opponents were but a refuge insofar as the women were only safe when they were demonstrating."[11]

While the government paid no attention, news of the Mothers of the Plaza de Mayo spread outside of Argentina. Countries without media censorship reported on their protests, raising awareness of the brutality of the Dirty War.[12] Human rights groups offered up resources to help the group achieve more.

With increased support came increased pushback. The Argentine government began to target the Mothers, and a number became desaparecidos themselves. A policeman fired a machine gun at them during one protest.[13] The founders of the movement were murdered, and the ultimate fate of some members is still unknown. But they refused to back down because they were safer in the public eye, not out of it.

Once the Dirty War came to an end in 1983, the Mothers knew their fight was far from over. They still needed to know the fate of their children and wanted those who murdered them or were responsible for orders that led to deaths to face the consequences. Mothers whose children were pregnant at the time of their disappearances wanted to trace their grandchildren. To date, over 850 people have been charged with crimes committed during the Dirty War, and over 120 stolen children[14] have been identified and reunited with relatives.[15] DNA testing has helped to identify bodies from mass graves.

By taking advantage of their power as a peaceful group, the Mothers of the Plaza de Mayo managed to help change things in Argentina. Nothing they did could bring their children back, but they could hope that it prevented others from losing theirs, and it could bring them closure. Their methods inspired similar groups around the world. While their initial intention was to find out what happened to their children, their protests had larger effects, such as calling the wider world's attention to the regime's abuse of power. They helped undermine the regime's sense of its ability to control people's thinking.

As a group, the Mothers possessed properties none of them had as individuals. They were visible, and that visibility made them counterintuitively less vulnerable to harm. Oppressive regimes thrive when people are too scared to be seen opposing them. Visible opposition inspires more people to ask questions and to join in fighting oppression. That's why the government at the time went to such lengths to prevent dissent.

What the Mothers achieved was not inevitable. Many other similar groups failed to provoke change. The fact the Mothers did was a novel property. Finally, the story can teach us that you don't always need to plan things all the way to the end. If you have a simple starting point on the right trajectory, surprising things can pan out through the power of emergence.

Social innovation

Knowledge sharing can often produce unexpected results. We start to work together; I bring an understanding of x, and you contribute experience with y. Combining our knowledge means we have x and y covered, but sometimes we are also able to create z. Using the lens of emergence, we can look at learning in humans and highlight that social interaction matters as

14
Abuelas, "Another Grandson Recovers His Identity and His Life Story," Abuelas de Plaza de Mayo, August 3, 2018, accessed August 23, 2019, https://abuelas. org.ar/idiomas/english/press/ news_2018-08-03.htm.

15
"World Report 2019: Rights Trends in Argentina," Human Rights Watch, January 17, 2019, https:// www.hrw.org/world-report/2019/ country-chapters/argentina.

Joseph Henrich - (b. 1968).
Henrich is currently a professor
and department chair of human
evolutionary biology at Harvard
University. His work explores the
interplay between genes and
culture in human evolution, with
a focus on cumulative cultural
learning—and incorporating ideas
from fields such as psychology,
economics, and ethnography. In the
field, Henrich has studied people in
the Peruvian Amazon, rural Chile,
the South Pacific, and Fiji.

16
Joseph Henrich, *The Secret of Our
Success* (Princeton: Princeton
University Press, 2016).

17
Henrich, ibid.

much as, if not more than, individual smarts if we want to ramp up innovation.

As a species, we can do more than any one human brain is capable of because of cultural learning. We don't need to reinvent the wheel each generation. We have evolved social networks that allow us to learn from our elders and to pass on that knowledge to our children. What is important for humans, though, is that we all don't need to know everything. Look around and you will see many items that you cannot build but that you can use. Cultural learning produces products that are emergent properties of human collective organization.

In describing the role of cultural learning for humans, Joseph Henrich*, in *The Secret of Our Success*, explains that "the striking technologies that characterize our species, from the kayaks and compound bows used by hunter-gatherers to the antibiotics and airplanes of the modern world, emerge not from singular geniuses but from the flow and recombination of ideas, practices, lucky errors, and chance insights among inter-connected minds and across generations."[16] Basically humans create things as a group that no one person is capable of.

Furthermore, as cultural learning gets passed from generation to generation, "our cultural learning abilities give rise to 'dumb' processes that can, operating over generations, produce practices that are smarter than any individual or even group."[17] Thus it is not just the knowledge that accumulates but our abilities to learn from and teach others that grow and give rise to emergent properties.

Think of it this way: Could you build a pyramid or a telephone? Even if you worked with the five or ten smartest people you know? How about survive in a forest? How many people would you have to bring with you to guarantee one of you knew how to start a fire? There is so much knowledge that has accumulated in the history of humanity, it isn't possible to know all of it. Henrich explains that the "practices and beliefs [of cultural learning] are often (implicitly) *much* smarter than

Humans are highly motivated to teach their children, passing on information and continuing the cultural learning process. These cumulative educational efforts are believed to be unique to humans and enable us to adapt to a wide range of environments.

18
Henrich, ibid.

19
Robert Boyd and Peter J.
Richerson, "Culture and the
Evolution of Human Cooperation,"
*Philosophical Transactions of the
Royal Society B: Biological Sciences*
364, no. 1533 (2009): 3281–88.

20
Henrich, ibid.

we are, as neither individuals nor groups could figure them out in one lifetime."[18] Cultural learning has produced a cultural mind: an emergent property allowing human knowledge to be far beyond the scope of any individual.

How does cultural learning work? In their paper "Culture and the Evolution of Human Cooperation," Robert Boyd and Peter J. Richerson look at living in the Arctic as one example and explain:

> Arctic foragers could make and do all the other things that they needed because they could make use of a vast pool of useful information available in the behavior and teachings of other people in their population....Even if most individuals imitate most of the time, some people will attempt to improve on what they learn. Relatively small improvements are easier than large ones, so most successful innovations will lead to small changes. These modest attempts at improvement give behaviors a nudge in an adaptive direction, on average. Cultural transmission preserves the nudges, and exposes the modified traditions to another round of nudging.[19]

Humans are generally very good at sharing our improvements and insights with those around us. Furthermore, we find it natural to learn from other people. Thus, although innovating is important in terms of adaptability and survival, what makes humans unique is our social networks that encourage the sharing and uptake of innovation.

Henrich also makes the point that "cultural evolution is often much smarter than we are."[20] It is part of the natural selection process. No one guides cultural learning. It's not prescribed. There is no authority setting out what we will learn every generation. And for most of what we do, we have no idea why it works.

Henrich traces the development of cultural learning in

the human line. Compared with our nearest relatives, chimpanzees, we learn from more individuals right from birth. He suggests that "once individuals evolve to learn from one another with sufficient accuracy (fidelity), social groups of individuals develop what might be called *collective brains*."[21] It is these collective brains—products of large, interconnected groups with strong social norms—that have the potential to generate emergent properties and propel a society to increased sophistication in technological complexity.

Language is a great example of the collective brain propelling the development of complexity. When it comes to language development, Henrich says that "no single individual does much at all, and no one is trying to achieve this [development] as a goal. It's an unconscious emergent product of cultural transmission over generations."[22]

Henrich explains how cultural learning has put selection pressures on humans, changing both our bodies and our instincts. Thus, we start out in life not as a total blank slate but with a huge amount of cumulative cultural evolution behind us. In his paper "The Pace of Cultural Evolution," Charles Perrault concludes, "Culture allows us to evolve over timescales that are normally accessible only to short-lived species, while at the same time allowing us to enjoy the benefits of having a long life history, such as a large brain, an extended juvenile period, and long life span."[23]

When explaining the power of cultural learning, Henrich says, "The first thing to realize is that you are much smarter than you would otherwise be because you've tapped into and downloaded an immense repository of mental apps from a vast pool of culturally inherited knowhow and practices."[24] People specialize because no one can know everything. Then they interact. And in that system in which the interaction occurs, something happens that otherwise wouldn't.

He argues that "innovation does not take a genius or a village; it takes a big network of freely interacting minds."[25]

21
Henrich, ibid.

22
Henrich, ibid.

23
Charles Perrault, "The Pace of Cultural Evolution," *PLoS ONE* 7 no. 9 (2012): e45150, https://doi.org/10.1371/journal.pone.0045150.

24
Henrich, ibid.

25
Henrich, ibid.

Innovation then is not the product of one-off smarts but is the result of the emergent property that our cultural learning has produced.

Conclusion

If all outcomes could be planned for by mixing specific components together, the world would be a boring place. Emergence reminds us that not all capabilities are obvious, and the innocuous can combine and surprise us. Using this mental model is not about trying to predict emergent properties but rather acknowledging they are possible. So don't always stick with what you know. Learn new skills, interact with new people. Working and sharing with others can create unexpected possibilities.

Chaos Dynamics

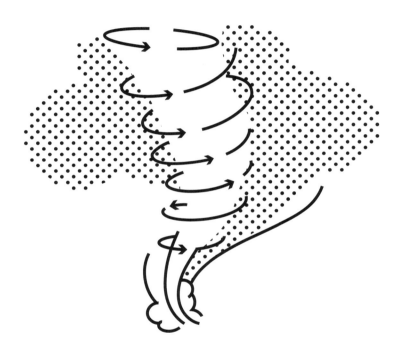

« Most systems behave linearly only when they
are close to equilibrium, and only when we don't
push them too hard. »

Steven Strogatz[1]

Chaotic systems are sensitive to initial conditions. This sensitivity gives rise to a phenomenon known as the butterfly effect, so named for the work of MIT meteorologist and mathematician Edward Lorenz. In the 1950s, Lorenz was working on weather prediction computer models. One day he entered data into a program and left to get a coffee. When he returned, he found the predictions were completely different from when he'd entered the same data earlier that day. At first he thought there was some sort of technical error. Then Lorenz realized he'd accidentally entered a rounded-up number for one of the variables. The discrepancy was tiny, yet the differences in the results were stark.[2]

From this accident, Lorenz discovered chaos dynamics, or the butterfly effect. He found that it wasn't just weather; other chaotic systems exhibited the same sensitivity to initial conditions. It explained why predicting the weather was such a challenge. In later research and talks, Lorenz compared the difference to the change in air pressure produced by the flap of a butterfly's wings.

Predicting the future behavior of chaotic systems is difficult or impossible because modeling outcomes requires perfect understanding of starting conditions. Any inaccuracies will result in incorrect—perhaps drastically so—predictions. As we progress further into the future, the impact of such deviations is magnified further and further, so predictions become exponentially less accurate.[3]

The butterfly effect is significant because it contradicts many of our assumptions about the world. We tend to assume systems are deterministic and tiny differences shouldn't matter too much. In a lot of what we encounter in our day-to-day life, that's true. But it's false for chaotic systems. Without perfect accuracy, we can't make useful, comprehensive predictions about them. It's often only possible to make probability-based predictions, hence why you might hear that there's a 60% chance of rain tomorrow.

Since Isaac Newton first codified laws explaining the functioning of the universe at a fundamental level, people wondered whether it would one day be possible to completely understand the world. Could we one day identify all of the relevant laws and be able to predict everything? In 1814, the mathematician Pierre-Simon Laplace declared Newton's laws would enable us, should we know the position and velocity of every particle in the universe, to predict anything, forever. Over a century later, computers made it seem as though we could put Laplace's prediction to the test.[4]

The butterfly effect suggests otherwise. Even when we can identify deterministic rules, we cannot make perfect predictions. In the face of chaos, we should expect to be surprised. We may know the rules governing a chaotic system's behavior, but we cannot know its precise initial conditions. When we look at the behavior of chaotic systems, we are in fact seeing the outcomes of deterministic rules. Even if we cannot predict their future behavior, it still has its own logic.

« For want of a nail the shoe was lost;
For want of a shoe the horse was lost;
For want of a horse the battle was lost;
For the failure of battle the kingdom was lost—
All for the want of a horseshoe nail. »

Anonymous

1
Steven Strogatz, *Sync: How Order Emerges from Chaos in the Universe, Nature, and Daily Life* (New York: Hachette Books, 2015).
2
Peter Dizikes, "When the Butterfly Effect Took Flight," *MIT Technology Review*, February 22, 2011, https://www.technologyreview.com/s/422809/when-the-butterfly-effect-took-flight/.
3
"Sensitivity to Initial Conditions," Vanderbilt University, accessed January 15, 2020, https://www.vanderbilt.edu/AnS/psychology/cogsci/chaos/workshop/Sensitivity.html.
4
Mitchell, ibid.

What Popular Culture Gets Wrong about the Butterfly Effect

The image of a butterfly flapping its wings and causing a typhoon is a vivid one, and it's no surprise it went on to inspire endless films, books, songs, and motivational quotes. It's unusual for a mathematical idea to become so mainstream. The idea of a tiny thing having a big impact on the world is powerful.

But this is a misreading of the actual meaning of the butterfly effect.[1] It's not that the wing flap *causes* the typhoon; it's that the difference in starting conditions between a world where the butterfly flaps its wings and one where it doesn't is sufficient to mean a typhoon in one and not the other. Chaotic systems are so sensitive to starting conditions that the minutest differences can lead to highly divergent outcomes. We cannot, however, look at an outcome and say that a particular change in conditions caused it. Within chaotic systems, no moment is any more significant than any other. Every single moment changes everything that happens after.

Some systems are very sensitive to their starting conditions, so that the tiny difference in the initial push you give them causes a big difference in where they end up. And there is feedback, so that what a system does affects its own behavior.
—John Gribbin[2]

1
Étienne Ghys, "The Butterfly Effect," *The Proceedings of the 12th International Congress on Mathematical Education* (2015): 19–39.
2
John Gribbin, *Deep Simplicity* (London: Penguin Books, 2005).

Irreducibility

—
As simple as possible but no simpler

Irreducibility

Albert Einstein's idea was that it is possible to reduce any theory down to a certain level that makes it as understandable as possible to as many people as feasible, but past a certain point, it would lose its meaning. That point is where a theory is irreducible.

« It can scarcely be denied that the supreme goal of all theory is to make the irreducible basic elements as simple and as few as possible without having to surrender the adequate representation of a single datum of experience. »

Albert Einstein[1]

Using irreducibility as a model has an echo of first principles thinking. It's a tool for thinking through to the basics: the minimum amount of time, or components, or structure required to maintain the overall qualities. What is the minimum amount necessary for a thing to still be that thing? Irreducibility is about finding the point beyond which you will inevitably change the fundamentals so that you can recognize when you are changing the system to something different.

There are certain irreducible limits to any system past which the system ceases to function as intended. One of the challenges is being able to identify those limits and not get sidetracked by what you think ought to be there.

Irreducibility is exemplified in the parable of the goose and the golden eggs. In this story, a farmer finds a goose that lays a solid-gold egg each day. The farmer grows tired of waiting for just one egg each day and cuts the goose open, imagining it will be full of gold. Instead it dies, and the farmer is left with no more gold because emergence is irreducible. The parts

1
Andrew Robinson, "Did Einstein Really Say That?" Nature News, April 30, 2018, https://www.nature.com/articles/d41586-018-05004-4.

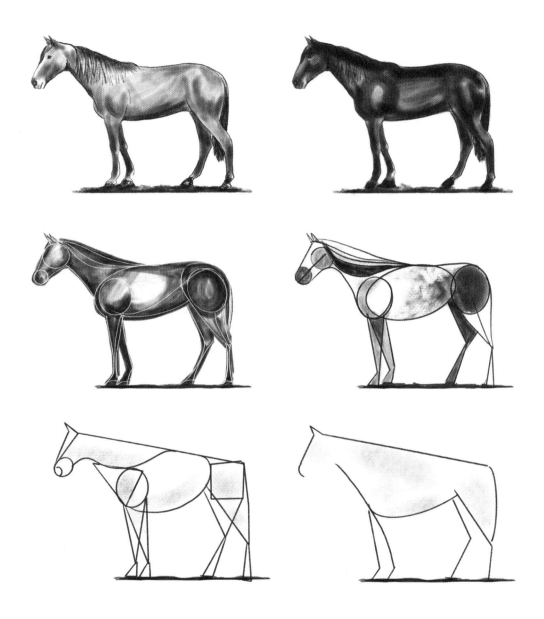

Like Plato's idea of forms, there are certain elements that a thing must possess in order to be considered that thing. We only need to see these minimum elements to be able to identify the object.

of a system with emergent properties do not display those properties, only their aggregate does. If you disassemble such a system, like the farmer cutting open the goose, it loses its emergent properties.

Loose lips sink ships

At what point is a drawing of a horse no longer recognizable as the animal? It's an interesting experiment to figure out the least number of pencil strokes needed to convey representation. When we consider irreducibility, it's often this minimum amount we are looking for. In communications, to get to the essence of the thing is important because simple communications are easier to understand. They contain less ambiguity and give fewer options for interpretation. Wartime propaganda posters are an excellent example of using few words and images to convey complicated information. Poster artists sought the minimum number of words and images they needed to depict their message.

Propaganda posters from World War I and World War II often contain simple images with few words that nonetheless convey an incredible amount of information. Just consider the slogan "Loose Lips Might Sink Ships." These five words were often paired with a simple image of a boat sinking. Together the words and images impart a lot of meaning. They ask people not to talk about anything that could negatively impact the war effort. They suggest that spies are circulating within the home population. The poster also suggests that the war could be compromised if everyone is not on the same page in terms of offering vocal support.

In addition to the messages implying that the words of civilians can derail the war, the posters also convey broader themes. They communicate that everyone is in it together and everyone has a role in the war effort. The posters also serve to condition people to think behavior changes are needed for their side to come out successful. If we imagine being a poster artist,

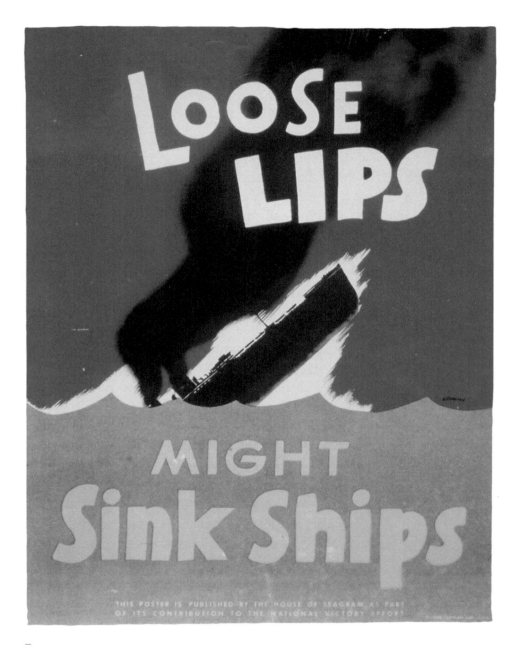

Wartime posters such as this one are considered "white" propaganda. They are definitely trying to influence beliefs, opinion, and actions, but the intentions are overt and can be perceived by observers.

Abram Games - (1914-1996). Born
Abraham Gamse, as a graphic
designer he was responsible for
many of the most famous images
in British history. As an official war
artist for the British government
during WW2, he pioneered
extraordinary new approaches
to conveying complex messages
through simple images. The over
100 posters Games designed to
encourage people to do everything
from joining the Air Force to
donating blood are remarkable as
memorable works of art in their
own right.

2

"Abram Games and the Power
of the Poster," National Army
Museum, accessed November 12,
2020, https://www.nam.ac.uk/
explore/abram-games-designer.

3

"Abram Games and the Power of
the Poster," ibid.

we can understand how difficult it is to convey complex themes
and messages like these in simple graphics and slogans.

Poster artists have to consider the minimum number
of elements to be drawn in order to still communicate their
intended message. Posters that read more like novels or that
are filled with multiple complicated images are not effective.

Abram Games[*] was a graphic designer and the official
war artist for the British during World War II. Many of his posters
are visually stunning and are excellent examples of going right
to the edge of irreducibility. The British National Army Museum
describes his technique: "Always keen to derive maximum
meaning from minimum means, his use of clever symbolic
devices and simplified forms resulted in some of the most
arresting and powerful posters of the era."[2] The images may
have been uncomplicated, but the message was clear. His posters were an effective means of communicating complex topics.
They were not so simple as to introduce ambiguity or confusion.

His posters covered a range of topics, from inspiring
patriotism to "instilling desirable habits and behavior in soldiers and civilians alike." The National Army Museum explains,
"Among other things, his posters encouraged people to avoid
waste, give blood, buy war bonds, handle weapons and ammu-
nition properly, avoid gossip, and maintain fighting fitness."[3]
To promote this wide spectrum of behavior change, Games not
only used few images but often reduced them to simple forms.

Wartime posters make use of common symbols and
symbolic representations. These types of symbols are often
culturally specific, such as an eagle to represent the United
States, or red to represent warning or danger. The use of
symbols is a critical component of being able to simplify the
message. The less you have to explain, the more you can communicate in any one poster.

Joseph Kaminski, in the paper "World War I and Propaganda Poster Art," provides an analysis of one recruiting
poster for the American Air Service. Two servicemen against

a backdrop of a plane midflight implore readers to join. The phrase "Give 'em the gun" is centered, and the words "learn" and "earn" are highlighted at the bottom. Kaminski explains that *learn* and *earn* "are meant to appeal to the individual's self-centered interest of learning a useful skill and making money so they can live comfortably after the war."[4] Thus the poster appeals to those who want to belong and those who want to fight, and shows how war experience can be useful later on. None of that messaging is explicit. The poster doesn't spell out what you will learn or how it will help you earn. But the placement of the words on a recruiting poster, in addition to their large size, is the minimum amount needed to still convey the complex message.

Using the lens of irreducibility on wartime posters demonstrates why in communication it can be so effective to find that minimum amount needed to not compromise comprehension. Simplicity can convey a powerful meaning. But too much simplicity conveys no meaning at all.

Typography

The mental model of irreducibility also teaches us that when we simplify or change things past a certain point, they cease to work or have meaning. There are limits to how much we can reduce while maintaining the important qualities making a thing what it is. Being aware of those limits allows for experimentation and creativity.

Designers of all kinds often have to pay attention to the irreducible components of whatever they're designing. If they want to make things simpler or be creative, they need to consider how they can do so while still being comprehensible. Designers need to identify what makes something what it is so they can ensure the irreducible components are present. If they remove or change into an unfamiliar form something that is essential for users to understand what they're looking at, the result is useless. Recognizing those limits is a key part of good

4
Joseph Jon Kaminski, "World War I and Propaganda Poster Art: Comparing the United States and German Cases," *Epiphany Journal of Transdisciplinary Studies* 7, no. 2 (2014).

Eric Gill - (1882-1940). Sculptor,
engraver, and designer, he is best
known for creating the Gill Sans
typeface. His book, *An Essay
on Typography*, uses a font he
designed especially for it, called
"Joanna." In recent years, Gill's
artistic legacy has become an
uneasy one due to diaries revealing
his abuse of his children.

5

Eric Gill, *An Essay on Typography*
(London: Penguin Modern Classics,
2013).

6

Gill, ibid.

7

Gill, ibid.

user-friendly design. Subverting the limits can be bad design—
but it can sometimes also be an exercise in finding new ways to
represent the same thing or in challenging expectations.

Typography is one area we can look at through the lens
of irreducibility. Take a look around you at all the different fonts
in your vicinity as well as their variant sizes, spacing, colors,
and so on: in this book, on food packaging, on billboards, street
signs, clothing labels, newspapers, slogan T-shirts, and so on.
They all vary a great deal, yet you can still read them. Whoever
designed the font retained the irreducible elements of each
letter. Despite the differences in overall design, they figured
out what makes each letter recognizable as itself.

Eric Gill's[*] 1931 *An Essay on Typography* is an ideal starting point for considering irreducibility in typography. At their
core, Gill explains, "Letters are signs for sounds....Letters are
not pictures or representations....They are more or less abstract
forms."[5] We have created them as signifiers, and we can modify them to suit new mediums or social demands. Letters have
changed a great deal over time, yet each generation of designers aims to identify the irreducible elements of older forms, to
hold on to them, and to ensure their type remains legible.

The letters of the English alphabet do not directly sym-
bolize the sounds of the language. A designer must "take the
alphabets we have got, and we must take these alphabets in all
essentials as we have inherited them."[6]

There are three core versions of the English alphabet:
lowercase, uppercase, and italic. Each forms letters differently, but each is still recognizable because it contains the
same irreducible elements. It is possible to change parts of the
design without losing these elements. Gill writes, "A Roman
capital A does not cease to be a Roman capital A because it
is sloped backward, or forward, because it is made thicker or
thinner, or because serifs are added or omitted; and the same
applies to lowercase and italics."[7] It is possible to change those
elements because they are not irreducible—certain features

8
Gill, ibid.

9
Gill, ibid.

10
Gill, ibid.

11
Paul Felton, *The Ten Commandments of Typography/Type Heresy* (London: Merrell, 2006).

12
Felton, ibid.

of the letter's shape are. Looking at a text mixing all three alphabets highlights that each has its own irreducible element. Capitals should be larger than lowercase when used together, and italics should be narrower and sloping.[8] These are irreducible elements of the alphabet, not the letters themselves.

For a designer, identifying and retaining those irreducible elements of each letter is an important, rare skill: "Everybody thinks that he knows an A when he sees it, but only the few extraordinary rational minds can distinguish between a good one and a bad one, or can demonstrate what constitutes A-ness. When is an A not an A? Or when is an R not an R? It is clear that for every letter there is some norm."[9]

Gill explains that the irreducible elements of a letter may be different depending on its context. For example, "A square or oblong with its corners rounded off may, by itself, be more like an O than anything else, but in conjunction with a D made on the same principles there is not much by which to recognize which is which, and from a distance the two are indistinguishable."[10] The irreducible elements of a system are not fixed and depend on the context and goals of that system.

In the book *Type Heresy*, Paul Felton explores how experienced designers who know the rules can break them while still getting a message across.[11] It comes down to understanding the irreducible elements of that component of type and how they vary between contexts.

The most important feature of a headline, for example, is that it is the first thing a reader notices and therefore reads when looking at the page. Convention states the easiest way to achieve this is to make the headline much larger than the rest of the text and to place it at the top of the page. Felton illustrates that the eye will also naturally go first to the boldest text on the page if everything is the same size, so it is also possible to differentiate a headline by making it bold, in which case it can be positioned anywhere.[12] What might appear to be an irreducible element is in fact not. The irreducible element of a

A letter can be stripped of every flourish, and its components manipulated, but there is a point beyond which too much change renders it no longer the symbol it once was. Typography designers must balance creativity and comprehensibility.

headline is that it is immediately noticeable, not that it is larger than the rest of the text.

Sometimes irreducible components are fairly obvious. As famously attributed to Warren Buffett, you can't produce a baby in one month by getting nine different women pregnant. Natural selection has resulted in an irreducible pregnancy process. Irreducibility, however, is not always this clear. Typography shows us the importance of identifying irreducible components. Each letter has elements that need to be present for legibility. The same goes for the overall way you lay out text on a page. When we mistake the irreducible components and then jettison the rest, we change the nature of the system, which often results in a new system. Fonts that fail to retain the irreducible elements necessary for readability move into the domain of visual art as opposed to being about communication.

— Sidebar: Gall's Law

Conclusion

Understanding the irreducible components of a system means you won't waste your time trying to change what is unchangeable. You can master the minimum elements, then explore. Using irreducibility as a lens helps you shed the nonessential, giving you options for adjusting or pivoting.

Gall's Law

Gall's law, put forward by author and pediatrician John Gall in *The Systems Bible*, states that complex systems that work invariably evolve from simple systems. Attempting to build a complex system from scratch tends to be ineffective. It takes consistent, incremental progress from something basic that works. Although not foolproof, we can see examples of Gall's law everywhere. A convoluted bureaucratic process in an organization probably began with something simple, a single form that served its purpose. Complex organisms like tigers and whales evolved from single-celled bacteria. Sprawling cities started off as small towns with a handful of inhabitants. Complex technologies like airplanes evolved from simpler ones like bicycles. Gall's law explains we cannot always establish how a complex system works by looking at its parts. It also teaches us to avoid trying to design complex systems from scratch.

Law of diminishing returns

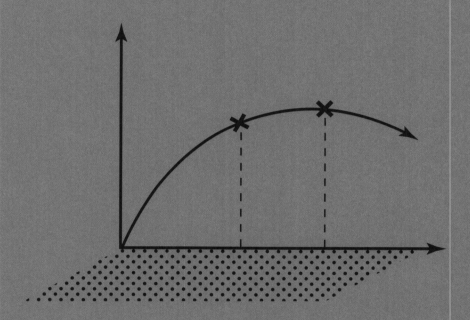

Hard work stops paying off

The Law of Diminishing Returns

When we put more effort or resources into something, we usually expect to get more out of it. Work more hours, be more productive. Exercise more, become fitter. Assign more people to a project, complete it sooner. Using the law of diminishing returns as a model shows us that the relationship between inputs and outputs in systems is not always linear. Past a certain point, diminishing returns almost always set in.

The law of diminishing returns posits that inputs to a system lead to more output, up until a point where each further unit of input will lead to a decreasing amount of output. In other words, at that point more effort leads to less return. Progress even further despite diminishing returns, and more inputs may reduce the amount of total output.

Diminishing returns apply in almost any system. In economics, it is a specific term for the fact that increasing inputs, like materials and labor in production processes, increases outputs, but not indefinitely. Past a certain level, more inputs will lead to lower increases in outputs, until the inputs start to become a hindrance. A classic example is the number of workers in a factory. Hire more people, and production goes up. Hire too many people, and the factory gets crowded, people get in each other's way, and there isn't enough equipment to go around. Each additional worker then contributes less to the factory's output.

One early application of the law of diminishing returns was to farming, with the advent of artificial fertilizers in the 19th and 20th centuries.[1] Farmers found that adding more nutrients to their soil increased crop yields at first, making plants grow bigger in less time. But past a particular ratio of fertilizer to soil, adding more means less corresponding increase in yield. Adding even more means less yield in total, as the soil becomes overloaded.[2]

Diminishing returns are everywhere. Working an extra

1
Darrell A. Russel and Gerald G. Williams, "History of Chemical Fertilizer Development," *Soil Science Society of America Journal* 41, no. 2 (1977): 260–65.

2
Paul M. Johnson, "Diminishing Returns, Law Of," A Glossary of Political Economy Terms, Auburn University, accessed August 15, 2019, http://www. auburn.edu/~johnspm/gloss/ diminishing_returns_law_of.

3
John Pencavel, "The Productivity of Working Hours," *The Economic Journal* 125, no. 589 (2014): https://doi.org/10.1111/ecoj.12166.

hour overtime might make you more productive; working an extra three might mean more mistakes, so less work gets done per hour.[3] Tweaking the little details of a project might improve it, but doing so for too long might mean the improvements aren't worth the time invested. Receiving enough funding to get off the ground might be a godsend for a new company, but receiving too much might mean decreasing benefits as proving profitable for investors takes precedence over serving customers. When you're learning a new skill, early practice sessions have a huge impact on your abilities, then subsequent hours of practice lead to diminishing improvements in performance.

The law of diminishing returns teaches us that outcomes are not linear and not all inputs to a system are equal. Often we focus on the trivial at the expense of the meaningful. An extra worker in a factory with ten employees is not equivalent to an extra worker in the same factory with 100. An extra hour of work at 9:00 p.m. is not the same as an hour of work at 9:00 a.m. The advantage to understanding the law of diminishing returns is being able to calculate where that point is for different systems so we know how best to interact with them.

— Sidebar: The Diminishing Returns of Homework

The Viking raids of Paris

Diminishing returns happen because systems adapt. They become accustomed to certain inputs and stop responding to them in the same way. The law of diminishing returns teaches us that a way of interacting with a system that produces desirable results at first can become less and less effective over time. No matter how impressive the initial windfall may be, we should anticipate eventually getting less for our effort.

In 814, the Holy Roman emperor and king of the Franks, Charlemagne*, died. The death of the ruler of Francia (now France) left a sudden power void in Europe. Throughout his life, Charlemagne led successful military campaigns against the Saxons and Vikings. Europe had no other leader of equivalent

The Diminishing Returns of Homework

Homework is a standard part of modern schooling. It's so ubiquitous few people—parents, teachers, and students alike—rarely question its value. However, homework is subject to diminishing returns. Research suggests it has no benefit for children younger than high school age, though a small amount may be beneficial for high schoolers. But each additional hour of after-school study carries fewer benefits, especially if it involves reiterating the same material.[1] This is even more of an issue for students who may have other responsibilities, like caring for siblings or helping with chores, meaning they don't get enough time for leisure or sleep. In this case, homework can have negative returns.

Ineffective or counterproductive practices, like schools giving hours of work to be completed every night, are often the result of us not recognizing the existence of diminishing returns. We can end up assuming that more effort always leads to more rewards—even when evidence contradicts that. As far back as 1950, research has shown that compulsory homework does not improve performance enough to be worthwhile.[2]

1
Vicki Abeles, Grace Rubenstein, and Lynda Weinman, *Beyond Measure: Rescuing an Overscheduled, Overtested, Underestimated Generation* (New York: Simon & Schuster Paperbacks, 2016).
2
Harris Cooper, "Synthesis of Research on Homework," *Educational Leadership* 47, no. 3 (1989): 85–91, https://eric.ed.gov/?id=EJ398958.

might to fill his role of keeping them confined to Scandinavia. His successor Louis the Pious didn't inspire the same fear as the leader who once massacred 4,500 captive Saxons in one go.[4]

> « The Vikings were never defeated; rather they allowed themselves to be assimilated. »
>
> Neil Oliver[5]

The first little fleet of Viking ships sailed up the river Seine in 820, looking to test Paris' defenses. Frankish guards beat them back without much trouble. But this was only a pilot raid. The first notable raid occurred in 841, when the Vikings targeted the Abbey of Saint-Denis, as churches tended to hold the most wealth at the time. It proved to be a profitable attack. Viking leader Asgeir enriched himself by taking a large number of hostages, returning some for ransom, and selling the rest as slaves.[6] After the initial success, the Vikings soon launched more raids.

The Viking leader Reginfred, who conducted the most notorious raid of all in 845, is so shrouded in mystery that historians are unclear if he was a single individual or a composite. He is sometimes also known as Reginherus, Reginhero, or Ragnar Lodbrok. Under his command, 120 ships carrying thousands of Vikings advanced up the river Seine toward Paris.[7] Guessing they would target Saint-Denis, the Frankish leader Charles the Bald[*], grandson of Charlemagne, placed one half of his army on either side of the river. His plan was misguided. By dividing his force, he allowed the Vikings to concentrate theirs, targeting one half at a time. Any soldiers they didn't slaughter they took as prisoners.[8] Then the Vikings demanded a ransom of 7,000 French pounds of silver and gold.

The 845 raid of Paris was not an attempt to take control of the city—it was about profit. Their pockets full, the Vikings left, ransacking a few villages along the way. Villagers viewed

[*] Charlemagne - (742/748-814). Also known as Charles the Great, Charlemagne became king of the Franks in 768 and king of the Lombards in 774. In founding the Carolingian Empire, he became the first person to rule over western Europe since the fall of the Western Roman Empire. As a result, he sparked the beginning of the Carolingian Renaissance, a period of accelerated cultural activity beginning in the late eighth century.

[*] Charles the Bald - (823-877). The grandson of Charlemagne, Charles the Bald was king of West Francia and Italy, as well as emperor of the Carolingian Empire. A general lack of support meant Charles struggled to retain power at times.

4 Alexander Mikaberidze, *Atrocities, Massacres, and War Crimes: An Encyclopedia* (Santa Barbara: ABC-CLIO, 2013).

5 Neil Oliver, *The Vikings* (London: Weidenfeld & Nicolson, 2012).

6 Joshua J. Mark, "Viking Raids on Paris," Ancient History Encyclopedia, November 13, 2018, https://www.ancient.eu/Viking_Raids_on_Paris/.

7 Martina Sprague, *Norse Warfare: The Unconventional Battle Strategies of the Ancient Vikings* (New York: Hippocrene Books, 2007).

8 Sprague, ibid.

According to chronicles and archeological evidence, Vikings explored
a large part of the globe. They were the first Europeans to reach North
America, stopping in present-day Newfoundland, Canada, over 1,000
years ago. One theory is that their polygynous society was a motivation
for expansion.

the raids as some sort of divine punishment for their sins.[9]

Historians remain divided on whether the ransom was a wise choice or not. It was certainly controversial among the people who had to pay for it.[10] Charles the Bald paid it because it got the Vikings to leave without inflicting further damage, saving him the expense of mobilizing an army again. He was also contending with divisions within Francia and was unsure whom to trust.

But in doing so, he set a dangerous precedent. Paying the ransom encouraged more Viking attacks.[11] Between 845 and 926, the Franks paid an estimated total of 685 pounds of gold and 43,000 pounds of silver to the Vikings.[12] Buoyed by the success of the 845 Paris raid, they continued to besiege any towns that held enough wealth to be of interest.[13]

The Franks did not just sit back and let this happen. Walls went up around Paris to withstand attacks. They built bridges across the Seine to block ships from reaching the city. Towers equipped with hundreds of guards capable of pouring boiling wax and oil on any Vikings below added to the protection.[14] Unable to get close to the city, the Vikings resorted to sitting out lengthy sieges, which taxed them in terms of resources, morale, and human life due to disease. They tried setting fire to boats and pushing them toward the bridges, but they sank without causing damage.[15]

Diminishing returns set in for the Vikings. Raiding Paris resulted in smaller and smaller ransoms at a higher cost. It became difficult and time-consuming relative to the rewards. In 886, a weakened Viking leader requested just 60 pounds of precious metals in exchange for leaving. In 911, the Viking leader Rollo[*] received an enticing offer from Frankish king Charles the Simple[*]. Rather than gold, Charles offered to give him land, a title, and his daughter's hand in marriage. There was one condition: Rollo had to protect the area from any further Viking attacks. They shook on it and thus founded Normandy.[16]

The Viking raids of Paris show us that we cannot keep

[*] Rollo - (846/860-930). Rollo was the first ruler of Normandy in France after Charles the Simple gifted the land to him in exchange for an end to Viking raids. Descendants of Rollo and the fellow Vikings he settled with were referred to as "Normans" and would go on to control significant areas of Europe. Rollo was the great-great-great-grandfather of William the Conqueror.

[*] Charles the Simple - (879-929). Known for his straightforward manner, Charles the Simple ruled over the area that is now France during the time of the Viking raids. Although Charles lacked the strategic insight of some of his predecessors, the deal he arranged with chief Rollo had a significant impact on European history.

[9] James T. Palmer, *The Apocalypse in the Early Middle Ages* (Cambridge: Cambridge University Press, 2014).

[10] Simon Coupland, *Carolingian Coinage and the Vikings: Studies on Power and Trade in the Ninth Century* (Burlington: Ashgate, 2007).

[11] Coupland, ibid.

[12] Angus A. Somerville and R. Andrew McDonald, *The Vikings and Their Age* (Toronto: University of Toronto Press, 2013).

[13] Sprague, ibid.

[14] John Haywood, *Northmen: The Viking Saga, AD 793–1241* (New York: Thomas Dunne Books, 2016).

[15] Haywood, ibid.

[16] Ben Hubbard, *Bloody History of Paris: Riots, Revolution, and Rat Pie* (London: Amber Books, 2018).

17
Mark Kurlansky, *Salt: A World History* (London: Vintage, 2003).

18
Hubbard, ibid.

performing the same actions and expecting the same results. Things change. When we first try something new, the returns can be dramatic. We might be tempted to keep repeating ourselves, expecting to reap the same benefits. But we're likely to end up expending more effort for less return. When that happens, it's time to change tack. During the first few attacks on Paris, the Vikings extracted large ransoms because people were unprepared, lacking appropriate defense mechanisms. Over time, they built up their ability to withstand attack.

« The main body of Vikings were given lands in the Seine basin in exchange for protecting Paris. They settled into northern France and within a century were speaking a dialect of French and became known as the Normans. »

Mark Kurlansky[17]

In addition, the areas simply began to run out of wealth to extract. The Franks stopped rebuilding their holy buildings so the Vikings would have less incentive to attack them. Finding new villages meant going further afield, which cost more and carried greater risk. Due to the distances traveled, the Vikings began to spend months at a time in Europe to avoid sailing during the winter. Eventually it made sense for them to just settle for good. Once the returns weren't worth the effort, Rollo took the opportunity to benefit from Europe in a different way. His choice teaches us that noticing diminishing returns means it's time to try something new.

Only after the raids stopped did Paris as we know it today begin to take shape, as the Franks found the courage to begin grand construction projects like the Notre Dame cathedral. It would take a long time for the memory to fade and the area to recover.[18]

— Sidebar: The Diminishing Returns of Mass Incarceration

The Diminishing Returns of Mass Incarceration

Incarcerating people has a long history as a means of punishing criminals and, in theory, making society safer. But incarceration has diminishing returns. Taking the most dangerous, violent individuals in a society off the street makes everyone else much safer. After all, most violent crimes are the work of a tiny minority of the population. However, the more people a society incarcerates, the less everyone benefits. As we punish more minor crimes with prison sentences, the safety gains decrease.[1] If incarceration continues increasing, it may reach the point of diminishing returns where the benefits are outweighed by the cost to taxpayers and by the inability of incarcerated individuals to contribute to society. Mass incarceration rests on the assumption that locking up people who commit crimes is always a good idea. But that belief has a logical end point.

French sociologist Emile Durkheim argued that a certain amount of crime is inevitable in any society because what is considered criminal is based on the "collective sentiments" of a society. As long as people are divergent and have many different ideas about the correct ways to act and live, in any group, there will be individuals whose actions will not follow the norms and will be labeled as criminal. Durkheim did not condone crime but did argue that it is impossible to conceive a society without it.[2] This is not to say that acts we currently label as criminal are merely divergent behavior, but that divergent behavior that people end up labeling as criminal is inevitable.

Even in a hypothetical world where none of the acts we condemn by law occurred, there would still be variations in behavior that some would consider criminal. Preventing the worst sorts of crimes does not create a perfect society. It just means people attach greater significance to crimes that are more minor. Continue this process, and you end up with a world where someone might be, say, put to death for spitting their gum on the ground because it is the worst conceivable infraction.

New opinions are always suspected, and usually opposed, without any other reason but because they are not already common.
—John Locke[3]

1
Steven Pinker, *The Better Angels of Our Nature: Why Violence Has Declined* (New York: Penguin Books, 2012).
2
Walter A. Lunden, "Pioneers in Criminology XVI—Emile Durkheim (1858–1917)," *Journal of Criminal Law and Criminology* 49, no. 1 (1958): 2.
3
John Locke, *An Essay Concerning Human Understanding* (Oxford: Clarendon Press, 1979).

19
Warren Buffett and Lawrence A.
Cunningham, *The Essays of Warren
Buffett: Lessons for Corporate
America* (Durham: Carolina
Academic Press, 2013).

20
Randall Clark, *At a Theater or Drive-
in Near You: The History, Culture,
and Politics of the American
Exploitation Film* (London:
Routledge, 2016).

« What the wise do in the beginning, fools do in the end. »

Warren Buffett[19]

Exploitation films from the 1950s to the 1970s

Our reactions to novel things are subject to diminishing returns. Enjoyable things tend to become less enjoyable if we're exposed to them a few times. The first snowfall of the year is beautiful. By March, you can't remember why you choose to live in a cold climate. The first time you go on a roller coaster, it gives you a thrill. After a dozen rides, you get bored. If you want people to pay attention, you need to keep raising the bar.

One area where this habituation is apparent is in films. A new technique that terrifies millions in a horror movie is a dull trope the dozenth time another director copies it. A film that kept someone awake at night when they were a teenager might end up being something they show their kids on a weeknight. A powerful advertising campaign might seem quaint after it becomes a convention. By looking at the history of exploitation films, we can see how the mental model of diminishing returns makes us nonchalant about things that used to provoke a reaction.

First of all, what exactly is an exploitation film? The simplest definition is a film made with the intention of getting as many people as possible to buy tickets without much regard for aesthetic or cultural merit, or for edifying audiences. Exploitation films capitalize on whatever viewers find titillating, often profiting from societal trends or moral panics. Virtually all have low budgets and tend to feature an unknown cast and crew.[20] During the heyday of exploitation films, from the 1950s to the 1970s, they were often defined by one thing: they featured what Hollywood couldn't or wouldn't feature.

As soon as the film industry began to take shape in the 1910s, people panicked about the morality of the medium.

Some worried the content of films could corrupt viewers and pressed for censorship. In the 1930s, this concern led to the Motion Pictures Production Code, which placed restrictions on what Hollywood could include in films. At the time, Hollywood was the film industry. Major studios owned the means of cinematic production, distribution, and exhibition, giving them full control over the movies the public saw.[21]

In 1948, a landmark US Supreme Court ruling declared that the big Hollywood studios were violating antitrust laws and could no longer remain vertically integrated. Around the same time, network television was taking hold, and theaters were looking for new ways to get audiences through their doors. Into the mix came the rise of youth culture, as entertainment industries began to cater more to the tastes of young people. These three main factors laid the foundation for the exploitation film industry.[22]

As Ric Meyers writes in *For One Week Only,* "Fools and filmmakers rushed in where wise men feared to tread. They pored over the various rules and regulations that controlled the motion picture industry until they fell through a loophole."[23] These types of films began with the "nudist camp" pictures of the 1950s, which claimed to be documentaries. With the rise of grindhouse theaters and drive-ins, exploitation films took off. Low-budget studios churned out films to meet the demand for shocking content.

« Horror is fear of the unknown. Terror is fear of the known. »

Ric Meyers[24]

To look at the history of exploitation films during this era is to see a repeated pattern of audiences responding strongly to one film, then directors and studios hastily copying its distinguishing features—on and on until the impact was lost.

21
Ric Meyers, *For One Week Only: The World of Exploitation Films* (Guilford: Emery Books, 2011).

22
Meyers, ibid.

23
Meyers, ibid.

24
Meyers, ibid.

25
Meyers, ibid.

26
Meyers, ibid.

27
Meyers, ibid.

Audiences couldn't be as surprised the tenth time they saw a possessed child or a group of campers being picked off one by one. They needed to see more deaths, more graphic gore, more taboo subjects, more nudity. Everything had to turn up a notch each time or diminishing returns set in.

Sometimes titles were copied. The 1962 film *Whatever Happened to Baby Jane?*, an acclaimed Academy Award winner, was soon followed by *Whatever Happened to Aunt Alice* (1969), *What's the Matter with Helen* (1971), and *Who Slew Auntie Roo* (1971). Similarly, we have *Don't Look in the Basement* (1974), *Don't Open the Window* (1976), *Don't Go in the House* (1981), and *Don't Answer the Phone* (1981). When making a new film with a copycat title was too much of a stretch, production companies were not averse to rereleasing an old one with a new name and poster. Any successful exploitation film would see its basic premise replicated ad nauseum until the effect wore off.[25]

Advertising materials were fair game too. After *Color Me Blood Red* (1965) used the tagline "You must keep reminding yourself it's only a motion picture!" on posters, similar sentiments followed for films lacking the clout to warrant it. *Last House on the Left* (1972) advised viewers, "To avoid fainting keep repeating, it's only a movie…only a movie…only a movie…" Hallmark then reused essentially the same marketing for *Don't Look in the Basement* (1973) and *The Horrible House on the Hill* (1974).[26] Makers of exploitation films had to keep coming up with new ideas to get a response. Any part of a film that got a reaction was fair game for copying, which deadened future responses and made viewers more skeptical of marketing materials. A clever new title structure might be a surprise to audiences at first, but copies wore them out.

Despite occasional later freak successes for low-budget, shocking films like *The Blair Witch Project* (1999), exploitation films as they existed from the 1950s to the 1970s are largely dead.[27] As we mentioned before, their key characteristic was covering content mainstream cinema couldn't or wouldn't

There are dozens of subgenres of exploitation films, including nudist films, spaghetti westerns, and Canuxploitation. There was the odd commercial success, such as *The Good, The Bad, and The Ugly*, but most are long forgotten, and many films from the 1930s have no known surviving copies.

28
Meyers, ibid.

29
Feona Attwood, I. Q. Hunter,
Sharon Lockyer, and Vincent
Campbell, *Controversial Images:
Media Representations on the Edge*
(Basingstoke: Palgrave Macmillan,
2013).

30
Meyers, ibid.

touch. But times have changed. Viewers are no longer easily shocked. Fringe themes have been absorbed into the mainstream. Meyers writes, "The major movie studios, who once spit on the very idea of making money off sex and slaughter, now bank on it."[28] It takes much higher budgets to interest audiences, and with less censorship, mainstream films have become less tame and audiences more desensitized.[29]

Ric Meyers explains, "Exploitation films were the price we pay for, essentially, living a lie. Once upon a time, many would like others to think that they were well-adjusted, considerate, intelligent people who would never enjoy—even revel in—the suffering of others." But exploitation films were an extension of the same urges that drove people in the past to watch gladiators slaughter each other or accused witches burn. The films were an unabashed recognition of those urges and thus "they allowed one to receive the perverted pleasure of looking at a car wreck without the guilt of knowing the victims are real."[30]

Our reactions to shocking content diminish over time, and we have to seek out something worse to get the same reactions. That's why exposure therapy can be an effective means of overcoming phobias. Exploitation films show that strong reactions cannot continue indefinitely. We return to being unsurprised after we've seen the same thing a few times. Exploitation films may seem an unimportant footnote in cinematic history, yet they reflect the cycles culture goes through as the fringe becomes a banal part of the mainstream.

Exploitation films changed what we considered "average" in films. To produce content at the far end of the spectrum, films had to respond to continually changing standards. Diminishing returns is an interesting model through which we can explore why we become jaded by novelty and thus always push the boundaries to experience the rush of finding something new.

— Sidebar: Diminishing Returns and Societal Collapse

Conclusion

When your results consistently take a nosedive and your past successes seem distant memories, diminishing returns have likely set in. We cannot expect that if we keep doing things the same way, we will always get the same remarkable results. This model reminds us that change is an essential element of moving forward. Even if it's not broken, there is always something to fix. Don't let early success make you complacent. Plan for diminishing returns, and you just might avoid them.

Diminishing Returns and Societal Collapse

Why do complex societies, like the Roman Empire, collapse? One theory, advanced by Joseph A. Tainter in *The Collapse of Complex Societies*, is that it comes down to diminishing returns. As societies grow and develop, they become more complex and require more and more "energy flow" to stay intact.[1] With increasingly advanced networks between individuals, "more hierarchical controls are created to regulate these networks, more information is processed, there is more centralization of information flow, there is increasing need to support specialists not directly involved in resource production, and the like." More complex societies extract an exponentially higher amount of energy from individuals just to stay intact than simple ones. At a certain point, the cost may exceed the benefits individuals derive from being part of that society. When this happens, it may begin to disintegrate.[2] Being complex no longer carries benefits, and it makes sense to return to a simpler level of organization.

1
Joseph A. Tainter, *The Collapse of Complex Societies* (Cambridge: Cambridge University Press, 2017).
2
Tainter, ibid.

Mathematics

What is mathematics? It is only a systematic effort of solving puzzles posed by nature.

Shakuntala Devi[1]

Mathematics

1
Shakuntala Devi, *Puzzles to Puzzle
You* (India: Orient Paperbacks,
2005)

Supporting Idea:
Distributions

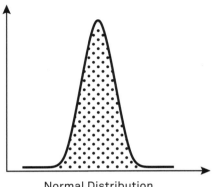

Normal Distribution

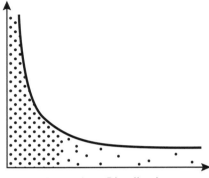

Power Law Distribution

Distributions help you contextualize what to expect given a certain data set. They help you make predictions about the probability, frequency, and possibility of future events. There are many different types of distributions. The four characteristics that will most determine the type of distribution you are dealing with for any given data set are:

1. Is the data made up of discrete values, or is it continuous?
2. Are the data points symmetric or asymmetric?
3. Are there upper and lower limits on the data?
4. What is the likelihood of observing extreme values?[1]

Distributions are often idealized (unrealistic) representations of a data set. According to a New York University document, "Raw data is almost never as well behaved as we would like it to be. Consequently, fitting a statistical distribution to data is part art and part science, requiring compromises along the way. The key to good data analysis is maintaining a balance between getting a good distributional fit and preserving ease of estimation, keeping in mind that the ultimate objective is that the analysis should lead to better decisions."[2]

The distribution we are all most familiar with is the normal distribution, and it is one of our most important lenses for looking at the world. Its influence is everywhere from education to medicine, even if it is often invisible. But it's also a mental model that is easily taken too literally, and you end up trying to fit reality to the model, not vice versa. Reality rarely fits into a neat normal distribution, and we miss a lot of important nuance and variation when we try to make it do so.

A set of data points is normally distributed if the majority of values cluster around a midpoint, with a few falling on either side. The farther from the midpoint, the fewer values show up. The midpoint is simultaneously the mean, mode, and median value. When plotted on a graph, normally distributed data forms a characteristic symmetrical shape known as a bell curve. Leonard Mlodinow, writing in *The Drunkard's Walk,* summarizes it as such: "The normal distribution describes the manner in which many phenomena vary around a central value that represents their most probable outcome."[3]

Many common measurements are normally distributed, such as height, IQ, blood pressure, and exam results. This normal distribution tends to be the case for values that are subject to certain physical constraints, such as biological measurements. Normal distributions usually also characterize the price of common household goods. If you have an idea of the average price of toothpaste, you can use an estimation of the distribution to tell you if you are paying too much for the one in front of you or if you are getting a good deal.

In a normal distribution, the more extreme a value is, the less likely it is to occur. However, it's important to note that the tails in most distributions, even normal ones, go on forever. The probabilities of these values get smaller but are not impossible.

We refer to values far from the mean as long-tail values. Seeing as they are highly unlikely, we tend to forget about them. But if we get too caught up in seeing the world as normally distributed, we can forget that long-tail values tend to have an outsized impact. If you commute to work, it probably takes roughly the same time each day with minor variations. Once in a while, though, there might be a major issue like a road closure or broken-down train, which means it takes significantly longer, with the corresponding knock-on effects for your day.

Normal distributions can be contrasted with power law distributions. The values in a power law distribution cluster at low or high values. Even though the distribution might cover a large diversity of potential values, the vast majority of points on the curve will represent a comparably small subset. Wealth follows a typical power law distribution. Although the range of the possible wealth of an individual is quite large, most people cluster around a small range of values at one end of the curve. There are exponentially more people with $1,000 in assets than $1 billion. In our wealth curve, excessive wealth may be rare relative to the entire population, but there is no real cap on the wealth any one person can accumulate. In *Algorithms to Live By*, Brian Christian and Tom Griffiths say that power law distributions "are also known as 'scale-free distributions' because they characterize quantities that can plausibly range over many scales: a town can have tens, hundreds, thousands,

tens of thousands, hundreds of thousands, or millions of residents, so we can't pin down a single value for how big a 'normal' town should be."[4]

« Something normally distributed that's gone on seemingly too long is bound to end shortly; but the longer something in a power law distribution has gone on, the longer you can expect it to keep going. »
Brian Christian and Tom Griffiths[5]

Being able to identify when you are in a power law distribution situation can help you be realistic about the effort required to break out of the end cluster. It also forces you to consider the diverse range of potential values you have to contend with. When imagining future wealth, a diversity of possible data points can be motivational, but the opposite is true if your power law distribution is about potential calamities.

There are other distributions. Geometric distributions give you intuition as to when a particular success might happen, and binomial distributions can suggest how long it will take to get particular numbers of successes. The Poisson distribution can give you an idea of the distribution of rare events in a large population. And understanding memoryless distributions can make you feel better when you have to wait a while for the next bus.

You never really know if you have the right distribution for your data. You can test your distribution against the ideal and conclude that they are similar with a high degree of confidence, but future data points may change the distribution.

1
"Statistical Distributions," accessed October 2020, http://people.stern.nyu.edu/adamodar/New_Home_Page/StatFile/statdistns.htm.
2
"Statistical Distributions," ibid.
3
Leonard Mlodinow, *The Drunkard's Walk: How Randomness Rules Our Lives* (New York: Pantheon Books, 2009).
4
Brian Christian and Tom Griffiths, *Algorithms to Live By* (Toronto: Penguin, 2016).
5
Christian and Griffiths, ibid.

The Good Life

One philosophy that has been misunderstood since it was first articulated is that of Epicurus. Writing around 300 BCE, he came after Plato and Aristotle and was a contemporary of the early Stoics. One of his core ideas centered around the value of pleasure. Epicurus argued that pleasure is the only realistic measure we have of evaluating our lives. When we experience pleasure, things are good, and thus the pursuit of pleasure ought to be the driving force behind our choices.

At first glance, his philosophy seems to promote a life of selfish indulgence. Criticized for promoting a hedonism that would lead to the breakdown of society, Epicurean philosophy has endured much maligning over the millennia. However, a complete read of his philosophy reveals how pursuing the Epicurean ideal of pleasure actually leads to a very sedate, mindful life. Using the lens of a normal distribution curve helps us understand why and thus suggests modern uses for this ancient philosophy.

In his *Letter to Menoeceus*, Epicurus writes that "no pleasure is a bad thing in itself. But the things which produce certain pleasures bring troubles many times greater than the pleasures."[1] These latter types of pleasures are the ones we should avoid, because what positive feeling we gain in the short term is outweighed by the ensuing negative experience.

An excellent way to thus capture Epicurus's idea of pleasure is the bell curve. If we imagine those things that cause us great pain being the values on the far left and those things that cause us great pleasure as being on the far right, where we want to be is in the middle. The ideal state is one of neither pleasure nor pain. As Daniel Klein writes, for Epicurus, "happiness is tranquility."[2] The state we should aim to be in is at the top of a normal distribution curve—a life free from pain and also free from the negative consequences of excess pleasure.

Far from promoting the pursuit of indulgence in all things pleasurable, Epicurus writes, "For we are in need of pleasure only when we are in pain because of the absence of pleasure, and when we are not in pain, then we no longer need pleasure."[3] For Epicurus, "'pleasure' is the logical opposite of 'pain.' In other words, for him pleasure meant non-pain."[4] His conceptualizing of pleasure is what lends itself well to imagining life events plotted along a normal distribution curve. There are extremes at either end that are possible, but the most rewarding life is one that hovers around the middle, experiencing neither too much pain nor pleasure.

How does one achieve this midpoint, and what does life look like there? Epicurus said, "Therefore, becoming accustomed to simple, not extravagant, ways of life makes one completely healthy, makes man unhesitant in the face of life's necessary duties, puts us in a better condition for the times of extravagance which occasionally come along, and makes us fearless in the face of chance."[5] He believed that living a simple life was the best way to avoid pain, which is a pleasure in itself. Albeit a very sedate, mindful one.

It is the focus on pain reduction that gives us indicators on the value of aiming for the median of the normal distribution curve of life. As Catherine Wilson explains in *How to Be an Epicurean*, Epicurus "stated clearly that the best life is one free of deprivations, starting with freedom from hunger, thirst, and cold, and freedom from persistent fears and anxieties."[6] Thus conceptualizing pleasure as a life free from pain demonstrates why the extreme pleasure end of the curve would be well worth avoiding. Excess pleasure of the indulgent kind results often in pain. From the more visceral experiences of pain, such as a stomachache from too much rich food, to the painful psychological consequences of always choosing what feels right now at the expense of future satisfaction, when we focus on immediate gratification, we often sacrifice the happiness and contentment of our future selves.

For Epicurus, paying attention to the knowledge we gain from our experiences is critical for achieving a pain-free life. We need to be in tune with ourselves, noticing how our actions impact our bodies and psychological states. We also need to actively perform second-order thinking, considering the effects of the effects of our actions.

Epicurean philosophy thus invites us to reconceptualize what we consider pleasure in order to attain that pain-free median at the top of the curve. Wilson explains that "regardless of the trouble other people can cause for us, Epicurus believed close human relationships to be the greatest source of pleasure in life."[7] Pleasure is not then about the attainment of things, status, and stuff, but the interactions we have and the knowledge we gain from them. It is a philosophy of experience rather than consumption.

1
Epicurus, "Letter to Menoeceus," in *Classics of Western Philosophy*, 4th ed., edited by Steven M. Cahn (Indianapolis: Hackett, 1995).
2
Daniel Klein, foreword to *Epicurus: The Art of Happiness* (New York: Penguin Books, 2012).
3
Epicurus, ibid.
4
George K. Strodach, introduction to *Epicurus: The Art of Happiness* (New York: Penguin Books, 2012).
5
Epicurus, ibid.
6
Catherine Wilson, *How to Be an Epicurean: The Ancient Art of Living Well* (New York: Basic Books, 2019).
7
Wilson, ibid.

Compounding

—
Play the long game

Compounding

Compounding follows a power law, and power laws are magical things. Knowledge, experience, and relationships compound. When it comes to our personal capabilities, there are few limits to the possibilities suggested by this model. As with compound interest, most of the gains come at the end, not at the beginning. You have to keep reinvesting your returns to experience the exponential growth that is compounding.

Albert Einstein supposedly described compounding as the eighth wonder of the world. While he probably didn't, whoever did wasn't far off the mark. Compounding is an immensely powerful and often misunderstood force.

The most visible form of compounding is compound interest: when the interest on a sum of money, if reinvested and untouched, goes on to itself earn interest. This means the total sum of money grows faster and faster, like a snowball rolling down a hill. Even a small amount of money can compound into a fortune over a long enough time span.

« Play iterated games. All the returns in life, whether in wealth, relationships, or knowledge, come from compound interest. »

Naval Ravikant[1]

1
Tweet by Naval Ravikant (@naval), Twitter, May 31, 2018, 1:26 a.m., https://twitter.com/naval/status/1002103908947263488?lang=en.

2
Bill Fay, "How Compound Interest Works: Formula & How to Calculate," Debt.org., July 16, 2018, https://www.debt.org/blog/compound-interest-how-it-works/.

In the same way that money compounds and grows by earning interest, debt can compound too, even to the point where it becomes essentially impossible to pay off. Many people who get into debt fail to realize just how powerful compounding can be over time. As Debt.org[2] puts it, "Compound interest is a powerful tool for building wealth. It's also a devastating tool that can destroy wealth. It just depends on which side of the financial equation you use it."

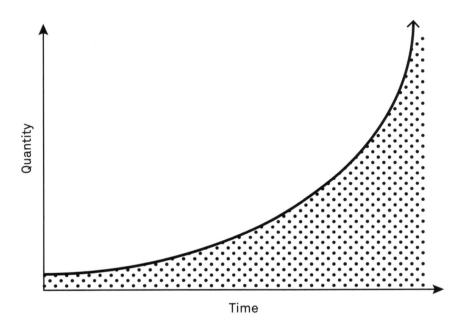

Exponential gains increase more dramatically the longer
we leave them to compound.

3
C. S. Lewis, *Complete C. S. Lewis
Signature Classics* (London:
HarperCollins, 2012).

Compounding is a crucial, versatile mental model to understand because it shows us that we can realize enormous gains through incremental efforts over time. It forces us to start thinking long term because the effects of compounding are only remarkable on a long timeline and most of the gains are realized near the end. Money isn't the only thing that compounds. Everything from knowledge to relationships has the ability to grow exponentially if we keep adding to it and reinvesting the returns. All that matters is making continuous progress, no matter how small.

Exponential functions are hard to envision, so it's no wonder we tend to underestimate the power of compounding. We're used to thinking in terms of linear dynamics, but compounding is nonlinear. Of course, other forms of compounding are not literal, and it's not like we can use a formula to calculate how something like knowledge builds upon itself. But we can use the concept as a metaphorical lens for thinking about how things grow.

« An apparently trivial indulgence in lust or anger today is the loss of a ridge or railway line or bridgehead from which the enemy may launch an attack otherwise impossible. »

C. S. Lewis[3]

In a process akin to money compounding, the impact of decisions we make early on in any endeavor grow in their impact over time. They can have a greater impact than decisions made later on because their consequences compound. For instance, imagine a new graduate who takes a job that is disconnected from their true interests. It might seem like a temporary, harmless choice, but it increases the chances the next job they get will be in the same area. The more experience they accrue, the better they're likely to be, and before they know it, switching is a challenge. It's important to consider how the consequences of our choices can multiply over time.

You don't always know the payoff

When we invest in things that compound, we don't always know how we will be able to leverage our compounding interest. Think of investing your money. If you know how much you will put into an account and the interest rate under which it will accrue, you can estimate how much money will be in your account in 20 years. What you cannot predict is what you will be able to do with that money. At the outset, you may imagine you'll buy yourself your dream home. But 20 years from now, you might leverage the money to make a different career choice. The security of having it in the bank might mean that you can take bigger risks to pursue your dreams.

Small investments over time in areas like relationships or learning have immediate benefit, which is usually what prompts us to undertake the initial commitment. But one of the most fascinating properties of using compounding as a lens is that it illuminates how investments now can give us opportunities later that we can't even imagine now.

One example of how compounding knowledge creates options can be seen by looking at the long-term effects of Jewish education norms. In *The Chosen Few*, Maristella Botticini and Zvi Eckstein trace the role of education in the Jewish religion and show how it was an investment that gave the Jewish people incredible opportunities.

In the first century of the Common Era, Jewish scholars and religious leaders "issued a religious ordinance requiring all Jewish fathers to send their sons from the age of six or seven to primary school to learn to read and study the Torah in Hebrew. Throughout the first millennium, no people other than the Jews had a norm requiring fathers to educate their sons."[4]

Botticini and Eckstein make it clear that there was no

4

Maristella Botticini and Zvi Eckstein, *The Chosen Few: How Education Shaped Jewish History, 70–1492* (Princeton: Princeton University Press, 2012).

5
Botticini and Eckstein, ibid.

6
Botticini and Eckstein, ibid.

7
Botticini and Eckstein, ibid.

plan in the early days of Jewish education that this practice would offer advantages down the road. As they explain, in the beginning "sending children to school to learn to read and study the Torah was a sacrifice with no economic returns in the agrarian economies in which Jews lived." Following the rule to educate was costly both in terms of maintaining the educational infrastructure and productive time lost. Initially the only tangible benefit to following the rule was probably something like spiritual satisfaction.[5]

When the norm of education was instituted, Jewish people were primarily farmers. Within a few centuries, they had given up farming for more lucrative professions as craftsmen, merchants, and moneylenders. Botticini and Eckstein demonstrate that "the direction of causality thus runs from investment in literacy and human capital to voluntarily giving up investing in land and being farmers, to entering urban occupations, to becoming mobile and migrating."[6]

The authors argue that "learning to read helps people learn to write. It also helps develop numeracy and the ability to compute prices, costs, interest rates, and exchange rates, and thus to keep account books." Therefore, literacy creates opportunities. Jewish people did not have to be farmers, a profession with less earning potential than those options available in the growing urban centers. Not only does literacy give you a competitive edge to be, say, a moneylender or merchant, but it also "raises productivity and earnings in these professions."[7]

First in the Muslim caliphates, and then in medieval Europe, Jewish people were consistently able to move into more financially rewarding professions at a significantly higher rate than non-Jewish people. "The literacy of the Jewish people, coupled with a set of contract-enforcement institutions developed during the five centuries after the destruction of the Second Temple, gave the Jews a comparative advantage in occupations such as crafts, trade, and moneylending." So while "most of the population in medieval Europe consisted mainly of

Hebrew persisted as a written language of the Jewish people from the beginning of the common era to the present, though it fell out of use as a spoken language for a long period. Throughout the centuries, this meant that Jewish people from different areas could share knowledge, such as rabbinic literature, in geographically diverse communities.

8
Botticini and Eckstein, ibid.

9
Botticini and Eckstein, ibid.

10
Botticini and Eckstein, ibid.

illiterate peasants, sharecroppers, and agricultural laborers," Jewish people were able to leverage their literacy (and other aspects of their culture) to specialize in lucrative professions.[8] Jewish people took advantage of the opportunity their education gave them by moving into professions that paid well.

Just because you don't anticipate all the opportunities an investment will give you down the road doesn't mean you don't take advantage of them when they arise. From very early days, Jewish people invested in education. At first, likely for spiritual reasons, but the investment nonetheless later allowed them to capitalize on changes in the world economy. Their literacy allowed them to be the first movers when new professions arose that required and thrived on an understanding of words and numbers. Botticini and Eckstein explain that "the Jewish community reaped the benefits of their investment in literacy by selecting into urban skilled occupations."[9]

We cannot know all the opportunities that will arise as a result of the investments we make today. Botticini and Eckstein conclude that "high levels of literacy and the existence of contract-enforcement institutions became the levers of the Jewish people." And they used these levers to "continue to search for opportunities to reap return from their investment."[10]

The lesson of applying the lens of compounding to Jewish education norms is to invest in things that provide you with benefit. For the early Jewish people, they received from their investment in literacy a benefit in terms of their religious commitment. As time continued, the knowledge they accrued compounded, giving later generations exceptional opportunities. Recognizing that knowledge compounds helps us be mindful about how we can leverage our investment in the future and to look for the opportunities compounding will open up.

Reinvesting experience

Experience also compounds. If we choose to build on the skills we've developed by using them in new situations, we are significantly more capable later in life. Using compounding as a lens to look at personal experience isn't about proving an equation. Rather, this model can give us insight on what it means to reinvest what we learn through experience.

In 2008 Mireya Mayor*, a scientist and explorer for National Geographic, participated in an expedition to retrace the path of Henry Morton Stanley, the man sent to find Dr. David Livingstone in Tanzania. Livingstone, the 19th century rock star explorer of his generation, had gone missing, and Stanley was sent by an American newspaper to try to locate him. Mayor was part of a team of four who were filmed trying to complete the treacherous journey with the same equipment Stanley would have had in 1865. Despite challenging terrain, illness, and a variety of dangerous animals, she and the rest of the group completed the challenge. How she was able to do things like trek for hours in incredibly hot, humid temperatures while battling dysentery can be illuminated through the lens of compounding.

One of the key components of financial compounding is the reinvestment. When the money you have invested earns interest, you can't take it out and go buy a new pair of shoes. You have to reinvest that interest into the original investment, so you increase the amount of funds earning interest.

We can think of using what we've learned in a similar way. The insights we get from experiences will pay off more if we reinvest them into further experiences.

Exponential gains from what we've learned aren't standard. Not everyone who has a degree in journalism wins the Pulitzer. Not everyone who has a lemonade stand as a kid ends up running a national juice chain.

Humans have evolved to be pretty good at using past experience to guide future decisions, so a lot of knowledge compounding happens naturally over time, especially when we are young. But sometimes we get stale. We stop reinvesting that interest because we stop challenging ourselves. We stop

*
Mireya Mayor - (b. 1973). In 1999 she became the first female wildlife correspondent for National Geographic's Ultimate Explorer series. Part of a team of researchers who identified a new species of mouse lemur in Madagascar, she convinced the prime minister of the country to designate its habitat a national park.

11
Mireya Mayor, *Pink Boots and a Machete* (Washington, D.C.: National Geographic, 2011).

12
Mayor, ibid.

compounding our learning. Twenty years of living become the same year repeated 20 times.

To gain insight and eventually wisdom, we need to reinvest our knowledge and let it compound. One way to do that is to be more deliberate about identifying how our past experiences can improve our chances of success in future ones.

Getting back to Mireya Mayor, it's unlikely she would have been successful on her Tanzanian expedition if it had been her first. It was tough. The conditions and the team dynamics were brutal. But she had years of insights from previous expeditions to draw on and apply.

Her first expedition was to Guyana in 1996, where she started doing the field research necessary to become a primatologist. She recounts how she packed for this expedition to study a rare species of monkey: "I purchased my plane tickets, the impractical teddy-bear backpack, and a pair of trendy hiking boots."[11] Her luggage also included a sleeping bag, tweezers, and a little black dress. She learned that the sleeping bag was unusable due to the deadly creatures that crawled around the forest floor and that hiking boots need to do more than look good. But she also learned that tweezers are invaluable on field expeditions because they can be used to remove a variety of small organisms that like to lodge in the skin.

In reflecting on her knowledge about packing gained from fieldwork, she writes, "By the time I had a few other trips to remote places under my belt, I had become an expert at packing minimalist." It was expertise gained through experience and included insights on the value of packing mirrors (for signaling and tick checks), tampons (for starting fires), and Windex (for neutralizing flesh-eating bacteria).[12]

Beyond what to pack for survival in the jungle, Mayor's story suggests further reinvestment of experiences compounding into her eventual success. Granted, she doesn't use the words *deliberate reinvestment*, but the stories she shares demonstrate a conscious reflection on how to use

Mouse lemurs are the smallest primates, having a total length of less than 27cm. There are over 24 different species of mouse lemur, and all are critically endangered largely due to habitat loss.

13
Mayor, ibid.

14
Mayor, ibid.

past knowledge. For example, before she was an explorer and primatologist, she was a cheerleader for the Miami Dolphins American football team. At first glance one might think there was no useful knowledge that could be applied from one job to another, but Mayor writes, "Working under pressure is nothing new to me. Even when I was an NFL cheerleader, I had to perform under the gun. Dancing in front of more than 75,000 screaming fans, remembering to smile, and making sure my hair remained in place in scorching heat after twisting an ankle—that's pressure."[13]

Mayor made numerous trips to Madagascar to study small primates that are unique to the island, like Perrier's sifaka. Over time she built relationships with everyone from other primatologists, organizations with grant money, and the locals she relied on to navigate the island and support the expeditions. After years of fieldwork, she became a wildlife correspondent for National Geographic. She says that "years before I appeared on television pointing out little-known facts about snakes or describing the mating behaviors of gorillas, I was putting in the legwork."[14]

This legwork gave her the knowledge to take on a vast array of assignments for National Geographic, from diving with sharks and giant squid off the coast of Mexico to working with leopards and giraffes in Namibia. Following Mayor through the journey of her career, from cheerleader and graduate student to television host, explorer, and primatologist, it's clear that her early experiences allowed her to take on increasingly complicated and dangerous challenges.

Which brings us back to Tanzania and the expedition to re-create the journey of Stanley's ultimately successful search for Livingstone. The journey was dangerous right to the final day. This is her description of the end:

> Back in canoes, we paddled up a tributary that ran
> through a swamp; it was slow going. A blood-red torrent

of unknown origin came out of the swamp and reminded me of descriptions in Stanley's journals. When we couldn't go any farther, we stepped out into the swamp. There were snakes and crocs everywhere. We were treading through mud up to our waists when suddenly my bad cheerleading ankle gave out on me. I tore a toe-nail off as I landed face first in the mud. This was no spa treatment. In the process I lost my shoe and would have to walk through the swamp barefoot, getting slashed by razor-sharp grasses while being sucked into the mud. Tanzania had already kicked my ass, but it was nothing compared to these last few miles.[15]

Mayor's success at completing the arduous expedition is testament to her ability to reinvest the knowledge accrued from past experiences and capitalize on the resulting growth. A career like Mayor's reveals the power of using the lens of compounding to shape how we use our hard-won insights to allow us to take on exponentially greater challenges.

Compounding relationships

Relationships are another thing that compound, becoming stronger over time if we keep investing in win-win dynamics. Imagine a network of nodes that connect to each other at random. The likelihood of any given node receiving an additional connection is proportional to the number of connections it already has. Through randomness, a small number of nodes will end up receiving most of the connections—a phenomenon called preferential attachment.

Preferential attachment is a type of compounding that occurs when a certain thing (such as money or friends) is more likely to accrue to individuals or entities that already have more of it. For instance, people who have many friends tend to keep making more and more. They have more opportunities to meet new people through the ones they already know.

Sidney Weinberg - (1891-1969).
Weinberg started working at the
age of ten, selling newspapers
and shucking oysters. As head of
Goldman Sachs, he oversaw Ford's
initial public offering, the largest
ever at that time. Famous for his
relationship-building abilities and
warm nature, he never tried to hide
his unusual outsider origins.

16
Michael J. Mauboussin, *The
Success Equation: Untangling
Skill and Luck in Business, Sports,
and Investing* (Boston: Harvard
Business Review Press, 2012).

For someone to gain a serious cumulative advantage, it's not even necessary for them to have dramatically different starting conditions to their peers. Michael J. Mauboussin writes in *The Success Equation* that small differences in the economic climate when someone graduates from college can compound. For each additional percentage point higher the unemployment rate is when someone graduates, they can expect to earn 6% to 7% less in their career.[16] To graduate during a recession means having a serious disadvantage, regardless of how smart someone is or how hard they work.

Thus where you start in life may have a huge impact on where you end up, but it doesn't have to define it. Some people can achieve extraordinary things against the odds by understanding and leveraging the concept of cumulative advantage. Such people grab hold of one tiny advantage and get every additional possible benefit out of it. Then they keep repeating that process until they get where they want to be. One way of doing this is through networking. Each person you know has the potential to lead you to additional people. The stronger your network, the more influential or interesting the people you could get introduced to are. Professional and social networks build upon themselves. Some people have an uncanny ability to take a connection with one person and use it to accelerate their careers.

Sidney James Weinberg[*] was not your typical Wall Street banker—not by today's standards, nor even by the standards of the early 20th century when he rose to the pinnacle of the banking world. For a start, there was his background. Weinberg didn't come from an illustrious family. He didn't have a top-tier education or a long list of credentials. He didn't get a leg up from well-positioned Wall Street contacts either. Instead, he was the son of a Polish liquor dealer and one of 11 children. His education didn't stretch beyond his 13th year, when a teacher deemed him ready to enter the workforce. By that point, he'd already been working for several years selling newspapers and doing other menial jobs.[17]

Nor did he particularly look or sound the part of a Wall Street success story. Weinberg was just five feet, four inches tall and was usually dwarfed by the other bankers around him. His back was marked with knife scars from childhood street fights.[18] He never made any effort to disguise his distinctive Brooklyn accent or lie about his background, even going as far as to proudly keep the spittoon he polished when he first got his start doing low-level work at Goldman Sachs.[19] Weinberg was famously outspoken and always willing to make jokes at his own expense.[20]

Yet despite his unorthodox background, Weinberg became one of the most powerful people on Wall Street, holding the position of Goldman Sachs CEO for 39 years. What set him apart was his understanding of cumulative advantage. His greatest assets were the relationships he carefully built and then continued to build upon to form more relationships. He understood that the more people he knew, the more people he could meet. By focusing on strengthening and then leveraging his relationships, Weinberg achieved remarkable success.

He started off on Wall Street aged about 15. These being the days before security was a thing, he picked a skyscraper and went from office to office, looking for any available work. Eventually he earned a menial job as a janitor's assistant at Goldman Sachs for a few dollars a week.[21]

One day Weinberg was tasked with taking a delivery to Paul Sachs, the founder's son. Sachs was charmed by him and had him promoted to the mailroom. Having a sudden opportunity to prove himself, Weinberg made an impression by reorganizing the mailroom to be more efficient, convincing Sachs he had potential in a banking role within the company. Sachs paid for Weinberg to take his first banking course and mentored him through university. When Weinberg returned to Wall Street after serving in World War I, his hard work paid off: he was now a salesperson. Eight years later, he was a securities trader.

17
William D. Cohan, *Money and Power: How Goldman Sachs Came to Rule the World* (New York: Anchor Books, 2012).

18
Adam Baldwin, *Heroes and Villains of Finance: The 50 Most Colorful Characters in the History of Finance* (Hoboken: John Wiley & Sons, 2015).

19
Jonathan A. Knee, *The Accidental Investment Banker: Inside the Decade That Transformed Wall Street* (New York: Random House, 2007).

20
Cohan, ibid.

21
Baldwin, ibid.

2970—The "Bulls and Bears" of Wall Street, New York City.
Copyright 1907, by Standard Scenic Company.

Wall Street has a difficult, controversial history, having profited
from slavery and due to its role in financial crises.

Another three years after that, Weinberg was the CEO. While we don't know exactly what happened during those years, everything began with that lucky meeting with Paul Sachs, which gave him a chance to prove himself. From there, Weinberg was able to get a better role in the company, giving him access to even more people and more opportunities for promotion.

We can understand Weinberg's phenomenal rise if we consider the ways in which he worked to build beneficial relationships that offered him accruing influence and opportunities throughout his entire career. We can see clues as to how he managed this further on in his career. One way that Weinberg built relationships was by serving on the boards of corporations—at one point over 30, for which he attended over 250 meetings per year. He befriended every CEO he could by being as helpful as possible. Board meetings weren't a distraction from his main job; they were a way to further it.

When Franklin D. Roosevelt ran for president, he was an unpopular candidate with Wall Street. Weinberg saw a chance to stand out by supporting him and raising campaign funds, bridging business and politics. He already had influence on Wall Street, which he was able to convert into political influence. After Roosevelt won the election, Weinberg organized an advisory board of corporate executives, all carefully chosen to align with his own business interests.[22] He knew that giving the executives such a high-status position would ensure their patronage later on. Many indeed became clients of Goldman Sachs.

It's worth noting that Goldman Sachs was not the giant it is today, meaning Weinberg's political influence was unusual and likely the result of his relationship-building.[23] He always declined offers of political roles; Wall Street was his world, and politics served simply as means of building relationships. Throughout his career, he advised a total of five US presidents, using the entry point of Roosevelt's campaign.

Building lasting relationships with Goldman Sachs,

22
Charles D. Ellis, *The Partnership: The Making of Goldman Sachs* (London: Penguin, 2009).

23
"How Goldman Sachs Landed on Top," *The Week*, August 13, 2009, https://theweek.com/articles/502831/how-goldman-sachs-landed.

24
"Business: Everybody's Broker Sidney Weinberg," *Time*, December 8, 1958, http://content.time.com/time/subscriber/article/0,33009,864550,00.html.

clients was also an important part of Weinberg's work. But he didn't just help people who were of direct use to him. One story tells of him sending $100 a week to a business rival who fell on hard times. As he told others, friendship should always come before business.[24]

Weinberg saw both the number of his relationships and their durability compound over time. His conscientious approach to his interactions with people suggests he invested in his relationships. When we aim to make our relationships reciprocal, seeking to give us as much as possible before we take, we can reap the benefits of compounding. The more we strengthen and deepen relationships, the more they build on themselves. The Wall Street of Weinberg's heyday was built on relationships. These days, we're not likely to see another Sidney Weinberg because the old system of reciprocity is no longer sufficient. When we create societies where starting conditions matter more than capacity and effort, we narrow the range of who can reap the benefits of compounding even if they start from nothing. That initial foot in the door upon which relationships build can be the hardest part.

— Sidebar: Basic Income and Death Taxes

Conclusion

Compounding is an incredibly useful mental model because it requires us to think long term about our knowledge, experiences, and relationships. It suggests to us that continual reinvestment of what we learn and in the people around us is the best way to set ourselves up for reliable, steady gains. The majority of success doesn't happen by accident, and the lens of compounding illuminates the investments we need to make to get there.

Basic Income and Death Taxes

Compounding and preferential attachment are so powerful that societies often have rules to mitigate the exponential accumulation of advantage.

One system that tries to level the playing field by supporting network development for those who don't—or can't—start building these networks early enough is basic income. Sometimes we need to disrupt the power of a preferential attachment cycle, whether it's to improve equity or just the flow of ideas, by increasing the number of people who can contribute.

There is no one definition of basic income. In some definitions it is income distributed to everyone within a geographic region regardless of other income or assets. In other definitions it is given out on a scale that factors in other wealth. Sometimes it is presented as a taxable income; other times it is put forward as a tax-free benefit. Regardless of the particular definition, "the one fundamental defining characteristic of a basic income of any type is that it must be unconditional."[1] The recipient of a basic income does not have to do anything to justify the continued receipt of the income if they stay in the same geographical region.

In this sense basic income is very different from welfare, which is a conditional income often dependent on job searches, ability to work, and neither owning nor accumulating any assets. It is subject to the discretion of caseworkers and thus is inherently unstable and subjective.

One of the arguments for basic income, as presented by Philippe van Parijs and Yannick Vanderborght in their book on the subject, is that "much of what we earn must be ascribed not to our efforts, but to externalities which owe nothing to them."[2] Although we may tell ourselves that our success is solely the result of our efforts, a significant contributing factor is the number of connections we have. Some of these connections seem obvious, like family connections to jobs or educational connections to information. Others, though, many of us take for granted. If we think of the network we engage with in order to work, connections to dentists and other health services, to quality child care, or to landlords and banks for housing security, we can see that success means leveraging a large network composed of many nodes.

Often the connection to a node is solely a matter of money. Education costs money, and so do dentists. It's harder to get a job with minimal education, or poor dental hygiene, or a lack of reliable access to a shower. Basic income programs are usually designed to provide enough money to meet these core requirements in order for people to have the option of pursuing meaningful work or social contribution. We can

think of people using basic income to increase their access to nodes in a network that will then accrue opportunities.

Studies of basic income have demonstrated that both education and health outcomes improve when people receive it. Economist Evelyn Forget examined basic income studies to show that it often results in young people obtaining more education and less use by recipients of the local health care system. She also argues that "basic income has been found to support social solidarity in various places around the world," leading to better social outcomes in communities.[3] Possibly this is because more connections by more people lead to a more stable network.

By giving people a predictable, secure income, they can increase their connections with nodes that accrue benefit, such as education. In *The Case for Universal Basic Income*, Louise Haagh references the work of Brian Barry, who says that "basic income is a way to abate cumulative disadvantage." It gives people access to power and "can contribute to the erasing social distinctions linked with insecurity and lack of status."[4]

Parijs and Vanderborght are careful to note that a basic income does not aim to equalize outcomes. "Rather, it aims to make less unequal, and distribute more fairly, real freedom, possibilities, and opportunities."[5] Essentially, it aims to equalize the benefits of preferential attachment.

While basic income attempts to give everyone a better starting point, societies have also developed ways to try to reduce the extent to which advantages accumulate to existing winners across the generations. If nothing is certain in life except death and taxes, then death taxes are the surest thing of all. As an umbrella term for inheritance and state taxes, this refers to deductions that governments make from the assets individuals leave behind after they die, even if those same assets were already taxed during their lifetime. Death taxes are typically a percentage of assets over a certain value with reductions or exemptions depending on whether someone leaves their estate to a spouse or partner, their level of charitable donations, and so on. This may be deducted from the entire estate before it goes to any heirs or from individual inheritances.

In theory, such charges help prevent wealth from becoming increasingly concentrated in the hands of a few families and force the richest people to make a sizable contribution to society after their deaths. Inheritances provide heirs with advantages they haven't worked for but that still provide a way to gain further advantages. The idea behind death taxes is to mitigate that, even if only in part.

1
Evelyn L. Forget, *Basic Income for Canadians* (Toronto: James Lorimer, 2018).
2
Philippe van Parijs and Yannick Vanderborght, *Basic Income* (Cambridge: Harvard University Press, 2017).
3
Forget, ibid.
4
Louise Haagh, *The Case for Universal Basic Income* (Cambridge: Polity, 2019).
5
Parijs and Vanderborght, ibid.

Supporting Idea:

Network Effects

Network effects occur when the utility of a product or service increases as more people use it. More users mean more value for all users. An obvious example is the telephone. If you own one but none of your friends do, it's not much use. But with each additional friend who gets one, the utility increases.

Network effects may also be indirect, as when a group of people using something for one purpose generate value for a group using it for a different purpose. For instance, more drivers joining a ride-sharing app means more utility for riders.

Network effects set off a reinforcing feedback loop wherein the added value attracts new users, who in turn create new users. Getting network effects started can be difficult, as certain types of products and services have little use until they reach a critical mass of users. But once this occurs, it creates a strong competitive advantage over new entrants to the market, even if they have a better product.

However, first movers are not always the most successful in a market, as later movers can learn from the early mistakes. Ultimately network effects can lead to a winner-takes-all market, where one product or service captures most of the users. Competitors can only secure a negligible share. Users become reluctant to switch to an alternative because of the advantages created by network effects. Once network effects take hold, a product or service will continue to grow in popularity even without additional marketing.

The single most important factor behind the rise of many of the most significant technologies over the last two centuries is network effects. It not only contributes to the success of new technologies; it also secures it long term. For this reason, companies put a lot of effort into attracting early users in the hopes of reaching the critical mass requisite for network effects to take hold. Often, it is a matter of luck.

Network effects don't just occur for technology. We can apply the concept to any situation where the value of something increases the more people use it. If a large number of skilled workers live in an area, it will attract companies offering well-paid jobs that use their skills, attracting yet more workers. Stores of value like gold are subject to network effects. The more people hold them as a long-term store of value, the more stable their prices become and the more appealing they are to future investors.

But network effects cannot continue forever. More users only build more value up to a certain point, past which negative network effects set in. This occurs when user base growth results in *less*, not more, value. Negative network effects can take several forms. A product or service may become overloaded and unable to serve its users as before. For instance, a public train network may benefit from a growing user base. More users mean more investment in infrastructure, more frequent service, and possibly lower cost. However, if too many people use it, the trains may become overcrowded and dangerous. If there isn't space to build more train lines, this may reduce value for users.

Negative network effects can also occur when too many users change the fundamental nature of something. A small online forum may have a tight-knit user base with high standards for posting. If there is an influx of new users, they may change its norms and dilute its value, destroying what attracted them in the first place.

Sampling

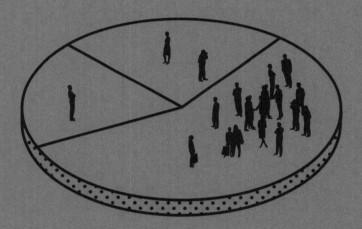

—

Your samples become your reality

Sampling

Understanding the influence and importance of sampling is a fundamental key to understanding the world better. The mental model of sampling is a first principle for a number of concepts in mathematics, especially in statistics. Seeing as we often use statistics to gain a picture of reality, taking sampling into account will broaden your knowledge of other areas involving measurement, such as psychology. It will also help you think about risk and reward while delineating luck from skill.

> « Numbers are intellectual witnesses that belong only to mankind. »
>
> **Honoré de Balzac**

When we want to get information about a population (meaning a set of alike people, things, or events), we usually need to look at a sample (meaning a part of the population). It is usually not possible or even desirable to consider the entire population, so we aim for a sample that represents the whole.[1] We use samples to tell us about the world. The exception is a census, which aims to include everyone, not just a sample.

Sample size refers to the number of people, things, or events we look at from a population. It can have an enormous influence on the results we get. According to the law of large numbers, the larger the sample size, the more the result obtained will converge with the true value. For instance, the likelihood of getting any of the numbers from one to six when you roll a fair die is one in six. If you roll a die six times, it would be unusual for each number to show up once. If you roll it 600 times, the frequency of each number would be closer to one in six, and even closer if you roll it 6,000 times or 60,000 times.

Sampling gives you an idea of the possible values in your data set. The law of large numbers helps identify the

[1]
Supriya Bhalerao and Prashant Kadam, "Sample Size Calculation," *International Journal of Ayurveda Research* 1, no. 1 (2010): 55.

2
Bhalerao and Kadam, ibid.

probability of any of those values occurring.

As a rule of thumb, more measurements mean more accurate results, all else being equal. Small sample sizes can produce skewed results. If your sample for assessing the color of swans is the white birds in your neighborhood pond, you might deduce all swans are white. But if you looked at a larger sample of swans from different places, you'd discover some are black. Even if you took a small sample from your local pond dozens of times, it might not be representative and would always mislead you. Small sample sizes can fail to include rare or outlier results, making it seem like they don't exist. If you are once again just looking at the birds in a particular pond, you might ascertain that all swans have two legs. But if you took a much larger sample (or visited a wildlife sanctuary), you may well discover a swan that has been in an accident and only has one leg.

One area where sampling is especially salient is in scientific studies of people, in which case the sample size is the number of participants. The larger the sample, the lower the margin of error and the higher the sampling confidence level, meaning the more probable it is the results will generalize to the whole population.[2]

But we have to make trade-offs. Studies with small sample sizes are not useless. Managing the funding and logistics for a larger study might be impractical, so a small one can provide evidence that further research is worthwhile. Researchers can combine a number of small studies in a meta-analysis to get a broader overview. If the costs of a study are high, such as a psychological study in which participants are subjected to a great deal of distress, a small sample may be more ethical. Researchers have to consider a range of factors to establish the right sample size, including the expected effect size and the expected dropout ratio.

In addition to being an appropriate size, samples need to be random to be representative of a varied population. This

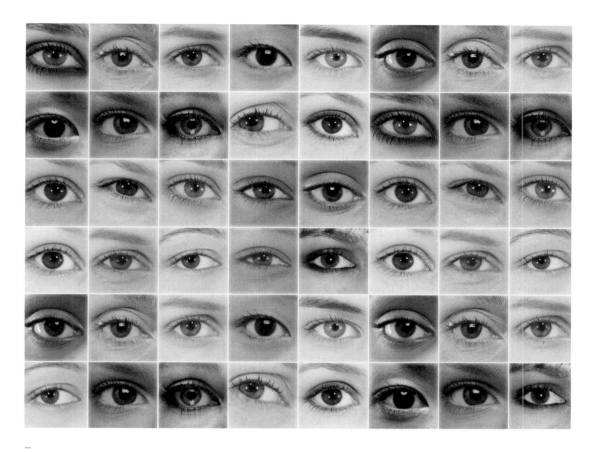

Choosing an appropriate sample size for research is complicated. Factors include the minimum required to get statistically meaningful data, how much funding is available, and the ethics of subjecting people to the research.

means every person, thing, or event within the population has an equal chance of ending up in the sample.[3] George Gallup[*], who could be called the inventor of the opinion poll, once gave a useful analogy for the necessity of a random sample. He said you can decide if a pot of soup needs more seasoning by tasting a single spoonful—provided you've stirred it well first.[4]

A large sample size is only certain to be more accurate if it is representative, which makes it important to be aware of sampling biases. For instance, the healthy worker effect refers to how people who are unwell are less likely to be in employment, meaning that workers within a field or for a company will be, on average, healthier than the general population. If you're trying to measure the impact of a dangerous chemical on factory workers who handle it, a sample of those currently employed in that type of factory will not be representative—no matter how large. You'll need to factor in those whose health has been damaged so much they no longer work or have moved to another field.[5]

Thinking about sampling can help us overcome some forms of bias. For example, we tend to place too much emphasis on anecdotes, in particular those coming from people close to us or that make good stories. We're all the more inclined to respect anecdotes if they confirm what we already believe. An anecdote is a sample size of one, and we should collect more data points if possible. The exception is when one result indicates something is possible. The first person to survive a heart transplant was more than an anecdote.

Thinking about your samples also teaches that sometimes what you need to do to see the world in a more accurate way is to obtain a larger or more representative sample. Traveling, living in a big city, or otherwise finding a way to meet more diverse people may make you more tolerant. Exposing yourself to a broader range of ideas through interdisciplinary, far-reaching reading may make you more open-minded. Learning more about the history of your industry and accumulating

[*] George Gallup - (1901-1984). Once a professor of journalism, he founded his polling company, the American Institute of Public Opinion, in 1955. The company later became Gallup, which is still in operation today. He also wrote about improving education and founded Quill and Scroll, an international honor society for high school journalists.

[3] Bhalerao and Kadam, ibid.

[4] David Spiegelhalter, *The Art of Statistics: Learning from Data* (London: Pelican, Penguin Books, 2019).

[5] Divyang Shah, "Healthy Worker Effect Phenomenon," *Indian Journal of Occupational and Environmental Medicine* 13, no. 2 (2009): 77.

6
Simon Winchester, *The Professor and the Madman* (New York: Harper Collins, 2005).

7
Winchester, ibid.

more experience may make you more risk aware as you learn about rarer yet more extreme possibilities.

Defining a language

It is important to recognize when one measurement isn't enough. The making of the first *Oxford English Dictionary* (OED) is a story that demonstrates the value of increasing sample size, in terms of the increased accuracy many measurements can bring.

It's hard to imagine the effort required for the first dictionary of a language to be created. We have grown up in a post-dictionary world, where all words are catalogued with their definitions and history. In looking through any dictionary, it's easy to find words that have multiple meanings. Does *dove* refer to a bird or the past action of jumping into a pool? To capture the entire history and use of a language, the first dictionaries must consider hundreds of thousands of data points. The OED, although not the first English dictionary, was the first to accomplish the feat of a thorough cataloguing of the English language.

Talk of the OED first got underway in 1856. At the outset, the purpose of the OED was described thus: "A dictionary should be a record of all words that enjoy any recognized lifespan in the standard language." The group instigating the task felt that a proper dictionary should not just show contemporary usage of words, but they "had to have, for every word, a passage quoted from literature that showed where each word was used first."[6]

What would producing this kind of record entail? As Simon Winchester explains in *The Professor and the Madman*, it "would mean the reading of everything and the quoting of everything that showed anything of the history of the words that were to be cited. The task would be gigantic, monumental, and—according to the conventional thinking of the times—impossible."[7] Essentially, to produce the OED, all books ever

THE NEW ENGLISH DICTIONARY.

Special quotations wanted for H.

LIST I.   Dec. 1896.

Where the date stands *before* a word, an earlier quotation is wanted; where the date *follows*, a later instance is wanted; for words without a date all quotations will be welcome. Every quotation should be furnished with an exact reference to date, author, work, edition, volume, chapter, page, etc., and sent to the Editor, addressed, 'Dr. Murray, Oxford.'

H.

1530. H.
1822 h-bone 1822
1893 h-less
1777 haar
hab
habeck
habena, -ar
habeury
habennla, -ar
1634 haberdash, v. 1644
1593 haberdashery
1530 haberdine
1610 habick
1860 habitant
1809 habitat
1819 habit-maker
1834 habit-shirt
1818 habitué
habrocome
habromania, a.
habroneme, a.
habrothrix
1822 hachel 1822
1885 hachure
1808 hacienda
1857 hack (*Football*)
hack (of boar)
hack (axe)
1740 hack (horse)
1792 hack (drudge)
1781 hack, a. (trite)
1673 hack, v. (chap) 1673
hack (cough)
1796 hackberry
1868 hackle (*Herald.*)
1616 hackle, v. (flax)
1862 hackler (of flax, etc.)
hackling-knife
hackling-machine
1845 hackmatack
1635 hackney-coach
1851 hack-work
1859 hack-writer
1849 haddock (pile of hay, etc.)
1736 hadji
1612 hadji
1647 hæcceity
1876 hæmaglobin
1840 hæmal, a.
1854 hæmapophysis
hæmatal
1865 hæmatein
hæmatherm
1842 hæmatic
1819 hæmatin

HÆMATITE

1567 hæmatite
1796 hæmatitic
1873 hæmatized
hæmato- and hæmo- compounds, generally
1876 hæmatoblast
1882 hæmatoblastic
1852 hæmatocele
1761 hæmatocyst
1803 hæmatode
1866 hæmatogenous
hæmatoglobin
1874 hæmatoid
hæmatology
1865 hæmatose
1866 hæmatothermal
hæmogastric
1854 hæredipety
hæreslarch
hæresiography
hæresiology
haffet (of a lid)
1832 haffle, v.
1835 hag (fish)
1855 hag (white mist)
1828 hag (brushwood)
hag (bird)
hag-a-bag 1725
1874 hagadah, haggadah
1866 hagadic, haggadic
1837 hagberry
1600 haggard
1420 haggis
1819 haggis-bag
hag-gull
1874 hagiocracy
hagiograph
1649 Hagiographa
1812 hagiography
1875 hagiolater, -ous
1805 hagiolatry
hagiology, -ist
1875 hagioscope
1886 hagiotypic
hag-moth
1866 hag-ridden
1886 hag-rope
1855 hag-snare
hag's-teeth
1845 hag-weed
1631 hag-worm
ha-ha!
ha-ha, sb.
1797 haik
1571 hail, sb. (health)

HAIL

1825 within hail
1836 out of hail
1804 hail (goal)
hail, a. = hale
1841 hail from
1611 hail-Mary
1818 hail-storm
1785 hain, v. (save)
1742 split hairs
1761 hair-dresser
1870 hair-oil
1839 hair-pin
1663 hair-powder
1584 hair's-breadth
1756 hair-shirt
1850 hair-splitting, -er
hair-spring
1840 hair-streak
1836 hair-trigger
1706 hake (a hook)
1846 hake (of plough)
1768 hake (frame)
1602 haking (fish) 1602
1881 halacha, -ist
1881 halation
1557 halberdier
1793 halberts (*Milit.*)
1650 halcyon
hale, v. intr. 1727
halecine, a.
halecoid
half (side) 1600
1658 by half
1821 to cry halves
1817 half-past . . . o'clock
1758 half-and-half
1635 half-blood
1791 half-breed
1798 half-caste
half-curlew
half-deal
1626 half-deck
half-deck (limpet)
1732 half-faced 1732
1621 half-hearted
1631 half-holiday
1565 halfly 1674
1627 half-moon
1860 half-mourning
1669 half-pay
1720 half price
half-snipe
1865 half-timer
half-wit 1678
1601 halibut
halichondroid

written in the English language would have to be read in order to pull out not only all the words the language has ever produced, but their first instances, their multiple uses, and their evolutions.

At what can be regarded as the kickoff meeting, Winchester describes that, with a sensibility that was out of step for their place and time, the group of men who sought to produce a dictionary of the English language realized the only way it would ever be achieved would be to enlist the help of large numbers of people "to peruse all of English literature—and to comb the London and New York newspapers and the most literate of the magazines and journals—must be instead the combined action of many."[8] In effect, production of the dictionary required combing through millions of pages of words.

Why wasn't it enough to just note the common usage of a word and carry on? Let's briefly consider the word *take*. It's fairly common and likely one we use every day. But to define it based on one example of usage would be a mistake. It has at least four definitions:

1.   To remove something (e.g., I take that away from you)
2.   To hold something (e.g., I take my mother's hand)
3.   A recorded scene from a movie (e.g., We shot that in one take)
4.   The amount of something gained from a source (e.g., taxation or being paid off; he was on the take)

To get a complete understanding of the word *take*, you need to factor in all of these possible uses. In order to include *take* in the dictionary, all of these uses need to be found. And you need to make sure there aren't any more.

An army of volunteers read through every book in the English language, preparing submissions for the editorial group. As Winchester describes, "Each volunteer would take a slip of paper, write at its top left-hand side the target word, and

Insurance

Insurance, as a concept, is predicated on the idea of reducing uncertainty by spreading the cost of adverse events between groups of people, companies, and other entities, and across time. It's impossible to predict if a given individual will get their laptop stolen or break their leg, or if a particular company will have a factory burn down or cause an oil spill, and so on. But with a large enough sample size, it's possible to predict with reasonable accuracy the expected number of payouts per year. Insurance companies use this information to calculate how much to charge. Each customer pays much less than they would if they were to face a calamity uninsured, but most never receive a payout.

Insuring a small group of customers tends to be high risk, and a big group is usually low risk. With enough customers, an insurance company can effectively eliminate the uncertainty. Individual risks are uncertain; aggregate risks are predictable.[1] In order for a risk to be safely insurable, it must show some uniformity across the population.

Occasionally insurers are blindsided by extreme or unforeseen events. The 1906 San Francisco earthquake was one of the most severe natural disasters in US history, leading to insured losses of over $6.3 billion in today's money. Such an earthquake (with an estimated magnitude of 7.7 to 8.3) is only expected every 200 years, making it a surprise for insurers. Around 14 insurance companies went bankrupt as a result of the payouts, and the losses were equal to all profit the industry earned over the prior 47 years.[2] Due to the earthquake's rarity and the extent of the damage, much of it caused by subsequent fires, sample size didn't help in this case.

In other cases, an event can essentially be the first of its kind and be so extreme and rare that no sample size makes it safe to insure. Following the 9/11 terrorist attacks, which led to payouts of $31.6 billion, the US government had to intervene to ensure companies continued offering terrorism risk insurance.[3]

1
Parimal Kumar Ray, *Agricultural Insurance* (Oxford: Pergamon Press, 1966).
2
"The San Francisco Earthquake of 1906: An Insurance Perspective," Insurance Information Institute, accessed January 27, 2020, https://www.iii.org/article/san-francisco-earthquake-1906-insurance-perspective.
3
"What Impact Have Terrorist Attacks Had on the Insurance Industry?," Investopedia, October 9, 2019, https://www.investopedia.com/ask/answers/050115/what-impact-have-terrorist-attacks-had-insurance-industry.asp.

9
Winchester, ibid.

10
Winchester, ibid.

11
Joseph Henrich, Steve J. Heine,
and Ara Norenzayan, "The Weirdest
People in the World?," *Behavioral
and Brain Sciences* 33, no. 2–3
(2010): 61–83.

below, also on the left, the date of the details that followed: these were, in order, the title of the book or paper, its volume and page number, and then, below that, the full sentence that illustrated the use of the target word."[9]

Entries poured in from across the world. Winchester states that "in the end more than six million slips of paper came in from the volunteers."[10] The vast numbers of books and magazines being investigated meant not only that the entirety of the language was being covered but also that the accuracy of the history and definitions of each word were quite refined. The editors could cross-reference ideas and sources to produce a final product verified against all written sources of English.

The first OED was finished on December 31, 1927. It contained 12 volumes with 414,835 words defined and 1,827,306 illustrative quotations. It is the most complete chronicle of the English language ever produced. It is also a testament to the value of considering what sample size you need to get accurate results.

— Sidebar: Insurance

Not all samples sizes are created equal

One of the most important considerations with sample sizes is their representative diversity. The insights you get from a large number of data points are only going to be as good as the range of possibilities they cover. If, for example, you want to know how effective airbags are in preventing serious injury in car passengers, but you've only collected information on drivers, no amount of that data will give you a useful answer to your question.

The authors of "The Weirdest People in the World?" explain that "behavioral scientists routinely publish broad claims about human psychology and behavior in the world's top journals based on samples drawn entirely from Western, Educated, Industrialized, Rich, and Democratic (WEIRD) societies."[11] They go on to demonstrate that the people in WEIRD

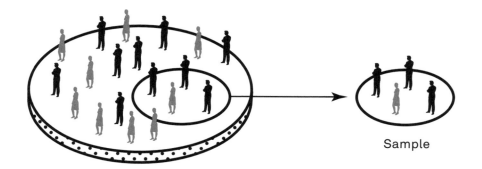

Sample

It is important to study samples representative of the overall population. However, it can also be important to study subsets with different features that might not be apparent from averages.

Caroline Criado Perez - (b.
1984). Criado Perez is a writer,
broadcaster, and campaigner. Her
book *Invisible Women* received
the Financial Times and McKinsey
Business Book of the Year Award in
2019. She has led many successful
campaigns to increase the visibility
and recognition of women in the
UK, resulting in representation on
banknotes and commemorative
statues.

12
Caroline Criado Perez, *Invisible
Women* (New York: Abrams Press,
2019).

13
Criado Perez, ibid.

societies are outliers in many ways; therefore, we probably shouldn't be using studies based entirely on the behavior of WEIRD subjects as representative of the entire human population.

If we want to uncover universals about the behavior of human three-year-olds, we don't need to study more children in California. Adding to the numbers we already have with more studies using the same subject set is not going to help us gain insights with broad applicability. If we want to say something meaningful about human nature, then our data set ought to contain information from a sample of humans that represent the diversity found on the planet.

In the book *Invisible Women*, author Caroline Criado Perez[*] explores how data sets that are often used to make decisions that impact women don't actually contain any information about women. She argues that "when your Big Data is corrupted by big silences, the truths you get are half-truths, at best."[12]

Data needs to be collected in order to be analyzed, so you need to ask yourself if you have the right mechanisms to collect the data that will give you the fullest picture possible— or at least enough to make a good decision with the potential for good outcomes. Criado Perez reports that over 90% of people who experience unwanted sexual behavior on public transportation in New York and London don't report it. Nor do female metro users in Azerbaijan. So if someone were to conclude, based on official police reports, that safety for women isn't an issue in these places, they would be dead wrong.[13] Therefore, making rules and changes based on data needs to look hard at the data being used.

Not including women creates a data set that eliminates half the human race. Criado Perez gives examples of when this is annoying, like phones too big for the average female hand, and when it creates serious negative outcomes for women, such as in medical treatment. She explains that "nearly all pain studies have been done exclusively on male mice," and many clinical trials done exclusively on men will have their results applied equally to women, despite women having different physiognomies.[14]

The majority of clinical trials (at least for prescriptions used by everyone) produce results applicable to a 200-pound adult. There's also the consideration of ethnicity to consider in the sample size: for example, African American, Latino, Asian, and Caucasian populations each have their own unique metabolic and enzymatic profiles, thus leading to many medications behaving differently in each population. To obtain sufficient diversity in a sample size is often far too costly for pharmaceutical companies. Therefore, many medications are launched with suboptimal data or never reach the market because a subset of the larger sample showed unexpected adverse events.

One of the problems with assuming that a large sample size alone gives us a good data set is that we can undermine the very problems we are trying to solve. For example, no number of samples will be sufficient if you can't acknowledge that you have biases, and volume on its own won't help you overcome them. Criado Perez writes, "If you aren't aware of how those biases operate, if you aren't collecting data and taking a little time to produce evidence-based processes, you will continue to blindly perpetuate old injustices."[15]

Criado Perez argues that "the introduction of Big Data into a world full of gender data gaps can magnify and accelerate already-existing discriminations."[16] It is not a big leap to conclude that Big Data based on narrow data sets can exacerbate many different discriminations. As the authors of "The Weirdest People in the World?" conclude, "We need to be less cavalier in addressing questions of human nature on the basis of data drawn from this particularly thin, and rather unusual, slice of humanity."[17] The lesson is that deep data on a homogenous population is only relevant to that population. If a data set is being used to describe the broad category of "human," then it needs to be representative of the diversity of the species.

14
Criado Perez, ibid.

15
Criado Perez, ibid.

16
Criado Perez, ibid.

17
Henrich, Heine, and Norenzayan, ibid.

18
Criado Perez, ibid.

Why should we care about the quality of our samples' sizes? Because, as Criado Perez explains, "having an accurate measure is important because data determines how resources are allocated."[18] We tend not to draw conclusions from samples for fun but to make meaningful, sometimes critical decisions that can have a wide impact. You will reduce your chances of a good outcome if the data you collect is not representational of the people affected by the decisions you make. Yes, large sample sizes are better than small sample sizes for decision-making, but it's critical to remember that not all data sets are created equal.

Conclusion

What this model teaches us is that sample size is often an invisible component of what we think we know about the world. In most situations, increasing our sample size gives us valuable information that lets us see our situation in a new light. But to have representative samples takes work. Using this model means taking the time to explore what isn't obvious and being aware of how easy it is to corrupt our samples with bias.

Randomness

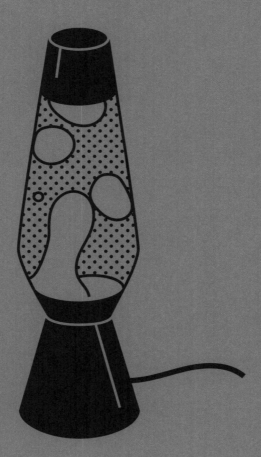

—
Predictability is often an illusion

Randomness

Randomness can be a hard model to use because humans aren't great at comprehending true randomness. When we look at the world, we tend to see order. We notice patterns and sequences, like thinking the world is out to get us because a few bad things happened in a row. Yet our sense of predictability and order is an illusion. Much of what we encounter day to day is random; we just don't perceive that. Using randomness as a model means being willing to accept that it exists and looking for situations where it can help us.

  The dictionary definition of randomness is "proceeding, made, or occurring without definite aim, reason, or pattern."[1] It is the opposite of predictability and order, something we aren't wired to conceptualize. Randomness goes against the way we like to view the world. Yet it's not an anomaly or a rarity; randomness is the rule, not the exception. We misunderstand randomness any time we attribute causality where none exists. Although we cannot tame it, we can learn to work with—not against—randomness.

« [T]he human mind is built to identify for each event a definite cause and can, therefore, have a hard time accepting the influence of unrelated or random factors. »

Leonard Mlodinow[2]

1
"Randomness," Dictionary.com, accessed August 23, 2019, https://www.dictionary.com/browse/randomness.

2
Leonard Mlodinow, *The Drunkard's Walk: How Randomness Rules Our Lives* (New York: Pantheon Books, 2009).

One reason randomness can be challenging is that it makes the universe seem less friendly and comprehensible than we might wish. It's hard to accept that much of what happens in our lives is chance, not ordained in any way. It's like the world throws random dots at us, and humans are constantly trying to draw lines between them, even if none exist. Randomness thus forces us to confront our lack of control over outcomes in many situations.

« The history of ideas is a history of gradually discarding the assumption that it's all about us.»
Paul Graham[3]

Similarly, we can forget that the past was as random as the future will be. In hindsight, history can seem ordered and logical. When we open a history book, we see structured narratives. Events have a beginning, a middle, and an end. It only seems this way in retrospect. Not only are past events random, so is the information we have about them. Historical documents survive at random, and it's also up to chance whether a particular researcher comes across them or even how they interpret them.[4] Documents get lost, destroyed by fire or water, or thrown away because no one recognizes their value. Others get ignored or are hard to interpret. The further back in time we look, the more incomplete the information we have becomes.

Randomness, however, is not something to be afraid of. It's a tool at our disposal. For example, our immune systems have to contend with a vast variety of possible pathogens. To deal with new and varied threats, our bodies produce differently shaped lymphocytes at random, meaning each has the potential to fight different pathogens.[5] Similarly, when ants forage for food, they all move around at random. If one finds food, it leaves a pheromone trail to it. Other ants will find that trail at random and follow it, making it stronger. Without any central control, this enables ants to coordinate themselves.[6] "It appears that such intrinsic and probabilistic elements are needed in order for a comparatively small population of simple components to explore an enormously large space of possibilities, particularly when the information to be gained from such explorations is statistical in nature and there is little a priori

3
Paul Graham, "See Randomness," April 2006, http://www.paulgraham.com/randomness.html.

4
"Professor Chris Wickham," University of Oxford, accessed August 23, 2019, http://www.ox.ac.uk/research/research-in-conversation/randomness-and-order/chris-wickham.

5
Mitchell, ibid.

6
Mitchell, ibid.

Jane Smiley - (b. 1949). Pulitzer
Prize–winning author of novels
including *A Thousand Acres* and
The Greenlanders, Smiley also
writes on a variety of nonfiction
topics and children's books.

7
Mitchell, ibid.

8
Christian and Griffiths, ibid.

knowledge about what will be encountered."[7]

Randomness is a fundamental part of the universe, and embracing it instead of trying to fit order where it doesn't belong can help us do two things: be less predictable and be more creative.

— Sidebar: What Are the Odds?

« Making use of chance can be a deliberate and effective part of approaching the hardest sets of problems. »

Brian Christian and Tom Griffiths[8]

Serendipity and creating

A question authors always seem to be asked in an interview is, "Where do you get your ideas?" More than a few have gone on record stating how much they hate this question. Why? Because it implies there is an idea bank, or a creativity app, or some defined source authors can access. When they are faced with a blank page, they can purchase or otherwise pull out an idea from this source, and away they go.

The reality is far messier. Ideas come from everywhere with great inconsistency. What is inspiring to one author one day may not inspire them the next time they are looking for an idea. And a particular source of inspiration is unlikely to work for another author in exactly the same way. When one's creativity feels blocked or when interesting ideas seem inaccessible, the introduction of randomness can come to the rescue.

Author Jane Smiley*, in her book *Thirteen Ways of Looking at the Novel*, reflects on her creative process in developing her works of fiction.

I hadn't ever had much of a theory of creativity beyond making a cup of tea or opening a can of Diet Coke and

What Are the Odds?

One situation where we misunderstand randomness is when equally likely random events happen in a sequence. We sometimes think what happened last time dictates what happens next time. For instance, in a sequence of random events, we may think it is unlikely for the same thing to happen multiple times in a row. If you flip a coin six times and it's heads every time, it might seem like it's not a fair coin. But seeing as the outcome of each flip is equally likely to be heads or tails regardless of the last result, HHH-HHH is as probable as any other specific sequence, say, HTTHTH.

Casinos take advantage of getting people to bet on random events while ensuring the odds are always to their benefit. Whether a given gambler wins any particular round is random, but on average everyone loses. One major fallacy casinos profit from is the mistaken belief that what happened in the last round affects what happens in the next one. Assuming no tampering, any particular outcome of a roll of the dice or the spin of a roulette wheel is equally likely each time. The past does not influence it.

In 1913, the roulette wheel in a Monte Carlo casino landed on black 26 times in a row. Gamblers lost millions when they kept betting large sums of money on it being red next. The fallacy was that each time the wheel landed on black, the chances of the next spin being red increased. But the probability of getting red is always 50%, and the previous results have no impact on that. The gamblers had no reason to bet more in that situation than any other. While a roulette wheel landing on black so many times in a row is remarkably unlikely, it doesn't change the probability of any given spin being black.

9
Jane Smiley, *Thirteen Ways of
Looking at the Novel* (New York:
Alfred A. Knopf, 2005).

10
Smiley, ibid.

11
Smiley, ibid.

sitting down at the typewriter or computer. The first and last rules were "get on with it." But perhaps that getting on with it that I had taken for granted for so many years was dependent upon those half-attentive ruminations during diaper changes and breadmaking and driving down the road?[9]

She makes it clear that although ideas definitely come from somewhere, an author can never know precisely where that might be. And so randomness—in this case understood as unpredictability—is a very useful tool when trying to create.

The writing process for fiction is far from formulaic. Sometimes you start with the whole plot in your head, and sometimes you don't. Sometimes you plan out every chapter before you start writing, and sometimes your characters unexpectedly steer your story in a different direction. Sometimes you have enough ideas to give you momentum to reach the end, and sometimes you get stuck halfway through. Smiley recalls how she dealt with a challenging time writing a story: "Rather than planning and working out in advance, as I had done with most of my earlier novels, I willingly entered a zone of randomness."[10]

Making your characters do something unexpected by writing a scene you hadn't planned is one way to work around a creative block. These scenes aren't always amazing, and you may cut it later. But sometimes just seeing your characters having an unplanned experience can give you insights into how to use their attributes to keep your story going.

Writing a work of fiction is not a linear process. As Smiley describes in one experience: "One day I waited for inspiration, got some, went off in a completely new direction, then had second thoughts the next day and tried something new."[11] Often an author will have to try a variety of options for a particular scene in order to determine the best way forward.

When you begin a novel, where you start is often not

where you end up. You may have certain ideas going into it, but your research demonstrates you've made some erroneous assumptions, and you have to change your plot or your setting. Or a character turns out to be more interesting than you imagined, and they end up carving out a bigger role for themselves.

In Smiley's description of the novel-writing process, she makes it clear that there are very few universals. "Some novelists write by obligation, others by desire. These are questions of temperament. There is no intrinsically better way, since the only standard of achievement to begin with (and for quite a long time) is the accumulation of pages."[12] Which brings up another important point with regard to the value of randomness in novel writing: authors are by no means universal themselves. The experiences, desires, assumptions, and goals of those telling the stories are just as varied as the stories themselves.

In exploring the history of the novel, Smiley looks at the works of Daniel Defoe, like *Robinson Crusoe,* and says, "Defoe's nonconformist religious training gave him a sense of sympathetic connection with subjects not previously given serious literary treatment—prostitutes, servants, criminals, working men and women, courtesans, adventurers of all stripes."[13] And Defoe is but one example. We can imagine that all novelists draw on their own lives for inspiration, and their particular backgrounds determine what they see in the world around them. The unique intersection of experience and temperament, combined with the unpredictability of how one feels at any given moment when writing, means that it is very hard to trace a line of cause and effect in the writing of a story.

Even with an interesting story developing in the brain, with plot points and characters pushing to get out and onto the page, sometimes authors get stuck. Instead of waiting to get unstuck as if by magic, the better solution is to add an element of randomness and see where it takes you.

Smiley advises as a remedy "to find out more—read more, travel to the spot where your novel is set and spend a

12
Smiley, ibid.

13
Smiley, ibid.

Robinson Crusoe surprising the three Englishmen.

Wildly popular right from its release, *Robinson Crusoe* by Daniel Defoe was a distinct step in the evolution of storytelling. Though Defoe likely drew inspiration from various true accounts, it was very much the product of his imagination and spawned a new genre.

few days there, ask questions, look for original documents, engage your senses to gain more knowledge of what you are writing about. If you are bored with your subject, it is fatal to try to think your way out of it."[14] Instead you must experience your way out of it. If you are stuck, it means that everything you currently think cannot help you. You must get out into the world and experience the serendipity of stumbling into new things. One of these new things will help you continue your story, and you have no way of knowing in advance which thing it will be. So get out there and see what you run into.

Although it's impossible to know for sure, it seems unlikely that all great novels haven't benefited from their author's exposure to a random event. Why? Great novels aren't a formula. You cannot copy exactly what others have done and achieve the same results.

Perhaps most importantly, there is no precise definition of what makes a novel great anyway. As Smiley explains to a novelist as they begin their creation, "As you aim for perfection, don't forget that there is no perfect novel, that because every novel is built out of specifics, every novel offers some pleasures but does not offer some others, and while you can try to achieve as many pleasures as possible, some cancel out others."[15] A particular novel cannot be all things to all people.

One of the greatest and most frustrating elements of creativity is its imprecision. One can neither master creativity nor be creative all the time. When you are stuck while pursuing the nebulous task of trying to achieve creative output, introducing an element or two of randomness can help you make new connections to move past the block you are pushing against.

Two perspectives on randomness

To understand true randomness, we need to distinguish it from pseudorandomness.

Pseudorandomness is the appearance of randomness due to our inability to predict or detect a pattern although there

14
Smiley, ibid.

15
Smiley, ibid.

Chan Canasta - (1920-1999). Born
Chananel Mifelew, he became the
first television celebrity magician
in the early 1950s. He retired from
that career at the height of his
fame and went on to become a
successful landscape painter.

are underlying causal influences.

True randomness is different. It is still coupled with probability distributions but is completely detached from any causal factor, meaning there's no explanation that we could apply to even approximately guess a more or less likely outcome for the next trial.

Our tendency to create a narrative to order and organize the world makes us predictable. We are also highly suggestible, remembering the most recent things we were exposed to. Thus humans often behave in a pseudorandom manner, a fact that can be exploited.

Professional magicians exploit our availability bias and narrative tendencies in some of their tricks. If you're asked to think of a random number or pick out a random card from a pack, you might not realize there is an order to your choices. Your choice is not truly random, merely pseudorandom.

Chananel Mifelew, better known by his stage name Chan Canasta*, became famous for his magic tricks in the 1950s and '60s. His tricks were typically simple, performed using little more than a pack of cards or a book, but with a flair that earned him the nickname "a remarkable man." Canasta's tricks had an experimental air, as they tended to rely on taking chances. It was not unusual for them to go wrong during live performances.

Yet failures only highlighted Canasta's lack of trickery. Sometimes he took wild chances if he believed it was worth the risk. In one trick, Canasta asked a panel to each come up with a random word, then combine them into a sentence that he would predict in advance. Canasta was completely wrong, but he explained that it was worth trying. The chance of him getting it right was higher than you might imagine because of the way we misunderstand pseudorandomness as randomness. When someone picks a "random" word, the chances of them picking any particular word in the dictionary are not equal. In reality, certain words are much more likely to come up than others.

Unlike many modern magicians, Canasta didn't pretend he was performing magic. Instead he took advantage of his impressive memory and his ability to give the impression of randomness.[16] For instance, in one trick, he would ask a volunteer to pick three random cards from a pack, then place each in a different pocket, again at random. He was able to subtly influence which cards they took and where they placed them. But the volunteer felt it was random and was unaware of his influence. Even if it didn't always work perfectly, it was impressive when it did.[17]

Canasta went on to inspire other mind readers who took advantage of the same psychological trick—making people think their choices were random when they were pseudorandom.

When we're asked to make a random choice, especially if we're under pressure, we tend to fall into certain patterns.[18] Asked to name a random vegetable, most people say carrot. After George Bush declared his hatred of broccoli, that briefly became the more popular choice. Asked to name a shape, mentalist Banachek[*] writes that most people will opt for a square. For a flower, they will usually say a rose. For a number between one and five, most will name three, and for one to ten, the usual choice is seven. The typical "random" color people name is blue, and the piece of furniture is a chair.[19] Performed with enough flair, simple tricks like this can seem like mind reading. It works because we don't recognize we're not making random choices.

Our inability to predict in Canasta's type of magic tricks comes from seeing only one instance of the trick instead of seeing hundreds. The magician takes advantage of the seeming randomness of a single trial, while few people would think it was purely random if they watched it performed a thousand times with different audiences. That's because it's not truly random; it's only pseudorandom.

Generating randomness is hard. Ask someone to give

[*] Banachek - (b. 1960). One of Banachek's earliest tricks was fooling a team of scientists at Washington University into believing he had psychic abilities. An entertainer and mentalist, he has been involved in extensive work to disprove bogus psychics.

16 Roberto Forzoni, "Chan Canasta," ForzoniMagic, accessed November 17, 2020, http://forzonimagic.com/mindreaders-history/chan-canasta/.

17 David Britland, "Chan Canasta Triple Card Coincidence," Cardopolis, January 27, 2010, http://cardopolis.blogspot.com/2010/01/chan-canasta-triple-card-coincidence.html.

18 Banachek, *Psychological Subtleties* (Houston: Magic Inspirations, 1998).

19 Banachek, ibid.

Originally from Poland, Chan Canasta volunteered with the Royal Air Force during World War II. He moved to England in 1947 and later became a citizen.

you a string of random numbers, and they'll end up following a form of order. Generating genuine disorder for things like data encryption requires unpredictable physical processes, like radioactive decay, atmospheric noise, and the movement of lava lamps.[20] When generating true randomness is essential, we have to find a method that overrides the way our brains work. One way that people throughout history have achieved this is through divination rituals that provide random data. Although people attributed success of these practices to magic or divine wisdom, that's not why they worked. Rather, despite the narrative of divination, the rituals generated truly random results that were far more useful than the pseudorandom data our brains often generate.

The Naskapi foragers in Labrador, Canada, needed a way to come up with hunting paths at random so the caribou wouldn't learn to anticipate their routes and avoid them.[21] They achieved this through a ritual involving heating the shoulder bone of a caribou over hot coals until the surface was covered in cracks. Then they used the cracks as a map to tell them where to hunt. Beaver pelvises, skinned otters, and fish jaws also served similar purposes.[22] Although they saw it as a form of divination, it worked by giving them hunting routes more random than any human could manage.

True randomness is detached from any causal factor, which is why no one could predict where the next hunting area was going to be before the bones were heated.

Conclusion

Randomness as a model reminds us that sometimes our pattern-seeking, narrative-building tendencies can be unproductive. Using randomness as a tool can help us get a fresh perspective and lift us out of the ruts we have built. It also gives us an appreciation of the value that the unpredictable or the unexpected can sometimes have.

20
Mads Haahr, "True Random Number Service," Random.org, accessed August 23, 2019, https://www.random.org/randomness/.

21
Henrich, ibid.

22
Shona L. Brown and Kathleen M. Eisenhardt, *Competing on the Edge: Strategy as Structured Chaos* (Boston: Harvard Business School Press, 1998).

Supporting Idea:

Pareto Principle

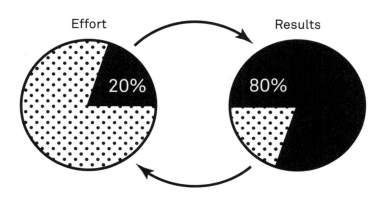

In 1906, the Italian polymath Vilfredo Pareto was researching wealth distribution in Italy. He noticed that 20% of the population owned 80% of the land and of the wealth. He is also said to have observed the same distribution in the pea plants he grew, wherein 20% of plants produced 80% of the peas. In the 1940s, quality control consultant and engineer Joseph M. Juran noted that 80% of manufacturing defects are the result of 20% of production issues. Juran applied Pareto's name to the principle he defined as a result: In systems, 80% of outputs are typically the result of 20% of inputs. The other 20% of outputs are the result of the remaining 80% of inputs.

We can apply the Pareto principle to numerous areas where this type of distribution holds roughly true: 20% of researchers in a field produce 80% of published research; 20% of words in a language are used 80% of the time; 20% of the population uses 80% of health care resources and public services; 20% of a company's customers create 80% of its profits. We often generate 80% of our personal results from 20% of our efforts. Of course, such distributions tend to be approximate, not precise. The Pareto principle is a rule of thumb, not a law of nature. However, the true split is often surprisingly close to 80/20.

Inputs and outputs are not evenly distributed. Not all inputs lead to the same sort of output. Not all the time you put into a project will be equally productive. Not all the money you put into a retirement fund will have the same impact on the final amount. Not all of the employees in a company will be responsible for the same amount of its annual profits. Knowing this can teach us where to focus time and energy. If a company knows 80% of users of a piece of software will only ever touch 20% of its features, they know to make those as effective and user-friendly as possible.

« That is all there is to the 80/20 rule. We tend to assume that all items on a list are equally important, but usually, just a few of them are more important than all the others put together. »
Hans Rosling[1]

1
Hans Rosling, Ola Rosling, and Anna Rosling Rönnlund, *Factfulness: Ten Reasons We're Wrong about the World—and Why Things Are Better Than You Think* (London: Sceptre, 2019).

Regression to the Mean

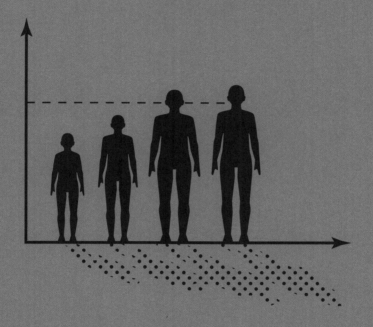

—
Moderate outcomes follow extreme ones

Regression to the Mean

When we have success in life, we are often faced with a challenge. Successes are great, and no doubt we want to repeat them, but we have to consider how much of our initial success was skill and how much was luck. Did we succeed mostly on our own merit, thanks to preparation and hard work? Or was our success on account of a massive stroke of luck, such as our competitors making poor choices? If we had faced stronger competition, would we have had more average results? The model of regression to the mean is a tool to understand where individual experiences fit on the spectrum of possibility.

« When the gods intend to make a man pay for his crimes, they generally allow him to enjoy moments of success and a long period of impunity, so that he may feel his reverse of fortune, when it eventually comes, all the more keenly. »

Julius Caesar[1]

Luck is random. So outlier results with a luck component are probably followed by more moderate ones. This is regression to the mean: when data far above or below the mean is more likely to be followed by data close to it. Outlier results in situations like exam scores tend to normalize if measured multiple times as we perform to what is average for us over multiple iterations. Where luck is a factor, some successes and failures always come down to randomness.

The statistician Francis Galton[*] identified the concept of regression to the mean in the late 19th century while comparing the heights of parents and their children. He found that unusually tall or short parents tended to have children of a more average height. It was as if nature were trying to maintain an

[*] Francis Galton - (1822-1911). An English polymath who coined the phrase "nature versus nurture," Galton contributed to fields as diverse as meteorology, with the first popular weather maps, and criminology, with the uniqueness of fingerprints. He was also an explorer, writing *The Art of Travel*, which is still in print. His legacy is overshadowed by his development and support of eugenics.

[1] Julius Caesar, *The Conquest of Gaul* (London: Penguin Books, 1982).

average height by returning to the average after outlier results.[2]

The same is true for other phenomena we experience in our lives. Extreme events and results tend to be balanced out. Extraordinary successes are often followed by average results as we perform to our true capabilities. From a single result, we can't distinguish luck and skill. An athlete who bombs one competition will likely perform at their regular skill level in the next one. A warm day in the winter might be followed by an average cold one. You will make both profitable and poor investment decisions, with most generating average returns corresponding to your knowledge and experience.

Failure or success is usually followed by a result closer to the mean, not the other extreme.

« The larger the influence of luck in producing an extreme event, the less likely the luck will repeat itself in multiple events. »

Wikipedia[3]

Regression to the mean is beneficial for differentiating between luck and skill. As you progress through any venture, be it investing in stocks, reading minds, or growing vegetables, it is inevitable you will have both good and bad luck. With repeated iterations, results will converge more toward your true ability level. It's unwise to place too much emphasis on the initial few outcomes because they're unlikely to be truly representative. Beginner's luck is a real thing, because beginners who fail spectacularly are less inclined to continue.

A further lesson from regression to the mean is that if you keep trying something, most of your results will be average, but with repetition you might get an exceptional outlier. For example, if you write a blog post every week for years, most will get roughly the same number of readers, yet you might end

2
Stephen Senn, "Francis Galton and Regression to the Mean," *Significance* 8, no. 3 (2011): 124–26.

3
Wikipedia. 2020. Regression toward the mean. https://en.wikipedia.org/wiki/Regression_toward_the_mean

Outlier results are often followed by average ones.

The *Sports Illustrated* Curse

Athletes refer to the "*Sports Illustrated* curse," wherein those who appear on the cover of the magazine experience a sudden decline in their performance afterward. Regression to the mean offers an explanation. Athletes featured tend to be at the very top of their game—something that is partly due to skill and partly due to luck. From there, they're most likely to regress to the mean and return to more average performance.[1]

An athlete who reaches the level of success necessary to appear on the magazine's cover probably has nowhere to go but down. It's usually outlier success that gets athletes on the cover of magazines, and outlier success always has a component of unreliable good luck to it. An athlete will probably regress to their mean in the next season, while someone else will have some lucky success.

Serious injuries bring an end to many athletic careers. Again, the more times someone plays a sport, the more opportunities they have to sustain an injury. Age-related wear and tear from doing something so physically demanding further compounds the role of bad luck. Just as good luck might lead an athlete to do exceptionally well one season, bad luck may lead them to break a bone the next. In baseball, players who win the Cy Young Award for pitching tend to later experience a downward turn for the same reason.[2]

The best way to assess someone's abilities is to consider their track record, not their greatest achievements. An extreme result is not necessarily the start of a new trend; we need a larger sample size to make an accurate assessment. While an athlete achieving something incredible during one season or game is for sure impressive, it doesn't mean they'll keep performing like that forever.

The same is true in our lives outside of the sports world, and for both positive and negative events. After having a bad experience in a job at a company with terrible culture, the company you work at next is likely to have a more normal, reasonable culture. After being in an amazing relationship, you might find that your next one is less extraordinary. The key is to recognize when luck is a factor. Whether things are going better than normal or worse than normal, they may well not continue that way. Life has its ups and downs, but most of the time you'll find yourself somewhere around the mean.

1
Thomas Gilovich, *What Isn't So: The Fallibility of Human Reason in Everyday Life* (New York: Free Press, 1991).
2
"Are Cy Young Award Winners Jinxed?: Injuries to Cubs' Rick Sutcliffe Seem to Credence to the Belief," *Los Angeles Times*, August 11, 1985, https://www.latimes.com/archives/la-xpm-1985-08-11-sp-2900-story.html.

4
Peter Carlson, "The Flop Heard
Round the World," *Washington
Post*, September 4, 2007, http://
www.washingtonpost.com/wp-
dyn/content/article/2007/09/03/
AR2007090301419_pf.html.

5
Jamie Page Deaton, "Why the
Ford Edsel Failed," How Stuff
Works, July 8, 2015, https://auto.
howstuffworks.com/why-the-ford-
edsel-failed.htm.

up writing one that attracts a lot of attention. Your skill will
have improved, and you'll have more chances for luck to play
a role too. Just as one extreme result is not always the start
of a new pattern, lots of average results do not preclude the
occasional big success.

— Sidebar: The *Sports Illustrated* Curse

The Ford Edsel was just a car

Not every effort we make is going to produce rare and spectacular results. There's always an average. So often we put so
much pressure on ourselves to knock it out of the park all the
time that average results can seem like failures. Regression to
the mean is a useful model for helping us put our averages in
perspective. We have some influence over what our personal
average is. We can work hard to get that mean comparatively
high. But we will always have an average and cannot expect
outlier success all the time. Appreciating the average is one
way to consider the story of the Ford Edsel.

In 1957, 16-year-old Don Mazzella skipped class for a
rather unusual reason. He wasn't off to smoke cigarettes in the
local park or meet a girlfriend. Mazzella and a couple of friends
were sneaking off to see a car.[4] They didn't plan to buy or joy-
ride it. They just wanted to know what it looked like.

Why were they so excited about this particular car? The
vehicle in question was the Edsel, launched dramatically by
Ford on what the company dubbed "E-day." Named after Henry
Ford's son, it might well have been the most hyped product
released during the 1950s.

Everyone knew about the Edsel before its release; no
one knew what it looked like. Ford preceded its release with
a lavish two-year advertising campaign. Its name was everywhere, but none of the adverts depicted the car itself.[5] Aiming
to build anticipation by shrouding the vehicle in mystery, they
only showed small details or unrelated images accompanied
by bold claims.

Ford made big promises about the Edsel. They said it was to be the greatest car ever made. Cars were a huge deal for Americans in the 1950s. In the postwar era, owning one went from being a luxury to something attainable for the average person. Mainstream car ownership literally changed the landscape of America with the construction of motorways and surrounding infrastructure like gas stations and motels. People took pride in their vehicles, viewing them as the linchpin of a new form of freedom and prosperity. So the Edsel captured their imagination, and the notion of it being something revolutionary seemed plausible. If cars had already changed the country, why couldn't a new car model prove transformative again?

Millions were spent on the Edsel's advertising. Ford's initial idea was to make a strategic move into the new market for medium-priced cars, which their main competitors dominated at the time. Following the wild success of the Ford Thunderbird a couple of years earlier, Ford management were confident they couldn't fail with the Edsel. If the Thunderbird had sold so well, surely the Edsel could only sell better with a bigger advertising budget.[6] They already had the brand name and the trust of consumers.

There was a queue at the local showroom to see the Edsel. Mazzella and his friends waited in line to peek around a corner. As soon as their eyes fell on the Edsel, they went through the same realization as the rest of America. The Edsel was just a car. For many who saw it, it wasn't a particularly attractive one at that. Its huge, vertical front grille looked odd and distorted, like a grimacing mouth.[7] The excitement bubble popped. Americans viewed the Edsel as a disappointment and didn't buy it in anywhere near the expected numbers.

Part of the problem was that the Edsel was so over-hyped, it could only ever fall short. Too much advertising drummed up so much excitement that it made the car seem worse than it was in comparison to people's expectations. In

6
Mark Rechtin, "The T-Bird: Whoever Did It, Did It Right," *Automotive News*, June 16, 2003, https://www.autonews.com/article/20030616/SUB/306160815/the-t-bird-whoever-did-it-did-it-right.

7
Richard L. Oliver, *Satisfaction: A Behavioral Perspective on the Consumer* (Oxfordshire: Routledge, 2010).

The Edsel was named after Edsel Ford, son of company founder Henry Ford. The reasons for its failure were complex, but it is now a valuable item for collectors due to the scarcity of certain models. Even toy models of the Edsel can be relatively valuable.

addition, its launch wasn't flawless. Early vehicles had some technical issues that, though minor, tarnished its image. When Ford hadn't managed to invent something truly revolutionary, they settled for marketing the Edsel as something it wasn't.

Within two years, Ford stopped selling the Edsel.[8] Some—possibly exaggerated—estimates put the total losses at $2 billion in today's money. Ford had tried to make it more desirable than it was through advertising. They ended up making it less desirable. As David Gartman writes in *Auto-Opium: A Social History of American Automobile Design,* "The Edsel was indeed different, but it protested its novelty so loudly that its exhortations rang hollow."[9]

Thomas E. Bonsall, writing in *Disaster in Dearborn: The Story of the Edsel,* takes a similar view: "People are mesmerized by the mighty brought low....The *Titanic* became a modern morality play. Man has reached too far, gotten too arrogant, and had, inevitably, been given a comeuppance. So it was with the Edsel."[10] People reveled in the schadenfreude of seeing Ford fail at last. (Ford didn't stay down for long, following up the Edsel with the Mustang in 1964.)

Many car models have failed over the decades, many in an even more spectacular fashion than the Edsel. Yet it remains the most famous car failure of all. In an ironic twist, today surviving Edsels are worth a great deal due to small production numbers. Failure made Edsels more popular among collectors of 1950s vehicles, some of whom delight in the almost comically distorted front grille.

The story of the Edsel is complicated. There wasn't one reason for its failure. There is no doubt that the prerelease hype caused consumer expectations to be high. And the higher expectations are, the harder it is to fill them. But there were also issues within the Ford Motor Company during the development of the Edsel that contributed to many poor decisions.

One way to understand the enduring fascination with the story of the Edsel is through the lens of regression to the

8
Eliot A. Cohen, *Military Misfortunes: The Anatomy of Failure in War* (Riverside: Free Press, 2012).

9
David Gartman, *Auto Opium: A Social History of American Automobile Design* (London: Routledge, 1994).

10
Thomas E. Bonsall, *Disaster in Dearborn: The Story of the Edsel* (Stanford: Stanford General Books, 2002).

Trung sisters - (circa 14-43).
Vietnamese heroes whose lives
are largely shrouded in mystery,
the Trung sisters continue to
be important historical figures
and are held up as exemplars of
strong leadership. They have many
temples dedicated to them, and
there is a national holiday in early
February commemorating their
legacy.

mean. Businesses are under constant pressure to have every release achieve a new level of success. But sometimes new products are just average. Ford had spectacular success with the Thunderbird before the Edsel and the Mustang after. When judged against those vehicles, the Edsel seems like a massive failure. It wasn't really, though. It ran okay. Some people liked it. It was just an average car useful for a mother taking her kids to baseball practice or an insurance salesman headed to work.

When you look at the spectrum of cars produced by Ford over time, some sold amazingly and others hardly registered, with everything else falling in the range in between. The more cars the company releases, the more it is statistically likely that some will be average sellers. The problem for the Edsel was the investment made in the marketing suggested brilliance. When the result turned out to be average, the disappointment was in the contrast.

Fighting back

Throughout history, extreme and unusual events have often been followed by more average ones. The highlights are what we study, with the many more mundane occurrences not even recorded. Regression to the mean is thus an interesting lens to use to look at historical change, because it suggests that we be cautious about making assumptions about the future based on the immediate past.

History is far too complicated to use a simple statistical concept to try to demonstrate a decisive pattern in complex and often random interactions. Rather, using regression to the mean as a model helps you put extremes of success and failure into perspective. An extreme event is not necessarily the start of a new trend. Dramatic events do not always change what follows them.

The Trung sisters*, Trung Trac and Trung Nhi, were born in rural Vietnam. While we don't know exactly when they were born or died, they are best known for their activities between

39 and 43 CE, when they earned a lasting legacy as Vietnamese national heroes. As daughters of a lord at a time when women in their country enjoyed unusual freedom, they experienced a relatively privileged upbringing.[11] Vietnamese women were able to inherit property and take on political, legal, commercial, and military roles. By some accounts, Vietnam at the time may even have been a matriarchy, although this may be an exaggeration to highlight the contrast with patriarchal China.[12]

At the time, Vietnam had been under Han Chinese rule since 111 BCE—a period of control that would last over a thousand years, with just a few intermissions of independence. The Chinese attempted to enforce their way of life based on Confucian philosophy, alongside other unpopular measures like harsh taxation. In 39 CE, Thi Sach, lord of Chau Dien and Trung Trac's husband, protested against the rising taxes and was executed as a result. Rather than going into mourning as expected, Trung Trac turned her anger and grief into fuel. Together with her sister, she rallied an army of 80,000 consisting mostly of ordinary Vietnamese people without training or much equipment. They assigned mostly women as generals and are often depicted riding elephants into battle.

According to legend, Trung Trac killed a man-eating tiger and wrote her intentions on its skin. Then their army fought back against the Chinese. Another legend tells of a soldier who went into battle nine months pregnant, gave birth on the field, then strapped her baby to her back and continued fighting. While the story is not altogether plausible, it says a lot about how the army was viewed.[13] Their attack was so unexpected that they succeeded in pushing the Chinese from 65 cities and establishing an independent state.

For three years the sisters ruled together and helped restore fairer conditions for the Vietnamese people—including doing away with the heavy taxes that led to their rebellion. In addition they revived aspects of Vietnamese culture the Chinese had replaced with their own, such as the traditional

11
Lynn Reese, "The Trung Sisters," Female Heroes of Asia: Vietnam, Women in World History Curriculum, accessed November 18, 2020, http://www.womeninworldhistory.com/heroine10.html.

12
Kathleen Barry, *Vietnam's Women in Transition* (London: Macmillan Press 1996).

13
Paige Whaley Eager, *From Freedom Fighters to Terrorists: Women and Political Violence* (London: Taylor and Francis, 2016).

Temples dedicated to the Trung sisters can be found all over Vietnam, with some dating back over 1,500 years. The sisters have been recast as heroes who defied gender roles, but some historical texts can be interpreted as mocking them and blaming their failure on unsuitability for leadership. It's important to understand that our view of figures from ancient history can say as much about the world today as about what truly happened.

language and literature. However, their rebellion proved to be an outlier. The Chinese were initially taken by surprise, so part of the sisters' success was due to the poor preparation of the Chinese. Because they were still far more powerful, the Chinese rebounded quickly. Their next efforts against the Vietnamese were more in line with the Chinese mean for military capability.

In 43 CE, the Chinese took back full control of the country and violently punished the rebels. In addition to slaughtering supporters of the Trung sisters, they sought to override Vietnamese culture with their own. Devastated by the loss and seeing no hope, the sisters are said to have leapt into a river together. Their army didn't have the strength to hold off the Chinese long term. China would ultimately control Vietnam for nearly a thousand years, but by some accounts, Vietnam wouldn't still exist as a country without the Trung sisters. Today they're commemorated throughout Vietnam and remain a source of inspiration.[14]

14
"Trung Sisters," Britannica.com, accessed November 18, 2020, https://www.britannica.com/topic/Trung-Sisters.

15
Patricia M. Pelley, *Postcolonial Vietnam: New Histories of the National Past* (Durham: Duke University Press, 2002).

« All the male heroes bowed their heads in submission / Only the two sisters proudly stood up to avenge the country. »

15th-century Vietnamese poem[15]

Using regression to the mean as a metaphorical lens, rather than pure math, can provide the insight that great, unusual success isn't usually followed by more of the same. The actions of the Trung sisters were outliers in their time. What they accomplished was not the start of a new standard. When you are new to something, it's a good idea to try to ascertain where the mean lies so you know if your early results are representative or not.

Conclusion

Regression to the mean is a great lens through which to look at the world because it helps you put success and failure into context. We all have an average. When luck is a factor, instead of trying to replicate an unusual success or giving up after an exceptional failure, we can instead try to find the mean and build from there.

Multiplying by Zero

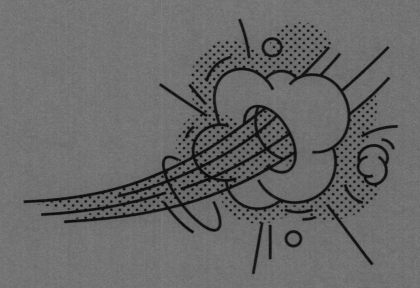

—
The ultimate destroyer

Multiplying by Zero

This mental model is useful for teaching us to look for the zero—the weak part of any system that threatens to bring the whole thing down. Any number multiplied by zero equals zero. This is basic math we all learn early in life. Within a multiplicative system, there is no point in optimizing the other components if we ignore the zero. It's always worth investing effort in the weakest part because nothing else can compensate for it. It doesn't matter if you multiply zero by 100 or 285,490,940, you still get the same outcome.

As commonplace as zero might seem now, it's extremely easy to forget it is a remarkable number. Without it much of modern mathematics would be impossible. Early numerical systems couldn't progress further without a means of representing nothing—a number that you can multiply by another number and still get nothing.

« Multiplication by zero destroys information. This means there cannot be a reverse process. Some activities are so destructive they cannot be undone. »

Paul Lockhart[1]

It doesn't matter if you have two zeros or five billion zeros. See, in multiplicative systems each number says something about the properties of the other numbers in that system. For example, 2 x 3 says of the number 2 that there are 3 of them (2+2+2), and of the number 3 that there are 2 of them (3+3). It follows that 2 x 0 says of the 2 that there are none of them, and of the zero, that there are 2 of them. No twos is nothing. Two zeros is also nothing. So in a multiplicative system with a zero, you will always have a total of zero. No matter how many zeros you add

[1]
Lockhart, ibid.

together, they will always add up to zero. And the rest of the numbers in that system are effectively nothing.

The principle of multiplying by zero applies outside of math. Any multiplicative system is only as strong as its weakest link. A zero in a system has the power to negate everything that comes before it. For instance, in a competent, well-organized team, one unmotivated person who complains nonstop can bring everyone else down. A company might have strong branding, a large user base, and a useful product, but a CEO who publicly makes racist comments has a good chance of canceling all that out. You might have a fancy security system in your house, but it's useless if you leave the front door open.

The value of this mental model is in learning to identify where the zero might be, how to avoid introducing one, or how to transform an existing one. Imagine you're trying to design an ideal dining experience for customers of a restaurant. What would create a zero for you as a customer? You go to a restaurant to eat. The most important component of the restaurant system for the customer is good food. Beautiful decor, attentive service, good atmosphere—none of these will compensate for tomato-soup pasta sauce or fish that has gone off. This restaurant could serve the water in gold glasses and be located in a charming French château, but if the food is tasteless and unimaginative, you will never go back. Bad food is the zero of the restaurant's system. Great food can compensate for slow service. But the sexiest, most attentive waiter will not make up for undercooked chicken.

East German technology theft

We all work in systems. Whether they're large or small organizations employing thousands of people or just one, we spend most of our time trying to make our systems better. Many of the decisions we make at work are about improving our system, whatever that means for us: higher sales, more flexibility, better outcomes for our clients. Deciding where to invest,

VEB Kombinat Robotron, headquartered in Dresden, was the biggest
East German electronics manufacturer in the 1980s. They assembled
most of the computers made in the country.

what to research, how to develop ourselves and others—these can be done by evaluating the strength of the components of our system.

Work environments are multiplicative systems. Whether you work for the government, a local brewery, a high-tech multinational, or as a freelance artist, the properties of each component of your system interact in the whole. Understanding sales means understanding marketing, which necessitates a firm grasp of R&D, which in turn draws from finance. If any one of these isn't working, there will be a negative impact on the rest of the system.

Therefore, you have to be able to identify if there are any zeros in your system—a part of the system that isn't producing at all. Putting time, effort, and resources into the other elements of a system will produce no results if any part of the system is a zero. Having a zero in a multiplicative system creates a mirage. You see all these other big numbers and think they are strong enough to compensate for this zero, but they aren't.

A great example of ignoring a zero is the East German quest to build a computer at the end of the Cold War. In the 1970s and '80s, the computer was seen, understandably, as an important technology, a critical element in the ongoing technological development race between East and West. The East Germans had a goal, which was, as Kristie Macrakis explains in *Seduced by Secrets*, "nothing less than constructing an indigenous self-sufficient computer industry."[2]

However, they were nowhere near developing computer technology for themselves. Decades into a social experiment that eventually proved untenable, they had created a system that punished creativity, innovation, and collaboration. It was hardly ideal for developing a computer industry.

In addition, because of the political climate, the East Germans couldn't partner with Western technology companies to build their computer industry either. By the late 1970s, most Western technology was under embargo; it could not be sold or

2

Kristie Macrakis, *Seduced by Secrets* (Annapolis: Naval Institute Press, 2008).

3
Macrakis, ibid.

4
Macrakis, ibid.

5
Macrakis, ibid.

distributed to Eastern Bloc countries.

The East German solution was to steal what they wanted. Carried out by the Ministry for State Security, commonly referred to as the Stasi, East Germany proceeded as they had for much of the Cold War. Using their networks of agents, Stasi officials worked around the embargo and proceeded to steal the information and technology required to build computers. They obtained everything from blueprints to hardware and reverse-engineered the technology in order to build it themselves. The East Germans spent billions of marks on theft, illegal smuggling, and espionage.[3]

In one example, "rather than conducting its own research and development work, East Germany would import the know-how and production facilities of a complete factory to produce 20 to 30 million 256K RAM circuits yearly."[4] "Import" here meant paying far more than the market price to try to bring in embargoed technology through elaborate illegal routes. This factory never came to pass.

Overall the attempt to build a computer industry in East Germany was a complete failure. Why? Because they didn't develop anything on their own. They didn't let their scientists travel to participate in research efforts or to obtain knowledge to build the desired technology in-house. Their whole computer industry was to be built on a foundation of theft. Money that could have been spent on research and development was instead poured into elaborate schemes to bring in embargoed technology. As Macrakis sums up, "That was the main contradiction the Stasi presents us with: On the one hand, they vigorously supported state programs by acquiring the needed embargoes or secret technology. On the other hand, security concerns made them work against their own interests by restricting the needed international travel of scientists and by imposing other harmful security measures."[5] Consequently, despite years of trying, the East Germans never met their technology production goals.

6
Macrakis, ibid.

We can understand their failure by considering that innovation does not just happen out of thin air. The history of invention shows us that smart people fail dozens of times before they succeed. They build on the failures of others by testing their own hypothesis, tinkering and refining, and learning a remarkable amount in the process. They learn not only how to make things work but why those things work in the first place. Therefore, when things go wrong, they have a deep store of earned knowledge to draw on. They can troubleshoot, adapt, and ultimately improve.

The East Germans had none of the knowledge that is earned in development and failure. "Even with their highly perfected espionage system and seasoned embargo smuggling operations, East Germany forgot one thing: A scientific establishment based on pirated and cloned technology can never be a leader." Because they didn't develop the knowledge themselves, they were not able to troubleshoot, adapt, and most importantly innovate. Macrakis says that "often machinery did not work when it arrived. Because it was acquired illegally, calling a service repairman was a problem. Sometimes only bits and pieces of information were available, when the whole puzzle was needed intact. But more fundamental problems arose because of secrecy. The [Stasi's] cult of secrecy clashed with the scientific ethos of openness."[6]

The lack of collaboration and knowledge gained from experience was their zero, the part of their system that reduced the rest of it to nothing. More spies, more theft, and more money were thrown at the problem, but increasing the value of the rest of the properties in a multiplicative system does nothing if that system contains a zero.

How do you find the zeros in your system? Zeros don't hide. In fact, they are usually quite obvious when you draw your perspective back, allowing you to see your system as a whole. They are usually what we deliberately ignore, naively hoping that they will "fix themselves" or that someone might come

The Kombinat VEB Zeiss Jena company was split after World War II, with parts continuing to operate in both East and West Germany. Although the company is predominantly known for their innovations and manufacturing of high-quality lenses, it worked on microchips during the Cold War.

along who can magic a solution. Zeros are persistent, structural flaws that intimidate us. If we avoid them, this is when we fall prey to snake oil salesmen who promise they have an easy (and often expensive) solution based on the latest technology/psychology/accidental success of someone else.

Changing a zero to a one is not going to happen overnight. But for all required components, all zeros can be turned into ones. In trying to build the computer, what the Stasi were missing was at least one person who had earned the knowledge required for the endeavor, someone who had studied, apprenticed, or worked beside others who knew what they were doing. Why didn't they have that one person?

They didn't have that one person because they hadn't created a culture that would allow someone like that to exist. Inventors ask questions, explore options, and challenge the status quo. These were all behaviors that were not encouraged in Cold War East Germany. For the Stasi to have turned their zero into a one, they would have had to modify their culture to support innovation. They would have had to build a team or an organization that would support the development of the creative people they needed. In effect, they would have produced more than one person to solve their problem. And this is the magic of changing your zero into a one. The result is a capitalization of all the other strong numbers you have in place.

It is hard. For the Stasi to implement structural changes of this sort would have amounted to an acknowledgment of the failures of their particular brand of socialism. It's understandable that they didn't own this and instead threw money at the other components of their system.

However, most people understand that success is complex and has many contributing factors. There is no one secret to a good marriage or a profitable business. These systems have many components, all of which have to be working to some degree of efficiency to achieve success. But critically it can often be just one thing that determines failure. If one

7
"Stuttering," Mayo Clinic,
accessed November 18, 2020,
https://www.mayoclinic.org/
diseases-conditions/stuttering/
symptoms-causes/syc-20353572.

essential component of the system is neglected, then the whole thing breaks down.

— Sidebar: Crop Diversity

Transforming zeros

Sometimes we feel like we have a zero in our personal equations: a characteristic, quality, or condition that serves to undermine our efforts in other areas. It can be frustrating when we work hard to develop skills and capabilities only to feel like they are negated by just one part of who we are. This feeling is common for stutterers. Sometimes it can seem like their struggle to verbalize words reduces the perception of the value of their knowledge and experience. In overcoming the limits that stuttering may place on them, many stutterers have found varied techniques and treatments to effectively manage their stuttering. Dealing with a stutter is often not just about addressing the condition itself but about overcoming the sense of inadequacy other people place on those who stutter early in life. There are many fascinating stories of the various ways people have turned their perceived zero of stuttering, and all its often-negative consequences, into a one.

Stuttering is defined as "a speech disorder that involves frequent and significant problems with normal fluency and flow of speech."[7] Stutterers may repeat words or syllables, or have a hard time articulating certain sounds. One of the major frustrations for stutterers is that their difficulty in speaking is not representative at all of what is going on in their head or of their intelligence. They know what they want to say. It is the disconnect between having an idea and being able to express it in the course of conventional conversation that causes issues. There is nothing intrinsically wrong with stuttering. It's just a different way of talking and therefore harder for other people to understand.

For many stutterers the physical condition has further consequences. It can lead to poor self-esteem and increased

Crop Diversity

When the consequences of failure are high, it's important to do everything you can to avoid multiplying by zero and negating your prior efforts. One place where this is apparent is in agriculture, where maintaining crop diversity is vital.

Crop diversity refers to the practice of using a variety of types of plants in agriculture, both in terms of different species of the same plant as well as variations within species. It applies to individual farmers, to communities, to nations, and to the world as a whole. Crop diversity is also relevant both in terms of the plants we are currently growing and those we have the capacity to grow, as well as referring both to domesticated and wild strains. Being dependent on a single crop is a bad idea because something could go wrong and leave you with no harvest, such as a plant disease, a parasite, or unfavorable weather conditions. For a subsistence farmer, that means having nothing to eat. On a larger scale, if most people in the world eat the same thing, a crop failure could mean widespread hunger or even political instability. There are other risks to crop homogeneity, like soil depletion and erosion.

Unfortunately, crop diversity is decreasing over time as more of the world comes to depend on wheat, rice, and potatoes.[1] The mental model of multiplying by zero helps illustrate the importance of not creating situations where the impact of one thing going wrong could wipe everything else out. Having crop diversity is like having multiple different equations: if one is multiplied by zero, it doesn't negate the others.

The Irish Potato Famine, beginning in 1845, is a classic example of the risks of lacking crop diversity. When a fungus affecting potato plants spread throughout the country, over a third of the population lacked their main food source for up to five years.[2] Not only were many people dependent on potatoes alone, there was also a lack of genetic variation within the species. Propagating these vegetatively meant the plants were all clones—that is, genetically identical. When a fungus came along targeting this particular plant, all were equally susceptible. There was no genetic diversity to ensure some plants had resistance.[3]

The mental model of multiplying by zero highlights the importance of not creating excessive dependency on one thing that could fail.

1
Mark Kinver, "Crop Diversity Decline 'Threatens Food Security,'" BBC News, March 3, 2014, https://www.bbc.com/news/science-environment-26382067.
2
Jim Donnelly, "History–British History in Depth: The Irish Famine," BBC, February 17, 2011, http://www.bbc.co.uk/history/british/victorians/famine_01.shtml.
3
"Monoculture and the Irish Potato Famine: Cases of Missing Genetic Variation," Understanding Evolution, University of California, Berkeley, accessed August 12, 2020, https://evolution.berkeley.edu/evolibrary/article/agriculture_02.

Marilyn Monroe - (1926-1962).
She was an iconic legend who
starred in multiple hit films. Tired
of being typecast and knowing
she had more to offer as an
actor, she co-founded her own
production company in 1955. She
was captivating on camera, a
talented comedic actor, and was
very sensitive to the sexist double
standards in Hollywood. She would
no doubt have contributed much
more to history had she not died
so young.

8
Mayo Clinic, ibid.

9
Maurice Zolotow, *Marilyn Monroe*
(New York: Perennial Library,
HarperCollins, 1990).

anxiety as everyday situations become huge challenges due to the judgment of other people. The Mayo Clinic says, "Stuttering may be worse when the person is excited, tired, or under stress, or when feeling self-conscious, hurried, or pressured. Situations such as speaking in front of a group or talking on the phone can be particularly difficult for people who stutter."[8] Daily interactions that most of us don't even register can become ongoing sources of stress and tension for stutterers, which can lead them to avoid needed social interaction and relationships.

There is no cure for stuttering. It is a condition that can be greatly improved by speech therapy and other types of therapy, such as cognitive behavioral. But stuttering never goes away completely and thus must always be managed.

One result of stuttering is often the feeling that, regardless of the effort you put into other areas of your life, the condition negates them all. No matter how much you know, how witty you are, or how much wisdom you've gained from your experiences, the struggle to verbally articulate negates the value of anything you have to say.

Stuttering affects millions of people. What many find surprising is the list of stutterers who have achieved success in very public speech roles. From James Earl Jones to King George VI of England, Carly Simon to Winston Churchill, many stutterers have found ways to effectively manage their stuttering in certain public situations.

Marilyn Monroe* was one of the first famous people to talk openly about how stuttering affected her life. In a 1955 discussion with the American columnist Maurice Zolotow, Marilyn recalled, "I guess you could say I gave up talking for a long while. I used to be so embarrassed in school. I thought I'd die whenever a teacher called upon me. I always had the feeling of not wanting to open my mouth, that anything I said would be wrong or stupid."[9] Yet she worked through this limitation to achieve success in the film industry.

—
In an interview with Richard Meryman, first published in *Life* magazine on August 17, 1962, Marilyn Monroe said, "It's nice to be included in people's fantasies but you also like to be accepted for your own sake. I don't look at myself as a commodity, but I'm sure a lot of people have."

Emily Blunt - (b. 1983). Blunt is a contemporary actor who has displayed a wide range of skill in many engaging films, including *Edge of Tomorrow* and *Mary Poppins Returns*.

B. B. King - (1925-2015). Nicknamed "The King of the Blues," he was inducted into the Rock and Roll Hall of Fame in 1987. In 1970, he recorded *Live in Cook County Jail*, which went on to earn great acclaim. Inspired by that experience, King co-founded the Foundation for the Advancement of Inmate Rehabilitation and performed for free in prisons for the rest of his life.

Rubin Carter - (1937-2014). A boxer and victim of one of the most famous miscarriages of justice, he spent 18 years in prison after being falsely accused of murder. After the verdict was overturned, he moved to Canada, became a sought-after speaker, and received two honorary doctorates of law. Carter was the inspiration for the Bob Dylan song "Hurricane."

10
"Putting It Bluntly," *W Magazine*, October 1, 2007.

11
B. B. King, *Blues All Around Me: The Autobiography of B. B. King* (New York: HarperCollins, 1996).

12
"The Turbulent Life of Rubin 'Hurricane' Carter," Stuttering Foundation, accessed November 18, 2020, https://www. stutteringhelp.org/content/ turbulent-life-rubin-hurricane-carter.

Many actors who stutter have spoken about how the notion of taking on a role helps them step away from their speech impediment and thus help them manage it. For example, Emily Blunt[*] is described in an article in *W Magazine* as developing "a stutter so debilitating that she could barely hold a conversation, let alone elbow her way into the limelight. 'I was a smart kid, and I had a lot to say, but I just couldn't say it....It would just haunt me. I never thought I'd be able to sit and talk to someone like I'm talking to you right now.'"[10] Then one of her teachers at school suggested acting lessons, and it was this experience that helped her manage her stutter.

Another fascinating thing about stuttering is that it often goes away while singing. Many stutterers find the words come much easier if they are put to sound. In his 1996 autobiography, B. B. King[*] wrote:

> I struggle with words. Never could express myself the way I wanted. My mind fights my mouth, and thoughts get stuck in my throat. Sometimes they stay stuck for seconds or even minutes. As a child, I stuttered. What was inside couldn't get out. I'm still not real fluent. I don't know a lot of good words. If I were wrongfully accused of a crime, I'd have a tough time explaining my innocence. I'd stammer and stumble and choke up until the judge would throw me in jail. Words aren't my friends. Music is. Sounds, notes, rhythms. I talk through music.[11]

Singing also played a role in how Rubin "Hurricane" Carter[*] was able to, over time, effectively manage his stutter. The Stuttering Foundation has a profile on Carter, among many other stutterers, that tells us, "From an early age, Rubin Carter had to fight so much due to abuse he received because of his stuttering that he developed into a great fighter and was urged by people to consider a career as a boxer."[12] In a 2006 interview with Nicholas Ballasy on his show *On the Issues*, Carter said,

"My first eighteen years of my life, I couldn't talk. I stuttered very badly. So fighting became just a natural thing for me because if you are going to attack people when they laugh at you, you better damn well know how to fight or you're gonna get your butt whooped. So that's what got me into fighting."[13]

In his 1974 autobiography *The Sixteenth Round: From Number 1 Contender to Number 45472*, which was written in prison, Carter writes openly about his stuttering. He says, "I couldn't speak to save my life. I had always been told that as I became older, my speech would eventually straighten itself out, but it did not happen that way with me. Any effort I made to talk made my speech worse, and therefore my habit was to speak as little as possible."[14]

His speech began to change when he discovered that he didn't stutter while singing. The Stuttering Foundation shares a summary from the book *Hurricane: The Miraculous Journey of Rubin Carter* by James S. Hirsch: "Carter worked hard on trying to replicate that relaxed fluidity from singing into his everyday speaking patterns. Over time he also diligently practiced cadences and forced himself to speak before groups, becoming a compelling speaker." Relaxing while speaking and changing up the cadence of speech are two of the core practices of speech therapy, which has helped millions of stutterers gain a measure of control over their stuttering.

Managing a stutter will not always lead to such visible success, but that isn't the point. Too often we think of certain conditions as inherently limiting, zeros that will always render the rest of our personal equations useless. Zeros, however, can form us and challenge us to develop new skills and qualities. How some people have managed their stuttering is a great example of the power of transforming a zero. As stuttering can never be completely "cured," it is not about getting rid of the zero. Stutterers have found many ways to shift the zero just enough to turn it into a one, thereby activating the power of the rest of their equation.

13
Rubin "Hurricane" Carter, interview by Nicholas Ballasy, *On the Issues*, accessed November 18, 2020, https://www.stutteringhelp.org/content/turbulent-life-rubin-hurricane-carter.

14
Rubin Carter, *Sixteenth Round: From Number 1 Contender to Number 45472* (Chicago: Chicago Review Press, 2011).

Conclusion

We often treat our lives as multiplicative equations. We want our skills and experience not to solve isolated problems but to increase values in many areas of our lives by multiple factors. We want to take our hard-earned knowledge and use it to support a variety of efforts. A zero in any multiplicative equation will reduce it to nothing, and so this model shows us that we have to be mindful of the zeros that will negate our other efforts. If we believe we have a zero, our most critical task is to turn it into at least a one.

Equivalence

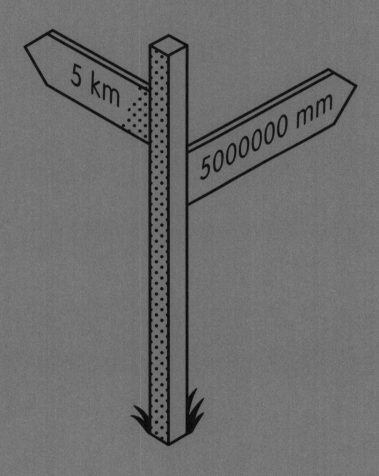

—

Equal doesn't mean same

Equivalence

Things do not have to be the same to be equal. Equivalence as a model helps us see that there are usually many paths to success. One of the ways equivalence is most useful as a model is when our traditional solution to a problem is no longer viable. We know we must now do things differently, yet we wish to achieve an equivalent result. It also reminds us to not focus on apparent differences but to look for the underlying equality of experiences if we want to better connect with others.

In math, one of the most basic equivalency concepts is "if A = B and B = C, then C = A." We can infer that A, B, and C need not be the same; after all, they are represented by different symbols. But for the purposes of comparison in at least one aspect, they are equivalent. It is often true in mathematics that different symbols can provide an equal answer to a question.

« The art of doing mathematics consists in finding that special case which contains all the germs of generality. »

David Hilbert[1]

The world is full of things that seem different yet are in some way equivalent. Take the case of human universals. We are, as a species, unimaginably diverse. Despite this, cultures across the world often solve the same problems in equivalent ways.[2] According to anthropology professor Donald Brown, these universals include taboo language, a distinction between how people behave when they are in full control of themselves and when they are not, making promises, rules surrounding inheritance, attempts to predict and influence the weather, and bodily adornments. While these features and behaviors manifest in different ways, they have equivalent purposes across cultures.[3]

1
Constance Reid, *Hilbert* (New York: Copernicus, 1996).

2
"Human Nature: Six Things We All Do," *New Scientist*, accessed August 23, 2019, https://www.newscientist.com/round-up/human-nature/.

3
Donald E. Brown, *Human Universals* (Philadelphia: Temple University Press, 1991).

4
George Eliot, *Scenes of Clerical Life: Janet's Repentance* (Boston: Lauriat Comp, 1908).

Sometimes things recur in equivalent yet different ways. Historical recurrence is the phenomenon wherein seemingly equivalent events happen more than once at varying points throughout history. It's a cliché that history repeats itself, but the similarities can be uncanny in events like the assassinations of Lincoln and Kennedy and the invasions of Russia by both Napoleon and Hitler. People in similar situations facing similar incentives are likely to behave in similar ways.

« History, we know, is apt to repeat herself, and to foist very old incidents upon us with only a slight change of costume. »

George Eliot[4]

Multiple discoveries

There's a powerful myth surrounding scientific discoveries and inventions. We imagine a solitary genius toiling away in their laboratory or workshop, performing experiment after experiment. Then one day, lightning strikes. They shout, "Eureka!" as a new idea is born and the sum of human knowledge grows in one swoop. The idea gets named after them, they receive awards and patents, and their name goes in the history books. Should they have been felled by a falling piano a day prior, the idea may never have come into existence.

Except invention and discovery rarely work that way in reality. Most discoveries are the product of the cumulative work of many people inching toward the conclusion. Often multiple people or teams reach an equivalent result independently at around the same time. In the past it was possible for this to occur even without them being aware of each other's work. Steel, slingshots, and the abacus are some of the many examples of inventions and discoveries that occurred in multiple places and multiple times in history.

There are many ways to represent the same mathematical concepts.
Various arithmetic systems developed independently all over the world,
from Egypt and Rome to China and India.

« Because everything arises from steps, not leaps, most things are invented in several places simultaneously when different people walk the same path, each unaware of the others. »

Kevin Ashton[5]

None of us live in full isolation from the ideas of others or the context of our time. New discoveries are the product of broad scientific and cultural landscapes, and often of recombining existing ideas.[6] We all draw upon what we are exposed to. The work of a researcher is the product of a lifetime spent absorbing the work of others.[7]

To give some of the many, many examples of simultaneous discovery, both Charles Darwin and Alfred Russel Wallace conceived of natural selection without knowledge of each other's work. Chemist Carl Wilhelm Scheele discovered oxygen in 1772 but didn't publicize his discovery for three years, by which point two other chemists, Joseph Priestley and Antoine Lavoisier, knew of its existence.[8] Both Louis Ducos du Hauron and Charles Cros presented similar methods for color photography in the 1860s.[9] Their work differed, as du Hauron used pigments and Cros favored dyes. Nettie Stevens and Edmund Beecher Wilson independently demonstrated that specialized chromosomes (X and Y) determine biological sex.[10] Takaaki Kajita and Arthur B. McDonald's research ended up sharing the 2015 Nobel Prize in Physics for demonstrating that neutrinos have mass.[11]

A misunderstanding of how invention truly works is apparent in patent law, which suggests patents should go to the inventor of something nonobvious.[12] The implication is that, as its source, they deserve to profit from it. So it's often the case that the person who profits isn't truly the sole source of innovation. They're one of many; they just happen to be the one who files a patent first or who gets it accepted. The

5
Ashton, ibid.

6
Steven Johnson, *Where Good Ideas Come From: The Seven Patterns of Innovation* (London: Penguin, 2011).

7
William F. Ogburn and Dorothy Thomas, "Are Inventions Inevitable? A Note on Social Evolution," *Political Science Quarterly* 37, no. 1 (1922): 83–98, https://www.jstor.org/stable/2142320.

8
Julian Rubin, "The Discovery of Oxygen," February 2018, https://www.juliantrubin.com/bigten/oxygenexperiments.html.

9
Saman Musacchio, "The Birth of Color Photography," CNRS News, August 23, 2018, https://news.cnrs.fr/articles/the-birth-of-color-photography.

10
"Nettie Stevens," Britannica.com, accessed November 25, 2020, https://www.britannica.com/biography/Nettie-Stevens.

11
Nobel Media, "The Nobel Prize in Physics 2015," press release, October 6, 2015, https://www.nobelprize.org/prizes/physics/2015/press-release/.

12
Mark A. Lemley, "The Myth of the Sole Inventor," Stanford Public Law Working Paper No. 1856610 (July 21, 2011), https://ssrn.com/abstract=1856610 or http://dx.doi.org/10.2139/ssrn.1856610.

Oxygen is colorless, odorless, and normally a gas that is essential
to life on earth. It is element number 8 on the periodic table, and in
liquid form it is light blue.

components of a steam turbine were described by Taqi al-Din in 1551 in Syria, long before the first patent was awarded in England for an early steam engine in 1698.[13]

The phenomenon of multiple discoveries shows us how things can be equivalent, even if not precisely identical. While they may differ in their details, the underlying principles and concepts are the same. They solve the same problem. In most cases, we only credit a well-known discovery or invention to the person who popularized it. We thus miss out on a rich understanding of the full process of innovation and often fail to hear the stories of those working outside the mainstream. In particular, female and minority scientists and inventors often have a hard time publicizing their work. Credit may go to someone else at a later date. Once a particular individual becomes well known, they're even more likely to receive credit, even if someone else had the same idea previously.

— Sidebar: Madeleine Vionnet and the Bias Cut

How we deal with the universal of death

Death is a reality all humans have in common. We know our lives will one day be over, and at some point we will have to process the death of a loved one. Due to our social natures, we form strong attachments to people in our lives. Our families and friends mean a lot to us, and when they go, it hurts. The need to process the death of someone we care about is a state all of us experience. How we choose to go about that processing varies widely across cultures. Equivalence is a useful lens through which to look at the various death rituals that exist in the world because it demonstrates just how many ways there are to get the same outcome.

Writing in *Do Funerals Matter?*, William G. Hoy says, "Just as death is a universal event, the desire of groups to make sense of death through ceremonies seems also to hold a universal appeal."[14] There is a wide variety of after-death practices in the world. Some are religious based, such as the

13
Salim Ayduz, "Taqi al-Din Ibn Ma'ruf: A Bio-Bibliographical Essay," Muslim Heritage, June 26, 2008, https://muslimheritage.com/taqi-al-din-bio-essay/.

14
William G. Hoy, *Do Funerals Matter?* (New York: Routledge, 2013).

Madeleine Vionnet and the Bias Cut

Up until the early 20th century, for many Western women corsets were part of their standard daily attire. Often containing boning, corset design evolved over the centuries to shape the female body to whatever was considered attractive at the time. Gradually corsets became less fashionable, partly driven by the restriction on material during World War I. In response to the changing trends, designer Madeleine Vionnet came up with a truly novel approach to dressmaking and demonstrated that there is more than one way to look good in clothes. "Vionnet's unique solution was to make the movement of the body part of the movement of the remarkably fluid shapes she was working on. No more boning, no more rubber, no more elastic to give support."[1]

As most of us can verify quite easily in our homes, if you hold a square of fabric—say, cotton—at the center of its edges and pull outward in opposite directions, the material will only stretch a little. However, if you hold it at the corners and pull, the material will stretch significantly more. In 1922 Vionnet exploited this property of fabrics, called the bias cut, to stunning effect in the design and construction of clothes.

As J. E. Gordon describes in *Structures*: "She realized intuitively that there are more ways of getting a fit than by pulling on strings or straining at hooks and eyes [of corsets]. The cloth of a dress is subject to vertical tensile stresses both from its own weight and from the movements of the wearer; and if the cloth is disposed at 45 degrees to this vertical stress, one can exploit the resulting large lateral contraction so as to get a clinging effect."[2]

As explained by Colin McDowell in his online biography of Vionnet, "Starting with studying classical Greek statues, she became obsessed with the soft flattery of clothes that 'moved like water.' From there, she made her great step forward by cutting fabric on the bias (previously used only for collars)

and, by doing so, created a completely new shape, which could be called free-form geometric. In her own words, it was 'to free fabric from the constraints that other cuts imposed on it.' She had found her road and, for the rest of her design life, she tackled the whole question of dress with an almost scientific rigor."[3]

The bias cut has become a staple of fashion. It looks nice, it easily clings to different body shapes, and it uses less fabric to achieve its effects. Vionnet's bias cut demonstrated that there is more than one way to shape a silhouette in fashion.

1
Colin McDowell, "Madeleine Vionnet (1876–1975)," Business of Fashion, accessed June 22, 2020, https://www.businessoffashion.com/articles/news-analysis/madeleine-vionnet-1876-1975.
2
J. E. Gordon, *Structures* (Cambridge: Da Capo Press, 1978).
3
McDowell, ibid.

—
Ancient Egyptians often used funerary boats, in which all participants accompanied the deceased to their final resting place across the Nile. They believed the dead would become immortal, provided the correct procedures were performed.

15
Hoy, ibid.

16
James Gire, "How Death Imitates
Life: Cultural Influences on
Conceptions of Death and Dying,"
*Online Readings in Psychology and
Culture* 6, no. 2 (2014): https://doi.
org/10.9707/2307-0919.1120.

Jewish custom of sitting with the body until burial or the Hindu tradition of constructing a pyre on which the deceased is cremated. Other practices are community centered, such as sharing food and drink at a gathering or parading with the deceased in a procession. Hoy continues, "Humans have an undeniable need to make sense of death; funeral rituals are created by social groups as potential scripts to achieve this end."[15]

« When Darius was king, he summoned the Greeks who were with him and asked them what price would persuade them to eat their fathers' dead bodies. They answered that there was no price for which they would do it. Then he summoned those Indians who are called Callatiae, who eat their parents, and asked them (the Greeks being present and understanding by interpretation what was said) what would make them willing to burn their fathers at death. The Indians cried aloud, that he should not speak of so horrid an act. »

Herodotus, *The Persian Wars*

Losing someone you love is painful. Across all human culture, crying, anger, and fear are standard reactions. We grieve for the life that is over, and we mourn their loss from our lives. Rarely do we deal with this pain alone; the ceremonies we perform, diverse as they are, serve the function of helping us deal with a death. In "How Death Imitates Life," James Gire explains, "In whatever form they may take within a given culture, funerals and burial rights are ways that each society tries to help the beloved with the death of a loved one."[16] Or as Colin Murray Parkes, Pittu Laungani, and Bill Young put it in *Death and Bereavement across Cultures*, "Times of death and bereavement are times when people need people."[17] We all have the same needs when processing the death of a loved one. There are just many different ways of meeting them.

One further aspect of death that the accompanying ceremonies address can be thought of as the closure of the deceased's experience of life. Parkes, Laungani, and Young conclude that "all societies see death as a transition for the person who dies."[18] The way we engage with that transition is varied, but the fact of engaging with it is pretty much ubiquitous across cultures. Hoy summarizes, "The concepts of eventual rest and reward for the dead are common in death rituals, transcending religious beliefs and cultural customs."[19]

The funeral is one such death ritual. Gire explains, "Funeral and burial rites vary significantly across cultures and are influenced by each culture's conceptions of life and dying."[20] Some funerals are somber affairs, with everyone dressed in dark colors and voices kept to a murmur. Others are lavish and colorful. Some include singing. Others dancing. Still others incorporate stories of the deceased. And the ways in which funerals treat the body are just as varied. Some end in burial, others in cremation. Tibetan Buddhists chop human remains and leave them on a mountain to return to the elements, and South Koreans turn the ashes into colorful beads. What ties together the variety of traditions is the intent behind them: consoling the living and dealing with the dead. On the subject of the funeral, Gire concludes that "death is the final life transition. The funeral is often considered as a celebration of a rite of passage for both the deceased and the living."[21]

We all have a need to process death. The traditions and ceremonies we practice are a means of activating that process, allowing us to grieve for lost loved ones as well as have reassurance in what will happen after our passing. The lens of equivalence shows that there are many ways to meet our need. None are the same, but all are equal in the ways they help people.

17
Colin Murray Parkes, Pittu Laungani, and Bill Young, *Death and Bereavement across Cultures* (London: Routledge, 1997).

18
Parkes et al., ibid.

19
Hoy, ibid.

20
Gire, ibid.

21
Gire, ibid.

Conclusion

Being equal doesn't mean being the same. Different inputs can produce identical results, and there is more than one way to solve most problems. Using equivalence as a lens helps us appreciate the richness of the solution space. We can better appreciate the efforts of others who took a different path and find a common language to share information and experiences.

Order of Magnitude

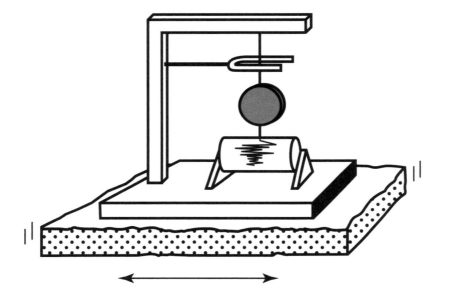

Representing very large or very small numbers can be a challenge. Our brains struggle to conceptualize them. Writing them out can be unwieldy. Primitive counting systems past and present sometimes progress from one and two to "many" because those are the figures needed for day-to-day life.[1] But today we also sometimes need to handle numbers on scales that aren't straightforward to depict. Science is essentially all about measurements. As it advances, its scale expands to include values like the weight of a cell and the size of a galaxy.

Orders of magnitude are a form of notation used to represent large or small numbers in a compact fashion. To say a number is an order of magnitude larger than another number is to say that it is ten times larger (a power of ten). To say it is an order of magnitude smaller means it is a tenth the size. So, 10 is an order of magnitude smaller than 100, and 1,000 is an order of magnitude larger. We write out orders of magnitude using the smallest possible power of ten. Science, mathematics, and engineering are disciplines for which this form of notation can be crucial.

One reason orders of magnitude are useful is that they enable us to make comparisons between numbers to give them context, such as stating how many orders of magnitude greater the weight of the Earth is than the weight of a car. We also use powers of ten when handling imprecise numbers and making estimations.

In our day-to-day lives, we might easily be able to imagine a group of 20 people, but what would a crowd of one million look like? We can picture $1,000 in one-dollar or one-hundred-dollar bills, but how big would a stack of a billion dollars be? If we sacrifice perfect accuracy, learning to conceptualize orders of magnitude can help us compare numbers. For instance, spending a dollar a second, it would take you just over 11 days to spend a million dollars and about 32 years to spend a billion. The difference between the two is three orders of magnitude.

The Richter scale is an earthquake measurement system using orders of magnitude. Created by seismologists Charles F. Richter and Beno Gutenberg, it measures the size and destructive power of earthquakes and was designed with the Southern California region in mind.[2] Although other systems are in use, "the Richter scale" tends to serve as an umbrella term for any means of categorizing and comparing earthquakes by magnitude. Using orders of magnitude is a shortcut for showing the size difference between seismic events.

The Richter scale ascends from 0 (with negative numbers being available on more advanced seismometers) to 10. In theory it could continue higher, but there has never been a recorded earthquake measuring 10 or more. Each step on the scale means an earthquake has ten times the ground motion effect of the prior step, which in turn means it releases 32 times as much energy. The largest earthquake recorded to date occurred in Chile in 1960, reaching 9.5 on the Richter scale. Most earthquakes are at the bottom end of the scale, too small for anyone to notice or measure them. Each year there are about 1.3 million measuring between 2 and 2.9, but only one at 8 or higher.[3]

As Richter himself explained in his original paper on the topic:[4]

Precision in this matter was neither expected nor required. What was looked for was a method of segregating large, moderate, and small shocks, which should be based directly on instrumental indications, and thus might be freed from the uncertainties of personal estimates or the accidental circumstances of reported effects.

Comparing the destructive potential of earthquakes going up the Richter scale is one tool for understanding orders of magnitude.

1
Tim Radford, "One, Two,... Er, Too Many," *Guardian*, August 20, 2004, https://www.theguardian.com/world/2004/aug/20/highereducation.research.
2
"The Richter Scale," Earthquake Magnitude: The Richter Scale (ML), accessed August 23, 2019, http://www.johnmartin.com/earthquakes/eqsafs/safs_693.htm.
3
"Earthquake Facts," US Geological Survey, accessed September 11, 2019, https://earthquake.usgs.gov/learn/facts.php.
4
Kirtley F. Mather and Shirley L. Mason, *Source Book in Geology, 1900–1950* (Cambridge: Harvard University Press, 1970).

Surface Area

—

Know your exposure

Surface Area

In general, we can think of surface area as the amount of something that is in contact with, or able to react to, the outside world. A teaspoon of loose sugar will dissolve much faster than a cube because the surface area is larger. As a model, surface area is about recognizing when increasing our exposure will help us and when it will cause us problems. Sometimes we want a large surface area, such as when we are trying to increase our exposure to new ideas. But large areas come with risks, so when we want to protect ourselves, shrinking our surface area might be the answer.

In chemistry, the greater a reactant's surface area, the faster a reaction is likely to occur, as there are more collisions between particles. So the same material in powdered form will produce a faster reaction than when in lumps. It's easier to start a fire with many small sticks than a few logs.

In biology, living things evolve to have a greater or smaller surface area for achieving different aims, either on the whole or in different parts of their bodies. Our lungs and intestines have a huge surface area to increase the absorption of oxygen and nutrients. Animals living in cold regions tend to have a lower surface-area-to-volume ratio than those in warmer regions to reduce heat loss, and vice versa. When you're cold, you probably scrunch up your body without thinking to reduce your surface area.

Surface area is useful when considering the amount of dependencies or assumptions something has. A program whose code has little surface area is much more likely to age well and be robust than a piece with many dependencies. The same goes for projects. If a project depends on ten teams, it's much less likely to finish on time than one with less surface area.

Circus schools and increasing creativity

Sometimes, as individuals or as organizations, we have a creativity problem. We need some fresh ideas but have a hard time coming up with them. We rely on what we already know and often end up with more of the same. When we need to spur innovation, we can try increasing our surface area of exposure to new disciplines. More surface area can give us more diversity, which is sometimes what we need in order to innovate and create.

One short period in the history of circus development provides an excellent example of why multidisciplinary learning can be so powerful. The circus has been around for a long time in various forms. Records of people juggling or doing acrobatics in a public space go back to the Middle Ages. The circus has evolved since then in response to changes in the social environment, and eventually it coalesced into the form that seems to represent the archetype: the big tent with a ringmaster, animals, clowns, and the flying trapeze.

Iconic circuses like Barnum & Bailey, with trains traveling around the country and setting up the big top for a few days of shows at every stop, became the definition of circus. The performers would live in the circus and raise their kids in the circus environment, and often those children would grow up to become circus performers. Duncan Wall explains in *The Ordinary Acrobat* that "during the eighteenth and nineteenth centuries, well after the rise of public education, circus performers continued to educate their children themselves." This resulted in a situation where "they didn't just learn their skills, they *lived* them, an intuitive experience that translated into astonishing ability."[1] From very young ages, circus performers could accomplish the amazing feats presented in a circus show.

However, this family system led to a problem. Circus acts became predictable. They may have required great athleticism, but they were always the same. As Wall describes, "Beholden to tradition, each generation mindlessly duplicated the work

1
Duncan Wall, *The Ordinary Acrobat* (New York: Vintage Books, Random House, 2013).

2
Wall, ibid.

3
Wall, ibid.

4
Wall, ibid.

of the last," creating an artistic bubble where "technical ability continued to rise, but the art as a whole stagnated, [and] a cheap uniformity ensued."[2]

Eventually the circus became synonymous with nostalgia and directed its marketing at children because they were the only group to whom the circus was new and exciting. Overall ticket sales went down, and the circus was well on its way to becoming history.

How did this decline happen? One of the reasons was that, as Wall explains, "the family system defined the circus for centuries. But while it provided the source for much of the circus's strength and allure, it also had a fundamental flaw. Ruled by families, the circus was what physicists call a closed system. Although the troupes traveled widely, they remained almost totally isolated from the outside world."[3] The surface area of the circus community was small. The borders were not around individuals but the whole unit. Interactions with anyone outside the circus were kept to a minimum. Thus there were minimal opportunities for creative reactions to occur.

Today it's a different story. Circuses are vibrant and diverse. Commercially, companies like Cirque du Soleil have wide appeal and earn into the billions of dollars. The shows are nothing like the traditional circus. In many, the animals have disappeared. Circuses are performed in a variety of venues, from stand-alone theaters to open-air spaces under the stars. Audiences go to see what is new and dynamic in both tricks and artistry. The creativity has exploded in the last 50 years. And one of the reasons is the increased surface area of the new circus education.

Duncan Wall writes that "the story of how the circus finally extracted itself from [its] creative hole is, in large part, the story of the development of circus education. It begins in Russia."[4] After the Russian Revolution in 1916, many of the circus families left due to the political uncertainty. Russians, however, still wanted to go to the circus. So the Russian

President George Washington watched the first circus performance in the United States, on April 3, 1793 in Philadelphia. The Circus Hall of Fame is in a building that formerly housed the winter home of the Hagenbeck-Wallace Circus, which, at its peak, was the second largest circus in America.

5
Wall, ibid.

6
Wall, ibid.

7
Wall, ibid.

government, deciding that maintaining and improving the circus could improve the people, re-created the Russian circus and opened a school.

These actions proved momentous in the evolution of the circus. Wall explains how circus performer education was changed by the Russians: "Based largely on Russia's famous ballet schools, the program took an interdisciplinary approach to education." Students learned traditional techniques, but they also learned philosophy, physics, math, and chemistry to "develop their intellects" and serve as sources of inspiration.[5]

Complementing this new education, the Russians took a fresh look at other aspects of the circus. "To encourage innovation, the state invited revered artists from other disciplines" to develop circus content, and "in circus 'labs' around the country, artists and scientists developed new circus methods and equipment."[6]

The results were incredible. "During the fifties and sixties, while the critics were lamenting the death of the circus in the West, the Soviet circus was soaring....They developed what was known as 'The Studio,' a sort of circus production house, in which artists from all disciplines teamed up to devise original circus material. The work coming out of such institutions was unparalleled in artistry and professional polish." Eventually the shows filtered out from behind the Iron Curtain. Soviet circuses toured abroad to critical acclaim and sold-out shows wherever they went. They established dozens of permanent circus theaters at home, selling a hundred million circus tickets every year.[7]

The new multidisciplinary approach to circus education did not go unnoticed, and many countries started their own schools. One of the most notable is the national circus school in France. They too teach a wide variety of subjects to their students. The French school culminates with the creation of an original work, giving students experience in all facets of a production. Wall explains why when he writes, "It trained the

8
Wall, ibid.

students to *create* new work, not just *perform* work, in order to keep the circus evolving."[8]

Therein lies the difference between the family approach that almost rendered the circus obsolete and the way circus education is taught now. Students are expected to come up with innovations to move the art in new directions. It is no longer enough to repeat what came before. Both audiences and performers expect new ideas to push the art forward.

Having the core of circus education be multidisciplinary is effectively increasing the surface area to promote more creative reactions, increasing the pace of innovation. When you have a narrow knowledge set to draw on, it's harder to come up with new ideas. Exposure to different disciplines sets up circus performers to be creative in the execution of their art. Increasing our own knowledge surface area is a solution when lack of creativity or fresh ideas is a problem.

Guerilla warfare

Sometimes reducing your surface area is important. Decreasing your exposure can make you less vulnerable to influence, manipulation, or attack. Designing security measures is one area where surface area needs to be as small as possible without compromising functionality.

In internet security, surface area refers to the number of opportunities an attacker has to gain unauthorized access. Every additional entry point increases the surface area. For instance, employees who have access to important information in a company increase the surface area, as an attacker could gain control of their accounts. Or the more connection points your network has to the internet, the more attack vectors an adversary has. While perfect security is impossible, having the smallest possible surface area reduces the risk of breaches.

Far from being a modern concept, we can also see the application of reduced surface area for security when we

9
Max Boot, *Invisible Armies* (New York: Liveright, 2013).

10
Robert Greene, *The 33 Strategies of War* (New York: Penguin, 2006).

consider the narrow slit windows of medieval fortifications or walled cities with only a few guarded entrances. There is a natural relationship between surface area and defense. The smaller your area of exposure to an adversary, the more you can concentrate your resources on a powerful defense of those exposure points.

A small surface area is not only a defensive strategy but also a possible offensive one as well. Guerilla warfare is essentially the use of small attack groups against larger, more conventional standing armies. Those who engage in guerilla warfare reduce their surface area in two dimensions. First, they operate in small autonomous units, and second, they aren't attached to occupying and holding a given territory. Both factors provide little surface area for their adversaries to attack.

The use of guerilla warfare can be traced back to ancient times when the guerillas were nomads fighting against the rulers in a particular region. In *Invisible Armies*, Max Boot explains one of the advantages that small, mobile bands of attackers had: "Having no cities, crops, or other fixed targets to defend, nomads had little cause to worry about enemy attack, making them hard to deter."[9] When you aren't defending a territory or other fixed structures, you give your adversary far fewer points of vulnerability.

As those types of fighters evolved into more contemporary guerilla warriors, the basic principle of a reduced surface area continued to define their tactics. As Robert Greene explains in *The 33 Strategies of War*, "Early guerilla warriors learned the value of operating in small, dispersed bands as opposed to a concentrated army, keeping in constant motion, never forming a front, flank, or rear for the other side to hit."[10] It's harder to attack small groups of people with no attachment to the territory they occupy.

Guerilla warriors keep their infrastructure to a minimum, as mobility is always a factor. Although a guerilla organization has leaders, they tend to organize offensive efforts around

Fidel Castro's rebel hide-out Comandancia La Plata in the rainforest of the Sierra Maestra at Cuba's eastern tip remains preserved for visitors. His two room cabin is still intact, with the original armchairs, double bed, and bullet-punctured refrigerator.

Fidel Castro - (1926-2016). Leader
of Cuba from 1959 to 2008 as the
head of a one-party communist
state, Castro overthrew the
previous government alongside
Ernesto "Che" Guevara. He was a
polarizing figure who aligned Cuba
with Russia and other socialist
governments, and was actively
opposed by the United States.

*

Fulgencio Batista - (1901-1973).
President of Cuba from 1940 to
1944, Batista led a successful
military coup against the
incumbent, resulting in his heading
a dictatorship from 1952 to 1959,
before he was removed from
power in the Cuban Revolution. His
leadership during this time was
marked by widespread corruption
and worsening income inequality.

11
Boot, ibid.

12
United States Army Special
Operation Command, Case Studies
in Insurgency and Revolutionary
Warfare: Cuba 1953–1959 (Fort
Bragg: Special Operations
Research Office, 1963). Available at
www.soc.mil.

small groups that can act independently. Guerilla warfare
maintains such a small surface area because it is critical
if they are to have any success. As Boot explains, "Guerilla
tactics always have been the resort of the weak against the
strong. That is why insurgents wage war from the shadows; if
they fought in the open, they would be annihilated."[11]

Perhaps one of the most famous examples of successful
guerilla warfare was that carried out under the leadership of
Fidel Castro[*] in Cuba in the 1950s. His rebel group operated out
of mobile bases in the highest mountains in Cuba and was dedicated to overthrowing the regime of Fulgencio Batista[*]. Their
eventual success came as a result of more than just the guerilla warfare tactics they employed, but those were textbook.

Castro started out in the mountains with only about 20
men. The United States Army Special Operation Command
produced a document entitled Case Studies in Insurgency and
Revolutionary Warfare: Cuba 1953–1959. The report makes it
clear that Castro's available manpower was only ever a small
fraction of Batista's: "Castro has revealed that he had only 180
men with him in April 1958" (Batista's regime fell on January
1, 1959), and that "the two columns that were given the single
biggest operation in August 1958 (by Castro) amounted to only
220 men."[12] Contrast these numbers with the thousands of
trained military personnel Batista commanded, and the surface area of the Cuban rebels seems incredibly small.

This small number of guerillas operated in tiny tactical
units that, in classic guerilla warfare style, chipped away at
Batista's infrastructure. They obviously never attacked the
Cuban military directly; they didn't have the resources for that.
Instead, they went after vulnerable, isolated units or relatively
unguarded parts of the communications infrastructure or
supply chains.

Castro's rebels were also mobile. They operated out of
bases deep in the heart of mountainous territory that was hard
to access. But they were not attached to any particular piece of

When You Can't Tell the Whole Truth

Maps are a great example of both the dangers and opportunities of reducing a surface area. All maps present "a chosen aspect of reality."[1] When we choose which details to include in a map, we are deciding which view of the territory to present. Thus all maps show a smaller surface area than the corresponding territory they represent. We are not talking about a geographical surface area but rather a conceptual one. Maps cannot capture every point of detail in a territory, and that is not their function. By necessarily omitting some details, a map reduces the number of information points about a given area. It is this reduction that we are referring to by saying maps reduce the surface area of a territory.

In *How to Lie with Maps*, Mark Monmonier explains, "A good map tells a multitude of little white lies; it suppresses truth to help the user see what needs to be seen.... But the value of a map depends on how well its generalized geometry and generalized content reflect a chosen aspect of reality."[2]

A clear example of the need to simplify a territory in order to make a useful map is the London Underground (known as "the Tube") map. It's instantly recognizable, popping up on T-shirts, mugs, posters, and souvenirs. It's been the inspiration for countless underground maps across the world. As a design, it's beautiful and elegant. Yet part of what makes it so successful is the fact that it doesn't represent reality.

The original design for the Tube map comes from Harry Beck, a humble electrical draughtsman. Lacking any relevant formal design training, Beck took his knowledge of drawing circuit diagrams and applied it to a new domain. As an outsider, he was able to approach the problem of conveying the relative locations of stations and lines in a fresh manner. Ignoring geographical accuracy, he portrayed the Tube lines as simple colored lines, with circles representing stations.[3] In reality, neither is laid out in a logical manner.

Beck unveiled his radical design in 1933 and was met with unequivocal derision. The Underground's publicity department couldn't imagine commuters using it. After all, it wasn't a map in the usual sense of the word. Beck ignored the actual scale of the city. He portrayed the distance between stations as almost exactly equal. He conveyed the Tube lines as a grid, ignoring the true way they twist and turn beneath the ground. He showed the line intersections as 45-degree angles to indicate where to change trains.

Yet as soon as they made a trial print run of the Tube map, people fell in love with it. Harry Beck opened up the city in a new way. The first prints were snapped up by commuters, for whom the simplicity mattered far more than geographical accuracy. Despite numerous changes to the transport system, the modern map retains the spirit of Beck's original design.

Seeing as a map is always a simplification, it must omit a large amount of unnecessary detail and nuance. The London Underground map excludes a number (some estimates run as high as 50) of abandoned stations that were closed due to low passenger numbers or never opened in the first place. There's no need to include these on the general public's map. It would just confuse people and prompt requests to visit them, which isn't allowed. A few can be briefly glimpsed if you look out the window at the right moment.

The tube map reduces the surface area of London to a few points of information to communicate for a single purpose. Thus, when we communicate, it might be helpful to reduce surface area to provide useful content. Monmonier writes, "The map must omit details that would confuse or distract."[4] We cannot cover everything at once.

1
Mark Monmonier, *How to Lie with Maps*, 3rd ed. (Chicago: University of Chicago Press, 2018).
2
Monmonier, ibid.
3
Amar Toor, "Meet Harry Beck, the Genius Behind London's Iconic Subway Map," *The Verge*, March 29, 2013, https://www.theverge.com/2013/3/29/4160028/harry-beck-designer-of-iconic-london-underground-map.
4
Monmonier, ibid.

13
Boot, ibid.

territory. Thus they could easily move around, evading capture and giving their adversary minimal surface area to attack.

The lens of surface area demonstrates how a small one can be both a defensive and offensive strategy. One of the most famous guerilla warriors, T. E. Lawrence—who led small groups of Bedouins against the Turks, wrote foundational literature on guerilla warfare, and became famous as Lawrence of Arabia—explained the essence of the strategy thus: to become "a thing intangible, invulnerable, without front or back."[13]

— Sidebar: When You Can't Tell the Whole Truth

Conclusion

The surface area model helps us identify situations where increasing our exposure would be beneficial and times when it might hurt us. It teaches us that increasing our diversity quotient can give us fresh ideas and help us innovate. The model also reminds us, however, that in many ways, the more we expose ourselves, the more vulnerable we are. Different situations require different surface areas.

Global and Local Maxima

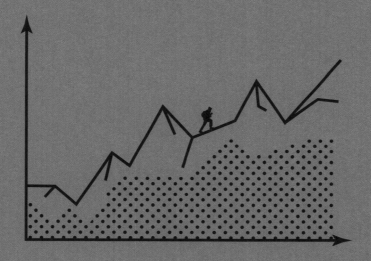

—
Embrace the peaks and valleys

Global and Local Maxima

The maxima and minima of a mathematical function are the largest and smallest values over its domain. Although there is one maximum value—the global maximum—there can be smaller peaks of value in a given range—the local maxima. Using global and local maxima as a model is about knowing when you have hit your peak, or if there is still potential to go higher. It reminds us that sometimes we have to go down to go back up. The model can also help us understand that to optimize and reach our peaks, we need to align the large components before we refine the details.

« We may need to temporarily worsen our solution if we want to continue searching for improvements. »

Brian Christian and Tom Griffiths[1]

One of the characteristics of maxima is that there is an increase before and a decrease afterward. Thus, they occur at a critical point of change.

The algorithm that produces the global and local maxima graph is known in computer science as "hill climbing," as Brian Christian and Tom Griffiths explain "since the search through a space of solutions, some better and some worse, is commonly thought of in terms of a landscape with hills and valleys, where your goal is to reach the highest peak."[2] We go up and down hills and valleys our entire lives as we work through challenges and develop new expertise.

One of the challenges with climbing a hill is how to know we are climbing the highest peaks. The value of using global and local maxima as a model is that it pushes us to consider if and how we could do better. Even when things are going well,

1
Christian and Griffiths, ibid.

2
Christian and Griffiths, ibid.

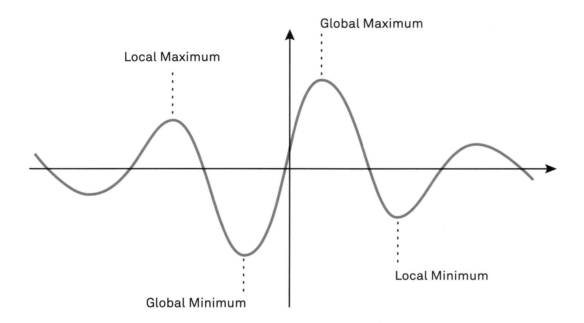

The hill climbing graph looks much like our experience of life:
a lot of time spent navigating between highs and lows.

Lisa Lindahl - (b. 1948). Co-inventor
of the Jogbra, she he is also
the co-inventor of the Bellisse
Compression Comfort Bra
designed to support breast cancer
patients as they are going through
treatment. Two of the original
Jogbras are in the Smithsonian.

3
Dave Rael, "Escaping Local
Maxima," October 30, 2015,
https://simpleprogrammer.com/
escaping-local-maxima/.

we are often just at a local maximum. In the article "Escaping Local Maxima," Dave Rael explains that the "chasms between where we are and where we could be [are] opportunities to improve by finding ways of moving from a place where progress is flat to find a new slope to climb."[3]

Getting to a new peak means change—changing what you know, changing the way you are doing things. At a local maximum, things are as good as they can get with the current structure. To get to the peak of a higher hill requires us to walk through a valley as we go back to being neophytes in some ways. Or it requires us to step back, broaden our view, and determine if we are heading in the right direction. But as we learn new skills, partner with new people, or make big jumps in our optimization, we start climbing back up to reach the next maximum.

Navigating the hills

The story of a new product, from conception to widespread use and high market share, is usually one of ups and downs. There are so many facets of business to learn, from production to sales to marketing, that for novice businesspeople trying to turn their great idea into a successful sales story, there are usually a few mistakes along the way. In addition, we often have to manage traversing our own peaks and valleys while trying to ensure that our current capacities don't limit our ability to climb a higher peak. Using the lens of global and local maxima shows that often in bringing a new product to market, there are many times the owners reach a peak of success only to have to go down to a local minimum as they take on the next challenging climb.

The story of the development of the sports bra is a great example of the hills and valleys one is likely to experience taking a product from conception to market success. In 1977 Lisa Lindahl* loved running, but she had a problem. The motion of running caused her breasts to hurt, but she didn't want to give up on a pastime she found so physically and psychologically rewarding. So Lindahl and her friend Polly Smith[*] designed the first sports bra based on the requirements Lindahl noted when running, things like straps that don't dig in, seams that don't rub, and support that minimizes breast movement.[4] Forty years later, sports bras were everywhere. Reading Lindahl's story makes it clear that a graph of the eventual success of the sports bra looks less like a 45-degree line that just keeps climbing up and more like the hills and valleys of reaching and moving past local minimums and maximums.

After many experiments with different designs and fabrics, Smith constructed a one-off sports bra. Lindahl wore it running, and it worked. But as anyone who has prototyped a new product knows, what you do to get the first one isn't scalable to turning it into a business.

Lindahl entered into a partnership with another woman who had been around during the initial design phase, Hinda Schreiber. Together they tried to develop the sports bra prototype into a business. Calling it the Jogbra, Lindahl and Schreiber had to figure out production, sales, logistics, and marketing. Where could they source the very specific material needed? Where could they get the bras sewn? How would they bring them to market? Who would sell them? How would they let women know the product was available?

Lindahl reflects in her memoir *Unleash the Girls* that "starting and running this business was always about learning, gaining information, then accruing the knowledge to apply it correctly."[5] This cycle is often filled with mistakes, as part of accruing knowledge is learning what doesn't work as much as it is about figuring out what does.

Part of what makes Lindahl's story interesting is that the development of the Jogbra company required her to work through personal local maxima and minima to reach a higher global maximum.

Lindahl describes how growing the Jogbra company required her to push herself out of the comfort zones of early

[*]
Polly Smith - (b. 1949). Emmy and BAFTA award-winning costume designer, Smith has clothed hundreds of Muppets. She also created the first Jogbra by sewing two jockstraps together.

4
Lisa Z. Lindahl, *Unleash the Girls: The Untold Story of the Invention of the Sports Bra and How It Changed the World (and Me)* (United States of America: Eugenie Z. Lindahl, 2019).

5
Lindahl, ibid.

6
Lindahl, ibid.

security. She went back to college in her late twenties, despite being intimidated, because she realized that in a sense, she had maxed out atop the hill she was on. In order to go higher, she had to start climbing another hill, "challenging many old, ingrained limitations that had held [her] back in the past."[6]

Another factor that required dedicated effort to address was her epilepsy. Lindahl had epilepsy since childhood, and she writes of how it shaped her early choices and understanding of her capabilities. For instance, she was conditioned to be afraid of living alone due to the risks associated with having a seizure, and thus she chose early marriage as a result. Part of Lindahl's attachment to running was the better connection it gave her to her own body. It was this connection that helped Lindahl not let her epilepsy stop her from looking for ways to reach her global maxima. Her epilepsy was a factor in her life, but she recounts how she often made decisions so that it wasn't a limiting one (it became a one instead of being a zero).

When it came to the Jogbra business, Lindahl's description of some of the early choices she made makes it clear that she was looking at what was needed to scale the highest peak. For example, Lindahl made the decision to sell it in sporting goods stores as a piece of sports equipment instead of the more obvious choice of the lingerie section of department stores. She recounts how during the late 1970s, women in the United States were starting to get into sports in unprecedented numbers due to legislative changes that mandated equal access to athletics. And the Jogbra was the only product on the market to give women the flexibility and support needed to participate. She felt that putting the Jogbra out there as lingerie would limit its sales, especially seeing as bra sales in general were on a downward trend. It was, however, by no means obvious to the mostly male sales reps and owners of sports stores that the Jogbra was a piece of athletic equipment. She and her small team had to work hard to convince them that Jogbras for women were as essential as jockstraps for men.

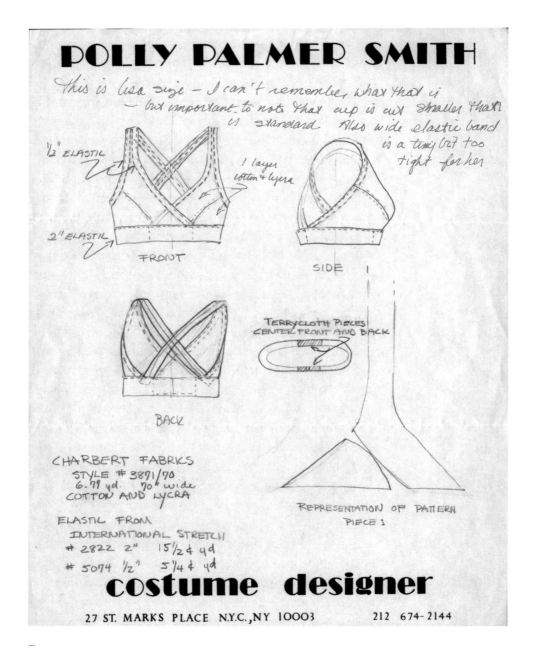

POLLY PALMER SMITH

This is lisa size — I can't remember what that is — but important to note that cup is cut smaller than is standard. Also wide elastic band is a tiny bit too tight for her

½" ELASTIC

1 layer cotton & lycra

2" ELASTIC

FRONT

SIDE

BACK

TERRYCLOTH PIECES CENTER FRONT AND BACK

REPRESENTATION OF PATTERN PIECES

CHARBERT FABRICS
STYLE #3871/70.
6.79 yd. 70" wide
COTTON AND LYCRA

ELASTIC FROM
INTERNATIONAL STRETCH
#2822 2" 15½ & yd
#5074 ½" 5¼ & yd

costume designer

27 ST. MARKS PLACE N.Y.C., NY 10003   212 674-2144

—

Lisa Lindahl wore the Jogbra prototype while Hinda Schreiber jogged backward in front of her to see how much her breasts bounced, verifying that the new bra offered more support than conventional bras.

7
Lindahl, ibid.

8
Lindahl, ibid.

She recounts their first full year of business:

> Already articles had been written about the product, about us, and there was never a lack of orders. So, yes, the perception both publicly and personally that Jogbra was a success came right away. Right. Away. And the perception was supported by some impressive numbers. We were profitable in our first full year in business and had no idea that this was unusual.[7]

It was an awesome start, and very quickly they hit a local maximum. The end of their first year, though, wasn't a global maximum, and Lindahl often references the learning she had to do to keep the company growing.

Do you go back down a hill when you learn something new? In a lot of ways, yes. If you've never done marketing, you're probably going to have to be bad at marketing for a while before you get good at it. And before your company can lever-age marketing to reach a new local maximum, you're going to have to start near the bottom of the marketing hill.

Lindahl describes the many mistakes the company made as they were developing both their product line and their brand. There were poor naming choices, awful colors, and styles that didn't sell. She says, "In those early years, we got off track quite a bit. But we were learning. We were learn-ing the importance of *not* being a one-product company." She describes the Jogmit—mitts to wear while jogging—as a failure but the foray into a men's line as a success. "The line evolved over time, some products came and went; some became staples. And some...some should have just stayed on the drawing board."[8] Using the lens of global and local maxima, we can see that experimentation, with its inevitable failures, is part of achieving success. Going down sometimes is a part of going up, but if you can improve, you know you haven't reached your global maximum.

9
Lindahl, ibid.

10
Lindahl, ibid.

Product failures taught the Jogbra team to be aware of their niche, and over time they got better and better at exploiting it. As the company grew, there were continued downs and ups. Expansion required new expertise—and often new capital. The partnership went through challenges. Competition increased. Eventually, as Lindahl describes, "the looming need for capital to fund our continually climbing sales growth" led to her and Schreiber selling the Jogbra company to Playtex.[9] For Lindahl, this was just another hill and valley that led to her exploring other life maxima.

Reflecting on her experience with the invention of the sports bra and the development of the Jogbra company, Lindahl writes, "You make your plans looking upward toward you goal, only to reach it and find that what you thought was the pinnacle, the ceiling of your endeavor, was in fact only the floor of your next level."[10]

Using the model of global and local maxima helps us remember that we often cannot reach our full potential if we aren't willing to stretch ourselves, take risks, and fail once in a while.

— Sidebar: Optimization

Using new partnerships to optimize

We don't have mathematical functions to determine subjective states in our life, such as whether we've reached a global or local maximum on our success potential. We have to perform an analysis of events to determine if we've gone as far as we can within the parameters we've set up, or if we need to regroup and change the scale of how we're optimizing in order to find a higher peak.

Using the model of global and local maxima helps us identify when and how to find a higher peak. Sometimes we know we're close and just need to fine-tune, like rolling the basketball in the sidebar example. And sometimes we need to get out the giant ball because we have the feeling we're not

Optimization

Another use of the global and local maxima model is in optimization. It helps you know how and when to optimize, and when to avoid overoptimization.

This is actually easier to explain if we start by talking about minima instead.[1]

Let's suppose you want to identify the lowest point in your hometown (the point from which everywhere else is uphill). How would you go about doing this?

One way to solve this problem could be to take a ball (let's pick a basketball), set it down, and watch where it rolls. We expect it to roll downhill, at least if it's on a hill, but since your town is probably pretty large and the ball is unlikely to navigate all of the routes, it's improbable that it will stop at the absolute lowest point. Instead it might stop on the lowest point of your street—a local minima. Could we improve this?

What if we took a giant ball, say a quarter mile in diameter. Forget for a minute the liability of such a plan and the cost of producing it. How would it roll? It could easily roll over houses with such a large size, and it's much more likely to find something approaching the global minima, but it'll never find the global minima itself. Why is that?

The scale is simply too large. The true global minima probably fits underneath such a large object, which never quite gets down there. Now that we're close, though, we could switch back to our basketball. Finally we may have found the true global minima (or at least we're close enough—we've already destroyed a lot of houses in our pursuit).

This story tells a lesson about scale in optimization. We need to make the big changes first, before we try to optimize the details. There is just no other practical way to do it. We also need to be mindful of the directionality of the changes. The feedback mechanism of the ball rolling tells us which way to look. We're not just randomly sampling different locations to try to predict which way will give us the greatest optimizations. The other major lesson in this thought experiment is that local minima (or maxima) act as a sort of trap. Our little basketball gets stuck too soon. Stepping back and making a bigger jump by using a bigger ball gives us a better indication of where the global minima is.

1
Thank you to Nathan Taggart for suggesting and developing this sidebar.

11
Mark Hodkinson, *Queen: The Early Years* (London: Omnibus Press, 2009).

in the right place at all. Changing the scale at which we are optimizing gives us perspective on where to go and how to get there. For rock bands, we can think of the members of a band like the giant balls and individual chords like the basketballs. There is no point in changing the chord in one particular song to get out of a local minimum if your bass player isn't a good fit and is leading you in the wrong direction. Before bands start tinkering with their image or style, they first need to have the optimal people in the group.

Who hasn't heard of the band Queen? Who can't sing along to at least one of their 25 top-ten hits? They are a rock band who unequivocally made it. They seemed to create hit after hit, entertaining millions and inspiring many musicians. It's easy to think it was all luck, but it wasn't. Queen was the product of years of experimentation, development, and many failed bands. Before they came together as Queen, each member of the band spent years learning how to try to optimize for success in the music business.

Each of the members of Queen—Freddie Mercury, Brian May, John Deacon, and Roger Taylor—were members of bands before. Many of these bands weren't total failures. They had gigs in decent-size venues, fans, and even a record contract. However, we can look back and see that each band before Queen was a local maximum.

John Deacon, the bassist, "who had been strumming the acoustic guitar he bought with his early morning round paper wages since the age of twelve," formed a band called the Opposition with some friends before he turned 14.[11] They played together for four years, and during that time they went through ten members. Some left to pursue other interests; some were asked to leave on account of inferior play or not gelling with the rest of the group. John was noted as a perfectionist in both playing and arranging, and the Opposition had many gigs in their home region of Leicester. As Mark Hodkinson writes in *Queen: The Early Years*, "This was John Deacon's musical

12
Hodkinson, ibid.

13
Hodkinson, ibid.

14
Hodkinson, ibid.

apprenticeship, and it was extraordinarily thorough."[12] In addition, just before joining Queen, he briefly formed another band with some friends simply called Deacon.

Roger Taylor started out on guitar before settling on the drums. He was part of three bands. His third band, the Reaction, had some longevity. With six different members over the years, this band, too, experimented with group dynamics. It was a learning process, a continual effort to understand what promoted cohesion and creativity as well as what undermined group success. Taylor "evolved into the natural leader. He was barely seventeen years old…but he willingly shouldered most of the responsibility for running the group."[13] These were lessons that he applied later to success with Queen.

Brian May also started strumming guitar in his school days. Captivated by science as well as music, "it was fated that Brian would fuse his interest in music and technology, and along with a school friend…he began to record songs." He and friends formed a band, called 1984, which over the years had eight members. With one of them, Tim Staffell, he wrote songs. These were harmonies that later turned into Queen songs, and "during these raw formative days, there was already evidence of ideas which would be developed many years later."[14] The band 1984 didn't have the right members to help the sound take off, but the process of trying to write songs gave May an indication of the type of people who might be needed to optimize them.

May played guitar and did backing vocals on the recordings of other groups, and with 1984 he gained exposure to some of the components that are required of a successful band: stage setup, sound checks, band etiquette and industry quirks, and the need for patience. This was information that was useful for figuring out the essentials of the minimum needed for success: who a band needed to develop style, sound, and songs.

In the late 1960s, Brian May and Roger Taylor formed the

Queen are the most successful act in the UK's album chart history, having spent more time on the chart than any other musical act.

15
Hodkinson, ibid.

16
Hodkinson, ibid.

17
Hodkinson, ibid.

18
Hodkinson, ibid.

band Smile with Tim Staffell. Smile worked hard to try to put together what each member had learned to find a higher peak. "The coyness and ready conformity was gone forever, and Brian and Tim's ideology reflected these changes. Individuality was everything and in support of this free expression, their new group would mainly write their own material, or interpret others from a unique panorama."[15]

Smile got a record deal and steady gigs—definitely a local maximum in the music business. They recorded tracks and tried to be an "albums band," but they found their record deal was going nowhere. They pivoted, and "with laudable fortitude resolved to find a niche as a live band."[16] Smile learned there is little predictability in the music business, and their studio-recorded album was never released. However, "elements which were later brilliantly realized by Queen were already present."[17]

Freddie Mercury, the man who became the legendary front man of Queen, was born Farrokh Bulsara and grew up in Zanzibar and India before moving to England in his late teens. Although he loved music and sang covers as part of his school's unofficial band, Mercury also cultivated a prescient understanding of another key component of musical success: image. The Freddie Mercury who rocked Live Aid in 1985 spent years, like every other member of the band, developing as an artist. He was a member of the group Ibex and then joined the band Sour Milk Sea. Playing with these groups helped him refine and polish both his vocals and his stage presence. Mercury was described as having "a certain tenacity, a single-mindedness,"[18] and reading his story reveals a man who paid a lot of attention to the details, absorbing the dynamics of the environment he intended to succeed in.

Before Queen could start producing hits, first the members had to find each other.

Changing who you play with in a band is like rolling the big ball. You already have a decent sense of the territory and

19
Hodkinson, ibid.

have an educated guess about which direction the ball is likely to roll. But the emergent properties of playing music as a group means that you can never exactly predict what sound certain individuals will make when they come together. You don't know if a group might have settled over the global maximum at least until they start playing together.

In 1970 May, Taylor, and Mercury, who had been friends for a while, decided to form a new band. Putting in all the knowledge they had gained over the years, they first had to roll that big ball to find a bass player. They went through three bassists before they found John Deacon, who turned out to be an excellent fit.

Once they thought they were in the general territory of the global maximum, they refined element by element. They played shows. They wrote music. "They openly solicited their friend's comments about performances and were not afraid of criticism."[19] Through constant learning and a willingness to incorporate feedback into developing new functions aimed at optimizing to reach their global maxima, the members of Queen became one of the most dynamic and memorable rock bands of all time.

Conclusion

Global and local maxima as a model can be used in different ways to help us make the changes we need for success. It encourages us not to see achieving our goals as a steady upward trajectory but as a path full of peaks and valleys. Understanding that sometimes we have to go down in order to climb even higher helps us make short-term sacrifices to play the long game. This model also offers insight on how to optimize to find our global maxima. It's more powerful to make the big changes before we try to optimize the details.

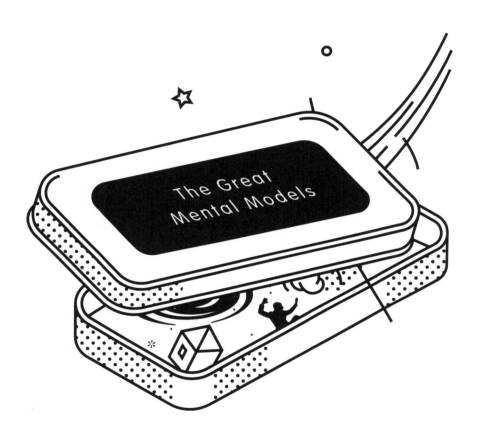

Now What?

You've finished reading the third volume of *The Great Mental Models* series. You now have almost 50 models from these books in your toolkit. We hope you have found our exploration of each model interesting and insightful. But now you may be wondering, what next? How can you take these seeds of ideas about timeless knowledge and grow them to make improvements in all areas of your life?

Exposing yourself to new ideas is always the first step in learning. But in order to develop wisdom, what you learn needs to be put to the test. When it comes to mental models, you can't just passively read about them and hope that one day you will notice a positive change in your life. You need to use them.

Pick a model, maybe one per week, and start looking at your life through that lens. What do you notice? What looks different? Write down or record your observations. Take the time to reflect on your experiences using each model, because it is through reflection that the most valuable knowledge builds. Note where you make a different choice based on the insight provided by the model. Pay attention to what worked and improved your outcomes. Learn from your mistakes. Over time you will build knowledge of where each model is most useful and most likely to help you.

As you practice using more models, you will begin to build a latticework. You will see connections and notice that some models give the best insight when paired with certain others. Eventually your latticework will be comprehensive enough that you will be able to use it in every situation, reducing your blind spots and preventing problems.

Using mental models is a lifelong journey, and this book is just one step on that road. The next volume in the series will cover the foundational ideas from new disciplines, which will give you another set of tools for your toolbox.

Improving our lives means seeing the world as it is and learning to work with the fundamental principles that govern it. Having a diverse set of thoughtful mental models that reflect how the world works is a critical component of making better decisions and ultimately living a more meaningful life.

As the series goes out into the world, we will continue to create resources on fs.blog/tgmm to help you integrate these models into your thinking. As we wrote in volume 2, before long, when it comes to using mental models, you will be capitalizing on the powerful momentum you have created. These ideas will become such an integral part of the fabric of your thinking that it will become impossible to view any situation without the valuable lenses they provide.

Afterthoughts

Thanks for picking up *The Great Mental Models, Vol. 3*. I love how this series continually evolves—and how, by applying its principles, so can we. The GMM series meets our evermore urgent need to understand our increasingly complex world and make significant decisions with confidence. In this volume, we learned how the Pareto principle can help us decide where to focus our work energy. How "finding the zero" can keep our businesses afloat. And why things really *do* get worse before they get better. (It's not an illusion, it's a mathematical principle, so hang in there!)

If you like solving problems and learning about new ways of thinking—if you're the kind of person who not only devoured this book, but enjoyed it so much that you're even reading this end page—have I got a job for you. Come join us at Automattic, Inc., where we've been democratizing publishing and commerce since 2005.

We're the people behind brands like WordPress.com, Tumblr, Jetpack, WooCommerce, and more—innovative products that help people express themselves *and* earn a living. Our workforce is distributed all over the globe, but we're united by a passionate desire to build a better web and world. And we're growing rapidly, as our mission is more important than ever.

Working with great people at Automattic, you can have a real impact, shaping an operating system for the open web: over 40% of the world's top ten million websites have chosen WordPress to be their foundation, more than ten times the second-largest platform in the market. Above all, working at Automattic means connecting your career to the power and sustainability of Open Source, not tying your fate to the evolutionary dead end of proprietary software.

Automattic's extremely flexible work environment empowers you to perform at your very best, while our fluid company structure and culture of individual autonomy means you can have a *huge* influence here—not just be part of a machine. If you're idealistic yet realistic, and if you believe changing the world and earning a living are compatible goals, this just may be the place for you. Why not apply? Hope to see you soon!

https://automattic.com/gmm

Jeffrey Zeldman | Designer, WordPress.com

Acknowledgments

Books are never the product of one mind. I am always so grateful for the people who share their wisdom and insight during the development of *The Great Mental Models* books.

First, to Rosie Leizrowice, who is an excellent writing partner. From her willingness to tackle any topic to her dedicated attention to detail, her contributions to this book are invaluable.

To our book designer Garvin Hirt and illustrator Marcia Mihotich: each volume seems more beautiful than the last. Thank you for your willingness to push until it all looks perfect.

We have so many wonderful contributors and reviewers. Thank you Simon Hørup Eskildsen, Jeff Annello, Tara Small, Tina Cantrill, Nathan Taggart, Tim Bragassa, Yves Colomb, Rick Jones, Ran Klein, and Dr. Gregory P. Moore for your inputs and insights. Without such a thoughtful community who is willing to take precious time to challenge and discuss our ideas, these books would be much less useful.

Thank you to our editor Kristen Hall-Geisler for diving fearlessly into the material to make sure the clarity and flow carried through the whole manuscript.

Our proofreaders Cooper Lee Bombardier, Sarah Currin, and Jenn Zaczek Kepler—I am humbled and appreciative of how much you catch and correct.

And to Vicky Cosenzo, thank you for taking the books the last mile and mastering the logistics of sales.

Gratitude to Shane for his commitment to the series. Your vision of the value of mental models continues to inspire the approach to the books and shapes the content.

Finally, I would like to thank all of our readers. Farnam Street is lucky to have such an engaged audience who are excited to explore mental models with us. I truly appreciate your support of the books we write and the work we do.

Rhiannon Beaubien
Co-author of *The Great Mental Models*

Picture Credits

In order of appearance:

Feedback Loops

Coke in a glass; TheCrimsonMonkey
/istockphoto.com

Thumbs up and down; BonNontawat
/istockphoto.com

Street performers; Borut Trdina
/istockphoto.com

Dessin 1918; Wassily Kandinsky

Equilibrium

Balancing rocks; Arctic ice/Shutterstock.com

Hand with cards; Tatiana Popova
/Shutterstock.com

The Biosphere 2 in Arizona; Joseph Sohm
/Shutterstock.com

Bottlenecks

TSR Poster; Intourist Poster/Russian State
Library

Metal Truss Railroad Bridge; Sergei Mikhailovich
Prokudin-Gorskii

Nylons; Kabardins photo/Shutterstock.com

Scale

Crumbling can; Africa Studio/Shutterstock.com

Can; Africa Studio/Shutterstock.com

Seigantoji temple and Nachi waterfall; Amstk
/Shutterstock.com

Mouse; Eric Isselee/Shutterstock.com

Pony; Artorn Thongtukit/Shutterstock.com

Gasometer and gas purification system;
Marzolino/Shutterstock.com

Margin of Safety

Dropper and liquid; Fotaro1965
/Shutterstock.com

The International Space Station; NASA

Artwork in transit during the war; Courtesy
National Archives, photo: Lady with an Ermine

Churn

Synanon members; San Francisco Chronicle
/Hearst Newspapers via Getty Images

Dangerous bend; Oliver Hoffmann
/Shutterstock.com

Algorithms

Pirates; duncan1890/istockphoto.com

Ching Shih; MR1805/istockphoto.com

Streptococcus pyogenes; Kateryna Kon
/Shutterstock.com

Critical Mass

Votes for Women; H.M. Dallas

Madeline Pollard; C. M. Bell, Library of Congress
Prints and Photographs Division

Stroget in Copenhagen; poludziber
/Shutterstock.com

Aerial View of Pilot Plan of Brasilia City; Donatas
Dabravolskas/Shutterstock.com

Emergence

Termite mound; Belikova Oksana
/Shutterstock.com

Chess knight; me4o/istockphoto.com

Mothers from missing people in Buenos Aires;
Gerardo C. Lerner/Shutterstock.com

People on swings; Ljupco Smokovski
/Shutterstock.com

Chaos Dynamics

Butterfly; Vladimirkarp/Shutterstock.com

Irreducibility

Loose Lips Might Sink Ships; Office for
Emergency Management. Office of War
Information.

Historic flying machines; ZU_09
/istockphoto.com

Law of Diminishing Returns

The Barques of the Northmen; Alphonse de
Neuville

Studying; State Library of Queensland

Chewing gum; OlegDoroshin/Shutterstock.com

Exploitation films movie poster; Devil's Harvest
(1942) Poster, US

House of cards; Anterovium/Shutterstock.com

Distributions

Good life glass of wine; RomoloTavani
/istockphoto.com

Compounding

RAMAT GAN, ISRAEL; Roman Yanushevsky
/Shutterstock.com

Mouse lemur; GUDKOV ANDREY
/Shutterstock.com

Sidney Weinberg; Library of Congress Prints and
Photographs Division

The Bulls and Bears of Wall Street; Library of
Congress Prints and Photographs Division

People sitting on coin stacks; Hyejin Kang
/Shutterstock.com

Network Effects

Bandwagon; Pixabay

Sampling

Eyes; sirtravelalot/Shutterstock.com

1896 'desiderata'; oed.com

Collapsed buildings; Everett Collection
/Shutterstock.com

Randomness

Roulette wheel; Vector-3D/Shutterstock.com

1865 Groombridge and Sons edition of Robinson
Crusoe; Alexander Frank Lydon

Chan Canasta; National Portrait Gallery

Regression to the Mean

Carrot 1; Anna Kucherova/Shutterstock.com

Carrot 2; Africa Studio/Shutterstock.com

Edsel Pacer green and white car; Eric Bascol
/istockphoto.com

Vietnamese sisters on postage stamp; Oldrich
/Shutterstock.com

Multiplying by Zero

Robotron KC 85/1; Enrico Grämer

Carl Zeiss Jena; Peter Liebers from
Bundesarchiv

Seedling; Japril17/Shutterstock.com

Marilyn Monroe filming The Seven Year Itch;
Published by Corpus Christi Caller-Times-photo
from Associated Press

Equivalence

Illustration from Margarita Philosophica, 1503;
Gregor Reisch (author) / illustrator unidentified
/Houghton Library

Oxygen bubbles; Alena Ohneva/Shutterstock.
com

Bias cut dress; Evening Dress (1931) by
Madeleine Vionnet from the National Gallery of
Victoria

Funeral Ritual in a Garden, Tomb of Minnakht;
Charles K. Wilkinson/Rogers Fund, 1930

Surface Area

The Great Wallace Shows circus poster; Courier
Litho Company

Fidel Castro mural; gary yim/Shutterstock.com

Global and Local Maxima

Jogbra; Records, Archives Center, National
Museum of American History, Smithsonian
Institution

Basketball; Lightspring/Shutterstock.com

Queen; Michael Ochs Archives

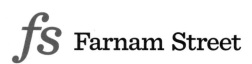